This collection of essays by Philippine evangelicals who have grappled with rule by democratically elected strongmen in their own country is spiritually mature, timely, and worthy of attention far beyond the Philippines. The authors propose a form of respectful public engagement grounded in deep theological reflection that transcends the common Christian choices of withdrawal from the public square or unquestioning submission to government, neither of which embodies God's call to love our neighbors and seek justice for all. The authors argue decisively that genuine faith and politics are interlinked, with implications that politically engaged Christians in particular should not ignore. Those who question the political implications of these essays have an obligation to take up the challenge of responding with equally thoughtful Christian arguments rather than retreating to their own echo chambers.

Bruce Barron, PhD
Executive Editor and Communications Consultant,
World Evangelical Alliance

The Philippines boasts to be the only Christian nation in Asia, and the fifth largest Christian nation in the world. While evangelicals only represent a small fraction of this majority, their engagement in politics offers unique insight for other Christian societies in Asia. Students of Christianity and politics have observed, with great interest, the evolving Filipino evangelical involvement in politics in the overall Philippine context, especially since the People Power Revolution in 1986. The Asia Evangelical Alliance enthusiastically welcomes the publication of *Faith and Politics: Filipino Evangelical Insights in Political Theology*. The book is timely and critically important, as Filipino evangelicals revisit the scripture for articulating fuller expression of holistic faith and worship in the current political reality.

Bambang Budijanto, PhD
General Secretary,
Asia Evangelical Alliance

Politics and Christian faith in one same breath? Yes! Both contextually rooted and globally significant at the same time? Yes! The book in your hand offers a rich Filipino spread that will surely nourish Christians who yearn to see the embrace of justice and peace in their places during these troubling days.

Ruth Padilla DeBorst, PhD
Richard C. Oudersluys Associate Professor of World Christianity,
Western Theological Seminary, Michigan, USA
Networking Team Coordinator,
International Fellowship for Mission as Transformation

This is a welcome addition to the development of political theology that is formed and shaped by local contexts of the church, state, and society. In this edited volume, some of the most prominent scholars of Filipino evangelical political theology discuss pertinent political themes in the contemporary Philippines, such as church-state relations, justice, governance, violence, and peacemaking. The strength and uniqueness of this volume lies in the fact that the contributors do political theology from an evangelical perspective and therefore make a distinctive contribution to our understanding of theological engagement in politics. This volume of *Faith and Politics* is meaningful for evangelicals who find it difficult to integrate faith and politics and an important reading, together with the literature regarding the "theology of struggle," offering ways and means to respond to political oppression in the Philippines, as well as in other contexts.

Sebastian C. H. Kim, PhD
Academic Dean, Korean Studies Center,
Robert Wiley Professor of Renewal in Public Life,
Fuller Seminary, California, USA

Through a multiplicity of voices, *Faith and Politics* grapples with the Christian imperative to make theologies of struggle, to speak to power, to resist violence, to dismantle hierarchies of predation, and take the side of the victims. This volume is a proclamation of diverse voices in the evangelical church – critical, decolonizing, prophetic, radical, and incarnational. As such, it is an invitation toward a continuing, transformative journey through theologies of liberation that are rooted in Filipino realities, bodies, and identities. More importantly, *Faith and Politics* demands its reader to be in solidarity with those who need God the most, here and now, in a nation with over 500 years of Christianity and yet one of the dangerous places to be in the world today, the Philippines.

Lizette Tapia-Raquel, PhD
Academic Dean,
Associate Professor of Christianity and Culture,
Union Theological Seminary, Philippines

If you want to know why the common belief that Christians are not to be involved in politics is bad theology, then read this book. *Faith and Politics* assembles faith-based interdisciplinary voices from the Philippine context that make a compelling case for faith-informed political engagement and politically engaged faith. The God of justice and mercy demands we do justice and love mercy to validate our worship, and vice versa: we worship and praise God to do justice and love mercy by a power not our own. We are indebted to the Filipino Christians represented in this book for showing us the way toward faithfulness in the public square.

Al Tizon, PhD
Affiliate Associate Professor of Missional and Global Leadership,
North Park University, Illinois, USA

As a young man, my heart burned with a passion for national transformation. I believed policies and leaders could shape my country's future. But when I met Jesus Christ in 1984, I realized that no system, policy, or governance structure – no matter how noble – can truly change a nation unless the hearts of its people are transformed.

Yet my dream wasn't wrong – it was simply incomplete. Discipleship and nation-building are not opposites but inseparable. That's why *Faith and Politics* is such a crucial read. It challenges the false divide between faith and governance, calling the church to reclaim its prophetic voice.

While not every detail in this book may align with my personal convictions, I find the discussions compelling and necessary. This book is thought-provoking and bold, offering fresh insights into how believers can engage in politics without losing sight of the more known side of Christ-given mission. Whether you're a church leader, policymaker, or believer, this will stretch your thinking and inspire you to engage with conviction and wisdom.

Cris Uy, PhD
President,
International Graduate School of Leadership, Philippines
Global Vice President for Southeast and South Asia,
Campus Crusade for Christ International

Many societies today are still mired in poverty, injustice, and corruption, and often lacking adequate legal frameworks and institutions to protect the weak and marginalized from the strong and powerful. As Majority World churches continue to grow and mature, they are inevitably confronted with the challenge of how the gospel can bring a significant contribution to the task of socio-political transformation and nation-building. Within Asia, partly because of their history, Filipino evangelicals have been in the forefront of engaging with this crucial question in the past few decades, both in practice and theology. This fine collection of essays represents one more step in their highly commendable efforts to demonstrate that Christ's Lordship carries serious socio-political implications. Read this and you will find much here that points to answers to similar challenges in your own context!

Hwa Yung, PhD
Bishop Emeritus,
The Methodist Church in Malaysia

Faith and Politics

Pananampalataya at Politika

Faith and Politics

Filipino Evangelical Insights in Political Theology

Edited by
Aldrin M. Peñamora and David S. Lim

© 2025 Aldrin M. Peñamora and David S. Lim

Published 2025 by Langham Global Library
An imprint of Langham Publishing
www.langhampublishing.org

Langham Publishing and its imprints are a ministry of Langham Partnership

Langham Partnership
PO Box 296, Carlisle, Cumbria, CA3 9WZ, UK
www.langham.org

ISBNs:
978-1-83973-785-5 Print
978-1-78641-288-1 ePub
978-1-78641-289-8 PDF

Aldrin M. Peñamora and David S. Lim hereby assert their moral right to be identified as the Author of the General Editor's part in the Work in accordance with sections 77 and 78 of the Copyright, Designs and Patents Act 1988.

All rights reserved. No part of this publication may be reproduced, stored in a retrieval system or transmitted, in any form or by any means, electronic, mechanical, photocopying, recording or otherwise, without the prior written permission of the publisher or the Copyright Licensing Agency.

Requests to reuse content from Langham Publishing are processed through PLSclear. Please visit www.plsclear.com to complete your request.

Scripture quotations marked (ESV) are taken from The Holy Bible, English Standard Version® (ESV®), copyright © 2001 by Crossway, a publishing ministry of Good News Publishers. Used by permission. All rights reserved.

Scripture quotations marked (NASB) are taken from the New American Standard Bible®, Copyright © 1960, 1962, 1963, 1968, 1971, 1972, 1973, 1975, 1977, 1995, 2020 by The Lockman Foundation. Used by permission.

Scripture quotations marked (NIV) are taken from the Holy Bible, New International Version®, NIV®. Copyright © 1973, 1978, 1984, 2011 by Biblica, Inc.™ Used by permission of Zondervan.

Scripture quotations are from the New Revised Standard Version Bible, copyright © 1989 National Council of the Churches of Christ in the United States of America. Used by permission. All rights reserved.

British Library Cataloguing-in-Publication Data
A catalogue record for this book is available from the British Library

ISBN: 978-1-83973-785-5

Cover & Book Design: projectluz.com

Langham Partnership actively supports theological dialogue and an author's right to publish but does not necessarily endorse the views and opinions set forth here or in works referenced within this publication, nor can we guarantee technical and grammatical correctness. Langham Partnership does not accept any responsibility or liability to persons or property as a consequence of the reading, use or interpretation of its published content.

Para sa Diyos, Iglesiya, at Bayan
(For God, Church, and Country)

Contents

Foreword xiii

Acknowledgments xv

Introduction 1

Part I: Church, State, and, Governance

1 Political Theology of the Prophets 13
   Abigail R. Teh

2 How Shall the Righteous Govern? Contextualizing Jesus's Transformation Politics for Nation-Building and World Peace 33
   David S. Lim

3 State Power and the Church in Society 55
   Melba P. Maggay

4 *Pamathalaan*: A Filipino Indio-Genius Idea of Governance 73
   Marie Joy D. Pring-Faraz

5 Enigmatic Formation of Separation of Church and State and De-politicization of Filipino Evangelicals 87
   Nestor M. Ravilas

6 Not the Janus-Faced State: (Re-)Reading the Decalogue as Basis for Normative Politics 107
   Romel Regalado Bagares

7 Transforming the Trauma of State Perpetrated Violence: Companioning Towards Healing and Justice 129
   Annabel Manzanilla-Manalo

8 The Voice of the Victim: A Reading of 2 Samuel 13 Using René Girard's Mimetic Theory 151
   Wilfredo A. Laceda

Part II: Contemporary Issues, Challenges, and Prospects

9 Decolonial Imagination and Political Theologizing 175
   Rei Lemuel Crizaldo

10	Feel-Good Christianity 195
	Jayeel S. Cornelio
11	Breaking Bread, Breaking Spiritual-Political Dichotomy:
	Eucharist, Forgiveness, and the Marcos Legacy 209
	Aldrin M. Peñamora
12	Remembering Truthfully: Memory, Justice, and the Problem of
	Conflicting Historical Narratives 231
	Athena E. Gorospe
13	The Cross and the 1986 People Power Revolution:
	Cultivating an Ethic of Peace 257
	Aldrin M. Peñamora and Emil Jonathan L. Soriano
14	Grassroots Evangelical Political Theology 279
	Jack Dosejo Alvarez
15	Restoring the Productive Capacities of Filipinos:
	The Biblical Way 299
	Alvin Ang
16	Theologized Context: Theological Education and Politics 319
	Dick O. Eugenio
17	How Shall the Righteous Elite Govern? Indigenizing
	Transformation Politics for Nation-Building and World Peace 341
	David S. Lim
	List of Authors 365

Foreword

It is a privilege to be invited to write the foreword to this collection of essays on Filipino evangelical political theology. It is an impressive volume covering a wide range of areas on Christian political theology.

My connection with evangelical political activists and scholars in the Philippines began in 1978 with the formation of the Institute for Studies in Asian Church and Culture (ISACC) and continued with close engagement through the EDSA Revolution up to the end of the 1980s. Filipino evangelical scholarship for me, as this book clearly demonstrates, is marked by creativity, biblical depth, incisive cultural and political analysis, and theological nuance. I have always enjoyed reading it and reflecting on it.

My context in India, however, is very different. It is a deeply Hindu country with eighty-five percent of its 1.4 billion population seeing themselves as proud Hindus. Christians constitute less than three percent of the population. This is in sharp contrast to the Philippines, a majority Christian nation.

Indian Christian political theology was first shaped by the movements of the freedom struggle against British colonial rule since the 1880s. After independence in 1947, the struggle widened to the liberation from oppression and poverty, particularly of the lowest caste orders of Indian society and tribals who constituted a quarter of the population. The challenge for Christians is how to develop social-political engagement that brings transformation through finding common grounds with the Hindu and Islamic Indian religious traditions. In the past two decades, the focus has been on cultivating a common understanding of humanity that all religions in India can resource and support.

Similar to this volume, Indian evangelical political theology has kept the kingdom of God as its central theme. Nearly all social and personal space in India is shaped and saturated by religion. To identify religious spaces where the seed of God's kingdom can take root and flourish and avoid stony and thorny ground is one key challenge for evangelical Christian social activism.

I am pleasantly surprised to note that one of the central theological themes of *Faith and Politics* is also about struggle, which has also been significant in Indian Christian political theology.

I trust this work will be widely read.

Vinay Samuel

Acknowledgments

The seed for this book was planted back in 18 September 2021 in an online "Call to ALL" conference, that sought to challenge the Philippine church to fulfill the Great Commission holistically. In the workshop on "Political Engagement" that we were part of, together with other evangelical leaders, Bishop Noel Pantoja, the national director of the Philippine Council of Evangelical Churches (PCEC) suggested to both of us to write a book that could help clarify the nature and role of Christians in the political and public square.

The idea appealed to me (Aldrin) personally since about that time, the manuscript of a book I co-edited, *Faith and Bayan: Evangelical Christian Engagement in the Philippines*, was already in the final stages of completion. It was a book dealing with the Philippine political context, mainly focusing on issues raised by the Duterte presidency. After the online conference, David and I got in touch and explored the possibility of coming up with a book on political theology in the Philippine context from an evangelical viewpoint that is interdisciplinary, which would allow us to cover a wide range of issues in theology and politics. Also giving us further motivation was the fact that talk of politics was raging at that time, with the May 2022 Philippine presidential elections just around the corner.

Those crucial May elections resulted in the landslide victory of the leading tandem of the son of a former dictator, now President Ferdinand "Bongbong" Marcos Jr., and the daughter of another strongman, now Vice-President Sarah Duterte, for the top two positions in the nation. Like the rest of the Filipinos in the country, evangelicals also got entangled in heated discussions on politics that sadly caused many friendships to go sour, even to the point of "cancelling" or "unfriending" others on social media platforms such as Facebook. We both felt all the more that this book is urgently needed to help equip our fellow believers in navigating the political terrain based on our evangelical moorings.

At the start of this project, we approached Dr. Federico Villanueva, Langham Publishing's commissioning editor for Asia, who also co-edited *Faith and Bayan* to see what he thought of our plan. We also asked him to be our co-editor, but due to his commitments he couldn't take on this role. We are thankful to Dr. Rico and Langham Publishing, especially to Dr. Mark Arnold and Luke Lewis, for their enthusiastic response to our proposal and agreeing to have it published. We also thank Megan Lowe for the very well designed book cover.

Politics deals with a wide array of subjects and questions related to the activities and governance of the *polis* for the flourishing of the nation and its people. And so, we agreed it would be beneficial for the book to have multiple authors with expertise from various fields. We are pleased with the interdisciplinary nature of this volume, with contributors specializing not only in the different subdisciplines in theology, but also in sociology, law, economics, psychology, anthropology, and education. Our goal is to provide the reader with a broad range of topics that will contribute to a deeper understanding of the interaction between our worship of God and politics, enabling us to participate in transforming our nation in God-honoring ways.

We express our most profound gratitude to the following contributors who gave of their time and shared their expertise to make this book possible. Listed here in the order of the place of their respective chapters in the book:

- Dr. Abigail R. Teh
- Dr. David S. Lim
- Dr. Melba P. Maggay
- Dr. Marie Joy D. Pring-Faraz
- Prof. Nestor M. Ravilas
- Atty. Romel. R. Bagares
- Dr. Annabel Manzanilla-Manalo
- Prof. Wilfredo A. Laceda
- Prof. Rei Lemuel P. Crizaldo
- Dr. Jayeel S. Cornelio
- Dr. Aldrin M. Peñamora
- Dr. Athena E. Gorospe
- Ptr. Emil Jonathan L. Soriano
- Ptr. Hesed Jack D. Alvarez
- Dr. Alvin P. Ang
- Dr. Dick O. Eugenio

To help us contributors think through and develop our chapters for the book, David and I organized a series of webinars entitled "Faith and Politics," launching the first session on 9 February 2022, in special coordination with Asian Theological Seminary's "Theological Forum"; the series ended on 28 August of the same year. Giving their responses to the presentations of our writers were highly-regarded leaders, scholars, and practitioners from the

Roman Catholic, Mainline Protestant and Evangelical traditions. Truly, our deepest thanks to our guest resource persons:

- Bro. Karl M. Gaspar, CSsR
- Fr. Albert E. Alejo, S. J.
- Former Chief Justice Ma. Lourdes P. A. Sereno
- Sr. Mary John Mananzan, OSB
- Dr. Edicio G. Dela Torre
- Prof. Eric P. Baldonado
- Dr. Muriel Orevillo-Montenegro
- Atty. Gilbert T. Andres
- Dr. Erlinda N. Senturias
- Fr. Daniel Franklin Pilario, CM, PhD, STD
- Rev. Eyriche C. Cortez
- Bishop Rex Resurreccion B. Reyes Jr.
- Rev. Dr. Mariano C. Apilado
- Rev. Dr. Ferdinand Ammang Anno
- Bishop Noel A. Pantoja, DMin
- Bishop Reuel Norman O. Marigza
- Dr. Federico G. Villanueva
- Rev. Callum R. Tabada
- Archbishop Antonio J. Ledesma, S. J., DD
- Shk. Abdulhadie Ibn As-Shahced Gumander
- Rev. Dr. Melanio L. Aoanan
- Dr. Victor R. Aguilan
- Prof. Hadje C. Sadje

We would also like to express our appreciation to ISACC (Institute for Studies in Asian Church and Culture) and Dr. Melba Padilla Maggay for assigning personnel to help in broadcasting the webinars. We are thankful to Dr. Marie Joy Pring-Faraz who served as the main host of the webinars, and to Catherine Valdez and Kuya Efren Pallorina for serving as hosts at various times. Thanks also to ISACC and FEBC's Cross-Currents for broadcasting the sessions on their FB pages. We deeply appreciate Light TV for broadcasting our sessions on their channel. Our appreciation also goes to our two other main sponsoring organizations, Langham Publishing, for donating books as prizes for our selected webinar participants, and PCEC Justice, Peace and Reconciliation Commission.

We also thank our webinar audience and participants who gave their insights and comments to our presenters and responders, and all who journeyed with us and prayed for us. We thank all those who gave us encouragement and support during the several months in 2022 when we held the Faith and Politics webinars, and also during the entire process of writing this book.

May each chapter in this book about our Christian worship and politics help you, our dear readers, to have a deeper understanding of God's kingdom and the holistic nature of God's salvation in Jesus Christ, our Lord and Savior, so that we can participate more fully, confidently, and even radically as Jesus did, in what God is doing in the world, of which the political sphere is a crucial dimension.

David S. Lim and Aldrin M. Peñamora

Introduction

This book is, first and foremost, about worship, it is about *pananampalataya sa Panginoon* (faith in God). Second, it concerns politics or *politika*, referring to the political context that shapes, and is itself shaped by, the worship given by Christians to God. It is simply about the interrelationship between *pananampalataya at politika* (faith and politics) that unfolds in the context of Philippine political realities.

Views from a Minority

For most evangelical Christians in the Philippines, the relationship between our Christian faith and politics is often viewed in terms of an antithesis or a dichotomy that leads to adopting a posture that is basically non-participative in social-political matters. Certainly, there are times when evangelical communities unite and become more involved because of overriding concerns for a particular political issue, but it is more often the case that believers choose to not be involved since they see faith as taking place on a plane that seldom intersects with politics. Faith and politics, in this sense, belong to very distinct paths with very distinct concerns.

Needless to say, with all the contributors in this volume engaged in the political expression of their faith which they strive to ground in biblical teachings and principles, this book presents the views of a minority within the Philippine evangelical tradition. However, it is a minority that is growing as more evangelicals are becoming aware through personal reflections, learning from their pastors, attending conferences, and through classes in Bible schools and seminaries, that the Bible has much to say about government, human dignity, freedom, social justice, corruption, wealth distribution, human rights – or in one word, *politics*. Vital, too, are the examples set earlier by certain leaders in the evangelical community.

A Glance at the Beginnings of Evangelical Engagement in Politics

The beginnings of Filipino evangelical engagement in politics can be traced to the National Conference of the InterVarsity Christian Fellowship-Philippines in 1970, which had plenary sessions on the themes "Christians as Nationalists" and "Christian Response to Communism."[1] Thereafter, the Institute for Studies in Asian Church and Culture (ISACC) was founded by Dr. Melba Maggay and her ministry partners in 1978, for the main purpose of giving an evangelical response to the authoritarian rule of the Filipino dictator, Ferdinand Marcos Sr. During the People Power revolutions of February 1986 and January 2001, ISACC led the evangelical presence in the streets of EDSA.[2] Since its inception, Dr. Maggay has articulated ISACC's position on major national issues through its magazine *Patmos* and news bulletin *Isip Isak*.

Another evangelical leader who helped raise the consciousness of the church about its vital role in political engagement is Bishop "Brother Eddie" Villanueva, who founded one of the most prominent evangelical movements in the country, the Jesus is Lord Church or JIL. The television program "*Diyos at Bayan*" (God and Nation) that Bro. Eddie has been hosting since he founded it in 1998 has also been a significant platform in raising the political awareness of the church. But perhaps it was Brother Eddie's candidacy especially in the 2004 presidential elections that gained much of the attention of the country's evangelical community as they reflected and argued about his decision to run for political office, which was strongly considered taboo back then for a religious leader, especially one of his stature, to enter the political arena. Bro. Eddie presently serves as a deputy speaker of the House of Representatives while his son, Joel, also one of JIL's leaders, serves as one of the country's senators. Even today, JIL is an exception, for in most evangelical denominations the pastor or bishop is usually not permitted to run for political office.

A unique engagement in politics was also demonstrated by the late Rev. Absalom Cerveza, a pastor from the Christian and Missionary Alliance Churches of the Philippines (CAMACOP), who served as the official spokesperson for the Muslim revolutionary group, Moro National Liberation Front (MNLF). He advocated for the political, economic, and social rights of Muslims at a time when the prejudice between Christians and Muslims was very

---

1. Dr. Isabelo Magalit gave his "I Have a Dream" speech then, https://ivcfphil.org/cool_timeline/the-ivcfdream/, which included the call for "politicians and social reformers who meet around the Word of God . . . planning to meet those needs through political and social action. Such men include justices, governors, congressmen, industrialists, barrio captains and social workers. This is not hopeless idealism: we have a prototype in the Clapham Sect of nineteenth-century, England . . . ," Andrea Roldan, "Isabelo Magalit (1970): I Have a Dream," (August 15, 2023).

2. David Lim, "Consolidating Democracy: Role of Evangelicals in Deepening Democracy in the Philippines from 1986–1998," in *Evangelical Christianity and Democracy in Asia*, ed. David H. Lumsdaine (Oxford: Oxford University Press, 2009), 241–42.

high. Influential also were former PCEC executive director, Rev. Jun Vencer and theology professor David Lim, co-editor of this volume, who published books and articles arguing biblically for evangelical participation in the political sphere. PCEC has also undertaken some concrete initiatives that interfaced with politics from its early days under Rev. Vencer, which continued under the succeeding PCEC national directors, Bishop Efraim Tendero, and currently Bishop Noel Pantoja. In those early days, too, PCEC issued politically relevant official statements on national issues drafted by the Theological Commission chaired by Dr. Isabelo F. Magalit, and afterwards by Dr. Rodrigo D. Tano.

Political Theology

As the subtitle of this book suggests, this collection of essays also deals with the subject of political theology. In its modern usage, the term political theology is often attributed to Carl Schmitt. The term was first used in the modern sense, however, by the Russian anarchist Mikhail Bakunin.[3] According to Bakunin, whom Schmitt considered as one of his main theoretical antagonists, blending religion and politics leads to metaphysical abstraction that brings about an absolutist state that curbs the progressive impulses of humanism, atheism, materialism and revolutionary socialism.[4] Bakunin therefore sought to strip the sovereign state of any theological legitimation. Schmitt rejected Bakunin's anarchist ideas, and all the other formulations that undermined the sovereignty of the state. Addressing the rising secularization theories of his day, Schmitt remarks that "All significant concepts of the modern theory of the state are secularized theological concepts."[5] His ardent theoretical defense of sovereignty, however, led him to become the premier legal theorist of the Nazi regime.[6]

After the Second World War, a new political theology arose led by Johann Baptist Metz, Dorothee Sölle, and Jürgen Moltmann, who were critical of Schmitt's views, and who programmatically reflected on the complicit par-

---

3. Saul Newman, *Political Theology: A Critical Introduction* (Cambridge: Polity Press, 2019), 5, 21.

4. Newman, *Political Theology*, 21–22. The ancient origins of political theology, says Jürgen Moltmann, can be traced to Stoic philosophy, Plato, and Augustine. Moltmann, "Political Theology," *Theology Today* 28, no. 1 (1971): 9.

5. Carl Schmitt, *Political Theology: Four Chapters on the Concept of Sovereignty*, trans. George Schwab (Chicago: University of Chicago Press, 2005), 36.

6. For a good historical account of Schmitt's career in Hitler's government, see Joseph J. Bendersky, *Carl Schmitt: Theorist for the Reich* (Princeton: Princeton University Press, 1983).

ticipation of Christians in the Holocaust.⁷ This "theology after Auschwitz" has influenced subsequent theologies that aimed to provide an analysis and critique of social inequalities for the creation of just social structures informed by Christian faith perspectives. Of these approaches, liberation theology is perhaps the most well-known.⁸

Indeed, political theology is often understood and identified with liberation theology. These two are certainly distinct in terms of their origin, context, orientation, and *raison d'etre*, but each has had an impact on the other.⁹ Thus, political theology and liberation theology share key features, such as the primacy of praxis, commitment to social justice, political participation to transform the political process, and the conviction that the gospel is a call for social transformation.¹⁰ In the Philippines, those features can also be ascribed to the *Theology of Struggle* (TOS) that mainline Protestants and Catholics developed¹¹ to confront the realities presented by the Marcos dictatorship.¹²

Political theology then can be understood narrowly in light of its "original" European origins and in its engagement with modern society and secularism, or it may be viewed more broadly to include 19th century iterations in Latin America and other contexts, and even from much earlier periods such as the time of Augustine or the Reformers.¹³ For what is crucial in political theology, according to Moltmann, is its crucicentric nature, the iconoclastic task of which is to struggle against religious superstition, political idolatry, and all forms of alienation so humans may be returned to their true likeness to God.¹⁴ As Moltmann states further:

> A Christian "political theology" wants to bring the Christians as Christians, that is, as liberators, to the place where they are being waited upon by the crucified one. In the suffering and con-

---

7. Ruben Rosario Rodriguez, "Preface," in *T&T Clark Handbook of Political Theology*, ed. Ruben Rosario Rodriguez (London: T&T Clark, 2020), xix. For a good overview of the lives and key themes of the works of these three political theologians, see Vincent Lloyd, "Christian Responses to the Holocaust," in Rodriguez, *Handbook of Political Theology*, 17–28.

8. Rodriguez, *Handbook of Political Theology*, xx.

9. Paul F. Lakeland, "Theological Trends: Political and Liberation Theology I," *The Way* 25, no. 3 (1985): 225.

10. Lakeland, "Theological Trends: Political and Liberation Theology I," 224–27.

11. Lisa Asedillo, "The Theology of Struggle: Critiques of Church and Society in the Philippines (1970s–1990s)," *Indonesian Journal of Theology* 9, no. 1 (July 2021): 62.

12. Eleazar S. Fernandez, *Toward a Theology of Struggle* (Eugene: Wipf and Stock, 2009), 20–30.

13. Rodriguez, *Handbook of Political Theology*, xx.

14. Jürgen Moltmann, "Political Theology," *Theology Today* 28, 1 (April 1971): 20.

demned ones of this earth Christ is waiting upon his own and their presence.[15]

It is in this broad, Christ-centered understanding of political theology that we are situating the essays in this volume. And while the writers may have written from various disciplines and sub-disciplines, what is clear among them is the conviction that *pananampalataya* and *politika* belong intrinsically together.

Toward an Evangelical Posture in Politics

As earlier mentioned, there have been significant strides made through the years in the engagement of evangelicals in politics. Yet, it must be acknowledged that the default public posture of the majority of Filipino evangelical believers in matters of politics remains non-participative and/or passive. One often hears that the church only needs to be submissive to governing authorities, with Romans 13 usually cited as *the* authoritative biblical teaching on the subject. This book presents an alternative position to shed light on a more robust understanding of the interrelationship between worship and politics.

It does not mean, however, that this book is presenting or even attempting to present a finished product called "Filipino evangelical political theology." What one can expect in this volume is similar to the forging of the Theology of Struggle "in" and "of" struggle, or out of the very situations of struggle.[16] In reading the chapters, one will be able to discern certain postures, principles, and values emerging as a result of the writers' struggle to understand what the Bible teaches in light of their own contexts and political engagements. Hopefully, fellow evangelicals will recognize these contributions as part of their evangelical heritage and so inform their engagement in the political and public square. As with the early Reformers who understood that the church is always reforming (*ecclesia semper reformanda est*), this book therefore sees the interrelationship between *pananampalataya at politika* with a "towards orientation" that never arrives fully at its destination. *Pananampalataya at politika* will always be a journey for God's people who are deeply yearning to see demonstrated in all societies and nations the politics of God's kingdom that has already been inaugurated in and through Christ.

---

15. Moltmann, "Political Theology," 23.
16. Fernandez, *Theology of Struggle*, 27.

Book Outline

Our book is divided into two parts. Part I consists of essays on topics about the church, state, and governance; Part II is composed of essays on contemporary political issues, challenges, and prospects for evangelical political engagement.

To underline the prophetic stance of this book, we begin with Abigail Teh's essay on what evangelical Christians can learn from the political theology of the biblical prophets. In her introduction in **Chapter 1**, Teh gives a disquieting observation on how the Philippines fell from being an exemplar of democracy and nonviolent change demonstrated in the 1986 People Power Revolution to becoming supporters of tyranny, first by electing as president an authoritarian figure in Rodrigo Duterte in 2016, then in 2022 by overwhelmingly voting for Bongbong Marcos, the son of a former dictator. This turnaround, according to Teh, shows how moral transformation also requires strong institutional transformations, which were lacking in the post-People Power years. Lacking too was the voice of the church to guide the Filipinos. Teh insists it is essential for the church to learn from the political theology of the biblical prophets so that evangelicals can take part in transforming political structures and be bastions of justice and good governance in the country.

Chapter 2 is David Lim's first of two chapters in this book. He expounds on the political theology of Jesus as contextualized in the New Testament for the Philippine context of a republic governed by a corrupt elite. He shows that Jesus's claim to be the Messiah who could demand allegiance to the kingdom of God brought him into conflict with both the political and religious authorities of the Jews and the imperial authority of Herod and Pilate who represented Caesar. This resulted in his death under the "powers and authorities" of his time. Yet his resurrection gives us hope for God's sure victory. Jesus's "transformation politics" was faithfully taught and obeyed by his disciples and their converts as they risked their lives to implement his governance in their hearts, homes, neighbors, and state/empire. And so must we as the governed or as his "righteous elite."

Melba Maggay addresses in **Chapter 3** the relationship of the church and the state based on Romans 13 that many evangelicals use to justify non-participation in the political realm in submission to the government. Drawing from a biblical view of the passage, Maggay points out that government is not the highest power demanding absolute obedience; that power belongs to God from whom government itself receives its mandate, which is to uphold justice. Knowing this, says Maggay, enables the church to properly fulfill its own mandate that includes entering the political space and creating a "hermeneutical community" that biblically addresses social and political concerns.

The next essay in **Chapter 4** is from Marie Joy Pring-Faraz, who highlights the contextual dimension of political theology as she talks about a government rooted in Filipino culture. This indigenous concept of government, *pamathalaan*, is anchored on three values that are central for its actualization: *kaloob* (insight), *patototoo* (commitment), and *kalinisan* (purity). Pring-Faraz appreciates the richness of this indigenous conception and its potential for a deeper Christian understanding of government, so she sets out in this chapter to provide a theological understanding of *pamathalaan* by introducing the Christological "entry point" of the *mathal*. By using the concept of *mathal*, a more robust understanding of *pamathalaan* in terms of Christ's governance emerges, as well as a notion of the church called to embody the values of the *pamathalaan* as demonstrated in Christ the *mathal*.

In **Chapter 5**, Nestor Ravilas gives an overview of the origins of the principle of the separation of church and state that has led believers to be politically unengaged. Ravilas rejects this principle and the response it has generated through the years. He shows how particularly in the Philippines, church-state separation was realized through the imposition of a few wealthy *ilustrados* and through American colonization. He calls for a reassessment of this concept, and shows also a more appropriate reading of a well-known biblical passage about Jesus and the question of paying taxes to Rome (Matt 22:15–21; Mark 12:13–17; Luke 20:20–25) which, like Romans 13, is often used to justify political apathy. Furthermore, Ravilas points out that the said passage is actually describing the contrary.

In **Chapter 6**, Romel Bagares discusses the state and normative politics in view of a wider creational reality. He draws from the Neocalvinist tradition which holds that all of life is interconnected under God who created all things, which makes all of life religious in nature and all human actions a form of response to the Creator. Bagares points out how this creational standpoint has crucial implications in understanding that the Decalogue is more than just a moral law, that the church's participation in politics is her response to creational norms, and that the state is not absolute but is called to uphold justice and fairness to attain a harmonious society.

If the previous chapter talks about the importance of the creational mandate of the state as a bearer of justice, Annabel Manalo's essay in **Chapter 7** demonstrates how the state in President Duterte's "War on Drugs" has become the bearer of violence and injustice. According to Manalo, state-sponsored violence (SPV) affects persons and communities deeply and can perpetuate the cycle of violence and trauma even across generations. SPV can be averted, however, through initiatives aimed to cultivate resilience and resistance, as exemplified in actual stories that Manalo shares. The author also calls on the church to condemn the state's wrongful acts, and to come alongside the victims so they can experience God's healing and compassion.

Chapter 8 by Fred Laceda underlines the plight of victims in his attempt to construct a political theology based on the story of Tamar in 2 Samuel 13 utilizing René Girard's mimetic theory. Showing that David's reign was marked by self-serving politics and sexual violence as demonstrated in the rape of Tamar, which did not receive justice through David or the monarchy's judicial institutions, the Bible nonetheless gave voice to Tamar signifying how God is on the side of victims. This perspective from the victims is a key feature of political theology, for Laceda, in view of the violence and injustices in Philippine politics that are often perpetrated by the state.

Part II of the book begins with Rei Crizaldo's essay in **Chapter 9** about the importance of decolonizing evangelical political engagement in the Philippines. For Crizaldo, the 2022 presidential elections serve as a good barometer of evangelical colonial mentality as Filipino believers mirrored the political concerns of their counterparts in America. A deeper contextualization of political theology is needed, Crizaldo insists, pointing to some pathways based on inroads already paved especially by Emo Yango, Melba Maggay and Timoteo Gener. The author shows us a pathway that uses local cuisine as contextual lens, reminding us of the importance of meals in the Bible. He also underscores the revolutionary spirituality evangelicals are called to in political theologizing.

In **Chapter 10**, Jayeel Cornelio looks at the phenomenon of "feel-good" Christianity that is prevalent among Filipino evangelical Christians. He warns against the consequences of this phenomenon that not only makes believers numb to urgent social-political questions assaulting society, but even supportive of tyrannical figures and narratives, as evident in the support of many evangelicals to the candidacy of now president, Ferdinand "BBM" Marcos, Jr. To counter "feel good" Christianity, Cornelio proposes bringing to the fore of evangelical Christianity the prophetic task of truth-telling and engaging in reimagined ecclesial practices that can lead to solidarity with people struggling against injustice and oppression.

Aldrin Peñamora's essay in **Chapter 11** points to the Lord's Supper as a powerful political act that Christians need to recognize in confronting their political apathy. The Lord's Supper is often understood as nourishing only one's spiritual well-being, not realizing that it cultivates political virtues, such as the virtue of forgiveness. This is important in view of the notion of forgiveness espoused by the current president, Bongbong Marcos, in relation to Martial Law, a notion that justifies oppression and makes victims invisible to the rest of society. For Peñamora, understanding forgiveness in light of the political Lord's Supper means confronting and acting against all forms of injustice, for in the Supper it is Jesus and his righteousness, not tyrants and their oppressions, that believers remember and celebrate.

In **Chapter 12**, Athena Gorospe raises the problem of how one can adjudicate between conflicting narratives. As an example, she compares the narrative of the 1986 EDSA revolution that ousted Filipino dictator Ferdinand Marcos and the version being peddled by his son BBM, which glorifies Marcos and the Martial Law era. For Gorospe, the concept of memory is crucial in this adjudication process, so she turns to Paul Ricoeur's insightful understanding of memory and to the Book of Deuteronomy to formulate key criteria that could guide in knowing which is truthful between the competing narratives.

Cultivating an ethic of peace is the focus of **Chapter 13**, co-written by Aldrin Peñamora and Emil Jonathan Soriano. To these writers, the supportive stance of many Filipinos and evangelical Christians to Duterte's "War on Drugs" and BBM's distortion of the Martial Law era is a cause of great concern, for they believe it cultivates an ethic of violence and dehumanization. To construct a counter-ethic that brings peace and humanization to Philippine society, Peñamora and Soriano look to the cross-event for the theological grounding, and to the 1986 EDSA Revolution for the historical, wherein crucial values are embodied in Jesus's cross. These Filipino values are *kapwa* (shared identity) and *malasakit* (deep compassion and empathy).

In **Chapter 14**, Jack Dosejo Alvarez writes his reflections based on his personal journey in developing a grassroots theology as an evangelical pastor in a local church among the urban poor. He also traces the historical roots of rampant corruption in patronage politics and bad governance by political dynasties, and how these relate to the actual situation in his parish. Alvarez then enumerates three recommendations for pastors and others who care to be politically involved for the welfare and development of urban poor dwellers. He concludes with a plea to help transform communities by doing theology and engaging politically at the *barangay* level.

As an evangelical economist, Alvin Ang in his essay in **Chapter 15** discusses how to restore the productive capacities of Filipinos in the biblical way. He provides statistics to show that the Philippines is going backwards rather than forward. And this, he writes, is not just an issue of economic capacity deficiency but also a worsening retrogression that instead of expanding opportunities, these are becoming limited and short-sighted, benefiting only a few. Ang challenges Filipino churches to help their members become more productive both in the material world and in the spiritual one, to dispense social justice in their family, workplace, and community, which will contribute significantly to their personal self-worth and our national productivity.

In **Chapter 16**, Dick Eugenio tackles the issue of how politics and religion interact in educational settings, particularly in theological education institutions which are the main venue for discussions on the church's role in politics. He discusses possibilities on how seminaries can equip students for relevant ministry in church and society, while responding critically to their religio-cultural heritage and socio-political-economic reality. Eugenio ends with the challenge to provide theology graduates with the skills to navigate their socio-political environment, so they can effectively interact with policymakers, community leaders, and civil society organizations to promote policies and initiatives that uphold the principles of well-being, social justice, and peace.

Our book ends with **Chapter 17**, by David Lim. Using the depiction of the New Jerusalem in Isaiah 65:17–25, he outlines the four agenda of "transformation politics" for indigenizing kingdom communities on earth. As we confront the various issues generated by the dysfunctional political order dominated by the corrupt elite, we need a multi-pronged approach to attain political, economic, cultural and ecclesiological transformation. Lim enumerates some major initiatives for equipping an enlightened citizenry able to raise and elect qualified people to constitute the righteous elite that will lead our people to achieve the goals of nation-building in the Philippines, and peace (*shalom*) in the world.

May you, our readers, gain a better understanding on how to live out a political theology that considers *Pananampalataya* as *Politika* (Faith *as* Politics) and *Politika* as *Pananampalataya* (Politics *as* Faith) so that all individuals and all organizations in all nations will see and experience the glorious kingdom of God on earth as it is in heaven.

Part I

Church, State, and, Governance

1

Political Theology of the Prophets

Abigail R. Teh[1]

"For the LORD is a God of Justice." (Isaiah 30:18)[2]

Introduction

Nearly forty years ago, the Philippines was the toast of the entire world. In February 1986, four days of massive people support for rebel soldiers ousted Pres. Ferdinand Marcos Sr. after twenty years of being in power. The peaceful uprising was hailed by the world as the "Smiling Revolution" or "People Power Revolution." The Church, in particular the Roman Catholic Church, played a pivotal role in those four days, with Manila Archbishop Jaime Cardinal Sin calling for people to support the embattled military defectors. Though smaller, the evangelical community was present at EDSA as well as an ecumenical coalition.

Why was such a revolution necessary? The dominance of a small group of wealthy and influential families who consolidate their fortunes by entering politics was first critiqued in the 1960s by political scientist Dante C. Simbulan.

---

1. This talk was first given on 5 May 2022 as part of the "Faith and Politics" webinar series sponsored by the Institute for Studies in Asian Church and Culture, Langham Publishing, among others. Author's note: "As a seminary professor who has been teaching the Old Testament for more than two decades, it has puzzled and pained me that the prophetic literature is seldom preached or taught in church pulpits systematically. If it was, churches would be shocked at how much the God of the Bible yearns for justice and righteousness."

2. All Scripture quotations are taken from the New Revised Standard version, unless otherwise indicated.

> [A] small upper strata minority . . . characterized by economic and social prominence . . . [is] the dominant source of political leaders in the country. . . . Possessing the key values [of] . . . wealth, education, prestige, and skills, it now adds power. . . . In office, the elite politician seeks to maintain, not only his position, but also to advance his interest or the interest of his class.[3]

Under Marcos's presidency, democratic values were disregarded for political favors. The term "crony capitalism" was coined by then *Time Magazine* business editor George M. Taber to refer to the 1980s martial law economy of Ferdinand Marcos Sr. The "distortion of the capitalist system . . . [and] the free market . . . benefited a few and kept the masses in poverty."[4]

Martial law rule also brought human rights abuses and the plunder of government coffers, with various reports that the Marcos family amassed as much as $10 billion while in office in the twenty-one years Marcos was president. In 2021, the Philippine Commission on Good Government reported that P174 billion had already been recovered from the Marcos plunder, with P125 billion still to go. Amnesty International reported that over fifty thousand people had been arrested and detained under Martial Law from 1972–1975, including church workers, human rights defenders, legal aid lawyers, labor leaders, and journalists. Thousands more met the same fate in the years from 1976 to 1986.[5] The people had suffered enough, and then the People Power Revolution happened.

Yet barely forty years later, the son of the dictator surprisingly won the 2022 presidential elections. Analysts say that this was in large measure due

---

3. Dante C. Simbulan, "A Study of the Socio-Economic Elite in Philippine Politics and Government, 1945–1963" (PhD diss., Australian National University, 1965), xiv, xvi. It was later published as *The Modern Principalia: The Historical Evolution of the Philippine Ruling Oligarchy* (Quezon City: University of the Philippines Press, 2005).

4. George M. Taber, "The Night I Invented Crony Capitalism," *Knowledge at Wharton*, 3 November 2015, accessed 21 October 2022, https://knowledge.wharton.upenn.edu/article/the-night-i-invented-crony-capitalism/. William Safire, "On Language: Crony Capitalism," *New York Times Magazine*, 1 February 1998, accessed 21 October 2022, https://www.nytimes.com/1998/02/01/magazine/on-language-crony-capitalism.html.

5. Nick Davies, "The $10bn Question: What Happened to the Marcos Millions?" *The Guardian* (May 7, 2016); accessed at https://www.theguardian.com/world/2016/may/07/10bn-dollar-question-marcos-millions-nick-davies; accessed on 21 October 2022; Lian Buan, "Breakdown: P174B recovered from Marcos loot, P125B more to get," *Rappler* [29 September 2021]; accessed at https://www.rappler.com/ newsbreak/iq/breakdown-billions-recovered-marcos-ill-gotten-wealth-by-pcgg-more-to-get/; accessed 21 October 2022; Amnesty International, "Five things to know about Martial Law in the Philippines," April 25, 2022; accessed at https://www.amnesty.org/en/latest/ news/2022/04/five-things-to-know-about-martial-law-in-the-philippines/; accessed 21 October 2022.

to his family's political machinery, a massive disinformation campaign, and suspected poll fraud. Filipinos cannot help but fear that this will be a return to the abuses of the past. Not even a year after the national elections, the Philippine Legislature moves towards a constitutional reform, the goal of which is believed to remove any obstacles to their continued stay in power and plunder of the nation's resources. Unlawful killings in the drug war have continued along with unjust red-tagging of community and church workers, carry-overs from the repressive policies of the Duterte administration.[6] And lest one think that crony capitalism is a thing of the past, a study using the *Economist*'s index on crony capitalism published in March 2022 showed the country ranking number four in the whole world, just behind Russia, Malaysia, and Singapore.[7]

Quo Vadis, my Philippines?

Political analyst Richard Heydarian mourned the victory of Marcos Jr. as "the death of the old liberal order"[8] of democracy. His analysis is disheartening: The 1986 People Power Revolution that ousted the dictator and the nearly four decades intervening failed to bring much-needed structural change to the Philippines.

Where will the Philippines go from here? It seems the country has just gone full circle. That political change – a change of leaders – is not enough has become painfully apparent. More profound reforms are required to correct failures in governance and massive graft and corruption. How will the church in a country that still prides itself as "the only Christian nation in Asia" take leadership of the much-needed change in identity and values of the Filipino people?

---

6. "Unlawful killings, repression continue in PH under Marcos admin – Amnesty International," CNN Philippines, 28 March 2023, accessed 3 April 2023, http://www.cnnphilippines.com/news/2023/3/28/amnesty-international-report-ph.html; Cristina Chi, "House flexes supermajority power to approve con-con resolution on final reading," *Philippine Star*, 6 March 2023, accessed 23 March 2023, https://www.philstar.com/headlines/ 2023/03/06/2249732/house-flexes-supermajority-power-approve-con-con-resolution-final-reading?fbclid=IwAR0IB3UzQV3jbs-AAfA1m7jVawBaROD7woH4dlDVNBCTlbGKLbKHcmAndcU.

7. Ben O. de Vera, "PH ranked fourth globally in 'crony capitalism,'" *Philippine Daily Inquirer*, 31 March 2022, accessed 15 April 2022, https://business.inquirer.net/344745/ph-ranked-fourth-globally-in-crony-capitalism.

8. Richard Javad Heydarian, "The Return of the Marcos Dynasty," *Journal of Democracy* 33/3 (July 2022): 74.

Where is the Church in All This?

In ancient Israel, the prophets served as the conscience of the leadership of the land, at great risk to their lives. In the 9th century BC, God sent the prophet Elijah to decry King Ahab's killing of Naboth and seizure of the latter's ancestral land (1 Kgs 21:1–24). In the 8th century BC, Amos and Micah denounced the northern kingdom of Israel for the abuses by the powerful against the poor (Amos 2:4–16; Mic 2–3) and mourned the people's empty religiosity bereft of justice and righteousness (Amos 5:21–25; Mic 6:6–8).

How about in our time? Where is the preaching of the prophets from our pulpits? Where is the teaching of the prophets in the public square? In the presence of powerful people, has the Philippine evangelical church consigned itself to be silent?

In the Old Testament, Israel was a theocracy, with the king directly under God's authority. The Philippines today is a constitutional democracy; the people, not the president, are the true sovereign with the power to elect leaders. The political rights and responsibilities of citizens living in a democracy are also vastly different. "Those who live in a democracy are the government and can effect greater change than those living in a totalitarian state. The privileges of living in a democratic society . . . warrant greater responsibility to work within the system to bring about changes for good."[9]

In the case of the Philippines, bad governance hinders the nation's growth and the people's well-being.[10] When believers abandon the public arena, they guarantee bad governance.

Christians and Political Engagement

In the past, evangelical Christians had been ambivalent about political involvement. Filipino anthropologist Melba Maggay, founder of Institute for Studies in Asian Church and Culture (ISACC), wrote about the aversion of Filipino Christians to run for political office, not only because of the lack of "guns, goons, and gold" – traditional political weapons in the country – but also because of the real danger of being swallowed up by a corrupt system.[11]

---

9. John S. Feinberg and Paul D. Feinberg, *Ethics for a Brave New World* (Wheaton: Crossway Books, 1993), 395.

10. Miriam Coronel Ferrer, "The Philippines: Governance Issues Comes to the Fore," *Southeast Asian Affairs* 2000: 241–55.

11. Melba Padilla Maggay, "Faith in Politics," *Philippine Daily Inquirer*, 7 September 2021, accessed 9 April 2023, https://opinion.inquirer.net/143880/faith-in-politics.

A much deeper issue is faulty theology that sees a dichotomy between the sacred and the secular, between evangelism and social action. Church leaders encourage individual Christians to vote according to their conscience and participate in social and political movements, but the priority remains evangelism and discipleship. Romans 13 is often wrongly interpreted to defend a refusal to engage and critique government policies and actions.

Yet as Maggay explains, a Christian population does not automatically translate into social justice. Personal conversion does not always lead to national transformation.[12]

> [S]ociety is complex and does not lend itself easily to facile generalizations on how to change it. Would that the doing of justice were merely a matter of personal obedience. Unfortunately, there are entrenched powers and monstrous structures we need to address and contend with. There is such a thing as organized injustice, which calls for thoughtful social analysis and complex solutions.[13]

Politics is the use of power to organize groups and societies and allocate decision-making and resources. It can be a powerful tool in the hands of the right people. Pope Francis in his encyclical *Fratelli Tutti (Brothers All)* coined the term "political charity," seeing politics as "an act of love to strive to organize and structure society so that one's neighbor will not find himself in poverty [or suffering injustice]."[14]

> If someone helps an elderly person cross a road, that is a fine act of charity. The politician, on the other hand, builds a bridge, and that too is an act of charity. While one person can help another by providing something to eat, the politician creates jobs for many people.[15]

The call for the followers of Christ to be salt and light therefore needs to encompass the world of politics. What is needed is a better kind of politics.

---

12. Melba Padilla Maggay, *Transforming Society* (Eugene: Wipf and Stock Publishers, 2010), 9.

13. Maggay, *Transforming Society*, 9–10.

14. Pope Francis, *Fratelli Tutti* (October 2020), nos. 180, 186, accessed 15 March 2022, https://www.vatican.va/content/ francesco/en/encyclicals/documents/papa-francesco_20201003_enciclica-fratelli-tutti.html.

15. Pope Francis, *Fratelli Tutti*, no. 186.

Is God Political?: The Nature of Political Theology

Because all power and authority derive from God, politics is necessarily intertwined with ideas of the divine. Political theology looks into "the nature and relationship of divine power and human political power."[16] A more formal definition is "the analysis and criticism of political arrangements (including cultural, psychological, social, and economic aspects) from the perspective of differing interpretations of God's ways with the world."[17] Political theology, or the more recent term "public theology," is needed because of the intersection between state power and religious ideas and language.

> [A] religion is whatever acts like one. There is nothing *essentially religious* that is shared by Christianity and Theravada Buddhism and Hinduism on the one hand, and not by so-called "secular" phenomena like nationalism and Marxism and free-market ideology on the other.... [P]olitics never was drained of the sacred; the primary locus of the sacred merely shifted from church to nation-state and market... [T]he form of state sovereignty was borrowed from God's sovereignty, and the miracle morphed into the ruler's ability to decide on the extra-legal exception.[18]

Listening to the Prophets Today

Four important principles from the political theology of the prophets must guide believers' political engagement.

First, God uses his power on behalf of the poor, outcasts and marginalized in obtaining justice against all forms of tyranny and oppression. This answers the question of whether social justice should be part of the mission of the church.

The standard definition of the prophet is that he is the messenger, the mouthpiece of God. But J. Dunning wrote, "The prophets spoke on behalf of God, in turn, God's speech is on behalf of us!" God gives voice to the voiceless, the minority, the invisible, the underrepresented. God hears and acts on the cries of the oppressed.

---

16. Carol Newsom, "Political Theology in the Book of Daniel: An Internal Debate," *Review and Expositor* 109 (2012): 567.

17. William T. Cavanaugh and Peter Manley Scott, "Introduction to the Second Edition," in *The Wiley Blackwell Companion to Political Theology*, 2nd ed., eds. William T. Cavanaugh and Peter Manley Scott (Hoboken: John Wiley & Sons, 2019), 3.

18. Cavanaugh and Scott, "Introduction to the Second Edition," 2–3.

Justice and righteousness is foundational to God's character and his rule (Gen 18:19; Pss 33:5; 89:14; 97:2; 99:4; Jer 9:24). According to Micah 3:8, the telltale sign that one is filled with the Lord's spirit is zeal for the oppressed.[19] The same idea is expressed in Isaiah 61:1–2, quoted by Jesus at the start of his public ministry as his mission statement:

> *The Spirit of the Lord GOD is upon me,* because the LORD has anointed me; he has sent me *to bring good news to the oppressed, to bind up the brokenhearted, to proclaim liberty to the captives, and release to the prisoners;*
>
> to proclaim the year of the LORD's favor, and the day of vengeance of our God; to comfort all who mourn. (Luke 4:18–19; italics supplied)

There is therefore a close connection between the Holy Spirit and justice and righteousness. If we are Christ's followers, we should have the same mission as Christ. "[L]et justice roll down like waters, and righteousness like an ever-flowing stream" (Amos 5:24). Social justice is the source of life of a nation – as essential as an adequate water supply. Without true justice and righteousness, any nation will disintegrate. Micah 6:8 also reminds us of the most important of God's demands on His people – "*to do justice, and to love kindness, and to walk humbly with your God.*"

In Hebrew, *mishpat utsedeqah*, "justice and righteousness" is considered a hendiadys, that is, the expression of a single idea or a single referent by two words connected with "and." The two words joined in this way are the equivalent of a single word with modifiers.[20] A good way of translating the word-pair is "righteousness expressed in justice."[21]

The Relationship between Justice and God's Love, and Personal and Societal Sin

Believers who want to downplay the place of justice in the mission of the church argue: "Let's not talk about justice or punishment; God is wholly loving

---

19. Bruce Waltke, "Micah," in *The Minor Prophets: An Exegetical and Expository Commentary, Vol. 2: Obadiah, Jonah, Micah, Nahum, Habbakuk*, ed. Thomas E. McComiskey (Grand Rapids: Baker Books, 1993), 593.

20. Bill T. Arnold and John H. Choi, *A Guide to Biblical Hebrew Syntax*, 2nd ed. (Cambridge: Cambridge University Press, 2018), 158–59.

21. James Luther Mays, "Justice: Perspectives from the Prophetic Tradition," *Interpretation* 37/1 (1983): 8.

and forgiving. Love covers a multitude of sins, so we must forgive." However, the Bible teaches that justice is based on God's love. For the Jewish scholar Abraham Heschel, he cannot be a God of love without being against evil and wrongdoing. He cannot be good without doing something about sin.[22]

Social justice is simply God's love applied to systems, policies, and cultures. The prophets teach us that sin is not only individual and personal; it is also systemic, structural, institutional, corporate. Human sin permeates into every human institution. Thus repentance is not only individual and personal, but systemic and structural. "Social morality is a necessary condition for individual morality to flourish."[23] Sooner or later, the loss of social justice will affect our individual moral life.

The Work of Justice

The work of justice goes to the root of the problem, not just the symptoms. Charity and mercy ministries are needed, but sooner or later we need to break the cycle of poverty or injustice. A famous story in social justice circles attributes to Archbishop Desmond Tutu the saying: "There comes a point when we need to stop just pulling people out of the river. We need to go upstream and find out why they're falling in."[24]

Many years ago, I volunteered at *Samaritana*, a ministry for prostituted women. We ministered to the women, taught them the Bible and an alternative livelihood. Eventually though, *Samaritana* needed to get involved in advocacy work with government agencies. Why? Because as fast as we were taking women off the streets, there were others who would quickly replace them. Because of poverty and with the absence of alternatives, many women had been forced into prostitution. *Samaritana* advocated for the police not to arrest the women but to go after the bars where they worked that were owned by or had ties to policemen, businessmen, and politicians. Justice work needs to address the roots of our social ills.

---

22. Abraham Heschel, *The Prophets* (New York: Harper & Row, 1962), 283. In the New Testament, we have John 3:16 but we also have John 3:18, "those who do not believe [him] are already condemned." Cheap grace fails to appreciate what it cost the Lord Jesus Christ to win our salvation.

23. Vitaliano R. Gorospe, "Christian Renewal of Filipino Values," *Philippine Studies* 14/2 (1966): 192.

24. Ronald Rolheiser, *The Holy Longing: The Search for a Christian Spirituality* (New York: Doubleday, 1999), 168.

Divine justice is also restorative justice. It does not aim simply to punish, but to restore sinners to relationship with God and fellow men. It is a return to God's original intention for wholeness, well-being or *shalom* for humanity and the entire creation (Gen 1:26–28). God wants humanity to experience this even in this life (John 10:10; Mark 10:29–30). Injustice obstructs God's plan. Politics is a way to participate in God's restoration project, since Jesus came to save the whole person, not just the soul.

Second, divine power is exercised through human agents and human institutions. Since all power and authority are delegated from God, they remain subject and accountable to him.

Isaiah 1–39 illustrates the truism "As the king goes, so goes the nation." Twice in the 8th century BC, the city of Jerusalem was surrounded by hostile armies and faced crushing defeat. The first was during the reign of King Ahaz (Isa 7–8) and the second under his son Hezekiah (Isa 36–39).[25] Isaiah gave the same message: Trust God and his promises. One king trusted God; the other did not. Ahaz rejected God's promises and instead made an alliance with Assyria, thereby rendering Judah a vassal to Assyria and introducing Assyrian gods to the nation (2 Kgs 16:5–18). Approximately seventy years later, Ahaz's son Hezekiah made the right choice in trusting YHWH over the superior military might of Sennacherib (Isa 37:1–38; 2 Kgs 18:9–37). The city was miraculously saved. In being a righteous leader, Hezekiah saved his generation. As the leader goes, so goes the nation.

How can the church take a more active role in national transformation? By advocating for moral and competent leadership and helping to raise such leaders. Texts about the qualities of righteous rulers are scattered throughout the Old Testament, many in the Psalms and Proverbs. In the books of the prophets, there are two important passages – Isaiah 11:1–5 and Ezekiel 34. These are leadership traits that are much-needed to this day.

Isaiah 11 – The Spirit-led Leader

> The spirit of the LORD shall rest on him, the spirit of wisdom and understanding, the spirit of counsel and might, the spirit of knowledge and the fear of the LORD. (Isaiah 11:2)

---

25. In Ahaz's time, a coalition of Syrian and Israelite (Northern Kingdom) forces go up to dethrone the then 20-year-old king (Isa 7; 2 Kgs 16:1–18). This siege is dated 735–34 BCE. In 701 BCE, it was his son Hezekiah's turn to face the wrath of the Assyrian army during Sennacherib's reign (Isa 36–38; 2 Kgs 18:13–37).

Isaiah 11 is a prophetic oracle describing the rule of God's coming king. Verse 2 focuses on the three pairs of gifts from God's Spirit that will empower this person's rule. Verses 3–5 describe the impact of the leader's rule.

Long considered a Messianic text, if studied theologically, Isaiah 11:2 describes the kind of leader God wants for his people, by logical extension, the qualities that a godly leader must aspire for.[26] Elsewhere in the Scriptures, these same qualities are commanded for all leaders.

1. The Spirit of Wisdom and Understanding (also Isa 10:13; Jer 10:12; 51:15; Ezek 28:4)

The Hebrew terms *ḥokmah* and *binah* refer to the ability to see a situation in-depth and discern the right step to take. The godly leader is someone who knows the true condition and problems of the nation, who never stops listening to and learning from all stakeholders.

In Psalm 78:72, David is described as leading his people with "an upright heart" and a "skillful hand." The latter phrase is literally a "hand of understanding (*binah*)." In 1 Kings 3:9, Solomon's prayer for wisdom (*ḥokmah*) to discern good and evil to judge his people was commended by God. In contrast, "a ruler who lacks understanding (*binah*) is a cruel oppressor" (Prov 28:16).

2. The Spirit of Counsel and Might

The Hebrew word translated "counsel" here is *etsah*, which means "plan" "purpose" or "strategy." The word "might" is *geburah*, which is the forcefulness to implement plans, in contemporary language, "political will." The word *gibbor* "warrior" shares the same root. The English translations of Isaiah 36:5 in which the same two words appear, capture the proper sense: "*Do you think that mere words are strategy and power for war?*" (NRSV); "*strategy and military strength?*" (NIV).

The Spirit-led leader must have a concrete vision and strategy as well as a track record of leading successful organizations or movements, someone who acts decisively and effectively when crises arise.

3. The Spirit of Knowledge and Fear of the Lord

Da'at and *yir'eh YHWH* (the knowledge and fear of the Lord) anchor us in the basic truth that ultimately human leadership is always flawed. No human

---

26. Isaiah prophesied this 700 years before the coming of Christ. How would the original recipients have understood it? When Hezekiah or Josiah (both Davidic kings) read it, they may have asked: "Am I the one this is referring to?," and thus motivating them to strive to be this kind of leader. This is reading the text for its theology – what it says about God and what he wants for his people.

leader is perfect, thus we look for the one who will hold herself or himself accountable to a higher authority, someone who lives up to moral principles (2 Sam 23:3–4).

The leader who consistently upholds the qualities in Isaiah 11:2 will usher in a reign of justice and righteousness (11:3–5).

Ezekiel 34 – The Good and Bad Shepherds

In the Ancient Near East, "shepherd" is a metaphor for kings and even the deity. In Ezekiel 34:1–16, the prophet denounces Israel's kings for failing to discharge their duty to implement justice and righteousness. To reverse the situation, God himself will be the good shepherd to his people. Note how the duty of the king is delineated.

The Bad Shepherds' Failures (34:4) and What God Will Do (34:16)

    A   You have not strengthened the weak,
        B   you have not healed the sick, you have not bound up the injured,
            C   you have not brought back the strayed,
                D   you have not sought the lost.
                D' I [YHWH] will seek the lost,
            C' I will bring back the strayed,
        B' I will bind up the injured
    A' I will strengthen the weak.

This passage functions to evaluate any political agenda. National development goals may look good on paper, but the acid test is how a society treats its weakest and most vulnerable members. "How a society and its leaders treat those who struggle against disadvantages speaks volumes about that society's true values – not the one it professes to hold, but those revealed in policy and action."[27]

Ezekiel's Remedy for Structural Sin

God is concerned not only about godly rulers but also godly institutions. As mentioned earlier, sin is both personal and institutional. The remedy for personal sin is repentance and conversion; the remedy for structural or corporate

---

27. Katheryn Pfisterer Darr, "Ezekiel," in *The New Interpreter's Bible*, Vol. 6 (Nashville: Abingdon, 2001), 1, 467.

sin is structural and legal reform. There is a passage in the prophetic literature that outlines structural reforms – Ezekiel 40–48. It is the only law code outside of the Pentateuch, and the only one not attributed to Moses.

As a member of the Zadokite priestly line that served in Jerusalem, Ezekiel was a first-hand witness to the profligacy of the royal and priestly leaders. The Babylonian Exile became a space for Ezekiel to imagine a renewed Temple and a renewed nation where monarchic and priestly abuses would be addressed. Laying out his reform agenda in Ezekiel 40–48, the prophet –

- Limited the power of the king, whom he called *nasi* "prince" instead of *melekh* "king" (45:7–8, 13–15).
- Removed the Temple from the control and supervision of the palace (45:1–8).
- Allowed priests to own agricultural lands, thus giving them an independent means of income, unlike before when the priests were in the payroll of the king (45:1–8).
- Separated the capital city of Jerusalem from the royal domain. The city would represent the twelve tribes, and would be run by people from all the tribes, not just Judeans (45:1–8).
- Refocused sacrificial rituals on holiness and purgation (45:17; 46:4–5).
- Instituted land reform by redistributing the land for the tribes (47:14; cf. Num 33:54).

Structural and Cultural Reform

Maggay observed that a Christian population does not necessarily equate to a just society, more is needed. That "more" is institutional and cultural renewal. As early as 1965, Simbulan already observed that "[t]he absence of any far-reaching economic change has meant the continuation of old economic and social relations."[28] Fr. Vitaliano Gorospe, S. J., a Jesuit educator in moral formation, came to the same conclusion:

> A change in the attitudes and values of the individual demands structured social changes in society. An individual or society will not change unless it is exposed to new experiences, new problems, and new challenges . . . Philippine society must set up new social structures in order to make such a change possible.[29]

---

28. Simbulan, "A Study of the Socio-Economic Elite," xv.
29. Gorospe, "Christian Renewal of Filipino Values," 224.

The Philippines's experience in the last forty years is a good test case for the principle that without genuine moral and socio-cultural transformation, political change will not lead to lasting gains for the majority of the people. The People Power Revolution did not lead to lasting national transformation. For transformation to happen, both idealist and materialist transformation must take place. Traditional cultural values on leadership and authority must give way to biblical values. Change of worldview must be accompanied by structural, institutional, and legal reform.

Transformation of communities and nations is an intentional mindful action and requires "a long obedience." In her book *Transforming Society*, Maggay outlined the four approaches historically taken by the Christian church to social transformation.[30] The Church has to participate if we are to break the cycle of bad governance that has for so long entrapped the Philippines.

Third, the prophets teach us that divine power is paradoxically often manifested in a veiled form in weakness and suffering. It is a warning to the church that can be easily seduced by worldly power.

Reflecting on the Servant of the Lord poems in Isaiah 40–55, theologian Reinhold Niebuhr warns that the church can fall into the temptation of grasping for worldly power.

> The contradictions of human existence . . . prevent power from ever being good enough to belong to the Kingdom and . . . equally prevent pure love from being powerful enough to establish itself in the world.[31]

---

30. The first is by being a set-apart "city on the hill." As an alternative, exemplary, and *countercultural community, the church* witnesses to the gospel and the kingdom by being salt and light. The Anabaptists and Mennonites and Quakers exemplify this approach.

The second is by building a Christian cultural consensus within society, in effect, a Christendom. This is done through the promotion of Christian ideals and principles. Christian political parties in the West take this approach.

The third is the approach of liberation theology, directly confronting and restructuring existing power relations for the goal of the liberation of the oppressed, marginalized, impoverished, and powerless.

The fourth is the developmental model, being a *compassionate presence* in the world. Catholic orders, like the Daughters of Charity of Mother Teresa, as well as multinational Christian aid and development agencies work for the sustainable upliftment of the most needy and powerless members of society (Maggay, *Transforming Society*, 47–60). See also chapter 1 of Graham Joseph Hill, *Salt, Light, and a City, Second Edition: Conformation – Ecclesiology for the Global Missional Community, Vol. 2: Majority World Voices* (Eugene: Cascade Books, 2020).

31. Reinhold Niebuhr, "The Suffering Servant and the Son of Man," in *Beyond Tragedy: Essays on the Christian Interpretation of History* (New York: Charles Scribner, 1965), 178.

All power in human history is too partial to be good, even the power that the church wants to exercise. Human frailty, even that of the church, limits all exercise of power. The Servant of the Lord figure in Isaiah models for us believers that the way to restoration will involve weakness, powerlessness, and self-sacrifice, even vicarious suffering. This is the way by which the Lord Jesus won us our salvation, not through military and political power.[32]

Is the world changed through a display of power or through sacrificial love? What can we learn from the examples of Mahatma Gandhi, Martin Luther King, Nelson Mandela, Archbishop Oscar Romero? In the Philippine experience, we have witnessed the heroism of Jose Rizal and Andres Bonifacio, Ninoy Aquino, and countless others who fought for justice and freedom at the cost of their lives. The supreme example is our Lord Jesus Christ, the Suffering Servant. These people changed the world.

Here, the book of Daniel can make a significant contribution. In terms of genre, Daniel is not considered prophetic but apocalyptic. But its portrayal of believers' relationship to government is invaluable to the present discussion. What does it mean for God's people to be subordinate to foreign rulers who do not believe in God? What does faithfulness to God look like? The Book of Daniel presents two paradigms of rulers or government and two types of responses from believers.[33]

In Daniel 1–6, the context is a government that can still respond to God; when confronted, the ruler backs down and even acknowledges the God of Daniel. The immediate cause of the confrontations vary: food (Dan 1); worship (Dan 3); the king's hubris (Dan 4); prayer (Dan 6). In such a situation, what are believers to do? Daniel's response is to work within the system and confront when the authorities do wrong. This presupposes that the authorities still have a sense of virtue and responsibility.

But in Daniel 7–12, the ruler is completely belligerent towards God and his people; there is oppression and persecution. What are believers to do? Cooperate? No, resist. In the New Testament, Romans 13 finds its counterpoint

---

32. This is the problem of the religious right that seek to impose their brand of morality on others – pro-life, anti-LGBTQ, anti-liberals – using political power, not moral persuasion or moral example. "Culture war" is what they call it. But they are creating a lot of polarization against the church. The church can also be an unjust and oppressive institution. The church grasping for power or being co-opted by the state is very dangerous.

33. John Goldingay, *Daniel*, Word Biblical Commentary, Vol. 30 (Dallas: Thomas Nelson Publishers, 1989), 329–34.

in Revelation 13.[34] Armed struggle? Daniel and Revelation never advocate violence; instead, the message is: Persevere, be faithful to God even to the point of death. The church comes in weakness, powerlessness, not grasping for worldly power.

We have to interpret what scenario we are in now or will be in the future. Sympathetic or belligerent government? Can we still work within the system, or resist through civil disobedience? Evil will never surrender to good, and that is why we must be willing to struggle in this task of rescuing our nation. The socio-economic-political elite will never voluntarily surrender their power. A theology of the cross leads us to a Christ-honoring, self-sacrificing, and loving confrontation with all that is opposed to God's teachings. In the end, when we think that all is lost, just like with the Lord Jesus Christ, the Suffering Servant, and Daniel and his friends, the God of reversals overcomes the evil that we cannot.

> Human power structures are subject to arrogance and the delusion that they are beholden to none . . . concentrated power inevitably manifests its monstrous nature. Only eschatological transformation can break its propensity to violence and sacrilege.[35]

Deliverance will come in his time, not ours. That is divine action.

Lastly, divine power will usher in the kingdom of God because the kingdom is both a gift and a task. This is to guard against our tendency to look for a human messiah in our elected officials.

The kingdom is both a gift and a task.[36] The fullness of the kingdom will not come about as a result of human efforts. The consummation of the kingdom will come only as a gift when God decides it is time. Before that happens, we will be disillusioned, disappointed, and there will be a lot of setbacks. No individual is meant to be a messiah. Only Jesus is the Messiah.

But it doesn't mean that believers are to be passive. We have a task; our mission is to reflect who our God is and what kind of world he wants for humanity. Our ministries, flawed and imperfect they may be, are making a substantial impact on these generations.

---

34. "Let anyone who has an ear listen: If you are to be taken captive, into captivity you go; if you kill with the sword, with the sword you must be killed. Here is a call for the endurance and faith of the saints" (Rev 13:9–10).

35. Newsom, "Political Theology in the Book of Daniel: An Internal Debate," 567.

36. John Fuellenbach, *The Kingdom of God: The Message of Jesus Today* (NY: Orbis Books, 1995), 205.

Our task is to witness to this presence of the Kingdom, to make it felt by our concern for "justice, peace, and joy" where we live and work, and to challenge every human society to restructure itself according to the Kingdom's principles. We will never build a perfect society where peace and justice are fully established. Our task is to set up signs on the way to the Kingdom; signs which radiate the vision of Christ into a world that looks, at times, so hopeless and doomed. By so doing we are called to provide a vision for which we can live, work, and die.[37]

The Church as God's Partner

The prophet Isaiah teaches us that "as the king goes, so goes the nation." As a counterpoint, Jeremiah teaches us that a righteous ruler is not enough; a critical mass of followers is also needed. Josiah, the last good king of Judah, instituted widespread religious and political reforms in the land, beginning in 626 BC (2 Kgs 22:1–23:20; 2 Chr 34:1–7). But after his untimely death in 609 BC, the reform movement quickly collapsed. No one rose up to continue his reform. Within twenty years after Josiah's death, Jerusalem fell to the Babylonians.

We witnessed the rise of volunteerism during the 2022 election campaign. The energy must be carried forward, participation drawn from all sectors of Philippine society, not only during election season. Being a good citizen should be part of discipleship training in our churches. Our country's pledge of allegiance to the flag provides an excellent framework: *Maka-Diyos, makatao, maka-bansa, maka-kalikasan* (For God, for fellowman, for country, for the environment).

Experts have said that many of the issues today – political dynasties, graft and corruption in the government, P14 trillion (and growing weekly) national debt, economic inequality, lack of universal health care, inadequate safety nets for the marginalized, homelessness, indigenous people rights, environmental disasters – will take decades to address; some even say fifty years. One six-year term of the president and vice-president is not enough. Nation-building is a long and arduous process.

What kind of country do we want for our children? What kind of government do we want to lead us? What kind of church does our country need?

---

37. Fuellenbach, *The Kingdom of God*, 206.

Nobel Laureate Amartya Sen, an Indian economist and philosopher, advocates for an approach to national development that does not focus on income levels or gross national product, but on people's "'capabilities' or freedoms, that is, their 'abilities to do valuable acts or reach valuable states of being' to enable people 'to help themselves and also to influence the world.'" "'Poverty' is understood as deprivation in the capability to live a good life, and 'development' is understood as capability expansion."[38]

Sen's moral vision of human development amazingly ties in with what the Scriptures say. Each person made in the image of God has a God-given calling and God-given talents and gifts. My vision is for each Filipino to live out his God-given calling to make a valuable contribution to his family and the world, for it not to be short-circuited by poverty, injustice, and lack of opportunities. As the prophet Micah pictured it: "But they shall all sit under their own vines and under their own fig trees, and no one shall make them afraid; for the mouth of the LORD of hosts has spoken" (Mic 4:4).

The prophetic stance calls us to re-imagine the world, re-imagine the Philippines. It all starts with seeing what does not yet exist – seeing with God's eyes, in other words, the eyes of faith. Without imagination, we cannot create a new world. Re-imagining the church and telling new narratives will help us to break the impasse of current ideologies, even ecclesiastical.[39] Maggay challenges us:

> [I]f there is any institution, any community that is truly global as well as local, it is the church. . . . [The church] seems to be the only countervailing force to all the failed institutions. . . . [The church is] global and can stand in solidarity together. [The church is] also at the grassroots; the history of social movements shows that when the church is truly herself, change happens, and it happens at that level where the narratives change.[40]

God has no other plan. He invites us to take part in what he is accomplishing in our country and in the world. May we sit at the table of suffering of our fellow Filipinos and share with them our vision of a table of plenty for all.

---

38. "Sen's Capability Approach," *Internet Encyclopedia of Philosophy*, accessed 23 October 2022, https://iep.utm.edu/sen-cap/.

39. This is the way that Jesus went about teaching kingdom values through parables – "beyond visible realities of Roman law and restrictive Jewish law, [it was] out of tradition, specific, open-ended, an alternative society of the 'kingdom of God.'" Walter Brueggemann, *Hopeful Imagination: Prophetic Voices in Exile* as cited by Maggay, "Re-imagining Church and Mission."

40. Melba P. Maggay, "Re-imagining Church and Mission," accessed 10 April 2023, https://www.allnations.ac.uk/sites/default/files/pictures/Re-imagining-Church-and-Mission-Webinar-Jun-2-2020_ Maggay.pdf.

Bibliography

Acemoglu, Daron, and James Robinson. "Cacique Democracy." Accessed 30 September 2022. http://whynationsfail.com/blog/2012/12/26/cacique-democracy.html.

Albertz, Rainer. *A History of Israelite Religion in the Old Testament Period, Vol. 1: From the Beginnings to the End of the Monarchy.* Louisville: Westminster John Knox, 1992.

Amnesty International. "Five things to know about Martial Law in the Philippines." 25 April 2022. Accessed 21 October 2022. https://www.amnesty.org/en/latest/news/2022/04/five-things-to-know-about-martial-law-in-the-philippines/.

Arnold, Bill T., and John H. Choi. *A Guide to Biblical Hebrew Syntax.* 2nd ed. Cambridge: Cambridge University Press, 2018.

Buan, Lian. "Breakdown: P174B recovered from Marcos loot, P125B more to get." *Rappler*, 29 September 2021. Accessed 21 October 2022. https://www.rappler.com/newsbreak/iq/breakdown-billions-recovered-marcos-ill-gotten-wealth-by-pcgg-more-to-get/.

Cavanaugh, William T., and Peter Manley Scott. "Introduction to the Second Edition." In *The Wiley Blackwell Companion to Political Theology*, 2nd ed., edited by William T. Cavanaugh and Peter Manley Scott. Hoboken: John Wiley & Sons, 2019.

Chi, Cristina. "House flexes supermajority power to approve con-con resolution on final reading." *Philippine Star*. 6 March 2023. Accessed 23 March 2023. https://www.philstar.com/headlines/2023/03/06/2249732/house-flexes-supermajority-power-approve-con-con-resolution-final-reading?fbclid=IwAR0IB3UzQV3jbs-AAfA1m7jVawBaROD7woH4dlDVNBCTlbGKLbKHcmAndcU.

Darr, Katheryn Pfisterer. "Ezekiel." In *The New Interpreter's Bible,* Vol. 6. Nashville: Abingdon, 2001.

Davies, Nick. "The $10bn Question: What Happened to the Marcos Millions?" *The Guardian*, 7 May 2016. Accessed 21 October 2022. https://www.theguardian.com/world/2016/may/07/10bn-dollar-question-marcos-millions-nick-davies.

De Vera, Ben O. "PH ranked fourth globally in 'crony capitalism,'" *Philippine Daily Inquirer*, 31 March 2022. Accessed 15 April 2022. https://business.inquirer.net/344745/ph-ranked-fourth-globally-in-crony-capitalism.

Feinberg, John S., and Paul D. Feinberg. *Ethics for a Brave New World.* Wheaton: Crossway Books, 1993.

Ferrer, Miriam Coronel. "The Philippines: Governance Issues Come to the Fore." *Southeast Asian Affairs* (2000): 241–55.

Fuellenbach, John. *The Kingdom of God: The Message of Jesus Today.* New York: Orbis Books, 1995.

Goldingay, John. *Daniel*. Word Biblical Commentary 30. TX: Word Publishers, 1989.

Gorospe, Vitaliano R. "Christian Renewal of Filipino Values." *Philippine Studies* 14/2 (1966): 191–227.

Heschel, Abraham J. *The Prophets.* New York: Harper & Row, 1962.

Heydarian, Richard Javad. "The Return of the Marcos Dynasty." *Journal of Democracy* 33/3 (July 2022): 62–76.

Hill, Graham Joseph. *Salt, Light, and a City, Second Edition: Conformation – Ecclesiology for the Global Missional Community, Volume 2: Majority World Voices*. Eugene: Cascade Books, 2020.

Maggay, Melba P. "Faith in Politics." *Philippine Daily Inquirer*, 7 September 2021. Accessed 9 April 2023. https://opinion.inquirer.net/143880/faith-in-politics.

———. "Re-imagining Church and Mission." Accessed 10 April 2023 https://www.allnations.ac.uk/ sites/default/files/pictures/Re-imagining-Church-and-Mission-Webinar-Jun-2-2020_ Maggay.pdf.

———. *Transforming Society*. Eugene: Wipf and Stock Publishers, 2010.

Mays, James Luther. "Justice: Perspectives from the Prophetic Tradition." *Interpretation* 37/1 (1983): 5–17.

Newsom, Carol. "Political Theology in the Book of Daniel: An Internal Debate." *Review and Expositor* 109 (2012): 557–68.

Pope Francis. *Fratelli Tutti*, October 2020. Accessed 15 March 2022. https://www.vatican.va/content/ francesco/en/encyclicals/documents/papa-francesco_20201003_enciclica-fratelli-tutti.html.

Rolheiser, Ronald. *The Holy Longing: The Search for a Christian Spirituality*. New York: Doubleday, 1999.

Safire, William. "On Language; Crony Capitalism." *New York Times Magazine*, 1 February 1998. Accessed 21 October 2022. https://www.nytimes.com/1998/02/01/magazine/on-language-crony-capitalism.html.

"Sen's Capability Approach." *Internet Encyclopedia of Philosophy*. Accessed 23 October 2022. https://iep.utm.edu/sen-cap/.

Simbulan, Dante C. "A Study of the Socio-Economic Elite in Philippine Politics and Government, 1945–1963." PhD diss., Australian National University, 1965.

———. *The Modern Principalia: The Historical Evolution of the Philippine Ruling Oligarchy*. Quezon City: University of the Philippines Press, 2005.

Taber, George M. "The Night I Invented Crony Capitalism." *Knowledge at Wharton*, 3 November 2015. Accessed 21 October 2022. https://knowledge.wharton.upenn.edu/article/the-night-i-invented-crony-capitalism/.

"Unlawful killings, repression continue in PH under Marcos admin – Amnesty International." CNN Philippines, 28 March 2023. Accessed 3 April 2023. http://www.cnnphilippines.com/news/2023/3/28/amnesty-international-report-ph.html.

Waltke, Bruce. "Micah." In *The Minor Prophets: An Exegetical and Expository Commentary, Vol. 2: Obadiah, Jonah, Micah, Nahum, Habbakuk*, edited by Thomas E. McComiskey. Grand Rapids: Baker Books, 1993.

2

How Shall the Righteous Govern?

Contextualizing Jesus's Transformation Politics for Nation-Building and World Peace

David S. Lim

Introduction

"What are we in power for?" was the infamous quip signifying self-interest and corruption that has ailed the Republic of the Philippines, uttered by Jose Avelino, the first president of the post-World War II Senate (1946–1949).[1] Having been an active participant-observer in the political scenario of the Philippines since 1972 just before Martial Law was declared, allow me to share the perspectives that I used and the insights that I propose for a principled and enlightened engagement of Jesus-followers to resolve the challenge to good governance.

My political consciousness and theologizing was nurtured mainly by InterVarsity-Philippines in the early 1970s. I began articulating my advocacy for good governance for nation-building and world peace locally and globally[2] since 1978 when I taught "Church and Culture" at the Asian Theological

---

1. J. V. Abueva, "The Sociology of Graft and Corruption," *Philippine Sociological Review* 18, no. 3–4 (July–October 1970): 203. Abueva, an advocate for the working classes, made the quip as a rhetorical question in a party caucus, and it was used by his opponents to smear his reputation.

2. I've been privileged to publish mainly in international journals starting with "Responding to Philippine Realities Today" with Isabelo Magalit and Jun Vencer, *Transformation* 1.3 (July 1983): 6–10; "A Plea for an 'Ethics of the Cross,'" *Transformation* 3 (October–December 1986):

Seminary.³ I was blessed in journeying with a community of "radical evangelicals" in Asia (called Partnership in Mission-Asia, 1982), that helped organize the International Fellowship of Evangelical Mission Theologians (INFEMIT)⁴ in 1987.

I started to publish my political theology, which has been self-labeled "Transformation Theology," in three articles namely "The City in the Bible" (1989),⁵ "Church and State in the Philippines, 1900–1988" (1989),⁶ and "The Uniqueness of Christ for Justice and Peace" (1994),⁷ and two books entitled *Transforming Communities* (1992)⁸ and *Christian Patriotism* (1998).⁹

By 1996, I co-founded the National Coalition for Urban Transformation (NCUT) where I served as co-chairman with Fr. Ben Beltran, SVD and our Secretary General Corrie Acorda DeBoer, which also led to my co-founding of the *Ang Kapatiran* Party (Alliance for the Common Good) with Nandy Pacheco (known for his advocacy for "Gunless Society") and his friends in 2003, which almost got into a partnership with *Bangon Pilipinas*, the party of

---

1–5; and "The Living God in the Structures of Philippine Reality," *Transformation* 5 (April–June 1988): 1–7.

I was tackling local issues, too: "Towards a Christian Response to Communism," *Evangelical Thrust* 12 (November 1985): 12–14; "Why We Should Form an Evangelical Political Party," *Evangelical Thrust* 13 (August 1986): 12–13; and (September 1986), 14–15, 18–19; "A Biblical Theology of Christian Patriotism, Part 1," *Evangelical Thrust* 14 (September–December 1987): 4–7; "U.S. Military Bases: Out!," *Evangelical Thrust* 15 (July–August 1988): 18–19; "A Biblical Theology of Christian Patriotism, Part 2," *Evangelical Thrust* 15 (July–August 1988): 36–39; "Biblical Basis for National Sovereignty," *Isip-Isak* 3 no. 3 (December 1990): 4–5; and "Born to Debt? Reflections on the Debt Crisis," *Patmos* 7 no. 2 (1991): 16–20.

3. This course was renamed "Transformation Theology" in 1987, just before I became academic dean in 1988.

4. INFEMIT has been renamed "International Fellowship of Mission as Transformation." Its major works are compiled in Vinay Samuel and Chris Sugden, eds. *Mission as Transformation* (Oxford: Regnum, 1999). My close Filipino partner is ISACC's founder and president Melba Maggay who published her political theology in *Transforming Society* (Quezon City: ISACC, 1996).

5. Published in *Urban Ministry in Asia*, ed. Bong Rin Ro (Taichung: Asia Theological Association, 1989), 20–41.

6. Published in *Transformation* 6, no. 3 (July–September 1989): 27–32, which was a reflection on the first People Power Revolution (called EDSA 1, February 1986). Then I had another essay on EDSA 2 (January 2001) in "Consolidating Democracy: Role of Evangelicals in Deepening Democracy in the Philippines from 1986–1998," in *Evangelical Christianity and Democracy in Asia*, ed. David H. Lumsdaine (Oxford: Oxford University Press, 2009): 235–84.

7. Published in *The Uniqueness of Christ*, ed. Bruce Nicholls (Carlisle: Paternoster, and Grand Rapids: Baker, 1994), 214–30.

8. Published by OMF Literature (Mandaluyong City), out of print since 2001. I was labeled a Communist in one evangelical sector when this was first released.

9. Published by New Day Publishers (Quezon City), out of print since 2012.

Brother Eddie Villanueva who ran for the presidency in the national elections of 2004 and 2010.

Since 2002 I have also served as the president (now president emeritus) and professor of Asian School of Development and Crosscultural Studies (ASDECS), a faith-based graduate school that trains leaders for transformational development (or integral mission) in Southeast Asia and beyond. I remain optimistic that in spite of the real threats of global warming and economic inequality, humanity is still moving forward towards attaining world peace through the global vision summed up in the seventeen Sustainable Development Goals of the United Nations. The UN has Isaiah 2:4 inscribed in its headquarters: Nations "shall turn their swords into plowshares, and their spears into pruning hooks."

Yet since 2016, I have been alarmed that our progress towards world peace was being reversed by the rise of authoritarian populism in the Philippines and in many democracies worldwide. Populists have used social media to erode the trust of citizens towards one another and those in governance structures through disinformation by trolls, usually financed by ill-gotten wealth. I see that for the next two decades, we need to actively participate in mobilizing our generation to stop the backsliding to authoritarianism, so as to advance our advocacy for good governance in functional democracies that are truly of the people, by the people, and for the people.

We need to work for our country's fragile democracy's long-standing struggle against patronage politics embodied in elections and bad governance dominated by political dynasties that have joined forces and become more entrenched in their sociopolitical bailiwicks. The oligarchic syndicate of the winning candidates (led by the children of former presidents, Ferdinand Marcos Sr. and Rodrigo Duterte) in the May 2022 election was able to convince a large majority that the felt dysfunctions in our country had not been remedied by the Aquino wing (opponents of Marcos) after EDSA 1, the first People Power Revolution of 1986.[10] This trend was preceded by a huge tragedy when in 2016, Rodrigo Duterte, with a track record of impunity as a city mayor, was voted into power not only by the masses but also by many in the educated middle class and even the religious (including many evangelicals) sector.

In fact, the harsh reality of patronage politics has plagued the country since our Independence and First Republic in 1898, dominated by "goons, guns, and

---

10. Richard Javad Heydarian, "The Return of the Marcos Dynasty," *Journal of Democracy* 33, no. 3 (July 2022): 62–76.

gold" of kleptocratic governance of political dynasties. This is how one of our statesmen, the former Senate president, Jovito Salonga put it:

> The main problems of the Philippine society . . . are massive poverty, rampant corruption and uncontrolled criminality. They are interrelated. Our grinding poverty, the result of the concentration of too much wealth and power in the hands of a few – the so-called elite – leads to graft and corruption, a double standard of justice (one standard of justice for the poor and another standard of justice for the rich) and ever-rising criminality. Thefts, robberies, drug addiction, murders and assassinations are what we see and read in the media every day. There are the flaws in our cultural traits, such as *utang na loob*, *pakikisama*, the *kanya-kanya* syndrome and the lack of sense of community that tend to worsen the twin problems of corruption and criminality.[11]

Here I present the political theology that undergirded my activism through the years, which should give us hope to plan and act for the future. I will first share the theological basis of my political engagement, which is that of Jesus of Nazareth, and was contextualized by the New Testament (NT) writers. Then in the last chapter of this book, I will show what my colleagues and I have taught our constituencies in applying the "whole gospel" in the public square of the Philippines and the world (since up to today, even developed democracies still struggle with similar issues for sustaining good governance).

My Biblical Framework: Jesus's Political Theology

Affirming that the Bible is the final authority of faith and practice, I believe that the narratives in the Bible were written not just as history, but also as theology – which prescribe how the church should represent and present Jesus on earth. Scripture was revealed so we can be "thoroughly equipped for every good work" (2 Tim 3:16–17), as we follow the teachings and example of our Lord Jesus, the perfect human who is our incarnate God.

What is the political theology of Jesus of Nazareth? The gospels record that Jesus and his cousin John the Baptist were calling people to "repent for the kingdom of God is near." And after his resurrection, Jesus spent forty days teaching his disciples only one theme: the kingdom or government of God (Acts 1:3). He claimed to be the promised Messiah prophesied in the

---

11. Jovito Salonga, "A Letter to the Filipino Youth of Today," *The Task of Building a Better Nation* (Mandaluyong City: Kilosbayan, 2005), 18–19.

Old Testament (OT), as he used Isaiah 61:1–2 to declare that his mission was "to proclaim good news to the poor; to proclaim freedom for the prisoners, and recovery of sight for the blind, to set the oppressed free" (Luke 4:18–19).

When he affirmed, "these words are fulfilled in your hearing," he was referring to the fulfillment that was not the end of history but rather the start of the transformation of life in history. He came so that all can experience "the favorable year of the Lord" (Jubilee year)[12] or "abundant life" (John 10:10). He was actualizing the hope for "a new heaven and a new earth" on earth as depicted in Isaiah 65:17–25.

Yet from the beginning Jesus attracted opposition, especially from religious leaders. His townmates sought to kill him when they realized that his message of deliverance meant to include their enemies, not only to free their compatriots from Roman rule. "As his ministry gained traction, he began to run into opposition from defenders of the status quo who angrily schemed against him (Luke 6:11)."[13] What was Jesus's movement like, that led to his martyrdom as a political rebel against Caesar?

Jesus's Political Option: Transformation Politics/Ideology

What did Jesus do to establish God's kingdom in the Roman empire? Like all societies in human history, Judea as a Roman colony had a small ruling class while the rest were the ruled majority.

The political landscape in Judea was rich with diverse groups, each with their own beliefs and practices. Among them were the Herodians, Sadducees, Zealots, Pharisees, and Essenes. Why did Jesus choose to form his own movement?

The power establishment in Judea then were the Herodians and Sadducees. Jesus was clearly critical of Herod and his dynasty who were the appointed Jewish royal family to rule the Jews on behalf of the Roman empire. He called Herod a fox and did not obey his summons (Luke 13:32). Like most of his contemporaries, he rejected their subservience to Rome.

---

12. On the Jubilee fulfilled, see my "Jubilee Realized: The Integral Mission of Asian House Church Networks in Contexts of Religious Pluralism," in *Jubilee: God's Answer to Poverty?* eds. Hannah Swithinbank, et al. (Oxford: Regnum, 2020), 79–95.

13. Ted Grimsrud, "The New Testament as a Peace Book" (2013) at https://peacetheology.net/2013/12/05/the-new-testament-as-a-peace-book/. Accessed 20 June 2025. I have developed my argument here in conversation with Yoder and Wink, who are also discussed by Grimsrud at the website referenced here.

The Sadducees were the organic political elite, who constituted the Sanhedrin that managed the governance of their society and the Temple. These "elders of the people" were wealthy and influential with the priestly class. The priestly class held conservative and aristocratic views that focused on the literal interpretation of the Torah and rejected the oral traditions and resurrection beliefs of the Pharisees. Jesus's encounters with the Sadducees revolved around theological matters, such as the nature of marriage and the resurrection (Matt 22:23–33).

The masses had three ideological options. The first option was the Zealots who resisted Rome. They were a political and religious group driven by a passion for the liberation of Judea from Roman rule. They advocated for armed rebellion and were willing to use violence to achieve independence from Rome.

The second option was the Pharisees, a small (about six thousand) religious sect that believed that the kingdom will be brought into the world through faithful obedience to the Torah. They were zealous for religious purity and traditions that were added to the Torah that totaled 613 commandments, which they copied and taught. They represented the apolitical orthodoxy of Judaism that strongly influenced the people, since they strategically used the synagogues to teach during the Sabbaths. Jesus's interaction with the Pharisees was mainly adversarial; he rebuked them for using human tradition to nullify Scripture, and especially for outward piety while neglecting justice and mercy.[14]

The third faction were the Essenes, known for their ascetic and communal lifestyle. They practiced strict observance of the Torah, especially ritual purity. Though Jesus had no direct interaction with them, he may have been influenced by their emphasis on spiritual purity, recruiting a couple of John the Baptist's disciples to be his own, who chose to no longer withdraw from society. He also showed the inclusivity of his movement by adding a couple of Zealots to be his disciples.

Jesus disregarded the socio-political opportunism, conservatism, violence, legalism, and separatism of these five groups. Instead, he initiated a social movement that emphasized inner transformation of love (agape) – to "love God and love neighbors" (Matt 22:37–39) as the core ethic of God's kingdom (6:33), which valued social justice and mercy (23:23). He taught his followers to treat all neighbors fairly – to do to others what they want done to themselves (7:12).

He organized his followers into a new community of disciples who lived out the love ethic in their society. They were about five hundred by the time of his resurrection (1 Cor 15:6). Central to their understanding of God's kingdom

---

14. Matt 15:3–9; 22:18; 23:13, 23, 25–26, 29; and Luke 12:1.

was that it required new relationships: To love one another as Jesus loved them (John 13:34–45; 17:21–23), following the way of righteousness and justice (Matt 5–7, cf. Ps 89:14), beyond just loving neighbors as themselves.

In relation to the authorities, Jesus called for conversion from sins ("repent") to join this community of friends who love all humans (including their Roman oppressors, Matt 5:43–47). To join his messianic community, they were required to "carry the cross daily." Following him involved agreeing to share in his destiny as someone considered an enemy by both the Temple and the empire as well as being called "social radicals" in terms of righteousness and justice.[15]

As his disciples came to a fuller understanding of his messianic identity, Jesus made his way to Jerusalem for a decisive encounter. Greeted warmly by the crowds, he went on to the Temple to challenge the established leadership. By driving out the money changers, he heightened the conflict with those controlling the socio-political order. It was only afterward that his followers realized his mission was not a violent revolt but a distinct – and still political – form of resistance. When they asked about the obligation to pay taxes to Rome, a basic civic duty, he responded with two options: "Give to Caesar what belongs to Caesar and to God what belongs to God" (20:20–25), highlighting that loyalty to these two "lords" requires a choice between them.[16] He was hinting that the kingdom of Caesar is just a small circle (his image in a coin) within the big circle of God (the creator of all things).

At the end of his life, the charge that Jesus claimed kingship was crucial: he posed a political danger, which led to his execution by Rome. He died as a revolutionary figure, and his death served as a cautionary example. The official reason for his crucifixion was the title "king of the Jews," a claim the religious leaders rejected, insisting that Caesar was the only rightful king. This kind of fatal punishment was the fate of anyone who defied Roman authority.[17]

The conflict between Jesus and the authorities, along with their efforts to have him killed, revealed their true nature. By carrying out the execution of the Messiah, they demonstrated that their claimed positions as God's servants working for the good of humanity were deceptive. These supposed "servants

---

15. John Howard Yoder, *The Politics of Jesus,* 2nd ed. (Grand Rapids: Eerdmans, 1994), 22; and Ted Grimsrud, "Peaceable Politics and the Story of Jesus (Peace and the Bible #11)" (2013) at https://thinkingpacifism.net/2023/12/18/peaceable-politics-and-the-story-of-jesus-peace-and-the-bible-11/. Accessed 20 June 2025.

16. Grimsrud, "Peaceable Politics," 1.

17. Grimsrud, "Peaceable Politics," 1

of God" – comprising both religious and political leaders – were, in reality, openly his enemies. Yoder notes,

> Jesus demonstrated his ideology of freedom from the powers' domination system (cf. 1:52–53) by his commitment to the way of love even when they did acts of horrific injustice and violence against him. God's vindication of Jesus through his resurrection reveals that loyalty to the fallen powers contradicts loyalty to God.[18]

After the resurrection, the disciples continued to hope for the "son of David" who would bring in the kingdom with force: "We had hoped that he was the one who would redeem Israel" (Luke 24:21; Acts 1:6–8). They were still expecting a violent revolution to drive out the foreign empire. Yet he told them that in his life and teaching, including his rejection of the violent option in directly challenging the powers, God's kingdom was fully present in his self-sacrifice as the Messiah (cf. Mark 10:42–45).[19]

Jesus's crucifixion, which occurred from his clash with the established order, serves as the revelation of the characteristics of God's Kingdom. He showed love even to his adversaries, practiced a righteousness that exceeded that of the Pharisees, stood in solidarity with the marginalized, and forgave those responsible for his death. Thereby he revealed the fundamental principles of the new political reality he was sent to set up.[20] We label his ideology "Transformation Politics."

Yoder concludes thus: "Jesus was, in his divinely mandated (i.e., promised, anointed, messianic) prophethood, priesthood, and kingship, the bearer of a new possibility of human, social, and therefore political relationships. His baptism is the inauguration and his cross is the culmination of that new regime in which his disciples are called to share."[21]

NT's Political Theology: Contextualizing Jesus's Transformation Politics

The NT portrays the early Jesus-followers' political ideology in the empire as copying that of Jesus in Judea. This conviction focused on building communities with economies based fundamentally on mutual love and abolition of

---

18. Yoder, *Politics of Jesus*, 53; and Grimsrud, "The New Testament," 1.

19. Yoder, *Politics of Jesus*, 54.

20. Ted Grimsrud, *Arguing Peace: Collected Pacifist Writings, Volume Three: Biblical and Theological Essays* (Harrisburg: Peace Theology Books, 2014), 66.

21. Yoder, *Politics of Jesus*, 52.

all forms of violence. Jesus's cross served as the guiding model and principle that will achieve societal transformation, which is the tangible realization of God's kingdom on earth.

How did Jesus's "kingdom/government of love" through transformation politics among his Jewish contemporaries develop as his early followers spread across and into the Greco-Roman culture of the empire, applying to the governed masses and the governing elite?

For the Governed

For the masses (approximately 99 percent of the population in Judea and 98 percent in the empire), the early church followed Jesus by identifying with the poor, submitting to the empire, and building up themselves into a movement of change towards a regime of love. They were to identify with the poor, form communities of love, and serve society sacrificially.

Identification with the poor[22] = doing good works

As the apostles and the early church shared the good news of God's kingdom to the Gentiles in the empire, they proclaimed the sovereign supremacy of Jesus: "Jesus is Lord (Kyrios)," the title for Caesar. To declare "Jesus is Lord" was as much a political statement as a religious one. Jesus is consistently set against Caesar. Calling Jesus "Lord" meant accepting his authority to shape society differently than under Roman rule. This is why the early church attracted the empire's marginalized populations (1 Cor 1:26–29; 2 Cor 8:1–4; Rev 2:9), similar to the masses' embrace of Jesus when he entered Jerusalem.

They were just taking the position that Jesus took – as one of the governed:

> Jesus was not a Roman citizen. He was not protected by the normal guarantees of citizenship – that quiet sense of security which comes from knowing that you belong and the general climate of confidence which it inspires. If a Roman soldier pushed Jesus into a ditch, he could not appeal to Caesar [like Paul]; he would just be another Jew in the ditch . . . Unless one actually lives day by day without a sense of security, he [sic] cannot understand what worlds separated Jesus from Paul at this point.[23]

---

22. I use "the poor" in the biblical wider sense to include all who are marginalised or vulnerable, not simply those who are economically disadvantaged.

23. Howard Thurman, *Jesus and the Disinherited* (Nashville: Abingdon-Cokesbury Press, 1949), 33.

Jesus identified himself with the homeless, with "no place to lay his head on" (Luke 9:58). Just as he understood and had compassion on the masses ("helpless and harassed, lost like sheep without a shepherd," Matt 9:35–36), so should they (Acts 20:33–35; Jas 2:1–5; Gal 2:10). As a carpenter (Matt 13:55) living unnoticed in provincial Galilee, Jesus taught his disciples how to live in the way of righteousness (3:15; 22:37–39; 21:43), including to pay their taxes (22:17–21).

As Jesus practiced what he preached (Acts 10:38, cf. Luke 7:18–23), he trained and empowered his disciples to do the same across the rural villages of Galilee (Luke 9:1–6; 10:1–20) – to holistically minister among the poor. He also warned them that if they did not feed and clothe "the least of his brethren," they would be condemned eternally (Matt 25:31–46). The first of the three disciplines that he taught his disciples was almsgiving (6:1–4), so that their light will shine for God's glory to be seen (5:14–16).

Hence the leaders in his kingdom must prioritize the poor (Acts 20:33–35; Gal 2:10; Jas 2:1–5), and the "first" must serve as a slave of everyone (*doulos*, Mark 10:44, cf. 1 Cor 9:19–23). Slaves can find dignity and value in their status (1 Cor 7:21–24) and offer their labor as worship unto God (Col 3:22–24). The ethos and governance structure of God's kingdom are different from and opposite of Caesar's empire.

Formation of communities of love/reconciliation = doing koinonia

When the *euangelion* ("gospel" or "good news") crossed beyond Judea, "the kingdom has come" became "Jesus is Lord (*kyrios*)," even among the Jews (as in Acts 5:42; 8:35; 28:31).[24] To the Jews, it was the joyful announcement that God has finally acted to fulfill the promise of messianic salvation that they had long been hoping for (as in Acts 2:22–36; 3:13–25). It was the victorious proclamation that a new order of peace (*shalom*) has dawned on the world with the defeat of the evil forces through Jesus's resurrection (as in Acts 17:18), though its usage ran the risk of being misunderstood, since the term *euangelion* was similarly used in the imperial cult (cf. Acts 17:7).

This concept was developed fully in the Pauline Epistles. Drawing from his own background as a persecutor of Jesus' followers, Paul framed the work of Christ as the foundation of a new society composed of former enemies reconciled. For Paul, the core of the gospel lies in breaking down the wall of hostility that had long divided Jews and Gentiles. Just as Jesus emphasized the creation

---

24. On the absolute claim that "Jesus is Lord," see James D. G. Dunn, *Christology in the Making: A New Testament Inquiry into the Origins of Doctrine of the Incarnation*, 2nd ed. (Grand Rapids: Eerdmans, 1989).

of a counter-cultural community marked by Jubilee generosity in proclaiming God's kingdom, Paul likewise depicted the presence of God's Spirit dwelling within this reconciled community of once-hostile former adversaries.[25]

The gospel is not only about making individuals into a new creation (2 Cor 5:17), it is also about the creation of a new community (*ekklesia*, a political term for an assembly of Roman citizens).[26] Jesus's ministry of reconciliation centered primarily on the forming of kingdom communities that practiced mutual care (*koinonia*), where genuine *shalom* prevails. The gospel finds its most powerful expression precisely where former enemies are united together in a single fellowship, thereby breaking down and removing walls of enmity[27] as Jesus taught (Eph 3:1–12).

Jewish men in Jesus's time often recited a prayer thanking God that they were not Gentiles, slaves, or women. Yet in this new community, Paul boldly proclaimed that there was no longer Jew or Gentile, slave or free, male or female, for all were united as one in Christ (Gal 3:28). This signified that the deepest hostilities of their world were being overcome, as Jews embraced Gentiles as full brothers and sisters. It also meant the wealthy shared generously with the poor, and men treated women as true equals.[28] These new relationships in the *ekklesia* are showcases of the reality of God's rule on earth (Eph 4:1–16).

Paul built on Jesus's ideology to encompass his understanding that human societal systems – referred to as the "principalities and powers" – as both part of God's original good design and yet corrupted, thus frequently unable to fulfill their intended role of organizing society to promote human well-being. Paul recognized that Jesus engaged directly with these flawed structures of power. What set Jesus apart was his freedom from being enslaved by any of these forces. He lived independently of existing laws, traditions, institutions, values or ideologies. Even when faced with death at the hands of these powers, he chose to maintain his loyalty to God rather than submit to them.[29]

---

25. Grimsrud, *Arguing Peace*, 67.

26. The Roman *ekklesia* were political councils that ensured imperial policies were carried out, so Jesus's *ekklesia* should be the arm of God's government to enact heavenly decrees on earth. Thomas Sullivan, "History 101: Western Civilization 1: Ecclesia Origins, History and Importance." *Study.com* (2023), 1. https://study.com/academy/lesson/ecclesia-ancient-greece-history-facts.html.

27. Grimsrud, *Arguing Peace*, 68.

28. On Galatians 3:28, see Richard Longenecker, *New Testament Social Ethics Today* (Grand Rapids: Eerdmans, 1984).

29. Grimsrud, *Arguing Peace*, 68; and Walter Wink, *The Powers that Be: Theology for a New Millennium* (New York: Doubleday, 1998), 32.

Paul understood that Jesus's teachings on social conduct engage directly with tangible realities. Jesus exemplifies a social ethic grounded in freedom, bravery, and faith in the Creator of those powers, with the hope that they will ultimately be changed. His challenge to the powers demonstrates his claim about the dawn of God's kingdom – a political order where service takes the place of control. This kingdom becomes evident when servanthood overcomes domination, even if standing for this truth results in suffering and martyrdom.[30]

Deceit has been the primary tool used by the powers to control human life. They strive to trick people into believing they represent God's will for justice and peace in the world. Through this, they gain loyalty and trust, which strengthens their control. However, for those who truly understand the meaning of Jesus's life and teachings, this call for allegiance by the powers represents a deliberate attempt to replace God's rightful rule.[31]

The early church perceived the expansion of their house fellowships throughout the empire as the direct extension of the radical community that Jesus originally formed. These groups, known as *ekklesia* boldly declared that they were subverting the unquestioned dominance of worldly powers in society. They viewed the fellowships that met in their houses spreading throughout the Mediterranean region as being in direct continuity with the community that Jesus had set up. The presence of these small communities showed the world that the rule of the powers in society is being terminated.

Serve society with self-sacrifice = do diakonia

Rome was a relatively benign empire. Julius Caesar's successor Octavius had claimed the role of emperor. Though maintained by military force, the "peace of Rome" (*pax Romana*) provided an atmosphere of order and plenty. A good network of roads was maintained well for fast and relatively safe travel and communication. The Greek language with its developed philosophical vocabulary was widely used in the Mediterranean region, thus facilitating communication across various ethnic groups.[32]

In the margins of this empire, Jesus taught his disciples to pray "thy kingdom come" on earth where righteousness and justice will prevail. He expected that there would be a substantial victory by his *ekklesia* as they released people from the strongholds of evil (Matt 16:18–19). There would be setbacks along

---

30. Grimsrud, *Arguing Peace*, 69; and Wink, *The Powers*, 31–36.
31. Grimsrud, *Arguing Peace*, 69; and Wink, *The Powers*, 42–62 calls this deception "the myth of redemptive violence."
32. David Lim, "Evangelism in the Early Church," in *Dictionary of the Later New Testament and Its Development*, ed. Ralph Martin, et al. (Leicester: Inter-Varsity Press, 1997), 353–54.

the way, but they would be successful to share this good news to all nations before the end comes (24:3–14; 28:18–20). He assured them that "greater things you will do" after he leaves them (John 14:12). After all, he had already trained them and their disciples on how to transform wolf-dens into sheepfolds in Luke 10:3–17. The "little flock" will win through a non-violent "revolution of love" (12:32–36).

Paul followed Jesus who taught an ethic of engagement in the world, to proactively "seek the kingdom of God and his righteousness" (Matt 6:33). Paul envisioned the church as a fellowship of liberated individuals, each contributing their unique talents and skills to support one another – and ultimately to benefit all humanity. His concept of the *ekklesia* is the exact opposite of a temporary "aside" waiting for a chance to wield authority by force. Instead, like Jesus, he pictured the *ekklesia* as the present-day embodiment of God's kingdom, actively reshaping societal relationships. Within this community emerges a "new humanity" that demonstrates strength through servanthood rather than control, and that addresses disputes through forgiveness and reconciliation instead of violence.[33]

Jesus's triumph over the powers, achieved through his resurrection, is historically real. This victory was not an abstract cosmic event detached from history, nor simply the completion of a required ritual sacrifice. Rather, Jesus has overcome these powers by living a life liberated from their control, remaining steadfast in unwavering love even unto death, and through God's affirmation of this self sacrifice as the true expression of his sovereignty.[34]

Jesus's triumph thus serves as a paradigm for the church, shaping both its communal existence and its testimony against the powers. Through his life amidst complex human reality, God's reign is made manifest. When the *ekklesia* follows his transformation politics, it becomes a living demonstration of God's ongoing work of changing the kingdoms of this world into his kingdom (Rev 11:15).[35] They are expected to live transformed lives, and exhibit self-giving love that transcends ethnicity, social class, and gender (Gal 3:28), as shown in their inclusive agape feasts (cf. 1 Cor 11:17–34; Jude 12).

Paul's understanding on how Jesus's teachings apply to the political conduct of his followers are evident in his well-known remarks in Romans 13. He shared the worldview of the earliest Jesus-followers who clearly recognized that the state is fundamentally one of the fallen powers. The state was seen as

---

33. Grimsrud, *Arguing Peace*, 69.
34. Wink, *The Powers*, 128–30.
35. Grimsrud, *Arguing Peace*, 69–70.

operating under satanic control, as illustrated in Satan tempting Jesus with the offer of the political authority over the world to him.[36]

In Romans 12, Paul addresses the practical ethical behavior within the *ekklesia*, with the opening word "but" serving as a clear call to resist conformity. He summons the believers for "reasonable worship," which entails rejecting the corrupt ways of the empire and being transformed to faithfully discern and obey God's perfect will. He then expands on the alternative lifestyle exemplified by Jesus, encouraging his followers to live differently, and closes this chapter with an appeal to abstain from retaliation against adversaries. Following this, in Romans 13:8–10, he underscores – quoting Jesus – that the essence of the law is fulfilled through loving one's neighbor.[37]

In between these calls to non-retaliation, Paul elaborates his ideas on how the Roman Christians ought to relate to governmental authority. He could not have thought in 13:1–7 to call for subservience to the empire. He calls not for "obedience" in 13:1, but only for "subordination." This ordering reflects both the sense that the powers have delegated authority from God (thus free to obey or disobey God) and the sense that nonetheless, God uses the powers even in their rebellion to serve his purposes.[38]

In Romans 13:1–7, Paul employs terminology that suggests a certain type of order, but he does not literally instruct believers to "obey the state" unconditionally. He does not suggest that Christians must comply with state demands that contradict Jesus's teachings – such as non-retaliation and love for one's neighbor. He sees the *ekklesia* in Rome as occupying a critical role, tasked with bearing witness to Jesus's radical political vision at the very center of the Empire. This testimony involves acknowledging the existence and influence of imperfect governmental authority. Genuine Christian submission to such authorities includes recognizing the state's role in maintaining order – promoting social welfare and cohesion – while simultaneously rejecting any unconditional allegiance to these earthly powers when they do the opposite.[39]

Romans 12–13 reaffirms rather than conflicts with Jesus's teaching on self-giving love found in Matthew 5–7. Both texts urge his followers to embody love without retaliation and to refuse any desire for revenge. Furthermore, they are challenged to honor God's ordering of authority while simultaneously reject-

---

36. Grimsrud, *Arguing Peace*, 70, and Wink, *The Powers*, 88–93 on the "Christus Victor" ("Christ is Victor") motif.

37. Grimsrud, *Arguing Peace*, 70; and Wink, *The Powers*, 94–97.

38. Wink, *The Powers*, 88–89.

39. Grimsrud, *Arguing Peace*, 70; and Wink, *The Powers*, 90–93.

ing the use of violence to retaliate when unjustly punished.[40] From the start in Jerusalem, the earliest believers refused to let the authorities stop them from bearing witness to their Lord. They said to the Sanhedrin, "Whether it is right in the sight of God to listen to you rather than to God, you must judge, for we cannot but speak of what we have seen and heard" (Acts 4:19–20). Also, "We must obey God rather than human beings" (5:29).

Thus the early Christians willingly committed themselves to a specific code of behaviors that distinguished them from the broader culture around them. These unique behaviors were not motivated by mere eccentricity, but were deeply rooted in the compassionate values that defined their social morality. These qualities consciously positioned themselves in opposition to the prevailing norms of the empire, thereby establishing a new awareness and framework for political engagement[41] that may cost their lives – and many did lose theirs.

For the Elite/Leaders

How about those who belonged to the elite, privileged with wealth and power in the early church? Among the Jews there were elite converts who were Sanhedrin members, priests, chiefs of synagogues, tax collectors, and teachers (Pharisees). And among the Gentiles there were centurions, city officials, prominent women, and praetorian guards.

How were they expected to lead and govern? Were these righteous elite able to implement Jesus's revolution of love for societal transformation? In his time, Jesus did not ask publicans and centurions to resign. Neither did he rebuke those who aspired to be among his ruling elite; he only taught them how to exercise their governance of love when they gain power (Mark 10:35–45). They were challenged to do three main tasks: Build peace with justice, govern with self-giving love (mercy), and empower the poor.

Building peace with justice

The main task for those who govern is to transform the Babylons of this world into the heavenly city called New Jerusalem[42] on earth. They are called to use their power, skills, and resources to govern by building peace (*shalom*) with social justice for the common good, rewarding the good and punishing evil

---

40. Grimsrud, *Arguing Peace*, 71; and Wink, *The Powers*, 162–65.

41. Grimsrud, Arguing Peace, 63; and Wink, *The Powers*, 175–79, which shows historically miracles have happened indeed (192–98).

42. I started using this metaphor in my lectures since 1988 when I published "The City in the Bible," *Evangelical Review of Theology* 12, no. 2 (April 1988): 138–56.

(Rom 13:3-4). They should uphold the truth (Jesus's commandments, in Matt 28:19-20; John 3:5; 8:13-20, 32; 18:36-37; 1 Tim 2:3-4), and with strict rule of law (with "rod of iron," in Rev 2:27; 12:5; 19:15). The prayer and goal is for all to live quiet lives in peace (1 Tim 2:1-2).

The gospels highlighted how Jesus formed a group of twelve who were discipled to live righteously and propagate this lifestyle from village to village (Luke 9:1-6; 10:1-17). Their first converts (called "persons of peace") could transform their villages into model communities (10:5-17) that demonstrated (as salt and light, Matt 5:13-16) what God's kingdom looks like. Paul saw the Jesus movement as one where Jubilee was being modeled and promoted, following the Messiah's example (2 Cor 8:9), for building egalitarian communities (8:11-15).

As the early church grew and organized kingdom communities across the cities and villages of the empire, they were raising servant-leaders from among their converts in the ruling class as well as from among their internal coordinators called elders and deacons, especially bishops as chief elders and prophets and teachers as local leaders (Acts 13:1), as well as apostles and evangelists as itinerant leaders in the Gentile-majority house-church networks (Eph 4:11-13). These leaders were expected not to use honorific titles and official entitlements in true humility, since Jesus taught this publicly (Matt 23:1-12). He treated his disciples as siblings and friends (John 10:15; 15:15) and commanded them to love and serve one another (13:1-17, 34-35), not comparing with what others did (21:20-22).

Governing with self-giving love

Jesus taught that governance in God's kingdom must be by the way of the cross – with self-sacrificing love, not domination. Paul affirmed that Jesus has been "equal with God" (Phil 2:5) yet "emptied himself of such position and power to be incarnated as a slave (*doulos*, 2:6-8). Jesus taught that only those willing to take up their cross can follow him: God's kind of power, the power that ultimately rules God's universe, underwrites a discipleship and for leaders a governance of compassion and self-giving love.[43] Most dramatic was when two of his disciples asked to be his deputies in his realm. He taught them that the

---

43. Wink, *The Powers*, 82-93. "To follow Jesus does not mean renouncing effectiveness. It does not mean sacrificing concern for liberation within the social process in favor of delayed gratification in heaven, or abandoning efficacy in favor of purity. It means that in Jesus we have a clue to which kinds of causation, which kinds of community-building, which kinds of conflict management, go with the grain of the cosmos, of which we know, as Caesar does not, that Jesus is both the Word (the inner logic of things) and the Lord ('sitting at the right hand')." Yoder, *Politics of Jesus*, 246.

one who will be first must serve all the others (Mark 10:42–45), in an inverse pyramid as the "slave (*doulos*) of all," and even unto death self-sacrificially (v. 45). And he demonstrated it by washing the feet (like a slave) of his disciples, including Judas his betrayer.

The NT closes in Revelation 5 by depicting the Lamb – slain yet risen – as the only one worthy to break the seals on the scroll. Rather than wielding the sword of political power, it is the cross – along with the life that preceded it and its ultimate vindication through resurrection – that unveils the true purpose of history. Jesus-followers are summoned to trail the Lamb in all his ways, overcoming challenges not through domination but by embracing a self-sacrificing love that shapes their political witness.[44]

Thus Revelation echoes Jesus's optimistic hope that the small loving communities will turn kingdoms upside down: The "kings of the earth" will be transformed from former enemies of God to devoted worshipers who lead their nations into the glorious New Jerusalem (Rev 21:24–27). The *ekklesia* will triumph in history not by superior military firepower but through its loving obedience to the Servant-king (Matt 16:18–19; 24:14), joining the Lamb in his distinctive way of exercising power – as humble suffering servants (Mark 10:45).[45] All their leaders are expected to follow Jesus's model of accepting his fate as a non-conformist leader executed by the powers with the sign "King of the Jews" on his cross.

Struggling for and with the poor

The NT also teaches that just like its Lord, the church must identify with and live among the marginalized, the poor, the weak, the lonely, the refugee, and any others within society who suffer exclusion or injustice.[46] The righteous (even among the elite) should be willing to disobey and suffer for righteousness and justice (Acts 14:22; Phil 1:27; 2 Tim 3:12, compare Acts 5:29). They should not be corrupted by the love of mammon (Matt 6:24) in the world order that thrives on greed or materialism (1 John 2:15–17; see also: Jas 4:4; Rev 18–19), but rather be content (Phil 4:6–10). Even slaves should not aspire to set themselves free (Col 3:22–24), but if opportunity arises they should avail of it (1 Cor 7:21–24). Implied is the expectation that elite slave owners

---

44. Grimsrud, *Arguing Peace*, 71.

45. Grimsrud, *Arguing Peace*, 71; and Wink, *The Powers*, 98–111.

46. Moltmann, *The Church in the Power of the Spirit*, 97 avers that identification with the poor is a consequence of our identification with the crucified Jesus.

should free their slaves (Phlm), and freemen could accept opportunities for vocational advancement.[47]

As they rule with justice for the oppressed, the righteous elite could provide protection from persecution for the Jesus movement, similar to what Gamaliel and Gallio did (Acts 5:34–42; 18:12–17). Besides being accused of being traitors (refusing to confess "Caesar is *kyrios*"), the early believers were also accused of being atheists (non-worship of the gods), anti-social (attending secret meetings), and depraved (rumored to have practiced sexual immorality and cannibalism). Until Domitian (died AD 96), the persecutions were sporadic and largely in limited regions, mostly instigated by the Jews.[48] Nonetheless though these periodic "trials" seemed to be setbacks, they helped to keep the church pure, and its members' commitment level high.

Above all, the righteous elite should also expect marginalization and persecution. A prophetic church, which like its *kyrios* seeks to live in the world, incarnating itself within institutions and cultures will often encounter situations where believers (especially their leaders) will be required to follow Jesus's example of laying down his rights, power, and position to identify with the masses and the oppressed; to fearlessly and unashamedly bear witness to him and express as best as possible the social justice of God; and be willing to suffer and die for him.

Evangelicals Eschatologically Divided

For those theologically educated on evangelical eschatology, the theological framework of Transformation Politics depicted above is labeled "historic premillennialism,"[49] following the works of George Eldon Ladd, Christopher Wright, and N. T. Wright.[50] It holds that the "not yet" future eternal kingdom of God has been inaugurated "already" on earth in the life and ministry of Jesus of Nazareth. This was promoted at the Asian Theological Seminary since the 1970s, the Alliance Graduate School since the 1980s, followed by most evangelical graduate seminaries in the 2000s.

---

47. No one was asked to yield or resign from their elite roles (cf. 1 Cor 7:17, 20, 24), though those who were chosen to be in Jesus's elite (including Matthew, a tax collector) divested themselves of their possessions. What a way to recruit generals for one's "peace corps."

48. Acts 4:1–31; 5:17–41; 14:2; 17:5–9; 21:27–26:32; Jas 5:10–11; 1 Pet 4:12–19; Rev 2:9, etc.

49. Craig L. Blomberg and Sung Wook Chung, eds., *A Case for Historic Premillennialism: An Alternative to Left Behind Eschatology* (Grand Rapids: Baker Academic, 2009).

50. George Eldon Ladd, *The Presence of the Future* (Grand Rapids: Eerdmans, 1974); Christopher J. H. Wright, *Living as the People of God* (Downers Grove: InterVarsity Press, 1983); and N. T. Wright, *Jesus and the Victory of God* (London: SPCK, 1996).

However, their impact to influence their alumni in their constituent churches seems to be minimal, due to the dominance of two other eschatological paradigms. But they have gained close allies with the Roman Catholic and Ecumenical Protestant theologians and leaders who are mainly amillenarian and adherents of the "Theology of Struggle," which is the Filipino version of Liberation Theology.

The greatest challenge has been the conservative stance towards political engagement, nurtured by the pessimistic eschatological outlook of the Dispensationalist Theology. While Dispensationalism can have valid perspectives, it has limited its political action with its "postponed kingdom" framework, particularly that the church's mission in today's dispensation of grace is mainly if not exclusively soul-winning and church-planting. They emerge with prayer rallies and pastoral statements only when the traditional moral pro-life issues (against abortion, divorce, and gay rights) are contested in public. This continues to be the dominant reason why mainstream evangelicalism is among the laggards in political awareness and enlightened activism among the religious groups in the Philippines today.

The other evangelical group that has emerged in our political scene upholds Dominion Theology, which gained prominence when Eddie Villanueva[51] ran for president in 2004. Mainly postmillenarian, they believe that we should be politically engaged and aspire to be in governance positions to legislate and implement Old Testament laws, especially on pro-life issues, yet endorsing death penalty for heinous crimes, like those from the engaged Dispensationalist camp. Those among them who won electorally or got appointed to public posts have proven to be vulnerable to the compromises of patronage politics, often becoming enablers and allies of corrupt politicians, hardly able to serve in the opposition or at least go against the administration on issues of dishonest gains, disinformation, and human rights. We long for them to overcome these weaknesses and be partners in forming the righteous elite alongside the Transformation Theology camp.

Conclusion

Here then is the essence of the kingdom of God from the view of Transformation Theology: We seek to infiltrate, engage, and transform the whole Babylonic world into the New Jerusalemic society of peace where Jesus's love

---

51. See critique of Dominionism in H. Wayne House and Thomas Ice, *Dominion Theology: Blessing or Curse? An Analysis of Christian Reconstructionism* (Portland: Multnomah Press, 1988).

ethic prevails in righteousness and justice. Our mission is to demonstrate and proclaim this persuasively (not manipulatively nor coercively) to all peoples, including those with other political theologies and ideologies, with patient understanding, dialogue, and witness.

The gospel of God's kingdom invites humanity to be reconciled with God who calls everyone to join Jesus's community that rejects racism, sexism, and ethnocentrism. With this transformation paradigm of political engagement, we have tried to recruit and develop Jesus-like leaders (who will constitute the "righteous elite") to lead the church and the world in following Jesus's way of righteousness by building societies of justice and peace.

How have we applied this biblical ideology for nation-building and world peace? Please read my other chapter (ch. 17) in this volume on how my friends and I have been indigenizing (or localizing) the political theology of Jesus and the early church (in Roman imperial context) into doing "Transformation Politics" in the context of a multi-party democracy dominated by corrupt political dynasties in the Philippines and beyond.

"Our Father in heaven, may your name be glorified, your kingdom come, your will be done, on earth as it is in heaven. In the name of King Jesus. Amen."

Bibliography

Abueva, J. V. "The Sociology of Graft and Corruption." *Philippine Sociological Review* 18, no. 3–4 (July–October 1970): 203–8.

Blomberg, Craig L., and Sung Wook Chung, eds. *A Case for Historic Premillennialism: An Alternative to Left Behind Eschatology.* Grand Rapids: Baker Academic, 2009.

Bonhoeffer, Dietrich. *Letters and Papers from Prison.* London: Macmillan Press, 1967.

Coleman, Robert. *The Master Plan of Evangelism.* Old Tappan: Revell, 1964.

Grimsrud, Ted. "The New Testament as a Peace Book." *Peace Theology.* 12 March 2013. Accessed 20 June 2025. https://peacetheology.net/2013/12/05/the-new-testament-as-a-peace-book/.

Heydarian, Richard Javad. "The Return of the Marcos Dynasty." *Journal of Democracy* 33, no. 3 (July 2022): 62–76.

House, H. Wayne, and Thomas Ice. *Dominion Theology: Blessing or Curse? An Analysis of Christian Reconstructionism.* Portland: Multnomah Press, 1988.

Ladd, George Eldon. *The Presence of the Future.* Grand Rapids: Eerdmans, 1974.

Levinson, Bernard M. "Neglected Contributions to the Study of Kingship in the Pentateuch and the Deuteronomistic History." In *The Formation of Biblical Texts: Chronicling the Legacy of Gary N. Knoppers,* edited by Deirdre N. Fulton, et al., 33–40. Tübingen: Mohr Siebeck, 2024.

Lim, David S. "A Biblical Theology of Christian Patriotism, Part 1," *Evangelical Thrust* 14 (September–December 1987): 4–7.

———. "A Biblical Theology of Christian Patriotism, Part 2," *Evangelical Thrust* 15 (July–August 1988): 36–39.

———. "A Plea for an 'Ethics of the Cross,'" *Transformation* 3 (October–December 1986): 1–5.

———. "Biblical Basis for National Sovereignty," *Isip-Isak* 3 no. 3 (December 1990): 4–5.

———. "Born to Debt? Reflections on the Debt Crisis," *Patmos* 7.2 (1991): 16–20.

———. *Christian Patriotism*. Quezon City: New Day Publishers, 1998.

———. "Church and State in the Philippines, 1900–1988," *Transformation* 6, no. 3 (July–September 1989): 27–32.

———. "Consolidating Democracy: Role of Evangelicals in Deepening Democracy in the Philippines from 1986–1998." In *Evangelical Christianity and Democracy in Asia*, edited by David H. Lumsdaine, 235–84. Oxford: Oxford University Press, 2009.

———. "Evangelism in the Early Church," *Dictionary of the Later New Testament and Its Development*, edited by Ralph Martin, et al., 353–59. Leicester: Inter-Varsity Press, 1997.

———. "Jubilee Realized: The Integral Mission of Asian House Church Networks in Contexts of Religious Pluralism." In *Jubilee: God's Answer to Poverty?*, edited by Hannah Swithinbank, et al., 79–95. Oxford: Regnum, 2020.

———. "Norway: the Best Model of a Transformed Nation Today." *Missions and Vocations Journal* 2, no. 1 (2016): 12–14.

———. "Towards a Christian Response to Communism," *Evangelical Thrust* 12 (November 1985): 12–14.

———. "Transformational Education: Academic Mission to Marginalized Peoples." *Christian Higher Education & Globalization in Asia/Oceania: Realities & Challenges*, edited by J. Dinakarlal. Sioux City: IAPCHE, 2010.

———. "The City in the Bible." In *Urban Ministry in Asia*, edited by Bong Rin Ro, 20–41. Taichung: Asia Theological Association, 1989. Also in *Evangelical Review of Theology* 12, no. 2 (April, 1988): 138–56.

———. "The Doctrine of Creation and Some Implications for Modern Economics," *Transformation* 7, no. 2 (April–June 1990): 28–32; and 7 no. 3 (July–September): 21–23.

———. "The Living God in the Structures of Philippine Reality," *Transformation* 5 (April–June 1988): 1–7.

———. "The Uniqueness of Christ for Justice and Peace." In *The Uniqueness of Christ*, edited by Bruce Nicholls, 214–30. Carlisle: Paternoster, 1995.

———. *Transforming Communities*. Mandaluyong City: OMF Literature, 1992.

———. "U.S. Military Bases: Out!," *Evangelical Thrust* 15 (July–August 1988): 18–19.

———. "Why We Should Form an Evangelical Political Party," *Evangelical Thrust* 13 (August 1986): 12–13; and 14 (September 1986): 14–15, 18–19.

———, with Isabelo Magalit and Jun Vencer, "Responding to Philippine Realities Today," *Transformation* 1, no. 3 (July 1983): 6–10.

Longenecker, Richard N. *New Testament Social Ethics Today*. Grand Rapids: Eerdmans, 1984.

Maggay, Melba. *Transforming Society*. Quezon City: ISACC, 1996.

Moltmann, Jürgen. *The Church in the Power of the Spirit*. Minneapolis: Fortress Press, 1993.

Roldan, Andrea. "Isabelo Magalit (1970): I Have a Dream" (accessed 15 August 2023), https://medium.com/@aroldan_5444/isabelo-magalit-1970-i-have-a-dream-1020435debfe.

Salonga, Jovito R. "A Letter to the Filipino Youth of Today." In *The Task of Building a Better Nation*. Mandaluyong City: Kilosbayan, 2005.

Samuel, Vinay, and Chris Sugden, eds. *Mission as Transformation*. Oxford: Regnum, 1999.

Sugden, Christopher. *Fair Trade as Christian Mission*. Cambridge: Grove Books, 1999.

Sullivan, Thomas. "History 101: Western Civilization 1: Ecclesia Origins, History and Importance." *Study.com*, 2023.

Thurman, Howard. *Jesus and the Disinherited*. Nashville: Abingdon-Cokesbury Press, 1949.

Wink, Walter. *The Powers that Be: Theology for a New Millennium*. New York: Doubleday, 1998.

Wright, Christopher J. H. *Living as the People of God*. Downers Grove: InterVarsity Press, 1983.

Wright, N. T. *Jesus and the Victory of God*. London: SPCK, 1996.

Yoder, John. *The Politics of Jesus*, 2nd ed. Grand Rapids: Eerdmans, 1994.

3

State Power and the Church in Society

Melba P. Maggay

Introduction

These days, we are hearing anew powerful theological narratives about the so-called "separation of church and state." This theological export dates back from the conflict between fundamentalists and modernists that erupted in the US in the early decades of the 20th century.

As a recipient of American missions that came alongside colonization, our churches have been shaped by the narrative that we are to be subject to ruling authorities, even when they are oppressive. Romans 13 is usually bandied about as a flag under which political submission is enjoined when we are faced with tyrannical regimes.

In this chapter we clarify the meaning of Romans 13 based on its cultural and textual context.

We shall spell out some of its implications in our understanding of contemporary church and state relations.

For those already engaged in the political struggles of our time, we offer some hard-won insights from experience on what it means to enter the political space.

Subjection and Obedience in Romans 13:1–7

This text accounts for much of our reluctance to speak, to step straight into the political arena and fight the dragons there. Subjection to governing authorities has been largely understood as a call to lie supine and bear with the abuses and political conflicts raging in the world.

But read within its larger context, Romans 13:1–7 is an elaboration, an application of the principle of non-retaliation stated earlier.[1]

Early on, we are told that the right to avenge oneself is not part of the conquest of evil. We are to overcome evil with good. This social ethic speaks personally to those who have been at the receiving end of wrongdoing, and to those of us who are tempted to bear the sword in working for justice. We are to leave to God the retribution of evil. This principle is then applied in the next chapter to the Christian's relationship to political authority.

In a general way, our relationship to the state is defined as submission:

> Let every person be subject to the governing authorities. For there is no authority except from God, and those that exist have been instituted by God. Therefore whoever resists the authorities resists what God has appointed, and those who resist will incur judgment. (Rom 13:1, 2)

The submission enjoined is part of the general command to respect authority: "respect to whom respect is due, honor to whom honor is due."

Scholars say that this community of Roman Christians were likely to be more conscious of the power and abuses of imperial authorities. Whether they were mostly Jewish Christians as the Tubingen School surmised, or predominantly Gentile Christians, as C. K. Barrett and other scholars supposed,[2] this mix of Jews and Gentiles in the churches had memories of the disturbances that caused the expulsion of Jews from Rome following the riots of the late AD 40s.

Paul probably had this in mind when he wrote this letter about AD 57, almost a decade after Emperor Claudius, who reigned from AD 41–54, had "commanded all the Jews to leave Rome."[3] According to the account of the Roman historian Suetonius, the disturbances were apparently "at the instigation of Chrestus," an agitation possibly brought about by Jewish Christian teachers like Aquila and Priscilla.[4] The couple were forced to leave Rome in AD 49, and met Paul two years later at Corinth. It is possible that there was internal strife

---

1. Rom 12:14–21.

2. Joseph A. Fitzmyer, S. J., "The Letter to the Romans," in *The Jerome Biblical Commentary*, Vol. 2, eds. Raymond E. Brown, Joseph A. Fitzmyer, Roland E. Murphy (Englewood Cliffs: Prentice-Hall, Inc, 1968), 292.

3. Acts 18:2.

4. Suetonius, *Claudii Vita*, 25, as cited by Edwin Yamauchi, *The World of the First Christians* (Tring: Lion Publishing, 1981), 127.

between Jew and Gentile Christians, a tension that the authorities settled by expelling them.

By AD 60, however, a sizable group of Christians had once again grown in Rome. Under the shadow of empire, the Christians were under pressure to buckle down to having to offer sacrifices and do cultic practices viewed as signs of allegiance to the Emperor. Paul in this letter may have been addressing those who were conscious that they are citizens of another world and are free people in Christ.[5] For this reason they may have been inclined to question their relation to civil authorities, especially since they are in the hands of pagans.

This distrust of the powers may have been especially true of the Jewish Christians in Rome, who most likely were converts from Palestine, Syria, and Rome much earlier.[6] Many in Palestine hated the Roman occupation. Time and again revolts would erupt, from the Maccabees against the Seleucid rulers to the resistance movement of nationalists called the Zealots in the time of Jesus. This patriotic undercurrent finally broke out in the great war of the Jews against Rome in AD 66.[7]

Paul wrote this letter when Nero was reigning,[8] but official persecution had yet to happen. With the peace and order legacy of Augustus Caesar's Pax Romana as backdrop, he sets forth the reason why Christians should submit:

> For rulers are not a terror to good conduct, but to bad. Would you have no fear of the one who is in authority? Then do what is good, and you will receive his approval, for he is God's servant for your good. But if you do wrong, be afraid, for he does not bear the sword in vain. For he is the servant of God, an avenger who carries out God's wrath on the wrongdoer.

God has delegated to rulers the task of promoting good and preventing evil. Twice, Paul calls them "God's servants." They are in fact "ministers," the same Greek word – *diakonos* – used for church leaders *at iba pang alagad ng Diyos*.

Political institutions are there to establish order. Rulers bear the sword so as to carry out God's wrath on the wrongdoer. But note that the primary

---

5. Phil 3:20; Gal 5:1.

6. Acts 2:10–11.

7. It was during Nero's reign that the great revolt broke out in Palestine and eventually led to the destruction of the temple in AD 70, never to rise again.

8. AD 57; Nero reigned in the years AD 54–68.

function of this power is to strike terror to bad conduct: "To punish those who do evil and to praise those who do good."[9]

But what if it is the other way around – government rewards the wicked and punishes those on the side of the good, as is the experience of many peoples under despotic regimes?

First of all, submission here is not premised on the condition that government is behaving as it should. We are to be subject simply for this reason: "There is no authority except from God, and those that exist have been instituted by God." The book of Daniel tells us that this was the lesson the great Nebuchadnezzar had to learn in his humiliation, "that the Most High rules over the kingdom of men, and gives it to whom he will. . . ."[10]

It is the sovereign God who has allowed whatever government exists, whether they be absolute tyrants like Nebuchadnezzar, oppressive "vanguard of the proletariat" like the Chinese Communist Party, or authoritarian leaders posing as populists.

Secondly, it must be emphasized that "submission" here does not mean "uncritical obedience."

The Anabaptist scholar John Howard Yoder has helpfully observed that the central imperative in this passage is *subjection*, not *obedience*:

> The conscientious objector who refuses to do what his government asks him to do, but still remains under the sovereignty of that government and accepts the penalties which it imposes, or the Christian who refuses to worship Caesar but still permits Caesar to put him to death, is being subordinate even though he is not obeying.[11]

This leaves us free to dissent, to question the ends for which authority has been put to use, though we are not free to despise that authority when it exacts the personal cost of such a protest. We may engage in civil disobedience, refuse to follow an unjust law, though we must be prepared to suffer the penalty of disobeying such a law. In protesting, we perform our social duty. In upholding

---

9. 1 Pet 2:13.

10. Dan 4:17; 5:21

11. "The Greek language has good words to denote obedience, in the sense of completely bending one's will and one's actions to the desires of another. What Paul calls for, however, is *subordination*. This verb is based upon the same root as the *ordering* of the powers of God. Subordination is significantly different from obedience." John Howard Yoder, *The Politics of Jesus* (Grand Rapids: Eerdmans, 1972), 212.

the right of that authority to punish us, we affirm subjection as our proper personal response to political authority.

This is the reason why some Bible scholars propose that this passage be read primarily as a *personal, rather than a social ethic.*

When government behaves consistent with God's mandate for it as an institution, the rulers strengthen the state's security. When they use state power for their own vested interests, it puts to question their right to rule, and endangers the society's stability.

There is room for questioning the legitimacy of whoever is in power, but the conditionality on whether we are to obey or not can be found elsewhere, but not in this passage.

Evidence elsewhere, as in the case of Paul's mistreatment by the magistrates in Acts 16, tells us that we must call authorities to account when they themselves violate the law, either because of their careless and abusive use of power, or sheer indifference to issues of justice.

When the magistrates sent word that Paul and Silas were to be released, perhaps because of fear or superstition over the earthquake the night before, Paul refused:

> They have beaten us publicly, uncondemned, men who are Roman citizens, and have thrown us into prison; and do they now throw us out secretly? No! Let them come themselves and take us out.[12]

Note that Paul insists on proper procedure: they were beaten and condemned without trial. There was also an insistence on their political rights: they were treated, he tells authorities, in a way that violated their rights as Roman citizens. The appeal was based on a law that forbade under severe penalty the flogging of a Roman citizen.[13]

Paul not only demanded respect as a Roman citizen, he later invoked this right in demanding that his case be brought before Caesar in Rome, after languishing in jail for two years under the charge of Felix the governor, who was hoping for a bribe.[14]

---

12. Acts 16:35–37.

13. Richard J. Dillon, Joseph A. Fitzmyer, S. J., citing sources such as the Lex Porcia de provocatione, in *Livy, History* 10.9, 4; Cicero, *Pro Rabirio* 4.12–13, OCD 501, in *Acts of the Apostles*, The Jerome Biblical Commentary, Vol. 2, eds. Raymond E. Brown, Joseph A. Fitzmyer and Roland E. Murphy (Englewood Cliffs: Prentice-Hall, 1968), 198.

14. Acts 22:25–29; 25:11–12.

Similarly, Jesus also protested when he was struck before the High Priest while undergoing questioning: "If I have spoken wrongly, bear witness to the wrong; but if I have spoken rightly, why do you strike me?"[15]

When public injustice is done, even when we ourselves are the victims of the unfairness, we do not turn the other cheek.

Jesus likewise asserted the priority of his mission over and against threats from hostile powers:

> At that very hour some Pharisees came and said to him, "Get away from here, for Herod wants to kill you." And he said to them, "Go and tell that fox, 'Behold, I cast out demons and perform cures today and tomorrow, and the third day I finish my course. Nevertheless, I must go on my way today and tomorrow and the day following, for it cannot be that a prophet should perish away from Jerusalem.'"[16]

It is not clear whether this account, unique to Luke, refers to a plot to lure Jesus into Judea, where the Sanhedrin exercised more power than in Herod Antipas's territory. Or whether Herod, crafty and unprincipled as a fox, really intended to kill Jesus as he did to John the Baptist. Against this underhanded opposition, Jesus ignores the veiled warning and keeps to his messianic task, masterfully going about his work in his own time.

The phrase "today, tomorrow and the day following," according to a scholar, may be an oblique reference to the biblically symbolic number of "three and one half," as with Daniel's "for a time, times and half a time," which is the length of the terrible reign given to the last Beast. This indicates "a time of dark persecution that will certainly and gloriously end, but in God's time."[17]

What this tells us is that there are moments when our citizenship in this world takes a backseat to our citizenship in heaven. Loyalty to God and the values of his kingdom is the controlling principle in facing complex issues where state laws are in conflict with our beliefs. Our allegiance to what God has ordained for society may sometimes mean that we obey God rather than men, as Peter and John declared before the Sanhedrin.[18]

---

15. John 18:23.

16. Luke 13:31–33.

17. Carroll Stuhlmueller, "The Gospel According to Luke," in *The Jerome Biblical Commentary*, Vol. 2, eds. Raymond E. Brown, Joseph A. Fitzmyer and Roland E. Murphy (Englewood Cliffs: Prentice-Hall, 1968), 147. Note the number symbolism in Dan 7:25; 8:14; 12:12; Luke 4:25.

18. Acts 5:29.

It is unfortunate that subjection in Romans 13 has been absolutized as the locus of our relationship with the state. The very large body of prophetic literature, the admonition to those in power to be a voice to the voiceless and defend the rights of the poor and needy, the radical pessimism of Ecclesiastes which observed that power is always on the side of the oppressor – all these Old Testament texts indicate that even monarchies sanctioned by God are not beyond accountability.[19]

Revelation 13, in fact, raises the specter of the state apotheosizing itself. Written at a time when the reigning Emperor Domitian demanded that people address him as "Lord and God," both Jews and Christians who refused to regard him as divine were persecuted. The apostle John was banished to the island of Patmos, off the coast of present-day Turkey. There he saw visions of terror as well as comfort.

In the image of the Beast, we see the state exercising absolute control. The state here is no longer an instrument of God, but of Satan, controlling not just the economic life but the imagination of peoples, its alter ego deceiving them into bowing before the image of the Beast by performing signs and wonders and the mythology that it has been mortally wounded and yet lived, mimicking the Christ.

When the state exercises absolute control over every aspect of our lives, such as in totalitarian regimes, it has become a Beast and must be resisted.[20]

The laws of Israel served as a hedge against this tendency of rulers to assume the proportions of a deity. The Torah, given before they entered the promised land, defined what they were to be as a people, and how they were to conduct themselves as a nation.

Peculiar to Israel, says Walter Brueggemann, is the understanding that

> government is not ontological, i.e., not ordained for itself as a center of reality. Kingship is always an incidental arrangement carved out of historical opportunity, always in the service of another ontological principle. We forget that about institutions as they become ends in themselves rather than servants and agents of a deeper priority . . . the fundamental religio-political reality is

---

19. Prov 31:8–9; Eccl 4:1.

20. There is a very strong strand of gospel teaching that sees secular government as the province of Satan. This position is perhaps most typically expressed by the temptation story in which Jesus did not challenge the claim of Satan to be able to dispose of the rule of all nations. If one makes this perspective central, all the New Testament texts appear in another light." John Howard Yoder, *The Politics of Jesus*, 195.

not king but Torah, not human distribution of power, but divine vision for society.

The task of the king is to enforce the Torah:

> The king is to sit all day on his throne and read the Torah. And Torah, as you know, is talk about mispat and sedeqah, about justice and righteousness. The monarchy is understood, valued and legitimated according to the norms of Torah – justice and righteousness.[21]

We are not to absolutize kingship nor any form of government just because it is the established political arrangement. The idea that God is sovereign over all kinds of authority is not to be misused as an excuse to be passively acquiescent and surrender principle when the state veers towards unrighteousness. It is not true that "whatever rule there is, is right." This is logical positivism, not Scripture.

The doing of justice is the main reason government has been instituted. Justice is government's core business. It has been given power to wield the sword so that the state can enforce the law and execute penalties when the law is violated.

In sum, government exists to bring order and security to a community. Its authority, however, is not absolute; it is subject to the rule of law. Its core function is justice; it takes priority over strong-fisted rule in the name of order:

> When the royal order conflicts with God-willed justice, order must yield to justice, even if that creates a situation of disorder. God will risk chaos (as in the case of the exodus) in order to bring justice out of an unjust order.[22]

Without justice, according to St. Augustine, government is just a band of brigands.

On Church and State Relations

"The church is the church, the state is the state. They must be kept apart, for the former is spiritual, while the latter is temporal." This is the usual argument against the church involving itself in politics.

---

21. Walter Brueggemann, *Living Toward a Vision* (Philadelphia: United Church Press, 1976), 92–93.

22. Brueggemann, *Living Toward a Vision*, 108.

The English Lord Melbourne found the campaign of William Wilberforce to abolish slavery as quite distasteful in its religious underpinnings, and said: "Things have come to a pretty pass when religion is allowed to invade public life."[23]

Should religion and politics be separate? In what sense should the state be independent of the church and vice versa? In what sense is religion meant to "invade public life"?[24]

Historically, the doctrine now known as "separation of church and state" was a reaction of the early American colonies' experience of persecution under state-sponsored religions in Europe. The Puritan pilgrims who set sail on the *Mayflower* and landed in Massachusetts in 1620 were not only fleeing the persecution under James the First upon the death of Queen Elizabeth. They made a covenant "to combine ourselves together into a civil body politic...." Named the Mayflower Compact, this is said to be the beginning of the American constitutional government.[25]

As enshrined in the American Constitution, which we copied, the "separation of church and state" simply means "religious liberty," the freedom to worship without interference by the state, and tolerance and equal treatment for all religions.

Politically, it meant that the pope may not tell the king how to rule, and the king may not interfere with church matters. In more modern terms, the Dutch theologian and politician Abraham Kuyper conceived this as "sphere sovereignty." The artist, the politician, the religious leader, the scientist – all are sovereign in their own spheres of authority and competence. They are directly accountable to God. Neither the government nor the church has a right to censor nor dictate to the artist or scientist the aesthetic and scientific norms by which they are to do their work.

Kuyper's notion of sphere sovereignty was mainly concerned against the danger of the state having too much power and influence that it encroaches in the activities of other spheres. Sphere sovereignty implies that no one area of life or societal community is sovereign over another. Each sphere has its own created integrity. Neo-Calvinists hold that since God created everything

---

23. Elizabeth Knowles, ed., *The Oxford Dictionary of Quotations*, 5th ed. (Oxford: Oxford University Press, 1999), 504.

24. Melba P. Maggay, "Christians in the Political Arena," Paper Presentation, 2018 *Stott-Bediako Forum*, Manila, Philippines, September 14–15, 2018. Available from: https://infemit.org/christians-political-arena/.

25. Stephen McDowell and Mark Beliles, *Liberating the Nations*, (Charlottesville, VA: Providence Foundation, 1995), 67.

"after its own kind," diversity as seen in creation and various institutions must be acknowledged and appreciated.[26]

Note that the church and the state are to be separate *only* as *institutions*. The church or any religious institution may not dominate the state; this is clericalism. The state may not encroach on the church's beliefs and polity; this is totalitarianism.

As spheres of human action, both are under the rule of God.

There is an intrinsic tension in the fact that Jesus's kingdom is not *of* this world, but it is *in* the world. While the kingdom is bigger and cannot be identified merely in its institutional forms such as the church, the whole body of Christ is to bear witness to the lordship of Jesus over all human institutions. We are to make the presence of the kingdom felt in all of society. Whether we are aware of it or not, the Church is the incarnate presence of Christ on earth.

The church as an institution must limit itself to its own sphere. It is, however, the primary social context in which the saving power of God is made visible.

This calls for a distinction between the local church right around the corner and the entire visible church as it bears witness in all of life. The local church does not exhaust the meaning of the visible church.

As the Dutch philosopher Herman Dooyeweerd puts it, "The temporal revelation of the Corpus Christi, in its broadest sense . . . embraces all the social structures of our temporal human existence."

The *ecclesia visibilis* is not just the church at worship but the church in the marketplace, the academe, or in politics. Christians as individuals or as a corporate body may engage in politics or business or any vocation that serves notice that even in governance or in the marketplace, Jesus is Lord.

The late British theologian and pastor John R. W. Stott calls this the *church scattered*, as distinct from the *church gathered*, or the *ekklesia*.

The "church scattered" is meant to penetrate society, to be "salt" and "light" wherever God has placed them. Government as God's major instrument for ordering society is a critical institution that needs the ethical and prophetic presence of his people.

> A big part of the vocation of Christian lay people is their participation in politics in order to bring justice, honesty and defense

---

26. See Richard J. Mouw, *Abraham Kuyper: A Short and Personal Introduction* (Grand Rapids: Eerdmans, 2011), 23–26.

of true and authentic values, and to contribute to the real human and spiritual good of society.[27]

Entering the Political Space: Some Perspectives on Praxis

- Political participation is more than putting Christians into office, it involves transforming the use of power to serve God's purposes:

    Christian political life is not the accepted political life of the time being accomplished by Christian individuals.... it is doing the will of God as revealed in Holy Scriptures in the political sphere of human society.[28]

- We are called to critical solidarity: the kingdom cannot be identified completely with ideologies, whether bulwarks of orthodoxy like the church, or of orthopraxis like liberation struggles.

    The Church must not be caught up with the surface meaning of events and say, "Behold, here is the Christ!" She must discern God at work in history, but carefully, so as not to tie up the Church to the merely expedient.[29]

History is littered with the mistakes of churches identifying with false theologies such as the Hamitic curse which has given rise to apartheid in South Africa, Nazism in Germany, white supremacy in the American South, and various other causes espoused by elements in the Religious Right. On the other hand, there are also those who collaborate with movements whose ideological underpinnings seem to be consistent with our concern for justice and the poor, but ultimately prove to be as oppressive as the powers they replaced.

- Collaborate with others who are also working towards the common good. Again from Jacques Maritain:

    There is a distinction between political activity as exercised by Christians and political activity as inspired by Christian principles.... The latter does not need *all* Christians or *only* Christians, but only those Christians who have a certain philosophy of the

---

27. Pope Benedict XVI on receiving the Bishops of Paraguay in September 2008.
28. Jacques Maritain is a French Thomist scholar, a philosopher and political thinker who was part of the drafting of the UN Declaration of Human Rights in 1948. See, for instance, his *Man and the State*, CUA Press, 1998.
29. Yoder, *The Politics of Jesus*, 138.

world, of society and modern history and such non-Christians as recognize more or less completely the cogency of this philosophy.[30]

The image of God in all of us makes possible the universal longing for justice. The Christian has no monopoly of insight; anyone with a highly developed sense of fact can apprehend the integrity of creation and the reality that it presents to us. All truth is God's truth wherever it may be found, and so it is possible to walk with those who recognize the truth of who we are as sinners and saints and the complex nature of human society.

- The church participates in politics to work for "justice for all."

Months after Martial Law was declared in the country in September 1972, a prominent evangelical leader mounted the pulpit and declared, that we must praise God for Martial Law, because now our freedom to worship is secure. . . . that we are not going to turn communist like those countries that have been overrun by this ideology.[31]

I squirmed in my seat, my instinctive reflex telling me that this was wrong, even if I did not have at that time the theological tools needed to counter this narrative. It sounded to me that we were just like any other vested interest, only that what we were concerned about was our freedom to worship, never mind if there were so many languishing or being tortured in jail at that time without charges.

These days we assemble recruits for this or that cause that is of interest to us as Christian people. We insert ourselves into political space to gain power and safeguard our values against secularism. But we are silent when there is need to raise our voices for justice or poverty issues that affect the whole society. In which case we are merely lobbyists or power brokers, out to gain leverage and influence for our own interests.[32]

- Create a culture, a social climate that engages the "prince of the power of the air."

We live in a time when the state has in its hands the technology to deceive masses of people. It is not an accident that the first thing despots do to consolidate power is to muzzle the media.[33]

---

30. Quoted in Melba P. Maggay, "Christians in the Political Arena: Some Sociological and Theological Learnings From the Philippines," *Transformation* 39, no. 4 (2022): 250.

31. Maggay, "Christians in the Political Arena": 249.

32. Maggay, "Christians in the Political Arena": 249–50.

33. Melba Maggay, Kosta Milkov and Jack Sara, "Radical Politics," https://lausanne.org/report/hope/radical-politics.

Years ago, the French sociologist Jacques Ellul had sounded the alarm that we now live in what he calls "shadows." In a technologically-mediated social environment, much of what we think we know is not from lived experience but mediated to us by anonymous authorities sitting in newsrooms.[34] In our day, much of our collective unconscious is shaped by those in troll farms and computer terminals manipulating the algorithms. What we think as "fact" is fake news, and "truth" is what we make out of the bits and pieces handed to us in social media.

What Paul calls "the prince of the power of the air" is most likely the demonic that is now lodged and has entrenched itself in technologies that have power to spread and massify lies. In the same way that behind an evil government may be "principalities and powers," media can be one of these structures that could be taken over by what Scripture calls "the powers."[35]

It has been suggested earlier that in Romans 13, the "authorities" – *exousiai* – may have a double meaning, referring also to "invisible angelic powers that stand behind the state government" or to "the empirical state and to the angelic powers."[36]

Similarly, Walter Wink in *Naming the Powers* argues that systems and institutions have inner and outer aspects – the inner aspect being the spiritual character of corporate structures, the outer aspect being the visible and tangible manifestations of power, such as actual rulers, laws, systems and organizational structures.[37]

Those of us who live under repressive regimes know how palpable and cruel such manifestations of the demonic can be when the instrumentalities of the state are trained in full force against dissenters and critics.

Jeremiah a long time ago had coupled untruth with oppression. When truth has fallen in the public square, "oppression upon oppression, deceit upon

---

34. See, for instance, Jacques Ellul's book, *The Technological Society* (New York: Vintage Books, originally published in French in 1954, then in English in 1964).

35. Melba Maggay, Kosta Milkov and Jack Sara, "Radical Politics."

36. Oscar Cullman, *The State in the NT* (New York: Scribner, 1956), 191–210. Also see 1 Cor 2:8; 1 Pet 3:22.

37. Walter Wink, in his Introduction to *Naming the Powers* (Philadelphia: Fortress Press, 1984) argues that "the 'principalities and powers' are the inner and outer aspects of any given manifestation of power. As the inner aspect they are the spirituality of institutions, the 'within' of corporate structures and systems, the inner essence of outer organizations of power. As the outer aspect they are political systems, appointed officials, the 'chair' of an organization, laws in short, all the tangible manifestations which power takes. This hypothesis, it seems to me, makes sense of the fluid way the New Testament writers and their contemporaries spoke of the Powers."

deceit" grows. Those who bend their tongues to speak lies proceed from evil to evil.[38]

In a time of massive disinformation, we are to intentionally wage a battle for the heart and soul of our people. We engage the "prince of the power of the air," articulating persuasively God's norms for society in the public square. As our church communities transform into new patterns of culture, we spread these changes through the structures that organize our common life, just like the way the early church broke through barriers of class and race and gender and eventually tore the social fabric of Greco-Roman society, a civilization borne on the backs of slaves.[39]

Creating a culture and a social climate for good governance is more important, says the poet T. S. Eliot, than putting Christians into office who often are clueless on how their faith should influence their politics:

> What the rulers believed would be less important than the beliefs to which they would be obliged to conform. And a skeptical or indifferent statesman, working with a Christian frame, might be more effective than a devout Christian statesman obliged to conform to a secular frame. . . .
>
> It is not primarily the Christianity of statesmen that matters, but their being confined, by the traditions and the temper of the people which they rule, to a Christian framework within which to realize their ambitions.[40]

- Build a hermeneutical community.[41]

Change needs a "software" of values that will support the "hardware" or the structures and institutions that we seek to put in place.

These days we are seeing a resurgence of authoritarianism in many countries where democracy was supposed to have been restored. The cult of the

---

38. Jeremiah 9:3–6.

39. Scholars have noted that while early Christian teaching did not challenge the existing structures, Paul's vision of unity and equality in Christ in Galatians 3:28 put the relationships between Jew and Greek, male and female, slave and master on a new footing, and eventually contributed to the erosion of the social order. See Melba P. Maggay, "When Media Becomes the 'Prince of the Power of the Air,'" *Christianity Today* (October 25, 2023), available from https://www.christianitytoday.com/2023/10/melba-maggay-christian-philippines-media-oppression/.

40. T. S. Eliot's *The Idea of a Christian Society*, originally a series of lectures delivered in Cambridge in 1939. "I have tried to restrict my ambition of a Christian society to a social minimum: to picture, not a society of saints, but of ordinary men, of men whose Christianity is communal before being individual."

41. Maggay, "When Media Becomes the 'Prince of the Power of the Air.'"

caudillo, of the mythic strongman, persists. Part of the reason is the lack of congruence between the operative values in the culture and the established structures of governance. As the Guatemalan sociologist Bernardo Arevalo puts it, "We have the hardware of democracy, but the software of authoritarianism."[42]

Creating supportive patterns of culture that will make our systems work requires not just "consciousness raising" as social activists know well how to do, but the building of what I call a "hermeneutical community" – those who, like the tribe of Issachar, can discern the times and give guidance on where we can locate ourselves so as to have maximum impact and influence on society.

The first step to this is discipling the mind. We are told that transformation begins in the mind.[43] It begins when our thought patterns conform to the mind of Christ and gradually influence the way we live.

A major task given to us is to "make captive every thought to obey Christ." Unfortunately, this missional mandate has been sidelined by the massive energy put on shallow gospel proclamations that pass for "evangelism." We are trained to use the Bible on things like "how to get saved," but not on how the "whole counsel of God" can be applied to the many issues we face every day.

This means that we disciple our people in the pews in such a way that there is universal biblical literacy, the kind that is able to engage issues in the public square. We harness the professional gifts of those in the sciences and open their minds to the height and depth and breadth of the gospel's relevance to all of life.

The second step is to intentionally create a community, a critical mass of thought leaders who can integrate the Bible into the analysis of issues and articulate this in the public square.

I was struck by the necessity of this when, at the height of the struggle against the Marcos regime, our evangelical leaders kept criticizing ISACC – our small community of social scientists, development practitioners, writers, artists, and a handful of pastors and theologians – for being part of the surge of resistance against the continuance of his rule. We were convinced that the results of the 1986 snap elections that proclaimed him winner were fraudulent. He had no more right to rule and so we mounted a protest together with other movements.

The evangelical leaders then labeled this as "rebellion" and kept talking of Romans 13. But our reading of the times was such that we thought the relevant

---

42. Maggay, "When Media Becomes the 'Prince of the Power of the Air.'"
43. Romans 12:2.

text was not Romans 13 but Revelation 13. There are times when the state ceases to be a servant but assumes the proportions of a Beast and so must be resisted.[44]

This reading won the day. After People Power, some church leaders began to ask, "How come ISACC seems to have its finger on the pulse of where our people are and we missed it?"

We must intentionally build a hermeneutical community lest we miss our historical cues.

- Are we being prophetic or merely politicking?

Having learned that politics is "the art of the possible," Christians in office often find themselves neutralized by having to make concessions. Usually, choosing the possible good over and against an impossible better is the only option available within the limits of one's power and responsibility.

Compromise soon becomes a habit, however, and tears to shreds whatever idealism propelled one into taking office. Eventually, one is eaten up by the "system," and conforms to the way things are – *"ganyan talaga ang kalakaran dito."* One can no longer muster the courage to raise a prophetic voice against institutionalized corruption and violence.

When the state assumes the proportions of the demonic, the church must resist with the full force of its authority to speak a prophetic word:

> The Church is summoned in the course of human history to speak a discerning word to each concrete situation, "These are the rights of man here and now. This is what man may demand. This is what he needs to be protected from. . . .
>
> This discerning word is part of the Church's proclamation. In pronouncing it, the Church addresses itself to society and to the state. It is the mouthpiece of man's exigencies. Normally, the Church should not leave it to revolutionary movements to assert human rights. Rather, it should claim them before man is driven to despair. In the past, the Church had the courage to do it. But it has kept silent now for three centuries.[45]

---

44. Maggay, "When Media Becomes the 'Prince of the Power of the Air.'"
45. Jacques Ellul, *The Theological Foundations of Law* (New York: The Seabury Press, 1969), 132.

Afterword: Prophecy as Poetic Power

Those of us who are pastors and leaders in churches may not be aware that we have power to shape the political opinions of our people. Most of them may not have the same access to information or theological insight, and so are trusting us to give guidance. This "delegated discernment" is a great power and must be used responsibly.

"Power is always exercised in any situation," says Michel Foucault, "and the most dangerous is unacknowledged power."

We may feel that we are powerless before the overwhelming strength of systemic evil. But we have resources in our faith – the Spirit and the Word – to provide counter-narratives to the powerful lies that surround us. Like Jesus, we are to practice what Brueggemann calls "poetic imagination":

> Jesus's way of teaching parables invited his community of listeners beyond visible realities of Roman law and restrictive Jewish law, . . . [it was] out of tradition, specific, open-ended, an alternative society of the "kingdom of God." He had no blueprints nor programs, "but turns people loose from the givens of the day [so they can] live toward new social possibilities. . . .
>
> This is the most subversive, redemptive act that a leader of a faith community can undertake in the midst of exile. This work of poetic alternative in the long run is more crucial than one-on-one pastoral care or the careful implementation of institutional goals. . . .
>
> That is because the work of poetic imagination holds the potential of unleashing a community of power and action that finally will not be contained by any imperial restrictions and definitions of reality. . . .[46]

This is what prophets like Isaiah did for the despairing exiles in Babylon. As servants of the Word in these critical times, we can do this likewise.

Bibliography

Brueggemann, Walter. *Hopeful Imagination, Prophetic Voices in Exile*. Philadelphia: Fortress Press, 1986.

———. *Living Toward a Vision*. Philadelphia: United Church Press, 1976.

---

46. Walter Brueggemann, *Hopeful Imagination, Prophetic Voices in Exile* (Philadelphia: Fortress Press, 1986), 96–97.

Cullman, Oscar. *The State in the New Testament*. New York: Scribner, 1956.
Eliot, T. S. *The Idea of a Christian Society*, originally a series of lectures delivered in Cambridge in 1939.
Ellul, Jacques. *The Technological Society*. New York: Vintage Books, 1964.
———. *The Theological Foundations of Law*. New York: The Seabury Press, 1969.
Fitzmyer, S. J., Joseph A. "The Letter to the Romans." In *The Jerome Biblical Commentary*, Vol. 2, edited by Raymond E. Brown, Joseph A. Fitzmyer, and Roland E. Murphy. Englewood Cliffs: Prentice-Hall, 1968.
Maritain, Jacques. *Man and the State*. Washington, DC: CUA Press, 1998.
McDowell, Stephen, and Mark Beliles, *Liberating the Nations*. Charlottesville: Providence Foundation, 1995.
Stuhlmueller, Caroll. "The Gospel According to Luke." In *The Jerome Biblical Commentary*, Vol. 2, edited by Raymond E. Brown, Joseph A. Fitzmyer, and Roland E. Murphy. Englewood Cliffs: Prentice-Hall, 1968.
Wink, Walter. *Naming the Powers*. Philadelphia: Fortress Press, 1984.
Yamauchi, Edwin. *The World of the First Christians*. Tring, Lion Publishing, 1981.
Yoder, John Howard. *The Politics of Jesus*. Grand Rapids: Eerdmans, 1972.

4

Pamathalaan: A Filipino Indio-Genius Idea of Governance

Marie Joy D. Pring-Faraz

The interest in the movement toward sacred governance peaked during the term of the late President Fidel Valdez Ramos.[1] Under this administration, the Moral Recovery Program that aimed toward a national revival of the valor of Filipino cultural and spiritual values was initiated. Through this endeavor, *pamathalaan*, which means *pamamahala kasama si Bathala* (governing with God), was championed and introduced to the larger Filipino public.[2] Regrettably, the next president did not have the same enthusiasm about the program and the funding for this government project was discontinued.[3]

This chapter reflects on the indio-genius idea of *pamathalaan* and ascertains its relevance to the Christian faith.[4] It is an act of remembrance, an invitation not to forget to drink from our cistern of rich indigenous tradition and history. If nation-building is a journey, this, then, is looking back twice as much as we look forward that those who hope to build a better nation will learn from our past. Certainly, the Filipino adage, "*Ang hindi lumingon sa pinanggalingan ay hindi makakarating sa paroroonan* (Those who do not look back to where they came from will not be able to reach their destination), is

---

1. Serafin Talisayon, "Sacred Governance." *Center for Conscious Living Foundation* (January 2012): 1.
2. Talisayon, "Sacred Governance," 2.
3. Talisayon, "Sacred Governance," 2.
4. "Indio-genius" is a term used by National Artist, Kidlat Tahimik, who is the husband of Sikolohiyang Pilipino practitioner Katrin De Guia. The word is an acknowledgement of the exceptional intellect and creativity of local Filipino people – called by colonizers as *Indios* – that have been developed over centuries and passed from generation to generation.

not limited to the interpretation of the importance of *utang na loob* (debt of gratitude). It can also be applied to the idea of navigating the difficult road of a nation's political development.

There are three questions that this work aims to reflect on: (1) What can evangelical Christians learn from the Filipino IKSP (Indigenous Knowledge Systems and Practices) on governance?[5] (2) What theological entry point can be explored, if there is any?[6] (3) What are the practical implications that can be gleaned from Filipino IKSP for Christians who hope to move forward in the task of nation-building?

Pamathalaan

Pamathalaan is a portmanteau of the words *Bathala* (God) and *pamahalaan* (government). Put together, this Filipino word is often translated to English as sacred politics, sacred governance, or even more broadly, model leadership.[7] Consolacion Alaras, a renowned advocate of *pamathalaan*, identifies five other units of meaning connected to the word.[8] The first three are provided by former SVD seminarian, Marius Diaz: (1) *pamahalaan* (governance), (2) *thala* (from the native word for the God, *Bathala*), and (3) *taal* (indigenous). The other two words are provided by Ma. Milagros Laurel, a comparative literature expert: (4) *mathal* ("model" in the Arabic language), and (5) *laan* (destined). Alaras takes these five words and defines *pamathalaan* as "a sacred model government based on ancestral moorings destined in our (Filipino) history."[9]

Pamathalaan at its core means *pamamahala kasama si Bathala* (governing with God) – a government that submits to the supreme authority of God and conducts itself by divine guidance. *Pamathalaan* affirms that the nation, the city, and the *barangay* (village) are sacred spheres where God-inspired leadership takes place. Nonetheless, it is not only the leader's responsibility to

---

5. A chief reservation one may have about exploring *pamathalaan* for Christian theological cogitation is its association to the Filipino folk religion, *Kapatiran* (spiritual brotherhood), chiefly from the *Katagalugan* region. Nonetheless, a closer investigation of this indio-genius concept shows that no specific group is the sole source of *pamathalaan* knowledge and practice – it is also associated to groups of artists, public servants, and academicians. Hence, *pamathalaan* can also be a valuable point to engage in theological reflection, especially Filipino Christian theology.

6. The felicitous term "theological entry point" in considering the relationship of faith with politics is used by Christian ethicist and advocate, Philip Wogaman, in *Christian Perspectives on Politics: Revised and Expanded* (Louisville: Westminster John Knox Press, 2000), 164.

7. Katrin De Guia, *Kapwa: The Self in the Other* (Pasig City: Anvil Publishing, 2005), 347.

8. Consolacion Alaras, "Pamathalaan." *Diliman Review* 53 (2006): 265–73.

9. Alaras, "Pamathalaan," 265–73.

keep the sanctity of the governmental spheres. *Pamathalaan* is two-fold: It is leadership by grace as much as it is citizenship by grace.[10] *Pamathalaan* is not only a vision for the government but for the whole nation.

In this ancestral national vision, leadership and citizenry are energized by love for God, love for the *kapwa* (neighbor), and love for the *sangkalikasan* (creation).[11] *Bathala* is acknowledged as the source of all life, and thus, all of life is sacred. The *kapwa*, wherever they are in the social strata, is seen not as another entity but as an extension of oneself. Therefore, the idea of government is not to be above the neighbor but to live and thrive alongside them.

Also in the *pamathalaan* vision, the earth and the rest of creation are sacred. The land and its produce are not meant to be exploited and exhausted until it dries up. *Pamathalaan* upholds that the earth is *Bathala*'s gift that must be cultivated to become fruitful and to meet the needs of the community today, as well as that of the next generations of *kapwa*.

Pamathalaan puts forth a holistic understanding that everyone and everything is interconnected. The spiritual and the material, the commonplace and the supernatural, and the past, present, and future are all enmeshed in the sacred harmony of life. This notion gives way to a kind of leadership that has both inclusive and non-hierarchical orientation. Inclusive because the *kapwa* and *kalikasan* are treated as dignified co-bearers of the sacred gift of life from *Bathala*. Also, non-hierarchical since the leaders of *pamathalaan* are not part of the ruling few above others. Hence, a more accurate understanding of the leader's task is not *pamumuno*, which is ruling from the apex, but *pamamathala*, which is serving with God.

There have been attempts in the past to bring this indio-genius model of governance back into the consciousness of the Filipino citizenry. Following the 1986 EDSA Revolution, a joint inquiry into the Filipino culture and values was led by then-senator Leticia Shahani.[12] Resource persons from the Executive Branch of government and recognized experts in the fields of psychiatry, psychology, sociology, and other social sciences were invited to participate. What ultimately came out of this was the "Moral Recovery Program" report, and the vital Executive Order No. 319 passed by then-president, Fidel Ramos. Here, the government and all of society were enjoined "to lay the necessary

---

10. Alaras, "Pamathalaan," 269.

11. De Guia, *Kapwa*, 347.

12. Leticia Shahani, "Senate Resolution No. 10," in *Filipino Values and National Development: Readings on the Moral Recovery Program* (Manila: Kabisig People's Movement, 1993).

foundations of the moral recovery crusade for Filipino core value infusion into the organization's culture, systems and processes."[13]

One of the projects under this national effort was the piloting of a course on *pamathalaan*. Talisayon who was instrumental in crafting the course identifies seven key practices of sacred governance: (1) the practice of Abraham: watching and listening to life, (2) continuous revision of obsolete mental models, (3) glocality, (4) conscious and continuous learning, (5) watching and listening within, (6) sensing and co-creating the emergent, and (7) bridging leadership.[14] The promise of this innovative course was evinced when the publication, "God-centered Economics," was produced after a conference of economists and *pamathalaan* practitioners was convened.

Unfortunately, with the change of administration came the diminishing interest to recover the richness of the Filipino culture and its significance to wielding national development. The lack of support from Ramos's successor, most especially the curtailing of the budget for such a cause, proved to be detrimental to the moral recovery program and the *pamathalaan* course. This eventually led to the loss of vibrance in pursuing such cultural efforts at a national scale by the dawn of the 21st century.

While *pamathalaan* may have lost its spotlight in Philippine politics, there are still culture-bearers who sought to live out its ethos and see this concept thrive in their spheres of influence. From various social strata, *pamathalaan* principles have been celebrated and practiced by artists, folk religion members, and academicians. There are three concepts core to pamathalaan that have been commonly identified by its diverse practitioners and researchers: *kaloob* (insight), *patotoo* (commitment), and *kalinisan* (purity).[15] What follows now is an exploration of the three guiding principles of *pamathalaan*.

Kaloob

Kaloob has its root in the word *loob* (inside). The meaning of *loob* goes beyond that of geographical location or the inner feelings of a person. The human *loob* is a world within the horizon of all of existence, a world of meaningful

---

13. Fidel Ramos, "Executive Order No. 319." *The Law Phil Project*, 3 April 1996. Accessed 23 November 2020. http://www.lawphil.net/executive/execord/eo1996/eo_319_1996.html.

14. Talisayon, "Sacred Governance," 1.

15. De Guia, *Kapwa*, 347–53.

connections.¹⁶ The human *loob* or *kalooban* refers to the quality of a person's character concerning God, the neighbor, and creation. In sacred governance, one's legitimacy to lead is based on the person's *kabutihang loob* or goodness of character. The *pamathalaan leader*, otherwise known as *mathal*, displays *kabutihang loob* through integrity. There is no weaving of deceptive propaganda for public opinion, but oneness of speech and deed, and congruence between intentions and actions.

Kaloob is translated by *pamathalaan* practitioners as "insight" or "enlightenment."¹⁷ In the Filipino IKSP, enlightenment is understood from a holistic perspective that is spiritual as it is rational. To be enlightened is to exercise the intellect as well as intuition, to perceive in one's *loob* the natural as well as the supernatural. Since the life of all creation is from and is connected to *Bathala*, the *mathal* is expected to lead with the life source and insight from God.¹⁸

Pamathalaan practitioners note that *kaloob* or insight can be received when one learns to closely observe and listen to the movements of life. This is the daily practice of reading the "Living Book" or the patterns and cues whether micro or macro in one's life.¹⁹ Talisayon acknowledges the importance of engaging the Bible in practicing *pamathalaan*, but he also points out that just as Abraham was able to hear God even when there was no Holy Scripture, those who seek to lead with goodness and radiant *loob* can receive instructions from God directly and personally.²⁰

Pumathalaan upholds that God is omnipresent and immanent, and it is crucial in sacred governance to learn to notice and listen to God in the everydayness of life. This anticipation that God will reveal his *loob* must be coupled with openness. Anthony de Mello, an Indian Jesuit, once noted that the final barrier to receiving insight from God is one's own God concept; one misses God because he or she thinks they know God already.²¹ The *mathal* does not limit God to a mere mental or religious model. Instead, the *mathal* is always open to the possibility of receiving new insights through new means about

---

16. Albert Alejo, "Loob as Relational Interiority: A Contribution to the Philosophy of the Human Person," *Social Transformations: Journal of the Global South* 6 (2018): 32. Accessed 10 June 2021. 10.13185/2866.

17. De Guia, *Kapwa*, 347–48.

18. De Guia, *Kapwa*, 353.

19. Talisayon, "Sacred Governance," 11.

20. Talisayon's development of *pamathalaan* is largely influenced by the Holy Scripture and Christian theologians such as Anthony de Mello and Ben Swett. See "Sacred Governance," 11–12.

21. de Mello in Talisayon, "Sacred Governance," 12.

God's *kalooban* at every moment of life, whether it is about their personal life or the life of the nation.

Another aspect worth noting is how *pamathalaan* enshrines the *kaloob* of the poor. Sacred governance has an unambiguous bent toward the underside of society. The following line could be considered as a battle cry of *pamathalaan* practitioners: "*Hangga't hindi binibigyan ng patotoo ang kaloob naming mga maliliit at inaapi, hindi magkakaroon ng kaganapan ang bayang ito*" (Until we have truly proven our commitment to include the insight of the marginalized and oppressed, there will be no fulfillment in this country).[22] *Pamathalaan* upholds that until the *kapwa*, especially the vulnerable ones, are recognized, heard, and given importance, the greatness of a nation will not be actualized. De Guia notes that the metaphor of *katawan* or the body as a social organization can be discerned in this *pamathalaan* cry. *Ang sakit ng kalingkingan ay sakit ng buong katawan* (the pain of the pinky is felt throughout the whole body) – the failure of one is the failure of everyone, and the success of one is the success of all. This is why *pakikiisa* (solidarity) and *pakikibaka* (struggle) are close to the heart of *pamathalaan*, and a public leader is expected to be one with the *kapwa*'s struggles, as well as triumphs. Only in solidarity can the *loob* of the *mathal* become one with the *loob* of the people, and only through this genuine unity can the *mathal* and the nation forge a way forward together.

Patotoo

Patotoo is often translated as "commitment."[23] More accurately, it is the commitment to seeking, verifying, and upholding the truth in one's life and community. While there may not be modern devices in Filipino IKSP, it has several systematic verification processes that have been handed down through the ages. Talisayon identifies the use of phenomenological approach in establishing the validity of facts and intersubjectivity among observers.[24] Similar to the process of triangulation, the validity of a *patotoo* is strong if there are two or more sources that corroborate the information. In *patotoo* (committed witness), truth must be empirical as it is experiential, and objective as it is subjective.

Pamathalaan practices a democratic process wherein all members of the community, the *kapwa*, are invited to witness and are assured of a share in the truth-seeking endeavor. Furthermore, *patotoo* and truth-seeking include the

---

22. De Guia, *Kapwa*, 349; Alaras, "Pamathalaan," 265.
23. De Guia, *Kapwa*, 348.
24. Talisayon, "Sacred Governance," 17–20.

practice of discerning the divine *loob*. The community listening to God's *kalooban* is as crucial as listening to the *kapwa*. This indio-genius process of listening to God and the neighbor is later on adapted by Talisayon in the *pamathalaan course* and referred to it as "consensual sensing and discernment."[25] Consensual discernment within the *pamathalaan* framework includes Christian spiritual disciplines such as silence, prayer or inquiring of the Lord, and encounter with God's Word in the community.[26] *Patotoo* is a three-fold commitment: first, to the truth and the process of determining it; second, to the *kapwa* who is both the co-seeker and co-bearer of truth; and third, to God who is the source of all truth.

Pamathalaan upholds that *patotoo* is not just in truth-seeking, but most importantly, it is evidenced in one's way of life. *Patotoo* is an embodied commitment to noble ideals; truthful rhetoric is coupled with truthful actions. A *mathal* is validated by his or her commitment to a lifestyle that shows compassion to the *kapwa*. Connectedness and genuine concern for the *mathal*'s *sakop* (constituency) are characteristic aspects of this governance. A *mathal* is always ready to share their resources with their *sakop* (constituents). Looking at indigenous public leadership, a *mathal*'s home and pantry are always open to all who may need sustenance; personal needs and belongings are sacrificed for the good of the *kapwa*. The *ako* (myself) and *akin* (mine) fade into *tayo* (us) and *atin* (ours). A *mathal* has keen eyes to spot the needs of their *kapwa* and responds with swift and supportive actions. The *sakop* becomes a *mathal*'s extended family. From sharing their pantry to managing the fields and other communal resources, a *mathal* shows prudence and uprightness in the economy.

Patotoo in sacred governance also includes a commitment to a lifestyle of modesty.[27] Extravagance and excess are words unfamiliar to the paradigm of *pamathalaan*. Sacred governance understands that where extravagance and excess exist, the abuse of *kapwa* and *sangkalikasan* is not far away. A *mathal* is a leader of the people from the people, and genuine solidarity is not just in thought and consolatory messaging, but it is shown in the *mathal*'s humble inner resistance to the propensity to abuse their own authority and status. It is a moral misdeed in *pamathalaan* for a public leader to profit from the suffering of the *kapwa* and *sangkalisan* or elevate oneself and a few others through the lowliness of the desolate. Abundance cannot be true life-giving when it is

---

25. Talisayon, "Sacred Governance," 24–26.
26. Talisayon, "Sacred Governance," 25.
27. De Guia, *Kapwa*, 359.

gained through pillaging the neighbor and nature. A true *mathal* uses their power to increase the good of their *sakop* and the many others affected by the exercise of their authority. A life of truth, simplicity, and goodness is a *mathal*'s credible *patotoo* (witness), and in return, it becomes the *patotoo* of others about them.

Kalinisan

Kalinisan, while often used to refer to good hygiene, also largely stands for the irreproachability of character that reflects the essence of *Bathala*'s goodness in a person's private and public life.[28] A *mathal* is a person of *kalinisan*, who shines with altruistic values, and whose lifestyle is a guiding light to the *kapwa*. Honesty and transparency make the *mathal walang bahid* or untainted with duplicity and misconduct. Where other *pinuno* (heads) miserably fail – power politics and exploitation of public resources – a *mathal* vigilantly guards their integrity. A *mathal* sees power as a force to be shared among their *sakop*, and an asset to be leveraged for the achievement of the highest common good.

Even more, money does not lure a *mathal*, for not only is this public leader exemplary in generosity, but he or she also has an unattached view towards possessions. Money is simply a means to attain things and make arrangements to benefit their *sakop*. The *mathal* knows that money is as vulnerable and easily plucked as the fruits of a tree, and the roots, which signify *pakikiisa* (solidarity) and *bayanihan* (cooperation), are what endure and sustain the community.[29]

Freedom is key to keeping a *mathal*'s *kalinisan*, especially on the topic of public resources and funds. If a *mathal* becomes beholden to others or attached to material possessions, the preeminence of public interest and public good would be compromised for the benefit of oneself and of select individuals. Just like the Filipino mythic man who is "content with being-at-home-in-the-world and being-human," a *mathal*'s attitude to life is intuition-driven, spontaneous, and open.[30] Nonetheless, a *mathal*'s freedom is not the happy-go-lucky kind of liberty; it is with a great burden. For in exercising their freedom, the *mathal* stays mindful that *Bathala* is overall, and they remain accountable to the *kapwa* and the *sangkalikasan*.

---

28. De Guia, *Kapwa*, 352.

29. The image of the "Money Tree" hangs in an artists' hub, *Pugaran* (the Nest), is illustrated in De Guia's book. See *Kapwa*, 345.

30. Gonzales in De Guia, *Kapwa*, 4.

It is such freedom that keeps a *mathal* from the clutches of people and things that illiberalize. This freedom grounds a *mathal* and ties them to *katuwirang landas* (straight, righteous path). A *mathal* understands that *pamamathala* is a sacred calling, and it is no less than *Bathala* who calls one into this journey and establishes a *mathal*'s feet on the *katuwirang landas*. *Katuwirang landas* is a thorny and narrow path. A *mathal* faces many challenges on such a road: "The straight path implies the experiencing of trials and suffering with a serenity that comes from the control of the self (*loob*)."[31] Only through *kalinisan*, *kalooban*, and *patotoo* can a *mathal* walk and endure the *katuwirang landas* which is the only path to community building, healing, and wholeness.

Christ the *Mathal*: A Theological Entry Point

The task to relate Christian theology to political thought, especially indigenous political philosophy, is daunting but necessary. And while there is no one grand theological conception to illumine politics, there can be "theological entry points" relevant to particular political settings.[32] Considering the three key concepts of *kaloob*, *patotoo*, and *kalinisan* in *pamathalaan*, a Christological entry point surfaces, that is Jesus Christ as the model leader or the *mathal*.

Christ the Mathal *and* Kaloob

Christ the *mathal* is the epitome of *kabutihan* and *kabuohang loob* (good and integral character), for not only is Christ a proclaimer of truth but is the Word of Truth himself (John 14:6). In his proclamation of the truth, Christ the true *mathal* uses rich *talinhaga* (metaphor) and vision to convey his message.[33] Christ often uses the imagery of light and darkness, of openness and hiddenness, in teaching about truth and untruth (John 3:19–21; Luke 8:17). Those who live by the truth see clearly and walk in the path of light, but those who live by lies are misled and are walking in darkness.

Truth has often been unwelcome in politics.[34] Machiavellian public leaders are well-versed in thwarting what is real through a complete or partial tweaking

---

31. Reynaldo Ileto, *Pasyon and Revolution* (Quezon City: Ateneo de Manila Press, 1979), 127–28.
32. Wogaman, *Christian Perspectives on Politics*, 163.
33. De Guia notes that common among *mathal* is the use of imagery and *talinhaga* (metaphor) in their communication. See *Kapwa*, 357.
34. Alan Storkey, *Jesus and Politics: Confronting the Powers* (Grand Rapids: Baker, 2005).

of details. But Christ, the great *mathal*, warned hypocrites on their deceitful rhetoric and duplicitous deeds: There is nothing concealed that will not be disclosed, or hidden that will not be made known (Luke 12:2).

Truth-telling is a precarious affair within halls of political power. It was Christ's fearless proclamation of truth before Pilate that led to the crucifixion verdict (John 18). When Christ testified that he is indeed the Savior-king, the increasing jealousy and violent desire of the teachers of the law to end his life were masked by false accusations of insurrection and subversion. Yet even when Christ the *mathal* faced the most brutal death penalty devised by the Roman empire, he proved that the power of truth trumps lies and political influence. The power in Christ's proclamation that he is indeed the Messiah-king was conclusively demonstrated when he rose from the grave that first Easter. Christ the *mathal* shows that the true might of a public leader lies not with weaponizing the law or commandeering the military; it is with a leader's oneness with the truth.

The connection of Christ the *mathal* to the concept of *kaloob* is not only in his honesty but in the core of who he truly is: the full revelation of God's *loob* (relational will) to humanity and all creation (Col 1:15–20). God's *kalooban* is to reconcile all things on earth and in heaven into a loving fellowship with the Trinity through Christ who is the *kephale* (head, supreme authority). Since God has exalted Christ the *mathal* to the highest, his *sakop* is all of earth and heaven. Yet Christ's status was not achieved with propaganda, hi-jacking of power, or brute force, it was secured through his openness and obedience to God's will. A true *mathal*, Christ is exalted and his authority is established because of his humility to the purpose of God and sacrificial service to others, even to the point of giving his life as a ransom for many (Matt 20:27).

Furthermore, Christ the *mathal* enshrines the *kaloob* of the poor. *Pamathalaan* practitioners cry out that until the plight and contribution of the marginalized and oppressed are considered, the nation will remain unfulfilled. This cry finds a rejoinder in Christ's most celebrated teaching: "Blessed are you who are poor, for yours is the kingdom of God" (Luke 6:20). The veneration of the lowly is central to the governance of Christ; the *mathal* himself is not only pro-poor, but he also became poor for people's sake (2 Cor 8:9). Mary's song of praise at the dawn of the incarnation even proclaims the veneration of the poor: "He has cast down rulers from their thrones, and has lifted up the lowly" (Luke 1:52). When the eternal word of God was made subject to time and space and entered human history, a reversal has taken place: the pride of the *may mataas na loob* (arrogant) is leveled, and the humility of the *may kababaang loob* (lowly) is exalted. Such reversal is the mark of the governance of Christ the *mathal*.

Christ the Mathal *and* Patotoo

Christ the *mathal* demonstrated his *matapat na patotoo* (faithful commitment) to humanity through the *kenosis* (Phil 2:6–8). As an exemplary leader, Christ willfully divested himself of his divine privileges to become human for all humans. Christ the *mathal* exemplified what it is to be in solidarity with the *sakop*. Beyond mere words, Christ the *mathal* became one with the *sakop* in form and life. Christ the *mathal* sacrificed and became poor so that through his voluntary poverty, his *sakop* may become rich (2 Cor 8:9). Such is the compassionate generosity of the true *mathal* – he did not only share parts of his possessions but he gave up his own life so that his *sakop* may have life, life to the fullest measure (John 10:10).

Nonetheless, the absolute expression of Christ's *patotoo* is the cross. It is, first and foremost, his *patotoo* to humble obedience to God the Father. Even though Christ prayed for such a cup to be taken away from him (Luke 22:42), as a dutiful *mathal*, he still submitted to the will of the Father and walked the thorny *matuwid na landas* (righteous path). Secondly, the cross is Christ's *patotoo* to goodness and peace in the face of evil and discord. The dreadfulness of Christ's cross lies not only in the gore of its torture, but even more so in its insidious motivations: jealousy, control, coercion, and violence. The crucifixion represented the vileness and cruelty of human governance – pinning an innocent man to appease and protect the interest of the greedy. Yet that very cross which stood for all such vehement things, Christ, the good *mathal*, took upon his shoulders so that he may exchange good for evil, and peace for hostility. Therefore, the *patotoo* (witness) of the cross changed; to the unbelieving, it remains the symbol of horrid death, but to Christ's *sakop* it has become a symbol of life. Furthermore, the cross of Christ signifies a political hope that humanity is no longer confined to flawed governance. Christ the *mathal*, through the cross, initiated a new norm of leadership: justice, righteousness, mercy, and peace.

Understanding Christ the *mathal* and *patotoo* would be incomplete if the narrative ends at the cross and the resurrection is not recounted. The resurrection is the greatest affirmation of God's *patotoo* (commitment) to humanity. For when Christ conquered the grave, he became the *mathal* over death, and as he leads, his *sakop* also conquer all that separate them from the kingdom of God. The resurrection is the *patotoo* to the sovereignty of God – that all control, power, and authority are completely in God's hand. The *patotoo* of the resurrection has eternal and temporal implications: While it assures the *sakop* of Christ the *mathal* of his eternal reign, it also gives a definitive response to all perplexities brought by evil and injustice done to humanity and all of creation here and now. The resurrection is God's *patotoo* to those who are seeking justice and reparations – especially that which is similar to what Christ has experienced, state-sponsored violence and abuse of authority – a day of reckoning surely is to come and God's justice and righteousness ultimately prevails.

Christ the Mathal *and* Kalinisan

Kalinisan (purity), a *mathal* quality, is evidenced in Christ's character and leadership. Christ the *mathal* is incorruptible, and the narrative of the temptation in the wilderness demonstrates this (Luke 4:1–13).

When Christ was tempted to turn stones into bread, the accuser was on to the weakness of the human flesh (Luke 4:3–4). Being one who is real and substantially human, Christ the *mathal* is certain to suffer hunger after fasting. Despite this vulnerability, Christ chose steadfastness in obeying the heavenly Father and in seeking the welfare of others instead of momentary gratification.

The next temptation was that of power (Luke 4:5–7). The deceiver promised Christ the *mathal* the splendor and authority of all kingdoms of the world if he would bow to him in worship. But Christ the *mathal* is not lured by supremacy or dominion, for he knows that absolute power is only in God's hands, and therefore, it is only God who is worthy of worship and who has the authority to confer such power. Even more, Christ, the *mathal* is a gentle leader, the lamb on the throne. He invites obedience, not one who controls and overrides others' volition.

Finally, the devil taunted Christ's identity as the Son of God and tempted him to throw himself down from the pinnacle of the temple (Luke 4:8–12). However, Christ the *mathal* is not concerned about himself. His work is to do the will of the Father, and he shall not abandon his messianic task to save humanity. As a genuine *mathal*, Christ demonstrated that he places God, and then others, above himself.

A human for all humans, Christ the *mathal* confronted all temptations without being defeated. Thus, Christ's victory is won not only for himself but for his *sakop* as well. Christ effectively undid Satan's perversion of God's law, not only with his wise and correct understanding of the Scripture but also with his commitment to fear God and remain in the *katuwirang landas* (straight/righteous path). The *kalinisan* of *Christ* the *mathal* is not only because he remained sinless or spotless, but also because he was single-minded and wholeheartedly devoted to the *kalooban* of God and the common good of his *sakop*. Christ the *mathal*'s *katuwiran* (righteousness) became the very *katuwiran* of his *sakop* – the one that brought them healing and wholeness.

The Church as *Mathal*: Some Practical Implications

Pamathalaan's vision includes not only an exemplary leader but also a model community. Hence, if Christ is the *mathal*, his *sakop* – his Body, the church – is called towards *imitatio Christi* (imitation of Christ) by being a *mathal* community.

The church as a *mathal* community of *kaloob* (insight) must be a group that consensually discerns God's *kalooban* (will) through the revelation of God's fullness in the life and work of Jesus Christ, as well as the Holy Scripture. Instead of being insulated, the church must completely immerse in the life of the larger society – observing the cues of life in the nation and bringing such events, whether positive or negative, into the light of God's Word. For instance, it is necessary for the church to reflect on the previous administration's "War on Drugs." What does this reveal of our character as a nation? How does this affect our testimony of being the only Christian nation in Asia? Questions such as these must be confronted by a church that seeks God's *kalooban* here and now.

Christ the *mathal* also invites the church to follow his example of taking up the cross daily – a *patotoo* (commitment) to unyielding obedience to God and sacrificial love for the *kapwa* and *sangkalikasan* (creation). The church as *mathal* is called to self-abasement and *kababaang-loob* (humility) just as Christ the *mathal* practiced *kenosis*. As a major pillar of society, the church as *mathal* checks her privileges and leverages these as she advances not her agenda but the well-being and protection of others, especially the weak. Phineas Bresee, the founder of the Church of the Nazarene, has been known to remind Christ's followers to live a simple life, even keep the physical structure of the church modest so that the poor may not feel ashamed to enter and share in the life of the community. Our places of worship must reflect the heart of Christ for the poor – a place where the lowly can meet the Savior, not a place garbed with pompous excess that is out of tune with the poverty outside its gates. Furthermore, the church as *mathal* seeks to touch and heal the wounded, those that society rejects and considers unworthy.

Furthermore, to keep her *patotoo* (witness) above reproach, the church as *mathal* must steer clear of political power play and retain her skepticism on concentrations of power. The relationship of the church as *mathal* with political power is chiefly defined by her prophetic role – to speak God's word unequivocally so that the truth does not fall in the public square and righteousness, justice, and integrity are not outlawed (Isa 59:14). Truth-telling in a time of political white-washing and historical distortion becomes a holy mandate for the church as *mathal*.

Finally, the church as *mathal* is an example of *kalinisan* (purity) through her faithfulness in following God's *kalooban*. The church's devotion to God's way must persist even when the *katuwirang landas* (righteous path) is thorny and narrow, even when it means challenging and resisting systems and powers that are contrary to Christ's truth. By remaining in the *katuwirang landas*, the church is continuously purified and transformed into the likeness of Christ the *mathal* – the Lord who has gone through the same perilous path and whose light continues to illumine the way for those who follow. This truth is certain: It is the church as *mathal* – people of *kalinisan* (purity), who are *buo ang loob* (courageous) to embody their *patotoo* (commitment) to God, to the *kapwa* and to *sangkalikasan* – whom God will use to make illiberal empires crumble and succumb to Christ's sacred governance, and make the Risen Lord's rule flourish on earth as it is in heaven.

Bibliography

Alaras, Consolacion. "Pamathalaan." *Diliman Review* 53 (2006): 265–73.

Alejo, Albert. "Loob as Relational Interiority: A Contribution to the Philosophy of the Human Person." *Social Transformations: Journal of the Global South* 6 (2018): 32. Accessed 10 June 2021. 10.13185/2866.

De Guia, Kathrin. *Kapwa: The Self in the Other*. Pasig City: Anvil Publishing, 2005.

Ileto, Reynaldo. *Pasyon and Revolution*. Quezon City: Ateneo de Manila Press, 1979.

Ramos, Fidel. "Executive Order No. 319." *The Law Phil Project*, 3 April 1996. Accessed 3 November 2020. http://www.lawphil.net/executive/execord/eo1996/eo_319_1996.html.

Shahani, Leticia. "Senate Resolution No. 10." In *Filipino Values and National Development: Readings on the Moral Recovery Program*. Manila: Kabisig People's Movement, 1993.

Storkey, Alan. *Jesus and Politics: Confronting the Powers*. Grand Rapids: Baker, 2005.

Talisayon, Serafin. "Sacred Governance." *Center for Conscious Living Foundation* (January 2012): 1–26.

Wogaman, Phillip. *Christian Perspectives on Politics: Revised and Expanded*. Louisville: Westminster John Knox Press, 2000.

5

Enigmatic Formation of Separation of Church and State and De-politicization of Filipino Evangelicals

Nestor M. Ravilas

Introduction: Separation of Church and State in the Philippines

The Philippines is in turmoil and it is not a recent development. The country has been in this condition since I can remember, but now it seems to be rushing towards a precipice. The Rodrigo Duterte regime ended with almost thirteen trillion pesos national debt, and yet the incumbent is planning to add more to augment the 2023 national budget! Corruption is rampant and the amounts involved are obnoxious. The Philippine peso is weak. Inflation reached an all-time high of 8 percent. The spate of killings has not stopped, and many of those recently killed are environmental defenders and journalists.

What I describe above is a crisis in dire need of intervention. A few concerned Filipinos are aware of this crisis. They braved the odds and called out the country's leaders to shape up and the people to wake up. Prominent among them are religious leaders who have become influential among their flocks. Surprisingly, instead of heeding their call, the public signaled them to back off and just focus on their religious vocation. It was an audacious response. But I think it does not stem from people's insolence but from their understanding, albeit lacking, of the separation of church and state principle. This, they believe, should have been strictly observed by church leaders in the first place.

Take the case of Cardinal Antonio Luis G. Tagle of the Roman Catholic Church when he delivered a homily on the Palm Sunday of 2018. In his powerful sermon he rebuked political leaders for their abuse of power.[1] In an instant, angry netizens posted harsh criticisms of the cardinal and said he should stay away from politics and just mind his own religious business. What Cardinal Tagle experienced is neither an isolated case nor a unique phenomenon within the Catholic Church. From different religious groups, church leaders and laity alike are bashed on social media when they express their dissatisfaction and dismay over the mismanagement of our country's affairs and resources. They are told to stop infringing on matters of the state.

Evangelical groups are suffering from the same malady. Many group chats or "virtual meet-up places" designed for mutual edification have turned into war zones of political opinions. In many instances, group administrators themselves would call out and threaten to bar the politically savvy members posting about the latest issues. These members have been rebuked and demanded to stick with spiritual topics only, and keep their politics to themselves. I myself, and some of my friends have been reprimanded many times. We've been told to not confuse religion with politics; we've been warned to refrain from politicizing our religious social media groups.

In this context, this short essay will look into the formidable principle of the separation of politics and religion in the Philippine setting, and its de-politicizing impact on Filipino evangelical Christians. I am aware, on the other hand, that there are other factors besides the church-state separation that contribute to this malaise, but I will not touch on them in this essay. Given another opportunity, I hope to delve into those factors in the same manner that I did with the principle of separation of church and state, and how it may have caused the de-politicization of Filipino evangelicals.

Finally, if this essay by chance happens to implicate other religious groups, that is intentional rather than accidental. It is quite an ambitious attempt to contain in a 6,000-word chapter a colossal issue like the relationship of church and state. This, for sure, will generate more questions than answers. It is also this paper's objective to trigger the reader's interest to review, re-visit, and re-evaluate the principle of the separation of church and state and its impact on Philippine politics. To augment the discussion initiated here, more monographs will be written as soon as possible.

---

1. *Rappler*, "Cardinal Tagle hits violent, arrogant 'kings' on Palm Sunday 2018," 15 March 2018, https://www.youtube.com/watch?v=JDMAjwT9KYQ.

Wall of Separation in the Philippine Constitution

A major reason why the principle of separation is ensconced in Philippine culture is that it is enshrined in the country's constitution, which defines the relationship of politics and religion this way:

> Article III Section 5. No law shall be made respecting an establishment of religion, or prohibiting the free exercise thereof. The free exercise and enjoyment of religious profession and worship, without discrimination or preference, shall forever be allowed. No religious test shall be required for the exercise of civil or political rights.

As argued by legal pundits, the law directs the state on how it should govern its sovereign territory composed of different groups with various interests, worldviews, and religious persuasions. Perceived to be a liberal democratic state, the Philippines pays allegiance to a secular constitution designed to uphold impartiality to various faith traditions. In short, the Philippine democratic state should neither favor any religion nor prohibit its free exercise. It is vital for the state to legislate its impartiality in order to not embroil itself in religious rivalry and controversy, and to be able to stand its ground against religion's own hegemonic force.

The Philippine Constitution, however, does not stop there. It says further in Article II Section 6 that "The separation of church and state shall be inviolable."

This has muddled the issue of church-state relationship. The relationship of the two institutions was clearly defined by implying a metaphorical "wall of separation." That being said, the mandate to not breach the demarcation line defined by the law is given to both the state and the church. Despite this, however, some have remained adamant and have maintained that there is no separation of the two institutions in light of Article III Section 5 that I cited above. Christian Monsod, a constitutionalist and member of the constitutional commission that revised the Philippine Constitution a year after the People Power Revolt in 1986, scoffed on the separation in an interview and said it is impossible to conceive.[2]

On the other hand, Florin "Pilo" Hilbay, who served as the Philippine solicitor general during the time of President Benigno Aquino Jr., interpreted the provision in saying that, "The state should not meddle with the affairs of

---

2. CNN Philippines, "What the Law Says about Separation of Church, State," 3 June 2016, https://www.youtube.com/watch?v=BexoojxCrqQ.

religion and vice-versa."[3] To see the law as impossible to execute is one thing, but to have it enshrined in the Philippine Constitution is another. And that, in my opinion, is what Christian Monsod tried to dismiss.

The fact of the law cannot be denied. Separation of the two institutions was the clear intention behind the constitutional provision under scrutiny. Unknown to many, it was engraved in the First Philippine Constitution crafted by the revolutionary government of Emilio Aguinaldo, and ratified in January 1899, with the intention to separate the newly born Republic from religion. The "wall of separation" enshrined in the Philippine Charter clearly defines the boundary between the two institutions, to be strictly kept in order to uphold the law of the land.

Wall of Separation in the Bible

As has been observed, the majority of evangelical Christians observe the law with no scruples. The reason behind such acquiescence to the constitution is the alleged agreement of the Bible with the principle of the separation of church and state. The constitution was accorded biblical trappings in the words of Jesus, to give to Caesar what belongs to Caesar and to God what belongs to God (Matt 22:15–21; Mark 12:13–17; Luke 20:20–25). The divide implied by Jesus between civil authority and divine power is reinforced by his surprising declaration in the Gospel of John during his trial before Pilate, that his kingdom is not of this world (John 18:36). The two narratives are widely used to buttress the idea that religion is distinct from politics, and the two, therefore, should not be confused with each other.

Such flawed readings of biblical narratives have turned the political principle into a religious dogma that is donned with immense authority. Unfortunately, this short essay will not focus on the biblical narratives mentioned. However, it will go back to one of those stories later, in order to draw a brief theological reflection offering an alternative theological reading, and to guide us in conceiving a theology that is political. In the meantime, it's enough to say that those biblical stories did not make any mention of separation, and what seems to be the case is that we imported the principle of separation from them.

---

3. DZRH News Television, "Legal Minds: Separation of Church and State," 20 August 2019, https://www.youtube.com/watch?v=vEWfarPdTsA.

Separation as Default Relationship of Church and State

With both the constitutional and biblical underpinnings, the "separation" was accepted as the default and established as the natural condition of the relationship of church and state. As a result, evangelicals have been conditioned to use both the Constitution and the Bible as a starting point when responding to the question in regard to the relationship of church and state. Every discussion, therefore, on the role of the church in the country's political affairs will quickly crumble before the wall of separation.

De-politicization of Evangelicals and its Consequences

Since both constitutional and biblical materials are perceived to be colluded in ascertaining the truth of the separation, evangelicals have accepted it without questioning, much less to challenge its history, ideologies, logic, and validity. Evangelicals, therefore, have conducted themselves within the boundary set by the principle, making themselves highly de-politicized, and exposing themselves to unpleasant consequences in the process. Here are the following consequences:

- Evangelicals use the separation to excuse themselves from their socio-political responsibilities, and prohibit others, in the same way, from fulfilling their own societal duty.
- Evangelicals withdraw to their imagined cloisters and celebrate their faith and spirituality in seclusion, insulated from the socio-political realities in the country.
- Their non-engagement hampers the growth and maturity of their own theological discourses and spiritual disciplines.
- Exegetical methods they use in reading and interpreting the Bible are wanting in political sensitivity and awareness. Even the most touted liberal method of historical-critical is cautious not to dig deeper on the political and economic world of the Bible.
- In withdrawing, evangelicals miss out on their potential as vigilant citizens that monitor and call out bad political policies, unwise decisions, and mismanagement. As a result, they fail to contribute their share of wisdom and guidance in nation-building and in the realization of a democratic society.

Wall of Separation in History: An Inquiry on its Origin

The crises cited above compel us to address the situation with urgency before things get out of hand. The situation may not appear to some as critical enough to deserve serious attention, but careful analysis will lead us to their damaging contribution to many of the terminal problems the world is now facing (such as climate collapse, violence, terrorism, poverty, and the alarming decline of democracy, just to mention a few). As presently being observed, the surprising resurgence of religion from the belly of secularism,[4] proves that religions cannot be separated from public life. To welcome, therefore, religions to local and global conversations in making strategies and plans to save the planet from imminent collapse is a hopeful development.

With such urgency, an inquiry needs to be carried out. Is this "separation" the default relationship of politics and religion, or is it a recent invention? Truth has its own history, and so with the case of the separation. To have, therefore, a full view of the wall of separation is to look back to its own history, to find out how it began to achieve its indomitable force. We have to travel back to the period of its conception in order to examine forces and factors that created it, to look into the ideological context that shaped it, and to evaluate its validity as a formidable social formation.

How the Separation Started

There is confusion as to when and where the separation of politics and religion started. A few theories are offered in the field of political theology and sociology of religion that will help us navigate the problem. Jan Assmann, a known Egyptologist, suggests that a rudimentary form of the separation was initiated by the Egyptian pharaoh, Akenathen, in the 14th or 13th BC when he reformed both the politics and religion of Egypt.[5] In Greece, the short-lived democratic *poleis* in the 6th and 5th century BC can be considered a successful record of the split of the two institutions.[6]

---

4. Jose Casanova, *Public Religions in the Modern World* (Chicago: University of Chicago Press, 1994), 3–10. See also Jurgen Habermas, *Between Naturalism and Religion* (Cambridge: Polity Press, 2008), 114–16.

5. Jan Assmann, *Of God and Gods: Egypt, Israel and the Rise of Monotheism* (London, England: University of Wisconsin Press, 2008), 85–86.

6. Kurt A. Raaflaub, "Why Greek Democracy? Its Emergence and Nature in Context," in *A Companion to Greek Democracy and the Roman Republic*, ed. Dean Hammer (Chichester: John Wiley & Sons Ltd, 2015), 23–37.

Filomeno Aguilar Jr., a professor and historian, claims that the Philippines legislated the separation of church and state earlier than European countries, in the historic Malolos Congress in January 1899.[7] The claim was a bit brazen considering the Philippines is an Asian country and the historical process of separation of church and state has its provenance in the West. Although he intimated that the same legislation was made earlier in France in 1795, a few years after the historic French revolution, I wonder why Aguilar insisted on the Philippine primacy in the legislation of the separation. Aguilar could not unjustly deprive France of the honor on the basis that the life of the French Republic was cut short by Napoleon Bonaparte in 1799, considering that the Malolos Republic lasted for only two years, shorter than the French Republic.[8] In that case, conferring the honor to the Philippines is historically flawed or inaccurate.

Regardless whether Aguilar was fair on his assessment or not, the separation as a cultural formation has its origin on Western soil, particularly associated with the zealous campaign for religious freedom and toleration. The early recorded legislation of "implied" separation was traceable in Section 16 of the Virginia Declaration of Rights written in 1776. It says partly that, ". . . all men are equally entitled to the free exercise of religion, according to the dictates of conscience."[9]

By distancing itself from religion, the state ceased from deciding which Christian variant bears the true version of the Christian faith, which consequently promoted tolerance and peace.

This judicial concept was realized later in the United States Constitution written a few years after the Virginia Declaration of Rights. Apparently, the First Amendment, added in the US Constitution in 1791, was a distillation of Section 16 of the Virginia Declaration of Rights.[10]

Although the word "separation" was never mentioned there, it could have been its intention since the word came from Thomas Jefferson in his letter to a

---

7. Filomeno V. Aguilar Jr., "Church-State Relations in the 1899 Malolos Constitution: Filipinization and Visions of National Community," *Southeast Asian Studies*, 4, no. 2 (2015): 281, accessed 22 November 2022, http://englishkyoto-seas.org/.

8. Jean Bauberot, "A Brief History of French Laicite," in *Religion and Secularism in France Today*, ed. Philipp Portier et al. (London and New York: Routledge, 2022), 11–19.

9. "America's Founding Document," *National Archives*, accessed 4 December 2022, https://www.archives.gov/founding-docs/virginia-declaration-of-rights.

10. Philip Andrew Quadrio, "Locke, Secularism and the Justice of the Secular Solution: Towards a Self-Reflective Transcending of Secular Self-Understanding" in *Secularisations and Their Debates: Perspectives on the Return of Religion in the Contemporary West*, eds. Matthew Sharpe and Dylan Nickelson (New York; London: Springer, 2014), 46–47.

Baptist pastor in 1801.[11] Jefferson was a significant figure in the framing of the United States Constitution. Although he was not present during its penning, it was said that James Madison, the known father of the US Constitution, was in close contact with Jefferson who was in France that time serving as consul.[12] Separation was therefore embedded in the First Amendment.

Separation, a Recent Invention

Whether we assign the formulation of the separation to 1776 or to 1791 or to 1801, or to the Malolos Constitution in 1899, the fact of the matter is that the separation of religion and politics is just a recent invention. Contrary to what we assumed in the beginning of this paper, separation was neither the natural nor the original condition of the relationship of religion and politics. With this, can we assume, therefore, that prior to the separation of the two institutions in the recent past, the two were originally joined and closely impinging on each other's affairs? If that is the case, evangelicals should therefore suspend in the meantime their unqualified submission to the separation law until thorough re-investigation of the matter is carried out to clarify factors and events that prompted its creation in recent history.

In the Beginning: Union of Politics and Religion

In the study of political theology, one common trend among the definitions given to it is its power to legitimize political authority. With this, it appears that, traditionally, politics owes its legitimacy and authority from religion. If this is the case, religion did not infiltrate the political sphere as some might have been thinking. It was, rather, the other way around. Religion was summoned, befriended, and assimilated by politics to address its legitimacy crisis. What do I mean by that?

As its authority is sanctioned by transcendental power and is shored up by revelation, religion stands on secured ground. With this, religion can command loyalty, subordination and obedience from people.[13]

---

11. Daniel L. Dreisbach, *Thomas Jefferson and the Wall of Separation between Church and State* (New York: New York University Press, 2002), 1–4.

12. Carol Walker, "Thomas Jefferson," *The First Amendment Encyclopedia*, accessed 22 November 2022, https://www.mtsu.edu/first-amendment/article/1218/thomas-jefferson.

13. Jurgen Habermas, "'The Political': The Rational Meaning of a Questionable Inheritance of Political Theology," in *The Power of Religion in the Public Sphere*, eds. Eduardo Mendieta et al. (New York: Columbia University Press, 2011), 17–18.

The case of politics, on the other hand, is completely different. Political authority was less problematic where social groupings were composed of people related by blood. In such social groupings, respect, loyalty, and obedience were not hard to give to the oldest, and considered as the wisest and most experienced of the clan. This is not to say that religion did not play a significant role in their social organization. It was, for sure, an integral factor in their communal integration and formation. Nonetheless, political leadership recognized the most respectable, credible, and capable members of a clan as the tribe leaders rather than they were divinely chosen.

Development happened when larger communities started to form as a result of migration driven by wars and famines, among other causes. The merging into larger groups of people from various origins created a crisis in political leadership. On what ground would people gather and organize themselves under the leadership of someone who has no blood ties with them?[14] Despite the obstacle, society was pressed to organize themselves to pursue peace, prosperity, and survival. With this collective social aim, leadership position was crucial and vital.

This leadership crisis prompted people to summon religion into the political arena to address the legitimation deficiency of political leadership brought about by the larger society of nation-state.

Drawing from the Same Source of Power and Legitimacy

As a result, both religion and politics started sharing from the same source of power, authority, and legitimacy, which consequently resulted in the intersection of the two. This condition was best illustrated in the affairs of Samuel and King Saul in the book of 1 Samuel in the Old Testament. Samuel was reduced to a mere prophet and priest when political power was taken away from him and given to the newly appointed king, Saul. This resulted in the creation of two powers in ancient Israel; distinct but both legitimized by the same source, Yahweh (1 Sam 8:1–10:26).

This development brought politics and religion closely linked with each other, resulting in confusion, conflicts, and at times, horrific crimes caused by their collusion. Confusion as to which of the two is superior in power, conflicts whenever a contest over superiority went out of hand, and horrific crimes when the two connived to inflict injustice and violence to people. The religious wars that decimated Europe in 1522–1648 made people realize that

---

14. Habermas, "The Power of Religion," 17.

unless and until politics and religion were finally separated, all the conflicts, scandals, and crimes that their toxic marriage brings would never ever stop.

Divorce and the Birth of Secular Democratic State

Political thinkers in the early modern period observed that as long as religion and politics draw power and authority from the same source, the scandals and crimes their relationship has caused will never cease. The long history of religious wars that followed the disintegration of Christianity into various splintered groups, engendered by the Reformation of Martin Luther, ravaged Europe and left them with no choice but to seek a solution to stop the carnage.[15] It was later realized that it would be best for politics to disentangle itself from the infighting among Christian groups over the question of which of the variants they represent bears the true version of Christian faith. Politics and religion must then be separated. But this can only be done by leading one of them to another source of power and legitimacy. Since the sacred was originally allied with religion, it was politics that should leave and lead somewhere else to look for its own source of legitimation and power.

Thomas Hobbes was recognized as the first one who attempted to draw political legitimacy and authority from the people and who first collected legal materials. John Locke developed what Hobbes started, then other enlightenment thinkers followed.[16] A new source of legitimacy was found. A secular politics grounded on the consent of the people emerged, and a collection of laws agreed and ratified in a constitutional assembly was established to govern and guide nation building. Many consitutions are based on the principle of the sovereignty of the people, and found their governing authority in the people. These ideas began the separation of politics and religion.

Separation in the Malolos Constitution

The presence of the doctrine of separation in the Philippine Constitution is a bit surprising, considering that the doctrine and all its corollary principles such as enlightenment, secularism, and religious toleration have all their origin in the West. The common assumption is that the Americans brought the separation

---

15. Ross Harrison, *Hobbes, Locke and Confusion's Masterpiece: An Examination of 17th Century Political Philosophy* (Cambridge: Cambridge University Press, 2002), 8–12.

16. Victoria Kahn, *The Future of Illusion: Political Theology and Early Modern Text* (Chicago: University of Chicago Press, 2014), 26–37.

doctrine to the Philippines when they colonized the country in 1901. Official history, however, tells of an interesting variant of the story.

On the 25th of January 1899, the fledgling Philippine Republic that had just declared its independence from Spain, the colonizer of the country for more than three hundred years, ratified its charter. Among the important items carved in that constitution was the separation of church and state. It seems the Americans, who colonized the country a couple of years after, have nothing to do with the presence of the wall of separation in the Philippine Constitution. Where did our forebears get the principle, and how did it land in the first constitution that was crafted more than a century ago?

The country's independence from imperial Spain was declared in June 1898 in Kawit Cavite, at the balcony of the house of Emilio Aguinaldo, the first president of the Philippine Republic. The next logical step in envisioning the post-colonial community is to draw its national charter. Immediately, in September of the same year, one hundred ninety-three *ilustrados* (wealthy and educated natives) gathered in Barasoain Church in Malolos, Bulacan, to envision the newly born republic by carving its national charter.[17]

As reported, the future of the relationship of church and state, which was described by Teodoro Agoncillo as a thorny question, divided the Malolos Congress into two infighting groups.[18] The issue was scheduled for floor deliberation in October, but it was deferred to the following month, due to the anticipation that a fervid debate would erupt between the two contesting groups with diametrically opposing perspectives on the matter.[19]

Post-colonial Philippines in relation to religion was envisioned within two possible paths: a religious state with Philippine Catholicism embraced as the national religion, or a secular state that is free from any religion. The tension was debated intensely by the contesting groups of Felipe Calderon and Tomas Del Rosario, both *ilustrados*, both lawyers, and both from wealthy families. Calderon with his "unity" group pushed for the first option, patterned closely from *Patronato Real*.[20] On the other side, Del Rosario and his "separationist" group crusaded for a more radical reform, a republic free from religion.

---

17. Teodoro A. Agoncillo, *Malolos: The Crisis of the Republic* (Quezon City: University of the Philippines Press, 1960), 223–28.

18. Agoncillo, *Malolos*, 242.

19. Aguilar, "Church-State," 283.

20. *Patronato Real* or Royal Patronage is the agreement between the Vatican and the Spanish crown in which the latter sponsored and financially supported Catholic missionary work in Spanish colonies in exchange of the Spanish crown to have the deciding voice in the selec-

Both groups fervently defended their imagined national community. Due to limited space, this paper will only tackle briefly the arguments of both sides, which are crucial to the issue of the separation of church and state.

Anti-friars Sentiment

Anti-friar sentiment was the biggest argument made as to why religion should be barred from the newly born republic. There were no qualms about the accusation against the friars' abusive records during the Spanish colonial rule in the Philippines.[21] Interestingly, both contending parties attested to the veracity of the abuses, and both despised the friars.[22] The abuses were primarily blamed on *Patronato Real*, the collusion between the Vatican and the Spanish crown.[23] Under the protection of the Spanish state, the friars enjoyed not only ecclesiastical authority, but civil as well. No wonder that among the reasons the separationists wanted religious people out of the political arena was their usurpation of civil offices.

Friars and Land Grabbing

The power of the friars was seen in their greedy accumulation of wealth, particularly agricultural lands. Cesar Majul wrote about the many acres of land acquired by the friars. In the inquiry done in 1900, huge agricultural holdings were discovered under the control of the friars. The Taft report listed an estimated 403,713 acres while the 4th Report of the Philippine Commission had it at around 420,000 acres of agricultural land owned by the friars.[24] Felipe Calderon remarked at one point that the whole of Cavite was owned by the friars! The reason why Cavite was tagged as one of the hotbeds of uprisings and unrests was peasants' outrage.[25] Restoration, therefore, of the vast land of Cavite from the hands of the friars was among the goals of the new republic of Emilio Aguinaldo.[26]

---

tion of ecclesiastical personnel and the disposition of the local church's revenues, see Aguilar, "Church-State," 289.

21. Cesar A. Majul, *The Political and Constitutional Ideas of the Philippine Revolution* (Quezon City: University of the Philippines Press, 1967), 116–22.

22. Aguilar, "Church-State," 284–85.

23. Majul, *The Political and Constitutional*, 147.

24. Majul, *The Political and Constitutional*, 123–24.

25. Majul, *The Political and Constitutional*, 125–26.

26. Majul, *The Political and Constitutional*, 131.

Birthright of the Revolutionary Clergy

Despite the friar problem, Felipe Calderon's group campaigned and argued for the unity of the church and the state from a different perspective. Although they fully sympathized with the anti-friar sentiment, they valued more the contributions of the native clergy to the national revolution and considered it as enough reason to embrace Philippine Catholicism as the national religion of the new republic. Calderon's group wanted to acknowledge the birthright of the native clergy in the struggle for independence since the fight of the native clergy for the filipinization of the Roman Catholic church served as the catalyst for the struggle for national independence.[27] Jose Rizal himself, the Philippine national hero, recognized this birthright when he dedicated his second book, *El Filibusterismo*, to the three martyred native priests dubbed as Gomburza, implicated in the Cavite Mutiny of 1872.

Philippine Catholic Church and Restoration of Land

Moreover, the Calderon group believed that the unity of the Filipino Catholic church and the Philippine Republic would give them a chance to retrieve the acres of land grabbed by the friars. Although the "separation" faction of Del Rosario saw this as unlikely to happen, Calderon's group argued that a compact could be worked out with the Vatican later to make it possible.[28] In Calderon's view, to separate the church from the state is tantamount to losing those properties completely from the Republic.

By and large, the struggle for national independence was inextricably connected with the struggle for the filipinization of the Roman Catholic church. The revolutionary leaders were fully aware that as long as the church is controlled by foreign religious entities, the journey towards national liberation would be far from being realized. To say it bluntly, decolonization is possible *only* within the ambit of liberation of both the nation and the church.[29]

Separation Wins!

Finally, votes were cast after a long and heated debate on the floor. The "separation of church and state" won by one vote and thus found its way in the

---

27. Majul, *The Political and Constitutional*, 138.
28. Majul, *The Political and Constitutional*, 139.
29. Majul, *The Political and Constitutional*, 114.

First Philippine Constitution.[30] Article 5 of Title 3 says: "The State recognizes the equality of all religious worships and the separation of the Church and the State."

Deferment of the Implementation

Apolinario Mabini, chief adviser to Aguinaldo and prescient as ever, knew that this development was not good for the fledgling republic. The revolutionary clergy, who were expecting the new republic to embrace Philippine Catholicism as the national religion, and to serve at the same time in the new government, would be offended.[31] Mabini was aware that the relationship between the Philippine Republic and its American ally was volatile, that war between them could erupt anytime soon, and thereby the services of the revolutionary clergy would once again be badly needed.[32] With this fraught relationship with the Americans, the Philippine Republic could not afford to antagonize the Filipino clergy and cause them to withdraw their support from the cause of independence.

True indeed, when Father Gregorio Aglipay, a clergy-member of the Malolos Congress, arrived from an errand and was informed of the result of the voting, he got irritated and immediately petitioned Aguinaldo to suspend the law.[33] The separation law, therefore, was left unresolved when Aguinaldo, through the advice of Mabini, deferred its implementation due to the fear of backlash from the offended revolutionary clergy. He reasoned that the nation's condition was so volatile to implement such delicate legislation, but made a promise to return to the issue once the situation becomes stable.[34]

Aguinaldo and Mabini's scheme was smart not to antagonize any of the two contending groups. Aguinaldo deferred its implementation to appease the angered clergy, but he did not veto the law so as not to offend the pro-separationist group of Del Rosario. For political expediency, the newly born republic took the Roman Catholic Church as its national religion due to the temporary deferment of the law of separation, until such time as the law was revisited.

---

30. Aguilar, "Church-State," 283–84.
31. Aguilar, "Church-State," 301–3.
32. Majul, *The Political and Constitutional*, 144–45.
33. Majul, *The Political and Constitutional*, 143.
34. Aguilar, "Church-State," 301–2.

Separation and American Colonization

While the issue of separation was left unresolved, barely two months after the ratification of the Malolos Constitution the fledgling republic plunged into another war with a new colonizer. With the dominant force of America invading and the exhausted Philippine army just emerging from a fierce war against the Spaniards, the American colonizers subdued the land in barely two years.

The United States immediately installed its colonial bureaucracy and imposed its own laws in the land. Among the civil rights enjoyed by the colonized people, under the Organic Act (or Cooper Act) passed by the United States Congress as the framework of Philippine colonial government in 1902, was the freedom of religion patterned from the First Amendment of the American Constitution.[35] As a forerunner of the principle of the separation of church and state in the West, the Americans imposed the same policy in their newly conquered territory.

With this development, the newly born republic was never given a chance to return to the working table to further deliberate the separation as they had planned. The Americans technically hijacked the issue and implemented, under the pressure of colonial force, what the Philippine Republic failed to do. Were the Americans aware of the separation crafted but deferred in the Malolos Congress, and so they took it upon themselves to implement it? Or, was it serendipitous that the Americans happened to embrace the same principle that coincided with the Malolos Congress decision? Whatever the answer is to this question, the controversial law was once-and-for-all implemented by a colonial power without the chance for the Filipinos to re-examine and re-evaluate the validity of the law of separation, along with its pros and cons in regard to their struggle for an imagined national community.

Summary

- The relationship of the church and the state in the Philippine Republic was decided by less than two hundred members of the *ilustrado* class, and the separation was engraved into the constitution by the will of only twenty-six of these *ilustrados*.
- Even those who campaigned, and voted for the separation remained religious and averred their allegiance to the Catholic faith. Though they opted for the separation, they were not ready to be impartial

---

35. Aguilar, "Church-State," 305.

with religion, let alone embrace secularism, which is an integral component of liberal-constitutional democracy.[36]
- If the trauma of "religious wars" is the primary cause of the separation of religion and politics in the West, the Philippine case was instigated, however, by the abuses of the friars, which was less serious in comparison to the West to warrant a separation.
- The majority of revolutionary forces, ordinary soldiers, and the larger Philippine population were cordoned from participating in the convention; they were never consulted, informed, and oriented regarding the debate on the state and religion relationship and its implications on the envisioned republic.[37]
- The implementation was suspended due to the question of the rights of the revolutionary clergy in the new republic and the impending war with the Americans.
- The Philippine Republic was deprived of the chance to revisit and re-evaluate the pending issue of separation when the Americans colonized the fledgling republic and imposed their own laws, including the separation of church and state. It turned out, therefore, that on the first occasion, the principle was engraved in the constitution by the will of a few *ilustrados*, and on the second one, by imposition of imperial America. Technically, among other social formations, the separation was bequeathed to the Filipinos under the duress of imperial subjugation.
- The de-politicization therefore of evangelicals and other religious people is a product of an enigmatic historical development that is actually a recent phenomenon. Refusal to revisit and re-assess this ambiguous social formation is due primarily to its advantages to both the state and the church. On the side of the state, it weaponizes the principle by dodging the church's attacks and criticisms. On the side of the church, it enjoys various privileges that the separation has accorded it, such as tax exemption, which involves a huge amount considering the colossal properties owned by big and rich religions.

---

36. Ulrich Beck, *A God of One's Own: Religion's Capacity for Peace and Potential for Violence*, trans. Rodney Livingston (Cambridge: Polity Press, 2010), 20–21.

37. Ambeth R. Ocampo, "Revolution Perished at Malolos Meet," in *101 Stories on Philippine Revolution* (Pasig City: Anvil Publishing Inc, 2009), 111–13.

Conclusion: Theological Reflection

As I stated early on, the contentious incident where Jesus was asked a trap-question on the lawfulness of paying taxes to Caesar has often been used to buttress the separation of church and state, contributing to the de-politicization of Filipino evangelicals. Let me draw out, therefore, from the same narrative our theological reflection.

To begin with, some details are immediately noticeable that do not sit well with the dominant interpretation of the story, which would therefore demand its re-assessment. As already mentioned, the word "separation" was neither found nor intimated in the narrative. The idea was forced into it. More so, the concept of "separation" is a modern phenomenon that is being anachronistically read into the narrative. It appears that the narrative is being used to support a cultural formation that is alien to it.

Consider the surprising fact that this narrative was the only occasion where Jesus directly addressed Caesar or the Romans, and this direct naming of the emperor was associated with the practice of imperial taxation. Jesus's invocation of the the emperor's name and of imperial taxation happened right in Jerusalem, Judea, which was under the rule of Rome since AD 6, and was therefore being taxed by the emperor.[38] It was most likely that this allegedly subversive detail of the story made its way in all the synoptic gospels and was at the same time preserved in the Gospel of Judas and in Papyrus Egerton 2. The seeming popularity of the narrative speaks of its importance to the early Christian communities.[39] While for us, our lack of appreciation of this allegedly subversive material is due to ignorance of the onerous practice of colonization.

In this regard, Michael Given helps us understand how controversial and subversive is our narrative. Given emphasizes that imperial taxation is the "heart of colonization."[40] Imperial taxation and tributes do not only exploit and abuse the colonized by seizing away portions of the peasant's table food, they are also signs that people are under the yoke of foreign subjugation. If that is the case, the question thrown to Jesus, whether it is lawful or not for the Jews to pay taxes to Caesar, is essentially asking his opinion on the presence of Roman colonizers on Jewish soil.

---

38. David A. Fiensy, "Assessing the Economy of Galilee in the Late Second Temple," in *The Galilean Economy in the Time of Jesus*, eds. David A. Fiensy et al. (Atlanta, USA: Society of Biblical Literature, 2013), 168.

39. Sean Freyne, *Jesus, a Jewish Galilean: A New Reading of the Jesus Story* (London: T&T Clark International, 2004), 143.

40. Michael Given, *The Archaeology of the Colonized* (London: Routledge, 2004), 26.

Fully aware that imperial taxation is a delicate matter, Jesus knew that any reckless response could either ignite another round of uprising, or cause him to be thrown right away in jail on the charges of sedition. Discretion and wisdom, therefore, are needed in answering the trap-question to avoid bloodshed. Jesus smartly requested a denarius. Then he asked whose image was inscribed in it (to confuse his audience as to what he was really up to). Upon hearing that it was Caesar's image carved in the coin, Jesus said the enigmatic line, "Give to Caesar things that belong to Caesar and to God things that belong to God." What Jesus said gave the impression that he was in favor of paying taxes and tributes to the Romans. But it was a cryptic statement that any Jew who shared Jesus's worldview would not miss its true message. The coin belongs to the Romans as the emperor's image was engraved on it. What belongs to God, however, is the entire land of Israel. All the Jews in the scene knew very well, as covenantal people, that as far as the Sinai Covenant is concerned, the land and everything in it belonged to Yahweh, and given as a gift to the people of Israel. Nothing in the land belongs to Caesar, and nothing should be given to Caesar. This cryptic message was the context behind the accusation charged against Jesus during his arrest in Luke 23:2, that he opposed paying taxes to Caesar. It was what Jesus really meant, so it was what the Jews understood.

Far from understanding the story as instituting the divide between religion and politics, it should rather be viewed as an incident of intersection between the two institutions where a religious teacher, a rabbi, was speaking against the oppressive political power of the Roman empire. If any paradigm happened to be constituted by the narrative, it was the integration between the two institutions of church and state, of religion and politics. Jesus lives in and transcends both worlds, and to restrain him to one side is to make him subject to the contraptions of modern society. A re-consideration of the principle of the separation of church and state is therefore necessary and inevitable. It is much-needed, particularly in the Philippines where a significant majority of evangelical Christians have relinquished their rights and their duty to fight for, demand, and install a good, just, and righteous political culture.

Bibliography

Agoncillo, Teodoro A. *Malolos: The Crisis of the Republic.* Quezon City: University of the Philippine Press, 1960.

Aguilar, Filomeno V., Jr. "Church-State Relations in the 1899 Malolos Constitution: Filipinization and Visions of National Community." *Southeast Asian Studies*, 4, no. 2 (2015): 281. http://englishkyoto-seas.org/.

Assmann, Jan. *Of God and Gods: Egypt, Israel and the Rise of Monotheism*. London: University of Wisconsin Press, 2008.

Bauberot, Jean. "A Brief History of French Laicite." In *Religion and Secularism in France Today*. London: Routledge, 2022.

Beck, Ulrich. *A God of One's Own: Religion's Capacity for Peace and Potential for Violence*. Translated by Rodney Livingston. Cambridge: Polity Press, 2010.

Casanova, Jose. *Public Religions in the Modern World*. Chicago: The University of Chicago Press, 1994.

CNN Philippines. "What the Law Says about Separation of Church, State." 3 June 2016. Educational video, 1:55. https://www.youtube.com/watch?v=BexoojxCrqQ.

Dreisbach, Daniel L. *Thomas Jefferson and the Wall of Separation between Church and State*. New York: New York University Press, 2002.

DZRH News Television. "Legal Minds: Separation of Church and State." 20 August 2019. Educational video, 15:43. https://www.youtube.com/watch?v=vEWfarPdTsA.

Fiensy, David A. "Assessing the Economy of Galilee in the Late Second Temple." In *The Galilean Economy in the Time of Jesus*. Atlanta: Society of Biblical Literature, 2013.

Freyne, Sean. *Jesus, a Jewish Galilean: A New Reading of the Jesus Story*. London: T&T Clark International, 2004.

Given, Michael. *The Archaeology of the Colonized*. London: Routledge, 2004.

Habermas, Jurgen. *Between Naturalism and Religion*. Cambridge: Polity Press, 2008.

———. "'The Political': The Rational Meaning of a Questionable Inheritance of Political Theology." In *The Power of Religion in the Public Sphere*. New York: Columbia University Press, 2011.

Harrison, Ross. *Hobbes, Locke and Confusion's Masterpiece: An Examination of 17th Century Political Philosophy*. Cambridge: Cambridge University Press, 2002.

Kahn, Victoria. *The Future of Illusion: Political Theology and Early Modern Text*. Chicago: University of Chicago Press, 2014.

Majul, Cesar A. *The Political and Constitutional Ideas of the Philippine Revolution*. Quezon City: University of the Philippine Press, 1967.

Ocampo, Ambeth R. "Revolution Perished at Malolos Meet." In *101 Stories on Philippine Revolution*. Pasig City: Anvil Publishing, 2009.

Quadrio, Philip Andrew. "Locke, Secularism and the Justice of the Secular Solution: Towards a Self-Reflective Transcending of Secular Self-Understanding." In *Secularisations and their Debates: Perspective on the Return of Religion in the Contemporary West*. New York: Springer, 2014.

Raaflaub, Kurt A. "Why Greek Democracy? Its Emergence and Nature in Context." In *A Companion to Greek Democracy and the Roman Republic*. Chichester: John Wiley & Sons Ltd, 2015.

Rappler. "Cardinal Tagle hits violent, arrogant 'kings' on Palm Sunday 2018." 25 March 2018. Religious video, 12:36. https://www.youtube.com/watch?v=JDMAjwT9KYQ.

Walker, Carol. "Thomas Jefferson," *The First Amendment Encyclopedia*. (2009). https://www.mtsu.edu/first-amendment/article/1218/thomas-jefferson.

6

Not the Janus-Faced State

(Re-)Reading the Decalogue as Basis for Normative Politics[1]

Romel Regalado Bagares

Citizenship in early political communities is . . . as much a part of the revelation of God and of our identity as God's image bearer as are marriage, family, friendship, discipleship, and shepherding. . . . [i]n the Bible's light . . . the development of well-governed political communities is one of the important dimensions of our service to God and neighbors in God's kingdom. In the new heavens and new earth, there will be no curse, because there will no longer be any sin or disobedience to condemn; that will mean God's throne of justice has been fully established in our midst; it will not mean the end of government and political community. . . .[2]

In our concern today about political, economic, and social justice we should not lose sight of this progression in the revelation of God. The bondage of sin goes deeper than oppression or exploitation. Liberation goes beyond it. At

---

1. I am grateful to Archbishop (ret.) Antonio Ledesma, S.J, Bruce Wearne, James W. Skillen, the VU Amsterdam Christian Philosophy Reading Group, and the editors for their comments to earlier drafts of the essay.
2. James W. Skillen, *The Good of Politics* (Grand Rapids: Baker Academic, 2014), 37.

the same time, this progression is a deepening, not a negation. The bondage of sin does include all social injustice.[3]

The Decalogue as Moral Prolegomena to Politics

Five years ago, my family became members of a small confessional Presbyterian congregation in Metro Manila. Every Sunday, the congregation recites the Decalogue (Ten Commandments) before the liturgy leads them to public confession. It's not that I didn't know the Decalogue before, having been taught about it in Sunday school in a Protestant evangelical church in Mindanao where I came to faith in Christ.[4] Yet it was never part of the Sunday services of my childhood. I recall being taught at a Bible study in my teens that it had been superseded by the Two Greatest Commandments taught by Jesus in the New Testament. In contrast, I noticed that Roman Catholic churches displayed in their premises giant replicas of the Decalogue's two tablets. In many a national election that I can recall from my youth, Roman Catholic bishops would hold it as a measure of a candidate's fitness to hold public office. It was much later as an adult that I would come to know that both Christian traditions have historically embraced a common reading for it. Thomas Aquinas (ca. 1225–1274), the Angelic Doctor, taught that the Old Law embodied the moral law binding for all times and cultures but its ceremonial and juridical rules were applied only to Israel. This moral law – which belongs to natural law knowable by right reason – proceeds from the general precepts to love God and neighbor[5] (as Jesus would summarize the Decalogue into the Two Greatest Commandments in the gospels). After its Catholic counterpart, Protestant Scholasticism also considered the Decalogue a unified moral law inseparable from the basic commandment of Christianity.[6] The 1646 Westminster Confession of Faith, the

---

3. Henk G. Geertsema, "Higher Education as Service to the King," in *Homo Respondens: Essays in Christian Philosophy*, eds. Govert J. Buijs and Perry Huesmann (Grand Rapids: Paideia Press, 2021), 454.

4. The Protestant Reformed divide the Decalogue's two tables into five commandments each, the last one on the first table being the command to honor one's parents. Roman Catholics and Lutherans treat the first four as part of the first table, the rest, of the second. See David L. Barker, "Ten Commandments, Two Tablets: The Shape of the Decalogue," *Themelios* 30, issue 3 (Summer 2005): 6–22; and *New Advent*, "The Ten Commandments." https://www.newadvent.org/cathen/04153a.htm.

5. J. Budziszewski, *Commentary on Thomas Aquinas's Treatise on Law* (Cambridge: Cambridge University Press, 2014), 221–25.

6. Scholasticism is used here in two senses: how Greek thought from the ancient times shaped Christian thinking as it developed an *apologia* of God and the world, as well as the highly specialized academic technique of disputation by distinction employed by the professors

great mid-17th century Protestant summary of the doctrines of faith, echoed Aquinas's view of the Decalogue:

> The moral law binds all people at all times to obedience, both those who are justified and those who are not. The obligation to obey the moral law is not only because of its content, but also because of the authority of God the Creator, who gave it. In the gospel Christ in no way dissolves this obligation, but strengthens it.[7]

This majority view in the Christian tradition, founded on the merger of the Bible and Greek thought, held that the human mind is able to grasp a rational order created by a rational God, and therefore, its moral rules as well.[8] The Scholastics were certainly aware of a wide variety of practical normative obligations, but in reading the Decalogue, they understood the scope of the question of normativity of such obligations as chiefly moral. We owe much to the great intellectual and spiritual achievements of this tradition.[9] Moreover, in both Protestant Reformed and Roman Catholic thought and practice, I see the continuing relevance of the Decalogue to the Christian life that the larger communities of Filipino evangelicals have tended to neglect. In this essay I explore how the Decalogue may relate to the question of a "normative politics" and what Filipino evangelicals may learn from it as part of their Reformation heritage; to do that, I propose that we (re)read it from lenses wider than what both Protestants and Roman Catholics have traditionally used.

Reading the Decalogue Beyond the Moral

Here, I draw from a smaller stream of the Neocalvinist tradition, in particular, the "reformational" philosophical movement identified with the late Dutch

---

(the "schoolmen") of the medieval universities. Jeremy G. A. Ive, "The Covenantal Trinitarian Alternative to the Scholastic Dilemma," *In die Skriflig/ In Luce Verbi* 52 no. 3 (2018): a2304.

    7. Chad Van Dixhoorn, *Confessing the Faith: A Reader's Guide to the Westminster Confession of Faith* (Edinburgh: The Banner of Truth Trust, 2014), 246–47; and Richard A. Muller, "Scholasticism and Orthodoxy in the Reformed Tradition: Definition and Method" in *After Calvin: Studies in the Development of a Theological Tradition* (Oxford: Oxford University Press, 2003), 27.

    8. Budziszewski, *Commentary on Thomas*, xviii-xxi, 127. See also Brian Tierney, *The Idea of Natural Rights: Studies on Natural Rights, Natural Law, and Church Law: 1160–1625* (Grand Rapids: Eerdmans, 2001); and Richard Ross, "Distinguishing Eternal Law from Transient Law: Natural Law and the Judicial Laws of Moses," *Past and Present* (2012).

    9. See the four-volume Richard Muller, *Post-Reformation Reformed Dogmatics* (Grand Rapids: Baker Academic, 2003); also, *Aquinas Among the Protestants*, eds. Manfred Svensson and David Van Drunen (Hoboken: Wiley-Blackwell, 2018).

philosopher and jurist Herman Dooyeweerd (1894–1977) and his brother-in-law D. H. Th. Vollenhoven (1892–1973). Not to be confused with "new Calvinism," it is a late 19th century religious movement in the Netherlands, whose proponents sought to realize Calvin's doctrinal insights on the sovereignty of God in culture and society.[10] Neocalvinists of the reformational stripe began within the classical framework (the so-called "Logos speculation") but over time developed a deep commitment to the biblical worldview as a basis for philosophical systematics, even in their account of the God-creation distinction, thus:

> But the radicality and primordiality of that distinction in neo-Calvinism, which seeks to capture the force of the Isaianic passages on the incomparability and transcendence of Yahweh, has some unexpected implications. If rationality is creature, and there is no creaturely principle of continuity between the Maker and the made, then rationality disqualifies as that principle . . . Accordingly, the reformational philosophers break with the ancient Christian tradition . . . , which identifies the Logos of John 1 with the logos of Heraclitean and Stoic paganism.[11]

For them, the Protestant Reformer John Calvin decisively foreswore rationalistic scholasticism and its dualistic insistence on the distinction between nature and grace, where true knowledge of God (grace) may be gained autonomously through speculative natural theology (nature). "Calvin," writes Dooyeweerd, "radically rejected the speculative natural theology," calling it "an 'audacious curiosity' of human reason that seeks to intrude upon the '*essentiae Dei*,' which we can never fathom, but can only worship."[12] This insight is drawn from Calvin's description of God's relation to the created world: *Deus legibus solutus est sed non exlex* (God is not subject to laws but he is also not arbitrary).[13]

---

10. Albert Wolters, "Dutch Neo-Calvinism: Worldview, Philosophy and Rationality" in *Rationality in the Calvinian Tradition*, eds. H. Hart, J. van der Hoeven and Nicholas Wolterstorff (Eugene: Wipf and Stock, 1983), 113–31.

11. Wolters, "Dutch Neo-Calvinism," 126–27.

12. Herman Dooyeweerd, *A New Critique of Theoretical Thought*, Vol. I (Jordan Station: Paideia Press), 517 [hereinafter, *NC I*].

13. Dooyeweerd, *NC 1*, 517. Muller allows that Calvin did exhibit a complicated relationship to scholasticism; he overtly – and even vociferously – rejected some of its methods at the same time that in many of his works "there is also appropriation, sometimes explicit, but often unacknowledged." Richard A. Muller, *The Unaccommodated Calvin: Studies in the Foundation of Theological Tradition* (Oxford: Oxford University Press, 2009), 57.

For them, the notion of a rational order turned rationality into "something in itself, either within itself or as an ideal for the present world. This order then is related to God, but primarily to his mind. Order is still basically rational. As such it is interpreted in basically impersonal terms: essence, causal order, finality."[14] But the Bible stresses an order given by God and fully dependent on him.[15] Reluctant to speak of "natural law,"[16] the reformational tradition instead refers to differentiated laws and norms that are embodied in creation and creaturely life yet do not apply to the Creator.[17] In that way, it distinguishes its understanding of reality from the realist (natural law) and nominalist/constructivist (modern and postmodern) approaches.[18] This essay allows but a brief explanation of Dooyeweerd's philosophy. He identifies and distinguishes between and among fifteen mutually irreducible and inter-related aspects of our temporal reality: numerical, spatial, movement, physical and chemical, biotic (organic life), psychical feeling, logical analysis (reason), historical, linguistic, social, economic, aesthetic, juridical, moral (ethical) and the aspect of faith. These aspects account for basic diversity in reality and the unity and coherence that can be found within such diversity. They are not the concrete "what" of phenomena but are "the different modes of the universal 'how' which determine the aspects of our theoretical view of reality." All things or events in our world function in all these fifteen intertwined and yet distinct modes of being.[19]

All of Life is Religion

The Decalogue's central command, summarized by Jesus – "You shall love the Lord your God with all your heart, and with all your soul, and with all your mind," and "You shall love your neighbor as yourself" (Matt 22:36, 39 RSV) – *is of a religious, rather than of a merely moral character.*[20] Human existence is

---

14. Geertsema, "Higher Education," 466.
15. Geertsema, "Higher Education," 466–67.
16. Govert J. Buijs and Annette K. Mosher, "Introduction: Rethinking the Idea of Creation Order Among Humans: Beyond Natural Law and Constructivism" in *The Future of Creation Order*, eds. Govert J. Buijs and Annette K. Mosher, *The Future of Creation Order*, Vol. 2 (Cham: Springer, 2018), 5–12.
17. Albert Wolters, *Creation Regained: Biblical Basics for a Reformational Worldview*, 2nd ed. (Grand Rapids: Eerdmans, 2005), 1–51.
18. Buijs and Mosher, "Introduction," *supra* note 12, 5–12.
19. Dooyeweerd, *NC I*, 3.
20. Dooyeweerd, *NC I*, 60.

intended to be oriented and surrendered to God the Origin of all that is created.[21] The Decalogue addresses the heart of humans as whole persons, requiring from them an obedience expressed in all that they do. "Religion" embraces all aspects of the inescapably creaturely human experience and existence.[22] Thus, all of "life is religion":

> Because of God's all-encompassing creation order, human life in its totality is to be understood as *response* . . . not to be conceived of simply as a groping for truth, a pilgrimage in which some people get farther than others, with all of them traveling toward the same destination. . . . [but] the necessity and unavoidability of choosing a direction. Either man worships the Creator and turns to Jesus Christ, or he turns his back on the Creator by abasing himself before the creature and worshiping a vain idol.[23]

Its full meaning is given in creation,[24] with all the power and potential it embodies, and which we are to disclose and nurture in our religious calling to serve God and neighbor.[25] In the Garden of Eden, God entrusted to humans this responsibility over the entire temporal creation, placing it at the center of their existence,[26] indeed, of the human heart, out of which arise many issues of life (Prov 4:23). As *homo respondens*, humans are called by God to respond to his call for responsibility according to their diverse vocations and abilities.[27] This happens in the context of different but interrelated aspects of creaturely reality. Reason, morality, and faith are but some of the different correlated aspects of human existence that find their fullest sense and expression in their coherence and interdependence with one another. For Dooyeweerd,

---

21. Herman Dooyeweerd, *A New Critique of Theoretical Thought*, Vol. II (Jordan Station: Paideia Press), 302–3 [hereafter *NC II*].

22. Dooyeweerd, *NC II*, 303.

23. Theodore A. Plantinga, "The Christian Philosophy of H. Evan Runner," in *Life is Religion: Essays in Honour of H. Evan Runner,* ed. Henry Van Der Goot (Jordan Station: Paideia Press, 1981), 15.

24. Herman Dooyeweerd, *Reformation and Scholasticism in Philosophy*, Vol. II, in *The Collected Works of Herman Dooyeweerd Series A, Volume 5/2*, Gen. ed. D. F. M. Strauss (Grand Rapids: Paideia Press, 2014), 219.

25. Dooyeweerd, *Reformation and Scholasticism*, 219.

26. Dooyeweerd, *Reformation and Scholasticism*, 219.

27. Henk G. Geertsema, "The Answering Nature of Being Human," in *Homo Respondens: Essays in Christian Philosophy,* eds. Govert J. Buijs and Perry Huesmann (Jordan Station: Paideia Press, 2021), 57.

> The distinction between faith and religion is crucial.... While faith is an aspect of experience, religion encompasses all the aspects of experience. By distinguishing between faith and religion one is allowed to retain the particular "religiosity" of faith without limiting religion to faith.[28]

The ethical aspect is revealed in normatively different ways in relations between parents-and-children, husband-and-wife, friends, citizens in relation to their country, members of a church, a football club, a labor union, or a mechanical engineer's professional organization. Yet, these societal relations will also display norms proper to their nature. Parental (moral) authority is never an excuse for sexual abuse. Such abuses are subject to legal norms. Churches are certainly not mere social clubs; yet church membership may neither be a moral nor legal justification to use physical torture for church discipline. And who is the neighbor? It is every member of the "radical religious community of mankind in its central relationship to God,"[29] who created man – male and female – after his image.[30] Everyone who bears the *imago dei* (Gen 1:26-27) is a neighbor.[31] The second commandment, inseparable from the first, must be a Christian expression of one's love for God or else "it is not the neighborly love of a Christian, but the *Mitsmenschlichkeit* (co-human-ness) of the (secularized, God-estranged) humanist."[32]

Decalogue and the Cultural Mandate

The call to love God and neighbor then, is the root of human responsibility to heed the cultural mandate (Gen 1:28). Humans are revelatory of God's glory, created to love, serve, and reveal God through their friendships, marriages, families, development of the earth, education of young people, and governing of creation, according to Scripture.[33] Such revelatory tasks distinguished humans from other creatures, rather than by a particular characteristic or

---

28. Renato Coletto, "Wolterstorff's Critique of the Reformational View of Scholarship in his essay 'On Christian learning,'" *Koers* 74, no. 387 n8 (2009), citing Dooyeweerd, *NC II*, 303.
29. Dooyeweerd, *NC I*, 60.
30. Dooyeweerd, *NC I*, 60.
31. Dooyeweerd, *NC I*, 60.
32. SU Zuidema, *Communication and Confrontation. A Philosophical Appraisal and Critique of Modern Society and Contemporary Thought* (Assen/Kampen: Royal VanGorcum Ltd, 1972), 108.
33. Skillen, *Good of Politics*, 20-21.

function, whether reason, love, or spirit, or soul.³⁴ The cultural mandate shows that the Decalogue "cannot be reduced to the moral law."³⁵ As Albert Wolters argues: "[h]uman civilization is normed throughout."³⁶ "There is nothing in human life that does not belong to the created order," he writes. "Everything we are and do is thoroughly creaturely."³⁷ Language, art, music, the various sciences, family, friendships, marriage, emotions, sexuality, education, business, agriculture, technology, government (politics), church life – among many diverse human responsibilities – are subject to creational norms proper to their differentiated natures, at the same time that they answer in an analogical way to other correlated norms. Rather than restrict human freedom, they enable human flourishing. We are to disclose and develop these creational norms in a historical process of unfolding. The Creation Order

> *is a way to bring the human condition into play as something we do not make but belong to* . . . [I]t is not a call for an adoration of the present situation, the static status quo, but calls us to keep, till, maintain, develop, and, in summary: (1) gratefully preserve the shalom-enhancing elements in the depth of our present, the depth of reality, and (2) be attentive to the distortive elements, and (3) try to bend the distortive elements toward *a new and perhaps deeper flourishing* of humans and the earth.³⁸

Norms are not an external imposition on the nature of the relationship or practice they hold for but are part of its inner meaning.³⁹ Norms and the structures they enable are designed to allow humans to open up life to its fullness from its intrinsic quality.⁴⁰ In principle, Calvin's thought displays an acknowledgment that the subjection of Christians to the Decalogue is religious in nature, one embracing norms proper to civil law, economics, and the state as

---

34. Skillen, *Good of Politics*, 21. The dominant Thomist view has always read the *imago Dei* as (an imperfect) rational reflection of a rational Creator. See Etienne Gilson, *Thomism: The Philosophy of Thomas Aquinas*, trans. Laurence K. Shook and Armand Maurer (Toronto: Pontifical Institute of Mediaeval Studies, 2002, 6th and final edn.), 1–37.

35. Herman Dooyeweerd, *Encyclopedia of the Science of Law*, Vol. 1 in *The Collected Works of Herman Dooyeweerd Series A, Vol. 8/1*, Gen. ed. D. F. M. Strauss (Grand Rapids: Paideia Press, 2012), 98.

36. Wolters, *Creation Regained*, 16, 25.

37. Wolters, *Creation Regained*, 16, 25.

38. Buijs and Mosher, "Introduction," 12 (Emphasis added).

39. Geertsema, "Higher Education," 464.

40. Geertsema, "Higher Education," 464.

an institution.⁴¹ In contrast, the Radical Reformers (Anabaptists), losing sight of the religious root of human temporal life, absolutized the Sermon on the Mount and its doctrine of love, and opposed it to civil ordinances.⁴²

The Normative Structure for Statecraft – and Politics

Filipino evangelicals have not reflected much on the nature of the state, outside of the obligatory invocation of Romans 13:1–6 as a basis to argue for an almost unqualified support for whatever the government does. Yet how we do politics is directed by our theory of the state and the role it plays in the proper ordering of society. Not too long ago, Walden Bello, a noted Filipino sociologist-turned-politician, wrote about a Janus-faced Philippine state with "hard" and "soft" faces: an institution with a Dr. Jekyll-and-Hyde nature. One part of the state is good but there is that part, represented by security forces, that does evil. Thus, human rights laws are needed to rein in the apparently inherently evil part of the state.⁴³ Three problems with Dr. Bello's dualistic formulation come to mind. First, in both constitutional law and international law, the state is an integration of people and government, regardless of its particular form.⁴⁴ The acts of organs of the state are the acts of the state.⁴⁵ If so, which part here answers to the soft side and which one answers to the hard part, if the state is one such unity? Second, he seems to define evil chiefly in terms of human rights violations. What about graft and corruption, or gross negligence and incompetence? Finally, he speaks of a hard face of the state as inherent. This is a point in political theory with a long history, from the first anarchists, the Radical Reformers, who rejected the state as evil,⁴⁶ to contemporary Marxists and Anarchists, who speak in varying ways of the "overcoming" of the state.⁴⁷ It is characteristic of opposing opinions in modern humanistic social philosophy

---

41. Dooyeweerd, *NC I*, 517.

42. Dooyeweerd, *NC I*, 518; Skillen, *Good of Politics, supra* note 1, xvii.

43. Walden Bello, "Restraining Leviathan," in "Afterthoughts," *Philippine Daily Inquirer*, 2 September 2013. https://opinion.inquirer.net/60185/restraining-leviathan.

44. See Art. 1, "Convention on the Rights and Duties of States," 26 December 1933, 165 LNTS 19.

45. Rosalyn Higgins, *Problems and Process: International Law and How we Use it* (Oxford: Oxford University Press, 1994), 149.

46. See also Peter Marshall, *Demanding the Impossible: A History of Anarchism* (London: Hyper Perennial, 2008), 92–93.

47. See Ralph Miliband, "Marx and the State," *The Socialist Register* (1965): 278–96 and Philip Breed Dematteis, *Individuality and the Social Organism: The Controversy between Max Stirner and Karl Marx* (New York: Revisionist Press, 1976).

and social science that steadfastly deny enduring structural principles for the state.[48] The reformational tradition distinguishes between *structure* (Creation)[49] and its (religious) *direction*.[50] There is a God-ordained structure for human institutions, structures, and social relations – the state included – that is perverted or distorted by the directionality of humanity's sinful heart (Fall). This directionality is what the reformational tradition calls the "religious antithesis," or that deep, radical, absolute – not just ethical – struggle between good and evil in the human heart that also cuts across all human institutions, relations, and communities.[51] This antithesis "rages for the sake of created structure, in and for the concrete reality of earthly creation."[52] As Strauss explains:

> The Bible does not localize evil in a specific domain of reality, but in the apostate direction of the human heart, while salvation is equally a directional matter (first seek the Kingdom of God – in every sphere of life). If we look at philosophy (and the different existing special sciences) . . . *the most remarkable fact is that we are constantly confronted by what may be called a surrogate salvific appeal* . . . When the good-evil opposition (antithesis) is identified with distinct domains within creation, structure and direction is confused [italics supplied].[53]

Our belief on creational structures commits us to "seek and find evidence of lawful constancy in the flux of experience, and of invariant principles amidst a variety of historical events and institutions."[54] It is thus possible to participate in all the potentialities for human flourishing that God has placed in creation for his creatures, which are felt even in the most perverse and sinful of situations (Redemption). Christian-Fall-Redemption summarizes the basic outline of a biblical worldview encompassing the distinction between structure and direction.[55]

---

48. Herman Dooyeweerd, *New Critique of Theoretical Thought*, Vol. III (Jordan Station: Paideia Press, 1984), 397 [hereafter, *NC III*].

49. Wolters, *Creation Regained*, 87–100.

50. Wolters, *Creation Regained*, 88.

51. Dooyeweerd, *NC III*, 15.

52. Wolters, *Creation Regained*, *supra* note 16, 88.

53. D. F. M. Strauss, *Philosophy: Discipline of Disciplines* (Grand Rapids: Paideia Press, 2009), 40.

54. Strauss, *Philosophy*, 40.

55. Wolters, *Creation Regained*, 88.

Foundation of Reformational Politics: **Souvereinteit in Eigen Kring**

The reformational tradition begins with the *given-ness* of an ordered diversity – of various communities, relations, institutions, and individuals; it then weaves this structured plurality to allow for a harmonious development of society that keeps a right balance between diversity and unity and yet recognizes that the human beings as individuals are not to be defined solely in terms of the diversity of their relationships, institutions, and communities. Abraham Kuyper (1827–1920), one-time Dutch prime minister and founder of the *Vrije Universiteit Amsterdam*, popularized the idea of societal pluriformity with his sociological principle *souvereinteit in eigen kring* (literally, "sovereign in its own orbit"). But it can be traced much earlier to Johannes Althusius (1563–1638), a leading German-born Calvinist political theorist and jurist of his day, who is said to be the first thinker to realize that the state should not be understood as an all-embracing institution that reduces other societal institutions, as well as individuals, to mere parts of its supposed greater whole.[56] While he understood that provinces and municipalities are parts of the state, he also saw that "not every societal entity (such as families, churches etc.) is part of the state."[57] This insight is rooted in proper laws (*leges propriae*), by which "particular associations are ruled."[58]

For Kuyper, the principle serves as a guarantee of the independence of various spheres of life before God, from overextensions of state power. Sphere sovereignty is a fundamental principle of a Reformed theory of politics,[59] on which constitutional checks and balances against the abuses by any sphere, most importantly by the government, hangs.[60] Dooyeweerd expanded it into an ontological or a "cosmological'" principle for a systematic theoretical account of a universal modal structure of reality,[61] founded on the realization that God *created everything after its kind and with its own internal law for life*.[62] Society does not consist of part-whole relations, because reality has a complex, multi-functional and inter-related character, in which all human and non-human creatures and institutions exist and develop in history in different ways. Thus,

---

56. Strauss, *Philosophy*, 532.
57. Strauss, 533 n23.
58. Strauss, 533 n23.
59. Abraham Kuyper, *Lectures on Calvinism* (Grand Rapids: Eerdmans, 1999 reprint), 79.
60. Kuyper, *Lectures*, 97.
61. Dooyeweerd, *NC I*, 99.
62. *NC II*, 16 (cf. Gen 1:24). See also Roger Henderson, "The Development of the Principle of Distributed Authority, or Sphere Sovereignty," *Philosophia Reformata* 82, no. 1 (2017): 74–99.

the state, family, church, friendships, the market, and every institution display aspects of reality at the same time, but there will always be two aspects which will exhibit and define their particular identity.

These are an entity's foundational and qualifying functions. The "foundational" or "founding" function is the aspect qualifying the process of transformation of an entity in its variant historical forms in temporal experience.[63] The qualifying or "leading" function is the aspect that qualifies an entity's intrinsic purpose and internal structure.[64] But the human "I-ness" is not qualified by any of the (modal) aspects of reality and are not to be treated as part of an organic whole.[65] Society is pluriform, with a diversity of mediating structures that encourage and allow individuals to thrive in a wide variety of occupations, relations, and interests; such associational diversity provides citizens with a buffer zone extending beyond the political arena, insulating them from a "totalitarian statism."[66] For the reformational tradition, "God has a strong vested interest in a pluralistic structuring of the patterns of human interaction."[67]

The Inner Structural Principles of the State and its Task

Here, I follow Skillen's reformational reconstruction of Dooyeweerd's Augustinian account of the state, insofar as the latter posited it, as solely a post-Fall entity.[68] Skillen invokes the Thomist and Althusian basic intuition that government is an original part of the very nature of things, rather than an *ex post facto* divine intervention because of human sin.[69] Otherwise, Skillen agrees with Dooyeweerd's understanding of the shape taken by the state post-Fall; that is, of the inner structural principles of the state as a unity of power (its founding function) and (public) justice (its qualifying function).[70] Yet Thomists posit the state as an entity whose aim and purpose is the development of

---

63. Roy A. Clouser, *The Myth of Religious Neutrality* (University of Notre Dame Press, 2005), 263–67.

64. René van Woudenberg, "Theories of Thing-Structures" in *Philosophical Foundations I Reader* (International Masters in Christian Studies of Science and Society Program, VU Amsterdam, 2006–7), 6.

65. Dooyeweerd, *NC III*, 196; Clouser, "The Myth," *supra* note 63, 285–90.

66. Richard Mouw and Sander Griffioen, *Pluralisms and Horizons: An Essay in Christian Public Philosophy* (Grand Rapids: Eerdmans, 1993), 121.

67. Mouw and Griffioen, *Pluralisms and Horizons*, 122.

68. Dooyeweerd, *NC III*, 423.

69. Skillen, *Good of Politics*, *supra* note 1, 97, 117, 123.

70. Skillen, *Good of Politics*, 27–31.

virtuous citizens (the state as an entirely ethical entity).[71] Aquinas taught that members of society are "parts" of a greater whole, the "perfect society" that is the political community, insofar as Aquinas identifies the political common good as the virtuous life of the *civitas*.[72] But for Dooyewerd, "[t]he state is led by norms of justice, not ethics; the accomplishment of public justice is the structural principle of the state, not the enforcement of non-public morals."[73] As the state functions in all aspects, ethical norms are also correlated with the norms of public justice in a differentiated way. Skillen explains that,

> The idea of the state "cultivating virtue" in an undifferentiated sense has roots in the ancient Greek idea of the polis as "man writ large" (Plato) and the person as the "polis writ small." ... [But] in a differentiated society, the virtues that ought to be nurtured and exemplified in the relation of government to the citizens is "civic virtue." There is a lot of light on this subject in the Prophets' condemnation of the king and the people for not acting justly (Isa 1, for example). What should nurture civic virtue in people as citizens is seeing that public justice and fairness are held high in principle and impressed in the laws and enforcement of the laws. When citizens see that exemplified in leaders who truly seek the public welfare and not their own interests in power, prestige and wealth, then they will learn what it means to practice righteous public living and will support and vote for honorable persons for public office. . . .[74]

Power is foundational to creation of the state as a *res publica* of government and subjects within a territory.[75] Without the monopoly of the sword (founding function), public order is impossible. Yet the exercise of state power cannot be divorced from the qualifying normative task of public justice,[76] a unity distinguishing it from other entities in society.[77] State power is not subject to some supposedly external limit set by another institution but by its very nature,

---

71. John Goyette, "On the Transcendence of the Political Common Good: Aquinas versus the New Natural Law Theory," *The National Catholic Bioethics Quarterly* (2013): 133–55.
72. Goyette, "On the Transcendence," 135–55.
73. Clouser, "The Myth," *supra* note 63, 316.
74. James W. Skillen, personal email to the author, 27 July 2022.
75. Dooyeweerd, *NC III*, 437–38.
76. Dooyeweerd, *NC III*, 416.
77. Dooyeweerd, *NC III*, 434.

which delimits the public interest as its task.[78] Sphere sovereignty in relation to the state's task is expressed in the following description: "[d]ifferent social relationships have different characters, different kinds of law-making requirements, different foundations."[79] It is the state's duty to protect and nurture the differentiated responsibilities and distinctive integrity of non-state entities.[80]

The State Beyond Individualism and Collectivism

Politics derives from the state's many-sided functions as a public-legal community integrating citizens, communities, and institutions over a territory. Recognizing the state's inner structural principle as a unity of power and justice amidst the reality of societal pluriformity allows us to see beyond the two contending theories of political and social arrangement: *individualism* and *collectivism*. The former posits that society consists only of individuals abstracted from tradition, history, and relations. All other entities and relations are merely derivative of individuals. Thus, the state, understood as a collection of autonomous and free individuals under a social contract, exists merely to cater to individual rights and demands. In recent progressive liberal thought, the state's chief political purpose is focused on the individual's "choice enhancement."[81] The collectivist's view becomes the individualist's mirror image at the opposite end, in the sense that the state is seen as the sole individual that matters. These polar opposites override the diversity of societal relationships in distinct ways. The latter conflates society with the state, thus exhibiting strong totalitarian tendencies;[82] the former explains genuine communities as simply a collection of autonomous and free individuals.[83]

Some Implications

Let me draw out of the above discussion some implications. First, (re)reading and obeying the Decalogue as part and parcel of Christian life means understanding that political life is not something that we create out of nothing, and

---

78. Dooyeweerd, *NC III*, 438–39.

79. James W. Skillen, *Development of Calvinistic Political Theory in the Netherlands, With Special Reference to the Thought of Herman Dooyeweerd* (unpublished PhD diss., Duke University, 1973), 388. See also Dooyeweerd, *NC III*, 439–42.

80. Mouw and Griffioen, *Pluralisms and Horizons*, supra note 66, 163–64.

81. David Koyzis, *Political Visions*, 83.

82. Clouser, "The Myth," *supra* note 63, 284.

83. Clouser, "The Myth," *supra* note 63, 284.

to which we then somehow add meaning and purpose. Rather, the Christian confession is that we pursue the "good of politics" in response to purposive creational norms. The Bible is a story of "the whole of created reality, encompassing all that exists and all that humans will ever be and do. That is why . . . in the political cultures of our day, we must find ourselves in the biblical story."[84] This teleological view of the political community is not uniquely Protestant nor Christian but has ancient roots in Greek thought, notably that of Aristotle. It found its most elaborate expression in the 13th century in Aquinas, from which grew the Roman Catholic Social Teaching founded on the doctrine of the common good.[85] Yet, because the doctrine of the common good sometimes tended towards a "parts-whole" collectivist politics,[86] the reformational tradition has proposed a useful Protestant corrective in the norm of public justice.[87] But the claim that God is the ultimate origin of all human institutions necessarily implies a theocratic society, is plainly false.[88] The opposite is true: "all institutions – including political community – are limited in relation to each other. The authority assigned to each is restricted to the specific human purpose it pursues, and no one institution may usurp the authority to pursue, or even supervise the pursuit of, all such purposes."[89]

Second, and this proceeds from the first implication, creational norms for the state hold regardless of who is in office. Thus, Filipino evangelicals need to train the next generation of Josephs, Daniels, and Nehemiahs demonstrating faithful and competent presence – "civic virtues" – in public office. But from our ranks must also rise new Jeremiahs, Hoseas, and Amoses calling out governmental neglect of duty and abuse of power; yet the kind of leaders elected or appointed to public office certainly matters (see Deut 17:14–20; Judg 9:1–57). Elsewhere, I have critiqued how recently, many Christians ostensibly chose to elect into office a president under whose administration thousands of civilians were killed in a drug war, and whose reverberations are still being

---

84. Skillen, *Good of Politics*, *supra* note 1, xx.

85. Jonathan Chaplin, *Faith in Democracy: Framing a Politics of Deep Diversity* (London: SCM Press, 2021), 13.

86. See Herman Dooyeweerd, *Roots of Western Culture: Pagan, Secular, and Christian Options*, Series B. Vol. 15, *The Collected Works of Herman Dooyeweerd* (Grand Rapids: Paideia Press, 2012), 122–36; Jonathan Chaplin, "Subsidiarity as a Political Norm" in *Political Theory and Christian Vision: Essays in Memory of Bernard Zylstra*, eds. Jonathan Chaplin and Paul Marshall (Lanham: University Press of America, 1994), 81–100; and Skillen, *Good of Politics*, *supra* note 1, 137.

87. Chaplin, "Subsidiarity," *supra* note 85, 18–24.

88. Chaplin, "Subsidiarity," *supra* note 85, 17.

89. Chaplin, "Subsidiarity," *supra* note 85, 17.

felt today.⁹⁰ Normative politics is incompatible with power politics, in which leaders deign to have the sole power to define and act on behalf of a collectivity, without being subject to any form of legal restraint:

> Without a clear understanding of the normative limits of the state, politicians and citizens alike are in constant danger of enabling state overreach. Appeals to the lofty ideals of the public interest, the common good, human rights, equality, or even national security can all be used to expand the state's ability to crush opposition.⁹¹

With the state, the central command of love is expressed in a differentiated way in the state's pursuit of the public interest as defined by the norm of public justice, entailing such tender and complex work of statecraft. We cannot dispense with institutions, the state included. It is part of our response to God's call to responsibility to help build institutions in a manner that discloses and deepens the norms designed for our flourishing. The coming of Christ's kingdom did not obliterate this responsibility of political vocation.⁹² Rather, ". . . it calls us to the obedient exercise of political responsibility . . . turning from practices and institutions of injustice to practices and institutions of justice. . . ."⁹³ How might Filipino evangelicals gain competence in these practices and institutions? It will require of them deeper study beyond proof-texts of the Bible, as the last two implications show.

Third, normative politics according to sphere sovereignty relativizes both the state and the political. Humans are more than political creatures. As bearers of the revelatory image of God, they are gifted with abilities and vocations beyond the political.⁹⁴ The state's inherent structural principle demands that it honor the norm of public justice or its duty to harmonize the various spheres and interests in society, weighing their respective claims (*confessional pluralism*), and recognizing their intrinsic limitations and their rightful place in their particular social contexts (*structural pluralism*).⁹⁵ As *res publica*, the state must grant legal recognition and protection to independent, non-political responsibilities that belong to citizens, instead of monopolizing all responsi-

---

90. Regalado Bagares, "Power Politics in the Philippines: A Reformed Response to the Populism and Violence of Duterte," in *Reformed Public Theology: A Global Vision for the Life of the World*, ed. Matthew Kaemingck (Grand Rapids: Baker Academic, 2021), 135–48.

91. Bagares, "Power Politics," 144.

92. Skillen, *Good of Politics*, *supra* note 1, 12.

93. Skillen, *Good of Politics*, *supra* note 1, 12–13.

94. Skillen, *Good of Politics*, *supra* note 1, 119–20.

95. Skillen, *Good of Politics*, *supra* note 1, 125.

bilities to satisfy every possible need.[96] The state is not an institution whose only goal is to maximally ensure individual freedoms or economic prosperity, or a country's political power,[97] but "to uphold a healthy public commons in which the great diversity of human activities – as well as complex social and ecological balances – is maintained for the long-term wellbeing of everyone."[98]

Between times is the societal reality of "directional pluralism"[99] of competing visions of the good, or the plurality of visions of the good life.[100] Sphere sovereignty is compatible with "jurisdictional secularism,"[101] in which the state "acknowledges it has no jurisdiction to adjudicate among competing claims of ultimate truth nor does the state have the power to assess the legitimacy of secular beliefs."[102] The state must deal with competing theories of the good in an even-handed manner, laying the basis for religious toleration, religious freedom, and freedom of conscience[103] (or allowance for the expression of "*faithful conscience*"[104]). This in itself is also an expression of God's mercy and patience towards human disobedience,[105] which does not task public officials with the duty to punish unbelievers and their unbelief.[106] We must view present pluralisms against the ultimate horizon of the Divine, inviting dialogue among different directionally committed groups to promote associational diversity,[107] with a stance of humility.[108] Still, it is not the final measure of political life but a continuing signpost for collective discernment for a tentative consensus that will never achieve perfection in this life[109] but only in God as the ultimate Judge of history.[110] Until then, we are to exercise equal treatment of all people, regardless of their faith – including those of secular faiths. In fact, the state's

---

96. Skillen, *Good of Politics, supra* note 1, 125.
97. Center for Public Justice, "Guidelines for Government and Citizenship: Government" (undated).
98. Center for Public Justice.
99. Mouw and Griffioen, *Pluralisms and Horizons, supra* note 66, 16.
100. Mouw and Griffioen, *Pluralisms and Horizons*, 24.
101. Chaplin, "Subsidiarity," *supra* note 85, 64.
102. Chaplin, "Subsidiarity," *supra* note 85, 64.
103. Chaplin, "Subsidiarity," *supra* note 85, 65.
104. Chaplin, *Faith in Democracy*, 128–29.
105. Skillen, *Good of Politics, supra* note 1, 43.
106. Skillen, *Good of Politics, supra* note 1, 43.
107. Skillen, *Good of Politics, supra* note 1, 119–22.
108. Mouw and Griffioen, *Pluralisms and Horizons, supra* note 66, 103–9, 118.
109. Mouw and Griffioen, *Pluralisms and Horizons*, 175.
110. Mouw and Griffioen, *Pluralisms and Horizons*, 175.

recognition of "principled pluralism" – its respect for structural pluralism (differentiated responsibility and distributed authority of non-state spheres and communities) and confessional pluralism (the distinctive integrity of ultimate communal commitments) is our best defense against totalitarian projects of both the Left and the Right (Chaplin calls this state pursuit of principled pluralism, its embrace of *"faithful association."*[111]).

That being said, Filipino evangelicals must reject any imposition by the state of a thoroughgoing societal plurality, where subjective and radical relativism is presented as a normative or flourishing state of affairs[112] (or a "normative directional pluralism").[113] There really are comprehensive public goods that, regardless of competing visions, society needs to flourish: among many other things, marriage, family and the proper rearing of children, the protection of the life of the unborn, and the weak and disabled, ensuring the circumstances of the elderly. At stake is the very meaning and structure of reality and how it actually presses upon us a multi-generational responsibility to *faithfully* nurture and develop culture, science and technology, educational and political institutions, environmental practices, and so on. Filipino evangelicals need to work with all men and women of faith and goodwill who recognize that the good of the neighbor in the city, the nation, and the world is best assured by their common work together, in fighting anti-normative initiatives in the halls of Congress, government offices, and elsewhere (in Chaplin's terms, the exercise of *"faithful power"*[114]).

Fourth, Filipino evangelicals must expose and challenge a secular society promoted in contemporary liberal democratic discourse that is actually founded on faith commitments: on faith in human autonomy and a closed universe.[115] Secularism's adherents take for granted the institutional and social shaping power of modern secularist beliefs that have done so much to shape and organize all areas of public and not only personal life, in which religion other than itself is straight away classified as private.[116] As Chaplin notes:

---

111. Mouw and Griffioen, *Pluralisms and Horizons,* 128–29.

112. Mouw and Griffioen, *Pluralisms and Horizons,* 129.

113. Mouw and Griffioen, *Pluralisms and Horizons,* 18.

114. Chaplin, "Subsidiarity," *supra* note 85, 191.

115. James W. Skillen, "Is There a Place for 'Christian Politics' in America'?" (unpublished lecture, 2011), 1.

116. James W. Skillen, "How Far Does Charles Taylor Take Us in Developing a Christian Understanding of the Secular Age?" *Pro Rege* 43, no. 3 (2015): 5. See also, Clouser, "The Myth," *supra* note 61, 9–61, on the unavoidably religious nature of all belief systems, "secular" or otherwise.

Behind the last reason in any chain of substantive argumentation about the human good is a prior commitment either to religious "revelation" or to some secular substitute. Such a commitment will concern things as the nature of truth, the purpose of human life, the source of morality, the nature of justice, the meaning of history, the prospects for human progress or "salvation," the rationale of political community, or perhaps, the inscrutability of the absence of such things.[117]

Moreover, it is one whose imagination of society is limited only to an abrupt collection of atomized individuals without tradition, community, and beliefs, with no further commitments than the perpetuation of a society peopled by the same class of autonomous and free-standing individuals. A deepened and broadened reading of the Decalogue allows us to see that this secularist faith goes against societal and human flourishing.

Finally, there is much to endorse to Filipino evangelicals in the distinction between the differentiated roles of the institutional church and of the organic church, following the principle of sphere sovereignty. The Neocalvinist tradition differentiates between the institutional church and its organic manifestations. The former is the concrete community of faith gathered around word, sacrament, and discipline. The latter is the universal body of Christ, its members working out their respective vocations in the world[118] but which must not be separated from the concrete life of the institutional church. Neither are to be understood as an alternative polis supplanting the state and other institutions in this present life.[119] That is simply not the purpose of the body of Christ.[120] Yet, the organic church will have a huge role to play in ensuring that the state succeeds in its task to render public justice and the common good. In Asia, contextual difficulties underline the reality that the institutional church often has had to fulfill the duties of the organic church, for lack of resources and competent leaders.[121] How are Filipino evangelical educational institutions

---

117. Chaplin, "Subsidiarity," *supra* note 85, 59, citing Mark Lila, *The Stillborn God: Religion, Politics, and the Modern West* (New York: Alfred A. Knopf, 2007), 10.

118. Abraham Kuyper, *Rooted and Grounded: The Church as Organism and Institution* (Grand Rapids: Christian Liberty Press, 2013). See also Koyzis, *Political Visions*, *supra* note 81, 275–86.

119. Skillen, *Good of Politics*, *supra* note 1, 130–31.

120. Skillen, *Good of Politics*, *supra* note 1, 130–31.

121. Richard Mouw, "Culture, Church, and Civil Society: Kuyper for a New Century," *Princeton Theological Seminary Bulletin* 28, no. 1 (2007): 48–63.

training people towards building both the institutional and the organic church in a way that one is not sacrificed in favor of the other?

Bibliography

Bagares, R. R. "Power Politics in the Philippines: A Reformed Response to the Populism and Violence of Duterte." In *Reformed Public Theology: A Global Vision for the Life of the World*, edited by Matthew Kaemingck, 35–148. Grand Rapids: Baker Academic, 2021.

Barker, D. L. "Ten Commandments, Two Tablets: The Shape of the Decalogue." *Themelios* 30, no. 3 (2005): 6–22.

Bello, W. "'Restraining Leviathan.' Afterthoughts." *Philippine Daily Inquirer*. 2 September 2013. https://opinion.inquirer.net/60185/restraining-leviathan.

Budziszewski, J. *Commentary on Thomas Aquinas's Treatise on Law*. Cambridge: Cambridge University Press, 2014.

Buijs, G. J., and A. K. Mosher. "Introduction: Rethinking the Idea of Creation Order Among Humans: Beyond Natural Law and Constructivism." In *The Future of Creation Order*, Vol. 2, edited by G. J. Buijs and A. K. Mosher, 5–12. Cham: Springer, 2018.

Center for Public Justice (n.d.). "Guidelines for Government and Citizenship: Government." https://cpjustice.org.

Chaplin, J. "Subsidiarity as a Political Norm." In *Political Theory and Christian Vision: Essays in Memory of Bernard Zylstra*, edited by J. Chaplin and P. Marshall, 81–100. Lanham: University Press of America, 1994.

———. *Faith in Democracy: Framing a Politics of Deep Diversity*. London: SCM Press, 2021.

Clouser, R. A. *The Myth of Religious Neutrality*. Indiana: University of Notre Dame Press, 2005.

Coletto, R. "Wolterstorff's Critique of the Reformational View of Scholarship In His Essay 'On Christian Learning.'" *Koers* 74, no. 3 (2009): 387 n8.

Convention on the Rights and Duties of States, Art. 1, 26 December 1933, 165 LNTS 19.

Dematteis, P. B. *Individuality and the Social Organism: The Controversy between Max Stirner and Karl Marx*. New York: Revisionist Press, 1978.

Dooyeweerd, H. (1954). *A New Critique of Theoretical Thought*, Vol. 1, *The Necessary Presuppositions of Philosophy*. Translated by D. H. Freeman and W. S. Young. Amsterdam/Paris/Jordan Station: Paideia Press, 1984 (referred to as *NC I*).

———. (1954). *A New Critique of Theoretical Thought*, Vol. 2, *The General Theory of Modal Spheres* (referred to as *NC II*).

———. (1954). *A New Critique of Theoretical Thought*, Vol. 3, *The Structures of Individuality of Temporal Reality* (referred to as *NC III*).

———. *Roots of Western Culture: Pagan, Secular, and Christian Options.* Series B. Vol. 15, *The Collected Works of Herman Dooyeweerd.* General editor, D. F. M. Strauss. Grand Rapids: Paideia Press, 2012.

———. *Encyclopedia of the Science of Law,* Vol. 1, *The Collected Works of Herman Dooyeweerd* Series A, Vol. 8/1. General editor, D. F. M. Strauss. Grand Rapids: Paideia Press, 2012.

———. *Reformation and Scholasticism in Philosophy,* Vol. 2. *The Collected Works of Herman Dooyeweerd* Series A, Vol. 5/2. General editor, D. F. M. Strauss. Grand Rapids: Paideia Press, 2014.

Geertsema, H. G. "Higher Education as Service to the King." In *Homo Respondens: Essays in Christian Philosophy,* edited by Govert J. Buijs and Perry Huesmann, 454. Grand Rapids: Paideia Press, 2021.

———. "The Answering Nature of Being Human." In *Homo Respondens: Essays in Christian Philosophy,* edited by G. J. Buijs and P. Huesmann, 57. Jordan Station: Paideia Press, 2021.

Gilson, Etienne. (1924). *Thomism: The Philosophy of Thomas Aquinas.* Translated by Laurence K. Shook and Armand Maurer Toronto. 6th and final ed. Toronto: Pontifical Institute of Mediaeval Studies, 2002.

Goyette, J. "On the Transcendence of the Political Common Good: Aquinas versus the New Natural Law Theory." *The National Catholic Bioethics Quarterly* 13, no. 1 (2013): 133–55.

Henderson, R. "The Development of the Principle of Distributed Authority, or Sphere Sovereignty." *Philosophia Reformata* 82, no. 1 (2017): 74–99.

Higgins, Rosalyn. *Problems and Process: International Law and How We Use It.* Oxford: Oxford University Press, 1994.

Ive, J. G. A. "The Covenantal Trinitarian Alternative to the Scholastic Dilemma." *In die Skriflig/ In Luce Verbi* 52, no. 3 (2018): a2304. https://doi.org/ 10.4102/ids.v52i3.2304.

Koyzis, D. *Political Visions & Illusions: A Survey & Christian Critique of Contemporary Ideologies.* 2nd ed. Downers Grove: IVP Academic, 2019.

Kuyper, A. (1898). *Lectures on Calvinism.* Reprint, Grand Rapids: Eerdmans, 1999.

———. (1870). *Rooted and Grounded: The Church as Organism and Institution.* Translated by Nelson D. Kloosterman. Grand Rapids: Christian Liberty Press, 2013.

Marshall, P. *Demanding the Impossible: A History of Anarchism.* London: Hyper Perennial, 2008.

Miliband, R. "Marx and the State." *The Socialist Register* (1965): 278–96. https://www.marxists.org/archive/miliband/1965/xx/state.htm.

Mouw, R. "Culture, Church, and Civil Society: Kuyper for a New Century." *Princeton Theological Seminary Bulletin* 28, no. 1 (2007): 48–63.

Mouw, Richard, and Sander Griffioen. *Pluralisms and Horizons: An Essay in Christian Public Philosophy.* Grand Rapids: Eerdmans, 1993.

Muller, Richard A. *Post-Reformation Reformed Dogmatic: The Rise and Development of Reformed Orthodoxy, ca. 1520 tp ca. 1725*, 4 vols. Grand Rapids: Baker Academic, 2003.

———. "Scholasticism and Orthodoxy in the Reformed Tradition: Definition and Method." In *After Calvin: Studies in the Development of a Theological Tradition*, 27. Oxford: Oxford University Press, 2003.

———. *The Unaccommodated Calvin: Studies in the Foundation of Theological Tradition*. Oxford: Oxford University Press, 2009.

New Advent. "The Ten Commandments." 2024. https://www.newadvent.org/cathen/04153a.htm.

Plantinga, T. A. "The Christian Philosophy of H. Evan Runner." In *Life is Religion: Essays in Honour of H. Evan Runner*, edited by Henry Van Der Goot, 15. Jordan Station: Paideia Press, 1981.

Ross, R. "Distinguishing Eternal Law from Transient Law: Natural Law and the Judicial Laws of Moses." *Past and Present* 217, no. 1 (2012): 79–115.

Skillen, J. W. "Development of Calvinistic Political Theory in the Netherlands, With Special Reference to the Thought of Herman Dooyeweerd." PhD diss., Duke University, 1973.

———. "Is There a Place for 'Christian Politics' in America?" Unpublished manuscript of a lecture, 2011.

———. *The Good of Politics*. Grand Rapids: Baker Academic, 2014.

———. "How Far Does Charles Taylor Take Us in Developing a Christian Understanding of the Secular Age?" *Pro Rege* 43, no. 3 (2015): 5.

———. Personal email to the author, 27 July 2022.

Strauss, D. F. M. *Philosophy: Discipline of Disciplines*. Grand Rapids: Paideia Press, 2009.

Svensson, M., and D. Van Drunen, eds. *Aquinas Among the Protestants*. Hoboken: Wiley-Blackwell, 2018.

Tierney, B. *The Idea of Natural Rights: Studies on Natural Rights, Natural Law, and Church Law: 1160–1625*. Grand Rapids: Eerdmans, 2001.

Van Dixhoorn, C. *Confessing the Faith: A Reader's Guide to the Westminster Confession of Faith*. Edinburgh: The Banner of Truth Trust, 2014.

Van Woudenberg, René. (2006). "Theories of Thing-Structures." In *Philosophical Foundations 1 Reader*, 6. International Masters in Christian Studies of Science and Society Program, VU Amsterdam 2006–7.

Wolters, A. *Creation Regained: Biblical Basics for a Reformational Worldview*. 2nd ed. Grand Rapids: Eerdmans, 2005.

———. "Dutch Neo-Calvinism: Worldview, Philosophy and Rationality." In *Rationality in the Calvinian Tradition*, edited by H. Hart, J. van der Hoeven and Nicholas Wolterstorff. Eugene: Wipf and Stock, 1983.

Zuidema, S. U. *Communication and Confrontation: A Philosophical Appraisal and Critique of Modern Society and Contemporary Thought*. Assen/Kampen: Royal VanGorcum, 1972.

7

Transforming the Trauma of State Perpetrated Violence

Companioning Towards Healing and Justice

Annabel Manzanilla-Manalo

For over twenty-five years now, I have been involved with non-government organizations (NGOs) providing psychosocial services to survivors of political violence or state perpetrated violence (SPV). Throughout my years of engagement, I have listened to many horrifying stories of torture, enforced disappearances, and extrajudicial killings (EJKs) of human rights activists. Despite the exposure, I remain sensitive to the emotional toll of bearing witness to such violence. In recent years, I've also been involved with families affected by the Duterte administration's "War on Drugs,"[1] fueling my anger at the injustice and dehumanization they experienced. Their cry for justice echoes deeply.

It is hard to fathom the cruelties that some people are capable of inflicting on their fellow human beings and the pain that families must endure. Yet, what's remarkable is individuals' capacity not only to survive but also to thrive and resist the indignities they have suffered. Equally impressive is the strength that comes from survivors' solidarity and collective action.

This article gives voice to the lived experiences of families affected by EJK during the "War on Drugs." The questions I'd like to explore are: How is the

---

1. The War on Drugs campaign is a nationwide effort to eradicate illegal drugs and trafficking in the Philippines. It has been characterized by extrajudicial killings, mass arrests, and incarceration of thousands of suspected drug users and dealers. Since its launch in 2016, it has resulted in the deaths of thousands of people, including children and bystanders.

trauma of SPV experienced individually and collectively? How can trauma be transformed into positive actions for seeking justice? The narratives are drawn from the stories of individuals who participated in Balay Rehabilitation Center, Inc.'s[2] community-based Mental Health and Psychosocial Support (MHPSS) program from 2017–2019.[3] The participants are from an urban poor community that experienced one of the highest numbers of EJKs in Metro Manila.

The following sections offer a brief context on the "War on Drugs," narratives of EJK impact, and unique features of SPV that can shed light on the severity of trauma's impact. I will then cover trauma healing narratives and processes that facilitate healing. Lastly, I will present a theological reflection that can inform ethical responses to state violence and its implications for a healing and justice-sensitive response.

Political Context of the "War on Drugs"

EJK related to the "War on Drugs" is a form of state-perpetrated violence (SPV) that is carried out under the direction of legally constituted officials of the state or on behalf of the state (WHO, 2002).[4] It is organized and intentionally inflicted to sow fear and terror in urban poor communities.

Illustrating this brutality is Jen's story, a celebrated case that highlights the trauma inflicted on family members.

"No end to suffering" (Jen, 30 years old)

Jen's father, a drug suspect, earlier surrendered to authorities under "Oplan Tokhang."[5] During the 2017 "War on Drugs" campaign, around 9 p.m., armed masked men fired into their house killing four family members and three neighbors, during a birthday party.

The left-behind family suffered intense trauma and grief. "There is no end to our suffering. I kept crying until there were no more tears left. I was even

---

2. Balay Rehabilitation Center, Inc. provides psychosocial services to victims of human rights violations perpetrated by the state. See https://www.hhri.org/organisation/balay-rehabilitation-center/.

3. A total of 118 individuals participated in Balay's MHPSS program. Their informed consent to use the data for research and advocacy purposes was taken and pseudo-names were used to hide their identity.

4. "World Report on Violence and Health: Summary," *World Health Organization*, 2002, http://apps.who.int/iris/bitstream/handle/10665/42512/9241545623_eng.pdf;jsessionid=4378 282ED53BF2407D93AA7D081B7F38?sequence=1.

5. *"Oplan Tokhang"* is the term used to describe the anti-drug campaign in the Philippines that was launched in 2016 by President Duterte.

thinking of committing suicide. I wished I were gone too, never to wake up in the morning."

For more than a year they endured on-going insecurity, fearing future tragedies. "Because of fear we would leave at night and sleep in another house. If only we have the means, we would relocate and never return home because of the memory of what happened. We are afraid for the remaining family members because the killing in the community has not stopped."

The experience of having loved ones brutally killed inflicts deep wounds in mind, body, spirit, and relationships that may take a long time to heal. Even more so because there was intentional use of power or force, and it was part of a systematic, organized plan by the very institution that is supposed to provide protection and support.

The issue of drug addiction is a complex, multifaceted social and public health problem. However, the "War on Drugs" campaign in urban poor communities was implemented like it was primarily a law enforcement issue, with focus on criminalizing drug users.[6] It was carried out without basic due process and often resulted to summary execution of suspected small-time drug users and peddlers. The killings were in almost all cases justified as a response to the target fighting it out ("*nanlaban*") against the police operatives.[7] There were also killings committed by non-uniformed persons or vigilantes.

Dehumanizing drug users is a strategy that was used to gain public acceptance of EJKs and created fertile ground for political violence. The following quotes from the former president, Rodrigo Duterte can be interpreted as publicly encouraging or instigating killings of drug users and peddlers:

> "Many of the Filipino drug addicts are no longer viable as human beings."[8]

---

6. Simbulan, Estacio, Dioquino-Maligaso, Herbosa and Withers, "The Manila Declaration on the Drug Problem in the Philippines," *Annals of Global Health*, 5 March 2019, https://www.annalsofglobalhealth.org/articles/10.5334/aogh.28/#:~:text=The%20declaration%20includes%20an%20implicit,and%20psychological%20%5B16%5D.%E2%80%9D.

7. The International Criminal Court report estimates twelve thousand to thirty thousand were killed during the drug operations from July 2016 to March 2019. Many of these killings were perpetrated by either law enforcement personnel or vigilantes who may be working with police or local government officials (ICC, 2021).

8. "Duterte slams 'stupid' UN criticism of his war on drugs," *Aljazeera*, 18 August 2016, https://www.aljazeera.com/news/2016/8/18/duterte-slams-stupid-un-criticism-of-his-war-on-drugs.

> "Drug addicts are criminals . . . When you kill criminals, it is not a crime against humanity. The criminals have no humanity."[9]
>
> "The killing of innocent people/children is part of collateral damage – an unfortunate but an inevitable consequence of the war on drugs."[10]
>
> "Thirty-two were killed in a massive raid in Bulacan. That is good. If we could kill 32 everyday, then maybe we could reduce what ails this country."[11]
>
> "Hitler massacred three million [sic] Jews . . . there are three million drug addicts. I'd be happy to slaughter them."[12]

Framing the drug problem as a peace and order problem and drug users as a threat to public safety and security has legitimized the use of coercive force. What's worse is that the daily exposure to killings has desensitized the public to human rights violations and reinforces the view that the lives of the poor and even innocent children are mere collateral damage.

But while the "War on Drugs" has been ruthless and relentless against the urban poor, it has not been so against major players. The government was widely criticized as exercising leniency and protection of due process to drug lords, large scale distributors and their coddlers.

Trauma of State-Perpetrated Violence and its Emotional and Psychological Impact

The profound impact of state violence on individuals is exemplified by the story of Delia, whose husband and son were brutally killed by a group of armed men inside her house.

> *"A bucket of blood"* (Delia, 60 years old)

---

9. Leila Salaverria, "Duterte: Criminals have no humanity," *Philippine Daily Inquirer*, 2 March 2017, https://newsinfo.inquirer.net/876970/duterte-criminals-have-no-humanity.

10. "Duterte says children killed in the Philippines drug war are 'collateral damage,'" *The Guardian*, 17 October 2016, https://www.theguardian.com/world/2016/oct/17/duterte-says-children-killed-in-philippines-drug-war-are-collateral-damage.

11. Leila Salaverria and Nestor Corrales, "'That's good,' says Duterte on killing of 32 Bulacan druggies," *Philippine Daily Inquirer*, 16 August 2017, https://newsinfo.inquirer.net/923267/president-rodrigo-duterte-drug-war-bulacan-one-time-big-time-operation.

12. "Rodrigo Duterte vows to kill 3 million drug addicts and likens himself to Hitler," *The Guardian*, 30 September 2016, https://www.theguardian.com/world/2016/sep/30/rodrigo-duterte-vows-to-kill-3-million-drug-addicts-and-likens-himself-to-hitler.

"Early dawn before daybreak, armed men forcibly entered our house. I saw my husband on his knees, terrified, begging for mercy. My son stepped in and begged for his father's life. They mercilessly killed both of them . . . I couldn't believe what happened. I was not myself as I cleaned the floor. I almost filled a bucket of the mixed blood of my husband and son. Until now, their bloody corpses always come back to mind . . . I still couldn't believe they are gone. I miss them so much. I want to hug and hold them. I told myself I wouldn't cry anymore, but the tears kept flowing.

"For several months, I suffered from extreme fear and nervousness, with my whole-body trembling. I could not sleep or stay asleep. I just sit there, stunned, and could barely speak, just crying . . . It's so painful, I can't accept what happened. I try not to think about it, but the memory of what happened, and their bloody corpses keep coming back to mind."

"The effect on my daughter-in-law was also severe, as if she were going crazy. For almost a month, she would brew coffee for my son every morning as she awaits his arrival from evening work as a tricycle driver. She hardly ate and was always crying."

This story illustrates the deep and lasting impacts of trauma on the individual's psyche, leaving a range of physical, emotional, and psychological symptoms. *Trauma* is derived from a Greek word meaning a wound or injury that is violently inflicted and overwhelms the person's capacity to cope. Being exposed to a violent, life-threatening event overwhelms the brain's behavioral and emotional response center. It activates the emergency response system in the brain and causes hyper-arousal in our nervous system.[13] This makes it possible to fight, flight, and freeze, which are survival responses to life-threatening situations.

For Delia, the shock and terror of seeing armed men forcibly enter their home, made it difficult to fight or flee. The result was a freeze response of helplessness, inability to do anything or even escape the situation. She dissociated from her thoughts, feelings, and body ("*I was not myself . . .*") as a way of coping with the shock and disbelief. The image of them with disfigured, bloody corpses remained frozen in her memory and would intrude in her daily life

---

13. B. A. Van der Kolk, *The Body Keeps the Score: Brain, Mind, and Body in the Healing of Trauma* (New York: Viking, 2014).

in the form of flashbacks and nightmares. These traumatic memories are so painful that the smallest triggers can activate strong negative reactions.

Trauma can lead to a range of mental health issues including post-traumatic stress disorder (PTSD), anxiety and depression. In the case of Delia, the intense trauma energy that was trapped in her mind and body, has resulted in disabling post-trauma reactions. Thus, she would suffer, for the next several months, symptoms of PTSD: hyper-arousal such as hypervigilance, startled reactions, difficulty concentrating, and sleep disturbances; re-experiencing the trauma through flashbacks or distressing dreams; negative changes in thinking and mood such as feeling detached from others and decreased interest in activities; and, avoidance of thoughts, feelings or anything that would remind her of the trauma.[14] Consequently, her ability to function in daily life was significantly impaired.

The Impact of Traumatic Grief

The sudden, unexpected, and violent nature of the death of loved ones can result in *traumatic grief*, where there is an overlap of trauma and grief reactions. The difficulty of disentangling the traumatic stress elements of the grief makes it difficult to move through the natural grief process. The result is *complicated grief*, a prolonged, ongoing, heightened state of mourning that is disabling.[15] The bereaved is stuck in intense sorrow and pain, distressing preoccupations with thoughts of the deceased and circumstances of the death. What complicates the grief process are the unresolved issues, like no opportunity to say goodbye, no ceremonies/rituals to commemorate the deceased, no space/time to grieve together as a family, and lack of justice.

The families experience too many significant losses: loved ones, source of support, sense of safety and security, and sense of control over their lives. Experiencing excessive losses all at once or within a short period of time puts an individual in a state of grief overload. This not only prolongs grieving but also makes it difficult for them to function in their daily lives.

---

14. American Psychiatric Association, *Diagnostic and Statistical Manual of Mental Disorders*, 5th ed. (Arlington: American Psychiatric Publishing, 2013), 271–74.

15. R. A. Neimeyer, "Complicated Grief and the Quest for Meaning: A Constructivist Contribution," *Journal of Constructivist Psychology* 25, no. 4 (2012): 313–25.

The Impact of Ongoing Violence and Chronic Stress

The trauma of losing a loved one continues to weigh on left-behind families for a long time. More so if the victim was the breadwinner in the family. This means economic loss and subsequent adversities. They are faced with the daily challenges of meeting the family's basic survival needs for food, medical/health care, education, and livelihood. Carla, a widow in her early thirties, cries out: *"It's unbearably painful and I could not accept what happened . . . I don't know how to raise my seven small children."*

There is also the on-going exposure to threat of violence in the community. The lack of sense of safety in the privacy of their homes and the uncertainty about the future result to individuals feeling vulnerable and disempowered. It also impacts their sense of agency or ability to take action that can shape their lives.

The combined impact of trauma, grief, and other chronic stressors makes individuals constantly anxious or distracted, unable to attend to their needs for healing. It is important to note, however, that there are individuals who manifest post-trauma reactions but do not develop long-term disabling symptoms. There are many who evidenced resilient coping and were able to recover with appropriate psychosocial support.

Beyond Individual Trauma: Understanding the Social Impacts of State-Perpetrated Violence

The trauma of SPV goes beyond the individual and its psychological impact. It is *social trauma* because it not only affects the individual's cognitive functions and ability to regulate emotions but also the network of relationships of which the individual is a part. It is also, as in the case of neighborhoods where the EJK occurred, a collective experience that affects groups of people and disrupts the social fabric of the community.

Judith Herman explains that social trauma is characterized by three key features: First, it is the result of deliberate and systemic effort to undermine the social identity and survival of a particular group; second, it involves the violation of basic human rights and moral principles; and third, it is perpetuated through social and political structures that serve to maintain the power and dominance of the oppressor.[16]

---

16. J. L. Herman, "Social Trauma and the Healing of Communities and Individuals," *Journal of the American Academy of Psychoanalysis* 20, no. 1 (1992): 1–23.

The social and political contexts of SPV present unique challenges that are different from other kinds of trauma.

The Trauma of Stigma and Social Isolation

The political context of the "War on Drugs" involves the spread of misinformation and dehumanizing labels (e.g., addicts, criminals, inhuman, pests, etc.) that fuel discriminatory attitudes and behaviors against drug users. These create powerful stigmas against left-behind families and violate their dignity as human beings.

In urban poor communities, to be a drug-user is associated with criminality or threatening behaviors and thus the public perception that they are somehow at fault and deserve being killed. In the aftermath of the killing, what makes the pain more unbearable is the negative social attitudes (stigmatization) and "victim blaming" by neighbors. *"It hurts so much to hear my neighbors talking about my parents – that they were killed for being drug addicts. Sometimes I think of committing suicide whenever I hear them talk that way."* (Dina, 16 years old)

Furthermore, the prevalence of EJK creates a climate of mistrust, fear and insecurity that prevents community members from reaching out to express support and solidarity. For many it's the fear of being associated with drug users and being targeted by the police or vigilantes. For others it's the discomfort of not knowing how to provide emotional support. Lorie, 20 years old, lamented, *"Very few people came to my father's wake, maybe because they were afraid to get implicated."*

The impact of stigma can be severe and profound. Stigmatized individuals may experience shame and social isolation that can affect their ability to cope with adversities. It can also have a broader community impact, with the support structures, social cohesion, and sense of community severely undermined.

The Trauma of Betrayal of Public Trust and Injustice

SPV involves a betrayal of public trust as it runs contrary to the role and functions of the state: of protecting the interests of its citizens, governing with justice, upholding the rule of law, and accountability. It leads to a loss of trust towards authorities and institutions because the state, instead of upholding human rights standards, abuses its power and authority and inflicts harm against them. The inability to turn to any higher authority for justice results in people feeling helpless. "*I feel helpless and restless . . . I don't know what to do and have nowhere to go.*" *(Rosa, 51 years old)*

The left-behind families face huge barriers in accessing justice and reparations because the perpetrators are in positions of power. "*How can we obtain justice? Only the poor are targeted by the drug campaign . . . our husbands and children are the only ones getting killed. It is very difficult for us to obtain justice because we are poor, and the perpetrators are still in power.*" (Emma, 55 years old)

Victimization and the Cycle of Violence
The experience of injustice and impunity can prevent healing from trauma. Without assurance of justice, some individuals can get stuck in a victim identity that manifests in feelings of shame, self-harm, and suicidal ideations. It can create a deep sense of grievance, resentment, and revenge fantasies that may fuel aggressive behavior: "*I'm worried about one of my sons, because until now he is still thinking of avenging his brother's death. My neighbor also wanted revenge, so he tried to stab two men riding in tandem. But he was the one who got shot.*" (Amy, 50 years old)

The lack of justice can perpetuate a cycle of violence. Breaking this cycle involves being able to process trauma and obtain justice. For some individuals, however, getting justice does not mean much as it can never compensate the death of a loved one. "*When will we able to obtain justice? But even if the person who killed my son is imprisoned, it still doesn't mean anything to me because they can't bring him back to life.*" (Lea, 48 years old)

Collective Trauma and Its Inter-Generational Impact
SPV can result in collective trauma. Its impact can be particularly severe in urban poor communities where exposure to EJK is more prevalent. Direct or vicarious exposure to community violence can leave people feeling afraid for their safety and security. "*Many people are afraid for their family members who might be wrongly accused and get implicated . . . The killing is continuing, it is not yet over.*" (Rose, 40 years old)

The effects of collective trauma can be inter-generational, as individuals may pass down their trauma to their children and grandchildren. The trauma can impact the way family members interact with one another. A parent with unhealed trauma may be more distant and emotionally unavailable to their children, who are themselves trying to cope with the impact of trauma. The suffering of children is often unseen, rendering them more vulnerable to physical and mental health issues. It may also place them at greater risk of perpetuating the cycle of trauma and violence as adults. Nelson, six years old, did not appear affected by what's happening in the family but was inwardly grieving the loss of his brother. He said, "*I miss my brother so much . . . When I grow up, I want to be a policeman and I will kill those who killed him.*"

Experiences of victimization, unsafety, and other adverse conditions affect children's developmental trajectory. These experiences may negatively impact their view of self, others, and the world, and shape how they respond to life challenges as adults. Pain that is not healed can be transferred. This is one way by which trauma gets transmitted across generations.

Navigating the Path to Resilience and Resistance

After experiencing a traumatic event, individuals can embark on various paths – some leading to feelings of victimization, severe distress and decline in overall well-being, while others lead to resilience, healing, and growth. The pathway an individual follows depends on numerous factors, including their inner resources and social support.

The narrative of Emma and Nina illustrates individuals who demonstrated personal resilience, responded with courage, and engaged in resistance against EJK. "*Resistance in the face of threat.*" (Emma, 55 years old and Nina, 27 years old)

Emma's life was shattered when her 16-year-old son became one of the victims of a massacre by armed masked men searching for drug suspects. The incident resulted in seven casualties, including three teenagers and a pregnant woman, all considered by authorities as "collateral damage."

In the aftermath of this devastating event, both Emma and Nina became participants of Balay's Mental Health and Psychosocial Support (MHPSS) Program. This integrated community-based initiative included various activities, such as community healing ceremonies and liturgies, group psycho-education sessions (monthly "*kumustahan*" or storytelling gatherings), grief support sessions, case management and counseling, as well as advocacy efforts. These activities provided them a safe space to share their painful experiences, mourn their losses, and process their trauma reactions.

Emma emerged as a passionate advocate for justice on behalf of EJK victims. She declared, "I have become more active in my advocacy. I just want to obtain justice . . . I want someone to be held accountable, for the killings to stop. Despite my fear, I muster the courage to help prevent more killings. The violence in our community persists, and so when I speak to the media, my call is: Stop EJK ... Every time I hear of a killing, it fills me with anger. Many of those killed were innocent victims."

When asked about the wellspring of her courage for her advocacy work, Emma responded, "My family has endured numerous tragedies – imprisonment, death. I refuse to let these happen again. I won't allow my family to be oppressed, I am ready to fight for them ... I grew up in poverty and endured ridicule because we were poor. This taught me to fight, to be brave, to not just think of myself."

Emma also draws strength from the solidarity expressed by a local parish church and other human rights organizations. Her sense of belonging to a collective struggle strengthens her determination to seek justice: "*I am emboldened by the support I receive from various groups. Thus, the fight continues. It's not just for my family, it's for everyone.*"

Nina, Emma's daughter, shares her mother's commitment to the pursuit of justice. She finds inspiration in her mother's bravery, stating, "*My mother's courage is infectious. Despite our fear, we both fight ... I cannot accept what happened to my brother. To honor his memory, I dream of establishing a community organization to help drug users and sellers break free from drugs.*"

Emma and Nina both identify as activists. They participate in rallies, volunteer as community-based monitors to document human rights violations and killings, offer emotional support to other grieving families, and encourage them to join collective protest actions. Their story exemplifies that the trauma may never fully heal, but it can be transcended and transformed. Their experience of injustice motivated them to act to prevent others from experiencing similar harm. They were able to harness and channel their trauma energy into actions for justice.

This narrative offers valuable insights into navigating the journey towards resilience and resistance in the face of trauma and adversity.

Connecting to a Supportive Community
At the heart of the experience of trauma is the loss of safety, trust, and social connection. Reconnecting to others and being part of a safe, caring, and supportive community can provide a context conducive to healing. Some kind of healing starts to happen in relationships, as one allows others to become co-bearers of the burden. When burdens are shared, the pain becomes easier to bear. "*The burden is lighter. I feel like I have friends who I can share with, and I won't be judged. The support of the group was very helpful.*" (Nina)

Having a community or network of support creates a sense of belonging, connection and solidarity. It is deeply comforting and reassuring to know that one's suffering is part of a collective experience and common humanity. This makes it easier to process their complex emotions and transform their trauma.

Finding Courage to Tell One's Story
In the face of the on-going threat of violence and stigma, the resulting fear and shame can be paralyzing, making an individual maintain a safe social distance. Telling one's story is an act of courage and a form of resistance. It's a way of resisting a victim identity – a way of saying that they will not remain victims, be broken down and silenced.

Safe supportive spaces can facilitate storytelling. Deep wounds are tended when stories are received, acknowledged, and validated in the presence of a warm, empathetic, and supportive group. In hearing the stories of others, one begins to see the experience from a broader perspective. One realizes that trauma need not destroy the family's future, and that they can transcend trauma.

Storytelling can be done through verbal, written or other artistic means allowing one to organize fragmented painful memories and regulate the emotions attached to them.

Remembrance and Collective Grieving
It is a normal human tendency to avoid or suppress painful memories and emotions. Especially when one is faced with the demands of daily survival that require priority attention. However, grieving is important in trauma healing. This means acknowledging the reality of the loss, accepting the pain, expressing intense emotions, and remembering and honoring the loved one. Remembrance involves reminiscing relationships, positive moments, and the legacy of loved ones, and then saying the goodbyes.

A healthier way of coping with grief is to oscillate between grieving (allowing oneself to feel the pain and grief) and setting it aside to re-engage life.[17] This means experiencing grief in doses, at times facing the pain and at other times taking a break to resume daily life.

Joel, 28 years old, lost his youngest brother (a case of mistaken identity) and struggled with intense anger, guilt, and revenge fantasies. Participating in grief support sessions provided the time and space for him to grieve, which was crucial in releasing him from the burden of anger and bitterness. It helped ease

---

17. M. Stroebe and H. Schut, "The Dual Process Model of Coping with Bereavement: Rationale and Description" (2010), https://wendyvanmieghem.com/wp-content/uploads/2012/08/dual-process-model-by-M.-Stroebe-.pdf.

his pain and let go of revenge thoughts, and prepared him to move forward in life. He shared, *"For me the process was hard and long, but when I learned to face and accept what had happened, I felt relieved and had the courage to move forward."*

What can be a more powerful healing experience is when individuals come together to mourn and grieve collectively. This reaffirms connection to others and creates a sense of solidarity. It can help support people move through the natural/organic grief process.

Collective grieving can also be a form of resistance. Coming together to mourn and publicly speak about the trauma's impact on their lives can raise awareness on the issue of state violence.

Discovering Faith and Spirituality
Trauma can shatter an individual's assumptions about oneself and the world, leaving individuals feeling helpless, vulnerable, and isolated.[18] Faith and spirituality are important resources for healing these shattered assumptions. Reconstructing the belief that human beings have dignity and worth can be very empowering. It can restore an individual's sense of self-worth and identity, rebuild trust in others, and fuel work for justice. *"The church teaches that no human being deserves to die that way . . . I continue to fight for justice."* (Emma)

A faith perspective provides ways of making sense of adversities, enabling one to let go of unhealthy responses and develop healthy coping. It facilitates acceptance, perseverance, and hope during adversities. *"I have been strengthened by the adversities and oppression I have experienced . . . My faith in God has sustained me to struggle it out even when afraid."* (Emma)

Engaging In Advocacy and Collective Action
Being part of advocacy groups can empower individuals to resist and demand for accountability and justice. They gain power from a sense of solidarity and shared purpose among fellow survivors. They draw strength in numbers knowing that being part of a collective has more power and influence than being alone. *"I encourage others to come out and speak before the media. There are now many of us joining rallies and calling for the killings to stop . . ."* (Emma)

Engaging in advocacy activities such as protest rallies or demonstrations and media interviews provides the opportunity to express their outcries and anger over the injustice they experienced. It helps individuals find their voice

---

18. J. L. Herman, *Trauma and Recovery: The Aftermath of Violence – From Domestic Abuse to Political Terror* (New York: Basic Books, 1992).

and feel heard. Sharing their stories and experiences can create awareness on state violence and break down the stigma and feelings of dehumanization. *"When I speak in rallies and share my story, it's a big relief as I'm able to unburden what's inside me."* (Emma)

Reflections from a Faith Perspective: What Does the Lord Require of Us?

In the context of pervasive political violence, we can acknowledge the political sphere as a battleground where competing powers clash. Those who embrace the Christian faith can find inspiration from biblical principles and values and engage in actions that influence individual's well-being. This engagement can be guided by the following themes:

Respect For Human Life and Dignity

At the core of the Christian faith is the belief that all individuals are created in the image of God (Gen 1:26–27), endowing them with intrinsic worth and value simply by being bearers of God's image. This affirms that every individual deserves a life of dignity and underscores the preciousness of human life. According to Bedford-Strohm, this perspective on human dignity calls us to foster relationships founded on love and mutual respect.[19] As God's image-bearers, we have the responsibility to love one another and work towards a just and peaceful relationship with one another.

Moreover, the connection between human dignity and doing justice is implied in the way God is portrayed in the Scriptures. God is the God of justice, who cares for the oppressed and marginalized – those stripped of their humanity and whose rights to live with dignity have been greatly denied. This God requires us "to act justly, to love mercy, and to walk humbly with God" (Mic 6:8) and commands us "to do right, seek justice, defend the oppressed, take up the cause of the fatherless and plead the case of the widow" (Isa 1:17).

The notion of inherent dignity, along with equality of rights, is echoed in the United Nations Declaration of Human Rights – which states that all human beings have inalienable rights and are born equal in dignity and rights.[20] It can be inferred from the declaration that respect for human rights and equality derives from God-given human dignity.

---

19. Heinrich Bedford-Strohm, "Human Dignity: A Global Ethical Perspective," *Scriptura* 104 (2010): 211–20.

20. United Nations General Assembly (1948). *Universal Declaration of Human Rights.* Resolution 217 A (III). Paris: United Nations.

Bedford-Strohm further argues that the concept of human dignity is closely connected to the principle of preferential option for the poor, which is a strong theme in the Old and New Testament.[21] The poor, who are often the most marginalized and oppressed members of society, deserve special concern and protection. He highlights:

> God's response to the injustices which Israel has to endure is to promise them liberation. . . . It is the most decisive moment in the whole history of God and God's people. This God is not only a God of the poor in words. This God acts in history. This God changes history. This God leads the oppressed out of their situation of oppression into a life of dignity and mutual respect.[22]

This understanding is very relevant to the victims of the "War on Drugs," the majority of whom are from urban poor communities and do not have the means to defend themselves from any unjust actions of state agents. Helping them attain justice, while mainstream churches and institutions are turning a blind eye, is a concrete expression of preferential option for the poor. It shows that when there is conflict between the weak and their powerful oppressors, the Christian ethical option is to take sides with the weak to resist the powerful.

Religious leaders, however, can be complicit to state violence through the way they justify or legitimize it by using Scriptures. It is common to hear religious leaders invoking Romans 13:1–7 but focusing on submission to authorities and completely downplaying the need to hold the state accountable for the abuse of God-delegated power and mandate. In her article on this issue, Maggay asserts that submitting to governing authorities does not equate to uncritical obedience to the state.[23] This is evident when Peter declared, "We must obey God rather than men" (Acts 5:29). When the state violates its God-given purpose to uphold the moral order, it forfeits its claim to legitimate authority. In such a situation, it is the citizens' duty to resist in order to uphold what is morally right.

A frustrating footnote to this is to hear so many Christian leaders applauding the killings of the "War on Drugs" campaign. They echo Duterte's argument that it is necessary to protect the moral fabric of Filipino society. The irony of it is while they preach redemption, they tacitly support Duterte's declaration that

---

21. Bedford-Strohm, "Human Dignity," 216.
22. Bedford-Strohm, "Human Dignity," 216.
23. See Melba Maggay's chapter in this book.

drug users or addicts are beyond redemption. As a result, they have become apathetic to the plight of the victims.

An appropriate ethical response is to challenge the legitimacy of Duterte's unjust use of power, as well as the system and policies that perpetuate such. One way to do this is for Christian leaders to call out the prevailing dehumanizing narratives and help create space with which the voices of the victims can be heard, their perspectives seriously considered, and their resolve to seek justice strengthened.

Jesus himself set an example of resistance that defied oppressive religious authorities and prevailing beliefs that led to the suffering of marginalized individuals. For this, the religious leaders conspired to have him executed by the Roman government. He was arrested, tortured, publicly shamed, and finally executed on the cross like a common criminal.

Demonstrating Love of Neighbor

Jesus's command to love our neighbor (Mark 12:30–31) provides a framework for how Christians are to relate to others and respond to violations of human dignity. Loving others is not merely a feeling or sentiment, but it requires action. In his life and ministry, Jesus consistently demonstrated love of neighbors. He showed compassion for those on the fringes, the outcasts, and the sick. He fearlessly confronted the abuses of those in positions of authority and questioned the systems that perpetuated injustice. Ultimately, he exemplified this love through his selfless sacrifice on the cross. He rejected violence as a means of resistance against those in power, instead showing that true strength lies in acts of love and service.

Christians are called to model our lives after Jesus's example of sacrificial, self-giving love, and willingness to suffer for others. This call challenges us to demonstrate our love for others and actively address all forms of violations of human dignity. In this way we are embodying God's presence and active involvement in the world.

Implications for a Healing and Justice-Sensitive Response

Biblical and theological teachings on human dignity and love of neighbor have important implications to the faith community's life and praxis.

Being a Compassionate Trauma-Informed Community

Being a compassionate community involves bearing witness to the suffering of others and being present with them in their pain. It means creating a safe space where they can share their stories and feel validated. This involves listening without blame, judgment, and attempts to treat or fix them. The presence of a compassionate witness helps them feel seen, heard, understood, and valued as human beings with dignity and worth.

Compassion must be embodied in concrete actions such as offering emotional support, practical assistance, and resources to help them rebuild their lives. To avoid the risk of doing harm, however, it is important to be trauma-informed, which means utilizing processes and practices that are not re-traumatizing.[24] This approach recognizes the negative impact of trauma while also acknowledging resilience and strengths.

The faith community can learn from best practices of integrated support services from psychosocial NGOs. For example, Balay's MHPSS program[25] is a model of how trauma-informed care can be done. The program addresses the trauma healing needs of left-behind families and includes services that:

- Address safety and protection needs of left-behind families by providing sanctuary, welfare support, burial assistance, medical, and legal support.
- Address trauma's impact by helping them process their trauma, grieve their losses, and deal with other negative outcomes.
- Provide psychoeducation on trauma, grief, stress and coping, emotion regulation, child protection, human rights, and legal rights.
- Equip them with life-skills such as livelihood and basic literacy.
- Monitor and report human rights violations.
- Organize and mobilize community members for advocacy and collective action.
- Form support groups to nurture a sense of community grounded on the Filipino value of "*damayan*" (mutual help).

---

24. See Substance Abuse and Mental Health Services Administration, "SAMHSA's Concept of Trauma and Guidance for a Trauma-Informed Approach," *HHS Publication* No. (SMA) 14–4884 (Rockville: Substance Abuse and Mental Health Services Administration, 2014). SAMHSA's Concept of Trauma and Guidance for a Trauma-Informed Approach.

25. Balay Rehabilitation Center's community-based MHPSS program adheres to key principles outlined in WHO Inter-Agency Standing Committee guidelines, which include ensuring that services are provided in ways that uphold human rights and dignity of individuals, as well as the participation and empowerment of affected communities. See https://www.who.int/publications/i/item/iasc-guidelines-for-mental-health-and-psychosocial-support-in-emergency-settings.

- Provide referrals to address other practical and legal needs.

Companioning Courageously towards Justice-Seeking

Companioning individuals in their path towards justice-seeking entails providing support, walking in solidarity, and strengthening their resolve and capacity for seeking justice. This means creating safe spaces for voices of resistance and engaging in advocacy and activism on their behalf. This involves actions that:

- Support their needs for legal redress.
- Give voice to their stories in truth-telling forums and raise awareness on their plight.
- Challenge the prevailing narratives and policies that contribute to a fertile ground for SPV.
- Advocate for alternative narratives that emphasize the drug problem's public health and social dimensions, acknowledging the role of poverty in driving individuals into the drug trade.
- Counter the stigma associated with drug-users and left-behind families.
- Advocate for policies that protect human rights and prevent state violence.

It is difficult to address all the needs of left-behind families. Thus, the necessity of engaging in multidisciplinary, collaborative, and partnership work with other agencies, both government and non-government organizations. To be sustainable, compassion and justice-work must be part of a larger peacebuilding effort that addresses direct and structural violence in the community.[26]

Conclusion

The trauma of SPV creates profound psychological, emotional, and social impacts on individuals, families, and communities. The political context shapes the experience of trauma and can complicate the healing process. The journey of transforming this trauma is a personal and collective process that requires companioning survivors to take action towards healing and justice. By affirm-

---

26. Cf. Fermin Manalo Jr., "Community Development Animating Peacebuilding from Below: The Case of GiNaPaLadTaKa Space for Peace in Pikit, North Cotobato," *Philippine Journal of Social Development* 15 (2013).

ing human dignity and embodying love of neighbor, the Christian community can play a vital role in this process.

My experience in companioning trauma survivors has sensitized me to justice issues and transformed me into an advocate for peace and human rights. However, it has also stirred up spiritual and existential questions around themes of evil, finding meaning in suffering, and the seeming absence of God in the face of injustice. In these challenging moments, the support and non-judgmental reflection space provided by my spiritual director and mentors have proven to be invaluable. They have guided me in making sense of my experiences, embracing uncertainty, giving voice to my lament before God, and rediscovering purpose. Equally vital is the sense of belonging to a community that shares similar values and works towards common goals. I have also drawn inspiration from the stories of trauma survivors' "*sama-samang pagbangon*" (rising stronger together). These narratives strengthen my faith and inspire hope in God's mysterious actions and loving presence, even in the midst of darkness.

Moreover, it is crucial to follow a rhythm of contemplation and action. Following the wisdom of Charles Ringma, we are invited to imitate Jesus the contemplative-activist, who models the practice of contemplation inspiring action, and action leading to deeper contemplation and prayer.[27] This entails engaging in self-care and spiritual practices such as mindfulness, solitude and prayer, reflective reading of Scriptures, silent retreats, and spending time with nature. These contemplative practices serve as sources of inner strength and nourishment, preparing us to return to our work, fully renewed and ready to face the tasks ahead.

Through this journey, I have learned that compassion and justice-work present challenges that require us to nurture certain virtues such as courage, perseverance, and equanimity. Courage empowers us to confront difficult situations and take actions despite apprehensions. Perseverance strengthens our commitments in a faithful, sustained way. Equanimity fosters emotional calmness and stability, allowing us to remain steady in the face of others' trauma responses. By cultivating these virtues, we can embody God's healing presence and offer companioning over the long term.

As a faith community responding to God's call, we must persevere in companioning oppressed and traumatized communities on their journey towards healing and justice.

---

27. See Charles Ringma, "Contemplation in a World of Action," https://www.northumbriacommunity.org/wp-content/uploads/2015/06/Contemplation-in-a-World-of-Action.pdf, 2.

Bibliography

American Psychiatric Association. *Diagnostic and Statistical Manual of Mental Disorders*. 5th ed. Arlington: American Psychiatric Publishing, 2013.

Bedford-Strohm, Heinrich. "Human Dignity: A Global Ethical Perspective." *Scriptura* 104 (2010): 211–20.

Herman, Judith L. "Social Trauma and the Healing of Communities and Individuals." *Journal of the American Academy of Psychoanalysis* 20, no. 1 (1992): 1–23.

———. *Trauma and Recovery: The Aftermath of Violence – From Domestic Abuse to Political Terror*. New York: Basic Books, 1992.

Maggay, Melba P. "State Power and the Church in Society." In *Faith and Politics: Filipino Evangelical Insights in Political Theology*, edited by David Lim and Aldrin Peñamora. Carlisle: Langham Global Library, 2025.

Manalo, Annabel M. "Healing the Trauma of War and Internal Displacement: Exploring the Nexus of Trauma Healing and Reconciliation." In *How Long, O Lord?: The Challenge and Promise of Reconciliation and Peace*, edited by Athena Gorospe and Charles Ringma. Carlisle: Langham Global Library, 2019.

———. "Losses and Grief During Challenging Times: Understanding and Befriending Your Grief." In *This Season of Grief: Stories, Poetry, Prayers, and Practical Help*. Mandaluyong City: OMF Literature, 2021.

Manalo, Fermin, Jr. "Community Development Animating Peacebuilding from Below: The Case of GiNaPaLadTaKa Space for Peace in Pikit, North Cotabato." *Philippine Journal of Social Development* 15 (2013).

Mijares, Aileen P. "Rebuilding Lives Amid the Ruins of Duterte's War on Drugs." *Journal of Human Rights and Peace Studies* 6, no. 2 (2020): 255–82.

Neimeyer, Robert A. "Complicated Grief and the Quest for Meaning: A Constructivist Contribution." *Journal of Constructivist Psychology* 25, no. 4 (2012): 313–25.

Peñamora, Aldrin M. "Their Blood Cries Out from the Ground: An Ethic of Malasakit and the War on Drugs." In *Faith and Bayan: Evangelical Christian Engagement in the Philippine Context*, edited by Lorenzo Bautista, Aldrin Peñamora, and Federico Villanueva. Carlisle: Langham Global Library, 2022.

Rothschild, Babette. *The Body Remembers Casebook: Unifying Methods and Models in the Treatment of Trauma and PTSD*. New York: WW Norton & Company, 2003.

Simbulan, Estacio, Dioquino-Maligaso, Herbosa, and Withers. "The Manila Declaration on the Drug Problem in the Philippines." *Annals of Global Health*, 5 March 2019. https://www.annalsofglobalhealth.org/articles/10.5334/aogh.28/#:~:text=The%20declaration%20includes%20an%20implicit,and%20psychological%20%5B16%5D.%E2%80%9D

Stroebe, Margaret, and Henk Schut. "The Dual Process Model of Coping with Bereavement: Rationale and Description." 2010. https://wendyvanmieghem.com/wp-content/uploads/2012/08/dual-process-model-by-M.-Stroebe-.pdf.

Substance Abuse and Mental Health Services Administration. "SAMHSA's Concept of Trauma and Guidance for a Trauma-Informed Approach." *HHS Publication No. (SMA) 14–4884*. Rockville: Substance Abuse and Mental Health Services Administration, 2014.

United Nations General Assembly (1948). *Universal Declaration of Human Rights*. Resolution 217 A (III). Paris: United Nations.

Van der Kolk, Bessel A. *The Body Keeps the Score: Brain, Mind, and Body in the Healing of Trauma*. New York: Viking, 2014.

"World Report on Violence and Health: Summary." *World Health Organization*, 2002. http://apps.who.int/iris/bitstream/handle/10665/42512/9241545623_eng.pdf;jsessionid=4378282ED53BF2407D93AA7D081B7F38?sequence=1.

8

The Voice of the Victim: A Reading of 2 Samuel 13

Using René Girard's Mimetic Theory

Wilfredo A. Laceda

Introduction

The goal of this chapter is twofold. First, it seeks to introduce René Girard's mimetic theory to a broader evangelical audience by using it as a lens to interpret 2 Samuel 13, the story of Tamar. Second, it aims to explore the implications of the Girardian theory for the current religio-political context in the Philippines, and, by extension to outline the contours of a political theology based on mimetic theory. We begin by reading the story of Tamar through pertinent aspects of Girard's mimetic theory. By examining the literary cues, themes, and characterizations in Tamar's story with Girardian eyes, we seek to highlight how literature can reveal important aspects of the human condition.[1] Since Tamar's story is part of a larger narrative, we also explore the interplay between monarchical politics and personal tragedy, drawing on mimetic theory's explanation of the scapegoat mechanism. Next, we examine the relationship between law and justice, focusing on the precarious position of the victim. Finally, as a

---

1. Martha Nussbaum, "Narrative Emotions: Beckett's Genealogy of Love," *Ethics*, Vol. 98, no. 2 (January 1998): 226.

point of departure we use Girard's insight that the Bible reveals the perspective of the victim to help construct a political theology rooted in mimetic theory.[2]

Mimetic Desire, Violence, and 2 Samuel 13

A number of scholars view the books of Samuel as a compilation of disparate works that were stitched together to form the text that we have now. The story of Tamar, for example, falls under the broader theme of David's tumultuous reign as Israel's king. In 1926, Leonhard Rost proposed a hypothesis known as the "Succession Narrative," which argues that 2 Samuel 9–20 and 1 Kings 1–2 originally comprised a single work intended to defend Solomon's ascension to the throne.[3] Contemporary scholars who follow Rost's theory focus on thematic unity, dating, authorial intent, and literary structure.[4] However, recent scholarship suggests that the unity of the books of Samuel lies in its author's insightful exploration of the complexities of politics and sovereign power.[5]

A major point of interest in the books of Samuel is their themes, though scholars remain divided on this issue. For example, David Gunn argues that the themes of sex, intrigue, and violence are central to David's narrative.[6] Hans Jensen, likely the first to apply Girard's mimetic theory to the story of David, reinterprets Gunn's themes through Girard's framework: replacing sex with desire, intrigue with rivalry, and violence with collective violence.[7] The theme of desire is especially prominent in David's story. Here, Girard's concept of mimetic desire, the first tenet of his mimetic theory is particularly relevant.

René Girard (1923–2015) was a French literary critic whose oeuvre transcends disciplinary boundaries, from literary theory, anthropology, and religious studies, to name a few. Throughout his career, Girard developed and

---

2. Although mimetic theory is our main theoretical framework, we also borrow ideas from different theoretical backgrounds.

3. Richard G. Smith, *The Fate of Justice and Righteousness During David's Reign: Rereading the Court History and Its Ethics according to 2 Samuel 8:15b–20:26* (New York: T&T Clark International, 2009), 1.

4. The recent exchange between Joseph Blenkinsopp and John Van Seter is both instructive of the state and history of scholarship of the Succession Narrative. See Joseph Blenkinsopp, "Another Contribution to the Succession Narrative Debate (2 Sam 11–20; 1 Kgs 1–2)," *JSOT* 38 (2013): 35–58; John Van Seter, "A Revival of the Succession Narrative and the Case against It," *JSOT* 39 (2014): 3–14.

5. Moshe Halbertal and Stephen Holmes, *The Beginning of Politics: Power in the Biblical Book of Samuel* (Princeton: Princeton University Press, 2017), 3.

6. David M. Gunn, *The Story of King David: Genre and Interpretation* (JSOTSup 6; Sheffield: Sheffield Academic Press, 1978), 89.

7. Hans J. L. Jensen, "Desire, Rivalry and Collective Violence," *JSOT* 55 (1992): 44.

expanded his mimetic theory. In his early work, *Deceit, Desire, and the Novel* he identified a structural pattern in the great European novels, which he argued reveal the mimetic nature of human desire, challenging the modern notion of human autonomy. Girard analyzed characters across a wide range of literary works, demonstrating how their intricately entangled relationships form a pattern he calls "*triangular desire.*"[8] Later in the book, he refers to this as "*desire according to Another,*" and ultimately, as "imitated desire."[9] In doing so, Girard redefines the classical concept of desire as originary force, instead positioning mimesis as the true driving force behind human motivation.

In *Violence and the Sacred*, Girard calls this "*mimetic desire*" or simply "mimesis."[10] Mimetic desire is ultimately concerned about being. His term for this is metaphysical desire. "The reason," Girard writes, "is that he desires *being*, something he himself lacks and which another person possesses. The subject thus looks to that person to inform him of what he should desire in order to acquire that being."[11] This is a hint on the social character of the human subject's formation and how it generates social conflict. Desire, in other words, is always mediated via a third party; hence the almost symbiotic relationship between mimetic desire and violence. Moreover, the discovery of mirror neurons in the mid-1990s confirms that mimesis is built into the human brain, and bolsters the claim of mimetic theory from the field of neuroscience.[12] In his later overtures to the biblical materials, Girard would highlight the role of positive mimesis as exemplified by the idea of "imitating Christ."

The triangle of desire is reconfigured in various stages of the Davidic narrative. The first triangle comprises David, Bathsheba, and Uriah. David is the desiring subject, while Bathsheba is the object of desire, and her husband Uriah is the obstacle that stands against the actualization of David's sexual dalliance. To acquire the object, the obstacle must be eliminated. Uriah's death clears the way for David to appropriate Bathsheba. The triangle is recast in Amnon, Tamar, and Absalom. Amnon takes the role of the desiring subject, while his half-sister Tamar as the object, and Absalom functions as the obstacle.

---

8. René Girard, *Deceit, Desire, and the Novel: Self and Other in Literary Structure*, trans. Yvonne Freccero (Baltimore: Johns Hopkins Press, 1965), 2.

9. Girard, *Deceit, Desire, and the Novel*, 4, 21. Italics in the original.

10. René Girard, *Violence and the Sacred*, trans. Patrick Gregory (Baltimore: Johns Hopkins Press, 1977; repr. 1987), 146, 148. Emphasis in the original.

11. Girard, *Violence and the Sacred*, 146. Italics in the original.

12. Cynthia L. Haven, *Evolution of Desire: A Life of René Girard* (East Lansing: Michigan State University, 2018), 219.

Scholars have long noticed the thematic proximity of these two episodes.[13] Yet, there are marked differences between these two stories. One such difference is the overall tone and tenor of chapter 13 which one scholar describes as "the darker and more terrible."[14] In chapter 13 the characters are all members of the royal family, which makes the story even more intriguing. Although both episodes eventually ended in death, they differ in that the obstacle in the latter story becomes the killer. The last triangle involves Absalom, the throne, and David. Absalom wants what David has, that is, kingship. David, in Girard's terminology, functions as the model and Absalom acts as his double or disciple. When David becomes a rival or an obstacle, he is transformed as a threat to be eliminated and thus begins Absalom's quest to usurp the throne. Thus, to quote Girard: "The principal source of violence between human beings is mimetic rivalry, the rivalry resulting in imitation of a model who becomes a rival, or of a rival who becomes a model."[15]

The first two desires are sexual in nature while the last fits what Girard calls "mimetic desire."[16] Common in all three is the presence of rivalry, although not always explicit. Once mimetic desire is enacted, rivalry naturally develops which then leads to a violent conflict that typically culminates in a paroxysm of violence. A comparative analysis of the three rape scenes in the Old Testament reveals a "family resemblance" (Gen 34; Judg 19; and 2 Sam 13).[17] Common with these texts is that "the rape of a woman in the narrative prefigures a war between men."[18] A woman's rape disrupts the community, leading to social fragmentation.[19]

Within these texts Alice Keefe suggests a "common narrative expression" that inscribes meaning to the female body vis-à-vis Israel's self-understanding.[20] The phrase "that such a thing is not done" appears in all three texts.[21] A key

---

13. Mark M. Gray, "Amnon a Chip of the Old Block? Rhetorical Strategy in 2 Samuel 13. 7–15: The Rape of Tamar and the Humiliation of the Poor," *JSOT* 77 (1998): 40.

14. Gray, "Amnon a Chip of the Old Block?," 40.

15. René Girard, *I See Satan Fall like Lightning*, trans. James G. Williams (Maryknoll: Orbis Books, 2001), 11.

16. Girard, *Violence and the Sacred*, 148.

17. Frank M. Yamada, *Configurations of Rape in the Hebrew Bible: A Literary Analysis of Three Rape Narratives* (New York: Peter Lang Publishing, Inc, 2008), 5.

18. Alice A. Keefe, "Rapes of Women/Wars of Men," *Semeia* 61 (1993): 80.

19. Yamada, *Configurations of Rape*, 5.

20. Keefe, "Rapes of Women," 81.

21. Mignon Jacobs, "Love, Honor, and Violence: Socioconceptual Matrix in Genesis 34," in *Pregnant Passion: Gender, Sex, and Violence in the Bible*, ed. Cheryl A. Kirk-Duggan (SBL Semeia Studies 44; Atlanta: Society of Biblical Literature, 2003), 13.

term found in these three rape texts is the word *nebalah*, usually translated as "disgraceful folly," and it is linked to the disruption and destruction of communal life.[22] Susan Niditch commenting on the connection between sex and society in the Hebrew Bible says that "inappropriate or forced [sexual] alliances always lead to larger social disintegration."[23] Conversely, "Politics are written on the bodies of women. . . . War is written on women's bodies."[24]

Regina Schwartz points out that "sexuality and politics" are interconnected in David's house.[25] In this context, sexual assault – particularly the rape of women – catalyzes violence that spreads throughout the larger community.[26] Although rape has a consistent definition, its meaning can vary depending on cultural context. As with other human experiences, the significance of rape is culturally mediated.[27] In ancient Israel, rape was viewed as "an affair between men."[28] In this framework, it became the kinship duty of a father or brother to respond when a female family member was sexually violated. In this sense, the rape of a woman was also an assault on the men's honor.[29]

Schwartz[30] and Keefe[31] both inquire on the persistent connection between sexuality and politics. In *Purity and Danger*, Mary Douglas sheds an illuminating light on this link:

> The Israelites were always in their history a hard-pressed minority. In their beliefs all the bodily issues were polluting, blood, pus, excreta, semen, etc. The threatened boundaries of their body politic would be well mirrored in their care for the integrity of the physical body.[32]

---

22. Keefe, "Rapes of Women," 82.
23. Cited in Keefe, "Rapes of Women," 81.
24. Fewell and Gunn quoted in Gray, "Amnon a Chip of the Old Block?," 41.
25. Regina M. Schwartz, "Adultery in the House of David: The Metanarrative of Biblical Scholarship and the Narratives of the Bible," *Semeia* 54 (1990): 44.
26. Keefe surmises that perhaps the "stories of rape are not intended primarily as stories of personal tragedies, but of disruptions of community life in Israel." Keefe, "Rapes of Women," 83.
27. Mary Douglas, *Purity and Danger: An Analysis of the Concepts of Pollution and Taboo* (New York: Routledge, 1984), 129.
28. William H. Propp, "Kinship in 2 Samuel 13," *CBQ* 55 (1993): 41.
29. Propp, "Kinship in 2 Samuel 13," 42.
30. Schwartz, "Adultery in the House of David," 46.
31. Keefe, "Rapes of Women," 80.
32. Douglas, *Purity and Danger*, 125.

Simply put, the body serves as a symbolic representation of society.[33] However, it is more than just a metonym for society. As Judith Butler writes, "The body implies mortality, vulnerability, agency: the skin and the flesh expose us to the gaze of others, but also to touch, and to violence, and bodies put us at risk of becoming the agency and instrument of all these as well."[34] Butler highlights the body's public and political dimensions.[35] Thus, to anticipate a strand in our argument, Tamar's violated body is emblematic of the failure of David's dynasty to administer justice.

The absence of a successor is a recurring theme in the reign of David.[36] Nathan's prophesies of promise and judgment resonate throughout the narrative.[37] A key turning point comes with David's affair with Bathsheba, which provokes God's wrath.[38] The way this unfolds is, to say the least, intriguing. The author of the book of Samuel is a keen observer of political dynamics and power, displaying a deep understanding of the ambiguity inherent in unchecked human authority. This shifting balance of power, which places God at the margins of political life, reshaped not only Israel's political structure but also its theological outlook.[39]

Triangle of Desire

A transitional phrase opens our story: "Now it was after this . . ."[40] which signals that the narrative is embarking on a new episode. Absalom, David's third son, takes center stage, creating the expectation that this story is primarily about him.[41] The other key figure is Amnon, David's firstborn and the presumptive heir to the throne. Both are introduced as "David's son," which confers prestige and position of power, but also hints at a potential rivalry on who will ulti-

---

33. Douglas, *Purity and Danger*, 126.

34. Judith Butler, *Precarious Life: The Powers of Mourning and Violence* (London: Verso, 2004), 26.

35. Butler, *Precarious Life*, 26.

36. Gerhard von Rad, following Rost claims that Michal's lack of a child is the starting point of the Deuteronomistic historian's overall thesis. Gerhard von Rad, *From Genesis to Chronicles: Explorations in Old Testament Theology*, ed. K. C. Hanson (Minneapolis: Fortress Press, 2005), 133.

37. 2 Samuel 7:1–14; 12:7–12, 14.

38. 2 Samuel 11:27.

39. Moshe Halbertal and Stephen Holmes, *The Beginning of Politics*, 3–4.

40. All Scripture quotations, unless otherwise indicated, are taken from the NASB.

41. In the larger narrative, Absalom indeed occupies a central role, here, however, he is part of the supporting cast. See van Dijk-Hemmes, "Tamar and the Limits of Patriarchy," 138.

mately sit on the throne.[42] In contrast, Tamar, Absalom's sister, and Amnon's object of desire,[43] is described differently.[44] While her two brothers are clearly identified as David's children, Tamar is not referred to as David's daughter. Instead, she is introduced as "Absalom's beautiful sister" (v. 1) and it is only through inference that we can deduce her royal lineage.[45]

One cannot help but wonder about the implications of Tamar's exclusionary signification. On the surface, it may seem innocent from a stylistic or rhetorical perspective. However, in a story laden with both political and personal consequences, such omission is anything but innocent. Butler argues that certain discourses "effect violence" through exclusion or omission,[46] and in extreme cases this can serve as a precursor or a form of legitimation for dehumanization.[47] A pertinent example is the public rhetoric of former Philippine president, Rodrigo Duterte (2016–2022). During his war on drugs campaign, Duterte routinely referred to those he labeled as drug addicts as less than human. This language arguably conditioned the public to view the deaths of these individuals not as murder, but as something less significant. By being excluded from the category of "human," their dehumanization began in discourse, and physical violence soon followed.[48]

Tamar's exclusion constitutes a form of violence. Critical theory has expanded the meaning of "violence" to include categories that are often difficult to grasp phenomenologically, such as psychological, symbolic, structural, epistemic, hermeneutical, and aesthetic violence.[49] Whether in discourse or in real life, such "framing"[50] can lead to what Butler describes as "differential allocation of grievability,"[51] which implies a hierarchy in the valuation of persons. Additionally, rhetorical structures – the ring composition[52] and triangular

---

42. See Yamada, *Configurations of Rape*, 108.
43. Trible, *Texts of Terror*, 38; Keefe, "Rapes of Women," 87.
44. See Bar-Efrat, *Narrative Art*, 241.
45. van Dijk-Hemmes, "Tamar and the Limits of Patriarchy," 39.
46. Butler, *Precarious Life*, 34.
47. Butler, *Precarious Life*, 34.
48. See Butler, *Precarious Life*, 34.
49. Beatrice Hanssen, *Critique of Violence: Between Poststructuralism and Critical Theory* (Warwick Studies in European Philosophy; New York: Routledge, 2000), 9.
50. Judith Butler, *Frames of War: When is Life Grievable?* (London: Verso, 2009), 3.
51. Butler, *Precarious Life*, 12.
52. Phyllis Trible, *Texts of Terror: Literary-Feminist Readings of Biblical Narratives* (Philadelphia: Fortress Press, 1984), 38; Keefe, "Rapes of Women," 87.

design[53] – are used in the introduction of the characters, underscoring Tamar's significant, and perhaps precarious, position.

A clearer source of conflict is Amnon's desire for Tamar. I agree with those who prefer the term "desire" over "love" to characterize Amnon's feelings toward his half-sister.[54] As one commentator notes, Amnon's action "lacks romantic overtones."[55] Therefore, the concept of desire is more suitable for describing Amnon's thoughts and behaviors, offering greater explanatory power from a theoretical perspective. We have already discussed how desire, particularly in its acquisitive form, can spark rivalry and conflict. In a compelling convergence of ideas, Michel Foucault and René Girard both explore the connection between violence and desire. Foucault writes, "When there is desire, the power relation is already present: an illusion then, to denounce this relation. . . ."[56] While Girard suggests that violence can awaken desire[57] or ". . . in one way or another violence is always mingled with desire."[58] Foucault emphasizes desire's implicit link to violence, while Girard more directly connects the two. This proximity between desire and violence reaches its height in Girard's concept of "conflictual mimesis."[59]

To reiterate Girard's structure of desire, it always involves a subject of desire, an object, and an obstacle.[60] The characters in this story fit neatly into Girard's framework: Amnon is the subject, Tamar is the object, and Absalom represents the obstacle. The narrator does not reveal the motivation behind Amnon's obsessive, and perhaps lustful,[61] desire for his half-sister Tamar. However, we can surmise that it is Tamar's beauty that captivates him.[62] Amnon

---

53. Propp, "Kinship in 2 Samuel 13," 40; Cheryl A. Kirk-Duggan, "Slingshots, Ships, and Personal Psychosis: Murder, Sexual Intrigue, and Power in the Lives of David and Othello," in *Pregnant Passion: Gender, Sex, and Violence in the Bible*, ed. Cheryl A. Kirk-Duggan (SBL Semeia Studies 44; Atlanta: Society of Biblical Literature, 2003), 55; Jensen, "Desire, Rivalry and Collective Violence," 45. Jensen and Kirk-Duggan both utilize René Girard's theory of mimetic desire.

54. Trible, *Texts of Terror*, 38; Jensen, "Desire, Rivalry and Collective Violence," 45; Kirk-Duggan, "Slingshots, Ships, and Personal Psychosis," 54.

55. van Dijk-Hemmes, "Limits of Patriarchy," 139.

56. Michel Foucault, *The History of Sexuality Vol. 1: An Introduction*, trans. Robert Hurley (New York: Vintage Books, 1990), 81.

57. Girard, *Violence and the Sacred*, 144.

58. Girard, *Violence and the Sacred*, 145.

59. Girard, *Violence and the Sacred*, 187.

60. Girard, *Deceit, Desire, and the Novel*, 2.

61. Amit, "To Include or Not to Include?," 211.

62. Keefe hesitantly suggests that the inclusion of Tamar's physical description plays a crucial role in the development of the plot. See Keefe, "Rapes of Women," 87.

becomes increasingly frustrated, but the true source of his frustration is his impotence – he cannot act on his desire to the point that "he made himself ill" (v. 2). On the surface, there appear to be two obstacles hindering Amnon's pursuit: Tamar's virginity and their shared blood ties. These are external social barriers signaling that Tamar is off-limits.[63] However, such barriers can be overcome with a well-conceived plan.[64] One lesson from the David-Bathsheba episode is that acquisitive desire, whether sexual or otherwise, recognizes no limits, especially for those in a position of political power.[65]

In Girard's structure of desire it is Absalom who truly stands between Amnon and his appropriation of Tamar.[66] The world our characters inhabit is governed by cultural codes that make some actions normative while others are deemed as *nebalah*.[67] One such code is the belief that a woman's sexual purity is closely tied to the honor of the male.[68] In this context, violating Tamar becomes not only an assault on her but, perhaps more importantly, an affront to Absalom.[69] As a result, this violation awakens the dormant rivalry between Amnon and Absalom. However, Absalom's personal stake in the matter adds complexity to the situation. His claim to the throne shapes his actions and foreshadows the course he will ultimately take. Amnon's words in verse 4 all but confirm Absalom's role as the obstacle standing in his way. This, in turn, completes the triangle of desire.

The Royal Rape of Justice and the Sacrificial Victims

Amnon's obsessive desire has taken a toll on him. The narrator implicitly characterizes Amnon as pathetic, as his failure to act on his desire is a proof of his impotence. Jonadab finds Amnon in an almost desolate condition. Described as "a very shrewd man" (v. 3b), Jonadab is Amnon's confidant and cousin. His proximity to power, yet permanent exclusion from the line of succession, may have fostered in him a mix of resentment and envy. Jonadab will quickly

---

63. See Smith, *The Fate of Justice and Righteousness*, 150.
64. Smith, *The Fate of Justice and Righteousness*, 150.
65. See Jensen, "Desire, Rivalry and Collective Violence," 45; Kirk-Duggan, "Slingshots, Ships, and Personal Psychosis," 55.
66. Trible perceptively sees this even without the aid of Girard's mimetic desire. See Trible, *Texts of Terror*, 40.
67. Keefe, "Rapes of Women," 83.
68. Gary Stansell, "Honor and Shame in the David Narratives," *Semeia* 68 (1994): 72.
69. Esther Fuchs, *Sexual Politics in the Biblical Narrative: Reading the Hebrew Bible as a Woman* (JSOTSup 310; Sheffield: Sheffield Academic Press, 2001), 204.

change the direction of the story by devising a ruse to deceive David. He provides Amnon the blueprint to entrap[70] Tamar using the monarchy – both spatially and politically. Tamar's movement from her own dwelling place to Amnon's house, culminating in the crime in Amnon's inner chamber, is all confined to the royal palace.[71] Demonstrating his cunning, Jonadab creates a short-term plan based on a deceptively simple but crucial detail: that David, king and father of both Amnon and Tamar, will acquiesce to the request of the crown prince. The narrator uses repetition to highlight the shrewdness of Jonadab's advice.[72]

When the king came to see Amnon, he requested that his sister Tamar would prepare food and nurse him (v. 6). This verse advances the plot of our story, intertwining monarchical politics and domestic sexual violence. Verses 6–9 commence the action, blending the characters' dialogue with narration. A key aspect of this section is the movement of the characters, which begins and ends at Amnon's house.[73] Additionally, a critical element in the plot development would be the words of David. Tamar goes to Amnon's house at the behest of their father, David. However, David's words are not just of a concerned and doting father alone. As king, his words have gravitas. In fact, they bear the weight of royal power. What begins as advice gradually becomes a request and ultimately a royal imprimatur.[74] Tamar is trapped within the royal household, where the monarchy serves as both a tool of control and a source of legitimacy. In the end, her only choice is to obey.

David's role in the subsequent rape of his daughter is pivotal to the disintegration of both his family and his monarchy, crumbling like a house of cards. David, according to Gerhard von Rad, is "far from a simple character, whose life is a mass of contradictions."[75] Part of the ambiguity surrounding David's life is his role in the violation of Tamar. For many interpreters, he is seen as an unwitting accomplice,[76] and thus, he can easily be off the hook. However, for Esther Fuchs, the "real victimization" of Tamar began with David's command for her to go to Amnon's house.[77] David, who is accustomed to using others as

---

70. Trible, *Texts of Terror*, 42.
71. See Fuchs, *Sexual Politics in the Biblical Narrative*, 208.
72. Amit, "To Include Or Not to Include?," 212; Bar-Efrat, *Narrative Art*, 252–55.
73. Trible, *Texts of Terror*, 42.
74. See Trible, *Texts of Terror*, 43.
75. Von Rad, *From Genesis to Chronicles*, 143.
76. Van Dijk-Hemmes, "Tamar and the Limits of Patriarchy," 140; Gray, "Amnon a Chip of the Old Block?," 42; Yamada, *Configurations of Rape*, 113; Trible, *Texts of Terror*, 42.
77. Fuchs, *Sexual Politics in the Hebrew Narrative*, 205; Yamada, *Configurations of Rape*, 113.

instruments through his words, such as in the case of Uriah's death, became the instrument of one of his own sons. David's lack of foresight would have grave consequences for Tamar, highlighting the conflicting aspects of his character.[78]

Furthermore, Trible rightly notes the theme of wisdom as crucial in the story; however, I see wisdom as part of a larger theme: justice, or its distortion.[79] Therefore, I chose to retell Tamar's plight as what I refer to as the royal rape of justice. The act takes place curiously within the royal premises, marking the only instance in the Bible where such a violation occurs at the very seat of power. The perpetrator, enabler, and victim are all members of the royal family. Ironically, the person who should embody wisdom, justice, and righteousness becomes the instrument of Tamar's victimization.[80] David, paradoxically, has become the royal fool, or *nabal*.[81] Girard's comments on the ambivalence of kings in archaic societies aptly capture David's polarizing character: "He is the wisest and the most lunatic, the blindest and the most lucid of men."[82]

There was a time when David was commended for doing what was just and right for all his people (2 Sam 8:15). These just and righteous actions align with his mandate to administer justice and resolve conflicts, especially in relation to blood feud.[83] However, this time, David's complicity and passivity come sharply into focus. The glaring lack of any effort to bring justice for Tamar, despite David having the means to do so, is striking.[84] The conspicuous absence of justice in the violation of Tamar raises important questions. Girard in an article titled "Generative Scapegoating" elaborates on the three current usages of the term "scapegoat."[85] By broadening the meaning of scapegoat, we can better understand the unresolved situation surrounding Tamar's rape. In a sense, she functions as a scapegoat offered on the altar of political expediency. David's and Absalom's responses converge because they share the same politi-

---

78. Von Rad, *From Genesis to Chronicles*, 143.
79. Trible, *Texts of Terror*, 37.
80. See Ken Stone, *Sex, Honor, and Power in the Deuteronomistic History* (JSOTSup 234; Sheffield: Sheffield Academic Press, 1996), 112.
81. Schwartz, "Adultery in the House of David," 48.
82. Girard, *Violence and the Sacred*, 252.
83. Halbertal and Holmes, *The Beginning of Politics*, 7–8.
84. Smith, *The Fate of Justice and Righteousness*, 75.
85. A biblical one found in Leviticus 16, an anthropological meaning referring to various ritual sacrifices analogous to the biblical one, and the third one is the psychosocial meaning wherein contemporary victims of violence are blamed for some sin or misfortune of others. René Girard, "Generative Scapegoating," in *Violent Origins: Walter Burkert, René Girard and Jonathan Z. Smith on Ritual Killing and Cultural Formation*, ed. Robert G. Hammerton-Kelley (Stanford: Stanford University Press, 1987), 73–74.

cal motivations. One could argue that both David's and Absalom's reactions to Tamar's rape are guided by a form of sacrificial logic; this kind of scapegoating can still be seen in political violence.

The infamous drug war launched by the former Philippine president Duterte is structured as a scapegoat mechanism: a fabricated social crisis that demands an urgent solution, a group of people bearing the brunt of the sanctioned violence, and, finally, the promise of social harmony and unity through the annihilation of those who are blamed for such a societal plague. Most of the victims come from impoverished communities within Metro Manila. This is not a coincidence. A salient point of Girard's scapegoat mechanism is that the victims are incapable of reprisal.[86]

We have already noted how mimetic contagion escalates into a never-ending cycle of violence. Since archaic societies did not have a central judicial system, they required preventive mechanisms to quell violence. Prohibitions functioned as a deterrent, preventing violence from running amok, while ritual sacrifice provided an outlet to redirect violence into a controlled domain through ritual. Together, ritual sacrifice and prohibitions served as protective measures against violence in archaic societies.[87] Here, we see religion's fundamental role in ancient societies as a means of containing violence. This stands in contrast to the contemporary view that religion is the source of violence and conflict. This also represents the second tenet of Girard's mimetic theory: the scapegoat mechanism as the origin of culture and social institutions.

It's difficult to imagine that violence is at the heart and origin of human culture and institutions. Yet, Girard argues that the culture-forming power of violence can be traced through religion, social structures, and culture, all of which, he suggests, originate from what he calls the "founding murder." This event becomes the basis for the ritualized violence of sacrifice. The Bible also connects the murder of Abel to the founding of the first city by his brother Cain. It is here that Girard locates the emergence of the sacred, which he defines as the anthropological foundation of society. The institutions, myths, rituals, and prohibitions of the sacred all engage with the subject and containment of violence in various ways.

Sacrifice persists in different forms in our modern, secularized societies. The sacrificial logic that is essential for sustaining our culture and social structure is rooted in violence. In other words, our culture is maintained sacrificially through the victimage mechanism that originates from "the generative

---

86. Girard, *Violence and the Sacred*, 13.
87. Girard, *Violence and the Sacred*, 14–18.

mechanism of ritual execution as of all other institutions, whether totemic or not."[88] Girard even goes so far as to say that behind the first transcendental signifier lies the victim of collective murder.[89]

Girard seems to highlight two undeniable facets of the human condition: the pervasiveness of mimetic desire and the ubiquity of sacrifice as embedded in our culture and social structure. Both are linked to the significance of violence in our shared experience. Yet there is another dynamic at play, which we have already alluded to. In Mr. Duterte's speeches about the drug war, there is almost always a juxtaposition of the threat to kill with religious language. This juxtaposition can be a concoction of populism, power politics, and a form of political theology,[90] or, it could reflect a deeper affinity rooted in their shared origin in sacred violence.

Justice, Law, and the Conflicted Victims

Our narrative picks up when Tamar went to Amnon's place to prepare food for her brother (v. 8). While Tamar prepares food, the narrator says that Amnon is intently looking. This seemingly small detail is significant. It creates an atmosphere which from Amnon's focalization is nothing short of voyeurism.[91] Although Tamar is kneading and making bread, Amnon perhaps is imagining a different aroma: the smell of flesh. The considerable length given to Tamar's preparation of food is exegetically curious. As one scholar argues, this section is "replete with double entendre and sexual innuendo. . . ."[92] Within this reading, every detail of Tamar's movement is sexually construed by Amnon, while supine on his bed and aroused at the sight of his half-sister making bread. Thus, Amnon's request for Tamar to "come, lie with me, my sister" (v. 11) is not surprising but rather the culmination of his distorted sexual fantasy.

The narrative takes a repugnant turn. However, this scene also reveals perhaps the only bright spot in this tragic story: Tamar's capacity to reason and object at her brother's nefarious request. Interestingly, this is the first time

---

88. René Girard, *Things Hidden Since the Foundation of the World*, trans. Stephen Bann and Michael Metteer (Stanford: Stanford University Press, 1987), 108.
89. Girard, *Things Hidden*, 99–104.
90. Romel Regalado Bagares, "Power Politics in the Philippines: A Reformed Response to the Populism and Violence of Duterte," in *Reformed Public Theology: A Global Vision for Life in the World*, ed. Matthew Kaemingk (Grand Rapids: Baker Academic, 2021), 140.
91. See Trible, *Texts of Terror*, 43.
92. Gray, "Amnon a Chip of the Old Block?," 44.

we hear Tamar's voice, and it is a voice of wisdom and reason.[93] In a story almost devoid of wisdom, Tamar stands as its redeeming voice. In a rapid but measured succession, she articulates her discontent with Amnon's egregious request. She first appeals to him by addressing him as her brother, then cites social prohibitions to further dissuade him from continuing with his plan (v. 12). Tamar then turns to the repercussions that await them: for her, the consequence is utter disgrace and the accompanying humiliation, while she framed Amnon's fate as being "like one of the fools of Israel" (v. 13). Tamar's appeals, however, fall on deaf ears.

In essence, she wants Amnon to come to his senses. In a last-ditch attempt, perhaps driven by desperation, Tamar invokes David, believing the king will surely not withhold her from him. However, Amnon ignores her plea, driven only by his desire. The narrator quickly notes that "he violated her and lay with her" (v. 14). No details were given on how the deed was done. Tamar's words expose the true state of David's kingdom, revealing it to be filled with *nabals*. Although Amnon deserves full condemnation for his actions, we must place him within the larger power structure that enables the fullfilment of his desire. It is important to remember that this rape was issued with royal imprimatur. Moreover, it is Tamar, not David nor Jonadab, who displays wisdom in the story, which makes her desolation even more tragic.

Another twist in the plot is Amnon's sudden revulsion toward Tamar. After the rape, Amnon "hated her with a very great hatred" (v. 15). "Violence in turn discloses hatred, the underside of lust," writes Trible.[94] Trible links desire, violence, and hatred to explain Amnon's abrupt repulsion.[95] Jensen notes that Amnon's sudden and violent reaction has long baffled interpreters.[96] Girard's concept of the metaphysical nature of desire, that beneath our desire is a desire for being, captures Amnon's violent turn.[97] The object of desire, in most cases, is merely a pretext. Amnon craved Tamar; however, after violating her, nothing changed. He was still as pathetic as he was before, perhaps even more so. Amnon's abrupt violence was not caused by Tamar; rather it was self-inflicted.

What is certain, however, is the added insult to Tamar's injury in Amnon's demand for her to leave. Another confounding detail is Tamar's appeal that sending her "away is greater than the other that you have done to me" (v. 16).

---

93. See Trible, *Texts of Terror*, 46.
94. Trible, *Texts of Terror*, 46.
95. Trible, *Texts of Terror*, 46–47.
96. Jensen, "Desire, Rivalry, and Collective Violence," 49.
97. Girard, *Deceit, Desire, and the Novel*, 88.

Tamar's reasoning is likely framed by Israel's legal discourse.[98] In Deuteronomy 22:28–29, it is stipulated that when a man rapes a "virgin" he must marry her. Tamar's conflicted and complex perspective is captured by what Judith Butler calls as normative violence.[99] For Butler, there is an intrinsic violence in the norms that sustains us,[100] similar to the victimage mechanism as expounded by Girard. Butler locates this violence as prior to – and continues within – the formation of the subject.[101] In other words, we are always already bound by a set of norms, and the traces of their violence are inscribed within us. The violence of norms becomes most pronounced when one such norm attains the status of law. In an influential essay, Jacques Derrida argues "that law is always an unauthorized force, a force that justifies itself or is justified in applying itself, even if this justification may be judged from elsewhere to be unjust or unjustifiable."[102] This helps explain Tamar's conflicted view between her rape and Amnon's subsequent act of forcing her out of the room.

A law is violent, moreover, when it excludes other voices in its deliberations, such as when it silences the majority or, worse, the victims themselves. In *Women, Ideology and Violence*, Cheryl Anderson argues that there is an "inherent violence in biblical laws," particularly against women.[103] One example is that the normative viewpoint in biblical law is male-centered: "*a law is male if it embodies only the male experience.*"[104] This explains the lacuna of female experience in Israel's legal materials. In addition to the limited legal options, Tamar must also consider the role of social disgrace, especially in a context where honor and shame are the dominant cultural codes. As a rape victim, she must endure the humiliation that is upon her, a further round of victimization, this time by society at large.[105] Tamar's question, "where will she carry

---

98. Stone, *Sex, Honor, and Power in the Deuteronomistic History*, 115.

99. Judith Butler, *Gender Trouble: Feminism and the Subversion of Identity* (New York: Routledge, 2006), xxi, xxv.

100. Judith Butler, *Senses of the Subject* (New York: Fordham University Press, 2015), 5–7.

101. Butler, *Senses of the Subject*, 1–2. Elsewhere Butler made a similar claim: that "Subjects are constituted through norms. . . ." Butler, *Frames of War*, 3.

102. Jacques Derrida, "Force as Law: The "Mystical Foundation of Authority," in *Deconstruction and the Possibility of Justice*, eds. Drucilla Cornell, Michael Rosenfeld, and David Gray Carlson (London: Routledge, 1992), 5.

103. Cheryl B. Anderson, *Women, Ideology and Violence: Critical Theory and the Construction of Gender in the Book of the Covenant and the Deuteronomistic Law* (London: T&T Clark, 2004), 9.

104. Anderson, *Women, Ideology and Violence*, 86. Emphasis on the original.

105. See Fuchs, *Sexual Politics in the Hebrew Narrative*, 214.

her shame?" is a harrowing one, and it is a question that every rape victim, however difficult, is forced to ponder.

Political Theology and Rehabilitation of the Victims

Tamar is removed from the scene of the crime, and the narrator vividly portrays her grief (v. 20). In an unprecedented move in the biblical text, a rape victim is given voice to articulate her pain. Tamar's focalization after the rape represents a breakthrough in the biblical material. This is the final tenet of Girard's mimetic theory: the role of the Bible in exposing the violence inherent in myth. The Judeo-Christian Scripture moves beyond the archaic (violent) sacred, progressively revealing the sacrificial mechanism as a violent solution to violence. However, Girard acknowledges that certain mythological elements, such as the flood as plague, warring brothers, founding murders, the founding cities, and twin rivalry, are present in the Bible. The key difference is in how the stories are told. In myths, the victim is often portrayed as guilty, and the narrative is presented from the perspective of the perpetrators. In contrast, the Bible tells these stories from the point of view of the victims. By giving voice to the victims, the Bible subverts myth from within, exposing its violence. "In the Hebrew Bible, there is clearly a dynamic that moves in the direction of the rehabilitation of the victims" writes Girard. He sees the Bible as "a process under way, a text in travail." This trajectory reaches its climax in the gospels, where the full sacrificial mechanism is laid bare.[106]

By registering her protest and lament, Tamar creates a space for other raped characters – nameless, faceless, and voiceless – those stripped of signification and subjectivity. It is this space for lament and grief that must be created and sustained for contemporary victims of the war on drugs, war on terror, ethnic cleansing, and other deplorable acts perpetuated by those in power. The recent rise of strongmen with tyrannical tendencies in key political positions around the globe underscores the urgent need for a critical and creative space for public lament. Thus, victims from different contexts share several commonalities. Albert Memmi, an early voice in postcolonial critique, points that subjugated, oppressed, victimized individuals and groups share a common expression of their collective experience of suffering, pain, agony, and revolt.[107]

Tamar's mourning is categorized as a non-petitionary rite. The purpose of a non-petitionary ritual is to create "a ritual context in which they can enact and

---
106. Girard, "Generative Scapegoating, Discussion," 141.
107. Albert Memmi, *Dominated Man* (Boston: Beacon Press, 1968), 16.

communicate their sorrow, shame, and personal or corporate diminishment as well as create, affirm, or modify social relationships."[108] Tamar's mourning offers a glimpse into the profundity of her pain. When we lose someone, our common reaction is to grieve and mourn. The self undergoes a transition, a form of dispossession.[109] Tamar had lost her sense of self, her status as the king's virgin daughter, and now stared at a desolate future. Although grief is often seen as a private experience, it can also be understood as a "reorientation for politics," as Butler asserts.[110] For this to happen, Butler reframes ontology as *social* ontology – based on our shared precariousness[111] – which highlights the relational ties that bind us.[112] By using vulnerability as a point of departure, Butler makes grief and similar gestures as "resource for politics" – or as an "identification with suffering itself" – to foster solidarity with the victims.[113] There is power in naming our pain and the perpetrators that inflict it. Listening to the stories of the families affected by the former president Duterte's bloody drug war is one step toward identifying with suffering, and, hopefully, it helps create empathy, solidarity, and accountability.

Butler warns that this vulnerability "becomes highly exacerbated under certain social and political conditions, especially those in which violence is a way of life. . . ."[114] This makes mourning, as both public and political rite, imperative; especially in places like the Philippines, where violence is becoming intimately entwined with the people's way of life, and its twin – apathy – is fast becoming a social norm. A different, but related, caveat must also be noted: the reciprocal nature of violence is a social fact. As such, victims, or in the idiom of Paulo Freire – the oppressed – can easily become ensnared in the vengeful cycle of reciprocal violence.[115] The disparate analyses of Nietzsche, Weber, and Scheler share a similar insight: the symbiotic bond between the victim and *ressentiment*, the latter of which Girard defines as "the interioriza-

---

108. Saul M. Olyan, *Biblical Mourning: Ritual and Social Dimensions* (New York: Oxford University Press, 2004), 98.
109. Butler, *Precarious Life*, 28.
110. Butler, *Precarious Life*, 28.
111. Butler, *Frames of War*, 3, 13.
112. Butler, *Precarious Life*, 22–23.
113. Butler, *Precarious Life*, 30.
114. Butler, *Precarious Life*, 29.
115. Paulo Freire, *Pedagogy of the Oppressed*, trans. Myra Bergman Ramos (New York: Continuum, 2007), 44.

tion of weakened vengeance."[116] In this configuration the victim is sacralized and holds a powerful position. The contemporary sacralization of the victim[117] ignites the archaic mechanism of sacred violence. Any account of justice must therefore consider the role of ressentiment in its deliberations.[118]

Moreover, as Saul Olyan has noted, mourning rites have "profound social implications" because of their "continual creation and recreation of the social order and for its potential for transformation."[119] Further, mourning rites can disrupt the politics that silence victims by registering in a public space the narratives of those who have been victimized, subjugated, and oppressed, thereby creating a counter narrative – one that is from the point of view from below. Tamar's grief and lament disrupt the looming political confrontation between David and Absalom. It is Tamar, not David or Absalom, who gives herself a chance for justice through her gestures of protest and lament.

In hindsight, both David's and Absalom's reactions can be seen as acts of political self-preservation. Although deeply troubled, David did not act because he loved his firstborn son. Absalom, on the other hand, sought to avoid trouble, even asking Tamar to remain silent. Absalom sensed a political opportunity to strike Amnon, thereby using Tamar's rape as a political pretext. The subsequent death of Amnon cannot be considered justice for Tamar, especially when we consider that she remained desolate in her brother's house. Rather than justice, it was a step toward Absalom's political victory. The civil war that followed, precipitated by Absalom's rebellion and his attempt to usurp the throne, confirms this. Both David and Absalom were responsible for delivering at least some measure of justice for Tamar, yet both failed miserably to do so. They missed the opportunity to pursue justice, resulting in a gross miscarriage of justice.

Conclusion: Insights into Political Theology

Part of René Girard's anthropological insights regarding the Bible is that it moves away from the violence of the archaic sacred. For Girard, archaic society was held together by the trio of myth, ritual, and prohibitions. The myths that became the foundational texts of societies were always told from the perspec-

---

116. Stefano Tomelleri, "Ressentiment and the Turn to the Victim: Nietzsche, Weber, and Scheler," in *The Palgrave Handbook of Mimetic Theory and Religion*, eds., James Alison and Wolfgang Palaver (New York: Palgrave Macmillan, 2017), 331.

117. Jean-Pierre Dupuy, *The Mark of the Sacred*, trans. M. B. DeBevoise (Stanford: Stanford University Press, 2013), 169.

118. Dupuy, *The Mark of the Sacred*, 173.

119. Olyan, *Biblical Mourning*, 148.

tive of the perpetrators. Those who were sacrificed were always portrayed as guilty. This is the context in which the biblical materials emerged. The biblical distinction is that it introduced a perspective from the point of view of the victim. For Girard, this trajectory culminated in the Passion and death of Jesus. However, there are other biblical texts, non-sacrificial ones, that also point in this direction. Tamar's story is a prime example. By giving Tamar her subjectivity, we become attuned to the victim's perspective. Tamar, or the victim's voice, disrupts the narrative of those in power – those who have access to juridico-political authority. The story of Tamar creates opportunities for political theology to emerge from experiences of pain, suffering and being vulnerable. Often viewed as debilitating, these experiences can be harnessed as a foundation for political and theological action.

It is imperative to ground our attempt to construct a political theology in biblical material. Central to this is the keen insight of the author of the book of Samuel into the nature of politics. Particularly enlightening is the emergence of monarchy in Israel, as it reveals the inherent ambiguity of large-scale human political projects. The apprehensive tone of God and Samuel when Israel requests a human king highlights the Bible's ambivalent posture on politics as a sphere of human action.[120] However, the book of Samuel also tacitly acknowledges the necessity of self-sustaining polity in the form of human political structures, as we have seen in the establishment of the monarchy. This may explain why there is no single, explicit form of government that runs throughout the entire Bible.

Taken together, the Bible's reluctance to endorse a specific political regime, the inherent ambiguity in political projects, and its emphasis on giving redress to victims all reframe our attempt to construct a political theology. While the Bible does not endorse a particular political structure, it does present a social ethic directed toward the entire covenant community of God: to do justice, protect the weak, feed the poor, free the slave, and love the resident alien.[121] This is what the gospels exemplify. In this chapter, we have reoriented our attempt to construct a political theology by using Girard's mimetic theory to interpret 2 Samuel 13 and its broader context, thereby fleshing out insights into the nature of politics and power.

---

120. Halbertal and Holmes, *The Beginning of Politics*, 10–11.
121. Walzer, *In God's Shadow*, 209.

Bibliography

Amit, Yairah. *In Praise of Editing the Hebrew Bible: Collected Essays in Retrospect*. Sheffield: Sheffield Phoenix Press, 2012.

Anderson, Cheryl B. *Women, Ideology and Violence: Critical Theory and the Construction of Gender in the Book of the Covenant and the Deuteronomistic Law*. London: T&T Clark, 2004.

Bagares, Romel Regalado. "Power Politics in the Philippines: A Reformed Response to the Populism and Violence of Duterte." In *Reformed Public Theology: A Global Vision for Life in the World*, edited by Matthew Kaemingk. Grand Rapids: Baker Academic, 2021.

Bar-Efrat, Shimon. *Narrative Art in the Bible*. JSOTSup, 70. Sheffield: Sheffield Academic Press, 1989.

Blenkinsopp, Joseph. "Another Contribution to the Succession Narrative Debate (2 Samuel 11–20; 1 Kings 1–2)." *Journal for the Study of the Old Testament* 38 (2013): 35–58.

Butler, Judith. *Precarious Life: The Powers of Mourning and Violence*. London: Verso, 2004.

———. *Gender Trouble: Feminism and the Subversion of Identity*. New York: Routledge, 2006.

———. *Frames of War: When is Life Grievable?* London: Verso, 2009.

———. *Senses of the Subject*. New York: Fordham University Press, 2015.

Derrida, Jacques. "Force as Law: The 'Mystical Foundation of Authority.'" In *Deconstruction and the Possibility of Justice*, edited by Drucilla Cornell, Michael Rosenfeld, and David Gray Carlson. London: Routledge, 1992.

Douglas, Mary. *Purity and Danger: An Analysis of the Concepts of Pollution and Taboo*. New York: Routledge, 1984.

Dupuy, Jean-Pierre. *The Mark of the Sacred*. Translated by M. B. DeBevoise. Stanford: Stanford University Press, 2013.

Foucault, Michel. *The History of Sexuality Vol. 1: An Introduction*. Translated by Robert Hurley. New York: Vintage Books, 1990.

Freire, Paulo. *Pedagogy of the Oppressed*. Translated by Myra Bergman Ramos. New York: Continuum, 2007.

Fuchs, Esther. *Sexual Politics in the Biblical Narrative: Reading the Hebrew Bible as a Woman*. JSOTSup, 310. Sheffield: Sheffield Academic Press, 2001.

Girard, René. *Deceit, Desire, and the Novel: Self and Other in Literary Structure*. Translated by Yvonne Freccero. Baltimore: Johns Hopkins Press, 1965.

———. "Generative Scapegoating." In *Violent Origins: Walter Burkert, René Girard and Jonathan Z. Smith on Ritual Killing and Cultural Formation*, edited by Robert G. Hammerton-Kelley. Stanford: Stanford University Press, 1987.

———. *Violence and the Sacred*. Translated by Patrick Gregory. Reprinted 1987. Baltimore: Johns Hopkins Press, 1977.

———. *I See Satan Fall Like Lightning*. Translated by James G. Williams. Maryknoll: Orbis Books, 2001.

———. *Things Hidden Since the Foundation of the World*. Translated by Stephen Bann and Michael Metteer. Stanford: Stanford University Press, 1987.

Gray, Mark M. "Amnon a Chip of the Old Block? Rhetorical Strategy in 2 Samuel 13. 7–15: The Rape of Tamar and the Humiliation of the Poor." *Journal for the Study of the Old Testament* 77 (1998): 39–59.

Gunn, David M. *The Story of King David: Genre and Interpretation*. JSOTSup 6. Sheffield: Sheffield Academic Press, 1978.

Halbertal, Moshe, and Stephen Holmes. *The Beginning of Politics: Power in the Biblical Book of Samuel*. Princeton: Princeton University Press, 2017.

Hanssen, Beatrice. *Critique of Violence: Between Poststructuralism and Critical Theory*. Warwick Studies in European Philosophy. New York: Routledge, 2000.

Haven, Cynthia L. *Evolution of Desire: A Life of René Girard*. East Lansing: Michigan State University, 2018.

Jacobs, Mignon. "Love, Honor, and Violence: Socioconceptual Matrix in Genesis 34." In *Pregnant Passion: Gender, Sex, and Violence in the Bible*, edited by Cheryl A. Kirk-Duggan. SBL Semeia Studies 44. Atlanta: Society of Biblical Literature, 2003.

Jensen, Hans J. L. "Desire, Rivalry and Collective Violence in the 'Succession Narrative.'" *Journal for the Study of the Old Testament* 55 (1992): 39–59.

Keefe, Alice A. "Rapes of Women/Wars of Men." *Semeia* 61 (1993): 79–97.

Kirk-Duggan, Cheryl A. "Slingshots, Ships, and Personal Psychosis: Murder, Sexual Intrigue, and Power in the Lives of David and Othello. In *Pregnant Passion: Gender, Sex and Violence in the Bible*, edited by Cheryl A. Kirk-Duggan. SBL Semeia Studies 44. Atlanta: Society of Biblical Literature, 2003.

Memmi, Albert. *Dominated Man*. Boston: Beacon Press, 1968.

Nussbaum, Martha. "Narrative Emotions: Beckett's Genealogy of Love. *Ethics* 98, no. 2 (Jan. 1998): 225–54.

Olyan, Saul M. *Biblical Mourning: Ritual and Social Dimensions*. New York: Oxford University Press, 2004.

Propp, William H. "Kinship in 2 Samuel 13." *Catholic Biblical Quarterly* 55 (1993): 39–53.

Schwartz, Regina M. "Adultery in the House of David: The Metanarrative of Biblical Scholarship and the Narratives of the Bible." *Semeia* 54 (1991): 35–55.

Smith, Richard G. *The Fate of Justice and Righteousness During David's Reign: Rereading the Court History and Its Ethics according to 2 Samuel 8:15b–20:26*. New York: T&T Clark International, 2009.

Stansell, Gary. "Honor and Shame in the David Narratives." *Semeia* 68 (1994): 55–79.

Stone, Ken. *Sex, Honor, and Power in Deuteronomistic History*. JSOTSup, 234. Sheffield: Sheffield Academic Press, 1996.

Tomelleri, Stefano. "Ressentiment and the Turn to the Victim: Nietzsche, Weber, and Scheler." In *The Palgrave Handbook of Mimetic Theory and Religion*, edited by James Alison and Wolfgang Palaver. New York: Palgrave Macmillan, 2017.

Trible, Phyllis. *Texts of Terror: Literary-Feminist Readings of Biblical Narratives.* Philadelphia: Fortress Press, 1984.

Van Dijk-Hemmes, Fokkelien. "Tamar and the Limits of Patriarchy: Between Rape and Seduction (2 Samuel 13 and Genesis 38)." In *Anti-Covenant: Counter-Reading Women's Lives in the Hebrew Bible*, edited by Mieke Bal. JSOTSup, 81. Sheffield: Almond Press, 1989.

Van Seter, John. "A Revival of the Succession Narrative and the Case against It." *Journal for the Study of the Old Testament* 39 (2014): 3–14.

Von Rad, Gerhard. *From Genesis to Chronicles: Explorations in Old Testament Theology*, edited by K. C. Hanson. Minnesota: Fortress Press, 2005.

Yamada, Frank M. *Configurations of Rape in the Hebrew Bible: A Literary Analysis of Three Rape Narratives.* New York: Peter Lang Publishing, 2008.

Part II

Contemporary Issues, Challenges, and Prospects

9

Decolonial Imagination and Political Theologizing

Rei Lemuel Crizaldo

"We need to realize when even our wokeness is colonized."
– Andrea Little Mason

The evangelical church in the Philippines has been finding itself more and more involved in the arena of politics.[1] This is a significant departure from the *apolitical* stance that has so often characterized evangelicals in the country for many years. But what a turn it has been since the attempt of a popular evangelist in 2004 to win the presidency on the platform of restoring righteousness in governance. Almost two decades later, in 2022, the presidential election in the Philippines turned out to be a sad commentary on the state of political engagement from within the evangelical community.

What was at stake then was the return to the highest seat of power of the family of the dictator thwarted by the 1986 People Power Revolution. But this concern of immense historical significance was dwarfed by a list of religious agendas put forward as *the* electoral issue that should matter to a good Christian. Instead of sounding a rallying cry to unite against a regime that will support a blatant denial of human rights violations and stolen wealth during the dark days of Martial Law in the Philippines, the list that made rounds in social media enjoined *Pinoy* evangelicals to weigh their options on whose

---

1. I traced the development of this political engagement in a previous work. See Rei Lemuel Crizaldo, "Casting Your Vote for Christian Candidates," in *What About Philippine Politics: Thoughts and Reflections on Political Leadership, Good Citizenship, and the Christian Faith* (Mandaluyong: OMF Literature, 2016), 46–59.

candidate shall take a stand against bills that seek to legalize abortion, sexual orientation and gender identity expression (SOGIE), same-sex marriage, and divorce.[2] At the height of the debates during the campaign season, it was not surprising to hear how even devout evangelicals would be amenable to casting their votes for politicians whose character ranges from the dubious to the devilish provided that lends support for what is considered as a "Christian" political platform of governance.

So, what gives? A variety of answers can be given. This will include the likelihood of a dampened sensitivity to the horrors of state-sponsored abuse of its citizens so often characteristic of dictators in the history of politics. Add to this the split of priority between historic social injustice on one hand and contemporary gender-related issues on the other. But most glaring is how this pattern of electoral campaign starkly resembles that of the political landscape in the United States, that is, Moral Majority politics, if not a mirror-image altogether. This kind of evangelical political engagement reeks of imported religious agenda wrapped in a political theology and fails to discern the more pressing contextual reality for the people of the Philippines. It does not help that it is so easy, in the age of social media, for global conversations to suffer from "context collapse" – a phenomenon that can result in the transplanting of issues from one part of the world to the other regardless if the dynamics on the ground are similar or not. But all these variety of answers inevitably point to a problem much deeper and more pervasive than what digital technology has helped create – a kind of "wokeness" that is suffering from a mental disease called "colonial mentality."

Colonial Mentality

Totik Diesto Jr. suggests that "colonial mentality" is best understood as "a negative consciousness of societies who have experienced the oppression of colonial rule," and its main characteristic is "the tendency of the people to consider themselves and their culture as inferior to their former colonial masters and their culture. Consequently, indigenous culture becomes undesirable

---

2. It is worth noting that a study of "stories from the past, myths and legends in the Philippine archipelago reflected a society that valued equality and plurality in terms of gender." This is a remarkable kind of progressivism in the area of gender and sexuality that is in dissonance with the moral ideals of the conservative religious bloc in the United States that has been closely followed by evangelicals in the Philippines. See Jessica Bartolome and Margaret Claire Layug, "Our Progressive Past," *GMA News Online*, 29 December 2021, https://www.gmanetwork.com/news/specials/content/206/our-progressive-past/.

and needs to be abandoned in favor of the perceived superior culture."[3] This inferiority is deeply embedded in both the collective and individual mindsets of a people and influences their political choices, among others, and in the case of the religious, their theological convictions. The beloved Filipino evangelical writer, Evelyn Miranda-Feliciano, described with disturbing accuracy what this phenomenon looks like from within the evangelical community in the country,

> We are too colonially-minded . . . forgetting what is good and beneficial and constructive for ourselves as a nation. Nationalist historian Renato Constantino calls this our tragic mis-education. Our mis-education is so deeply entrenched that to many of us our Christian faith seems not like the Christian faith at all if not garbed in Western clothes, programs, liturgies, as well as money. The theologies predominantly taught to us are interpretations of Western minds of biblical truths as they relate to Western contexts. Yet, we gladly accept them *in toto*, as if they fit our own culture. We lap up all the methodologies and semantics uncritically, forgetting our people's sensibilities, culture, worldview, and spirituality. Too often, the so-called Christian leaders live, behave, and speak the language of their Western tutors or benefactors, altogether alienating themselves from the rest of their countrymen – if not physically and geographically, then in thought and perspective.[4]

The willing embrace of foreign insights, innovations, and issues among colonized people comes intertwined also with the unconscious process of internalizing "all the projections of the colonizers into their concept of self, of who they are in the world."[5] In other words, one would feel not only that the colonizer is better but also that his own, when put in comparison, is of little or no worth. The result is a tragic state of *destitution* with regard to one's own values and indigenous identity. It is a deep poverty of spirit rendered even

---

3. Genaro Diesto Jr., *The Effects of Colonial Mentality on the Religious Consciousness of Filipinos* (Iloilo City: College of Theology, Central Philippine University, 2011). He identified three major factors which he called the "unholy trinity" that brought about this mentality: military rule, dogmatic religion, and education. From within the field of psychology, E. J. R. David identifies that "colonial mentality is a specific form of internalized oppression that has its roots in colonialism and has been transmitted through the generations by more contemporary forms of oppression such as neocolonialism." See Eric John Ramos David, *Brown Skin, White Minds: Filipino-American Postcolonial Psychology* (Charlotte: Information Age Publishing, 2013), 74.

4. Evelyn Miranda-Feliciano, *Filipino Values and the Christian Faith* (Mandaluyong City: OMF Literature, 1990), 34–35.

5. Leny Strobel, *Decolonizing as a Spiritual Path*, 18 December 2014, YouTube video, 1:12:17. https://www.youtube.com/watch?v=u-_rxeCKyA8.

worse by a sustained pressure to adapt into the supposed well-developed, and therefore perceived as superior, conventions of the Western world. The social anthropologist Melba Maggay noted how this destitution has resulted in layers upon layers of maladaptive practices serving as coping mechanisms among the Filipinos in the face of colonial oppression, which include the severe form of "reverse ethnocentrism" described by Diesto and Feliciano above.[6] This condition all the more highlights the importance of understanding the multifaceted historical development that gave rise to the kind of colonial mentality that has developed as a result.

If anything, the recent 2022 election can be an interesting case for reflection on how evangelicalism in the Philippines continues to be haunted by this sticky malady. By way of using metaphors, it can be said that it resulted in a kind of "coconut political theology" – brown on the outside but is very much "white" on the inside. If not arrested with vigor, this form of theologizing will continue to fail in sifting through (*pagtatahip*) the complexity of political issues that the country faces. The unfortunate result will be the occurrence of "coconut political theologizing" – brown on the outside but is very much "white on the inside."[7] But how is one to move from a "coconut" to something that is thoroughly brown on the inside and out? A "*chico*" political theology, perhaps? This is the question that this chapter seeks to explore as a contribution to this volume's aim of developing an evangelical political theology that is rooted well in the context of Philippine political realities.

Undoing Coloniality

Confronting the sustained colonial influence in the country is a painstaking but nonetheless on-going struggle. It is a task that has been taken up in several disciplines and fields of study.[8] An important stream of work on *de*-colonization in the Philippines has been formed around the push for "indigenization" or

---

6. Melba Maggay, *Pagbabalik-loob: Moral Recovery and Cultural Reaffirmation* (Quezon City: Akademya ng Kultura at Sikolohiyang Pilipino, 1993), 4.

7. This is an adaptation of the metaphor first used by Hwa Yung, retired Methodist bishop of Malaysia, in his book *Mangoes or Bananas: The Quest for an Authentic Asian Christian Theology* (Oxford: Regnum, 1997). E. J. R. David also used brown-white dynamic to describe the phenomenon of colonial mentality among Filipino-Americans in the United States, in his *Brown Skin, White Minds*.

8. For a work that chronicles the contribution of notable Filipino intellectuals from the time the Philippines gained independence from the United States, see Charlie Samuya Veric, *Children of the Postcolony: Filipino Intellectuals and Decolonization, 1946–1972* (Quezon City: Ateneo University Press, 2020).

taking seriously the recovery of indigenous pathways, a body of work consolidated later on into what came to be called "indigenous knowledge, skills, practices, and spiritualities" or IKSPS.[9] This is a critical move since one of the debilitating effects of being under colonial rule is that the entire experience of oppression disparages whatever remains of people's pre-colonial heritage.[10] The recovery of indigenous pathways is a necessary step towards exploring a concrete grounding for the collective discourse that will seek to address the lingering effects of "coloniality" in the contemporary lived reality of Filipinos.

At this point, it would be necessary to distinguish colonialism from coloniality. The former refers to political colonization that properly ended in the birth of former colonies of the Western Empires into independent nation-states. The latter is the enduring impact of this colonial experience even in the present postcolonial era. Coloniality is now widely understood as a "colonial matrix" perpetuated to this very day through the following manifestations: (1) the coloniality of power, (2) the coloniality of knowledge, and (3) the coloniality of being – which includes the coloniality of faith.[11]

The phenomenon of "colonial mentality" in the Philippines is a concrete example of coloniality in its subtle but full operation even in the aftermath of the formal period of colonialism. Undoing this subservient disposition to the ways and means of the old colonial masters is the pressing task of *decoloniality* for Filipinos.[12] For evangelicals in the Philippines, this includes confronting

---

9. The indigenization movement in Philippine academia developed out of a resolve to go beyond mere reactionary stances of anti-colonialism. This includes the notable works of Virgilio Enriquez (psychology, *Sikolohiyang Pilipino*), Prospera Covar (anthropology, *Pilipinolohiya*), and Zeus Salazar (history, *Pantayong Pananaw*). See S. Lily Mendoza, "Theoretical Advances in the Discourse of Indigenization," *Mga Babasahin sa Agham Panlipunang Pilipino*, eds. A. Navarro and F. Lagbao-Bolante (Quezon City: C&E Publishing, 2007), 241–97.

10. Frantz Fanon explains, "Colonialism is not satisfied merely with holding a people in its grip and emptying the native's brain of all form and content. By a kind of perverse logic, it turns to the past of the oppressed people, and distorts it, disfigures and destroys it." Frantz Fanon, *The Wretched of the Earth* (New York: Grove Press, 1963), 210.

11. The matrix was first conceptualized by the Peruvian scholar Anibal Quijano. But for this particular configuration, see Raimundo Barreto and Roberto Sirvent, *Decolonial Christianities* (Switzerland: Palgrave Macmillan, 2019), 5.

12. Elsewhere in the world, similar efforts and initiatives have been described as "The Decolonial Turn." Maldonado-Torres explains, "The decolonial turn does not refer to a single theoretical school, but rather points to a family of diverse positions that share a view of coloniality as a fundamental problem in the modern (as well as postmodern and information) age, and of decolonization or decoloniality as a necessary task that remains unfinished." See Nelson Maldonado-Torres, "Thinking Through the Decolonial Turn," *TRANSMODERNITY: Journal of Peripheral Cultural Production of the Luso-Hispanic World* 1, no. 2 (2011): 2. Mignolo offers this description of the decolonial task: "It is a form of struggle and survival, an epistemic and existence-based response and practice – most especially by colonized and racialized subjects –

"theological coloniality" that manifests in the likes of US-based political theologizing peddled as normative elsewhere in the world.

While this would be an endeavor that involves forging a path towards emancipation, it also calls for a prior step of naming and understanding what binds the mind and holds captive the heart of the people. For this reason, recovering and re-embracing indigeneity, while important, will have to come with identifying what have suppressed and have continued to inhibit these indigenous ways. Among decolonial scholars, the European phenomenon of Modernity is considered to be the cradle of the era of Western colonialism that put into motion the imperialistic ventures of the Western world into the territories of Africa, the Americas, Asia and the Pacific.[13] To this very day, the ideals, logic, constructs, structures, and projects of Modernity remain at work in the world. Modernity serves as the bedrock of present-day forms of coloniality and sustains its impact. It is this sustained form of colonial hegemony and the drift towards the usual projects of Modernity at work in the postcolonial era that the growing field of decoloniality has sought to reject.

Intentional confrontation with the legacy of Modernity distinguishes decoloniality from postcolonial theories and criticism.[14] While the two have a shared aspiration for people's liberation from colonial imperialism, decoloniality rejects the continued reliance on epistemic assumptions and tools forged from within the logic of Modernity.[15] This rejection includes statist political

---

against the colonial matrix of power in all of its dimensions, and *for* the possibilities of an otherwise." See Walter Mignolo and Catherine Walsh, *On Decoloniality: Concepts, Analytics, Praxis* (Durham and London: Duke University Press, 2018), 17.

13. See Walter Mignolo, *The Darker Side of Modernity: Global Futures, Decolonial Options* (Durham and London: Duke University Press, 2011), 6–8. Rah and Charles trace this phenomenon in the enactment of the Doctrine of Discovery through a series of papal bulls starting in 1452. Soong-Chan Rah and Mark Charles, *Unsettling Truths: The Ongoing Dehumanizing Legacy of the Doctrine of Discovery* (Downers Grove: InterVarsity Press, 2019).

14. Postcolonial criticism and theory involve works that carry out the projects of anti-colonial scholars such as Edward Said, Gayatri Spivak and Hommi Bhabha whose frameworks were in turn informed by the philosophies of Michel Foucault, Jacques Lacan, and Jacques Derrida. Daniel Pilario identified the several ways postcolonial theories have been appropriated in contemporary theology. See Daniel Pilario, "Mapping Postcolonial Theory: Appropriations into Contemporary Theology," *Asian Christian Review* 1, no. 1 (2007): 74–75.

15. Madina Tlostanova's probing of this divergence is helpful: "Postcolonial theory stops at the level of changing the content but not the terms of the discussion. . . . Decolonial option performs a different epistemic operation. It does not start with Lacan or Butler, slightly modifying their theories to make them fit the analysis of the post/neocolonial reality, but rather focuses from the start on the genealogy of decolonial thinkers and their epistemic tools. . . . It is necessary not to build into the existing system by merely expanding it with new elements, as postcolonial studies have mostly been doing, but rather to problematize this system as such and offer other options as decolonial thought has attempted to do in the last two decades." Madina

projects like nation-state formation and social analysis using tools developed from the era of Modernity like Marxism and critical theory.[16] In the Philippines, for example, S. Lily Mendoza felt a deep questioning that is needed in particular towards the *nationalist project* that has become an intrinsic feature of the indigenization movement in the Philippines. She remarked, "Ironically, despite the theoretically articulated commitment to go beyond the stance of anti-colonialism (disavowed earlier as merely reactive to Empire) towards the construction of a discourse on knowledge that is finally 'by us, of us, and for us,' the prioritization of national unification appeared to have hitched the movement almost exclusively to a modernizing imperative."[17]

Decoloniality, by choosing to find its footing elsewhere, seeks to transcend the indebtedness and captivity to European thought. For theologians in the Philippines, in particular, decoloniality is uncoupling as well from the thinking coming out of the United States of America.[18] Decolonial sensibility heeds the haunting reminder of Audre Lorde, "For the master's tools will never dismantle the master's house. They may allow us to temporarily beat him at his own game, but they will never enable us to bring about genuine change."[19]

Tlostanova, "The postcolonial condition, the decolonial option, and the post-socialist intervention," in *Postcolonialism Cross-Examined: Multidirectional Perspectives on Imperial and Colonial Pasts and the Neocolonial Present*, ed. M. Albretch (New York: Routledge, 2019), 165–78.

16. This is an important point to emphasize considering the expansive presence of Marxism in the political revolutionary movements in the Philippines. Far too often, anything revolutionary is associated with the Communist Movement whereas the uprising against Spain in 1896, for example, is closely linked instead to the international anarchist network exemplified by the linkages of Jose Rizal and Isabelo delos Reyes to the anarchists in Spain and Cuba. The famed sociologist Benedict Anderson documented the non-statist political imagination that may have served as a key strand of the revolutionary history of the Philippines. See Benedict Anderson, *Under Three Flags: Anarchism and the Anti-Colonial Imagination* (Pasig City: Anvil Publishing, 2006).

17. See S. Lily Mendoza, "Transdiasporic Indigeneity and Decolonizing Faith," in *Decolonizing Ecotheology: Indigenous and Subaltern Challenges*, eds. S. Mendoza and G. Zachariah (Eugene: Pickwick Publications, 2022), 267. In particular, Mendoza critiques the *Pantayong Pananaw* and its embrace of the Tagalog-based Filipino language as national language for all to adopt and thus reliving the colonial experience for people of other languages in the archipelago. See S. Lily Mendoza, "Ang Usaping Pangwika sa Bagong Yugto ng Pantayong Pananaw: Ang Panloob na Hamon ng Pluralismo," *Social Science Diliman* 7, no. 1 (June 2011): 37–62.

18. In South America, this meant an act of "delinking" or the vehement refusal to continue abiding by the colonial ways of thinking and Modernist structures of thought. Walter Mignolo called for an "epistemic disobedience" and even a more radical "epistemic insurrection" by Enrique Dussel.

19. Audre Lorde, "The Master's Tools Will Never Dismantle the Master's House," in *Sister Outsider: Essays and Speeches* (Berkeley: Crossing Press, 1984), 112.

Pathways for Decoloniality in the Philippines

For those in the Philippines, what will be the "footing" that makes for the fundamental epistemic shift towards decoloniality?

The insights of the cultural anthropologist Emo Yango offer a helpful path to move forward in the work of confronting the mechanisms of colonial mentality. Of which, two things are worth noting for the purpose of this chapter.

First is his proposal of internalizing decoloniality as a deeply personal process of healing one's "decolonial wound." He refers to "decoloniality" as a consciousness able to "re-member" one's colonized past and to reframe a new path moving forward, freed from the hegemonic control of its colonized experience. The decolonial process involves recognizing the ongoing presence of colonial mentality at the collective and individual level, and the need for space that allows the colonized to confront the colonizers. It also involves creating fresh paths leading to stories of liberation from oppression and victimization, including the opportunity to dwell in a new state of freedom amidst the memories of colonial history. Yango's challenge for us as colonized people is to "find that space where we can identify our commitment and intentionality to begin to construct stories wherein our consciousness is no longer victimized and subjugated by our colonial mentality."[20]

Second is Yango's observation that there are shared characteristics between primal indigenous cultures like the one in Asia and the postmodern condition. He suggests that the conditions being observed and upheld in the aftermath of Modernity such as contextuality, plurality, diversity, and fluidity, among others, resonate well with "conditions" that have always been in Asia, thus predating the "postmodern outlook" that the West is still struggling to come to terms with.[21] If coloniality is closely intertwined with Modernity, then people in Asia, like those in the Philippines, have little need to go through the Western "shift" towards postmodernity. In order to overcome the mold of Modernity, they simply need to anchor themselves in their own indigenous cultures. In other words, to be comfortable being primal is a confident step to be deco-

---

20. Emo Yango, "*Decolonizing Colonial Mentality*" (paper presented at the annual Genaro "Totik" Diesto Jr. Memorial Lecture, Central Philippine University-College of Theology, Cebu City, 2017). Together with this personal dimension of decolonization, he also suggests a more public dimension which he termed as the "prophetic act of decolonization," 16. https://www.academia.edu/33565795/Decolonizing_colonial_mentality.

21. Emo Yango, "*An Anthropology for Decolonizing a Philosophy of Modernity when Constructing Asian Theologies*" (paper presented at the Asia Theological Association Theological Consultation, Manila, 31 July–2 August 2018). https://www.academia.edu/37034251/An_Anthropology_for_Decolonizing_a_Philosophy_of_Modernity_when_Constructing_Asian_Theologies.

lonial. For theologians, this means "to shift away from being a derivative of Modernity." This is a reminder he issued even to those working in contextual theology whose hermeneutical assumptions and exegetical methodologies remain largely influenced if not rooted in Western constructs.[22]

In the field of theology, Fr. Daniel Pilario, C. M., identified two possible forms of theologizing that will fit with what Yango described as non-derivatives of Western Modernity: (a) theological hermeneutics based on people's reading, and (b) hermeneutics based on identity concerns.[23] The former has to do with "non-specialists (i.e., members of grassroots communities) claiming the Bible for themselves and reading the significance of its message from the perspective of their present concerns. There is no talk of the need for proper exegesis or the overriding concern for orthodox readings. What was crucial is the applicability of the word and theological concepts to everyday concerns."[24] Of which, Ernesto Cardenal's "The Gospel of Solentiname" is a notable example. The other emphasizes the "significance of diverse cultural identities" such as women, indigenous peoples, and many more. Examples of this include the *Dalit* Theology in India and the *Burakumin* Theology in Japan. These two theological hermeneutics are part of the broader and subsequent development, following the suggestion of R. S. Sugirtharajah, in liberation theologizing which has its roots in what Pilario termed as "classic liberationist perspective." This is a theological position that he sees is "guilty of reductionism in its strong affiliation with Marxist economistic readings."[25] As mentioned in the earlier section of this chapter, Marxist theorizing is a derivative product of Modernist thought and therefore more broadly postcolonial than decolonial. It will be the two forms of theological hermeneutics that grew out of the classical liberation theologizing, identified by Pilario, that can offer a potential footing outside of Western Modernity.

---

22. Traces of what Yango has in mind can be found in the theological project of the book *Christologies, Cultures, and Religions: Portraits of Christ in the Philippines*, eds. Pascal Bazzell and Aldrin Peñamora (OMF Literature and ATA/AGST, 2016). Despite some attempts in some of the chapters to utilize local hermeneutics, Melba Maggay in her epilogue for the volume wrote the following observation, "I could not help but feel a bit hemmed in by the presence of the proverbial elephant in the room – the unseen yet obviously dominant partner in this conversation: the discourse on Christology as framed by centuries of reflection in the West. The presence is signaled by the continuing reference to categories like 'little' and 'big' tradition, 'popular' and 'formal' religion, and the postmodern idea of 'hybridity' as a label for this emergent form called 'Filipino Christology.' These and other conceptual tools are applied . . . ," 185.

23. Daniel Pilario, "Mapping Postcolonial Theory: Appropriations into Contemporary Theology," *Asian Christian Review* 1, no. 1 (2007): 74–75.

24. Pilario, "Mapping Postcolonial Theory," 74.

25. Pilario, "Mapping Postcolonial Theory," 73.

From within the evangelical theological community in the Philippines, liberation theologizing has not made much of an inroad. Suspicion of the use of Marxist tools of analysis and its association with Communist ideology had evangelical theologians maintaining a critical distance from the liberationist stream of theologizing.[26] Impulses of decoloniality will instead find footing from the works of two leading figures in developing contextual evangelical theology in the Philippines: Melba Padilla Maggay and Timoteo Gener.[27]

A social anthropologist specializing in the field of cross-cultural communication and development work, Maggay helped introduce insights and conceptual frames from these different disciplines to bear upon the missiological task of providing a non-Western witness to the gospel. Her approach has been credited to have offered "a new direction, even a new option for younger Filipino evangelicals."[28] Maggay's key insight is the necessity of "contextualization from within." It involves rejecting the usual process of contextualization that involves mere translation and re-interpretation of a fixed gospel formulated from outside the local context. She proposes instead a kind of theological re-rooting that constructs and communicates the gospel from the themes and categories of people's specific contexts.[29] For her, this process is captured in the idea of *pagbabalik-loob* or a return to one's inmost being. The concern is to be in touch with one's *loob* as the place to meet with Christ and allow him in such depths to convey healing and wholeness. In other words, it is to embark on a journey of finding one's way home after having made a wrong turn that causes wandering like a lost soul (*naligaw ng landas*).[30] Maggay gives an apt description of being led astray by colonial mentality and being conscious of

---

26. See for example, James Whelchel, *The Path to Liberation: Theology of Struggle in the Philippines* (Quezon City: New Day Publishers, 1995). A curious case for instance, Prof. Arsenio Dominguez, then president of the Philippine Missionary Institute in Silang, Cavite, offered what he called a "theology of bondage" to serve as a playful counter-suggestion for his fellow evangelicals to adopt, in contra-distinction to liberation theology. See Arsenio Dominguez, *Theological Themes for the Philippine Church* (Quezon City: New Day Publishers, 1989).

27. Aside from Maggay and Gener, I have traced impulses of decoloniality from other evangelical theologians in the Philippines. See Rei Lemuel Crizaldo, "Pathways for Decolonization in Philippine Evangelical Discourse" (paper presented at the Philippine Studies Association National Conference, online, August 25–27, 2021). https://www.academia.edu/99842421/Pathways_for_Decolonization_in_Philippine_Evangelical_Discourse.

28. Timoteo Gener, "Re-rooting the Gospel in the Philippines: Roman Catholic and Evangelical Approaches to Contextualization" (Master of Theology thesis, Institute for Christian Studies, 1998), 95.

29. Melba Maggay, *A Clash of Cultures: Early American Protestant Mission and Filipino Religious Consciousness* (Mandaluyong City: Anvil Publishing, 2011), 179–80.

30. Maggay, *A Clash of Cultures*, 189.

the need to undo it. For her, "to incarnate Christianity more genuinely within the context of Filipino culture is to become not only perhaps more Christian but also more truly Filipino."[31]

Timoteo Gener, a leading scholar on local theologizing in the Philippines and in Asia, builds upon the proposal of Maggay and suggests theological "re-routing" as a subsequent and complementary step to theological re-rooting. His idea is captured by the picture of *pagbabagong-loob* or the change of one's innermost being as a move to both affirm local culture and at the same time make space for its renewal. This aims to "re-assert 'transformation' or 'conversion' as the pivotal missional concept for cultivating Filipino theology" that points to the experience of *pagbabagong-buhay* (new life) as a major criterion for genuine encounter with Christ.[32] Gener's proposal is important considering that the decolonial process is not just an exercise of "remembering" but also one of re-imagining.

Yango rightfully pointed to a possible pathway for decoloniality, one that reaches within the depths of a Filipino's being and becoming. The complementary proposals by Maggay and Gener illustrate the kind of footwork needed as a tenable way forward for evangelical theologizing.

Re-imagining Evangelical Political Theology

How and where can be a good start for an evangelical theologian in the Philippines to hit the road of *pagbabalik-loob* (re-rooting) and *pagbabagong-loob* (re-routing) in developing a decolonial political theology? Contrary to the usual remarks that such an endeavor of reaching into a people's storied past is an exercise in futility, one can discover that the seeds to a decolonial process are within reach. But this process has to begin with expanding the capacity to imagine differently. It will be good to start with concerns nearest to people's minds, and therefore wise to heed the wisdom behind a local saying whenever someone shrugs off something as unimportant with *malayo sa bituka* (far from one's belly). For something to make sense and be of an immediate concern, it has to be connected to the *kalam ng sikmura* (hungry stomach), of which the primary antidote is food on the table.

Speaking of food, it provides a rich resource for *Pinoys* when thinking about the experience of colonization. Elsewhere in the world, food has been a

---

31. Melba Maggay, *The Gospel in Culture: Contextualization Issues through Asian Eyes* (Mandaluyong: OMF Literature, 2013), 56.

32. Timoteo Gener, "Re-rooting the Gospel in the Philippines," 122.

principal tool of colonization. But it has also been, at the same time, a primary means of resistance. In the Philippines, cuisine presents an interesting area of contestation and negotiation with regard to the country's relentless struggle with colonial powers. A good illustration would be the "Filipino spaghetti":

> Filipino spaghetti is a rebellious version of the Italian pasta. Its noodles are somewhat overcooked. It has a striking red color and is sweet and spicy. To make it even more absurd, chopped hotdogs, ground pork, onions, and garlic are mixed into the thick sauce made with banana ketchup and tomato paste. A generous helping of cheddar cheese is sprinkled on top of the spaghetti. The resulting catastrophe is a celebration of sweet, salty, and sour flavors that puncture the palate, true to a dish that is remarkably Filipino.[33]

Rather than the Philippines being "Italianized," the Italian pasta was indigenized by the distinct taste and flavor for food of most *Pinoys*! The sweet spaghetti that has been a staple of many parties and fast-food chains is a testament to people's latent but potent capacity to confront and subvert a remarkable serving of foreign influence. In this and in other cases, food represents critical issues of both identity and history.

"There is history in every dish, a story in every bite," writes Felice Prudente Sta. Maria.[34] In a pioneering work on using food in the context of writing Philippine history, she notes the simplistic and limited paradigm of Christian Europe with regard to culinary arts during the time of its colonial conquests in Asia. Its tragic handicap rendered it unable to grasp the luxury and opulence ever present at the royal tables of India, China, and Persia.[35] In the Philippines, for example, she emphasizes that "food was the first Filipino gift to the first Europeans in Philippine territory" and functioned as the point of diplomacy "being a language of possible friendship or tolerance."[36] Jars of coconut wine,

---

33. Mario Alvaro Limos, "The Crazy History of Filipino Spaghetti," *Esquire Philippines* (2020), https://www.esquiremag.ph/long-reads/features/filipino-spaghetti-history-a00293-20200610?utm_source=Facebook-Esquire&utm_medium=Ownshare&utm_campaign=20220617-fbnp-long-reads-filipino-spaghetti-history-a00293-20200610-fbold&fbclid=IwAR3NLvyZcuCk3l4A-gjD3ninuOcKX7YQs8b4hJTITYdPo2Ar1pOPrk-Xcbs.

34. Felice Prudente Sta. Maria, *Pigafetta's Philippine Picnic: Culinary Encounters During the First Circumnavigation, 1519–1522* (Manila: National Historical Commission of the Philippines, 2021), x.

35. Sta. Maria, *Pigafetta's Philippine Picnic*, 8–15.

36. Sta. Maria, *Pigafetta's Philippine Picnic*, 39, 41.

rice, and swine were served on porcelain plates to Ferdinand Magellan and his crew.[37]

In her meticulous study of the culinary heritage of the country, Doreen Fernandez observed that the Philippine cuisine "provides a key to the understanding of national identity . . . the study of food as culture within the context of colonization leads to an understanding of the fate of the local culture under hegemony of the dominant culture of the colonizers."[38] She was convinced that in not a few instances, the culinary heritage in the Philippines survived colonization, "either unchanged in its traditional ways (indigenous), or slightly changed in its contact with dominant culture (through the indigenization of foreign influences)."[39] And for her, such culinary heritage offers much hope for a whole lot of other forms of local heritage which "many have feared are too fragile to survive Modernity and global tides."[40]

Gastronomic imaginative reflections like these can enrich, inform, and hopefully transform the doing and development of political theology. If taken as a point of departure for a renewed sense of political and spiritual consciousness, there is much in the staples of *Pinoy* tables that can be explored. Consider the following:

1. *Sapin-sapin*: This sticky but colorful rice-cake illustrates that there can be diversity even in unity. In a country of more than seven thousand islands and more than three hundred languages, it will be more proper to speak of diverse evangelical political "theologies" instead of the singular monolithic "theology" that has been characteristic of much of colonial "Modernist" theologizing. In other words, not only that a pursuit of a "Filipino political theology" is unhelpful, it will also be harmful to the intrinsic diversity of the people of the archipelago. A good practice with regard to this plurality of voices in political theologizing is the evangelical think-tank *Pananaw Pinoy*. The group is composed of different and differing theological voices whose body of works comprises decades-long radio commentaries

---

37. Sta. Maria, *Pigafetta's Philippine Picnic*, 38, 44.

38. Doreen Fernandez, *Tikim: Essays on Philippine Food and Culture*, revised and updated (Pasig City: Anvil Publishing, 2020), 196. Binamira highlights the importance of Fernandez's culinary historiography, "We really need to go back as far as possible to the roots of a dish. Because if we understand the soul of a dish then you can play with it with abandon and you can play with it in a way that seems more honest." Joel Binamira, "Pre-Colonial Recipes," *Facebook*, 3 June 2022, https://www.facebook.com/watch?v=396057878953498.

39. Fernandez, *Tikim*, 205.

40. Fernandez, *Tikim*, 205.

and newspaper editorials on pressing political issues written from a faith perspective.⁴¹ The commentaries and editorials are all written and delivered in the vernacular.

2. *Halo-halo*: This popular ice dessert is the *Pinoy* counterpart to "fruit shakes" wherein the ingredients get mashed and fused with one another in a blending machine. The *halo-halo*, on the other hand, while also mixing everything together, yet it keeps the character of every individual ingredient distinguishable: the beans, the fruits, and the jellies. This delicacy invites an imaginative shift from the usual tendency to integrate diverse theological thinking towards a model of theological multiplicity wherein each is affirmed without the pressure to fit within a schematic whole. A good example of this spirit of multiplicity at work is the book *BOBOto Ba Ako? How to Think Smart and Vote Right* that offers a range of different perspectives, including that of a Christian anarchist's. The book is written in a mix of English and the *Tagalog* vernacular (*Taglish*).⁴²

3. *Adobo*: This beloved dish is actually more of a method of food preparation and preservation than a culinary trick. With the use of vinegar and salty seasoning as base ingredients for marinade, the *Pinoy adobo* inhibits bacterial growth and thus prevents food from spoiling.⁴³ But the complexity of the dish lies elsewhere. Chef Claude Tayag writes in a definitive *adobo* book, "To say there are seven thousand six hundred forty recipes of our *adobo* is an understatement. There are as many kinds of *adobo* as there are households!"⁴⁴ The *adobo* opens up an instructive piece of reflection on how and why theologizing, when embraced by the notion of fluidity, can step into the space of re-imagining orthodoxy as a dynamic process

---

41. For an initial assessment of this initiative, see Rei Lemuel Crizaldo, "Pananaw Pinoy: An Expression of Doing Theology in Public" (paper presented at the Asia Theological Association Theological Consultation, Manila, July 31–August 2, 2018).

42. See Rei Lemuel Crizaldo, Caloy Dino, Ronald Molmisa, Bryan Paler, Mighty Rasing, and Emil Jon Soriano, *BOBOto Ba Ako? How to Think Smart and Vote Right* (Mandaluyong City: OMF Literature, 2015).

43. Mario Alvario Limos, "Filipinos Were Eating Adobo Before the Spaniards Came, Says Spanish Culinary Scientist," *Esquire*, April 10, 2019, https://www.esquiremag.ph/long-reads/history-of-adobo-a2017-20190410-lfrm?utm_source=Facebook-Esquire&utm_medium=Ownshare&utm_campaign=20220817-fbnp-long-reads-history-of-adobo-a2017-20190410-lfrm-fbold.

44. Claude Tayag, *The Ultimate Filipino Adobo: Stories through the Ages* (Manila: Foreign Service Institute, 2022).

rather than a mechanism to produce a static product. A recent initiative is the panel on "Christianity and Decoloniality: Evangelical Perspectives" at the National Conference of the Philippine Studies Association (PSA) on the theme "500 years of Christianity in the Philippines," held on August 25–27, 2021.[45] The papers presented in the panel explored a multi-faceted decolonial pathway for an alternative and a more well-rounded evangelical discipleship that includes political life: "Churches as Agents of Indigenous Response to Social Justice" by Arla Fontamillas, and "Christian Ethics and Filipino Values" by Bernard Moreno Bragas, among others.

These examples are just a few among the *vistas* that food can open for fresh decolonial reflections. Sta. Maria put it well when she said that "People decide, even against greatest odds, how they and their communities will live. Food choices are expressions of human resolve and relish." Decoloniality is not a metaphor. Yes, but sure it has to be edible too!

"But culinary insights in theologizing, how serious can this be?" one may ask.[46] It is good to start by considering how from the standpoint of the Bible, food is a central theological issue. Those who will say otherwise have not paid a careful attention to how issues of eating and drinking have occupied much attention in the pages of both the Old and New Testaments.[47] At the very least, the most powerful theological instruction that Jesus left his disciples to remember with regularity came by way of bread and wine (Luke 22:7–19). Jesus settled for a gastronomic visual imagery for the act of reflecting on his redemptive work.

What this chapter sought to show is the potential of a decolonial pathway: culinary-infused reflections that can open up fresh and exciting trails for theologizing on political issues and engagement. The initiatives cited alongside the imaginative culinary themes outlined above hopefully serve as a positive response to Totik Diesto Jr.'s lamentation that: "The crisis in Filipino theology

---

45. More information about the conference is available at https://www.philstudies.com/2021-national-conference/.

46. This is different from, in fact the opposite, of taking a "theological approach to food," by Norman Wirzba, which was aimed at deploying theological resources to help navigate the complex world of food: the very act of eating, issues of justice in food production, among others. See his "Food for Theologians," *Interpretation: A Journal of Bible and Theology* 67, no. 4 (2013): 374–82.

47. The apostle Paul, for instance, was writing letters to churches all over the Greek civilization, with questions about food on the table as among the most important inquiries he needed to address.

is nothing less than fundamental: it speaks in a foreign language, while at the same time using an alien methodology to reflect on problems not related to its own culture nor relevant to the struggles of its people."[48]

Conclusion

If one of the marks of decoloniality is to "dwell in a new state of freedom amidst the memories of colonial history" (Yango), then a chapter like this can only end by looking forward to exploring more pathways. The immediate implication of which is to be wary of political issues and ideas that are foreign (and harmful!) to the context and culture of the Philippines, like the Moral Majority politics from the US. The pursuit will demand a painful but fruitful coming to terms with one's coloniality and the healing process that it requires. And the journey is by no means a solitary endeavor. The advances in local theologizing among *Pinoy* evangelicals are waiting to be utilized in developing a kind of Christianity that is no longer derivative of what was forged in the West.[49] But, this will require stepping into the space of a festive, at times gastronomic, but surely a more constructive type of theologizing instead of the typical doctrinal arena of puritanical, assembly line, systematics.

By way of recommendation, two things are worth looking into for further research on evangelical political engagement in the country:

Rediscovery of a "spirituality of revolution": Within the history of the Philippines is the story of brave peoples bent on waging uprisings anchored not merely on aspirations for freedom but also from deep spiritual convictions. The most notable is the successful armed revolution against the Spanish Empire compelled and animated by a strong spiritual foundation (cf. Reynaldo Ileto's *Pasyon at Rebolusyon*). We should therefore raise our eyebrows at any notion of apolitical Christianity being imposed in the Philippine archipelago.

Embrace of a heritage of "revolutionary spirituality": Within the ecclesial history of the Philippines is a resistance and refusal, as a community of faith, to be subservient to foreign control. This includes the one led by Nicolas Zamora, grandson of one of the three priests famed for their martyrdom at the hands of the Spaniards (the *GOMBURZA*). It led to the founding of the *Iglesia Evangelica*

---

48. Diesto, *The Effects of Colonial Mentality*, 130.

49. Many times in this chapter, the term *Pinoy* has been used to refer to the inhabitants of the Philippine archipelago. For a helpful explanation of this terminology, see Rodrick de Ocampo Jr., "Defining Pinoy through T-shirts" (College thesis, University of the Philippines Diliman, 2009). On how it relates to theologizing, see Ian de Ocampo, "On Pinoy Theology," *Every Square Inch* (blog), 14 March 2021. https://www.facebook.com/notes/858139061703743/?_rdc=1&_rdr.

Metodista En Las Islas Filipinas or the IEMELIF (The Evangelical Methodist Church in the Philippine Islands) in 1909 – an indigenous church organization that continues to flourish to this very day.[50]

With such a legacy of radical and subversive spirituality, there is insufficient reason for theologians with evangelical sensibility to inhibit themselves from charting a truly liberating direction for faith communities in the Philippines. It is wise to heed Sta. Maria's remarks about the first successful resistance to European colonial ventures in the archipelago: "People with a passion for freedom and a mastery of their strengths can overcome invasion, injustice, and disrespect."[51]

Bibliography

Anderson, Benedict. *Under Three Flags: Anarchism and the Anti-Colonial Imagination.* Pasig City: Anvil Publishing, 2006.

Barreto, Raimundo, and Roberto Sirvent. *Decolonial Christianities.* Switzerland: Palgrave Macmillan, 2019.

Bartolome, Jessica, and Margaret Claire Layug. *Our Progressive Past.* GMA Network, 29 December 2021. https://www.gmanetwork.com/news/specials/content/206/our-progressive-past/?fbclid=IwAR2CTf6QrVnpBaAZp5q7x7xADcN5i9GXSfO1BREaGuOMER51eFRAOFQEpKQ.

Binamira. "Pre-Colonial Recipes," Facebook, 3 June 2022. https://www.facebook.com/watch?v=396057878953498.

Bulatao, Jaime. "Split-Level Christianity." *Philippine Sociological Review* 13 no. 2 (1965): 119–21.

Crizaldo, Rei Lemuel. "Casting Your Vote for Christian Candidates." In *What About Philippine Politics: Thoughts and Reflections on Political Leadership, Good Citizenship, and the Christian Faith*, 46–59. Mandaluyong City: OMF Literature, 2016.

———. "Pananaw Pinoy: An Expression of Doing Theology in Public." Paper presented at the Asia Theological Association Theological Consultation, Manila, July–August 2018.

———. "Pathways for Decolonization in Philippine Evangelical Discourse." Paper presented at the Philippine Studies Association National Conference, Manila, August, 2021.

---

50. See Ruben Trinidad, *A Monument to Religious Nationalism: History and Polity of the IEMELIF Church* (Quezon City: Iglesia Evangelica Metodista en las Islas Filipinas, 1998). Other religious movements born at the time of the revolution against Spain and the United States are the *Iglesia Filipina Independiente* or the IFI (established in 1902) and the *Iglesia Evangelica Unida de Cristo* or the UNIDA (established in 1932).

51. Sta. Maria, *Pigafetta's Philippine Picnic*, 52.

Crizaldo, Rei Lemuel, Caloy Dino, Ronald Molmisa, Bryan Paler, Mighty Rasing, and Emil Jon Soriano, *BOBOto Ba Ako? How to Think Smart and Vote Right*. Mandaluyong City: OMF Literature, 2015.
de Ocampo, Ian. "On Pinoy Theology." *Every Square Inch* (blog), 14 March 2021. https://www.facebook.com/notes/858139061703743/?_rdc=1&_rdr.
de Ocampo, Rodrick. "Defining Pinoy through T-shirts." College thesis, University of the Philippines Diliman. Quezon City, Philippines, 2009.
Diesto, Genaro, Jr. *The Effects of Colonial Mentality on the Religious Consciousness of Filipinos*. Iloilo City: College of Theology, Central Philippines University, 2011.
Dominguez, Arsenio. *Theological Themes for the Philippine Church*. Quezon City: New Day Publishers, 1989.
Fanon, Frantz. *The Wretched of the Earth*. New York: Grove Press, 1963.
Fernandez, Doreen. *Tikim: Essays on Philippine Food and Culture*. Revised and Updated. Mandaluyong City: Anvil Publishing, 2020.
Gener, Timoteo. "Re-rooting the Gospel in the Philippines: Roman Catholic and Evangelical Approaches to Contextualization." Master's thesis, Institute for Christian Studies, 1998.
———. "Re-imaging Conversion in the Lowland Philippine Setting: The Perspective of Gospel Re-rooting." *Journal of Asian Missions* 3, no. 1 (2001): 43–77.
Limos, Almario. "The Crazy History of Filipino Spaghetti." *Esquire Philippines*, 2020. https://www.esquiremag.ph/long-reads/features/filipino-spaghetti-history-a00293-20200610?utm_source=Facebook-Esquire&utm_medium=Ownshare&utm_campaign=20220617-fbnp-long-reads-filipino-spaghetti-history-a00293-20200610-fbold&fbclid=IwAR3NLvyZcuCk3l4A-gjD3ninuOcKX7YQs8b4hJTITYdPo2Ar1pOPrk-Xcbs.
———. "Filipinos Were Eating Adobo Before the Spaniards Came, Says Spanish Culinary Scientist." *Esquire Philippines*, 10 April 2019. https://www.esquiremag.ph/long-reads/history-of-adobo-a2017-20190410-lfrm?utm_source=Facebook-Esquire&utm_medium=Ownshare&utm_campaign=20220817-fbnp-long-reads-history-of-adobo-a2017-20190410-lfrm-fbold.
Lorde, Audre. "The Master's Tools Will Never Dismantle the Master's House." In *Sister Outsider: Essays and Speeches*. Berkeley: Crossing Press, 194.
Maggay, Melba P. *A Clash of Cultures: Early American Protestant Missions and Filipino Religious Consciousness*. Pasig City: Anvil Publishing, 2011.
———. *The Gospel in Culture: Contextualization through Asian Eyes*. Mandaluyong City: OMF Literature, 2013.
———. *Pagbabalik-loob: Moral Recovery and Cultural Reaffirmation*. Quezon City: Akademya ng Kultura at Sikolohiyang Pilipino, 1993.
Mendoza, S. Lily. "Theoretical Advances in the Discourse of Indigenization." In *Mga Babasahin sa Agham Panlipunang Pilipino*, edited by A. Navarro and F. Lagbao-Bolante, 241–97. Quezon City: C&E Publishing, 2007.

———. "Transdiasporic Indigeneity and Decolonizing Faith." In *Decolonizing Ecotheology: Indigenous and Subaltern Challenges*, edited by S. Mendoza and G. Zachariah, 259–79. Eugene: Pickwick Publications, 2022.

———. "Ang Usaping Pangwika sa Bagong Yugto ng Pantayong Pananaw: Ang Panloob na Hamon ng Pluralismo." *Social Science Diliman* 7, no. 1 (June 2011): 37–62.

Mignolo, Walter. *The Darker Side of Modernity: Global Futures, Decolonial Options*. Durham: Duke University Press, 2011.

Mignolo, Walter, and Catherine Walsh. *On Decoloniality: Concepts, Analytics, Praxis*. Durham: Duke University Press, 2018.

Miranda-Feliciano, Evelyn. *Filipino Values and Our Christian Faith*. Mandaluyong City: OMF Literature, 1990.

Pilario, Daniel. "Mapping Postcolonial Theory: Appropriations in Contemporary Theology," *Asian Christian Review* 1, no. 1 (2007): 48–78.

Sta. Maria, Felice Prudente. *Pigafetta's Philippine Picnic: Culinary Encounters During the First Circumnavigation, 1519–1522*. Manila: National Historical Commission of the Philippines, 2021.

Strobel, Leny. "Decolonizing as a Spiritual Path." 18 December 2014. YouTube video, 1:12:17. https://www.youtube.com/watch?v=u-_rxeCKyA8.

Tlostanova, Madina. "The Postcolonial Condition, the Decolonial Option, and the Post-Socialist Intervention." In *Postcolonialism Cross-Examined: Multidirectional Perspectives on Imperial and Colonial Pasts and the Neocolonial Present*, edited by M. Albretch, 165–78. New York: Routledge, 2019.

Torres, Nelson Maldonado. "Thinking Through the Decolonial Turn." *TRANSMODERNITY: Journal of Peripheral Cultural Production of the Luso-Hispanic World* 1, no. 2 (2011): 1–10.

Trinidad, Ruben. *A Monument to Religious Nationalism: History and Polity of the IEMELIF Church*. Quezon City: Iglesia Evangelica Metodista en las Islas Filipinas, 1998.

Veric, Charlie Samuya. *Children of the Postcolony: Filipino Intellectuals and Decolonization, 1946–1972*. Quezon City: Ateneo University Press, 2020.

Whelchel, James. *The Path to Liberation: Theology of Struggle in the Philippines*. Quezon City: New Day Publishers, 1995.

Wirzba, Norman. "Food for Theologians." *Interpretation: A Journal of Bible and Theology* 67, no. 4 (2013): 374–82.

Yango, Emo. "An Anthropology for Decolonizing a Philosophy of Modernity when Constructing Asian Theologies." Paper presented at the Asia Theological Association Theological Consultation, Manila, July–August 2018.

———. "Decolonizing Colonial Mentality." Paper presented at the Annual Genaro "Totik" Diesto Jr. Memorial Lecture, Manila, July–August 2017.

Yung, Hwa. *Mangoes or Bananas: The Quest for an Authentic Asian Christian Theology*. Oxford: Regnum, 1997.

10

Feel-Good Christianity

Jayeel S. Cornelio

Introduction

To feel good is at the center of contemporary Christianity. There is enough evidence to show that this is the case.[1]

Around the Philippines, many Christian circles echo the same mantra: "I'm blessed," "I'm favored," "I'm loved," and "I'm saved." Christians are also taught they have a purpose, and it makes them feel good too. God, believers are reminded, has a purpose for everything and for everyone.

Blessed, favored, loved, saved, and purpose-driven. Nobody will doubt the power of these words to make people feel good, especially those facing uncertainties. It is no wonder then that they are found even in the very names of local churches and their fellowships. It does not matter if these congregations are evangelical or Catholic, charismatic or otherwise. Many of us can readily identify them.

Many worship songs, the most efficient conduit of theological thought, are all about feeling good too. Those of us exposed to compositions from Western churches know that many of them lyricize the triumph of the self over personal troubles.

One way or another, these religious expressions speak of personal breakthrough, happiness, and success, all couched in theological language. In fact, they are now taken for granted even in non-religious settings. The public finds

---

1. Some parts of this piece are derived from my early articles for *Rappler*:
https://www.rappler.com/voices/thought-leaders/opinion-problem-feel-good-christianity/;
https://www.rappler.com/voices/thought-leaders/opinion-marcos-and-the-church/;
https://www.rappler.com/nation/elections/opinion-message-to-christians-voting-bongbong-marcos-elections/.

so much inspiration listening to motivational speakers, often with Christian backgrounds, who tell us that it is God's will for all of us to find meaning and happiness in life.

The message is to feel good and be fulfilled. Not necessarily aware of it, many Christians consider this to be the central ethos of their Christian life. To point this out is of course not to dismiss its validity, especially for those who are undergoing personal struggles.[2] Instead, this chapter is an invitation for Christians to take a step back and critically reflect on what it might mean in relation to faith in public life. The working premise is that theological discourses shape public consciousness.[3] This has been demonstrated in other countries, but certainly true in the Philippines where competing religious perspectives have been offered on the role of the Christian with respect to elected leaders and divisive issues.[4] Feel-good Christianity may appear to be individualistic and depoliticized, but it can, as I will show below, prove instrumental in enabling Christian support for unaccountable leaders.

In what follows, I will first spell out specific cases of feel-good Christianity. I explain this in the light of emerging scholarship about toxic positivity and "Christianity Lite."[5] I then explain how feel-good Christianity builds on the influencer culture that celebrates well-being and happiness but also on the prosperity ethic espoused by some of the most influential churches today.[6]

In the second part, I will turn to the social consequences of feel-good Christianity, in particular its complicity with the rise of regimes that evade public accountability. In feel-good Christianity, one loses sight of faith's relevance in the hardcore issues affecting our society. The chapter ends with a reflection on truth-telling and solidarity. The antidote to toxic Christianity, I believe, is to recognize suffering as part of our collective Christian walk. Doing so ultimately calls for solidarity with one another and those who have been left behind.

---

2. Russell P. Johnson, "The Gospel and the Prosperity Gospel: Joel Osteen's Your Best Life Now Reconsidered." *Theology* 121, no. 1 (2018): 28.

3. Paul Hanson, "The Bible and Public Theology," in *A Companion to Public Theology*, eds. Sebastian Kim and Katie Day (Leiden: Brill, 2017), 25.

4. Jayeel Cornelio and Robbin Dagle, "Weaponising Religious Freedom: Same-sex Marriage and Gender Equality in the Philippines," *Religion & Human Rights* 14, no. 2 (2019): 65.

5. Glen Berteau, *Christianity Lite* (Lake Mary: Passio, 2013), 8.

6. Erron Medina and Jayeel Cornelio, "The Prosperity Ethic: Neoliberal Christianity and the Rise of the New Prosperity Gospel in the Philippines," *Pneuma* 43, no. 1 (2021): 72.

What is Feel-Good Christianity?

My take-off point is Glen Berteau's pastoral reflections on what he refers to as Christianity Lite. In the course of his work as a pastor, he has encountered many sermons that focus mainly on the "friendly, pleasant, fun, accepting, and exciting aspects of Jesus's life and message" but ignore "the parts that make us feel uncomfortable."[7] Thus a big part of his book exposes Christianity Lite's theological inadequacies. He is very critical of seeker-sensitive messages that downplay the demands of repentance and obedience.

Christianity Lite has a material dimension too. Congregations that are consciously seeker-sensitive make decisions based on the concerns of potential converts. When Berteau was invited to speak at a local congregation, he was specifically asked to not conduct an altar call "because it makes people feel uncomfortable."[8] This also explains why church leaders go to lengths to redesign their halls, enhance the sound system, and play with the lighting to enhance people's sensory experience.[9] Often, by accommodating the aesthetics of concert halls, the objective is to minimize the churchy feel. Nathan Cruz, a Filipino sociologist who has studied megachurches, refers to these practices as the "spectacle of worship."[10] For many pastors, Christianity Lite dismisses the cost of discipleship. They are bothered by what they feel are the compromises of many churches today.

Reflections on Christianity Lite also have sociological value. While the pastoral insight focuses on its theological inadequacy, the sociological perspective pays attention to its underpinning ethos and implications on public life.[11] For this reason, I turn to "feel-good Christianity" as a heuristic label for the religious discourse that draws on Christian values and teachings to emphasize well-being as the mark of an authentic Christian. Through the repetitive use of positive messaging and practices that make people feel comfortable about their existence, it in effect calls for the denial of one's difficult circumstances.

---

7. Berteau, "Christianity Lite," 121–22.

8. Berteau, "Christianity Lite," 2.

9. Dick Staub, *The Culturally Savvy Christian: A Manifesto for Deepening Faith and Enriching Popular Culture in an Age of Christianity-Lite* (San Francisco: John Wiley & Sons, 2007).

10. Joseph Nathan Cruz, "A Spectacle of Worship: Technology, Modernity and The Rise of the Christian Megachurch," in *Mediating Piety*, ed. Francis Khek Gee Lim (Leiden: Brill, 2010), 113.

11. Zygmunt Bauman and Tim May, *Thinking Sociologically*, 2nd ed. (Oxford: Blackwell, 2014).

Through sermons, worship songs, and other congregational practices, Christians are exhorted to claim blessings, comfort, and happiness for oneself.[12]

And yet the consequence of feel-good Christianity is even more far-reaching. From my point of view as a sociologist, the issue is not only how it shapes congregational life. Feel-good Christianity's emphasis on personal well-being has implications on how Christians are to tackle public issues.[13] As a religious discourse that limits negative confessions, feel-good Christianity is unable to draw on the riches of the faith to read the signs of the times and offer a Christian response that comprehensively addresses issues of the day. Old Testament scholar Rico Villanueva, in his chapter in the volume *Faith and Bayan*, asserts the following point when he notes the absence of complaining in churches.[14]

> If there is anything on complaining, the emphasis is on its prohibition, using as an example the murmuring and complaining of the Israelites in the desert and how they were punished by God as a warning. The New Testament text that says, "Do everything without grumbling or arguing" (Phil 2:14) is always cited.

He then goes on to show how complaints are legitimate in the prophetic tradition, especially when the issues at stake affect the weak in society. It is for this reason that Christians need to take it with a grain of salt whenever pastors and public figures invoke unity, harmony, and peace. Couched in the language of feel-good Christianity, these ideas are often used to silence every form of dissent, including legitimate ones.

In the months leading up to the 2022 elections, many Christians did exactly that. On his highly followed IG account, one evangelical figure listed down eight reminders for Christians. A notable one reads as follows: "Promote your

---

12. Its resonances with the prosperity gospel are unmistakable. When pastors call on their members to confess only good things, they often refer to material well-being. Health and wealth are thus commonplace in these confessions. But in a way, what I consider feel-good Christianity also goes beyond the prosperity gospel. One reason is that in this worldview, one can only feel good if the totality of one's existence is comprehensively good. Thus, while health and wealth are important, other aspects are also crucial, including discovering one's purpose. Thus, economic poverty is not the only enemy. Other issues that one needs to actively reject are depression, hopelessness, and every other form of suffering. For more on new developments in the prosperity gospel in the Philippines, please see Medina and Cornelio, "The Prosperity Ethic."

13. Hadje Sadje, "What Does Theology Do, Actually? (Un)Doing Filipino Theologies," in *What Does Theology Do, Actually? Observing Theology and the Transcultural*, eds. Matthew Robinson and Inja Inders (Leipzig: EVA, 2020), 45.

14. Federico Villanueva, "Why the Church Needs to Learn How to Complain and Not Just 'Trust and Obey,'" in *Faith and Bayan: Filipino Evangelical Responses to Contemporary Social Issues*, eds. Lorenzo Bautista, Aldrin Peñamora, and Federico Villanueva (Carlisle: Langham Global Library, 2022), 77.

candidate by sharing their merits, not by destroying their opponents. It is not appropriate for us who claim to follow Christ to make other candidates look bad just to make our candidates look good."[15]

As many of us know, this was not an isolated incident. In a viral tweet, Henry Espiritu, a philosophy professor, recounted his encounter with a "BBM [Bongbong Marcos] apologist pastor." He "asked me why can't I forgive, move on and forget Martial Law. I told him that the great theologian Luther taught that offense against God can be forgiven by God's mercy but God can only forgive offenses against humans if justice is served and reparation is given."[16] Judging by the comments he received on Twitter, many could relate to Espiritu's experience in their own congregations.

I too have my own story to share. Months before the elections, I wrote an open letter to Christians voting for Bongbong Marcos.[17] My message was simple. While reconciliation and forgiveness are pillars of the Christian faith, neither Bongbong Marcos nor his supporters can haphazardly invoke them, as they have time and again. Drawing on these virtues, they castigate BBM's critics for digging up the past and take comfort in the man's message of national healing. In the words of BBM himself, "haters gonna hate."[18]

But their message of forgiveness, I proposed, is inadequate. Every time they bring up forgiveness, they in effect dismiss the atrocities of the past as if they were all an inconsequential blip in our history. They conveniently forget too that an intimate relationship exists between forgiveness and justice. As theologians in conflict settings have shown, these virtues are not antithetical to one another and both require truth-telling.[19] Especially in the light of reconciliation and the need to confront wrongdoing, this lesson should be basic to any Christian.[20]

---

15. Jeel Monde, "Hayden Kho Shares Christian Traits During Election Campaign," *Philippine News*, 12 February 2022, https://philnews.ph/2022/02/12/hayden-kho-shares-christian-traits-during-election-campaign/.

16. https://twitter.com/HenryFrancisBE1/status/1518811584306442240.

17. Jayeel Cornelio, "To Christians Voting for Marcos," *Rappler*, 17 October 2021. https://www.rappler.com/nation/elections/opinion-message-to-christians-voting-bongbong-marcos-elections/.

18. Nicole Curato, "The Philippines: Erasing History through Good Vibes and Toxic Positivity," *HBS Southeast Asia*, 28 March 2022, https://th.boell.org/en/2022/03/28/philippines-good- vibes-toxic-positivity.

19. Stephen J. Pope, "The Convergence of Forgiveness and Justice: Lessons from El Salvador," *Theological Studies* 64, no. 4 (2003): 812.

20. Paul S. Fiddes, "Restorative Justice and the Theological Dynamic of Forgiveness," *Oxford Journal of Law and Religion* 5, no. 1 (2016): 54.

Given our politically charged divisions, it was meant to be a respectful appeal. But based on the comments online and the many private messages I received, I know that my piece affected many in the faith community. One person even called me "un-Christian" for maligning BBM's reputation. Others dismissed the entire piece and accused me of promoting "hatred and unforgiveness."

This appeal to forgiveness is repetitive. We find it on social media and in everyday discourse. We hear it too in our own congregations. Pastors and Christian celebrities tend to be their most influential conduits. In these contexts, to forgive is the duty of the Christian, no questions asked. With respect to Martial Law, it means going past it. In the spirit of feel-good Christianity, calling for accountability from the Marcos family reeks of bitterness, which true Christians, according to them, must not encourage.

Enabling Authoritarian Nostalgia

In effect, feel-good Christianity enables strongman rule and demonizes critical dissent. As Anthony Lawrence Borja puts it, "Hopeful and reconciliatory as it may sound, it is premised upon an electoralist condemnation of a supposed 'politics of division.'"[21] In 2019, anthropologist Melba Maggay brought together her contemporaries to write about their experiences during Martial Law. But the collection, *Dark Days of Authoritarianism*, is also a reading of the signs of the times for the faith community: "An enduring legacy of the martial law years has been the mystique of the strongman, fed by the mythology that the culture is, at bottom, authoritarian. The people need – and want – a strong iron hand. Nothing gets done, it is said, because the country suffers from 'too much democracy.'"[22] In the literature, this disposition to be governed by a strongman is referred to as "authoritarian nostalgia." With respect to the Philippine context, it builds on myths about a golden past under the dictatorial rule of Ferdinand Marcos Sr.[23]

---

21. Anthony Lawrence Borja, "The Rise of Anti-Politics: 'Unity' in Curbing Dissent in the Philippines," *Rappler*, 27 September 2022, https://www.rappler.com/voices/imho/opinion- rise-anti-politics-unity-curbing-dissent-philippines/.

22. Melba Maggay, "By Way of a Prologue" in *Dark Days of Authoritarianism: To Be in History*, ed. Melba Maggay (Carlisle: Langham Global Library, 2019), xiv.

23. Adele Webb, "Why Are the Middle Class Misbehaving?: Exploring Democratic Ambivalence and Authoritarian Nostalgia," *Philipine Sociological Review* 65, no. Special Issue: Imagine Democracies (2017): 77; Bobby Benedicto, "The Place of the Dead, the Time of Dictatorship: Nostalgia, Sovereignty, and the Corpse of Ferdinand Marcos," *Environment and Planning D: Society and Space* 39, no. 4 (2021): 722; Jayeel Cornelio, "Marcos, Christianity, and the Seduc-

The virtuous discourse of feel-good Christianity has enabled this nostalgia, one that Bongbong Marcos's campaign has taken advantage of to present itself as a noble cause. The cause is to make the Philippines great again, and the message is unity. Marcosian distortionism, according to scholarly accounts, depicts the dictator as a "benevolent patriarch" who punished "troublemakers" and rewarded "law-abiding citizens."[24] Bongbong Marcos does not come across as a treacherous dictator precisely because of his redemptive narrative; the Philippines was once great until it lost its glory when his dictator father was ousted, and he is now in the business of reclaiming that status. In his viral interview with Toni Gonzaga, Bongbong Marcos described himself as the "son of the longest-lasting president who brought the Philippines into the modern world, really . . . and who brought to the Philippines a sense of nationhood . . . when we were proud to be Filipino."[25]

Speaking before his supporters at the Philippine Arena, Marcos appealed to the best in the Filipino: "*Nasa puso at ugali ng mga Pilipino ang maging mabait. Di naman tayo pala-away, di naman tayo naghahanap ng gulo. Ang hanap lang natin ay magkaroon ng disenteng buhay para sa ating sarili, para sa ating pamilya at para sa ating bansa.*"[26] [It's in the heart and character of Filipinos to be kind. We're not quarrelsome. What we're looking for is a decent life for ourselves, families, and country.] The remark is noble and it would be difficult to disagree with the man. After all, Filipinos do desire to lead decent lives. As *Ambisyon 2040* puts it, Filipinos aspire to build families that are "*matatag, maginhawa, panatag*"[27] [strong, comfortable, peaceful]. By appealing to positive Filipino sensibility, this message of unity is deeply moral. And by appealing to the welfare of the nation, it too is a patriotic call.

To be sure, the message of unity originates from the campaign itself and has a longer history. In 2016, when he ran for vice-president, Marcos Jr. expressed confidence in the promise of unity for national progress: "The situation in the Philippines will not improve and we will not be able to address our problems

---

tion of Authoritarian Nostalgia," in *The Marcos Era: A Reader*, eds. Leia Castañeda Anastacio and Patricio Abinales (Quezon City: Bughaw/Ateneo de Manila University Press, 2022), 335.

24. Victor Felipe Bautista, "The Pervert's Guide to Historical Revisionism: Traversing the Marcos Fantasy," *Philippine Studies: Historical & Ethnographic Viewpoints* (2018): 282.

25. Toni Gonzaga Studio, "The Greatest Lesson Bongbong Marcos Learned From His Father," YouTube, 13 September 2021, https://www.youtube.com/watch?v=1EwMAiqLUhM&t=930s.

26. Kristine Joy Patag, "It's 'Unity, Unity, Unity' for Uniteam's Presidential Bet Marcos," *Philippine Star*, 9 February 2022, https://www.philstar.com/headlines/2022/02/09/2159653/its-unity- unity-unity-uniteams-presidential-bet-marcos.

27. NEDA, "About Ambisyon Natin 2040," *Ambisyon Natin 2040*, http://2040.neda.gov.ph/about- ambisyon-natin-2040/.

if we are not united in working to move forward."[28] On social media, networks of disinformation – what we might refer to informally as trolls – capitalized on positive messaging too. During the events that led to the burial of Ferdinand Marcos Sr. in the *Libingan ng mga Bayani* (Heroes' Cemetery), online campaigns called for national healing, forgiveness, and unity. Run by some of the most experienced PR agencies in the country, these campaigns appealed to the best in the Filipino. In the report "Architects of Disinformation," Ong and Cabañes have observed that the campaign "included heart-tugging graphics with biblical verses and life quotes that emphasized Filipino culture of *bayanihan* (community spirit) and religiosity."[29]

What makes feel-good Christianity an effective enabler of authoritarian nostalgia? Several reasons may be offered. The first is that it builds on an already pervasive influencer culture. On social media, celebrities and influencers gain traction through feel-good messages that appeal to well-being, happiness, and the good life. In politics, this has proven to be an effective technique to evade difficult questions during the elections. Among the celebrities who supported Bongbong Marcos, Bible quotes accompanied their social commentaries. In the words of one: "If we choose a harsh tone and unkind words, it's going to be hard for those around you to see God's grace at work in your life."[30] The other reason is that feel-good Christianity readily resonates with what may be characterized as the dominant religious mood, at least in Christian circles in the country. This is nowhere more evident than in the massive success of the prosperity gospel that one can readily discern in many Christian churches. As Medina and Cornelio have shown, the prosperity gospel has effectively displaced social and political teachings that used to define theological reflections in the 1970s and 1980s.[31] And in recent decades, the prosperity gospel is taking on new forms that appeal not just to disenfranchised Filipinos but also aspirational ones through positive thinking, self-care, and financial skills.[32]

And yet feel-good Christianity is entrapped by its own irony. It purports to be concerned about the welfare of the public, but ultimately resists it. For

---

28. Carla Gomez, "Marcos: Message of Unity, Cooperation Pushed Me to Top of Surveys," *Philippine Daily Inquirer*, 13 April 2016, https://newsinfo.inquirer.net/779255/marcos-message-of-unity-cooperation-pushed-me-to-top-of-surveys#ixzz7RdbSnNXc.

29. Jonathan Corpus Ong and Jason Vincent A. Cabañes, "Architects of Networked Disinformation: Behind the Scenes of Troll Accounts and Fake News Production in the Philippines" (2018): 58.

30. Curato, "The Philippines."

31. Medina and Cornelio, "The Prosperity Ethic," 72.

32. Medina and Cornelio, "The Prosperity Ethic," 65.

depicting resistance as "un-Christian," "harsh," and "unkind," feel-good Christianity commits what may perhaps be among the gravest of sins: thoughtlessness. This is what happens when it mislabels the concerns of other people, some of which may be legitimate in their own right, as sowing disunity. Without them realizing it, feel-good Christians are committing to the "tyranny of idiocy." For the ancient Greeks, idiocy is the placing of "private interests and concerns above the common good."[33] It becomes tyrannical not just as a result of coercion. The protection of political interests is compelling enough to abandon one's moral and social duties in a democratic space. And it becomes far more convincing if expressed as both Christian and virtuous. Forgiveness, peace, and unity are thus deceitful.

Conclusion

There is so much wisdom in confronting feel-good Christianity today. I see at least two considerations.

First, doing so reclaims the cost of discipleship.[34] It is a reminder for many Filipino evangelicals who are drawn to the "spectacle of worship" that informs much of their congregational life today.[35] In fact, confronting feel-good Christianity may in the end be an encouragement to small congregations. As they free themselves from the compulsions of rapid growth, they can rediscover that Christ's ministry was, in the words of Bishop Noel Pantoja, "the growth of the kingdom of God."[36]

Second, confronting feel-good Christianity is an invitation to reflect on why many Christians feel that talking about corruption, inequality, and injustice is divisive. Lest I be misunderstood, this is not to deny the many social contributions of Christian churches. One of the strengths of local congregations is their readiness to address local concerns especially in times of crisis.[37] One can argue that those are expressions of their civic responsibility, driven by compassion and prompted by their faith. But why do many Christians, in

---

33. Cristopher Britt and Eduardo Subirats, *Intellectuals in the Society of Spectacle* (Cham: Springer, 2021), 139.

34. Berteau, "Christianity Lite," 87.

35. Cruz, "A spectacle of worship," 113.

36. OMF Lit., *Passion & Power: Pulpit Messages from the Filipino Heart* (Mandaluyong City: OMF Literature, 2017), 215.

37. Emma Tomalin, *Religions and Development* (London: Routledge, 2013), 218; Jayeel Cornelio, "Religion and Civic Engagement: The Case of Iglesia ni Cristo in the Philippines," *Religion, State & Society* 45, no. 1 (2017): 23.

the name of relational peace, choose to be silent over issues of abuse even in their own circles?

Third, it brings us to perhaps the most important question: What then is the way forward?

I believe the answer lies in turning feel-good Christianity on its very head. If feel-good Christianity is the rejection of everything that makes us feel bad about ourselves and our society, then the antidote is to recognize all of it as part of our Christian walk. To this end we can draw tremendously on the spirituality of suffering. In the face of suffering and injustice, the Christian is called to respond with a spirit of redemption, which Charles Ringma characterizes as a "transformational reality."[38] Christians are to participate in this transformation by putting an end to oppression whether at the personal, congregational, or societal level. He then concludes that "when the least – the poor, the marginalized – are served well, then the God of justice dances with delight."[39]

From this point of view, the Christian response is not only charity or aid, even if that may be important especially in moments of humanitarian crisis.[40] To recognize people's suffering demands truth-telling, especially when it comes to inconvenient realities affecting a person's life or the life of a people.

Truth-telling, at one level, is an introspective act. It raises questions about the character of Christian discipleship in many congregations today. As discussed above, Filipino Christians are reminded by their pastors, the preachings they listen to, and the books they read that peace among the brethren must be maintained at all costs.[41] To exercise truth-telling is to reclaim the heroic Christ from the passive one that valorizes passivity. This is an invitation to ministers and their congregations around the country to assess how much of their discipleship programs echo toxic Christianity and how much foster spaces for accountability in our own Christian circles.

Beyond our congregations, truth-telling is much needed in our collective life as a Filipino people. It rejects not only historical distortions but also theologies that silence the cries against injustices. As it confronts abuses of power, truth-telling opens up the space for justice, forgiveness, and even reconciliation. Truth-telling can of course cause of a lot of discomfort to the powers that

---

38. Charles Ringma, "Liberation Theologians Speak to Evangelicals: A Theology and Praxis of Serving the Poor," in *The Church and Poverty in Asia*, ed. Lee Wanak, 7–53 (Mandaluyong City: OMF Literature, 2008), 19.

39. Ringma, "Liberation Theologians Speak," 19.

40. Patty Sison-Arroyo, "Seek Justice: A Witness of Courage in a Suffering World." In *The Church and Poverty in Asia*, ed. Lee Wanak (Mandaluyong City: OMF Literature, 2008), 163.

41. Villanueva, "Why the Church Needs," 77.

be and those in alliance with them. This is why truth-telling is fundamentally antithetical to toxic Christianity, which ultimately serves the interests of the powerful. When Christian communities engage in truth-telling, they in effect engage the wrongdoers to "confess their guilt, express contrition, do their penance, and make amends."[42]

It is for this reason that truth-telling cannot be the work of discrete individuals. It is only through solidarity that the people of God can effectively speak truth to power. As Aldrin Peñamora reminds us, participating in the Lord's Supper is not only a symbolic rite.[43] It calls on the people of God to include in our fellowships the marginalized and bear in mind our possible complicity in their exclusion. Calling for "responsible remembrance," Peñamora asks fellow Christians to be ready "to confront memories of oppressions and be responsible for whatever may have been our part" in those moments.[44]

Concretely, this means re-imagining the practices in our congregations, as to whether they exclude marginalized sectors. Congregations, for example, may consider creating spaces where members who come from different socio-economic backgrounds can interact with one another and reflect on what God might be calling them to do to confront inequality and oppression. These activities may take place in the context of a small group, but also through community exposures. If solidarity is affinity with other people and their struggles, then the only way for it to happen is through direct encounter. In these encounters, members must also consider how leadership and governance are deeply implicated in the sufferings of others. As a result, these fellowships can conclude that charity work is not enough and take part in long-term community engagements. They may also get involved in advocacy work with other secular and faith-based organizations.

There are no shortcuts. The process of transforming churches in this manner takes a while and may encounter resistance. But ministers may find hope that as Christians learn from one another, they may arrive at a wider view of the kingdom of God.[45]

In effect, truth-telling and solidarity are inseparable from each other. In a society where injustices have been coddled by feel-good Christianity, both

---

42. Pope, "The Convergence," 834.

43. Aldrin M. Peñamora, "Eucharistic Justice: A Christ-Centered Response to the Bangsamoro Question in the Philippines," *AJPS* 19, no. 1 (2016): 31.

44. Peñamora, "Eucharistic Justice," 43.

45. David W. Swanson, *Rediscipling the White Church: From Cheap Diversity to True Solidarity* (Downers Grove: InterVarsity Press, 2020), 65.

are urgent. Both call for a change in the way evangelicals profess the relevance of their faith to people. Both demand a re-imagining of the practice of faith in the public sphere. Both demand intense soul-searching. And both demand an honest recognition of the seductions that have captivated our own people.

Bibliography

Bauman, Zygmunt, and Tim May. *Thinking Sociologically*. 2nd ed. Oxford: Blackwell, 2014.

Bautista, Victor Felipe. "The Pervert's Guide to Historical Revisionism: Traversing the Marcos Fantasy." *Philippine Studies: Historical & Ethnographic Viewpoints* (2018): 273–300.

Benedicto, Bobby. "The Place of the Dead, the Time of Dictatorship: Nostalgia, Sovereignty, and the Corpse of Ferdinand Marcos." *Environment and Planning D: Society and Space* 39, no. 4 (2021): 722–39.

Berteau, Glen. *Christianity Lite*. Lake Mary: Passio, 2013.

Borja, Anthony Lawrence. "The Rise of Anti-Politics: 'Unity' in Curbing Dissent in the Philippines." *Rappler*, 27 September 2022. https://www.rappler.com/voices/imho/opinion-rise-anti-politics-unity-curbing-dissent-philippines/.

Britt, Christopher, and Eduardo Subirats. *Intellectuals in the Society of Spectacle*. Cham: Springer, 2021.

Cornelio, Jayeel Serrano. "Religion and Civic Engagement: The Case of Iglesia ni Cristo in the Philippines." *Religion, State & Society* 45, no. 1 (2017): 23–38.

———. "To Christians Voting for Marcos." *Rappler*, 17 October 2021. https://www.rappler.com/nation/elections/opinion-message-to-christians-voting-bongbong-marcos-elections/.

———. "Marcos, Christianity, and the Seduction of Authoritarian Nostalgia." In *The Marcos Era: A Reader*, edited by Leia Castañeda Anastacio and Patricio Abinales, 335–52. Quezon City: Ateneo de Manila University Press, 2022.

Cornelio, Jayeel, and Robbin Dagle. "Weaponising Religious Freedom: Same-sex marriage and Gender Equality in the Philippines." *Religion & Human Rights* 14, no. 2 (2019): 65–94.

Cornelio, Jayeel, and Erron Medina. "The Prosperity Ethic: The Rise of the New Prosperity Gospel." In *Routledge International Handbook of Religion in Global Society*, edited by Jayeel Cornelio, François Gauthier, Tuomas Martikainen, and Linda Woodhead, 65–76. London: Routledge, 2020.

Cruz, Joseph Nathan. "A Spectacle of Worship: Technology, Modernity and the Rise of the Christian Megachurch." In *Mediating Piety*, edited by Francis Khek Gee Lim, 113–38. Leiden: Brill, 2010.

Curato, Nicole. "The Philippines: Erasing History through Good Vibes and Toxic Positivity." *HBS Southeast Asia*. 28 March 2022. https://th.boell.org/en/2022/03/28/philippines-good-vibes-toxic-positivity.

Fiddes, Paul S. "Restorative Justice and the Theological Dynamic of Forgiveness." *Oxford Journal of Law and Religion* 5, no. 1 (2016): 54–65.

Gomez, Carla. "Marcos: Message of Unity, Cooperation Pushed Me to Top of Surveys." *Philippine Daily Inquirer*. 13 April 2016. https://newsinfo.inquirer.net/779255/marcos-message-of-unity-cooperation-pushed-me-to-top-of-surveys#ixzz7RdbSnNXc.

Hanson, Paul. "The Bible and Public Theology." In *A Companion to Public Theology*, edited by Sebastian Kim and Katie Day, 23–39. Leiden: Brill, 2017.

Johnson, Russell P. "The Gospel and the Prosperity Gospel: Joel Osteen's Your Best Life Now Reconsidered." *Theology* 121, no. 1 (2018): 28–34.

Maggay, Melba P. "By Way of a Prologue." In *Dark Days of Authoritarianism: To Be in History*, edited by Melba P. Maggay, xi–xix. Carlisle: Langham Global Library, 2019.

Medina, Erron, and Jayeel Cornelio. "The Prosperity Ethic: Neoliberal Christianity and the Rise of the New Prosperity Gospel in the Philippines." *Pneuma* 43, no. 1 (2021): 72–93.

Monde, Jeel. "Hayden Kho Shares Christian Traits During Election Campaign." *Philippine News*. 12 February 2022. https://philnews.ph/2022/02/12/hayden-kho-shares-christian-traits-during-election-campaign/.

NEDA. "About Ambisyon Natin 2040." *Ambisyon Natin 2040*. http://2040.neda.gov.ph/about-ambisyon-natin-2040/.

OMF Literature. *Passion & Power: Pulpit Messages from the Filipino Heart*. Mandaluyong City: OMF Literature, 2017.

Ong, Jonathan Corpus, and Jason Vincent A. Cabañes. "Architects of Networked Disinformation: Behind the Scenes of Troll Accounts and Fake News Production in the Philippines" (2018).

Patag, Kristine Joy. "It's 'Unity, Unity, Unity' for Uniteam's Presidential Bet Marcos." *Philippine Star*. 9 February 2022. https://www.philstar.com/headlines/2022/02/09/2159653/its-unity-unity-unity-uniteams-presidential-bet-marcos.

Peñamora, Aldrin M. "Eucharistic Justice: A Christ-Centered Response to the Bangsamoro Question in the Philippines." *AJPS* 19, no. 1 (2016): 31–44.

Pope, Stephen J. "The Convergence of Forgiveness and Justice: Lessons from El Salvador." *Theological Studies* 64, no. 4 (2003): 812–35.

Ringma, Charles. "Liberation Theologians Speak to Evangelicals: A Theology and Praxis of Serving the Poor." In *The Church and Poverty in Asia*, edited by Lee Wanak, 7–53. Mandaluyong City: OMF Literature, 2008.

Sadje, Hadje. "What Does Theology Do, Actually? (Un)Doing Filipino Theologies." In *What Does Theology Do, Actually? Observing Theology and the Transcultural*, edited by Matthew Robinson and Inja Inders, 45–58. Leipzig: EVA, 2020.

Sison-Arroyo, Patty. "Seek Justice: A Witness of Courage in a Suffering World." In *The Church and Poverty in Asia*, edited by Lee Wanak, 163–70. Mandaluyong City: OMF Literature, 2008.

Staub, Dick. *The Culturally Savvy Christian: A Manifesto for Deepening Faith and Enriching Popular Culture in an Age of Christianity-Lite*. San Francisco: John Wiley & Sons, 2007.

Swanson, David W. *Rediscipling the White Church: From Cheap Diversity to True Solidarity*. Downers Grove: InterVarsity Press, 2020.

Tomalin, Emma. *Religions and Development*. London: Routledge, 2013.

Toni Gonzaga Studio. "The Greatest Lesson Bongbong Marcos Learned From His Father." YouTube. 13 September 2021. https://www.youtube.com/watch?v=1EwMAiqLUhM&t=930s.

Villanueva, Federico. "Why the Church Needs to Learn How to Complain and Not Just 'Trust and Obey.'" In *Faith and Bayan: Filipino Evangelical Responses to Contemporary Social Issues*, edited by Lorenzo Bautista, Aldrin Peñamora, and Federico Villanueva. Carlisle: Langham Global Library, 2022.

Webb, Adele. "Why Are the Middle Class Misbehaving?: Exploring Democratic Ambivalence and Authoritarian Nostalgia." *Philippine Sociological Review* 65, no. Special Issue: Imagine Democracies: 77–102, 2017.

11

Breaking Bread, Breaking Spiritual-Political Dichotomy

Eucharist, Forgiveness, and the Marcos Legacy

Aldrin M. Peñamora

Introduction

What has the Eucharist or Lord's Supper[1] to do with Philippine political realities? What has the Upper Room[2] in Jerusalem to do with Malacañang Palace?[3] The connection of the Eucharist to social and political realities has been frequently overlooked. Sadly, it is often considered a private and spiritual ritual between us Christian believers and God, which implies "withdrawal from the community's awareness, even to the point where we often hid our faces from each other."[4] Said from another perspective, the Lord's Supper is usually understood as inculcating only spiritual virtues that do not have relevance for Christian life in the *polis*.

---

1. The Lord's Supper and the Eucharist are two terms, among others, that are used in referring to the rite Jesus instituted during the Last Supper. The biblical term "Lord's Supper" was used by the apostle Paul in 1 Cor 11:20 in the context of a proper meal. "Eucharist," on the other hand, comes from the Greek expression *eucharistia* ("thanksgiving") and was used as a blessing that forms part of a meal where God is praised for his goodness (Cf. 1 Cor 10:30). I will primarily use the terms "Lord's Supper" and the "Eucharist" interchangeably in this paper.

2. Mark's and Luke's gospels tell us that the Last Supper was held in an upper room (Mark 14:15; Luke 22:12).

3. This is the official residence and office of the president of the Philippines.

4. Megan McKenna, *Rites of Justice: The Sacraments and Liturgy as Ethical Imperatives* (Maryknoll: Orbis, 1997), 111.

This chapter argues against such a notion of the Lord's Supper wherein the spiritual and the political are set in opposition to each other. Rather, this chapter seeks to illuminate how the Lord's Supper is inherently a social-political practice. When understood within its proper biblical-theological moorings it will be seen, as Brent Peterson points out, as the "most political act of the church."[5] Hence, it cultivates political virtues, or theologically grounded moral dispositions for the flourishing of the political community. Such is the virtue of *forgiveness*, which will be discussed in relation to how the dark legacy of the former Philippine dictator and president, Ferdinand Marcos Sr. is being reconstructed in a positive light through the claims of his son, the 17th and current president of the Philippines, Ferdinand "Bongbong" Marcos Jr.

Virtues and Philippine Politics

Politicians in the Philippines understand the public and political nature of virtues and use them often in political slogans to promote the values they stand for. For instance, business tycoon and former senator Manny Villar used "*Sipag at Tiyaga*" (Diligence and Perseverance) to highlight the virtues' importance in ending the nation's poverty. During the 2022 presidential elections, former vice-president Leni Robredo campaigned under the slogan "*Gobyernong Tapat, Angat Buhay Lahat*" (Honest Government, A Better Life for All), pointing to how honesty in political governance results in national flourishing. Perhaps one of the most compelling uses of virtues in Philippine politics was from the former president, Rodrigo Roa Duterte, the country's 16th president. In 2016 his campaign tagline was "*Tapang at Malasakit*" (Courage or Fearlessness and Compassion), a powerful slogan that struck a chord among the Filipino masses. It was ominously paired with another political mantra, "Change is Coming."[6] In light of his flagship program, the "War on Drugs" that aimed to put an end to the drug trade in the country through a, "*Tapang and Malasakit*" was implemented without fear – whether of law, man, or God. By August 2018, just a little more than two years after taking his oath of office as president, the war on drugs had already yielded a death toll of as high as twenty-seven thousand, according to human rights organizations, which included killings

---

5. Brent Peterson, "Eucharist: The Church's Political Response to Suffering and Vocational Empowerment to Suffering Love." *Wesleyan Theological Journal* 43, no. 1 (September 2008): 148.

6. Vicente L. Rafael, *The Sovereign Trickster: Death and Laughter in the Age of Duterte* (London: Duke University, 2022), 31.

through "EJK" (extra-judicial killing) or killings outside the law or official police operations.[7]

President Duterte's war certainly brought "change" to the Philippine nation, a change that led not only to thousands of brutal killings but also to a change in the Filipino's value system. As the Filipino-American historian and anthropologist Vicente L. Rafael asked, "But *tapang* – courage – against whom? Compassion for whom?"[8] In other words, were *tapang* and *malasakit* in the war on drugs truly virtues, or were they perhaps evil vices masquerading as virtues?[9] Here we need to be reminded of the negative side of political slogans, that they "generalize the idea in question, typically with the intent to evoke persuasive emotion from the listener, they encourage that a blind eye be turned towards the facts surrounding the issue."[10] Turn a blind eye many Filipinos did, and have continued doing.

Oppression and Moral Dichotomy

While many Filipino politicians have become adept in using virtue-language in their campaigns that connect the private and political spheres, still, this relationship has often been obscured and understood in terms of a private-public dichotomy. One can thus be a moral person in private while *at the same time* apathetic or supportive of oppressive and even evil political policies. Such dichotomy was exemplified by German participation in the Holocaust. In her essay "Organized Guilt and Collective Responsibility," Hannah Arendt points out how Germany's degradation between the two World Wars led the average German *paterfamilias* to myopically value the security of his family and private domain to the point of driving the private-public dichotomy extremely apart; so "when his occupation forces him to murder people, he does not regard himself as a murderer because he has not done it out of inclination but in his professional capacity."[11] This occurred, Arendt remarks, because Germany

---

7. Rappler.com, "In Numbers: The Philippines' 'war on drugs,'" 13 September 2016, updated, https://www.rappler.com/newsbreak/iq/145814-numbers-statistics-philippines-war-drugs/.

8. Rafael, *The Sovereign Trickster*, 61.

9. See Aldrin M. Peñamora, "Their Blood Cries Out from the Ground: An Ethic of *Malasakit* and the 'War on Drugs,'" in *Faith and Bayan: Evangelical Christian Engagement in the Philippine Context* (Carlisle: Langham Global Library, 2002), 115–31.

10. Newsome, "The Use of Slogans in Philippine Rhetoric": 23.

11. Hannah Arendt, "Organized Guilt and Universal Responsibility," in *The Portable Hannah Arendt*, ed. Peter Baehr (New York: Penguin Books, 2000), 152, 154.

failed to adequately address the dichotomy; as she says insightfully, "behind the facade of proclaimed and propagandized national virtues, such as 'love of the Fatherland,' 'German courage,' 'German loyalty,' etc., there lurked corresponding real national vices."[12] In a similar manner, the US civil rights movement leader, James A. Joseph spoke of white churches in Alabama during the 1960s which supported white supremacists in public office and their racial doctrines, while considering themselves moral people in the private realm.[13]

Mary Wollstonecraft who promoted women's rights in the 18th century rejected such a private-public bifurcation of morality based on a person's gender. In this arrangement, women's nature and virtues are seen to be appropriate only in the confines of the household, while the nature and virtues of men make them fit for public life. For Wollstonecraft, private and public are "mutually creating and reinforcing. . . . Private virtue is the foundation of public virtue, but public virtue is also a condition for private virtue."[14] As such, she saw women as not only suitable but just as necessary as men for public life.

Centuries earlier, the Greek philosopher Aristotle propounded such an integrated notion of the private-and-political nature of virtues (*arête*), which he defines as permanent dispositions of character acquired through habituation for the sake of living well (*eudaimonia*).[15] Virtues for Aristotle are inherently political, comprising the chief end of political activities. In the *Nicomachean Ethics*, he states: "The end of political expertise is best, and this expertise is dedicated above all to making the citizens be of a certain quality, i.e. good . . . the true political expert will have worked at excellence more than anything; for what he wants is to make the members of the citizen-body good, and obedient to the laws."[16] In this arrangement, while the ends (*telos*) of the individual are important, such ends are however only attainable through the political community which gives it prior importance. Thus, Aristotle says at the very outset of *Ethics*:

---

12. Arendt, "Organized Guilt," 153.

13. James A. Joseph, *Saved for a Purpose: A Journey from Private Virtues to Public Values* (Durham: Duke University Press, 2015), 30.

14. Virginia Sapiro, *A Vindication of Political Virtue: The Political Theory of Mary Wollstonecraft* (Chicago: University of Chicago, 1992), 180. It was pointed out that during the Enlightenment period, women were conceived to have a different but complementary constitution compared to men; women are more practical, emotional and passionate, while men are more rational, which is the precondition for public affairs. Genevieve Lloyd, *The Man of Reason: "Male" and "Female" in Western Philosophy* (Minneapolis: University of Minnesota Press, 1984), 74–85.

15. Aristotle, *Nicomachean Ethics*, I.2, I.10, II.1.

16. Aristotle, *Nicomachean Ethics*, I.9, I.13.

For even if the good is the same for a single person and for a city, the good of the city is a greater and more complete thing both to achieve and to preserve; for while to do so for one person on his own is satisfactory enough, to do it for a nation or for cities is finer and more godlike.[17]

Both Wollstonecraft and Aristotle therefore hold that individual virtues and flourishing are entwined with the collective. For the former, the collective is represented by the government, and for the latter by the *polis*. The end of government, says Wollstonecraft, is to pursue equality and destroy inequalities by protecting the weak;[18] for Aristotle, the *polis* is the citizen's natural setting for the cultivation of virtues that happens not simply by living in the *polis*, but more importantly by participating in its governance.[19]

Certainly, an integrated perspective of the private and public coheres with the biblical witness, as will be shown in our discussion about the Lord's Supper. Such a perspective points to a continuity between the two domains,[20] which creates the space for individual Christians and for the church to prophetically engage society and the powers that be. In contrast, a dichotomized morality leads to the abnegation of Christian responsibility toward one's neighbors and the broader community, which often has deadly consequences. As Tom Gregg remarks: "Political engagement is necessary for the church truly to be the church. This means that simple binary thinking about the secular and the sacred, a religious realm and a political realm, requires challenging . . . The question is not whether the church should be political, but what the wise way is in which the church should be political."[21]

---

17. Aristotle, *Nicomachean Ethics*, I.2. See also *Politics* I.2.

18. Sapiro, *A Vindication of Political Virtue*, 182.

19. Edward Halper, "Aristotle's Political Virtues," *The Paideia Project On-Line: Proceedings of the Twentieth World Congress of Philosophy*; e-publication, accessed 15 September 2023, https://www.bu.edu/wcp/Papers/Anci/AnciHal2.htm. Governance of the *polis* does not only refer to rulers like a monarch, but also to the manifold tasks of citizens. See Aristotle's *Politics* III.4 where he compares the different governing tasks of citizens to sailors who have various roles in a ship but having a common object.

20. See Peter Elbow, "The Use of Binary Thinking," *Journal of Advanced Composition*, 13, no. 1 (1993): 51–54.

21. Tom Greggs, *Theology against Religion: Constructive Theologies with Bonhoeffer and Barth* (New York: T&T Clark, 2011), 151.

A House Divided

Generally, like in other parts of the globe, evangelical Christians in the Philippines often demonstrate a dualistic view that cuts-off the private from the public, the sacred from the secular. This is not to disregard variations in doctrines, practices, trainings and approaches to social-political issues which can be readily discerned even among members of the main evangelical umbrella organization in the country, the Philippine Council of Evangelical Churches (PCEC).[22] While there have been times when evangelicals took to the streets to address a particular political concern, for instance in 2018 when an estimated thirty thousand believers publicly opposed the passage of the SOGIE bill,[23] such public demonstration is few and far between. Jayeel Cornelio and Ia Marañon's research on the responses of some church leaders and megachurch pastors to the "War on Drugs" points to the more common spiritual, quietist, and non-confrontational approach among Filipino evangelicals that often imply "submission to the governing authorities."[24] Sadly, on this particular concern, only a pocket out of the entire Filipino populace expressed public outrage to the brutal killings of drug personalities.[25] It is hard to recall the last time the Filipino people have been so much united in supporting, explicitly or implicitly, so great an evil.

The Filipino evangelical response to the "War on Drugs" of course did not emerge from a vacuum. Various resources have been embedded and cultivated in the Christian tradition that give justification to a spiritualized, bifurcated, and privatized ethical response. Speaking about evangelicalism in America that resonates in the Philippine context, Stephen Hart remarks that "When contemporary evangelicals are privatistic . . . they are drawing on deeply traditional elements of their heritage."[26] Among the Christian views that have often

---

22. PCEC is a network of evangelical organizations, with fifty-five thousand member-churches. See https://pcec.org.ph/.

23. Senate of the Philippines, 7 March 2018; https://legacy.senate.gov.ph/photo_release/2018/0307_04.asp. SOGIE stands for sexual orientation, gender identification and expression. The bill aims to prohibit discrimination against members of the LGBTQ, but evangelicals believe that the bill leads to discrimination against the religious community.

24. Jayeel Cornelio and Ia Marañon, "A 'Righteous Intervention': Megachurch Christianity and Duterte's War on Drugs in the Philippines," *International Journal of Asian Christianity* 2 (2019): 226–27; Jayeel Cornelio and Erron Medina, "Christianity and Duterte's War on Drugs in the Philippines," *Politics, Religion & Ideology* 20, no. 2 (2019): 151–69.

25. As cited by Cornelio and Marañon in "Righteous Intervention": 214, a 2017 Pulse Asia Survey showed that 88 percent of the Filipino people supported the drug war campaign, even as 73 percent believed extrajudicial killings were being committed.

26. Stephen Hart, "Privatization in American Religion and Society," *Sociological Analysis* 47, no. 4 (1987): 323.

been interpreted – many times erringly – as promoting a privatized form of Christianity are: Luther's doctrine of the "Two Kingdoms," which separates a private Christian morality ruled by love from a non-Christian public morality ruled by force;[27] the idea that religion is an internalized matter; a dichotomy between spiritual and material questions; and a voluntarism that emphasizes direct personal relationship and response to God.[28] While faith and worship have private dimensions necessary and beneficial to the believer, a privatized form of Christianity has a greater corrosive tendency to the individual and society. As Hart further points out, privatization leads to the impoverishment of the Christian life as it makes believers more self-centered and less able to articulate a public ethic.[29]

For many Filipino evangelicals, such dualistic morality has biblical basis. For instance, in the volume *Faith and Bayan*, Christopher Sabanal calls for a more careful and nuanced examination of biblical passages about the end-times based on his incisive observation that a commonly held evangelical posture toward political issues is disentanglement or apathy due to the notion that only Christ's *parousia* can solve all the world's ills.[30] In a similar manner, the Lord's Supper is often practiced without any reference to its social-political dimension or relevance, therefore reinforcing a non-public and self-centered ethic. A more robust understanding of this sacred meal is certainly needed.

The Political and Subversive Supper

Notwithstanding theological and liturgical variations, the main Christian traditions have consistently upheld the centrality of the Eucharist. Indeed, during the Protestant Reformation, this ordinance was so important and politically relevant that at the Marburg Colloquy, the formation of the urgently needed pan-Protestant political alliance that will fight the Roman Catholic powers,

---

27. See Alastair E. McGrath, *Reformation Thought: An Introduction*, 4th ed. (Oxford: Wiley-Blackwell, 2012), 211–12. William J. Wright points out, however, that Luther's use of the concept was not political. The consequences of misunderstanding the doctrine, such as by the Nazis, must not therefore be ascribed to the thoughts of the Reformer. See chapters 1 and 4 of William J. Wright's *Martin Luther's Understanding of God's Two Kingdoms* (Grand Rapids: Baker, 2010).

28. Hart, "Privatization in American Religion and Society," 321–25.

29. Hart, "Privatization," 332–33.

30. Christopher D. Sabanal, "'Your Kingdome Come, Your Will Be Done': Disclosing the Ethics of the New Testament's Parousia," in *Faith and Bayan*, 133–34. See also Aldrin M. Peñamora, "Asia and God's Cruciform and Eschatological Reign," chapter 6 in *All Things New: Eschatology in the Majority World*, eds. Gene L. Green, Stephen T. Pardue and K. K. Yeo (Carlisle: Langham Global Library, 2019).

depended on whether or not Martin Luther and Ulrich Zwingli would agree on their views about the Lord's Supper. More recently, the significance of this ordinance was underlined by the Vatican II document *Lumen Gentium* (Light of the Nations) where Pope Paul VI splendidly described the Eucharist as "the fount and apex of the whole Christian life."[31]

It is however lamentable how the discussions and practice of the Supper have developed to a point that it has often led to abstraction and social irrelevance. As Markus Barth says, in partaking of the Supper,

> the impression is created that it is only individual salvation and personal satisfaction that are sought . . . This salvation and satisfaction are so much restricted to the soul or to a life after death that little or no attention is paid to the body, to the present plight and needs of human society, especially to the people who exist in appalling poverty, and to the many suffering creatures all over the world.[32]

Not only has the Lord's Supper been understood as cultivating an ethic of indifference toward the poor, the suffering, and those who are outside the church, but for many believers with disabilities, it has also become a "ritual of exclusion and degradation."[33] For oftentimes, they are not able to partake of the elements with dignity; they encounter architectural barriers and experience being at the receiving end of disrespectful speech and bodily gestures from church members, which make the Supper for them a humiliating remembrance of their broken bodies.[34]

Apathy and exclusionary practices toward the poor, the oppressed and differently abled are not inherent to the Eucharist. But if we are to partake of this sacred meal in a way that is faithful to Jesus's remembrance (11:24, 25), then *at the table we first need to recognize its vision for justice and inclusion,* so that the Eucharist is not only for those that society deems "worthy," but also for the unworthy, which we all are.[35] The abovementioned shortcomings in celebrating the Eucharist show us the need to give serious attention not only to its outward

---

31. Second Vatican Council, *Lumen Gentium* (A Light to the Gentiles), 2, 11.

32. Markus Barth, *Rediscovering the Lord's Supper: Communion with Israel, with Christ, and Among the Guests* (Eugene: Wipf and Stock Publishers, 1988), 1–2.

33. Nancy L. Eiesland, *The Disabled God: Toward a Liberatory Theology of Disability* (Nashville: Abingdon Press, 1994), 113.

34. Eiesland, *The Disabled God*, 113.

35. Eiesland, 114; Anne Primavesi and Jennifer Henderson, *Our God Has No Favorites: A Liberation Theology of the Eucharist* (San Jose: Resource Publications, 1989), 35.

performance, but more importantly to what as an ecclesial practice the Lord's Supper means and cultivates, especially in relation to the oft-neglected other-centered and political virtues. As Lee Yearley reminds us, "If we are to thrive, or perhaps even survive, we must develop those virtues that will enable us to understand, judge, and deal with ideals of human flourishing that confront us but appear to differ markedly from our own."[36] Two interrelated biblical meal practices can help us toward understanding the public and political character of the Lord's Supper – *the Passover* and *the Lord's Supper at Corinth*.

As one of Israel's major festivals, the Passover celebrates God's miraculous and liberating acts during the exodus when the early Hebrews were set free from being slaves and a "non-people" under Egyptian oppression, to become God's people that freely worship God (Exod 4:22; 12–13). Indeed, it was through God's mighty acts that Israel's identity was formed as a holy and priestly nation, and as a new political community under the kingdom of God (Exod 19).[37] In this foundational event can be seen how worship and politics are closely interwoven.

Although there were times in Israel's history that its celebration was neglected,[38] the Passover remained an enduring source of an alternative and transformative national vision for Israel. Especially when Israel was threatened or was under foreign domination, the Passover was celebrated with political overtones, such as in king Josiah's time (2 Kgs 23:21–23), when its reinstitution symbolized resistance against Assyrian power,[39] and in Jesus's "triumphal entry" in Jerusalem (Matt 21:1–9; Mark 11:1–10; Luke 19:28–40; John 12:12–19) around the time of the Passover, an act that at the very least had indirect politi-

---

36. Lee H. Yearley, *Mencius and Aquinas: Theories of Virtue and Conceptions of Courage* (New York: State University of New York Press, 1990), 2.

37. R. Alan Streett, *Subversive Meals: An Analysis of the Lord's Supper under Roman Domination during the First Century* (Cambridge: James Clarke & Co., 2016), 59.

38. Barth, *Rediscovering the Lord's Supper*, 9. See also Streett, *Subversive Meals*. In chapter 3 he traces the practice of the Passover in Israel's history.

39. Douglas E. Oakman, *Jesus and the Peasants* (Eugene: Cascades, 2008), 273. See Gillian Feeley-Harnik, *The Lord's Table: Eucharist and Passover in Early Christianity* (Philadelphia: University of Philadelphia Press, 1981), 135–37; Walter Brueggemann, *Hope Restored: Biblical Imagination Against Empire* (Louisville: Westminster John Knox Press, 2023), chapter 3; e-book, https://ereader.perlego.com/1/book/4142475/13.

cal implications.[40] As Joachim Jeremias noted, it was during the Passover feast that political revolts against Rome repeatedly occurred.[41]

A crucial feature of the Passover that made it politically subversive and a source for Jewish political resistance was its conviction about the temporality of all earthly kingdoms over which, as exemplified in the exodus, God's kingdom will ultimately triumph. This commemoration-proclamation runs through the entire biblical narrative and was alluded to by Jesus during the Last Supper, when he spoke of drinking from the fruit of the vine again when the "kingdom of God comes" (Luke 22:18; Matt 26:29; Mark 14:25; 1 Cor 11:26). Recognizing this indelible link between the Passover and the gospel message, Paul McGlasson says incisively, "the gospel is political," pointing to God's opposition against all tyrannical powers for which reason he said that the "church cannot stand idly by. . . . To embrace the gospel – as instructed by the Passover – is to take a stand against oppression, and for the full civil rights and dignity of everyone."[42]

With its Passover origins, the Lord's Supper thus similarly rejects all forms of oppression and serves as an open invitation for upholding every person's God-given dignity. Such openness contrasts with the accent of the Passover commemoration, which is through strengthening traditional kinship bonds. Hence, the Passover is celebrated among family members while the Lord's Supper transforms and extends the concept of family, in some ways even breaking it apart, so those outside Israel's ethnic and national boundaries can be included.[43] As a paradigmatic ecclesial practice of inclusion, it therefore has crucial social-political implications. R. Alan Streett thus calls it a "subversive meal," and Andrea Bieler and Luise Schottroff describe it as "a counter-liturgy to violent state politics that deny the dignity of the human body."[44] A key pas-

---

40. Oakman, *Jesus and the Peasants*, 273; Richard A. Horsley, *Jesus and the Powers: Conflict, Covenant, and the Hope of the Poor* (Minneapolis: Fortress Press, 2011), 169. Horsley commented that Jesus's entry was an "act of political confrontation with at least a veneer of anonymity and disguise." See also Scot McKnight, "Extra Ecclesiam Nullum Regnum: The Politics of Jesus," in *Christian Political Witness*, eds. George Kalantzis and Gregory W. Lee (Downers Grove: IVP Academic, 2014), 71–72. An apolitical view of the entry is proposed by Brent Rogers Kinman in "The 'A-Triumphal Entry' (Luke 19:28–49): Historical Backgrounds, Theological Motifs, and the Purpose of Luke," *Tyndale* 45, no. 1 (1994): 189–93.

41. Joachim Jeremias, *The Eucharistic Words of Jesus* (London: SCM Press, 1966), 207.

42. Paul C. McGlasson, *Theological Exegesis of Scripture, Vol. 1: The Pentateuch* (Eugene: Cascade Books, 2022), 140.

43. Feeley-Harnik, *The Lord's Table*, 138, 144–45. Jesus thus celebrated his final Passover meal or the Last Supper with his disciples and not with his immediate family.

44. Andrea Bieler and Luise Schottroff, *The Eucharist: Bodies, Bread, and Resurrection* (Minneapolis: Fortress, 2007), 13; quoted in R. Alan Streett, *Subversive Meals*, 208.

sage among other biblical texts that brings out this social-political dimension is 1 Corinthians 11:17–33, wherein Paul admonished the Corinthians for their unacceptable version of the Lord's Supper (1 Cor 11:20).

Paul's rejection of the Corinthian Supper was due to its elitist approach that led to the poor's exclusion from the table. As expressed by the Greek term *synerchesthai* ("come together," vv. 18, 20), their worship gathering was supposed to be one of genuine unity.[45] With the Eucharist probably prepared in the form of a Graeco-Roman *deipnon* (dinner) wherein the poor are not typically invited to the main dinner,[46] *synerchesthai* meant for the wealthy believers sharing their food with the underprivileged. Such sharing would demonstrate concern for the poor and affirm the equal dignity of the members of the church. However, the Corinthians coming together failed to express genuine fellowship or *koinonia*. As Paul pointed out, some of them got full and drunk, while others remained hungry (v. 21). Brian Brock and Bernd Wannenwetsch thus asked in light of the exclusionary practice of the Corinthian church, "Is their gathering a proper eucharistic celebration or a partial Eucharist, a pseudo-Eucharist, or perhaps even an anti-Eucharist?"[47] And as Richard Hays reflected, "The meal that should be the symbol and seal of their oneness has in fact become an occasion for some of them to shame others (11:21–22)."[48]

Clearly, the Corinthian church was following the oppressive customary norms of a typical Graeco-Roman society that promotes hierarchy, unjust economic distribution, and social exclusion. For Paul, a community shaped by the Lord's Supper should be marked by hospitality, sharing, inclusion, and sensitivity to the downtrodden;[49] values that are counter-cultural. Yoder's remark is on point that the "Eucharist, substantially and historically, functionally understood, is the paradigm for every other mode of inviting the outsider and the underdog to the table."[50]

---

45. Julie Marie Land, "Remember as Re-membering: The Eucharist, 1 Corinthians 11:17–34, and Profound Intellectual Disability," *Studia Liturgica* 50, no. 2 (2020): 154.

46. Peter Lampe, "The Eucharist: Identifying with Christ on the Cross," *Interpretation* 48, no. 1 (January 1994): 40.

47. Brian Brock and Bernd Wannenwetsch, *The Therapy of the Christian Body: A Theological Exposition of Paul's First Letter to the Corinthians*, Vol. 2 (Eugene: Cascade Books, 2018), 49.

48. Richard B. Hays, *First Corinthians, Interpretation: A Bible Commentary for Teaching and Preaching* (Louisville: John Knox Press, 1997), 193.

49. Tony Kelly, *The Bread of God: Nurturing a Eucharistic Imagination* (Liguori: Liguori, 2001), 23; Raymond F. Collins, *First Corinthians, Sacra Pagina Series*, Vol. 7, ed. Daniel J. Harrington (Collegeville: Liturgical Press, 1999), 438.

50. John Howard Yoder, *For the Nations: Essays Evangelical and Public* (Grand Rapids: Eerdmans, 1997), 32.

With these in mind that clearly show the Lord's Supper's social-political significance, we now turn our attention to the virtue of *forgiveness* as cultivated through this ordinance. We will look at how forgiveness, as a political virtue, could be deployed in relation to the dark legacy of the Marcos dictatorship.

Eucharist, Forgiveness, and a Revolution

As an ecclesial social practice the Lord's Supper, as mentioned above, aims toward the formation of Christian identity by fostering solidarity with the Lord, with our fellow believers, and with our neighbors. In other words, the meal at the Upper Room prepares Jesus's followers for life and having meals with others in the *polis*. On this other-centered dynamic of the Supper, Stanley Hauerwas says:

> Our eating with our Lord is not different from our learning to be his disciples, his holy people. . . . who have learned not to fear one another and thus are capable of love. We do not just go ahead with our meals or our lives, but we wait for one another, so we may learn to live in the presence of others.[51]

Living in the presence of so many different others is certainly a great opportunity for sharing and living out the good news. It is inevitable, however, that living with others necessitates having the capacity to forgive.

This was exemplified even among Jesus's inner core of disciples, attested in the earliest liturgical formula of the Lord's Supper in 1 Corinthians 11 that begins with the words, "The Lord Jesus, on the night *he was betrayed*, took bread" (v. 23, emphasis added).[52] Judas's betrayal (Luke 22:1–6); the disciples' argument on which of them is the greatest (Luke 22:24); Peter's looming denial (Matt 26:69–75) – it was in light of these situations that Jesus enacted the Last Supper, a fitting continuation of the subversive meals he shared with sinners, the poor and outcasts throughout his ministry. What made these meals unifying and even celebratory in light of the brokenness of the participants was the possibility and bestowal of *forgiveness*. As the Matthean account of the Last Supper emphasizes (26:28), Jesus's shed blood of the covenant is for the forgiveness of sins; through Christ the paschal lamb, the offer of forgiveness became a reality that paved the way for the broken and sinful to have communion with

---

51. Stanley Hauerwas, *The Hauerwas Reader*, eds. John Berkman and Michael Cartwright (Durham: Duke, 2001), 386.

52. William C. Spohn, *Go and Do Likewise: Jesus and Ethics* (New York: Continuum, 1999), 168.

God.⁵³ Jesus's meals thus "enacted the forgiveness of sins, the welcoming home of the exiled, lost sheep of the house of Israel."⁵⁴

One who had an incisive perception of the political character of forgiveness is Hannah Arendt, who locates its origin in Jesus Christ. According to Arendt, "The discoverer of the role of forgiveness in the realm of human affairs was Jesus of Nazareth. The fact that he made this discovery in a religious context and articulated it in religious language is no reason to take it any less seriously in a strictly secular sense."⁵⁵ Indeed, there are many who reject assigning an important place to forgiveness in politics; among other reasons it is deemed as sentimental, utopian, irrational, sectarian that favors the Christian tradition among other religions, and does not satisfy the demands of justice.⁵⁶

But for Arendt, political life (*bios politikos*) can at any given time go wrong, which could bring about a vicious cycle in human relationships that she calls the "predicament of irreversibility." Only forgiveness can release people from such a predicament. According to Arendt, "Without being forgiven, released from the consequences of what we have done, our capacity to act would ... be confined to one single deed from which we would never recover, we would remain the victims of its consequences forever."⁵⁷ Miroslav Volf says similarly how "forgiveness breaks the power of the remembered past ... and so makes the spiral of vengeance grind to a halt."⁵⁸ This is to say that forgiveness gives both perpetrator and victim a chance to start anew. Dealing with the nature of memory, Paul Ricoeur insightfully says, "Forgiveness is a sort of healing of memory ... Delivered from the weight of debt ... Forgiveness gives memory a future."⁵⁹

Back in 1999, the Jesuit priest Fr. John J. Carroll pointed out that forgiveness mainly applies "to those who acknowledge their offenses and ask pardon,

---

53. William Hendriksen's remark is on point, "Without the shedding of blood, there could be no covenant, and no relationship of friendship between God and his people." Hendriksen, *The Gospel of Mark*, New Testament Commentary (Edinburgh: Banner of Truth, 1981), 575.

54. Spohn, *Go and Do Likewise*, 168.

55. Hannah Arendt, *The Human Condition*, 2nd ed. (Chicago: University of Chicago Press, 1998), 238.

56. See P. E. Digeser, *Political Forgiveness* (Ithaca: Cornell University Press, 2001), 11–18.

57. Arendt, *The Human Condition*, 25, 236–37.

58. Miroslav Volf, *Exclusion and Embrace: A Theological Exploration of Identity, Otherness and Reconciliation* (Nashville: Abingdon Press, 1996), 121.

59. Paul Ricoeur, "Memory, Forgetfulness, and History," *Iyyun: The Jerusalem Philosophical Quarterly* 45 (July 1996): 24.

not to those who arrogantly deny that they have done any wrong."⁶⁰ Carroll was referring to the ousted former Philippine president and dictator, Ferdinand Marcos Sr. who never acknowledged any wrongdoing, much more ask for forgiveness. Perplexingly, just a few months after the celebrated 1986 EDSA People Power Revolution that ousted Marcos, a survey was conducted showing that the majority of the Filipino people did not want the exiled dictator to be punished despite amassing billions of US dollars in ill-gotten wealth and despite his regime's horrifying violations of human rights.⁶¹

By 2022, thirty-six years after the revolution, the Filipinos have voted the former dictator's son Ferdinand "Bongbong" Marcos Jr., also known as "BBM" as the country's 17th president. By this time Marcos the dictator is being rebranded as Marcos the hero, who in 2016 was interred at the *Libingan ng mga Bayani* (Heroes' Burial Grounds). Attempts had also been made – and are still being made – to paint the Marcos dictatorship as the country's "golden age."⁶² BBM contributes to this move to revise history by not acknowledging his father's crimes and consistently defending the Martial Law regime.⁶³ Instead of asking forgiveness, especially to the thousands of human rights victims of that era who are still living, BBM spoke of his willingness to forgive those who ousted his family through EDSA, if they should ever want it.⁶⁴ With BBM's landslide victory in the elections, one can say that the Filipino people have now granted political forgiveness to the Marcoses and have moved on, or away from, remembering the legacy of the dictatorship. Perhaps, Johann Baptist Metz is correct that we are now living in an "era of cultural amnesia," where a

---

60. John J. Carroll, "The Philippines: Forgiving or Forgetting?" *Public Policy Journal* 3, no. 2 (April–June 1999): 90.

61. Carroll, "Forgiving or Forgetting?": 90. During the Marcos dictatorship from 1972 until his ouster in 1986, it was estimated that seventy thousand people were detained, thirty-four thousand tortured, and more than three thousand were victims of extrajudicial killing. Chad De Guzman, "The Philippines Once Celebrated Marcos' Fall. Under His Son, Has the Country Moved On?" *Time,* 21 February 2023, https://time.com/6257017/philippines-bongbong-marcos-people-power-revolution/.

62. Kurt Dela Peña, "Marcos Martial Law: Golden Age for Corruption, Abuses," *Inquirer.Net,* 21 September 2021, https://newsinfo.inquirer.net/1490968/marcos-martial-law-golden-age-for-corruption-abuses.

63. See Ayee Macaraig, "Marcos on Dad's Regime: What Am I to Apologize for?" *Rappler,* 26 August 2015, https://www.rappler.com/nation/103772-bongbong-marcos-regime-no-apologies/.

64. Argyll Cyrus Geducos, "No Need to Forgive Those who Caused Family's Exile – Marcos," *Manila Bulletin,* 18 November 2023, https://mb.com.ph/2023/11/18/marcos-no-need-to-forgive-those-who-caused-family-s-exile.

people's vision of human happiness is grounded in the capacity to forget the painful memories of the past.[65]

If the Filipinos, or at least a significant part of the populace, have indeed forgiven and/or forgotten Marcos and his tyrannical legacy, as Christians it is imperative for us to examine if such forgiveness conforms to the shape of forgiveness that is cultivated through the central practice of the Lord's Supper.

Eucharistic Forgiveness and the Marcos Legacy

During a hearing in the Philippine Congress on the 51st anniversary of Marcos's Martial Law declaration which marked the beginning of his dictatorship, House Representative Edcel Lagman gave this emphatic remark: "There can be no forgiveness without remorse and repentance from the surviving martial law implementers, perpetrators, and beneficiaries."[66] This is, of course, problematic, for as mentioned earlier, BBM has an entirely opposite view of his father and the Martial Law regime. Armed with more than eleven thousand testimonials from Martial Law survivors, the executive director of the Human Rights Violations Victims' Memorial Commission, Carmelo Crisanto, therefore sounded a call – "This is a battle for memory that we're in."[67]

The distortion or obliteration of memory is what lies at the center of Miroslav Volf's concern for the importance of the *moral obligation to remember truthfully*, for justice is entwined with truthful remembrance especially in cases of gross human violations.[68] As Volf points out, "When perpetrators 'remember' untruthfully, their stories are a continuation of wrongful deeds in an altered form. They add the insult of misrepresentation to the injury of the original violation."[69] Memories are therefore, according to Metz, dangerous, specifically memory situated in the Eucharist wherein Christ's passion is united with his resurrection (*memoria passionis, mortis et resurrectionis Jesus Christi*). It is dangerous because the narratives of the victims of suffering in history are

---

65. Johann Baptist Metz, e-book, *Remembering and Resisting: The New Political Theology*, ed. John K. Downey (Eugene: Cascade Books, 2022), Chapter 4.

66. Gabriel Pabico Lalu, "Lagman on Martial Law: No Forgiveness without Remorse from Implementers," *Inquirer.Net*, 21 September 2023, https://newsinfo.inquirer.net/1835044/lagman-on-martial-law-no-forgiveness-without-remorse-from-implementers.

67. Quoted in Althea Manasan, "Filipino Survivors of Martial Law Still Haunted by Abuses 50 Years After Declaration," *CBC Radio*, 23 September 2022, https://www.cbc.ca/radio/thecurrent/survivors-martial-law-philippines-abuses-50-years-later-1.6592042.

68. Miroslav Volf, *The End of Memory: Remembering Rightly in a Violent Word* (Grand Rapids: Eerdmans, 2006), 51–52, 55.

69. Volf, *The End of Memory*, 56.

united with Jesus's passion narrative that engenders liberative impulses; and it is subversive because it announces "an active presence in history of God's interruptive act of salvation at the end of history, when God will rescue those whom history has destroyed and forgotten."[70]

Yet, a crucial element missing in Metz's *memoria passionis*, says Joas Adiprasetya, is the element of forgiveness, which is a central feature of the Lord's Supper. While Metz's conception of *memoria* is adequate in fighting injustice especially when crimes and truth are neglected or "forgotten," it falls short, however, in effecting the important goal of reconciliation. What is needed, Adiprasetya points out, is a "forgiving memory," or a memory that holds together both justice and forgiveness.[71]

In the Eucharist as we have seen, forgiveness and justice are given emphasis, and the truthfulness of events that have transpired is taken seriously. Contrarily, by intentionally distorting history and disregarding the immensity of the sufferings caused by his father's dictatorial regime, BBM has rejected justice and truthfulness, and placed himself in the position of not someone who can dispense forgiveness to others – as he mistakenly believes – but one who is in dire need of the people's forgiveness. BBM can take heed of Anthony Bash's insightful remark that forgiveness and justice start from one's self:

> wrongdoers who repent, who are contrite and remorseful, and who (when appropriate) offer reparation demonstrate that they themselves have judged their actions and sought to put right what they can. They stand (as it were) self-condemned, and their self-imposed sentence is to admit and acknowledge the wrong and do what they can to restore the *status quo ante*.[72]

But outside of forgiving one's self, forgiving is a *right* that belongs to the victims, not to the perpetrators. As a right, it is likened to a creditor who can choose not to collect a debt payment. In this sense, victims may choose to not forgive their oppressors, which is usually conditioned by the demands of rectificatory justice. As P. E. Digeser points out, forgiveness can only be

---

70. Joas Adiprasetya, "Johann Baptist Metz's Memoria Passionis and the Possibility of Political Forgiveness," *Political Theology* (2016): 6; quoting Gaspar Martinez, *Confronting the Mystery of God: Political, Liberation, and Public Theologies* (New York: Continuum, 2001): 66; https://www.tandfonline.com/doi/full/10.1080/1462317X.2015.1131800. See also Bruce T. Morrill, S. J., *Anamnesis as Dangerous Memory: Political and Liturgical Theology in Dialogue* (Collegeville: Liturgical Press, 2000), 30–40.

71. Adiprasetya, "Metz's Memoria Passionis: 7–8, 11

72. Anthony Bash, e-book, *Forgiveness: A Theology* (Eugene: Cascade Books, 2015), Chapter 14.

meaningful when understood against the backdrop of rectificatory justice, whether its demands are met or not.[73] To the victims of Martial Law and to the Filipino people who value the truths about the country's history, acknowledging what has actually transpired is the most basic debt that BBM owes them. Acknowledgment is of course an essential beginning that needs to be supplemented by remorseful and concrete acts toward restoring the situation of the victims. The absence of such steps, says Volf, "*would* result in the suspension of forgiveness," for one's genuine reception of forgiveness should lead to further acts of restoration.[74]

The absence of restorative steps for the victim, nonetheless, cannot annul the gift of forgiveness that victims are called to extend to oppressors on account of the unconditional forgiveness the crucified Jesus extended to undeserving human beings.[75] As the apostle Paul powerfully puts it, "But God demonstrates his own love for us in this: While we were still sinners, Christ died for us" (Rom 5:8). In other words, an equally vital aspect of eucharistic forgiveness that complements its demand for justice is its unconditional character as an *offer*. This corresponds to Volf's symbolic gesture of opening one's arms in the "drama of embrace," wherein through forgiveness a space is created in one's self that draws the perpetrator to accept the offer.[76] Thus, Jesus commands us, "Love your enemies and pray for those who persecute you" (Matt 5:44). This means that forgiveness can be offered even to the worst of sinners and oppressors, and despite their not asking for it. Jacques Derrida's remark on this point is incisive:

> If one is only prepared to forgive what appears forgivable, . . . then the very idea of forgiveness would disappear. If there is something to forgive, it would be . . . the worst, the unforgivable crime or harm. . . . *forgiveness forgives only the unforgivable*. . . . there is only forgiveness, if there is any, where there is the unforgivable.[77]

Bestowing unconditional forgiveness to unrepentant oppressors should not mean that the wrongs done are suddenly relegated to the dustbins of history, and that perpetrators need no longer be called to account. We must not make

---

73. Digeser, *Political Forgiveness*, 38.
74. Volf, *The End of Memory*, 121.
75. Volf, *The End of Memory*, 121.
76. Miroslav Volf, *Exclusion and Embrace: A Theological Exploration of Identity, Otherness, and Reconciliation* (Nashville: Abingdon, 1996), 140–42.
77. Jacques Derrida, *On Cosmopolitanism and Forgiveness*, trans. Mark Dooley and Michael Hughes (New York: Routledge, 2001), 32–33.

the serious mistake of reducing political forgiveness to amnesia or some form of political therapy of reconciliation.[78] In the face of unrepentant perpetrators, the cross serves as a forceful symbol of protest against unaddressed injustice in a similar way that Abel's blood cried out to God from the ground (Gen 4:10). But when such cries are left unheeded, or when a community fails to oppose serious violations of their deepest values, there is a "grave danger that the community will no longer know what it stands for."[79] In other words, if Filipino evangelicals would not reject BBM's gross distortion of our nation's history as to the evil of the Marcos dictatorship, just as a great number of evangelicals have failed to protest the killings under President Duterte's "War on Drugs," then as evangelical Christians we will be, or perhaps we already are, in grave danger of not knowing our very identity and what it means to be followers of the crucified Christ.

Concluding Remarks

To many evangelical Christians in the Philippines, political and spiritual matters belong to separate realms, so that it is not the church's business to meddle into politics. While there is certainly a danger in being overly political, being apolitical is equally a great – if not a greater – danger to the church. More than sixty years ago the Jesuit priest Jaime C. Bulatao already discerned this phenomenon of bifurcated faith and morality and called it "split-level Christianity." One reason for this bifurcation, in my view, is the misunderstanding of the Eucharist or Lord's Supper, which as a central Christian practice powerfully shapes how Christians ought to act both in the private and public spheres.

Sadly, the Lord's Supper has often been understood mainly in terms of its private significance, of what God has done for the individual on the cross that leads to spiritual salvation. This focus on the spiritual, personal and individual dimensions of the ordinance has neglected the social and political dimensions that are also vital for the nourishment of the body of Christ. Hence, the virtue of forgiveness as cultivated in the Eucharist is usually understood spiritually. But, as Brueggemann remarks, forgiveness is also political pointing to "a redress of power in which the weak and the strong, the least and the greatest, really derive their life from each other."[80]

---

78. Derrida, *On Cosmopolitanism*, 45.
79. Carroll, "Forgiving or Forgetting?": 90.
80. Walter Brueggemann, "Covenant as a Subversive Paradigm," *The Christian Century* (1980): 1097.

Seen in relation to the deceptions and distortions of history about the Marcos dictatorship, the Eucharist can be a powerful practice that fosters a biblical stand against political injustice. In the Eucharist forgiveness is cultivated, which is a yearning for justice and reconciliation. It is an act that seeks culmination in the embrace of both victim and perpetrator that is reminiscent of the father embracing his long lost son (Luke 15:20).

Bibliography

Adiprasetya, Joas. "Johann Baptist Metz's Memoria Passionis and the Possibility of Political Forgiveness." *Political Theology* (2016): 1–16.

Arendt, Hannah. "Organized Guilt and Universal Responsibility." In *The Portable Hannah Arendt*, edited by Peter Baehr, 146–56. New York: Penguin Books, 2000.

———. *The Human Condition*. 2nd ed. Chicago: University of Chicago Press, 1998.

Aristotle. "Nicomachean Ethics." In *The Basic Works of Aristotle*, edited by Richard McKeon, 935–1126. New York: Random House, 1941.

Barth, Markus. *Rediscovering the Lord's Supper: Communion with Israel, with Christ, and Among the Guests*. Eugene: Wipf and Stock Publishers, 1988.

Bash, Anthony. *Forgiveness: A Theology*. Eugene: Cascade Books, 2015.

Bieler, Andrea, and Luise Schottroff. *The Eucharist: Bodies, Bread, and Resurrection*. Minneapolis: Fortress, 2007.

Brock, Brian, and Bernd Wannenwetsch. *The Therapy of the Christian Body: A Theological Exposition of Paul's First Letter to the Corinthians*, Vol. 2. Eugene: Cascade Books, 2018.

Brueggemann, Walter. "Covenant as a Subversive Paradigm." *The Christian Century* (1980): 1094–199.

———. *Hope Restored: Biblical Imagination Against Empire*. Louisville: Westminster John Knox Press, 2023. chapter 3. e-book, Perlego.

Carroll, John J. "The Philippines: Forgiving or Forgetting?" *Public Policy Journal* 3, no. 2 (April–June 1999): 83–92.

Cornelio, Jayeel, and Erron Medina. "Christianity and Duterte's War on Drugs in the Philippines." *Politics, Religion & Ideology* 20, no. 2 (2019): 151–69.

Cornelio, Jayeel, and Ia Marañon. "A 'Righteous Intervention': Megachurch Christianity and Duterte's War on Drugs in the Philippines." *International Journal of Asian Christianity* 2 (2019): 211–30.

De Guzman, Chad. "The Philippines Once Celebrated Marcos' Fall. Under His Son, Has the Country Moved On?" *Time*, 21 February 2023. Accessed 15 December 2023. https://time.com/6257017/philippines-bongbong-marcos-people-power-revolution.

Dela Peña, Kurt. "Marcos Martial Law: Golden Age for Corruption, Abuses." Inquirer. Net, 21 September 2021. Accessed 17 December 2023. https://newsinfo.inquirer.net/1490968/marcos-martial-law-golden-age-for-corruption-abuses.

Derrida, Jacques. *On Cosmopolitanism and Forgiveness*. Translated by Mark Dooley and Michael Hughes. New York: Routledge, 2001.

Digeser, P. E. *Political Forgiveness*. Ithaca: Cornell University Press, 2001.

Eiesland, Nancy L. *The Disabled God: Toward a Liberatory Theology of Disability*. Nashville: Abingdon Press, 1994.

Galagala-Nacion, Junette B. "Romans 13 and the Limits of Submission." In *Faith and Bayan: Evangelical Christian Engagement in the Philippine Context*, edited by Lorenzo C. Bautista, Aldrin M. Peñamora, and Federico G. Villanueva, 49–76. Carlisle: Langham Global Library, 2022.

Geducos, Argyll Cyrus, "No Need to Forgive Those who Caused Family's Exile – Marcos," *Manila Bulletin*, 18 November 2023. Accessed 17 December 2023. https://mb.com.ph/2023/11/18/marcos-no-need-to-forgive-those-who-caused-family-s-exile.

Hart, Stephen. "Privatization in American Religion and Society." *Sociological Analysis* 47, no. 4 (1987): 319–34.

Hauerwas, Stanley. *The Hauerwas Reader*. Edited by John Berkman and Michael Cartwright. Durham: Duke University Press, 2001.

Horsley, Richard A. *Jesus and the Powers: Conflict, Covenant, and the Hope of the Poor*. Minneapolis: Fortress Press, 2011.

Johann Baptist Metz. *Remembering and Resisting: The New Political Theology*. Edited by John K. Downey. Eugene: Cascade Books, 2022. e-book, Perlego.

Joseph, James A. *Saved for a Purpose: A Journey from Private Virtues to Public Values*. Durham: Duke University Press, 2015.

Kelly, Tony. *The Bread of God: Nurturing a Eucharistic Imagination*. Liguori: Liguori Publications, 2001.

Lampe, Peter. "The Eucharist: Identifying with Christ on the Cross." *Interpretation* 48, no. 1 (January 1994): 36–49.

Land, Julie Marie. "Remember as Re-membering: The Eucharist, 1 Corinthians 11:17–34, and Profound Intellectual Disability." *Studia Liturgica* 50, no. 2 (2020): 17–34.

Macaraig, Ayee. "Marcos on Dad's Regime: What Am I to Apologize for?" *Rappler*, 26 August 2015. Accessed 17 December 2023. https://www.rappler.com/nation/103772-bongbong-marcos-regime-no-apologies.

McGlasson, Paul C. *Theological Exegesis of Scripture, Vol. 1: The Pentateuch*. Eugene: Cascade Books, 2022.

McKenna, Megan. *Rites of Justice: The Sacraments and Liturgy as Ethical Imperatives*. Maryknoll: Orbis Books, 1997.

Morrill, S. J., Bruce T. *Anamnesis as Dangerous Memory: Political and Liturgical Theology in Dialogue*. Collegeville: Liturgical Press, 2000.

Oakman, Douglas E. *Jesus and the Peasants*. Eugene: Cascades, 2008.

Peterson, Brent. "Eucharist: The Church's Political Response to Suffering and Vocational Empowerment to Suffering Love." *Wesleyan Theological Journal* 43, no. 1 (September 2008): 146–64.

Rafael, Vicente L. *The Sovereign Trickster: Death and Laughter in the Age of Duterte*. London: Duke University, 2022.

Ricoeur, Paul. "Memory, Forgetfulness, and History." *Iyyun: The Jerusalem Philosophical Quarterly* 45 (July 1996): 13–24.

Sabanal, Christopher D. "'Your Kingdome Come, Your Will Be Done': Disclosing the Ethics of the New Testament's Parousia." In *Faith and Bayan: Evangelical Christian Engagement in the Philippine Context*, edited by Lorenzo C. Bautista, Aldrin M. Peñamora, and Federico G. Villanueva, 133–56. Carlisle: Langham Global Library, 2022.

Sapiro, Virginia. *A Vindication of Political Virtue: The Political Theory of Mary Wollstonecraft*. Chicago: University of Chicago, 1992.

Spohn, William C. *Go and Do Likewise: Jesus and Ethics*. New York: Continuum, 1999.

Streett, R. Alan. *Subversive Meals: An Analysis of the Lord's Supper under Roman Domination during the First Century*. Cambridge: James Clarke & Co., 2016.

Volf, Miroslav. *Exclusion and Embrace: A Theological Exploration of Identity, Otherness and Reconciliation*. Nashville: Abingdon Press, 1996.

———. *The End of Memory: Remembering Rightly in a Violent Word*. Grand Rapids: Eerdmans, 2006.

Yoder, John Howard. *For the Nations: Essays Evangelical and Public*. Grand Rapids: Eerdmans, 1997.

12

Remembering Truthfully

Memory, Justice, and the Problem of Conflicting Historical Narratives

Athena E. Gorospe

The advent and explosive growth of social media have made it possible to share and propagate multiple alternative accounts of a historical event. This in itself may not be a bad thing since this makes it possible to view an event from different lenses and from many angles. The result is a richer, fuller account, with multiple layers and viewpoints, and providing diverse insights that can deepen and broaden one's understanding of a past event.

The problem, however, is when radically conflicting narratives vie with each other in shaping the identity and soul of a nation, and influence not only public sentiment and election results, but also public policy and practices, including laws, institutions, and court decisions. Moreover, the conflict may not just be in terms of variations in recollection, or perspectives based on social location (e.g. a government official or politician vs. an ordinary citizen; a participant or eyewitness vs. an academic who has access to multiple sources). Rather, it is on the level of facts – whether a certain conversation or incident actually took place and at what time and in what place and for what reason – or when the order, length, or omission/addition of events are radically and deliberately altered in order to fulfill a certain personal/ideological agenda. Assigning agency and ethical responsibility to actions that have led to the loss of lives, health, livelihood, and dignity of people becomes complicated and contested.

One such conflicting narrative is the rendering of the Martial Law era of Ferdinand Marcos, Sr., former president of the Philippines.[1] After he was removed from office in 1986 through a People Power Revolution, several books were published afterwards documenting this period of the nation's history.[2] In these accounts of the years in which Marcos Sr. was in power, he is described as assuming dictatorial powers by revising the Constitution to extend his term indefinitely, placing broadcast and print media under government ownership, and controlling the legislative and judicial branches of government. In addition, his family is reported to have acquired massive hidden wealth, while his economic cronies were favored at the expense of competitors.[3] Those who dissented were jailed, tortured, or abused, while others disappeared, or were found dead.[4]

However, just a mere thirty years later, Marcos Sr.'s physical remains were buried in 2016 with full military honors at the *Libingan ng mga Bayani* (Heroes' Cemetery).[5] The Martial Law era is now being hailed as the golden age of Philippine history, when the streets were peaceful, the people disciplined, the economy booming, and roads and infrastructure built.[6] The new mantra is that there were no human rights abuses under Martial Law. Moreover, the independent commission tasked to recover the Marcoses' ill-gotten wealth was transferred to the Executive branch and most of the legal cases against

---

1. Marcos signed Proclamation 1081 on 21 September 1972, putting the entire Philippines under Martial Law.

2. Among these are Primitivo Mijares, *The Conjugal Dictatorship of Ferdinand and Imelda Marcos* (San Francisco: Union Square Publishing, 1976); Belinda A. Aquino, *Politics of Plunder: The Philippines under Marcos* (Quezon City: University of the Philippines, 1999); Raymon Bonner, *Waltzing with a Dictator* (New York: Vintage Press, 1988); Reuben Canoy, *The Counterfeit Revolution: Martial Law in the Philippines* (Manila: Philippine Editions Pub., 1980).

3. Jovito R. Salonga, *Presidential Plunder: The Quest for the Marcos Ill-Gotten Wealth* (Quezon City: Center for Leadership, Citizenship and Democracy, 2000).

4. There were more than seventy thousand victims of human rights violations, of which eleven thousand were awarded compensation after intensive interviews and documentation. Christian Esguerra, "11000 Martial Law victims to get compensation," *ABS-CBN News*, 9 May 2018, https://news.abs-cbn.com/news/05/09/18/11000-martial-law-victims-to-get-compensation/.

5. Marcos died in 1989 in Hawaii where he fled after being ousted. His remains were flown back to his hometown Batac in Northern Philippines in 1993 and was interred in the Marcos Mausoleum. However, his family kept hoping that he would be buried in the Heroes' Cemetery. Finally, their wishes were fulfilled by former president Rodrigo Duterte. Jodesz Gavilan, "From Hawaii to Ilocos Norte: The Long Journey of Ferdinand Marcos's Remains," *Rappler*, 11 September 2016, https://www.rappler.com/newsbreak/iq/143236-hawaii-ilocos-norte-ferdinand-marcos-body/.

6. Floyd Whaley, "30 Years After Revolution, Some Filipinos Yearn for 'Golden Age' of Marcos," The *New York Times*, 23 February 2016, https://www.nytimes.com/2016/02/24/world/asia/30-years-after-revolution-some-filipinos-yearn-for-golden-age-of-marcos.html.

the Marcoses have been dismissed.⁷ The Marcoses are now enjoying a political resurgence, with his son Ferdinand Marcos Jr. (Bongbong Marcos) becoming the 17th President of the Philippines, his daughter Imee Marcos becoming a senator, his grandson Sandro Marcos becoming congressman and elected as senior deputy majority leader of the House of Representatives, and the wife of Marcos Sr. herself – 94-year-old Imelda Romualdez Marcos – elected as well to the House of Representatives. More recently, the anniversary of the EDSA People Power Revolution, which ended the Marcos era and has been commemorated on February 25 since 1986,⁸ was no longer declared a public non-working holiday by the Marcos administration.⁹

The problem of conflicting narratives of past events is confounded when these events are dramatized in a film or TV drama, which is broadcasted to millions who may find it difficult to differentiate between fact and fiction.¹⁰ While poetic license is certainly allowed in artistic works, how much freedom is allowed so that it does not impinge on the right of individuals, groups, and the events themselves to be represented in a truthful manner, which would show clearly the injustices that were committed against them? While storytelling involves *selectivity* – so that not all events can be included – as well as *point of view* – so that events are told from a certain angle of vision – how can one distinguish when the story already verges on deception, manipulation, and the lack of responsibility for one's actions that have harmed others?

In this chapter, I will show the phenomenon of conflict of narratives in Scripture, particularly in relation to narratives that have great impact on the

---

7. Edu Punay, "SC junks P51 billion PCGG suit vs Marcos, cronies," *Philippine Star*, 20 June 2018, https://www.philstar.com/headlines/2018/06/20/1826270/sc-junks-p51-billion-pcgg-suit-vs-marcos-cronies.

8. In 1986, a People Power protest started at the Epifanio Delos Santos Avenue (EDSA), the main highway of Metro Manila. The protest was in relation to the anomalies in the results of the national election of president, which favored Ferdinand Marcos Sr. over Corazon Aquino. The protest mushroomed to more than a million people on EDSA, and was successful in pushing Marcos Sr. out of power, thus ushering the end of the Marcos regime.

9. Ian Laqui, "LIST: Philippine holidays for 2024 released, EDSA anniversary missing," *Philippine Star*, 13 October 2023, https://www.philstar.com/headlines/2023/10/13/2303435/list-philippine-holidays-2024-released-edsa-anniversary-missing/.

10. A recent film is "Maid in Malacañang," which depicts the Marcoses' last days in Malacañang, the presidential palace, before their exile in Hawaii as a result of the People Power Revolution in 1986. The film portrays them as victims of a political vendetta and characterizes the elder Marcos as soft-hearted, eschewing violence, who loved simple food, and who thought only of the good of the Filipino people. His eldest daughter, Imee Marcos, describes the film as a "work of truth." Camille Elemia, "What Martial Law? Marcoses Get Star Treatment in New Film," The *New York Times*, 10 August 2022, https://www.nytimes.com/2022/08/10/world/asia/philippines-marcos-movie.html.

collective life and political decisions of the people. I will then look at the admonitions from the book of Deuteronomy to "remember" and "not forget," especially in relation to founding events that have shaped the collective identity of the people. Based on the ideas of Paul Ricoeur and other works on memory studies, I will ground the conflict of narratives on the problems related to memory and remembering, and of the nature of historical works as belonging to the narrative genre.[11]

One area to be explored is what possible criteria may be applied to adopt what is a more "truthful" and "just" account. To do this, it is necessary to expound the terms "truthful," "just," and related words in relation to how Scripture understands them.

Conflict of Narratives in the Old Testament

Even in the biblical account, we can see a conflict of narratives, often between the narrator's account vs. one of the characters in the story. For example, in the story of the Levite and his concubine in Judges 19–20, what befell the concubine has two versions – the first one is from the narrator; the second, from the Levite's testimony.

For those who are unfamiliar with the story, there was a Levite – a religious leader – whose concubine left him (Judg 19:1–2).[12] The Levite and his concubine eventually reconciled (vv. 3–10). On the way home they stopped at Gibeah, a city of Benjamin, to rest for the night; however, nobody offered to put them up, except for an old man, a resident alien (vv. 11–21). At night, they were disturbed by a pounding at the door. This is where our text begins.

> The Narrator's Version (Judg 19:22–30)[13]
>
> While they were enjoying themselves, some of the wicked men of the city surrounded the house. Pounding on the door, they shouted to the old man who owned the house, "Bring out the man who came to your house so we can have sex with him."

---

11. Paul Ricoeur was a French philosopher and is considered as one of the giants of 20th century hermeneutic philosophy. His influence spans diverse fields – from biblical studies, theology, psychology, linguistics, literary theory, anthropology, and the rest of the human sciences. I will draw particularly from his work *Memory, History, and Forgetting* (Chicago: University of Chicago Press, 2004), henceforth cited as *MHF*.

12. A concubine in ancient Israel is not a mistress, but a legal secondary wife.

13. Unless otherwise noted, all Scripture quotations are from the NIV.

The owner of the house went outside and said to them, "No, my friends, don't be so vile. Since this man is my guest, don't do this outrageous thing. Look, here is my virgin daughter, and his concubine. I will bring them out to you now, and you can use them and do to them whatever you wish. But as for this man, don't do such an outrageous thing."

But the men would not listen to him. So the man took his concubine and sent her outside to them, and they raped her and abused her throughout the night, and at dawn they let her go. At daybreak the woman went back to the house where her master was staying, fell down at the door and lay there until daylight.

When her master got up in the morning and opened the door of the house and stepped out to continue on his way, there lay his concubine, fallen in the doorway of the house, with her hands on the threshold. He said to her, "Get up; let's go." But there was no answer. Then the man put her on his donkey and set out for home.

When he reached home, he took a knife and cut up his concubine, limb by limb, into twelve parts and sent them into all the areas of Israel. Everyone who saw it was saying to one another, "Such a thing has never been seen or done, not since the day the Israelites came up out of Egypt. Just imagine! We must do something! So speak up!"

The Israelite tribes called for an assembly and they asked the Levite for his testimony. However, the Levite's testimony in the Tribal Assembly is markedly different from the narrator's version.

The Levite's Version (Judg 20:4–7)

So the Levite, the husband of the murdered woman, said, "I and my concubine came to Gibeah in Benjamin to spend the night. During the night the men of Gibeah came after me and surrounded the house, intending to kill me. They raped my concubine, and she died. I took my concubine, cut her into pieces and sent one piece to each region of Israel's inheritance, because they committed this lewd and outrageous act in Israel. Now, all you Israelites, speak up and tell me what you have decided to do."

Obviously, the Levite's version is shorter because he omitted many details; at the same time, there are several significant changes to his version. First, there was no mention of his host the old man, who could have acted as an additional witness, nor did he mention that his host, in place of the Levite, offered the women of the household to the angry mob. Second, he omitted the detail that the men wanted to have sex with him; instead, he said that the men wanted to kill him. Rather than confining the crime to a few "wicked men of the city," he implicated the whole city by referring to the perpetrators as the "men of Gibeah." More significantly, he left out the part where he himself pushed his concubine out to the waiting men outside, and how he treated her harshly after she was gang raped all night, struggling to go back to their host's place. In his testimony to the rest of the Israelites, the Levite made it appear that the woman was murdered by the men after she was raped, instead of dying later.[14]

While variations in recounting are natural occurrences in oral and written traditions and are attested by Scripture itself in order to make the tradition relevant to changing contexts,[15] the Levite's omission and additions were not motivated by concerns for contextual relevance. Rather, these arose from a desire to shield himself from any responsibility regarding what happened to his concubine by putting the blame wholly on the men of Gibeah. Moreover, he presented himself as the victim, while his concubine merely became a prop for his desire to avenge his honor.[16]

What is disastrous is that the Israelite assembly unilaterally accepted the Levite's testimony without further investigation and verification of what really happened; thus, they decided to attack Gibeah (Judg 20:8–10). The result was a civil war that killed thousands of Israelites, fragmenting the whole Israelite society (vv. 12–48).

Here, we can see how one person's skewed narrative and lack of accountability resulted in grievous consequences for the whole community. "All Israel" –

---

14. See Athena E. Gorospe and Charles Ringma, *Judges*, Asia Bible Commentary (Carlisle: Langham Global Library, 2016), 264–65; Daniel Block, *Judges, Ruth*, NAC (Nashville: Broadman & Holman, 1999), 553–55.

15. The canonical process itself, according to James Sanders, is selective repetition of tradition and reinterpretation/resignification that contemporizes the tradition to the current generation. Thus there is both stability and adaptability in the passing on of traditions, including historical ones. See *Canon and Community: A Guide to Canonical Criticism* (Philadelphia: Fortress, 1984), 22–33. According to Gerhard Von Rad, Israel recounted the history of God's saving acts through confessional testimony, combining historical traditions with theological interpretation in light of the context of the present day. See *Old Testament Theology*, Vol. 1, study ed. (London: SCM Press, 1965), 105–21. Paul Ricoeur echoes this process in the passing on of tradition in his concepts of sedimentation and innovation. Sedimentation is what is typological or paradigmatic in a narrative, which remains stable and the same, while innovation is what deviates from the paradigm. See *Time and Narrative*, Vol. 1, trans. Kathleen McLaughlin and David Pellauer (Chicago: University of Chicago Press, 1984), 68–70, 76.

16. Gorospe and Ringma, *Judges*, 265–66.

referring to the eleven tribes – were all united against Benjamin (Judg 20:1–2, 8–11), their brother tribe, based on a distorted testimony, while the concubine, who was the real victim, was forgotten. There was unity, but on the wrong basis, "for every one did what was right in their own eyes" (17:6; 21:25), so that their preference and opinion, and not what really happened, became the standard for action. While it purports to bring justice to the violence committed against the Levite's concubine, it actually engendered more violence in society and injustice against a whole tribe. Moreover, as a result of the near extinction of one tribe of Israel, the elders of the other tribes responsible for their annihilation resorted to solutions that degraded the virgin women of Israel.[17]

If this is the impact of an individual's alteration of a domestic story, how much greater the consequences would be if the story involves the history of a nation, which has the capacity to form the collective identity of a people.

Memory, History, Identity

It is important first of all to show the links and the distinctions between memory and history.

Memory, according to Ricoeur, can be understood as an *object* or as *capacity*. As an *object*, memory has to do with what we remember – "an image we have of the past."[18] But memory can also be regarded as one of the *capacities of the self*. The capacity to remember – to recount my own story – is part of what constitutes personal identity.[19] It is through memory that we have the consciousness of the past so that we can't go back to the events of our childhood and see these as distinct, but continuing to the present. The act of *remembering* can be *passive*, as when an event or person comes to our mind involuntarily, or it can be *active*, as when we exert effort in trying to recall something.[20] Whether passive or active, memory assumes the passage of time.

However, memory is not only personal; it can also be collective. While memory has a fundamentally private character, one does not remember alone, and a social bond and a social context are inherent in any act of recollection

---

17. Gorospe and Ringma, *Judges*, 269–305.

18. *MHF*, 44. In Western philosophy, memory as image is expressed in the idea of *eikōn*, of representation.

19. Other capacities of the self are: the capacity to speak, to act, to say that I am the author of my actions and therefore I am accountable for them.

20. *MHF*, 4.

and recognition.²¹ Maurice Halbwachs makes the point that, while it is the individual who remembers, these remembrances are supported by an intersection of collective influences. Each member of a group may have partial images of a common event or place or time, but collectively they can have a fuller memory of what, where, and when it happened. Thus, apart from individual memory, there exists the phenomenon of group or collective memory.²² When a personal memory of a past event has receded or while living in a different milieu from one's parents or grandparents, one nevertheless has access to the past through the remembrances of close relations and in the mementos left in common places we live or frequent. It is in this sense then that we can speak of collective memory, not singular, but plural, since a person's recollection interacts with several groups' collective memories, thus forming intersecting and interconnecting relationships.²³

While memory starts off as individual images, memory becomes narrative through what Ricoeur calls "declarative memory."²⁴ The original perception of the experience, which could easily be forgotten due to the passage of time, is retained and restored by verbalizing it. When we share with others a memory-image, this becomes visible and public and is marked by the time of occurrence – "this memory happened a month ago or on my birthday." The process of recollecting the past involves a reflection that moves through time and demands a recounting of a succession of events. Thus an incipient narrative is born.²⁵

Because declarative memory has a reflexive character,²⁶ it takes the form of testimony: "I was there, and this was what happened."²⁷ When oral testimonies are written down, preserved, and classified, they pass into archives, which then

---

21. *MHF*, 93–96, 120–24. He draws from Maurice Halbwachs, *On Collective Memory* (Chicago: University of Chicago Press, 1992).

22. Halbwachs, *On Collective Memory*, 43–51.

23. Halbwachs, *On Collective Memory*, 63–78.

24. *MHF*, 129.

25. *MHF*, 42, 154. Although both image and narrative are representations of reality, what differentiates image from narrative is the temporal element. Ricoeur suggests that perhaps a temporal process can be recognized as such only as it is put into a story. See "On Interpretation," in *Philosophy in France Today*, ed. Alan Montefiore (Cambridge: Cambridge University Press, 1983), 176.

26. One remembers what one has seen, experienced or learned, *MHF*, 36.

27. *MHF*, 146.

provide the documentation for the writing of history.[28] Thus, "testimony constitutes the fundamental transitional structure between memory and history."[29]

Just as Halbwachs distinguishes history from collective memory,[30] Ricoeur also does not see an immediate equivalence between history and memory. He traces through an indirect route the threefold overlapping historiographical operations[31] by which memory becomes the base for history, but at the same time, takes off from it. First, documentary proof is established when declarative memory as testimonies are interrogated, written down, and systematized into archives.[32] Second, explanation/understanding seeks to make sense of the documentary proof by asking the question "why," seeking causal relationships that can interconnect the different traces of the past, whether in the form of testimony, archives, artifacts, or other material traces. It does this by using a variety of models drawn from the historical disciplines and the broader field of the social sciences. It is on this level, according to Ricoeur, that history is seen as an autonomous discipline and is most discontinuous from memory studies.[33] The third is the "representative phase," that is, the putting into writing the historian's representation of the past through the literary form of narrative.

History, as one of the two major narrative modes,[34] has the power to mold collective identity because of its narrative character and its links with collective memory. A narrative has the capacity to shape personal identity because

---

28. *MHF*, 166–69.

29. *MHF*, 21.

30. Halbwachs considers the end of a collective memory when the members of a group possessing the lived memories are no longer alive, and hence there is an impetus to write them down while there are still members who can recount them. History begins when the collective memory ends. *On Collective Memory*, 78–87.

31. This threefold operation should not be seen as chronological or successive. Rather, each part of the operation acts as the base for the others. See *MHF*, 136–37.

32. *MHF*, 146–81.

33. *MHF*, 182–233.

34. Fiction is the other narrative mode. According to Ricoeur, both history and fiction are rooted in narrative understanding. History requires the exercise of our narrative competence to be intelligible. History, like fiction, utilizes the imagination in reconstructing the past. For example, imagination serves history in remembering "epoch-making events" in the life of a community – those that provoke indignation, regret, or horror. There are some events (such as Auschwitz, for example) in which historical distance and ethical neutrality are no longer desirable. Fiction gives "eyes to see and weep" that would evoke the horror of the events, and ensure that it would not be forgotten. See *Time and Narrative, Vol. 3*, trans. Kathleen McLaughlin and David Pellauer (Chicago: University of Chicago Press, 1990), 187–89. Nevertheless, history differs from fiction in that it preserves an epistemological break so that the link with narrative understanding is only indirect, in *Time and Narrative, Vol. 1*, 175–79. Also see my discussion in *Narrative and Identity: An Ethical Reading of Exodus 4* (Leiden: Brill, 2007), 68–84.

it moves through time in the same way that the self moves through time. Both a story and the self has a before and an after in relation to the present, and so the focus is not just one point in time. Moreover, a narrative is made up of diverse events that are plotted together to form a whole, in the same way that the self consists of diversities and goes through change but remains the same self. As we read a narrative, our personal identity is formed as we interact with the diversity and coherence of the plot and, along with the characters, explore the possibilities and limits of our narrative identity.[35]

Nevertheless, the proximity between history and fiction as narrative modes, and history's use of narrative resources, such as selectivity and imaginative variations, means that historical narrative is vulnerable to abuse, especially if it is made to bear upon the formation of identity. Likewise, history's utilization of memory, which is associated with images of the past, leads to confusion between history as standing for the past versus something that is purely inventive. But before we look at the abuses of memory and historical narrative, let's look at some important injunctions on memory that Scripture brings to us.

Remembering in Deuteronomy

The genre of the book of Deuteronomy is not history, although it includes a recounting of past events and a repeated admonition to remember. The setting of Deuteronomy is at the boundary of Moab, before the Israelites crossed the Jordan into the promised land. After wandering in the wilderness for forty years, most of the old generation had passed away, and a new generation was about to possess the land. The book is structured around the last speeches or sermons of Moses before he died. The introductory speech (Deuteronomy 1–5), as well as other sections of the book, recounts the history of the past for the new generation, to guide them as they transition into a new life in the land.

The memory motif in the book of Deuteronomy has been highlighted by several authors.[36] This motif is most evident in the repeated admonitions

---

35. Gorospe, *Narrative and Identity*, 36–52.
36. Edward Blair, "An Appeal to Remembrance: The Memory Motif in Deuteronomy," *Int* 15 (1961): 41–47; Ernest Nicholson, "Reconsidering the Provenance of Deuteronomy," *ZAW* (2012): 535–38, drawing from Jan Assmann, *Religion and Cultural Memory: Ten Studies*, trans. Rodney Livingstone (Stanford: Stanford University Press, 2006); Jeffrey Arthurs, "The Lord's Remembrances," *JEHS* 14, n. 1 (March 2014): 35–37; Brian M. Britt, "Remembering Narrative in Deuteronomy," in *The Oxford Handbook of Biblical Narrative*, ed. Dana Nolan Fewell (Oxford: Oxford University Press, 2015), 158–60; 164–65.

of the book for Israel to "remember" (*zakar*)[37] and "not forget" (*lo shakakh*).[38] However, it is also seen in the memorialization of significant events through feasts, annual rites, and celebrations that provide opportunities to retell the people's story to the gathered family or community.[39] In addition, Deuteronomy also puts great emphasis on passing on to succeeding generations God's story with God's people, as well as God's commands and instructions.[40]

The command to remember mostly centers on Israel's experience of being slaves in Egypt and how the Lord liberated and redeemed them. The Israelites were repeatedly reminded: "Remember that you were slaves in Egypt and the Lord your God redeemed you" (Deut 15:15; cf. 16:12; 24:18). They were to look back at their time of oppression in Egypt and how God had brought them out with a mighty hand.

This remembrance should motivate their future actions. How? First, Israel's laws were grounded on their story. For example, because they had experienced what it means to be slaves and aliens, then they should extend compassion and practical help to slaves and aliens as well.[41] Moreover, the story served as motivation for their actions, warned them against future dangers, and formed in them important values and perspectives that they needed to imbibe once they cross over to the new land. Apart from the exodus, the wilderness experience was also something that they should remember (8:2; cf. 1:19), as well as God's establishment of the covenant and the giving of the law on Mt. Horeb (4:9–20; 5:1–33).

Distorted and Divergent Narratives

The corresponding action of remembering is "not to forget." Here, forgetfulness has to do with a distorted narrative. Rather than attributing their prosperity in the land to Yahweh who brought them out of their oppression in Egypt into an abundant land, they began to attribute their good life to their own merit and

---

37. Deut 5:15; 8:2, 18; 15:15; 16:12; 24:18, 22.

38. Deut 4:9, 23; 6:12; 8:11, 14, 19; 9:7; 25:19.

39. Blair, "An Appeal to Remembrance," 44. An example is the feast of Passover in which the head of the family retells the story of the exodus to the younger members of the family (Deut 6:20–25). Another one is the Feast of First Fruits in which the head of the family, while offering the first fruits of his harvest, recounts the story of the migration of the patriarchs, their slavery and liberation in Egypt, up to the time of their settlement in the land (Deut 26:1–10). Cf. Deut 31:9–13.

40. Deut 4:9–13; 6:4–10, 20–25; 11:18–21; 31:12–13; 32:46.

41. Deut 15:12–15; 24:17–18, 21–22.

their own efforts alone, without honoring the God who made it happen (Deut 6:10–12; 8:12–18; 32:15–18). Believing and propagating a story that magnified their own role, while minimizing God's part, eventually led to forsaking Yahweh and turning to other gods.

The story also reminded them to reflect on their past failures: "Remember and do not forget how you provoked the LORD your God to wrath in the wilderness" (Deut 9:7 NRSV). One instance is the incident at Kadesh Barnea, which is recounted in Deut 1:19–46, and is narrated in more detail in Numbers 13–14. The Israelites sent out spies to check out the land before entry. But ten of the spies gave a slanted report that magnified the challenges. As a result, the people complained and wanted to go back to Egypt.

> All the Israelites grumbled against Moses and Aaron, and the whole assembly said to them, "If only we had died in Egypt! Or in this wilderness! Why is the LORD bringing us to this land only to let us fall by the sword? Our wives and children will be taken as plunder. Wouldn't it be better for us to go back to Egypt?" (Num 14:2–3)

This longing to go back to Egypt is a recurring theme in Israel's complaints in the wilderness (Num 11:5–6), containing an implicit accusation that the reason God brought them out of Egypt is to leave them to die in the desert (Exod 16:3). And yet when we go back to the Exodus account, the impetus for God bringing them out of the land is because they cried out in their suffering and oppression.

> During that long period, the king of Egypt died. The Israelites groaned in their slavery and cried out, and their cry for help because of their slavery went up to God. God heard their groaning and he remembered his covenant with Abraham, with Isaac and with Jacob. So God looked on the Israelites and was concerned about them. (Exod 2:23–25)

> The LORD said, "I have indeed seen the misery of my people in Egypt. I have heard them crying out because of their slave drivers, and I am concerned about their suffering." (Exod 3:7)

The way the Israelites recounted their life in Egypt, as they were wandering in the wilderness, underwent a revision. It became the "golden years," instead of a time of slavery and oppression.

So, here again was a clash of narratives, and it influenced how the people reacted to their current situation. In this case, the threats had been magnified by their own compatriots, to the point that they forgot the oppression they experienced under the Egyptians. Also, when they were only eating manna in the wilderness, they only remembered the food in Egypt (Num 11:4–6) and it became more important than God's gift of freedom from slavery in Egypt.

Part of the "forgetfulness" is due to the failure of the Exodus generation to pass on the memory of the founding events to the next generation. Hence, there is an admonition in Deuteronomy 4:9 (NRSV):

> But take care and watch yourselves closely, so as neither to forget the things that your eyes have seen nor to let them slip from your mind all the days of your life; make them known to your children and your children's children.

Here, the emphasis is on the responsibility to faithfully pass on their story and their covenant with God to the future generations.[42]

However, the people failed in this responsibility. Thus, after the Joshua generation, "another generation grew up who knew neither the LORD nor what he had done for Israel" (Judg 2:10),[43] who "forgot the LORD their God" (3:7); because of this, they looked for their salvation and hope in other gods, in their own leaders, or in their own limited comprehension of the situation. Thus, in the book of Judges, we see a progressive deterioration of the socio-religious conditions of Israel and the decline in the moral fiber of the nation so that at the end of the book, there is rape, murder, rampant idolatry, and inter-tribal war.

The Abuse of Historical Narrative and Memory

As we see above, "forgetfulness" in Scripture is not described as the material obliteration of certain information in the brain. It is not that their knowledge of Yahweh has been erased. It is more that the memory of Yahweh's deeds has been distorted to the extent that the narrative that is being passed on to succeeding generations is no longer a faithful representation of God's central role in bringing Israel into being.

As mentioned above, history's basis in collective memory and its use of narrative as the mode of representation brings with it certain problems. First, memory has been associated with imagination from the beginning because

---

42. Cf. Deut 6:7, 20–21; 11:18–21; 31:12–13; 32:46.
43. "Not knowing" in this context does not mean ignorance or lack of knowledge, but rather not valuing or honoring what God has done for them (cf. Exod 1:8).

the representation of the past appears as an image.[44] This exposes memory to the constant confusion between memory, which deals with the remembrance of a prior reality, and pure imagination – which conjures up what is unreal.

Thus, one can sometimes be unsure whether what one remembers is accurate and faithful to the past. As Ricoeur remarks, "How are we to preserve the difference in principle between the image of the absent as unreal and the image of the absent as prior?"[45]

Second, history's narrative form involves selectivity in the highlighted events. This means that certain events can be omitted, magnified, and even distorted to achieve a certain ideological purpose. Moreover, historical narrative also uses the same rhetorical forms as fiction and utilizes the imagination to represent the past. In its search for readability, historical narrative must seek visibility, that is, give the readers the sight to see by the use of imagination.[46] All these obscure the differences between history and fiction, thus making historical narrative always open to the suspicion of having a "referential illusion."[47] In addition, the plot structure of narrative tends towards closure, which might result in the exclusion of any reference outside the story's world.[48]

These problematics of memory and narrative lend historical renditions vulnerable to ideological manipulation. Ideology can impose an "authorized" history that involves "a strategy of remembering" as well as a "strategy of forgetting."[49] Thus, elements of the collective history are selectively remembered or forgotten in order to support a collective identity that would maintain and perpetuate the socio-political base of the ones in power. I contend that this has been happening in the representation of Marcos's Martial Law.

Martial Law in Support of the Strongman Ideology

In 2018, during Rodrigo Duterte's term as president, the Philippine army branded the showing of films critical of Martial Law as part of a communist subversive plot to topple the Duterte government, despite the fact that Martial

---

44. *MHF*, 44.
45. *MHF*, 238.
46. *MHF*, 237, 251, 262–63.
47. *MHF*, 249–50.
48. *MHF*, 237, 247, 276.
49. *MHF*, 85, 448.

Law film screenings have been going on for decades.[50] In 1972, the army chief at that time also justified Marcos's declaration of Martial Law as necessary to deal with a nation in crisis.[51] Juan Ponce Enrile, Marcos's former chief of defense and an ally of Duterte, then claimed that there were no arrests or executions during Martial Law.[52] The more than seventy thousand claimants of human rights violations, of which eleven thousand were awarded compensation from the recovered ill-gotten wealth of the Marcoses, belie Enrile's claims.[53]

The revision in the recounting of Martial Law is central to Duterte's grand narrative that a strongman is indispensable to solving the nation's problems. The narrative goes this way: The Philippines faces festering problems, such as drugs, terrorism, corruption, insurgency, and many other problems because of the people's lack of discipline and the oligarchs' control of the system. Thus, a president who has the political will to fight the elités and instill discipline is needed. But in order to do this, he must be granted extraordinary powers to do the job, including the power to eliminate those who stand in his way. Thus, ideology takes the form of a narrative that resonates with Filipino culture and colonial history, while continually being reinforced by government propaganda through historical revisionism and social media memes that praise the strongman.

While Bongbong Marcos, the son of Ferdinand Marcos Sr., and the current president of the Philippines, does not seem so far to embrace the strongman ideology of his father and of Rodrigo Duterte, his election to power because of a revisionist rendering of Martial Law has resulted in certain consequences.[54] It has paved the way for the glorification of his father and of martial rule, the

---

50. Chad de Guzman, "AFP Official: CPP Recruits in Manila Schools through Martial Law Film Screenings," *CNN Philippines*, 3 October 2018, http://cnnphilippines.com/news/2018/10/03/Red-October-AFP-schools.html.

51. These include economic crisis, communist insurgency, worsening crime, and the uncontrolled power of the political elite at that time. Jonathan de la Cruz, "Martial Law: The Historical Narrative," *Manila Standard*, 26 September 2018, http://www.manilastandard.net/opinion/columns/crossroads-by-jonathan-dela-cruz/276419/martial-law-the-historical-narrative.html.

52. Pathricia Ann V. Roxas, "Enrile: No Massacres, No Arrests for Criticizing Marcos During Martial Law," *Inquirer.Net*, 21 September 2018, https://newsinfo.inquirer.net/1034796/enrile-no-massacres-no-arrests-for-criticizing-marcos-during-martial-law.

53. Jodesz Gavilan, "11,103 Victims of Human Rights Violations under Martial Law to Get Compensation," *Rappler*, 10 May 2018, https://www.rappler.com/nation/202033-human-rights-victims-claims-board-final-list-eligible-claimants-released/.

54. Saima Islam, "Revisionist Narratives and the Revival of the Marcos Family in the Philippines," *Asia Pacific Foundation of Canada*, 6 May 2022, https://www.asiapacific.ca/publication/election-watch-philippines-dispatch-6-marcos-legacy-and-youth.

silencing of the victims of Martial Law, apathetic disregard for human rights abuses, the implicit acceptance of nepotism and family dynasties, resignation towards graft and corruption, and disregard for the value of historical accounts based on documentary evidence.

Moreover, the denial or belittling of the economic plunder and human rights abuses under Martial Law has resulted in a culture of impunity. Because the Marcoses are not made accountable, other Duterte and Marcos allies have been able to escape responsibility for their crimes. Moreover, this culture of impunity has served as a fuel for the political resurgence of the Marcoses and their allies, even as the family has refused to take responsibility for how they gained their enormous wealth, their unpaid estate taxes amounting to 203 billion pesos, and their complicity in the political crimes committed under Martial Law.

However, according to Ricoeur, it is not only the ones who hold power that are responsible for the abuse of remembering. The social actors themselves are complicit in the act by a semi-passive, semi-active strategy of avoidance, in which through denial and evasion and by wanting not to know, they accept the identity defined and imposed by the prevailing power through a narrative of an ideologed memory.[55]

For example, a video interview of the next-generation millennials, who never experienced Martial Law, reveals that they consider Martial Law as good for the country, because discipline and law prevailed then. They were shocked when the interviewers – Martial Law victims – disclosed the torture and abuse they went through.[56] Even many adults who lived through that period believe that Martial Law was peaceful and prosperous, partly because of regional loyalties, but also because of government propaganda.[57]

The main issue, however, is not only *how* we should remember, but the more basic question is *who* should remember? When the ones in power manipulate memory in order to serve their ideological interests, a devious form of forgetting is at work, resulting from stripping the social actors of their original

---

55. *MHF*, 448–49.

56. Jodesz Gavilan, "Young Filipinos Shocked by Martial Law Stories," *Rappler*, 4 May 2016, https://www.rappler.com/move-ph/131716-history-martial-law-filipino-youth.

57. The government controlled the media; hence, people's knowledge was limited to what was reported in the state-controlled TV station and the one surviving newspaper. "Manila Imposes Strict Censorship on News Media," The *New York Times*, 29 September 1972, https://www.nytimes.com/1972/09/29/archives/manila-imposes-strict-censorship-on-news-media.html.

power to recount their actions themselves.[58] If memory is one of the capacities by which agency is exercised, wouldn't people be robbed of the power to form their own identity if they were not able to recount their own history? The basis for possible reconciliation is laid when the parties involved are given the power and the freedom to tell their own stories. This means that one party does not dominate the storytelling, and that all are given the space to recount what happened from their own perspective, without being interrupted or challenged.

However, as what often happens in many disputes, the narrative interpretations do not coincide, and so there is the problem of a conflict of narratives.

The Clash of Narratives and the Duty of Memory

What criteria do we use then to evaluate competing testimonies? Often the narrative that prevails is the one pushed by those with the most dominant voice or the most power – whether this is economic, social, religious, or persuasive power. Giving an adequate hearing to all the contending testimonies, as in a court of law, is a necessary first step before evaluating.

Ricoeur highlights the two aspects of testimony that distinguish it from other types of narrative. One, there is an assertion that the reported event is factually true, and two, the authenticity of the reported event depends on the trustworthiness of the witness. The judgment of trustworthiness, however, is only made possible because of a dialogical situation, in which the witness testifies before someone who evaluates the testimony, accepts it, and accredits it.[59] Ricoeur believes that it is only through the confrontation between testimonies that history can fulfill its function of "standing for" the past, not in the sense of an exact resemblance of the events that it recounts, but in a metaphorical and analogical relation to the past.[60] Thus, in the final analysis, "we have nothing better than our memory to assure ourselves of the reality of our memories – we have nothing better than testimony and criticism of testimony to accredit the historian's representation of the past."[61]

Nevertheless, Ricoeur gives a very crucial criterion, which he calls "the duty of memory." He asserts that "the duty of memory is the duty to do justice, through memories, to an other than the self."[62] He connects this idea of justice

---

58. *MHF*, 448.
59. *MHF*, 163–64.
60. *MHF*, 279.
61. *MHF*, 278.
62. *MHF*, 89.

to that of debt: "We are indebted to those who have gone before us for part of what we are."[63] In an earlier work, he talks of the writing of history as paying a debt to the past, particularly to the "victims whose suffering cries less for vengeance than for narration."[64] Thus, in judging conflicting historical narratives, one may ask which account best fulfills the duty of justice by identifying the victims and recounting their story. Ricoeur cautions, however, that "[t]he victim at issue here is the other victim, other than ourselves."[65] Otherwise, by assuming the status of victim, we take upon ourselves an "exorbitant privilege," in which everyone else owes us a debt, engendering an attitude of entitlement that continually demands reparation.[66]

Hence it is not enough just to say "remember," but to ask who needs to remember and how do we remember. In light of rival testimonies, greater effort should be given to tell the stories of Martial Law victims, especially since there is a concerted effort by the authorities to silence or discredit them. These individual stories, when shared, create an intersubjective bond that becomes "our" collective memory and common story, that can be passed on to the next generations, first through "close relations," then to the wider community, forming a collective identity.[67] Moreover, individual victims recounting their memories is an outworking of agency that can lead to the exercise of other capacities, such as the power to act and not be acted upon; in other words, to resist.

Truth and Faithfulness in the Biblical Story

In Scripture, we see how different narratives can be generated from the same event. In fact, major events in the Bible, such as the exodus, are retold in different ways, with certain elements being emphasized, depending on the context of the audience, and reinterpreted for a new generation. In the Chronicler's account of the reigns of David and Solomon, certain events mentioned in the

---

63. *MHF*, 89.

64. Ricoeur, *Time and Narrative, Vol. 3*, 139.

65. *MHF*, 89.

66. *MHF*, 86, 89.

67. As one Filipino writer puts it: "Only with a sense of history can history be the judge that is immune to the seduction of power and the eroding influence of time's passage. And herein lies our comfort: For as long as we bear the memories of injustice, the hope of a fair verdict remains." Gideon Lasco, "Memory as Resistance," *Philippine Daily Inquirer*, 17 May 2018, https://opinion.inquirer.net/113248/memory-as-resistance.

book of Kings were omitted.⁶⁸ The four gospels themselves show variations in the accounts of Jesus's life, death, and resurrection. This implies that, in Scripture, variations in narrative accounts do not necessarily mean that they are untruthful.

In the Old Testament, truth or *emeth* is related to the word for faithfulness (*emunah*).⁶⁹ Hence, it indicates what is reliable and trustworthy, and what one can depend on because of its constancy and stability through time. When used as an adverb, for example, "in truth, truly" (*beemeth*), the word connotes sincerity and lack of duplicity.⁷⁰

Moreover truth "always involves one's relationship to his fellow men and pertains to his speech and actions; *emeth* is that on which others can rely. To this extent, *emeth* involves a personal relationship. It is not merely an objective fact."⁷¹ It is also for this reason that *emeth* is often paired with *hesed*,⁷² translated as "lovingkindness," which has to do with mutual commitment and kindness, and springs from faithfulness to one's promises and mutual obligations in the context of a certain relationship.⁷³ Other important word-pairs with *emeth*, especially in the context of a court where one judges between competing accounts, are "righteous" (*tsedeq*) and justice (*mishpat*).⁷⁴

Hence, truth in the Old Testament has an objective element, as well as a subjective one.⁷⁵ On one hand, it refers to words, claims, reports, or charges that can be established as true, such as when evidence is diligently and thoroughly scrutinized and assessed to try to establish the truth.⁷⁶ On the other hand, it has to do with the character of a person, as someone who is trustworthy and faithful to words that he or she has uttered, and who is sincere in intentions and dealings with others.⁷⁷ This corresponds to Ricoeur's two aspects of a testimony, that it involves an assertion of a true statement or story, and a trustworthy

---

68. For example, David's sin with Bathsheba (2 Sam 11:1–12:25), the rebellion of Absalom (2 Sam 13:1–18:33) and the palace intrigues regarding David's successor (1 Kgs 1:1–53) are not mentioned by the Chronicler.

69. H. Wilderberger, "אמן," *TLOT* 1:135; Alfred Jepsen, "אָמַן," *TDOT* 1:309.

70. *HALOT* 1, study ed., 68–69.

71. *TDOT* 1:313.

72. Gen 24:49; 47:29; Exod 34:6; Josh 2:14; Ps 25:10; Prov 3:3.

73. H. J. Zobel, "חסד," *TDOT* 5:46–56.

74. Isa 15:5; 59:14–15; Jer 4:2; Ezek 18:8–9; Zech 8:16; Ps 89:14.

75. *TLOT* 1:155.

76. Gen 42:16; Deut 13:14; 17:4; 22:20; 1 Kgs 10:6–7.

77. Exod 18:21; Josh 2:12–14; 1 Kgs 17:24. Hence *emeth* is used to describe God and God's Word (Gen 24:27; Exod 34:6; Isa 61:18; Jer 10:10).

person giving the testimony. What the objective and subjective elements have in common is the characteristic of faithfulness (to what happened, to others) and stability through time, so that *emeth*, whether expressed as factual assertion or in a person's trustworthy character, is what is constant through time and demonstrates dependability and faithfulness.

Based on the OT understanding of truth, we can formulate some questions to discern what a truthful historical narrative is, even though there may be variations in the telling.

- First: Does it show an effort to be faithful to the past? A truthful historical narrative has a sense of obligation to the past, to the generations who lived beforehand. History's reference to the past can be described as "standing for" or "taking the place of." Historians have a feeling of indebtedness to the past, and the desire to do justice to the past. By writing history, they are able to pay their dues to the dead, the people of the past, and "to 'render its due' to what is and to what once was."[78]
- Second: Are the purported facts in the story consistent through time, that is, can they be verified again and again by succeeding generations?
- Third: Is the person writing the historical account credible and reliable? Do they have a record of misrepresenting events and persons? Do they have competent knowledge of what they are talking about?
- Fourth: Are the intentions of the supposed-to-be historiographer trustworthy, in the sense that there is no deliberate attempt to misrepresent and manipulate the past to protect or advance one's personal interest or promote an ideological agenda for one's benefit?
- Fifth: Does the account seek to do justice to the victims by ensuring that their stories are told and not buried in a desire to magnify the "achievements" by omitting the account of human cost and suffering?

Burying the Victims' Story

In 1981, several thousands of workers labored for six months to rush the construction of the Manila Film Center, a project of Imelda Marcos, who intended to showcase the Philippines as a cultural mecca and the film capital of Asia

---

78. Ricoeur, *Time and Narrative, Vol 3*, 143, 152, 157.

to the international community. The center was completed minutes before the First Manila International Film Festival opened on 18 January 1982. The twelve-day festival was considered a resounding success, bringing in three hundred international celebrities and showing films from thirty-nine countries, with the *New York Times* calling it "the most spectacular festival anywhere."[79]

However, beneath the imposing edifice and the glitter of the Hollywood stars who attended, there lay a horrible tragedy two months before the opening of the festival. With thousands of workers working round-the-clock to finish a massive building in such a short time, and with no adequate safety precautions in place, a mishap was bound to happen. The roof of the building collapsed, hurling workers into the ground of wet cement quickly drying, half-burying and killing some of them.

To this day it is not clear how many died in that accident. A news blackout was imposed soon after, and with government having full control of all news outlets, this was not surprising. An international news provider reported twenty-six fatalities at that time, while the government claimed only three,[80] but a New York film publication said two hundred persons died.[81] It took nine hours before ambulances were let in, and by that time, the cement had hardened, trapping the ones who fell. With the tight deadlines, some were left buried under the building while construction continued at a fast pace.[82]

A person who saw the scene immediately afterwards narrated:

> From a distance I could see people in stretchers being carried out, frozen in cement. When I got there, they were still digging out people; [the cement] was not completely hard . . .
>
> Jackhammers were employed hours later. There was a gruesome view of bodies sticking out of the pavement. The exposed

---

79. Pamela G. Hollie, "Manila Film Festival Proves All-Out Spectacular," *New York Times*, 7 February 1982, https://www.nytimes.com/1982/02/07/movies/manila-film-festival-proves-all-out-spectacular.html.

80. Fernando del Mundo, "26 dead in Philippines movie theater collapse," *UPI Archives*, 17 November 1981, https://www.upi.com/Archives/1981/11/17/26-dead-in-Philippines-movie-theater-collapse/8733374821200/.

81. Patrick F. Campos, "Manila by Night as Third Space," *Kritika Kultura* 19 (2012): 151, quoting Elliot Stein, "Manila's Angels," *Film Comment* 19.5 (1983): 48, https://journals.ateneo.edu/ojs/index.php/kk/article/viewFile/KK2012.01907/1412.

82. Martial Law Museum, "Edifice Complex: Building on the Backs of Filipinos: Manila Film Center," https://martiallawmuseum.ph/magaral/edifice-complex-building-on-the-backs-of-the-filipino-people/.

parts had to be tapered off and built over. The rule was they had to meet the deadline, no matter what happened.[83]

In some sense, the story of what happened at the Manila Film Center is a metaphor of how the stories of the victims of Martial Law are being buried in an edifice of glittering but distorted narrative, in which the "glories of Martial Law" are highlighted, while the injustice done to the victims is "tapered off and built over" – their stories silenced and forgotten. To remember truthfully is to bring to the surface these stories and to fulfill the duty of memory which is "to do justice, through memories, to an other than the self."[84]

Abbreviations

ABC	Asia Bible Commentary
HALOT	*Hebrew and Aramaic Lexicon of the Old Testament*, study ed.
Int	*Interpretation*
JEHS	*The Journal of the Evangelical Homiletics Society*
MHF	*Memory, History, and Forgetting*
NAC	New American Commentary
NIV	New International Version (2011 edition)
TDOT	*Theological Dictionary of the Old Testament*
TLOT	*Theological Lexicon of the Old Testament*
ZAW	*Zeitschrift für die Alttestamentliche Wissenschaft*

Bibliography

Aquino, Belinda. *Politics of Plunder: The Philippines Under Marcos*. Quezon City: National College of Public Administration and Governance, University of the Philippines, 1999.

Arthurs, Jeffrey. "The Lord's Remembrancers." *Journal of the Evangelical Homiletics Society* 14, no. 1 (March 2014): 32–45.

Assmann, Jan. *Religion and Cultural Memory: Ten Studies*. Translated by Rodney Livingstone. Stanford: Stanford University Press, 2006.

---

83. Nicai de Guzman, "The Mysterious Curse of the Manila Film Center," *Esquire Magazine*, 7 November 2019, https://www.esquiremag.ph/long-reads/features/manila-film-center-haunted-a1729-20191107-lfrm2.

84. *MHF*, 89.

Blair, Edward. "An Appeal to Remembrance: The Memory Motif in Deuteronomy." *Interpretation* 15, no. 1 (1961): 41–47.
Block, Daniel. *Judges, Ruth*. The New American Commentary. Nashville: B&H Publishing Group, 1999.
Bonner, Raymond. *Waltzing with a Dictator*. New York: Vintage Books, 1988.
Botterweck, G. Johannes, and Helmer Ringgren. *Theological Dictionary of the Old Testament*. 17 vols. Grand Rapids: Eerdmans, 1974–2021.
Britt, Brian. "Remembering Narrative in Deuteronomy." In *The Oxford Handbook of Biblical Narrative*, edited by Danna Nolan Fewell, 156–67. Oxford: Oxford University Press, 2015.
Canoy, Reuben. *The Counterfeit Revolution: The Uncensored Story of the Marcos Regime in the Philippines*. Manila: Philippine Editions Pub., 1980.
De Guzman, Chad. "AFP official: CPP recruits in Manila schools through martial law film screenings." CNN Philippines, 3 October 2018. https://www.cnnphilippines.com/news/2018/10/03/Red-October-AFP-schools.html.
De Guzman, Nicai. "The Mysterious Curse of the Manila Film Center." *Esquire Philippines*, 7 November 2019. https://www.esquiremag.ph/long-reads/features/manila-film-center-haunted-a1729-20191107-lfrm2.
De la Cruz, Jonathan. "Martial law: The historical narrative." *Manila Standard*, 26 September 2018. https://www.manilastandard.net/opinion/columns/crossroads-by-jonathan-dela-cruz/276419/martial-law-the-historical-narrative.html.
Del Mundo, Fernando. "26 dead in Philippines movie theater collapse." *United Press International*, 17 November 1981. https://www.upi.com/Archives/1981/11/17/26-dead-in-Philippines-movie-theater-collapse/8733374821200/.
Elemia, Camille. "What Martial Law? Marcoses Get Star Treatment in New Film." *New York Times*, 10 August 2022. https://www.nytimes.com/2022/08/10/world/asia/philippines-marcos-movie.html.
Esguerra, Christian. "11,000 Martial Law victims to get compensation." ABS-CBN News, 9 May 2018. https://news.abs-cbn.com/news/05/09/18/11000-martial-law-victims-to-get-compensation/.
Gavilan, Jodesz. "11,103 victims of human rights violations under Martial Law to get compensation." *Rappler*, 10 May 2018. https://www.rappler.com/nation/202033-human-rights-victims-claims-board-final-list-eligible-claimants-released/.
———. "From Hawaii to Ilocos Norte: The long journey of Ferdinand Marcos' remains." *Rappler*, 11 September 2016. https://www.rappler.com/newsbreak/iq/143236-hawaii-ilocos-norte-ferdinand-marcos-body/.
Gorospe, Athena. *Narrative and Identity: An Ethical Reading of Exodus 4*. Leiden: Brill, 2007.
Gorospe, Athena, and Charles Ringma. *Judges*. Asia Bible Commentary Series. Carlisle: Langham Global Library, 2016.
Halbwachs, Maurice. *On Collective Memory*. Edited and translated by Lewis Coser. Chicago: University of Chicago Press, 1992.

Hollie, Pamela. "Manila Film Festival Proves All-Out Spectacular." The *New York Times*, 7 February 1982. https://www.nytimes.com/1982/02/07/movies/manila-film-festival-proves-all-out-spectacular.html.

Islam, Saima. "Revisionist Narratives and the Revival of the Marcos Family in the Philippines." Asia Pacific Foundation of Canada, 6 May 2022. https://www.asiapacific.ca/publication/election-watch-philippines-dispatch-6-marcos-legacy-and-youth.

Jenni, Ernst, and Claus Westermann. *Theological Lexicon of the Old Testament*. 4 vols. Translated by Mark E. Biddle. Peabody: Hendrickson, 2004.

Koehler, L., W. Baumgartner, and J. J. Stamm. *The Hebrew and Aramaic Lexicon of the Old Testament*. Translated and edited under the supervision of M. E. J. Richardson. 5 vols. Leiden: Brill, 1993–2000.

Lagui, Ian. "LIST: Philippine holidays for 2024 released, EDSA anniversary missing." *Philstar.com*, 13 October 2023. https://www.philstar.com/headlines/2023/10/13/2303435/list-philippine-holidays-2024-released-edsa-anniversary-missing/.

Lasco, Gideon. "Memory as resistance." *Philippine Daily Inquirer*, 17 May 2018. https://opinion.inquirer.net/113248/memory-as-resistance.

Martial Law Museum. "Edifice Complex: Building on the Backs of the Filipino People." Martial Law Museum. Accessed 1 January 2024. https://martiallawmuseum.ph/magaral/edifice-complex-building-on-the-backs-of-the-filipino-people/.

Mijares, Primitivo. *The Conjugal Dictatorship of Ferdinand and Imelda Marcos*. San Francisco: Union Square Publishing, 1976.

Nicholson, Ernest. "Reconsidering the Provenance of Deuteronomy." *Zeitschrift für die alttestamentliche Wissenschaft* 124, no. 4 (2012): 528–40.

Punay, Edu. "SC junks P51 billion PCGG suit vs Marcos, cronies." *Philippine Star*, 20 June 2018. https://www.philstar.com/headlines/2018/06/20/1826270/sc-junks-p51-billion-pcgg-suit-vs-marcos-cronies.

Rappler.com. "Young Filipinos shocked by martial law victims' stories." *Rappler*, 4 May 2016. https://www.rappler.com/moveph/131716-history-martial-law-filipino-youth/.

Ricoeur, Paul. *Memory, History, Forgetting*. Translated by Kathleen Blamey and David Pellauer. Chicago: University of Chicago Press, 2004.

———. "On Interpretation." In *Philosophy in France Today*, edited by Alan Montefiore, 175–97. Cambridge: Cambridge University Press, 1983.

———. *Time and Narrative*. Vol. 1. Translated by Kathleen McLaughlin and David Pellauer. Chicago: University of Chicago Press, 1984.

———. *Time and Narrative*. Vol. 3. Translated by Kathleen McLaughlin and David Pellauer. Chicago: University of Chicago Press, 1990.

Roxas, Pathricia Ann. "Enrile: No massacres, no arrests for criticizing Marcos during martial law." *INQUIRER.net*, 21 September 2018. https://newsinfo.inquirer.net/1034796/enrile-no-massacres-no-arrests-for-criticizing-marcos-during-martial-law.

Salonga, Jovito. *Presidential Plunder: The Quest for the Marcos Ill-Gotten Wealth*. Quezon City: Center for Leadership, Citizenship and Democracy, 2000.

Sanders, James. *Canon and Community: A Guide to Canonical Criticism*. Philadelphia: Fortress Press, 1984.

Stein, Elliot. "Manila's Angels." *Film Comment* 19.5 (1983): 48. Quoted in Patrick Campos. "'Manila by Night' as Thirdspace." *Kritika Kultura* 19 (2012): 139–65. https://doi.org/10.13185/KK2012.01907.

The *New York Times*. "Manila Imposes Strict Censorship on News Media." The *New York Times*, 29 September 1972. https://www.nytimes.com/1972/09/29/archives/manila-imposes-strict-censorship-on-news-media.html.

Von Rad, Gerhard. *Old Testament Theology*. Translated by D. M. G. Stalker. 2 vols. Study ed. London: SCM Press, 1965.

Whaley, Floyd. "30 Years After Revolution, Some Filipinos Yearn for 'Golden Age' of Marcos." The *New York Times*, 23 Feb 2016. https://www.nytimes.com/2016/02/24/world/asia/30-years-after-revolution-some-filipinos-yearn-for-golden-age-of-marcos.html.

13

The Cross and the 1986 People Power Revolution

Cultivating an Ethic of Peace

Aldrin M. Peñamora and Emil Jonathan L. Soriano

Introduction

From the time Cain committed the cold-blooded fratricide of his brother Abel as recounted in Genesis 4, the earth has been continually submerged in violence and drenched in blood. Auschwitz[1] is surely one, if not the most, enduring symbol of the evil and injustice caused by violence that people are capable of committing toward each another. The current wars between Israel and Hamas, Ukraine and Russia, and many other conflicts in varying scales now taking place around the world seem to substantiate what the Babylonian myth *Enuma Elish* claims – that violence, of which murder is its foremost expression, is intrinsic to humanity's very nature.[2]

In the Philippines, the "War on Drugs" that former Philippine president, Rodrigo Roa Duterte led was undoubtedly one of the most brutal measures undertaken by the state against its own citizens. Sadly, a majority of the Filipino people, including many evangelical Christians, gave their approval or were

---

1. Auschwitz-Birkenau in Poland was the site of one of the largest concentration camps built by the Nazis during World War II where more than a million Jews were exterminated.

2. Walter Wink, *Engaging the Powers: Discernment and Resistance in a World of Domination* (Minneapolis: Fortress Press, 1992), 15.

indifferent to the "War on Drugs."[3] A more subtle expression of the oppressive use of violence, or one's support of it, is the denial by the current president, Ferdinand "Bongbong" Marcos of the tyrannical nature of Martial Law under his father, former president, Ferdinand Marcos Sr.[4] Not many Filipinos, especially from the evangelical tradition, voiced out their disgust or opposition to Bongbong's false historical narrative that denigrates the sufferings of the thousands of Martial Law victims. These two social phenomena, we argue, are powerfully contributing to the cultivation of an ethic of violence and dehumanization in Philippine society. Regrettably, the church is no stranger to this, as Mark Noll says based on the history of Christianity in the West, "the role of Christians in promoting the destruction of others, while acting self-consciously in defense of what believers openly claim as Christian principles, cannot be denied."[5]

We reject such ethic that promotes and cultivates violence and dehumanization, particularly in the church. In this chapter we seek to contribute toward the cultivation of a Christ-centered ethic of peace for transforming society. Just as the cultivation of violence through the drug war and historical revisionism are rooted in history, so too are we grounding this ethic that promotes life and peace in one of the most momentous events in the history of our Philippine nation, the 1986 EDSA People Power Revolution.[6] We hope this would remind our fellow Filipinos and our evangelical Christian community that at EDSA, we Filipinos compellingly demonstrated how social change can be attained through peace and nonviolence in a way that coheres with the peaceful ways of Jesus. Indeed, at EDSA we Filipinos proved the Maoist principle wrong – true power for social change does not lie in the barrel of a gun.

---

3. A 2017 Pulse Asia Survey shows that 88 percent of Filipino people indicated support to the drug war campaign, with 73 percent believing that extrajudicial killings were being committed. Jayeel Cornelio and Ia Marañon, "A 'Righteous Intervention': Megachurch Christianity and Duterte's War on Drugs in the Philippines," *International Journal of Asian Christianity* 2 (2019), 214.

4. See Helen Flores, "President Marcos: My Father Was Not a Dictator," *Philstar Global*, 15 September 2022 accessed 1 June 2024, https://www.philstar.com/headlines/2022/09/15/2209778/president-marcos-my-father-was-not-dictator.

5. Mark A. Noll, "Have Christians Done More Harm than Good?" in *Must Christianity be Violent? Reflections on History, Practice and Theology*, eds. Kenneth R. Chase and Alan Jacobs (Eugene: Wipf and Stock, 2003), 83.

6. EDSA is the acronym for Epifanio de los Santos Avenue ("Avenue of the Epiphany of Saints," where from 22–25 February 1986, civilians peacefully confronted the military forces of the Marcos dictatorship. While another peaceful revolution occurred several years later called EDSA 2, which also removed an incumbent President, we are focusing on the 1986 revolution, which was truly more revolutionary given the context that it fought against a dictatorship.

Cultivating Violence and Dehumanization through Political Apatheia and Amnesia

Crucial to the success of the brutality and excesses of the "War on Drugs" was the apathy of the Filipino people towards the victims of this so-called war. For this reason, during his presidential campaign and after being elected president in 2016, Duterte and his allies continuously proclaimed a narrative that dehumanized drug addicts and people involved in illegal drugs. Drug addicts, said Duterte, "have no redeeming value."[7] Duterte's secretary of justice, Vitaliano Aguirre once made this remark against the charge that the drug war was inhuman, "How can that be when your war is only against drug lords, drug addicts, drug pushers? You consider them humanity? I do not." Duterte similarly asks, "Crime against humanity? In the first place, I'd like to be frank with you: Are they humans?"[8] The aim of such a narrative is to cut off any concern or sympathy (*malasakit*) for drug addicts and create what Jürgen Moltmann calls *homo apatheticus*,[9] humans who have no sympathy or concern for their fellow human beings (*walang malasakit*).[10]

Such dehumanization of drug addicts was translated into the brutal killings and treatment of the bodies of the victims that became a "spectacle" for all to see, as the corpses were often dumped in public places with the head and the mouth, sometimes the entire body, wrapped in packaging tape with a placard tied around the neck saying, "*Adik ako*" or "*Tulak ako. Wag Tularan*" (I am a drug addict, or I am a drug pusher, do not imitate me).[11] For Duterte, *malasakit* applies only to Filipinos in good standing, for the future of the youth and the children, and for the country. Speaking about the "War on Drugs," Duterte said, "I did it because I want to protect your children and their future. . . . *Ginawa ko*

---

7. Al Jazeera, "Talk to Al Jazeera: Rodrigo Duterte Interview: Death, Drugs and Diplomacy," *Al Jazeera*, 16 October 2016, accessed 20 May 2024, https://www.aljazeera.com/program/talk-to-al-jazeera/2016/10/16/rodrigo-duterte-interview-death-drugs-and-diplomacy.

8. Agence France-Presse, "Criminals are not Human – Aguirre," *Inquirer.Net*, 1 February 2017, accessed 21 May 2024, https://newsinfo.inquirer.net/867331/criminals-are-not-human-aguirre.

9. Jürgen Moltmann, *The Crucified God*, trans. R. A. Wilson and John Bowden (New York: Harper & Row Publishers, 1974), 272.

10. See Aldrin M. Peñamora, "Their Blood Cries Out from the Ground: An Ethic of *Malasakit* and the War on Drugs," in *Faith and Bayan: Evangelical Christian Engagement in the Philippine Context*, eds. Lorenzo C. Bautista, Aldrin M. Peñamora, and Federico G. Villanueva (Carlisle: Langham Global Library, 2022), 126–29.

11. Danilo Andres Reyes, "The Spectacle of Violence in Duterte's War on Drugs," *Journal of Current Southeast Asian Affairs* 35, no. 3: 120–22.

lang ang trabaho ko kasi ayoko ngang masira ang bayan ko" (I just did my job because I do not want my country to be destroyed [because of illegal drugs]).¹²

Certainly, there are those within the main Christian groups – Roman Catholics, Evangelicals and mainline Protestants – who firmly rejected the killings. In fact, the Philippine Council of Evangelical Churches (PCEC) issued two official statements condemning EJK (extra-judicial killing) and the brutalities of the drug war.¹³ Sadly, a majority of the people in the church did not share the sentiments of the official statements. A study by the sociologist Jayeel Cornelio involving religious leaders in one of the villages that was most affected by the drug war in fact yielded that "for a majority of religious leaders *drug users are sinners whose 'wickedness' and criminal acts need to be eradicated.* Their view underscores an implicit religious underpinning for the popular support of the War on Drugs."¹⁴ Giving a religious legitimation of the "War on Drugs" was certainly one of the powerful ways that violence was being cultivated within the very walls of the church. Filipinos seem to have accepted the killings as the "new normal," as the Catholic bishop, Virgilio "Ambo" David further remarks:

> There is a dangerous virus that is spreading faster than the Corona Virus. *It is the virus of indifference.* It has already infected millions in our country. Symptoms include a deadened conscience that is silently convinced that extrajudicial killing is probably the most effective solution to the problems of criminality and illegal drugs in our country.¹⁵

---

12. Ruth Abbey Gita-Carlos, "Drug War's Only Aim is to Protect PH: Duterte," *Philippine News Agency*, 6 November 2021, accessed 21 May 2024, https://www.pna.gov.ph/articles/1158985.

13. See Bishop Noel Pantoja, "PCEC Statement on the Recent Upsurge of Drug-Related Killings," 1 September 2016, accessed 24 May 2024, https://pcec.org.ph/2016/09/01/pcec-statement-on-the-recent-upsurge-of-drug-related-killings/; and Bishop Noel Pantoja, "PCEC Statement on the Administration's Campaign Against Illegal Drugs," 17 January 2017, accessed 24 May 2024, https://pcec.org.ph/2017/01/17/pcec-statement-on-the-administrations-campaign-against-illegal-drugs/. One of the strongest official statements of the Catholic Church in the Philippines against the War on Drugs was from Archbishop Socrates B. Villegas. See "Lord Heal Our Land," *CBCP News*, 12 September 2017, accessed 24 May 2024, https://cbcpnews.net/cbcpnews/lord-heal-our-land/.

14. Jayeel Cornelio, "Popular Support for Duterte's War on Drugs: Investigating the Religious Dimension," *Hal Open Science* (2020): 4; https://hal.science/hal-03784795v1 (Emphasis added).

15. Ruben C. Mendoza, "The Performance of the Christian Faith under a Populist President: The Case of the Philippine Church under Duterte," *MST Review* 22 (2020): 30–31 (Emphasis added). Mendoza also says that while the leaders of the church were consistent in rejecting Duterte's drug war and its killings, "there were many Catholics, even members of the clergy, who found no problem with it and would even justify the government's approach," 24.

If the "War on Drugs" has cultivated an ethic of violence through *apatheia*, the ascendancy of Bongbong Marcos as the 17th president of the Philippines and his view of his father's tyranny, have promoted it by nurturing political-historical *amnesia*.

As of August 2023, there were 11,103 Martial Law victims that have been officially recognized by the government-mandated Human Rights Violations Victims' Memorial Commission, covering the years from 1972 when Marcos declared Martial Law, until his ouster in 1986 through the EDSA People Power Revolution. The Marcos regime "is widely documented for the gross human rights violations abuses perpetrated by State forces across various sectors of Philippine society."[16] Amnesty International gives a much higher number – more than three thousand killed; thirty-five thousand tortured, and seventy thousand incarcerated, for a total of more than a hundred thousand victims.[17]

Notwithstanding the differences in numbers, the unquestionable fact remains that during this dark period, gross human rights violations were committed by the State against its own people. Sadly, the current president of the country, Ferdinand "Bongbong" Marcos Jr., son of the erstwhile dictator, persistently denies that such violations happened during his father's regime. Despite the testimonies of Martial Law victims still living today and the mountains of evidence attesting to the historicity of the regime's brutality, as memorialized in the *Bantayog ng Mga Bayani* (Monument of Heroes) where the names of some of those killed are enshrined, Bongbong Marcos continues to turn a blind eye and depicts his father's authoritarian rule as the country's "Golden Age."[18]

This campaign or "tsunami of disinformation," as journalist Michael Beltran called it, employed various modes of communications and took years in the making. It was designed to sanitize the dark legacy of the Marcoses and put Bongbong Marcos in power. It propagated falsehoods that no one got arrested during the Martial Law era and that so-called "victims" only fabricated stories

---

16. Human Rights Violations Victims' Memorial Commission, "Historical Background," accessed 25 May 2024, https://hrvvmemcom.gov.ph/about-us/. See the Roll of Victims section of this website for a detailed breakdown of the violations committed.

17. Althea Manasan, "Filipino Survivors of Martial Law Still Haunted by Abuses 50 Years After Declaration," *CBC Radio*, 23 September 2022, accessed 25 May 2024, https://www.cbc.ca/radio/thecurrent/survivors-martial-law-philippines-abuses-50-years-later-1.6592042. See also Human Rights Violations Victims' Memorial Commission, *Essential Truths About Human Rights During the Martial Law Era (1972–1986)* (Quezon City: Human Rights Violations Victims' Memorial Commission, 2023), 10–19.

18. Artchil B. Fernandez, "The 'Golden Age,'" *Daily Guardian*, 2 July 2022, accessed 25 May 2024, https://dailyguardian.com.ph/the-golden-age/. See also the chapter I (A. Peñamora) wrote in this volume entitled, "Breaking Bread, Breaking Spiritual-Political Dichotomy: Eucharist, Forgiveness, and the Marcos Legacy."

of violations.[19] The majority of Filipinos were swayed by the new Marcos narrative and the promise of a new "Golden Age" so that they elected Bongbong Marcos to the presidency in the 2022 national election. Political amnesia had set in. More than twenty years ago, Fr. John Carroll made an insightful remark that seems to be most fitting today. He said, "we in the Philippines are in a state of denial with regard to the crimes of the Marcos regime. . . . the willingness to forget these massive crimes against the nation and against communities and against individuals reflects the weakness of the 'common conscience,' a weak sense of the nation and of the common good."[20]

Indeed, Bongbong Marcos's historical revisionism that has created political *amnesia* and Duterte's "War on Drugs" that has promoted political *apatheia* are powerful forces that have cultivated an ethic of dehumanization and violence among the Filipino people. If we Christians are to repel this kind of an ethic, then a counter-ethic that extols peace and respect for human dignity in line with the teachings of the Scripture need to be formed, and which hopefully, is also rooted in our nation's history. One such compelling historical event is the 1986 EDSA People Power Revolution.

The 1986 EDSA Revolution at a Glance

At the root of the EDSA Revolution was the tyranny of the Marcos regime. Along with human rights violations, as we have seen earlier, Marcos Sr.'s authoritarian rule was accompanied by an economic crisis that saw three out of four Filipinos living below the poverty level.[21] In contrast, the Marcos family and their cronies ran lucrative businesses and amassed great wealth both in the country and abroad as massive graft and corruption pervaded the government.[22] Meanwhile, thousands of Filipinos were being killed, tortured, and were languishing in prison for opposing the dictator.

---

19. Michael Beltran, "Disinformation Reigns in Philippines as Marcos Jr. Takes Top Job," *Al Jazeera*, 29 June 2022, accessed 25 May 2024, https://www.aljazeera.com/news/2022/6/29/disinformation-reigns-in-philippines-as-marcos-jr-takes-top-job.

20. John J. Carroll, "The Philippines: Forgiving or Forgetting?" *Public Policy Journal* 3, no. 2 (April–June 1999): 91.

21. Santos and Robles, 3–17 gives a more detailed account of the economic crisis in the country after the imposition of Martial Law up to the middle of the 1980s.

22. Santos and Robles, 10. The authors mention specific exposés made by a San Francisco-based newspaper, *The Mercury News*, and one based in New York, *The Village Voice*, which both relate how Marcos and many prominent Filipinos systematically depleted the country's treasury and poured vast amounts of wealth into other countries. In a 43-minute film exposé

Marcos's authoritarian hold on the country started to weaken, however, after August of 1983, when the nation heard a gunshot from the Manila International Airport. Indeed, it was the cold-blooded assassination of opposition leader, former senator Benigno "Ninoy" Aquino Jr., that planted the seed of EDSA. For over a decade, protests against the regime had ebbed, but with Aquino's death the protest movement once again came to the fore, with the "Justice for Aquino, Justice for All" (JAJA) movement leading the way.[23] From the August 31st funeral of Aquino up to April of the following year, almost two hundred mass actions took place in the country, not counting the boycotts and strikes organized by the labor and other sectors.[24]

The protesters were dubbed "street parliamentarians" who boldly took to the streets demanding Marcos to relinquish the presidency. Succumbing to internal and external pressures especially from his American allies, Marcos then announced on 3 November 1985 that a "snap" election would be held for both the offices of president and vice-president of the country. It was set on 7 February 1986, with the opposition choosing Cory, the widow of Aquino, to run against the powerful dictator. Courageously, Cory declared in Davidic fashion:

> You're coming against me with guns, goons and gold, but I come against you in the name of the Lord Almighty whom you've defied. Come February the Lord will put you in my power, I'll defeat you and your arrogant head will roll. Then the whole world will know that our God is alive and is in full control of human affairs. . . . This battle is the Lord's, and He will put you and all of your KBL lapdogs in our People Power.[25]

When the election finally came, the people voted for Cory, but the Marcos Administration resorted to corruption and violence in order to guarantee victory for the beleaguered tyrant. With the government about to announce victory for Marcos, three key events took place that led to the historic people's march to EDSA. First, the 9 February "walk-out" of thirty-five Commission on Elections vote tabulators in protest of the massive posting of fraudulent

---

by the UNIDO (United Nationalist Democratic Organization), properties were shown allegedly owned by Marcos and his cronies, located in New York, San Francisco and New Jersey, 12.

23. Ma. Serena I. Diokno, "Unity and Struggle" in Aurora Javate De Dios, Petronilo Daroy, and Lorna Kalaw-Tirol (ed.), *Dictatorship and Revolution: Roots of People Power* (Manila: Conspectus, 1988), 132.

24. Diokno, "Unity and Struggle" 136.

25. Villacorte, 18, 20. Cory's statement is certainly patterned after David's as seen in 1 Sam 17:45–47. KBL is the name of the political party of Marcos, which stands for *Kilusang Bagong Lipunan* (Movement for New Society).

returns.²⁶ Second, the February 22 resignations of Marcos's defense minister Juan Ponce Enrile and Armed Forces vice chief of staff General Fidel V. Ramos. And third, the appeal to the people on the same day (22 February) by Manila archbishop Jaime Cardinal Sin to march to EDSA and Camp Aguinaldo to protect and support Enrile and Ramos in a nonviolent manner, and to show solidarity with the ideals for which they gave up their posts.²⁷

The following day, 23 February, tanks came to disperse the "People Power" and assault Camp Aguinaldo where Ramos and Enrile were holed up. The people surrounded the tanks, knelt down and prayed. They would rather be crushed under the tanks than allow the regime's army to pass through. Seeing their resolve, the military withdrew from EDSA.²⁸ Similar events occurred on 24 February. The people peacefully defied the soldiers and even appealed to them to join the revolution. Some soldiers did. On 25 February, in separate venues both Cory and Marcos were inaugurated as the country's eleventh president, but on that fateful day too, it became clear to the once powerful strongman that he had lost the support of the people. By the evening of 25 February Marcos together with his family and closest cronies fled the country. After two decades during which oppression and violence reigned in the land, the darkness of the dictatorship was finally lifted. A new day had finally dawned on the Philippine nation through the miracle that was the EDSA People Power Revolution.

Toward a "People Power" Ethic
The Paradoxical Nonviolent Cross as Theological Foundation²⁹

In our world where greatness is defined by the attainment of worldly power, it is no surprise that humanity pays homage to the Alexanders, the Caesars,

---

26. Sider, *Exploring the Limits of Non-Violence*, 62. To see the group's statement and perspective after the event, see Reynaldo Santos Jr., "1986 Comelec walkout not about Cory or Marcos," *Rappler*, 15 February 2013, accessed 14 May 2024, https://www.rappler.com/nation/elections/22582-1986-comelec-walkout-not-about-cory-or-marcos/.

27. "LISTEN: Cardinal Sin's 1986 appeal for Filipinos to go to EDSA, support Ramos and Enrile," *Rappler*, 23 February 2022, accessed 14 May 2024, https://www.rappler.com/nation/audio-jaime-cardinal-sin-1986-appeal-go-edsa-support-fidel-ramos-juan-ponce-enrile/.

28. See Alfeo G. Nudas, *God With Us: The 1986 Philippine Revolution* (Quezon City: Ateneo University Press, 1986), 58–63, 77–79 for interviews and comments of some of the religious persons who participated directly or indirectly in stopping the tanks.

29. This section is drawn from Aldrin M. Peñamora, "The Power of Powerlessness: A Study of the Cross Motif as the Underlying Theological Principle of the 1986 People Power Phenomenon" (Master of Theology Thesis, Asia Graduate School of Theology, 2004).

and Napoleons of history. For the "will to power" is the very definition of what is good for humanity, as Friedrich Nietzsche asserts, and in contrast he defines what is bad as "all that proceeds from weakness."[30] The apostle Paul similarly observes how Jesus's cross is for the Jews a scandal or a stumbling block (Gk. *skandalon*), and for the Gentiles it is nothing but foolishness (1 Cor 1:23). From these perspectives, the cross epitomizes failure and weakness. It is understandably scandalous, but for believers it is also paradoxical that when "people meet the King on his throne, the throne is a cross."[31]

By choosing the cross as the *way* and the *place* of fallen humanity's redemption, Christ has manifested the paradoxical and mysterious nature of how God confronted worldly power, the normal expressions of which are violence, coercion, domination, and terror. Martin Luther pointed to this mystery during the 1518 Heidelberg Disputation when he said that true theology or knowledge of God can only be found in the theology of the cross (*theologia crucis*), not in the theology of glory (*theologia gloriae*).[32] That is to say, it is not through human rational and moral capacities and efforts which lead to self-glorification that one can know God,[33] but true knowledge of God can only be attained through knowing the suffering Christ, Christ on the cross, whom Luther called "the Hidden God" (*Deus Absconditus*). The cross therefore leads us to a profound enigma, according to H. E. Fosdick:

> The cross itself has in it a paradoxical duality: on the one side it is failure complete and awful; on the other it is power, the most impressive and moving power in man's ethical experience, the potency of a life that gets at the heart of the world by caring enough about the world to die for it. So one of the most colossal defeats of righteousness in history became one of the greatest triumphs righteousness ever won.[34]

Focusing on the nature of God's power that was revealed on the cross, C. S. Song's remark is also quite profound: "on the cross what was exposed was not

---

30. Friedrich Nietzsche, "The Anti-Christ," in *A Nietzsche Reader,* trans. R. J. Hollingdale (London: Penguin Books, 1977), 231.

31. Hans-Ruedi Weber, *Power:Focus for a Biblical Theology* (Geneva: WCC Publications, 1989), 61.

32. Martin Luther, "Heidelberg Disputation" in *Martin Luther's Basic Theological Writings*, ed. Timothy F. Lull (Minneapolis: Fortress Press, 1989), 31.

33. Paul Althaus, *The Theology of Martin Luther,* trans. Robert C. Schultz (Philadelphia: Fortress Press, 1966), 27.

34. H. E. Fosdick, *The Greatness of God* (London: Collins, 1958), 54.

the powerlessness of God but the powerlessness of the power of negation. *What was revealed was the power of the powerlessness of God . . . It was the triumph of love over hate, heaven over hell, and life over death. The world was saved by this powerlessness of God.*"[35]

Thus, in contrast to the worldly weapons of violence, the way of the cross introduces us to an altogether different kind of weapon, a revolutionary kind of violence that Jacques Ellul calls the "violence of love" which Jesus's followers are called to employ in waging battles against the injustices, sufferings, violence, and all forms of evil in the world.[36] The antithetical relationship between the use of physical violence and the way of the cross can be seen in the life of Jesus viewed against the background of the "peace" imposed through the *Pax Romana* (Roman peace). According to Martin Hengel, of all the ancient nations it was the Jewish nation that defended itself most stubbornly against the incursions and oppression brought by the military might of the Roman Empire.

There were three possibilities open to the Jewish people – open armed revolt, opportunistic compromise with Rome, or passive endurance.[37] Jesus rejected these options and instead chose to resist nonviolently, of which the cross was the most powerful expression. In teaching his followers to turn the other cheek, give one's undergarment, and walk the extra mile (Matt 5:38–42), Jesus was not endorsing passivity, defeatism or servility; he was teaching them a "way by which evil can be opposed without being mirrored, the oppressor resisted without being emulated, and the enemy neutralized without being destroyed."[38] It is, moreover, a way expressing love of enemies (Matt 5:44). As Walter Wink incisively explains, conflicts tend to dehumanize both victims and oppressors; nonviolence is a way that allows them to recover their humanity, allowing them to become more of what God intends them to be.[39]

---

35. C. S. Song, *Third Eye Theology: Theology in Formation in Asian Settings* (Maryknoll: Orbis Books, 1979), 167 (Emphasis added).

36. Jacques Ellul, *Violence from a Christian Perspective* (New York: The Seabury Press, 1969), 165–66.

37. Martin Hengel, *Victory Over Violence: Jesus and the Revolutionists*, trans. David E. Green (Philadelphia: Fortress Press, 1975), 45.

38. Walter Wink, *Engaging the Powers: Discernment and Resistance in a World of Domination* (Minneapolis: Fortress Press, 1992), 184, 189.

39. Wink, *Engaging the Powers*, 276.

The Cross and Filipino Values at EDSA[40]

Christ's sufferings, says Carmen Guerrero-Nakpil correctly, influenced "the religious character of the people's participation at EDSA in February 1986."[41] Indeed, a key characteristic of EDSA was the willingness of the people to suffer themselves but not to inflict suffering even toward their oppressors. In this section, we will look specifically at two crucial Filipino values, *kapwa* (shared identity) and *malasakit* (deep compassion or empathy), that were both exemplified during the revolution and that both cohere with Jesus's nonviolent way of the cross.

Kapwa (Shared Identity)

The term *kapwa* is usually translated in English as "other," a term that indicates the distinctiveness of the self's identity and autonomy from other persons. *Kapwa*, on the other hand, accentuates the "deeper sense of identification" of self and other.[42] Virgilio Enriquez defines it incisively as the "unity of the 'self' and 'others,' or simply 'shared identity.'"[43] Katrin De Guia has a similar understanding and defines *kapwa* as "shared Self," wherein the gap is bridged between the self and others, including strangers and enemies.[44] Community, rather than individuality, is therefore emphasized in *kapwa*, as expressed by the creative notion of "SelfOther."[45] This close identification between self and others of course doesn't abolish the notion of individual for the sake of community, *kapwa* rather situates the individual in the context of community, and vice versa. Kapwa is thus considered "the core Filipino value that serves as the base or the 'trunk' that drives and connects together the surface values."[46] In the relational culture of Filipinos, the concept of *kapwa* is the ethical standard orienting the person (*tao*) toward properly relating with others. The expecta-

---

40. See Peñamora, "The Power of Powerlessness," 96–111. There were four values analyzed in the thesis; we are drawing from two of those values for this section.

41. Carmen Guerrero Nakpil, *The Manila Times*, 3 March 1989, cited in Ileto, *Pasyon and Revolution*, back cover.

42. Virgilio G. Enriquez, "*Kapwa*: A Core Concept in Filipino Social Psychology," in *Philippine World View* (Singapore: Institute of Southeast Asian Studies, 1986), 11.

43. Enriquez, "*Kapwa*," 11.

44. Katrin De Guia, *Kapwa: The Self in Other: Worldviews and Lifestyle of Filipino Culture-Bearers* (Pasig City: Anvil Publishing, 2005), 28.

45. Merlinda Bobis, "Weeping is Singing: After the War, a Transnational Lament," in *At the Limits of Justice: Women of Colour on Terror*, eds. Suvendrini Perera and Sherene H. Razack (London: University of Toronto Press, 2014).

46. E. J. R. David, *Filipino-/American Postcolonial Psychology: Oppression, Colonial Mentality and Decolonization* (Bloomington: AuthorHouse, 2011), 130.

tion is for the *tao* to treat other *tao* as equal, which makes *kapwa* a wellspring of ethical behavior.[47]

This means that failure to regard the Other as a person who is an iteration of the Self leads to the negation of *kapwa*, that turns *pakikipagkapwa* (the act of being a *kapwa*) into a contradiction. Duterte's dehumanization of drug addicts and Bongbong Marcos's revisionist view of history that makes Marial Law victims invisible exemplify this contradiction. In such situations, as Dionisio Miranda points out, "The Thou has become an It . . . the I is left even poorer than what it was in its solitariness."[48] In other words, being *kapwa* is what makes us human, and its failure is what makes people enemies (*kaaway*). Miranda further avers, "*Kapwa* transformed into its opposite – *kaaway*, is more direct in its denial of the human: . . . it is the corruption of *pagkamakatao* (being *for* humans)[49] because it not only refuses to acknowledge its similarity in the *kapwa* but seeks to destroy what is clearly its own image in the other."[50]

At Calvary's cross, Jesus demonstrated fully what *kapwa* means. There, Jesus revealed God's love for creation, especially for those he endowed with his very image. If there is any abstraction in the concept of *imago dei* (Gen 1:27), Jesus's death gave it concrete meaning and exemplification. As Cornelius Plantinga Jr. stated, "You cannot spit on a person who wears a crown. . . . Such affronts as racism, sexism, and classism must accordingly be seen as insulting not only to humans but also to the God they represent."[51] Indeed by dying on the cross, Jesus showed not only that he is the Messiah, the Son of God; but he is also the paramount *tao*, the "*tao para sa kapwa*" (man for others).[52]

At EDSA, the Filipino people displayed in a truly marvelous way the value of *pakikipagkapwa* as they gathered peacefully and prayerfully to oppose Marcos's attempt to extend his authoritarian rule. Key to the success of the revolution was its *kapwa*-orientation that showed how the revolutionaries

---

47. Proserpina Domingo Tapales and Maricon P. Alfiler, "Harnessing Indigenous Values for Moral Recovery and Filipino Unity" in *Moral Recovery and Philippine Development: Proceedings of the Consultative Forum on Moral Recovery*, ed. Belinda A. Aquino (Metro Manila: Raintree Trading & Publishing, 1991), 61–62.

48. Dionisio M. Miranda, *Loob: The Filipino Within* (Manila: Divine Word Publications), 111.

49. Translation of *pagkamakatao* mine (Aldrin).

50. Miranda, *Loob*, 114.

51. Cornelius Plantinga Jr., "Images of God" in *Christian Faith and Practice in the Modern World: Theology from an Evangelical Point of View*, eds. Mark A. Noll and David F. Wells (Grand Rapids: Eerdmans, 1988), 64.

52. Vitaliano R. Gorospe, *Filipino Values Revisited* (Metro Manila: National Bookstore, 1988), 258. Translation mine (Aldrin).

were not animated by hatred or vengeance, but by *pakikipagkapwa* that necessitates freedom from tyranny. As *kapwa*, Marcos and the soldiers he sent to quell the revolution by force were therefore not treated as enemies to be vanquished, but as people with dignity to whom they can appeal for compassion and understanding.

To a large extent, Ninoy Aquino planted the seed of this *kapwa*-oriented revolution when he came home on that fateful day of 21 August 1983, knowing full well that his return could mean his assassination – and die by an assassin's bullet he did. His wife, Corazon "Cory" Aquino, who became the country's eleventh president through the EDSA People Power Revolution, thus recalled that "it was after his (Ninoy's) death that People Power blossomed in all its glory."[53] But while the manner of his death was crucial, at EDSA the people also remembered the reason for it. As Ninoy himself emphatically said in a speech he delivered in 1980, "I have carefully weighed the virtues and the faults of the Filipino and *I have come to the conclusion that he is worth dying for*."[54]

Pagmamalasakit (Deep Compassion and Empathy)

Because of the suffering and pain Filipinos have experienced throughout their history, it is no surprise that they attach great significance to the suffering and death of Christ.[55] No less than our Filipino national hero, Jose P. Rizal, who died a martyr's death in the hands of Spanish colonizers, had attached great importance to Jesus's suffering and death, when he said, "We are walking the way to Calvary, now Christ's Passion is better understood. He was nailed to a Cross; the bullets will nail me to the cross formed by the bones of my back."[56] Similarly, Ninoy Aquino was profoundly influenced by Christ's passion and death, as shown by a letter he wrote in solitary confinement:

---

53. From a speech by President Cory Aquino delivered at Waseda University, Tokyo, Japan on 12 November 1986, in Corazon C. Aquino, *In the Name of Democracy and Prayer: Selected Speeches of Corazon C. Aquino* (Pasig City: Anvil Publishing, 1995), 55.

54. Benigno S. Aquino Jr., "The Filipino is Worth Dying For" (speech delivered in New York City on 4 August 1980), *Manila Times*, 22 August 2010, accessed 29 May 2024, https://www.manilatimes.net/2010/08/22/special-report/the-filipino-is-worth-dying-for/638146#_=_ (Emphasis added).

55. See Douglas J. Elwood and Patricia I. Magdamo, *Christ in Philippine Context: Course Textbook in Theology and Religious Studies* (Quezon City: New Day Publishers, 1971), 6–7. On p. 6 the author writes, "The Christ of the Filipinos is pre-eminently a suffering Christ. He is the beaten, scourged, humiliated and defeated Christ."

56. Reynaldo C. Ileto, *Filipinos and Their Revolution: Event, Discourse, and Historiography* (Quezon City: Ateneo de Manila University Press, 1998), 171.

His life was to become my inspiration. Here was a God-man who preached nothing but love and was rewarded with death. Here was a God-Man who had power over all creation but took the mockery of a crown of thorns with humility and patience. And for all his noble intentions, he was shamed, vilified, slandered and betrayed.[57]

Many Filipinos, however, give excessive attention to the sufferings and death of Jesus to the point that he is perceived merely as the "Victim Christ" – powerless, weak, and defeated. Such image, says Benigno Beltran, neglects the resurrection event, thus leading to the cultivation of passivity and numbness among the people even in the face of injustice, and the acceptance of suffering and tragedy as an irreversible decree of fate.[58]

Far from being fatalistic or passive, however, at EDSA the people, just like Ninoy, viewed suffering as liberative. Manila Archbishop Jaime Cardinal Sin underlined this theme in his message during Ninoy's funeral, saying "[To Ninoy's challenge] our people are waiting for a reply [from the state]. They wait, no longer as timid and scattered sheep, but as men and women purified and strengthened by a profound communal grief that has made them one."[59] United in their suffering and grief, the Filipinos broke the chains of their passivity and fear of Marcos and demonstrated a profound sense of *malasakit* (deep compassion or empathy) for their country and for one another, for whom Ninoy died. At EDSA the Filipinos shared one another's pain (*sakit*). The People Power Revolution truly "was the consequence of *malasakit*, a concern for the humanization of a suffering *bayan* (people or nation) brought about by a solidarity in *sakit* (pain) due to the national economic, political, and social crises."[60]

Such deep concern for others that leads to liberating actions reflects God's *malasakit* for all the oppressed and suffering in this world. Jesus's ministry reflected the divine *malasakit* as he often visited the weak, the sick, the poor, and the oppressed in order to bring them the healing and freedom that emanates from God's kingdom that he inaugurated.[61] As Marites Redona says

---

57. Ileto, *Filipinos and Their Revolution*, 172.

58. Benigno P. Beltran, *The Christology of the Inarticulate: An Inquiry Into the Filipino Understanding of Jesus the Christ* (Manila: Divine Word, 1987), 138.

59. Ileto, *Filipinos and Their Revolution*, 173.

60. Allan J. Delotavo, "People Power and the Humanization of Society," in *Toward a Theology of People Power*, ed. Elwood, 72.

61. Peñamora, "Their Blood Cries Out from the Ground," 128.

thoughtfully, *malasakit* is the heart of God for the miserable, it is the "Filipino face of God's mercy."⁶²

From the foregoing we can see how Duterte and his "War on Drugs" and Marcos's revisionist account of Martial Law promote the perversion of the important Filipino value of *malasakit*. What their actions promote, clearly, is an ethic of *walang pagmamalasakit* (apathy or absence of deep concern or compassion) toward the victims of injustice and oppression, which seeks to blot out compassion from the face of the earth, even from their own memory. It is thus an ethic that fosters violence, injustice, and dehumanization, which rejects Jesus's *cruciform-and-transforming* ways. Keeping the memory of Martial Law and the "War on Drugs," and publicly remembering the victims are therefore crucial, for as Jürgen Moltmann warns, "where forgetfulness is the order of the day, the dead are slain once more and the living become blind."⁶³

Peace as a Way of Life

The 1986 People Power Revolution has aptly been called the "Filipino Exodus," describing the liberation of the Filipino people from suffering and oppression, by a mighty and compassionate God who ultimately became incarnate to be one with his people.⁶⁴ While People Power definitely led to a political upheaval, it also exemplified a moral revolution that saw how the way of violence and injustice were conquered by the way of nonviolence and peace that was undergirded by the people's trust in their *kapwa* and *malasakit* for them, and believing that God was fighting alongside them as the divine Kapwa. Like the Exodus event, the lessons of the miracle at EDSA were not supposed to simply be forgotten or treated as mere relics of history. As Vitaliano Gorospe correctly remarks, the cruciform way of "nonviolence is not just a tactic or strategy but *a way of life*."⁶⁵

This way of life has a fuller description in the Scripture, it is the way of *shalom/eirene*, or *the way things ought to be*, in terms of moral behavior, mate-

---

62. Marites Rano Redona, "*Malasakit*: The Filipino Face of God's Mercy," in *Fearful Futures: Cultural Studies and the Question of Agency in the Twenty-First Century* (Kobe, Japan: IAFOR, 2018), 97.

63. Jürgen Moltmann, *The Way of Jesus Christ: Christology in Messianic Dimensions* (Minneapolis: Fortress Press, 1993), 90.

64. Vitaliano R. Gorospe, "Power and Responsibility: A Filipino Christian Perspective," *Philippine Studies* 36 (1988), 84. Gorospe mentions the term "Filipino Exodus" which was first used by Antonio Lambino.

65. Gorospe, "Power and Responsibility," 84.

rial condition, and our various relationships[66] – between God and his creatures, between human beings and with themselves before God, and between humans and the environment where God had placed them.[67] As described in Isaiah 2:2–4, *shalom/eirene* serves as a "powerful symbol of God's purpose and will for our world."[68] And according to John Goldingay, with YHWH as creator of *shalom*, it stands "for all forms of well-being. It covers peace . . . that embraces much more than the absence of conflict; it suggests a community enjoying fullness of life, prosperity, contentment, harmony, and happiness."[69] The New Testament term *eirene* contains these meanings in conjunction with NT concepts such as righteousness (*dikaiosune*), grace (*charis*) and life (*zoe*) that like the OT concept of *shalom* applies holistically to a person.[70]

Indeed, the cultivation of *shalom* should be the way of life of every Christian and the church. Some evangelical Christian leaders who are actively involved in peacemaking and peacebuilding initiatives pointed to Jesus's ministry to the outcasts and oppressed and his nature as "Prince of Peace" as a vital influence.[71] In following Jesus, they sought to bring *shalom* to people such as the *Moros* or Muslim Filipinos who historically have been treated by the majority Christian Filipinos as enemies. For these Christian peace advocates, Muslims are also *kapwa* who deserve our *malasakit*, for they too share in God's gift of the *imago dei*.

Sadly, *shalom*-making and *shalom*-building are often considered a specialized ministry to which very few are called to do. It is even seen as belonging to the secular since it often interfaces with the political and public spheres. For many evangelical churches, evangelism and discipleship are paramount because of the view that the spiritual is far more important than, and can be completely separated from, the temporal. While there is some degree of truth

---

66. Perry B. Yoder, *SHALOM: The Bible's Word for Salvation, Justice, & Peace* (Eugene: Wipf and Stock Publishers, 1997), 16.

67. Mark DeVine, *Shalom Yesterday, Today, and Forever: Embracing All Three Dimensions of Creation and Redemption* (Eugene: Wipf and Stock, 2019), chap. 1, e-book, https://ereader.perlego.com/1/book/955428/7.

68. Yoder, *Shalom*, 16, 18.

69. John Goldingay, *Old Testament Theology, Vol. 2: Israel's Faith* (Downers Grove: IVP Academic, 2006), 79.

70. Apolos Landa, "Shalom & Eirene: The Full Framework for Health Care," *Christian Journal for Global Health* 1, no. 1 (June 2014): 58.

71. Several evangelical leaders and peace advocates were interviewed by Jon Emil Soriano. Among them were Bishop Mark A. Dimerin from Zamboanga City, Ptr. Daniel Calubiran from Cotabato City, and Engr. Renato Constantino from Manila. They are actively involved in building peace with Muslims.

to this, such perspective has led, however, to a dichotomized view of reality where the church only looks after spiritual concerns, while the state looks after the political, economic, social and all other "non-spiritual" matters. From this perspective, the church ought to submit to the state in all "non-spiritual" matters, in accordance with Romans 13.[72] Hence, very few evangelical leaders conveyed meaningful reaction and opposition against Duterte's "War on Drugs" even as the bodies killed through EJK continued to pile up. Similarly, most evangelicals have been silent with regard to Bongbong Marcos's distortion of a crucial juncture in Philippine history that has blatantly robbed Martial Law victims of their dignity.

This leads us to ask whether being apathetic or oblivious to the plight of victims of injustice and violence, especially *when committed by the state*, is the way of life that the church envisions for itself in the public or political sphere. Does this way of life contribute to the flourishing of God's kingdom and *shalom* on earth, or does it result in its withering? We evangelicals need to grapple honestly with such questions, for while the church may be doing well in spiritual areas such as evangelism, mission, and discipleship, we must take heed also of Melba Maggay's warning that "there is always this shadow side which accounts for the contradictions that develop in all the good work we wish to do."[73]

Concluding Remarks

Almost forty years have now gone by since the Filipino people regained their freedom at EDSA from Marcos's authoritarian regime. It was a revolution that was, simply, revolutionary. Perhaps, back then, the Filipinos on the streets and around the world who were one with the ideals of People Power believed that *vox populi, vox Dei* (the voice of the people is the voice of God) is, or can be, true after all. The many years that have passed may have drowned out such a voice, but clearly, there are many important things that we Filipinos and the church should not forget about the 1986 People Power Revolution. Foremost among these are the people who, like Ninoy, became victims of Marcos's tyranny. Their martyrdom, echoing Tertullian's adage, became the seed of the

---

72. For a biblical-theological perspective of this contentious passage, see Junette B. Galagala-Nacion, "Romans 13 and the Limits of Submission," in *Faith and Bayan: Evangelical Christian Engagement in the Philippine Context*, eds. Bautista et al. (Carlisle: Langham Global Library, 2022), 49–76.

73. Melba Padilla Maggay, ed. *Dark Days of Authoritarianism: To Be in History* (Carlisle: Langham Global Library, 2019), 195.

revolution. The values of *pakikipagkapwa* and *pagmamalasakit* also need to be emphasized in our national and ecclesial consciousness and practice. Enfolded in faith in the God who was crucified, these and other related values lead to acts of "delivering love,"[74] or love that delivers the *kapwa* from oppression and injustice through nonviolent means. People Power has taught us, moreover, that faith needs to be intertwined with concrete actions in the social-political sphere, for the public and political spaces do not belong to the state; they ultimately belong under God's domain.

With the ethic of violence and dehumanization, or the *ways of death* continuing to take root in Philippine society, of which Duterte's drug war and Bongbong Marcos's distortion of history are but two examples, we believe it is crucial for the evangelical church in the Philippines to not only confront its own shadows but to step out of its shadows, especially out of the shadow that the state has cast over the church. Against the way of death, violence, and dehumanization the church must once again take up the Filipino people's battle cry at EDSA, *"Tama Na! Sobra Na! Palitan Na!"* (It Is Enough! It Is Too Much! It Needs To Be Changed!). As David Lim incisively said, "Rather than just being reflectors or endorsers of the social and structural status quo, churches should be prophetic witnesses which stand for structures which are loving (humanizing, humanitarian), just and righteous, and fight against those which are not."[75] The road out of the shadows may be toilsome and difficult, but as John Ferguson reminds us "Christ showed us a new way, a way of life, a way of changing the world . . . It was the way of love, the way of the Cross . . . It is still the way He seeks to fulfill in us."[76]

Bibliography

Agence France-Presse. "Criminals are not Human – Aguirre." *Inquirer.Net*, 1 February 2017. Accessed 21 May 2024. https://newsinfo.inquirer.net/867331/criminals-are-not-human-aguirre.

Al Jazeera, "Talk to Al Jazeera: Rodrigo Duterte Interview: Death, Drugs, and Diplomacy." *Al Jazeera*, 16 October 2016. Accessed 20 May 2024. https://

---

74. Glen H. Stassen and David P. Gushee, *Kingdom Ethics: Following Jesus in Contemporary Context* (Downers Grove: InterVarsity Press, 2003), 336–38.

75. David Lim, "The Living God in the Structures of Philippine Reality," *Transformation* 5 (April–June 1988), 7.

76. John Ferguson, *The Politics of Love: The New Testament and Nonviolent Revolution* (New York: Fellowship Publications, 1979), 112.

www.aljazeera.com/program/talk-to-al-jazeera/2016/10/16/rodrigo-duterte-interview-death-drugs-and-diplomacy.

Althaus, Paul. *The Theology of Martin Luther*. Translated by Robert C. Schultz. Philadelphia: Fortress Press, 1966.

Aquino, Corazon C. *In the Name of Democracy and Prayer: Selected Speeches of Corazon C. Aquino*. Pasig City: Anvil Publishing, 1995.

Aquino, Benigno S., Jr. "The Filipino is Worth Dying For" (Speech delivered in New York City, 4 August 1980). *Manila Times*, 22 August 2010. Accessed 29 May 2024. https://www.manilatimes.net/2010/08/22/special-report/the-filipino-is-worth-dying-for/638146#_=_.

Beltran, Benigno P. *The Christology of the Inarticulate: An Inquiry Into the Filipino Understanding of Jesus the Christ*. Manila, Philippines: Divine Word, 1987.

Beltran, Michael. "Disinformation Reigns in Philippines as Marcos Jr. Takes Top Job." *Al Jazeera*, 29 June 2022. Accessed 25 May 2024. https://www.aljazeera.com/news/2022/6/29/disinformation-reigns-in-philippines-as-marcos-jr-takes-top-job.

Bobis, Merlinda. "Weeping is Singing: After the War, a Transnational Lament." In *At the Limits of Justice: Women of Colour on Terror*, edited by Suvendrini Perera and Sherene H. Razack, 237–62. London: University of Toronto Press, 2014.

Carroll, John J. "The Philippines: Forgiving or Forgetting?" *Public Policy Journal* 3, no. 2 (April–June 1999): 83–92.

Cornelio, Jayeel, and Ia Marañon. "A 'Righteous Intervention': Megachurch Christianity and Duterte's War on Drugs in the Philippines." *International Journal of Asian Christianity* 2 (2019): 211–30.

David, E. J. R. *Filipino-/American Postcolonial Psychology: Oppression, Colonial Mentality and Decolonization*. Bloomington: AuthorHouse, 2011.

De Guia, Katrin. *Kapwa: The Self in Other: Worldviews and Lifestyle of Filipino Culture-Bearers*. Pasig City: Anvil Publishing, 2005.

DeVine, Mark. *Shalom Yesterday, Today, and Forever: Embracing All Three Dimensions of Creation and Redemption*. Eugene: Wipf and Stock, 2019. https://ereader.perlego.com/1/book/955428/7.

Diokno, Ma. Serena I. "Unity and Struggle." In *Dictatorship and Revolution: Roots of People's Power*, edited by Aurora Javate-de Dios, Petronilo Bn. Daroy, and Loma Kalaw-Tirol, 132–75. Manila: Conspectus, 1988.

Ellul, Jacques. *Violence from a Christian Perspective*. New York: The Seabury Press, 1969.

Elwood, Douglas J., and Patricia I. Magdamo. *Christ in Philippine Context: Course Textbook in Theology and Religious Studies*. Quezon City: New Day Publishers, 1971.

Enriquez, Virgilio G. "Kapwa: A Core Concept in Filipino Social Psychology." In *Philippine World View*. Singapore: Institute of Southeast Asian Studies, 1986.

Ferguson, John. *The Politics of Love: The New Testament and Nonviolent Revolution*. New York: Fellowship Publications, 1979.

Fernandez, Artchil B. "The 'Golden Age.'" *Daily Guardian*, 2 July 2022. Accessed 25 May 2024. https://dailyguardian.com.ph/the-golden-age/.

Flores, Helen. "President Marcos: My Father Was Not a Dictator." *Philstar Global*, 15 September 2022. Accessed 1 June 2024. https://www.philstar.com/headlines/2022/09/15/2209778/president-marcos-my-father-was-not-dictator.

Fosdick, H. E. *The Greatness of God*. London: Collins, 1958.

Galagala-Nacion, Junette B. "Romans 13 and the Limits of Submission." In *Faith and Bayan: Evangelical Christian Engagement in the Philippine Context*, edited by Lorenzo C. Bautista, Aldrin M. Peñamora, and Federico G. Villanueva, 49–76. Carlisle: Langham Global Library, 2022.

Goldingay, John. *Old Testament Theology, Vol. 2: Israel's Faith*. Downers Grove: IVP Academic, 2006.

Gorospe, Vitaliano R. *Filipino Values Revisited*. Manila: National Bookstore, 1988.

Hengel, Martin. *Victory Over Violence: Jesus and the Revolutionists*. Translated by David E. Green. Philadelphia: Fortress Press, 1975.

Ileto, Reynaldo C. *Filipinos and Their Revolution: Event, Discourse, and Historiography*. Quezon City: Ateneo de Manila University Press, 1998.

Landa, Apolos. "Shalom & Eirene: The Full Framework for Health Care," *Christian Journal for Global Health* 1, no. 1 (June 2014): 57–59.

Lim, David. "The Living God in the Structures of Philippine Reality," *Transformation* 5 (April–June 1988): 1–8.

Luther, Martin. "Heidelberg Disputation." In *Martin Luther's Basic Theological Writings*, edited by Timothy F. Lull, 30–49. Minneapolis: Fortress Press, 1989.

Maggay, Melba Padilla, ed. *Dark Days of Authoritarianism: To Be in History*. Carlisle: Langham Global Library, 2019.

Manasan, Althea. "Filipino Survivors of Martial Law Still Haunted by Abuses 50 Years after Declaration." CBC Radio, 23 September 2022. Accessed 25 May 2024. https://www.cbc.ca/radio/thecurrent/survivors-martial-law-philippines-abuses-50-years-later-1.6592042.

Mendoza, Ruben C. "The Performance of the Christian Faith under a Populist President: The Case of the Philippine Church under Duterte." *MST Review* 22 (2020): 1–46.

Moltmann, Jürgen. *The Crucified God*. Translated by R. A. Wilson and John Bowden. New York: Harper & Row Publishers, 1974.

———. *The Way of Jesus Christ: Christology in Messianic Dimensions*. Minneapolis: Fortress Press, 1993.

Nietzsche, Friedrich. "The Anti-Christ." In *A Nietzsche Reader*, translated by R. J. Hollingdale. London: Penguin Books, 1977.

Nudas, Alfeo G. *God With Us: The 1986 Philippine Revolution*. Quezon City: Ateneo University Press, 1986.

Peñamora, Aldrin M. "The Power of Powerlessness: A Study of the Cross Motif as the Underlying Theological Principle of the 1986 People Power Phenomenon." Master of Theology thesis, Asia Graduate School of Theology, 2004.

———. "Their Blood Cries Out from the Ground: An Ethic of *Malasakit* and the War on Drugs." In *Faith and Bayan: Evangelical Christian Engagement in the Philippine Context*, edited by Lorenzo C. Bautista, Aldrin M. Peñamora, and Federico G. Villanueva, 115–31. Carlisle: Langham Global Library, 2022.

Redona, Marites Rano. "*Malasakit*: The Filipino Face of God's Mercy." In *Fearful Futures: Cultural Studies and the Question of Agency in the Twenty-First Century*, 103–12. Kobe, Japan: IAFOR, 2018. Accessed 15 May 2024. https://papers.iafor.org/wp-content/uploads/papers/accs2018/ACCS2018_41147.pdf.

Reyes, Danilo Andres. "The Spectacle of Violence in Duterte's War on Drugs." *Journal of Current Southeast Asian Affairs* 35, no. 3 (2016): 111–37.

Santos, Reynaldo, Jr. "1986 Comelec Walkout not about Cory or Marcos." *Rappler*, 25 February 2013. Accessed 14 May 2024. https://www.rappler.com/nation/elections/22582-1986-comelec-walkout-not-about-cory-or-marcos/.

Song, C. S. *Third Eye Theology: Theology in Formation in Asian Settings*. Maryknoll: Orbis Books, 1979.

Stassen, Glen H., and David P. Gushee. *Kingdom Ethics: Following Jesus in Contemporary Context*. Downers Grove: InterVarsity Press, 2003.

Weber, Hans-Ruedi. *Power: Focus for a Biblical Theology*. Geneva: WCC Publications, 1989.

Wink, Walter. *Engaging the Powers: Discernment and Resistance in a World of Domination*. Minneapolis: Fortress Press, 1992.

Yoder, Perry B. *SHALOM: The Bible's Word for Salvation, Justice, and Peace*. Eugene: Wipf and Stock Publishers, 1997.

14

Grassroots Evangelical Political Theology

Jack Dosejo Alvarez

Grassroots politics is the heart and soul of democracy.[1]
– Bart van Heerikhuizen

This statement from a well-known Dutch sociologist regarding grassroots politics is exhilarating and enlightening. Exhilarating because it animates and gives the poor excitement and hope for social change. Enlightening because in a democratic form of government, the grassroots or the poor, are privileged and less likely to be marginalized. Democracy, after all, is the rule of the poor.[2] And such a kind of politics is indeed the *raison d'etre* of democracy.

The Philippines is a democratic and republican state: "Sovereignty resides in the people and all government authority emanates from them."[3] The Philippines having such a political system is home for grassroots politics. But unfortunately, grassroots politics is scant in the Philippines. It is hardly felt if

---

1. Heerikhuizen taught sociology at the University of Amsterdam for more than forty years. See his *Grassroots as the Heart of Democracy*, accessed 8 March 2022, https://www.youtube.com/watch?v=OCVqAkPHc0Y.

2. Aristotle says in his *Politics*, "Where the poor rule, that is democracy." See *The Pocket Aristotle*, ed. Justin D. Kaplan and trans. W. D. Ross (New York: Pocket Books, 1958), 308. See also "The result in democracies the people have more power than the well off" in Carnes Lord, *Aristotle's Politics*, 2nd ed. (Chicago: University of Chicago Press, 2013), 192. Take note by the way that Aristotle distrusted democracy.

3. Constitution of the Republic of the Philippines of 1987, article II, section 1, accessed 25 January 2023, https://www.officialgazette.gov.ph/constitutions/1987-constitution/.

not for the *Makabayan* bloc[4] in the Philippine Congress. From my observation of Philippine society, the poor organizing to air out their grievances and advocating for their welfare in their cities, municipalities, and *barangays*,[5] is almost nonexistent. It is because Philippine politics is grossly dominated by the elite of the society. This is a reason why the *Makabayan* bloc is an evidence of grassroots politics. Lest of course one perceives the *Makabayan* as misrepresenting the poor and the marginalized, and that they are actually leftists using the *masang Pinoy*[6] for their own political interest. Even if this is true, they are nonetheless a solid evidence of grassroots politics in the Philippines.

This brief work on grassroots politics is mainly from the talk I gave at the Faith and Politics forum that Drs. David Lim and Aldrin Peñamora organized in late 2021. "*Ebanghelikong Theolohiyang Pulitikal sa Masang Pilipino*"[7] was aired on Meta on 10 March 2022. I am grateful to Edicio dela Torre, a well-known political theologian who was captured and tortured during the Martial Law years, for responding to my talk. Dela Torre was a religious priest. He is one among the Catholic clergy and laity who were imprisoned and tortured during Marcos Sr.'s brutal Martial Law. In this essay, I will first describe Philippine politics and give a sociopolitical and historical glimpse that is crucial for this task. Second, I will marshal that the poverty of the Filipino masses is caused by political corruption due to the influence of the few super-rich in the government. Third, I will venture to define what grassroots politics and grassroots evangelical political theology are. And fourth and last, I am positioning the locus of grassroots evangelical political theology in the local church. This includes three important interrelated recommendations to my fellow evangelicals, not to mention that we can love our neighbors through politics.

I am writing mainly as a pastor of a small urban church in the slums of Payatas. I am not a political scientist. However my deep interest in biblical and contextual theologies as well as my firm belief in Christ as Lord of all of life has plunged me into Philippine politics and society. Pastorally, I wish to address an elephant in the room, which makes tens of millions of Filipinos

---

4. The *Makabayang Koalisyon ng Mamamayan* (coalition of patriotic citizens) or more popularly known as the *Makabayan* bloc, is mainly composed of leftist party-lists in the House of Representatives.

5. The word *barangay* is usually translated as village. This Filipino word is derived from *balangay*, a boat used by precolonial inhabitants of the Philippine archipelago. *Barangay* is the smallest independent political unit in the Philippines. As of September 2022, there are 42,047 *barangays* throughout the Philippines.

6. Colloquial for the Filipino masses.

7. "Evangelical Political Theology in the Filipino masses."

poor and politically marginalized. And that elephant is none other than political corruption and bad governance. My prayer is that the scales blinding the eyes of many evangelicals regarding this matter would fall out. It is of utmost importance that we understand what makes the Philippines poor, ill, and awful so we can take concrete actions on how to transform it.

Philippine Politics

Perhaps the best way to understand Philippine politics is to describe it and identify some characteristics that pundits have been talking about. I list only three characteristics here. A quick look on precolonial roots of Philippine politics is included in this section.

Traditional Politics

This is perhaps the most prominent terminology people use in describing Philippine politics. This term has been shortened to *tradpol* and then *trapo*.[8] This is evident in people's frequent use of the term during election times. *Trapo* involves the society's elite as the ones always winning elections and occupying key governmental positions. This kind of politics is well-entrenched in Philippine society. It has become a culture and a tradition. If this is indeed the case of Philippine politics, it is not a democracy but "*cacique* politics."[9] Abinales and Amoroso observed that post-EDSA[10] *trapos* had lost national grounding. However, the Aquino revolutionary government failed to totally eradicate them, only to discover later that they had become localized and had forged coalitions with nongovernmental organizations (NGOs) and people's organiza-

---

8. There is word play here; *trapo* is actually a Bicolano and a Visayan (Cebuano, Hiligaynon, Waray, etc.) word for dirty rag that people use daily at home. The word is originally Spanish, so colonialism and oppression of the rich toward the poor also plays in and is imagined here.

9. "*Cacique*" is a Spanish transliteration of the Taino word *kasike*, meaning a king or a prince. In Philippine politics, this is characterized by a political boss. See Benedict Anderson, *Cacique Democracy and the Philippines: Origins and Dream*. https://newleftreview.org/issues/i169/articles/benedict-anderson-cacique-democracy-and-the-philippines-origins-and-dreams.

10. On 22–25 February 1986 – People Power Revolution, also known as EDSA Revolution, was a series of peaceful demonstrations of over two million Filipinos (civilians, political, and military groups) along Epifanio delos Santos Avenue (EDSA). This historical political event ended the twenty-year regime of Ferdinand Marcos Sr. Shortly after that, a revolutionary government under Corazon C. Aquino took over and restored democracy in the Philippines. Unfortunately, as Abinales and Amoroso and some critics would argue – Corazon Aquino's presidency did nothing to demolish *cacique* politics in the country.

tions (POs).¹¹ By the time of President Fidel V. Ramos who succeeded President Cory Aquino, the *caciques* who are pro-Marcos, had comfortably adjusted to the post-authoritarian era and had rejoined the "constitutional process."¹²

Dynastic Politics

This is also caciquism or political bossism except for the bigger imagery it exudes. Dynastic politicians' influence is deep and widespread. They have been in various government positions for decades. An example of this is the Joson dynasty in the province of Nueva Ecija in Central Luzon. For forty-eight years they were the governors in the province while some relatives and people close to the family occupied other key government positions. The Josons lost the gubernatorial position in 2007 and were replaced by the Umalis, another dynastic family. Another case is in the Science City of Muñoz where I grew up. It is also in the same province. The Alvarez dynasty has been in the mayoralty since 1992. The incumbent mayor and vice mayor are siblings while their nephew is a city councilor.¹³

Patron-Client Politics

The two political characteristics mentioned above result in patron-client politics. Politicians as patrons give many kinds of goods and services to their constituents, and vice versa. Oftentimes only those who supported elected officials in the recent elections can receive benefits from the government. An example of this is a neighbor of mine who campaigned for a popular personality and his son in Quezon City in the local elections of 2022. Her efforts paid off when her candidates won. She was given a job and she's now earning monthly from her government work. This exchange for the benefit of both parties is complex and comes in many forms. Some people call this kind of set-up *patronage politics* and *clientelism*.

---

11. Patricio N. Abinales and Donna J. Amoroso, *State and Society in the Philippines*, 2nd ed. (Quezon City: Ateneo de Manila University Press, 2017), 237–42.

12. Patricio N. Abinales, *Images of State Power: Essays on Philippine Politics from the Margins* (Quezon City: University of the Philippines Press, 1998), 156.

13. They are not my relatives. My family is originally from Negros Occidental while they are from Cavite.

Precolonial Roots

In precolonial social structures, the ruling class in North Luzon were called the *agturay* or *aris*. This class of people had the superior authority in the *ili* (town). Second to them were called *amaen* or *panglakayan*.¹⁴ Among the Ifugao, William Henry Scott notes that the *kadangyans* are a plutocracy while among the Ibanags, the *kammaranan* is the chief of the town.¹⁵ Among the Tagalogs, there were the *maginoo* and the *datus*. These were the heads of the barangays. Slave owners were called *panginoons* while those who own houses and boats were addressed as *may-ari*.¹⁶ In Bikolandia, Fray Marcos de Lisboa noted that preconquest Bicolano elites were the *datu* and *ginoo*. If one is prominent, he is called *maginoo* or *hiyangta*. *Kagduluhan* was the head of the community while a *namamanwa* was the ruler of a town. A *pono* was a senior among chiefs just like a *pono sa banwaan*.¹⁷

In the Visayas, the ruling elites were the *dato*, *pangulo*, and *kaponoan*. *Kadatoaan* were the chief leaders. Among them was a *pangulo*, a head or leader as well as the *kaponooan* who was the most sovereign.¹⁸ A *dato* who was autocratic, oppressive, courageous, and frightening is called a *pamalpagan* – from *palpag*, split and flattened bamboo. To the present Visayans, especially among the Hiligaynon, *palpag* means to strike the person down.¹⁹ In Mindanao, particularly in Maguindanao – the ruling elite were called *sultans*, *rajas*, and *orangkaya* (rich people).²⁰ In Sulu, the sultan was very much in connection with the sultans of Brunei and Sumatra. The *tuam* or *orangkaya* of Sulu were overlords to vassal chieftains of the Suban-on and Monobo tribes.

I wish to note how the late Renato Constantino, a well-known Filipino historian, somehow romanticized our precolonial ancestors. He mentions in one of his works that the elite mentioned above are not rulers but administrators,²¹

---

14. Juana Jimenez Pelmoka, *Pre-Spanish Philippines* (J. J. de Pelmoka and E. P. Ujano, 1996), 79.

15. William Henry Scott, *Barangay: Sixteenth-Century Philippine Culture and Society* (Quezon City: Ateneo de Manila University Press, 1994), 261, 267–68.

16. Scott, Barangay, 219–24. It seems that the honorific titles in Luzon are just confined among the Tagalog.

17. Scott, Barangay, 183.

18. Scott, Barangay, 127–28.

19. Scott, Barangay, 129.

20. Scott, Barangay, 176–78.

21. Renato Constantino, *The Philippines: A Past Revisited, Vol. 1* (Panay Avenue, Quezon City, 1975), 32–33.

and that slavery is a misnomer.[22] However, a more recent scholarship done by William Henry Scott tells us that there were lords and owners in precolonial Philippines. That a *pamalpagan* is a dreaded *dato* because he strikes down subjects who do wrong.

If these kinds and classes of peoples were the ruling elite before the coming of the Western powers to the archipelago, we can say for sure that they would not easily disappear in Philippine society. And so, Filipinos have witnessed historically that these ruling elite became the *cabeza de barangay* (head of the barangay), *gobernacillo* (town governor), and the *alcalde mayor* (provincial governor) in the Spanish-ruled Philippines.[23] "The old and new principalia are the basically the same, i.e., they both consist of the socioeconomic dominants in the society,"[24] says Simbulan and this is in the postwar setting. He concludes in his research that, "Philippine political parties were – and still are – elite parties."[25]

Poverty and Philippine Politics

According to the late senator, Jovito J. Salonga, Philippine society has three main problems: "*massive poverty, rampant corruption, and uncontrolled criminality. And these three are interrelated.*"[26] Salonga adds

> Our grinding poverty, the result of the concentration of too much wealth and power in the hands of a few – the so called elite – leads to graft and corruption, a double standard or justice (one standard of justice for the poor and another standard of justice for the rich) and ever-rising criminality. Thefts, robberies, drug addiction, murders and assassinations are what we see and read in the media every day. There are the flaws in our cultural traits, such as *utang na loob, pakikisama*, the *kanya-kanya*[27] syndrome

---

22. Constantino, *The Philippines*, 33–36.
23. Dante C. Simbulan, *The Modern Principalia* (Diliman, Quezon City: The University of the Philippines Press, 2005), 18–20.
24. Simbulan, *The Modern Principalia*, 76, 298.
25. Simbulan, *The Modern Principalia*, 299.
26. Jovito R. Salonga, *The Task of Building a Better Nation* (Mandaluyong City: Kilosbayan, 2005), 18 (Emphasis added).
27. *Utang na loob* (debt of gratitude that cannot be paid monetarily or materially, which could be used to take advantage of the person), *pakikisama* (going along with others despite the wrongdoing of the group), *kanya-kanya* (going each other's way and disregarding other people). These are some Filipino traits that are deemed to be negative and disadvantageous.

and the lack of sense of community that tend to worsen the twin problems of corruption and criminality.[28]

To reiterate Salonga: Poverty, corruption, and uncontrolled criminality are interrelated. However, this fact has eluded even the most educated Filipinos, especially evangelical leaders, myself included, despite fifteen years of pastorate in the slums of Payatas near the foot of a towering garbage dump. It was just recently that I have come to realize this interrelationship. This happened one time when I was walking the streets of *Lupang Pangako*.[29] It dawned on me that political corruption is the main cause of poverty of the *masang Pinoy* (the Filipino masses). I kept hearing Lady Wisdom[30] pointing out to me that the severe poverty of children playing on the dirty streets and the half-naked men drinking gin in front of their shanties has something to do with corruption. To a sociologist or a highly educated non-slum dweller living a comfortable life in a gated subdivision, this realization could be obvious. But to many of us, this is a case of "the elephant in the room." It's a daily reality that we have ignored or avoided to discuss. But, how come many of us cannot easily articulate the wide economic injustice between the poor and the rich? Even to us who have been used to poverty and a hard life, this is not easily realized. I suspect that the difficulty in discerning is because of some level of desensitization. After all, what is socio-economically normal to us is relative. And slum dwelling is actually a way of life.[31] I myself have been desensitized from it, even after fifteen years of residence in Payatas. Poverty has been normalized, it almost slipped my attention.

When I started looking for the connection between poverty and politics, little did I know that I had opened a kind of Pandora's box. A superficial look at poverty will not make nor mention the connection of the two. An example

---

28. Jovito R. Salonga, *The Task of Building*, 19. Those cultural traits mentioned by Salonga are in the negative and they contribute to the worsening of Philippine society.

29. *Lupang Pangako* is a slum area in Payatas. It is where I live. It is where the two towering dump sites of Metro Manila could be found, which the Philippine government eventually closed down in 2017 because it could no longer hold the influx of tons of garbage of Metro Manila. Ironically in English, *Lupang Pangako* is literally "promised land" – the land that *trapos* promised to the thousands of Filipino poor migrating to Metro Manila in search of a better life. In 10 July 2000, the first dump site of Payatas at Urban, *Lupang Pangako* collapsed, leaving many people dead. The government reported that seven hundred people died. Some people say that seven hundred people were buried alive. Still some people, who are actual residents, say that more than a thousand people were killed in that tragic trash slide.

30. Proverbs 8 challenges me to observe life in order to gain wisdom and understanding.

31. F. Landa Jocano, *Slums as a Way of Life* (Quezon City: University of Philippines Press, 1970).

of this was the 2009 Asian Development Bank report on poverty.³² Of the eight main causes of poverty in the country, nothing was linked to political malfeasance and bad governance. However, the "key findings" of the report did mention two factors relating to governance and institutional constraints and the weakness of the local government in implementing poverty programs.³³ I construe the report as somehow careful not to rock the boat. However, I applaud ADB's key recommendations that government agencies like the National Anti-Poverty Commission (NAPC), National Economic and Development Agency (NEDA), and other agencies should revise, reform, engage, and even examine the political economy of poverty. Also, that there should be close coordination among these agencies.³⁴ ADB's 2009 report on poverty in the Philippines may not be conversant of the political angle of why Filipinos are impoverished. Fortunately, it does include lots of governmental and political responsibilities in the medium and long-term economic solutions.³⁵

Perhaps the real perpetuators of why we often do not link corrupt politics to the poverty of many *Pinoys* are the textbooks on social issues being used in our schools.³⁶ But even the more recent work of Mooney, Know, and Schacht's *Understanding Social Problems* (eighth and international edition),³⁷ does not make a direct reference to political wrongdoings. Their sociological theories of poverty and economic inequality are reduced to structural-functional, conflict, and symbolic interactionist perspectives. These sociologists have yet to link bad governance and geopolitics as contributing factors that hamper people's prosperity and welfare.

My realization was confirmed when I started reading literature showing the connection. The works of Ronald U. Mendoza and his co-authors,³⁸ and

---

32. See Asian Development Bank, *Poverty in the Philippines: Causes, Constraints and Opportunities*. https://www.adb.org/sites/default/files/publication/27529/poverty-philippines-causes-constraints-opportunities.pdf.

33. ADB, *Poverty in the Philippines: Causes, Constraints and Opportunities*, 3.

34. ADB, 4.

35. ADB, 5–6.

36. See for example, Custodiosa A. Sanchez and Fe B. Agpaoa, *Contemporary Social Problems and Issues* (Mandaluyong City: National Book Store, 1997); Sison Q. Jarapa, Rafael B. Perez, and Tito S. Segarra, *Current Social Issues* (Sampaloc, Manila: Rex Book Store, 2001); Francisco M. Zulueta and Dolores B. Liwag, *Social Problems and Issues in the Philippines* (Mandaluyong City: National Book Store, 2001).

37. Linda A. Mooney, David Knox, and Caroline Schacht, *Understanding Social Problems* (Boston: Wadsworth Cengage Learning, 2013).

38. Ronald Mendoza, Edsel Beja Jr., Victor S. Venida, and David B. Yap II, "Political Dynasties and Poverty: Measurement and Evidence of Linkages in the Philippines," *Oxford Development Studies* 44 (2016): 189–201. See also Ronald U. Mendoza, Edsel Beja, Victor

Sheila S. Coronel and other investigative journalists at the Philippine Center for Investigative Journalism[39] exposed this sad reality. Political malfeasance that causes economic poverty to the tens of millions of Filipinos ranges from public works, textbook funds, public schools, expressways, fake court ruling and bribery, presidential and congressional links, local government, environment, etc. Coronel even made mention of "grand corruption."[40] Political corruption in the Philippines is staggering.

Socioeconomic Consequences of Corruption

Coronel listed five consequences of corruption. I think these would suffice to show that poverty in the Philippines is caused by political corruption and bad governance. Each one of these five consequences has data and explanation. However, I will just note them down here and leave it to the reader to internalize this reality.

- Corruption impedes economic growth
- Corruption worsens income inequity and poverty
- Corruption damages political legitimacy and stunts democracy
- Corruption endangers public order and safety
- Corruption results in bureaucratic inefficiency and demoralization[41]

So from the words of the late Senator Salonga, the findings of Simbulan, the works of Mendoza and Coronel and their co-authors – our country is run by corrupt politicians. These political dynasties are the elite of our society and they happen to be families and clans: husbands and wives, fathers and sons and daughters, and their close relatives in Malacañang, in Congress, and in the local government units.[42] There is no doubt that the main cause of grind-

---

Venida, and David Yap, *Political and Poverty: Chicken or the Egg*, https://www.kas.de/documents/275121/275170/7_file_storage_file_9551_2.pdf/e5a6f153-7de8-3611-50a5-4a0a0387cea9?version=1.0&t=1539679408792.

39. See Sheila S. Coronel, *Betrayals of the Public Trust: Investigative Reports on Corruption with Explanation of Reporting Techniques Used* (Quezon City: Philippine Center for Investigative Journalism, 2000). See also Sheila Coronel, ed. *Porks and Other Perks: Corruption and Governance in the Philippines* (Quezon City: PCIJ, 1998).

40. Sheila Coronel and Lorna Kalaw-Tirol, eds., *Investigating Corruption: A Do-It-Yourself Guide* (Quezon City: PCIJ, 2002), 12–13.

41. Coronel and Kalaw-Tirol, *Investigating Corruption*, 17–22.

42. For concrete examples, see Sheila S. Coronel, Yvonne T. Chua, Luz Rimban, and Booma B. Cruz, *The Rulemakers: How the Wealthy and Well-Born Dominate Congress* (Quezon City: PCIJ, 2004). See also Ronald U. Mendoza, Edsel L. Beja Jr., Victor S. Venida, and David B. Yap, "Political Dynasties and Poverty: Measurement and Evidence of Linkages in the Philippines, "

ing poverty in the Philippines is the dominance of the few super-rich in our society's political culture and our nation's economy. Another solid proof is the scandalous fact that the banking system in the Philippines is run by the elite, as Paul D. Hutchcroft reveals in his book, *Booty Capitalism: The Politics of Banking in the Philippines*.[43]

Barking at the Wrong Tree?

Walden Bello and his co-authors attempt "to puncture a powerful discourse that has seduced the most sophisticated analysts as well as the ordinary man on the street: that the Philippines is so poor because its leaders are corrupt."[44] They are saying that, "it is wrong for the easily demonstrable fact that so many other countries suffering from as much or even more systematic corruption than the Philippines have succeeded in developing and reducing poverty."[45] Instead, Bello and his co-authors fault the ruling oligarchy. They were making their case during the presidency of Joseph Estrada whose cronies – Lucio Tan, Mark Jimenez, Dante Tan, and Danding Cojuangco – benefited much.

So it is not the corrupt politicians that make Filipinos poor. It is the ruling oligarchy who marionette whoever is in the highest position. It is the few super-rich raping the country's economy and making the Filipino people perpetually poor. The thesis of Bello and his co-authors makes a lot of sense. Though it is somewhat reductionist and tainted with neo-Marxist ideology, it confirms what others have observed. We can posit that the main reason why tens of millions of Filipinos remain economically poor and politically manipulated is actually *the connivance, if not the conspiracy, of the super-rich and their political agents in government and other institutions of the Philippine society*. Perhaps, we should also consider and imagine the spiritual side of this: That greed is their idolatry[46] – the elite are exceptional in loving *mammon* (money),[47] to the

---

Oxford Development Studies 44, no. 2 (11 April 2016), 189–201, https://www.tandfonline.com/doi/abs/10.1080/13600818.2016.1169264.

    43. Paul D. Hutchcroft, *Booty Capitalism: The Politics of Banking in the Philippines* (Quezon City: Ateneo de Manila University Press, 2000).

    44. Walden Bello, Herbert Docena, Marissa de Guzman, and Marylow Malig, *The Anti-Development State: The Political Economy of Permanent Crisis in the Philippines* (Quezon City: Department of Sociology, College of Social Sciences and Philosophy, University of the Philippines, 2004), 243–323.

    45. Bello, Docena, de Guzman, Malig, *The Anti-Development State*.

    46. See Ephesians 5:3 and Colossians 3:5.

    47. 1 Timothy 6:10 and 2 Timothy 3:2.

detriment of millions of Filipinos. And Jesus's injunction to the rich young ruler[48] is still relevant today, as well as the apostle James's teaching on the rich and the poor.[49]

Grassroots Politics

Grassroots social movements are a phenomenon not easy to explain, but we can posit that humans by nature want to be liberated from any form of oppression and malevolence induced by any regime. Joerg Rieger points out that grassroots social movements are the combination of religion and politics in an organic fashion.[50] Referring to ordinary people, he observes, "Their horizons are rarely confined by the strict separation of religion and politics that is part of the history of modernity;"[51] history is being filled by the grassroots who were religious and at the same time political.[52] Until now, though some are seemingly less religious, people are rising up to fight sociopolitical injustices.[53]

Here in the Philippines, we can clearly see this kind of sociopolitical phenomenon in Reynaldo Ileto's *Pasyon and Revolution*.[54] He referred to the popular movements as "religiopolitical."[55] Serafin Talisayon says that Filipino revolutionaries are not only patriotic but religious as well.[56] Talisayon argues that Andres Bonifacio has been viewed as a spiritual hero; Bonifacio's *Dekalogo* (Ten Commandments) proves this. Not to mention the pop movements Ileto refers to in his book. Of the approximately two hundred reported grassroots uprisings against Spain in the Philippines, can we refer to them all as religiopolitical uprisings?

---

48. See Mark 10:17–31 and its parallel passages – Matthew 19:16–30 and Luke 18:18–30.
49. See James 1:9–11; 2:1–13; and 5:1–8.
50. Joerg Rieger, "Grassroots Social Movements" in *The Wiley Blackwell Companion to Political Theology*, 2nd ed., eds. William T. Cavanaugh and Peter Manley Scott (Hoboken: John Wiley & Sons, 2019), 562–64.
51. Rieger, "Grassroots Social Movements," 562.
52. Rieger, "Grassroots Social Movements," 564–65.
53. Joerg Rieger, "Grassroots Social Movements,"565–68.
54. Reynaldo Clemeña Ileto, *Pasyon and Revolution: Popular Movements in the Philippines, 1840–1910* (Quezon City: Ateneo de Manila University Press, 1979).
55. Ileto, *Pasyon and Revolution*, 1, 120, 185, and 209. Although the exact term is somehow scant, the interplay of religion and politics of the pop movements is what we can discern in Ileto's findings. This is tenable knowing that the *Pasyon* is a pop religious song that was the inspiration of the religious *masa* for political liberation.
56. Serafin Talisayon, "Ang Ulirang Pamumuno sa mga Pilipino" in *Roots of Filipino Spirituality*, ed. Teresita B. Obusan (Mamamathala, 1998), 270.

Grassroots social movements are obviously grassroots politics. The term grassroots politics is coined by Heerikhuizen in his social media lecture mentioned above. This term is originally of an American origin. Its earliest possible historical recorded use was in a political campaign strategy. Eli Torrance, Theodore Roosevelt's running mate, uttered the term in 1903.[57] However, the idea of political parties and democratic involvement of the grassroots – a coalition of poor farmers, city-dwelling laborers and Irish Catholics, could be attributed to Andrew Jackson and his kind of democracy.[58] When Alexis de Tocqueville arrived in the US in 1831, what he had observed was Jacksonian democracy. Heerikhuizen is right to term that kind of politics today as grassroots politics. Here in the Philippines, as mentioned in the beginning of this essay, the *Makabayan* bloc, despite how many Evangelicals keep their distance from this movement as being leftist, is the most visible evidence of grassroots politics.

Grassroots politics is obviously the fusion of two words. *Grassroots* connotes the masses, the ordinary people. They are the poor and the marginalized. The word is a metaphor of the people who are viewed as unrepresented and marginalized by the democratic system that should actually embody them. *Politics*, the second word in the term, is not easy to define. However, it is important to have a functional understanding of the word. So I follow Kari Palomen's definition that politics should be construed as a *sphere* and an *activity*.[59] Sphere is the spatial concept and demarcation of public and private life, but it means more on the public matter.[60] Politics is also an activity, which means that historically, temporal contingency on politics results in deliberative rhetoric. Conceptualization, democratization, and parliamentarization of politics are the results of such activities that include the *topoi* (areas) of politics – themes, conventions, rhetorical figures. Policy making as the notion of "play" and "game" also characterizes the undertakings of politics.[61] If Aristotle is foundational in political theory, politics is indeed the affairs of the people of the *polis* (city).

---

57. See *The Salt Lake Herald*, 6, Image 6, 25 September 1903, https://chroniclingamerica.loc.gov/lccn/sn85058130/1903-09-25/ed-1/seq-6/.

58. Sean Wilentz, *The Rise of American Democracy: Jefferson to Lincoln* (New York: W. W. Norton, 2005). See also Thomas Patterson, *The American Democracy* (New York: McGraw-Hill Companies, 2013), 228–29.

59. Kari Palomen, "Politics" in *The Encyclopaedia of Political Science*, Vol. 1–5, eds George Thomas Kurian, James E. Alt, Simone Chambers, Geoffrey Garrett, Margaret Levi, and Paula D. McClain (Washington, DC: CQ Press, 2011), 1299–1301.

60. Kari Palomen, "Politics," 1300.

61. Kari Palomen, "Politics," 1300–301.

If we have rightly described and defined politics, grassroots politics then is the coming together of the poor and marginalized to deliberately exercise their rights and responsibility to the state, especially to the locality where they are situated. Scores of books have been written with regard to the word "grassroots" in their titles. The term is frequently used by political activists, social justice advocates, and even theologians.[62] Unfortunately, despite the desire of many to realize social justice, there are malevolent people who counter the works of social justice. Astroturf is literally an artificial grass or lawn surface used in athletic fields or shopping malls. The word is used metaphorically to indicate fake grassroots movements. Corrupt politicians with their vested interests use astroturf to trick people. I have seen this in huge protest rallies like in the case of the former president, Gloria Macapagal Arroyo. The huge crowd in Commonwealth Avenue protesting against her regime were matched by a crowd of Arroyo supporters. They were just a small crowd but they managed to disrupt the line of protesters and get media attention. I personally know this because some of the protesters who were scouted by a political agent were my friends in Payatas. One of them complained to me about how their astroturf organizer did not pay their disguised work.

Defining Grassroots Evangelical Political Theology

How shall we then define grassroots evangelical political theology? What would be its "meaning" and expected "doing"? I hereby propose the idea that grassroots evangelical political theology is "talking about God" where *Christ's lordship is in the political aspect of God's order of creation* (which is total and absolute), and the *human agency* which is crucial for its reformative task in the world. This "God-talk" is essentially "evangelical," that is the good news of politics being created and redeemed by God through Jesus Christ and for Christ's glory.

I wish to emphasize that this God-talk necessitates active and energetic evangelical Christians who will walk and flesh it out in real life. Besides evangelical audacity on the Holy Scriptures and the exciting synergy of Christians in the wide spectrum of evangelicalism – grassroots evangelical political theology must be unabashedly for the poor and the marginalized in society. It

---

62. See for example, Terry Christensen and Tom Hogen-Esch, *Local Politics: A Practical Guide to Governing at the Grassroots*, 2nd ed. (London: Routledge, 2006); Carol Chetkovich and Frances Kunreuther, *From the Ground Up: Grassroots Organizations Making Social Change* (Ithaca: Cornell University Press, 2006); and Simon Chan, *Grassroots Asian Theology: Thinking the Faith from the Ground Up* (Downers Grove: InterVarsity Press, 2014).

must be strategic, prophetic, charismatic, practical, and incarnational. It must always seek the power and guidance of the Holy Spirit. And amid religious and ideological pluralism and a myriad of issues besetting our society, this God-talk and praxis must always be in conjunction with other individuals and peoples who have genuinely concerned themselves with human flourishing in the world today.

The Local Evangelical Church

The locus of grassroots evangelical political theology is the local church. It is so, not just because of the need to be socio-politically relevant today. It is so, because of the very fact that God, through Jesus Christ, is the creator of all governing powers. These powers are for Christ being its owner and Lord (Col 1:16).

The local church, after all, is essentially political. It is an *ekklesia* or assembly of people in Jesus Christ, that is an integral part of the *polis* and at the same time not *of* it. It is political not just because of the possibility of the messianic ethic and the political implication of the kingdom of God.[63] It is political due to the fact that it lives for Jesus Christ the *pantokrator* (ruler of all). Moreover, it has a biblical worldview and an integral philosophy that needs to be embodied in the world. And if this is indeed the case – the local church is a revolutionary community demanding political leaders, being God's *diakonos* (servants), to be fully just, righteous, and peaceful to all peoples in the *polis*. This proclamation is of course not coercive. It is through humble and excellent service and peaceful means.

A lot is to be thought about and said in regard to the political nature of the local church. And before I venture to recommend practical ideas to fellow Christians, especially evangelicals, I wish to remind the reader that my recommendations come from my realizations as a pastor who lives and ministers in a slum area. I became a social activist in early 2004 during the tumultuous times of the former president, Gloria Macapagal Arroyo. Ever since, I have become active not only in political protest rallies but also in studying the situations that have beset the *masang Pinoy*. Contextual theology taught me to grapple with biblical theologies and my Filipino life-situation. Below are my three interrelated practical political recommendations.

---

63. John Yoder, *The Politics of Jesus*, 2nd ed. (Grand Rapids: Eerdmans, 1994).

Practical Political Recommendations

Philip Flores's *A New Breed: Call for a New Generation of Pastoral Leaders*[64] beseeches for Christlikeness in the evangelical pastorate. Flores was scandalized by the attitude of some pastors. The evangelical pastorate, after all – and just like others – is not immune to blunders and scandals. I can personally testify on this sad reality (and sometimes wonder if I am part of it). I agree with what Flores is advocating, but I wish to include in Flores's clarion call the need for pastors and church leaders to be politically ethical. By this I mean embracing what is good and righteous in politics as well as shunning and condemning any form of evil that distorts its creational teleology. I tremble at the thought of power-mongering pastors. It is a fact that some pastors are close to corrupt politicians while unmindful of the poor and of public justice. So my first recommendation is to address in our pastorate the need to be *politically ethical* and not just have a pietistic "Christlikeness" that has nothing to do with our society.

Second, *political discipleship*. Discipleship programs in our local churches and denominations are pietistic, emphasizing Christian holiness yet missing the practical and missional side of transforming society and the world for Christ. It is high time for evangelicals to have a holistic worldview: a way of seeing the world as God's domain and locus of his kingship. I think Abraham Kuyper's 1880 speech at the opening of the Free University of Amsterdam that there's not a square inch in the whole domain of human existence over which Christ, who is Lord over all, does not exclaim, "Mine!" should also enter our evangelical imagination and vocabulary. Political discipleship is a must among evangelical Christians all over the world. I have been reading five important books on politics. I would like to suggest these titles to the reader. Jim Skillen's *The Good of Politics*[65] is an important book, while Al Wolter's *Creation Regained*[66] is foundational. Adding to these is David Koyzis's *Political Visions and Illusions*[67] which is vital in understanding political ideologies and their accompanying "soteriologies." I include Yoder's important book, *The Politics of Jesus* that I already mentioned and this is along with Ron Sider's *The Scan-*

---

64. Philip C. Flores, *A New Breed: Call for a New Generation of Pastoral Leaders* (Makati City: Church Strengthening Ministry, 2007).

65. James Skillen, *The Good of Politics: Biblical, Historical, and Contemporary Introduction* (Grand Rapids: Baker Academic, 2014).

66. Albert Wolters, *Creation Regained: Biblical Basics for a Reformational Worldview* (Grand Rapids: Eerdmans, 2005).

67. David Koyzis, *Political Visions and Illusions: A Survey and Christian Critique of Contemporary Ideologies*, 2nd ed. (Downers Grove: IVP Academic, 2003).

dal of Evangelical Politics.[68] Of course, we can engage these authors and their contexts without losing sight of Philippine socio-political realities. However, these authors' ideas on politics are all important. But the rubber needs to meet the road and so my next recommendation is apt and contextual.

Third and last, I am proposing, if not insisting, to my fellow evangelicals *the need to engage barangay politics*. It is my firm conviction that we evangelicals should penetrate the *barangay* with our reformational politics. Local pastors who are politically ethical and prophetic in their dealing with *barangay* chairs and leaders, are encouraged to let their *politically discipled* lay leaders run for the *barangay* government. If a pastor feels that they are called and competent to a political position, they must resign from their pastorate and work fulltime for politics while still being an active leader of their local church. This response considers "sphere sovereignty"[69] and the need to focus on the good of politics. After all, pastors who engage politics do not stop being Christ's *diakonos*, they only shift to another sphere of life. But before we should do this, keep in mind that the laity of the *Iglesia ni Cristo* are already occupying not just *barangay* positions but key political and institutional positions in Philippine society.

I hope and pray that my humble recommendations would somehow provoke our local churches to be theologically and ethically engaged in politics.

Conclusion: Loving your Neighbors through Barangay Politics

My three interrelated recommendations spring from the fact that we can love our neighbors through politics. I first learned from Stephanie Summers the wisdom of loving our neighbors through politics.[70] As a pastor, I wish to situate and embody it in the *barangay* where I reside and minister. I believe that those who have changed lives, biblical worldview, and political competence are the ones most qualified to be God's *diakonos* in the political sphere. We at Payatas Evangelical Movement are already doing it. One of our members is running for *barangay* council. And we are in coalition with people who we see as reputable and transformational. (They are not necessarily evangelicals or

---

68. Ronald Sider, *The Scandal of Evangelical Politics: Why are Christians Missing the Chance to Really Change the World?* (Grand Rapids: Baker Books, 2008).

69. In neo-Calvinism, *sphere sovereignty* is the philosophy that recognizes each sphere or sector of life (e.g. family, state, academe) as having its own distinct roles and norms that need to be observed, lest we jumble a particular sphere with others and lose its creational purpose in creation.

70. Stephanie Summers, "Reflections from a Reformed Activist" in *Reformed Public Theology*, ed. Matthew Kaemingk (Grand Rapids: Baker Academic, 2021), 179–80.

religious, but they are principled people and mindful of the poor and the need for political change in our *barangay*.) We believe that in order to holistically change our *barangay*, we need to have a grand strategy. And as far as we are concerned, politics is a key missional sphere that we need to ethically engage for the greater glory of God.

Bibliography

Abinales, Patricio N. *Images of State Power: Essays on Philippine Politics from the Margins*. Quezon City: University of the Philippines Press, 1998.
Abinales, Patricio N., and Donna J. Amoroso. *State and Society in the Philippines*. 2nd ed. Quezon City: Ateneo de Manila University Press, 2017.
Anderson, Benedict. *Cacique Democracy and the Philippines: Origins and Dreams*. Accessed 13 June 2023. https://newleftreview.org/issues/i169/articles/benedict-anderson-cacique-democracy-and-the-philippines-origins-and-dreams.
Asian Development Bank. *Poverty in the Philippines: Causes, Constraints and Opportunities*. Accessed 28 January 2013. https://www.adb.org/sites/default/files/publication/27529/poverty-philippines-causes-constraints-opportunities.pdf.
Bello, Walden, Herbert Docena, Marissa de Guzman, and Marylow Malig. *The Anti-Development State: The Political Economy of Permanent Crisis in the Philippines*. Quezon City: Department of Sociology, College of Social Sciences and Philosophy, University of the Philippines, 2004.
Chan, Simon. *Grassroots Asian Theology: Thinking the Faith from the Ground Up*. Downers Grove: InterVarsity Press, 2014.
Chetkovich, Carol, and Frances Kunreuther. *From the Ground Up: Grassroots Organizations Making Social Change*. Ithaca: Cornell University Press, 2006.
Christensen, Terry, and Tom Hogen-Esch. *Local Politics: A Practical Guide to Governing at the Grassroots*. 2nd ed. New York: Routledge, 2006.
Constantino, Renato. *The Philippines: A Past Revisited, Vol. 1*. Quezon City: Renato Constantino, 1975.
Coronel, Sheila S. *Betrayals of the Public Trust: Investigative Reports on Corruption, with explanation of reporting techniques used*. Quezon City: Philippine Center for Investigative Journalism, 2000.
———. *Porks and Other Perks: Corruption and Governance in the Philippines*. Quezon City: PCIJ, 1998.
Coronel, Sheila S., and Lorna Kalaw-Tirol, eds. *Investigating Corruption: A Do-It-Yourself Guide*. Quezon City: PCIJ, 2002.
Coronel, Sheila S., Yvonne T. Chua, Luz Rimban, and Booma B. Cruz. *The Rulemakers: How the Wealthy and Well-Born Dominate Congress*. Quezon City: PCIJ, 2004.
Flores, Philip C. *A New Breed: Call for a New Generation of Pastoral Leaders*. Makati: Church Strengthening Ministry, 2007.

Heerikuizen, Bart van. *Grassroots Politics as the Heart of Democracy*. Accessed 8 March 2022. https://www.youtube.com/watch?v=OCVqAkPHc0Y.

Hutchcroft, Paul D. *Booty Capitalism: The Politics of Banking in the Philippines*. Quezon City: Ateneo de Manila University Press, 2000.

Ileto, Reynaldo Clemeña. *Pasyon and Revolution: Popular Movements in the Philippines, 1840–1910*. Quezon City: Ateneo de Manila University Press, 1997.

Jarapa, Sison Q., Rafael B. Perez, and Tito S. Segarra. *Current Social Issues*. Revised ed. Manila: Rex Book Store, 2001.

Jocano, F. Landa. *Slums as a Way of Life*. Quezon City: University of Philippines Press, 1970.

Kaplan, Justin D., and W. D. Ross. *The Pocket Aristotle*. New York: Pocket Books, 1958.

Koysiz, David. *Political Visions and Illusions: A Survey & Christian Critique of Contemporary Ideologies*. 2nd ed. Downers Grove: IVP Academic, 2019.

Lord, Carnes. *Aristotle's Politics*. 2nd ed. Chicago: University of Chicago Press, 2013.

Mendoza, Ronald U., Edsel L. Beja Jr., Victor S. Venida, and David B. Yap. "Political dynasties and poverty: measurement and evidence of linkages in the Philippines." *Oxford Development Studies* 44, no. 2 (11 April 2016): 189–201. https://www.tandfonline.com/doi/abs/10.1080/13600818.2016.1169264.

———. *Political and Poverty: Chicken or the Egg*. Accessed 25 January 2023. https://www.kas.de/documents/275121/275170/7_file_storage_file_9551_2.pdf/e5a6f153-7de8-3611-50a5-4a0a0387cea9?version=1.0&t=1539679408792.

Mooney, Linda A., David Knox, and Caroline Schacht. *Understanding Social Problems*. Boston: Wadsworth Cengage Learning, 2013.

Palomen, Kari. "Politics." In *The Encyclopedia of Political Science*, vols 1–5, edited by George Thomas Kurian, James E. Alt, Simone Chambers, Geoffrey Garrett, Margaret Levi, and Paula D. McClain. Washington, DC: Congressional Quarterly Press, 2011.

Patterson, Thomas. *The American Democracy*. The McGraw-Hill Companies, 2013.

Pelmoka, Juana Jimenez. *Pre-Spanish Philippines*. J. J. de Pelmoka and E.P. Ujano, 1996.

Philippine Statistics Authority. *Poverty Threshold*. Accessed 25 January 2023. https://psa.gov.ph/content/poverty-threshold-pt-2.

———. "Proportion of Poor Filipinos was Recorded at 18.1 Percent in 2021." Accessed 25 January 2023. https://psa.gov.ph/poverty-press-releases/nid/167972.

Rieger, Joerg. "Grassroots Social Movements." In *The Wiley Blackwell Companion to Political Theology*, 2nd ed., edited by William T. Cavanaugh and Peter Manley Scott. Hoboken: John Wiley & Sons, 2019.

Salonga, Jovito R. *The Task of Building a Better Nation*. Mandaluyong City: Kilosbayan, 2005.

Sanchez, Custodiosa A., and Fe B. Agpaoa. *Contemporary Social Problems and Issues*. 3rd ed. Mandaluyong City: National Book Store, 1997.

Scott, William Henry. *Barangay: Sixteenth-Century Philippine Culture and Society*. Quezon City: Ateneo de Manila University Press, 1994.

Sider, Ronald. *The Scandal of Evangelical Politics: Why are Christians Missing the Chance to Really Change the World?* Grand Rapids: Baker Books, 2008.

Simbulan, Dante C. *The Modern Principalia.* Quezon City: University of the Philippines Press, 2005.

Skillen, James W. *The Good of Politics: A Biblical, Historical, and Contemporary Introduction.* Grand Rapids: Baker Academic, 2014.

Summers, Stephanie. "Reflections from a Reformed Activist." In *Reformed Public Theology*, edited by Matthew Kaemingk. Grand Rapids: Baker Academic, 2021.

Talisayon, Serafin. "Ang Ulirang Pamumuno sa mga Pilipino." In *Roots of Filipino Spirituality*, edited by Teresita B. Obusan. Quezon City: Mamamathala, 1998.

The Constitution of the Republic of the Philippines. 2 February 1987. Accessed 25 January 2023. https://www.officialgazette.gov.ph/constitutions/1987-constitution/.

The Salt Lake Herald. September 25, 1903, Last Edition, Page 6, Image 6. Accessed 29 January 2023. https://chroniclingamerica.loc.gov/lccn/sn85058130/1903-09-25/ed-1/seq-6/.

Wilentz, Sean. *The Rise of American Democracy: Jefferson to Lincoln.* New York: W. W. Norton and Company, 2005.

Wolter, Albert M. *Recreation Regained: Biblical Basics for a Reformational Worldview.* Grand Rapids: Eerdmans, 2005.

Yoder, John. *The Politics of Jesus.* 2nd ed. Grand Rapids: Eerdmans, 1994.

15

Restoring the Productive Capacities of Filipinos

The Biblical Way

Alvin Ang[1]

Introduction

Some months back, a fellow academic from Indonesia visited me in my office in regard to a potential research partnership on ASEAN, especially in relation to addressing issues that prevent member countries from reaching their development potential. I was floored when he asked me a straightforward question about why is it that all member-countries in Southeast Asia are bent on moving upward in the social status of their population while the Philippines seemed stuck and retrogressing. This discourse attempts to show that addressing social structures and governance, and exercising political will are not enough to push development forward. Development needs social justice, understanding of value and personal worth, and productivity as essential components that will help social structures, governance, and political will accelerate upward development. The former are micro-components that are the moving force in the latter.

In my view, social justice, personal worth, and productivity are three big concepts that are not only interrelated but also strongly connected to each other. In general, and based on logical anecdotal observation: When people have equal opportunities and feel that there is fair treatment, their personal

---

1. Professor and chair, Economics Department, Ateneo de Manila University; preaching elder, Capital City Alliance Church, Quezon City, Philippines.

valuation increases, which leads to a sense of self-worth. Confident people are likely to be productive in their work and can contribute better to their community and society. From the secular worldview, these three concepts define how an individual is able to respond to the overall living environment, allowing them to maximize their full potential as a human being or their "full productive capacity." However, in the biblical context, the interconnection of these three concepts is magnified as the expected outcome of a person reaching full productive capacity goes beyond the person himself. The interconnection reaches beyond the people of reachable influence, to the community and to the larger sphere of human interaction. The definition of "full productive capacity" extends beyond one's life on earth to how it matters till eternity. It would be interesting to juxtapose these three concepts into the *whys* of Philippine development. Our country is known to be "Christian" and yet it was called the "sick man of Asia."[2] Can an understanding of biblical productive capacity help Filipinos escape the "low level equilibrium"[3] and transcend beyond mere existing? We know that there is more to what the Filipinos have and can do today.

We will attempt to answer this question in the following sections: definitions, digression, descriptions, and directions.

Definitions

The challenge in bridging the secular mindset towards the biblical view is that these concepts defining productive capacities are not static, and they build upon each other in an interconnected manner. This section will look at the different concepts and tie them up into a framework that is pragmatically possible. Our approach will be to present the definitions first from a secular worldview, and then relate and integrate them to the extent possible, and then clarify them from a biblical view.

First, we define what is "productive capacities." Productive capacities refers to the abilities, skills, and talents that enable individuals to engage in productive activities and contribute to society. Our proposition posits that these capacities can only be maximized once the elements of social justice, personal worth, and

---

2. Adam Scwarz and John Kenneth Estiller, "Has Covid-19 Made the Philippines the 'Sick Man of Asia' Once More?" (Online, 24 June 2020); available from https://asiagroupadvisors.com/insights/has-covid-19-made-the-philippines-the-'sick-man-of-asia'-once-more%3F/18.

3. "Low level equilibrium" is a phrase I coined in trying to explain the seeming ease in pleasing the Filipino. Not really caring much about the future as long as there is work, even if it is not paying well, and as long as that work can buy food, and as long as government supports the education of their children.

productivity are intertwined with the institutions and social structures where they exist. These elements are defined below:

Social Justice

Any society that has someone being left behind in their economic, social, political life needs to strengthen their social justice system to help these people catch up. If left unchecked, a weak social justice system will worsen poverty and inequality. There will always be people in that society who will always be in need in every aspect of living. The National Association of Social Workers (NASW) defines social justice as "the view that everyone deserves equal economic, political and social rights and opportunities. Social workers aim to open the doors of access and opportunity for everyone, particularly those in greatest need" while the United Nations defines it simply as the fair and compassionate distribution of the fruits of economic growth. These definitions are summarized by the San Diego Foundation as "equal rights and equitable opportunities for all."[4]

Personal Worth or Value

Economics is primarily concerned with how people create value. Value is the equivalent amount in monetary or time that one is willing to give up to obtain a product or service being offered. Related to this, a person's value or worth is based on what they can produce or provide in terms of service that others are willing to buy or pay for since they will benefit from it. The world values persons based on the importance of their contribution, which in turn can be measured in terms of income, social stature, social capital, access to other goods and services. People who produce low value are unable to access many goods and services in society. If this situation persists, people can develop low self-value and become resigned to their state of low self-esteem, no longer wanting to compete to be the best.

---

4. SDF, "What is Social Justice?" *San Diego Foundation* (15 June 2024), online article, available at https://www.sdfoundation.org/news-events/sdf-news/what-is-social-justice/#:~:text=%E2%80%9CSocial%20justice%20is%20the%20view,Social%20justice%20encompasses%20economic%20justice.

Productivity

The concept of productivity can be understood as the number of eggs produced by a hen. The more eggs produced by the hen means that the hen is more productive than another hen that produces fewer eggs. Converting this to service, a car washer who can wash four cars in an hour with the same quality of work is more productive than another who can only wash three cars in an hour. From a business perspective, one will be willing to pay more for the service of the one who can clean more cars in the same time allotment. Productivity is the key to improving standards of living in any society. It explains efficient production of goods and services allowing those who are producing them to earn more. People become more productive if they are good at what they do and they can increase their valuation over time. As members of society become more productive, everyone desires to do things better and faster, and to get paid higher.

Integrated View

These three concepts respond directly to the definition of productive capacities. Social justice refers to the environment that nurtures productive capacities. It provides support to those who need to improve their productivity by training, education, and social services; it also creates the mechanism to heighten personal worth and valuation. The secular worldview focuses on making these three concepts work to maximize human potential.

However, despite decades of efforts to push low income and poorly developed countries out of the low level equilibrium trap, the world has remained highly unequal in terms of income and opportunities. The United Nations Commission for Trade and Development (UNCTAD) revealed in its 2021 Least Developed Countries (LDC) Report[5] that from its monitoring of fifty-one countries from about three decades now, only five countries have graduated from this category. A country is considered an LDC measuring income, human capital assets (education and health), economic and environmental vulnerability. This report tells us that despite all the knowledge, experience, and technology available to humankind, there are still many people worldwide who do not experience social justice and continue to exhibit low personal worth. They have been denied the opportunities to improve productivity and increase income and future valuation. Moreover, societies even in highly developed and

---

5. The Least Developed Countries Report 2021 – The least developed countries in the post-COVID world: Learning from fifty years of experience (unctad.org).

developing countries also have pockets or even regions of similarly situated people. This points to the reality that all human efforts to leave no one behind in opportunities and provide a better quality of life to all will always fall short.

Biblical View[6]

Christians are also in the world and many of them belong to societies struggling to provide social justice for all. Christians believe that social justice, personal worth, and productivity are important because each human being has the potential to live productively. Christians also believe that each person is equally valuable to God regardless of their material income level, education and knowledge, and stature in life. God sees everyone equally and everyone has human dignity as God created them all (Prov 22:2). As God commanded mankind to rule the earth and subdue it (Gen 1:28), each human being therefore has the responsibility to exercise their unique role in creation as stewards. The Bible is also clear that mankind is given the freedom to choose to exercise this mandate. To rule and govern the earth, humans are expected to use their God-given talents to nurture their dignity and self-worth. God's design for people, following the Trinitarian nature of God, is that they are communal in nature, that he created humans as social beings – physically, emotionally, and intellectually interdependent, with an inherent responsibility to care for one another.

However, the entry of sin into the world has prevented humans from expressing this communal nature in pursuing productive capacities that benefit oneself and others. For while God has allowed and empowered people to maximize the produce of the earth for our enjoyment (Eccl 5:19), nonetheless, there are people who have extended this power only for their own benefit, making it exploitative rather than creative. As the prophet Micah cried out, "Woe to those who plan iniquity, . . . because it is in their power to do it. They covet fields and seize them, and houses and take them." God, therefore, has always demonstrated his justice by intervening to correct the imbalance against the weak, poor, needy, and incapacitated (Exod 3:7–9; Isa 41:17; Ps 10:14). His intervening power is demonstrated in justice. As Stephen Mott and Ronald Sider said insightfully, "Justice provides the right structure of power. Without

---

6. This section draws heavily from: Mott and Sider, "Economic Justice: A Biblical Paradigm," *Transformation* 17, no. 2 (April/June 2000). Also in, *Christian Faith and Economics Revisited* 1 (April/June 2000): 50–63.

justice, power becomes destructive."[7] Justice ensures that what is essential in life is lived together in community and is based on specified rights and responsibilities of institutions in society.

Mott and Sider also viewed biblical justice from various perspectives, three of which are: (1) procedural justice – fair legal processes or the unbiased and equal access of rich and poor alike (Deut 10:17–18; Lev 19:15), (2) commutative justice – the fair, honest exchange of goods and services, such as in having honest weight and measures (Lev 19:35–36; Amos 8:5) and (3) distributive justice – the fair distribution of resources and power in society (Deut 24:19–22; Ps 146:7–9).[8]

Clearly, addressing productive capacity deficiency the secular way will not result to the desired outcome of pulling everyone up to a higher standard of living. The secular mindset of extreme individualism and rights-based context is contrary to the Creator's design of a sustained community with a dynamic restorative character defined by love and generosity. This implies that in a biblical setting, everyone has the opportunity for a dignified participation in the community, and we are to help people get back to sharing fully within one's capacity and potential. These are demonstrated in the Jubilee years in Leviticus 25 and in the canceling of debts in Deuteronomy 15, both of which are designed to help people catch up and get back.

Limitations of Secular Social Justice Efforts

Figure 1 (see below) illustrates the options often taken by secular authorities to address the issue of productive capacity deficiency. Much of the issue is wrong analysis of what prevents people from improving their capacities. Addressing this problem by addressing inequality will not solve the deficiency since the starting point in life is already unequal to begin with. Approaching it by providing continuous and sustained biased support to those who have less may solve the problem, but it is unsustainable. This approach is unsustainable because of the magnitude of the resources required regardless of the design chosen, whether in the form of a dole-out, or education, health and livelihood support, or a combination. Not only does this approach require resources but also time

---

7. Stephen Mott and Ronald J. Sider, "Economic Justice: A Biblical Paradigm," *Transformation* 17, no. 2 (2000): 53.

8. Mott and Sider, "Economic Justice": 51, 54–56.

and good governance in order to work effectively.⁹ These two approaches can generally fall into secular social justice programs. The third approach aligns closely to the biblical approach that addresses the cause of the deficiency – the barrier. The secular approach identifies various barriers but could not pinpoint exactly which one to address. The Bible clearly points this barrier as sin. Hence, true social justice is addressing the root cause of the deficiency, which is sin.

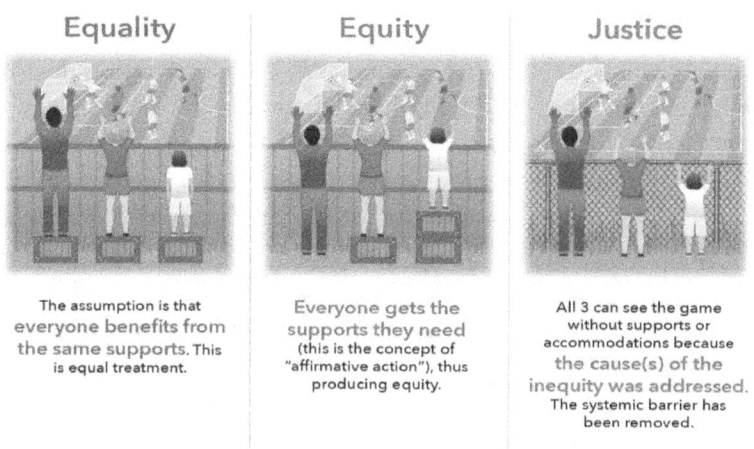

Figure 1. Equality, Equity or Justice¹⁰

As believers, we know that the basic precondition for any of these approaches to work is a reconciliation with God first before one can be reconciled with others. True social justice demands that every person be given the chance to access productive resources (land, capital, and knowledge) so they have the opportunity to earn a sufficient amount of material necessities and become dignified participating members of the community and the broader society. From a secular perspective, we know that countries with strong com-

---

9. The *Pantawid Pamilyang Pilipino* Program (4Ps) is a good example of an equity program formally known as cash transfer. While studies have shown its effectiveness in improving future human capital and reducing poverty, it took more than a decade of sustained investments in four million families. Nonetheless, this is a good model if it could be unbiasedly implemented and politically shielded from interference. The church can participate in this program actively through the Family Development Sessions (FDS). The PCEC and/or the evangelical seminaries can design modules to incorporate biblical productivity with that of secular human capital build up.

10. Source: MobilizeGreen (30 September 2018). *Environmental Equity Vs. Environmental Justice: What's the Difference?* Retrieved from https://www.mobilizegreen.org/blog/2018/9/30/environmental-equity-vs-environmental-justice-whats-the-difference.

munity and nationalistic values such as China, Japan, Singapore, and Korea are able to address social justice issues mainly through their Confucian heritage. While their secular efforts have worked, these are limited to earthly success. The Christian view is that a holistic productive life is anchored on God's purposes that naturally flow to personal value and self-worth, concern for others, and a contented life.

True Productivity

When an individual is truly free to express one's productive capacities, they are able to benefit the broader community. The preceding section clearly points to the fact that structures that nurture knowledge and skills beyond personal benefits can unleash the true productive potential of every human being. Economic theory and reality, however, show that it is impossible to accomplish it without God. In this section, we stress this point by considering an expansive explanation by Neil Cable regarding true productivity. He defined productivity as "making the best use of our God-given opportunities and talents for the glory of God and the eternal benefit of others."[11] His distinction of worldly from godly productivity clearly provides a pragmatic approach in dealing with productive capacity deficiencies. According to him, worldly productivity is measured by how much money one makes, what position one occupies, how many friends one has on social media, and how high is one's score in school exams. These are tangible measures by which people can compare and set standards. Godly productivity, on the other hand, is all about intangible matters like how strong are one's relationships and how much one's love for God has grown. These intangibles last for eternity. True productivity therefore is one where people work in the realm where outcomes are measured tangibly and at the same time produce intangible measures.

This approach to productivity also implies that macro-level approaches will only be able to provide superficial structures and institutions. Ultimately, it is a function of individuals in micro settings. To reach this kind of productivity, one must be able to transcend his or her current economic and social status, education, and resources by recognizing one's worth in the eyes of the Creator. This in itself is a process. According to Cable, the process of becoming productive entails the following – the promises of God one needs to believe; faith one needs to exercise; instructions one needs to obey; self-interest one needs

---

11. Brackenhurst Baptist Church, "True Productivity (Joshua 11:11–23)," 22 June 2014, https://brackenhurstbaptist.co.za/true-productivity/.

to put aside; the needs of others one needs to consider above selfish needs; dependence and humility one needs to develop. This explanation provides a working framework that even the biblical approach to social justice requires time and resources. However, it is not a top-down macro approach but bottom-up, requiring individuals to recognize their self-worth.

Reagan Rose[12] adds that Christian productivity is based on knowing one's unique advantages brought about by a personal relationship with Jesus. What Jesus has won for us on the cross has released so much productive power. Unfortunately, we fail to see its potential since we are too focused on what the productivity of the world defines in terms of the tangible representation of income, position, and fame. Christians cannot produce fruits on their own, only through Jesus. Philippians 2:13 clearly explains that it is God who is working in a Christian to will and act for his good purpose. Productivity for the Christian is not found in any technique or system, but if one is in Christ alone. According to 2 Corinthians 9:8, Christians are designed to "abound in every good work." Therefore, true productivity is not about being the strongest, smartest, or hardest working, it is about drawing on God's power to draw others to God and bring him glory.

Social Justice in the Philippines

Having set the tone, this section now considers the situation in the Philippines as we have presented in the introduction. Here we show descriptions of information on the state of social justice, personal worth, and productivity in the Philippines.

Life Aspirations

According to the *Ambisyon Natin* 2040 survey conducted in 2015,[13] the Filipino valuation of self-worth is simple and achievable. An overwhelming majority of about 80 percent are content to have a simple and comfortable life. This is defined as having a medium-sized home, having enough earnings to support everyday needs, owning at least one vehicle, having the capacity to provide for

---

12. Reagan Rose (n.d.), "The Source of Productivity: You Are Uniquely Gifted by God," Bible to Life, https://bibletolife.com/resources/articles/the-source-of-productivity-you-are-uniquely-gifted-by-god/.

13. National Economic and Development Authority, *Ambisyon Natin 2040*, 2016; available from https://2040.depdev.gov.ph/.

their children's college education, and going on local trips for vacation. As of this writing in 2023 and post-pandemic economy, many Filipinos have already achieved these "low-level aspirations." The post-pandemic economy opened five million more jobs than the pre-pandemic levels. Numerous motorcycles and e-vehicles have swamped small streets both in urban and rural centers. The Duterte government passed a law making college education free. Post-pandemic travel around the country reached new highs with airlines, buses, and shipping lines reporting levels that are all-time high. Across income levels, the definition of a comfortable life is about job opportunities, no poverty, and no one hungry.

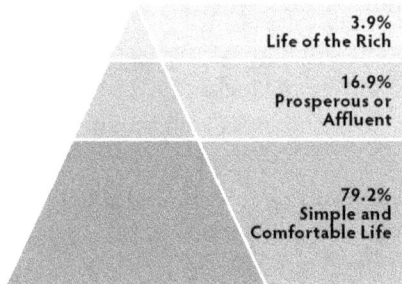

Figure 2. Idea of Desired Life Status

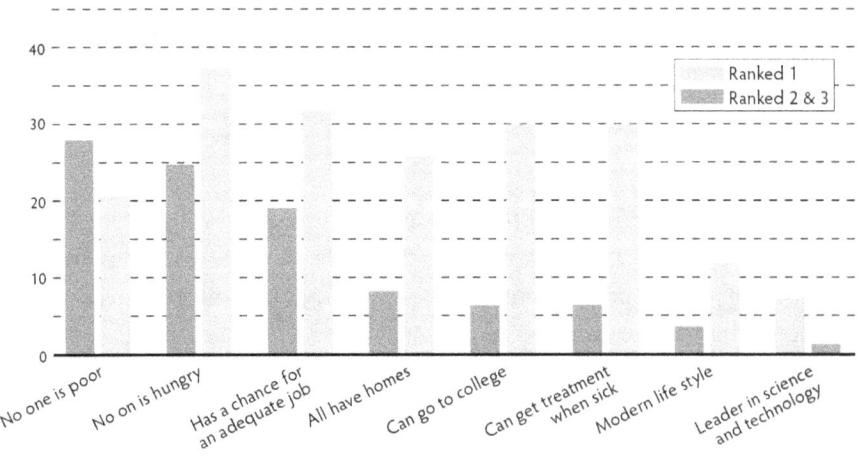

Figure 3. Most Important Conditions
Source: National Economic and Development Authority. (2016). *AmBisyon Natin 2040*. Retrieved from https://2040.neda.gov.ph/.

Personal Worth

Since there is no direct information about how people value themselves, we herewith consider the educational background of Filipinos based on income class. Data reveals that people with higher education have more chances and opportunities of getting jobs whether locally or abroad. That is why one of the aspirations of the Filipino is for their children to finish college education. This has become an inflationary cycle in itself, with people trying to get more education, thereby creating a huge educated class. However, since Filipinos are studying for the sake of a diploma rather than for a professional purpose or to acquire a skill, many are unable to maximize what they have learned with what they do for work. There is an educational mismatch, which does not really matter to many since having more education allows one to access more work opportunities for now, and as long as there is work to provide for current needs. The future, however, is not a priority. The lesser-income brackets dominate the lower education level, while the higher-income brackets have higher education. This explains the desire to acquire a college education. Also, those with less personal worth see education as an equalizer.

On the other hand, the same conditions apply for opportunities. Those with lower income have lower opportunities for business and employment.

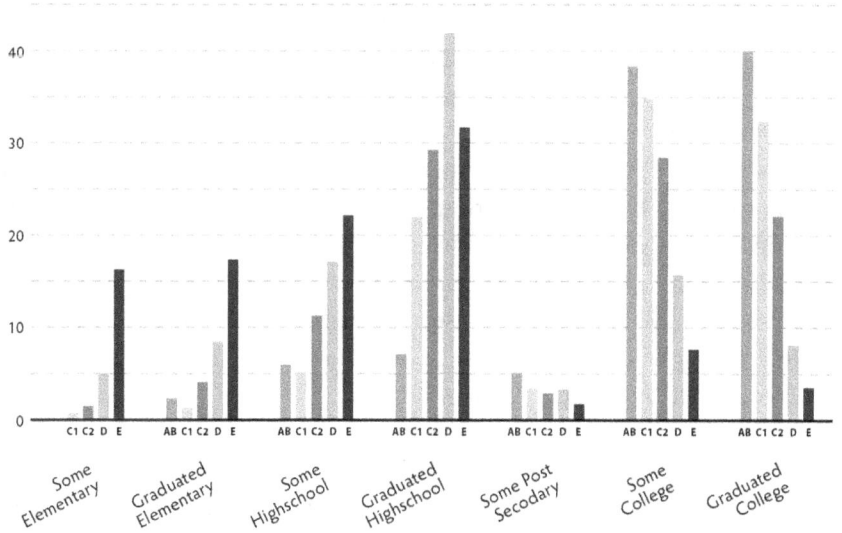

Figure 4. Educational Attainment of Filipinos by Income Class
Source: National Economic and Development Authority. (2016).*AmBisyon Natin 2040*. Retrieved from https://2040.neda.gov.ph/.
AB – High Income, C1 and C2 – Middle Class, D and E – Poor

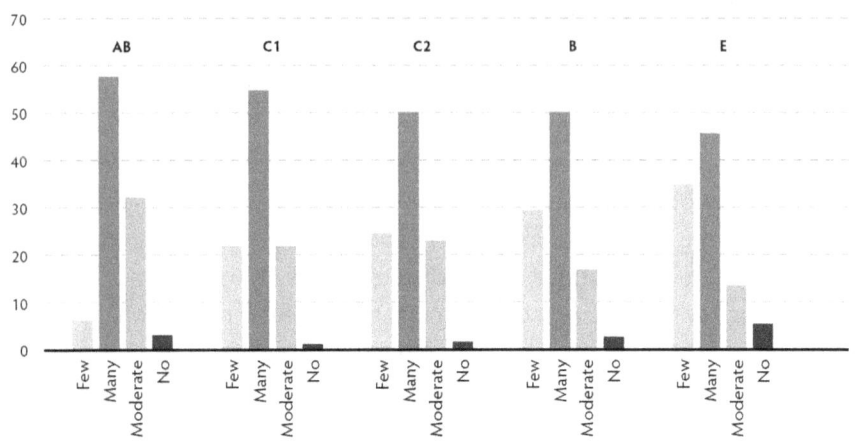

Figure 5. Opportunities for Business or Employment
Source: Author's estimates

Productivity

The last aspect of ascertaining the productive capacities of Filipinos is actual productivity based on economic sectors and outputs. I have estimated the productivity of sectors in the Philippines and found that the agriculture sector has the lowest productivity. This is concerning because the agriculture sector has the highest employment rate (dark gray bar in figure 6) among all industries in the country. This low productivity is also the reason why income is low in that sector. Note also other sectors with high employment such as wholesale/retail trading, construction, transportation, and accommodations; they also exhibit low productivity. These are sectors where most of the lower-income Filipinos are working. There are very few opportunities of increasing income unless people move to high-productivity sectors such as manufacturing, information technology, and finance. These sectors are mostly employing those with higher education. As a result, the poor are congregating in the low-productivity sector. Consider the figure from the Philippine Statistical Authority (PSA) on poverty incidence in the basic sectors. The figure shows that there has been an across-the-board decline in poverty from 2015 to 2018 and a slight uptick in 2021 due to the COVID-19 pandemic. It is critical however to note that poverty is congregating around fisherfolks and farmers and those residing in rural areas. This means that indeed their low productivity prevents them from increasing their incomes. Similarly, those who are self-employed and unpaid family workers belong to the high-poverty sectors. Self-employed people are usually those who cannot find opportunities in the existing jobs market and are forced to do selling as an informal enterprise. They are forced to take risks even if they will not be able to earn more since opportunities for them are limited.

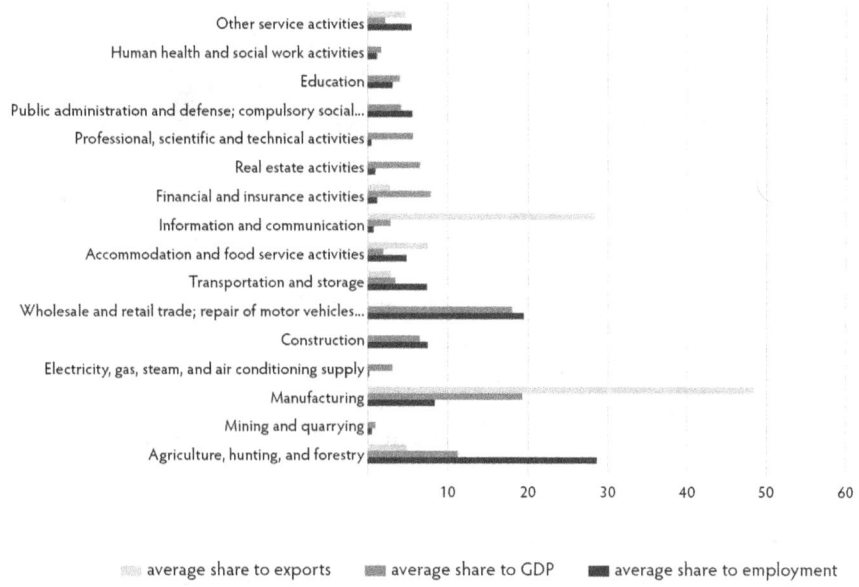

Figure 6. Comparative Shares in Exports, GDP and Employment 2010–2020

Combining these different conditions, it is clear that the Filipino is in a low-level equilibrium despite the various social justice programs the country has implemented over the decades. This condition is beyond the changes in the political climate and administration, as can be seen in the charts. Efforts to address these conditions cannot be short-term, nor can they be one-time attempts in macro-level activity. Experience has shown that over the years, this condition of not having a challenging long-term goal is not pushing Filipinos to use their God-given talents and opportunities to reach God's goal for the country. Consider this summary chart of Filipinos' description of their current life status. The richer class definitely are comfortable in their life status. Note, however, that what is consistent across income levels is that all have experienced being poor sometimes and being comfortable sometimes, at very high percentages. This implies that even the rich are unsure of consistency in their status of being comfortable.

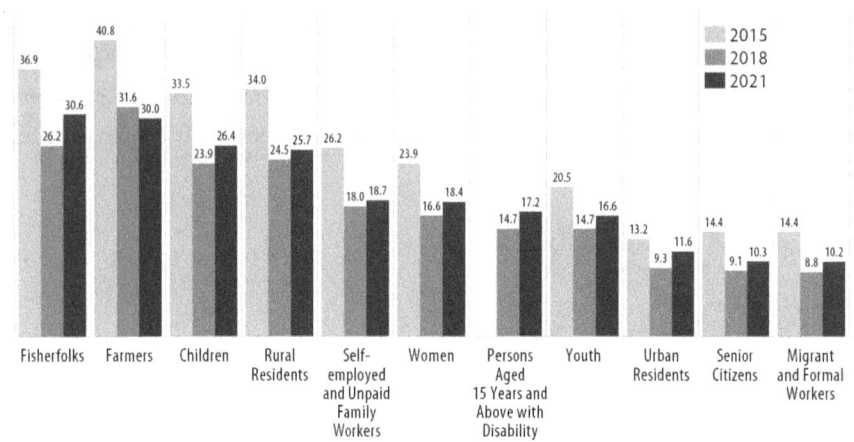

Figure 7. Poverty Incidence Among the Basic Sectors (%) 2015, 2018, and 2021
Source: Merged datafile of the 2015 Family Income and Expenditure Survey (FIES) and January 2016 Labor Force Survey (LFS), merged datafile of the 2018 FIES and January 2019 LFS and merged datafile of the preliminary 2021 FIES and January 2022 LFS, Philippine Statistics Authority

Meanwhile, the chart on the self-reported life satisfaction of nations puts the Philippines in the middle of the pack. It has a level of life satisfaction equal to Japan with an income difference of about US$42,000.00. This is what Filipinos colloquially call *"mababaw ang kaligayan"* or shallow happiness.

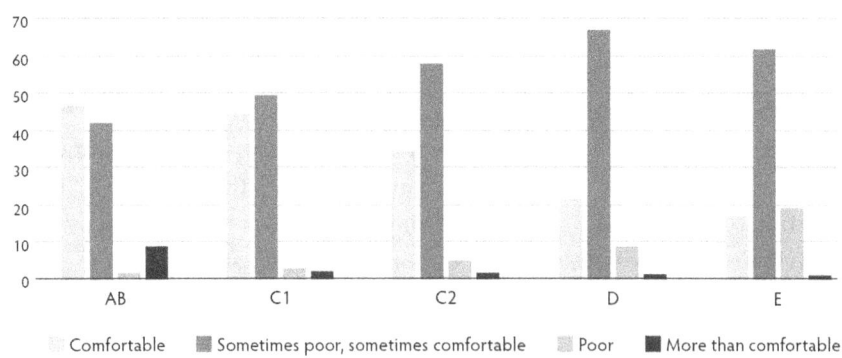

Figure 8. Current Life Status
AB – High Income, C1 and C2 – Middle Class, D and E – Poor

Source: National Economic and Development Authority. (2016). *AmBisyon Natin 2040*. Retrieved from https://2040.neda.gov.ph/.

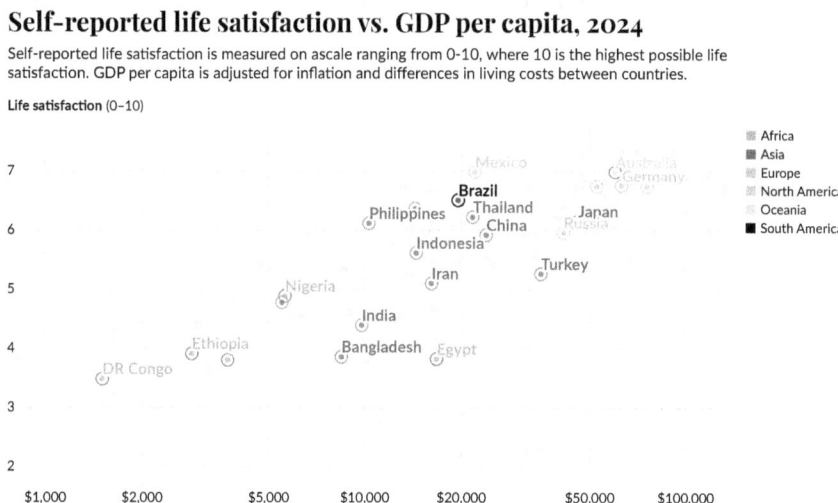

Figure 9: Self Reported Life Satisfaction

Other Critical Information

Apart from the data above, there are other pieces of information that will point to inconsistencies and lack of focus that have led to the low productive capacities of Filipinos. These have to do with inappropriate or weak use of power related to governance. Rep. Joey Salceda has a number of studies that show these weaknesses that have led to the country being pulled downward to a much lower level equilibrium than its neighbors in the region.[14] Among the findings of Rep. Salceda is that the Philippines has only 18 percent of its land that is arable and yet the land being presently cultivated is double this size. This means that we are cultivating more than we should. Worse, the country is irrigating only 6 percent of its land area, the lowest in Asia. This explains why productivity in agriculture is so low – it is weakly planned. Another data is about the perceived advantage of Filipinos in speaking English, a natural competitive advantage, with more than 95 percent of the population conversant in English. Unfortunately, the country also has the highest learning poverty in Asia at 91 percent, meaning Filipinos can read English but they do not

---

14. Joey Salceda, presentation, Ateneo Eagle Watch, August 2022.

understand what they are reading. Other comparative data rank the country lowest in Reading and second lowest in Math and English in Asia. This rank is traced to the low passing percentage in the board exams for teachers, which only averaged 28 percent for elementary and 37 percent for high school.

All told, these facts suggest that the Philippines is moving backwards rather than forward. Our situation is not simply an issue of productive capacity deficiency but a worsening retrogression that instead of opportunities expanding, these are becoming limited and short-sighted, benefiting only a few.

Directions

In summary, we are looking for pragmatic responses to address productive capacity deficiency beyond what secular governance can achieve. We considered that this deficiency can be traced at macro-level conditions and micro-level conditions interacting with each other. Social justice, personal worth, and productivity are the elements that can help people reach their productive potential. Nonetheless, decades of attempts to address these elements have revealed that their impact on expected productivity improvements of deficient people have remained inadequate. This is especially true among societies clustered as least developed nations. We are also aware that there are pockets of this deficiency within developed and developing countries. We understand that the limitations of these approaches vary according to resource availability and that the expected productivity outcomes take time, especially when dealing with extreme inequality in income and starting assets in life. Nonetheless, inconsistent applications of solutions and changing approaches often lead to stalling, and even worsening the desired outcomes of improving productivity. We take the case of the Philippines, once considered the "sick man of Asia." Although it is a society aware of the power of these elements to change and improve quality of life, it has continued to fall instead of move up the productivity ladder, thereby left behind by nations around it. The more than four hundred years of historical connection with the West and its supposed Christianized culture have not mattered much to make lives better for the majority of the Philippine population.

We looked at how the Bible deals with this human challenge that confronts us, and how the Word of God has transformed the lives of people who have adhered to its guidance. From God's point of view, all persons are equally given the same responsibility of subduing the earth, despite being unique individuals and not having similar resources. God has designed humans to be living together in a community, compensating for the differences of one another to reach a common goal. Considering the successes of the patriarchs like Joshua, we understand that once they put the goal of God ahead everything else, they are able to reap the harvests of tangible success such as victory in wars, bountiful harvests, relative peace, and progressive individual lives of the people. Joshua was able to rally his people to the goal of glorifying the Lord, and all else were added to them. This formula was clarified and simply explained by Jesus himself in Matthew 6:33, "Seek first the kingdom of God and his righteousness and all these things shall be added to you."

Process Check

The key difference between the secular and the biblical approach in addressing productive capacity deficiency is in the context of intervention. Secular intervention looks at a macro-level, standardized institutional approach in addressing this deficiency, while the Bible points to this as a micro-level individual decision. We know that a macro-level intervention requires the participation of individuals, and if these individuals implementing the interventions are themselves conflicted, they would falter and their efforts become unsustainable. The reason for the success of many countries using the macro-level approach is that a sense of national community exists among their people. This is complemented by a consistent and sustained national leadership that pushes for a national goal. The Philippines has tried to build this sense of nationalism and national goal in its *AmBisyon Natin 2040* program. Nonetheless, a tacit lack of concern for the nation prevails in the country. The majority are relegated to myopic dreams about something easily achievable that will only benefit themselves and are focused on living day-to-day rather than thinking about the future and the good of the nation and how they can contribute to achieve it. James Fallows writing in the Atlantic in 1987 observed this and called it "damaged culture" characterized by unconcern for one's nation and a lack of national pride. More than three decades hence, his observation continues to define Philippine society. This observation was technically captured by Alessandro Bocchi of the World Bank in 2008. He explained that the Philippine economy is at a low-level equilibrium of capital stock – meaning no one is willing to invest more than what they have already invested. Since people are not complaining and there are jobs anyway, no matter how low quality those are, there simply is no incentive to go beyond the status quo.

What Are We to Do?

We are faced with a tall order. We know that it is only by applying the biblical approach that we could help reverse the retrogression of Philippine economic and social life. It is the only way to restore the productive capacities of Filipinos. We also know that it is not going to happen at the national level using secular institutions and structures without addressing the micro level. The body of Christ in the Philippines is one with the whole society in wanting to see the improvement of this country. However, I have observed that the local body of Christ also wants to see an immediate national change and have become focused only on the tangible. The evangelicals have left governance and institutions to the secular authorities. Unlike their Roman Catholic counterpart, the evangelicals have become too focused on addressing the basic needs and situations of their flock and have failed to see our present situation in the broader and eternal context. Although there are social justice programs, most of them are either related to education only or are only short-term responses to disasters and calamities.

In this current situation of the Philippines, the role of the church of Jesus Christ has to be magnified beyond the day-to-day needs of the flock. The church must take up the cudgels and work together to seek the Lord's national agenda for the Philippines that every believer can participate in and be responsible for. It's not that there are no initiatives, but that they all dissipate after some time. There is a need for serious rethinking of how the Filipino church is shaping its flock and helping them be productive, both in the natural tangible world and in the intangible spiritual one. The following need to be considered by the different local congregations:

1. Repent as a church, for disconnecting from the Lord's national agenda for the Philippines.
2. Make national transformation part of the teaching and preaching agenda of the church.
3. Train pastors and church workers to develop a broad view of the church beyond their physical reach.
4. Change the metrics of church growth to include impact to society as observed through passage of laws, implementation of rules, poverty reduction, among others.
5. For individual churches, to be prophetic in the role of each believer and their responsibility to be a productive witness for Christ.

6. Transform the social justice and benevolence programs from one-time, short-term approaches to those that invest in the person's productivity materially and spiritually.
7. Connect with and participate in the community/workplace/school where they are planted, so that they can productively manifest the distinction that God is making.
8. Individual churches and organizations must engage with the larger body of Christ in corporate prayer and vision casting, and they must unite in accomplishing the work of God.

Final Word

God is not yet finished with the Philippines. Acts 17:26 says that God has determined the time and places of nations. I believe it is not an accident that I am a Filipino. I see the secular technical world from the lens of an economist, but deep within me I see God's amazing hands moving to see his work accomplished in my country, as I seek him everyday and ask him to work through me, to dispense social justice in my family, my workplace, my community – contributing to the self-worth and productivity of my fellow Filipinos.

Bibliography

Ambisyon Natin 2040. 2015. https://2040.neda.gov.ph/about-ambisyon-natin-2040/.

Ang, A. "Restoring the Productive Capacities of Filipinos God's Way." Webinar from Manila, Philippines, September 1, 2022. https://www.facebook.com/faithandpoliticsinitiative/videos/808595950273752/.

Barro, R., and R. McCleary. "Religion and Economic Growth." NBER Working Paper Series No. 9682. National Bureau of Economic Research, 2003.

Bocchi, A. (2008). "Rising Growth, Declining Investment: the Puzzle of the Philippines." Policy Research Working Paper No. 4472. World Bank, 2008.

Fallows, J. "A Damaged Culture." *The Atlantic Monthly*, November 1987.

Mott, S., and R. Sider. "Economic Justice: A Biblical Paradigm." *Transformation* 17, no. 2 (April/June 2000). Also in, *Christian Faith and Economics Revisited* 1 (April/June 2000): 50–63.

Salceda, J. Presentation at the Eagle Watch Economic Briefing, Ateneo Center for Economic Research and Development, Quezon City, August 2022.

United Nations Conference on Trade and Development. The Least Development Country Report 2021. United Nations, 2021.

16

Theologized Context
Theological Education and Politics

Dick O. Eugenio

The state does not mask its attempt to influence everything within its territory. Although there is a pronounced separation between the state and religion enshrined in Article II, Section 6 of the 1987 Philippine Constitution, the government possesses regulatory power even over theological education. Republic Act 7722 of 1994 mandated the creation of the Commission on Higher Education (CHED) while Republic Act 9155 of 2001 mandated the establishment of the Department of Education (DepEd). The former governs higher education, while the latter governs basic education in the country. Religious or theological education is inescapably implicated. In higher education, degree programs – undergraduate and graduate – must comply with the minimum standards set by the Commission through various CHED Memorandum Orders (CMO), including those related to religious or theological education. For instance, in as early as 2008, CMO 30, S. of 2008 had specified the policies, standards, and guidelines in offering a Bachelor of Science in Islamic Studies in the country. For master's programs in Catholic theological and religious education, CMO 12, S. of 2007 was released. There are also regulations governing religious education in basic education. The release of Republic Act 11476, for instance, stipulates the content standards in providing values education in the K-12 curriculum. Institutions seeking government recognition must comply with these regulations.

Theological education is indubitably impacted by the moods of the *polis*. Although no research has been conducted to determine the degree of influence, a cursory look at government policies indicates that the state's arms have long reached the hallowed grounds of theological education. But is the obverse also true? Does theological education also have an impact on political offices and state policies? What role does theological education play – directly or indirectly – in the political sphere? Do theological institutions, seminaries, and Christian universities make it as one of their goals to engage in political affairs? Do their institutional mission and vision include socio-political action? Does the curriculum of their various degree programs contain courses meant to equip their graduates with the knowledge and skills to engage politics? These are important questions because education, according to Liam Gearon and Arniika Kuusisto, is essential to bridging the gaps between governmental and religious authority.[1] Educational institutions are safe spaces where political and religious goals converge and influence one another. Although "the politicisation and secularization of religion in education"[2] in universities is an issue, theological education institutions (TEIs) may sacralize politics and integrate theological ideas into political discourse as well. This shows that there is a need for closer examination and understanding of how politics and religion interact in educational settings. Of course, theological education institutions are the optimal venue for discussions concerning the church's involvement in politics.[3]

Political Theology

There are many types of political theology, each influenced by unique continental concerns.[4] Political theology is an interdisciplinary field that explores the connection between religion and politics, and how theological ideas and beliefs impact political ideologies, institutions, and actions. There is a widespread allusion to Carl Schmitt's claim that "all significant concepts in the modern theory of the state are secularized theological concepts," which implies that the history of politics may be characterized as the "metamorphoses of

---

1. Liam Gearon and Arniika Kuusisto, "Researching Religious Authority in Education: Political Theology, Elite's Theory and the Double Nexus," *Power and Education* 10 (2018): 3.

2. Liam Gearon, "Paradigm Shift in Religious Education: A Reply to Jackson, or Why Religious Education Goes to War," *Journal of Beliefs and Values* 39 (2018), 358–78; Emerito P. Nacpil, *A Spirituality that Secularizes*, Vol. 3, *The Secularity of the Word* (Manila: Wesleyan College of Manila, 2017), 329.

3. Festus Omosor, "Theological Education and Socio-political Stability in Nigeria: The Role of Religious Leaders," *UNIUYO Journal of Humanities* 22 (2018): 115–31.

4. For example, within Europe, there are four types of political theology. See Jürgen Moltmann, "European Political Theology," in *The Cambridge Companion to Christian Political Theology*, eds. Craig Hovey and Elizabeth Phillips (Cambridge: Cambridge University Press, 2015), 4.

sacralization."[5] With this foundational assertion, political theology explores aspects such as the historical evolution of religious doctrines and their influence on governance, the involvement of religious institutions in shaping political authority and legitimacy, and the utilization of religious rhetoric by political leaders to rationalize their policies or actions. After all, "all conceivable human institutions rest on a religious basis, or else they pass away. Their strength and durability depend on how far they are divinized."[6]

Political theology functions as a prophetic voice against all forms of injustice in politics, whether directed to persons, institutions, or policies. Liberation theology, for instance, speaks against structural and systemic evil that creates and sustains poverty. Part of the agenda of political theology, therefore, is "the analysis and criticism of political arrangements (including cultural-psychological, social, and economic aspects) from the perspective of differing interpretations of God's ways with the world."[7] The emergence of political theology within the Roman Catholic Church was an important antidote to two problematic modes of thinking that have plagued Christianity for a while: (1) the relegation of religion as a private matter during the Enlightenment, and (2) the separation between the sacred and secular of Lutheran Pietism.[8] The deafening silence of many mainline denominations during the Third Reich's campaign reveals the intentional distancing of Christian faith from matters of politics. Today, although a few Christian groups occasionally express views on political topics, they have not completely positioned themselves as active players in modern political discussions. The hesitancy may arise from multi-

---

5. Carl Schmitt, *Political Theology:Four Chapters on the Concept of Sovereignty*, trans. G. Schwab (Chicago: University of Chicago Press, 1985), 36. Social philosopher Gillian Rose quotes Hegel: "In general, religion and the foundation of the state is *[sic]* one and the same thing; they are identical in and for themselves." See Gillian Rose, *Hegel Contra Sociology* (London: Athlone Press, 1981), 48.

6. Joseph de Maistre, *Considérations sur la France* (Euvres completes de J. de Maistre, 14 vols.; Lyon: Vitte et Perrussel, 1884–1886), t. I, ch. VI, 71; quoted in Anna Rowlands, "Teaching Political Theology as Ministerial Formation," *Political Theology* 13 (2012): 708. M. P. Adogbo similarly writes: "The relationship between religion and the society is so close that it is possible to trace the history of key social, economic and political development through the episodes of religious history," in "Religion as a Strategy for Socio-Political Development in Nigeria," *Abraka Humanities Review* 1 (2005): 1.

7. Peter Scott and William T. Cavanaugh, eds., *Blackwell Companion to Political Theology* (Oxford: Blackwell, 2007), 2.

8. Filipino Methodist theologian Emerito P. Nacpil addresses this throughout his four-volume series entitled *A Spirituality that Secularizes*. God is at work in the world, and genuine spirituality sacralizes every aspect of the world. See *Discerning the Trajectory of the Spirit in the Old Testament, Vol. 1* (2015), *The Secularity of Jesus, Vol. 2* (2016), *The Secularity of the Word, Vol. 3* (2017), and *The Secularity of the Resurrection, Vol. 4* (2021).

ple grounds, such as apprehensions about upholding spiritual integrity in the face of secular matters, a preference to steer clear of contentious issues, and prioritization of philanthropic or humanitarian endeavors instead of direct political involvement to fulfill their specific missional mandate. Nevertheless, the reluctance to participate in political activities also prompts questions regarding the untapped potential influence of Christian principles on urgent societal matters and governmental decisions.[9]

If, as John Gray suggests, "Modern politics is a chapter in the history of religion,"[10] then the problems of the state have deep religious backgrounds. Since current political challenges, especially in historical Christian nations, are rooted in religious interpretation gone awry, it is only apt that the Church be involved in rectifying the situation. Moreover, if, as Schmitt claims that "all significant concepts of the modern theory of the state are secularized theological concepts,"[11] then their re-deification cannot be the task of anyone else than the church. We cannot leave the state on its own because without intervention it will only pursue further secularization. While the church's separation from the state must be upheld, the church's abandonment of the state must be avoided[12] because the consequence would be dire, such as the concept of unlimited secular authority as totalitarian power explored by political theorists in the mid-twentieth century.[13]

Festus Omosor asks a crucial question: Is there something about the Christian faith that hinders it from being involved in politics?[14] The obverse question would be as important: Is there something in the Christian faith that man-

---

9. For examples of how the church may be involved in political issues, see Rula Khoury Mansour, "Just Peacemaking and Reconciliation," in *Asian Christian Ethics: Evangelical Perspectives*, eds. Aldrin M. Peñaroma and Bernard K. Wong (Carlisle: Langham Global Library, 2022), 301–25.

10. John Gray, *Black Mass: Apocalyptic Religion and the Death of Utopia* (London: Penguin, 2017), 1.

11. Schmitt, *Political Theology*, 32.

12. See Aldrin M. Peñamora, "God's *Basileia* in Asia's *Res Publica*: Situating the Sacred in Asia's Public Sphere," in *Asian Christian Theology: Evangelical Perspectives*, eds. Timoteo D. Gener and Stephen T. Pardue (Carlisle: Langham Global Library, 2019), 245–64.

13. See for example Raymond Aron, *The Opium of the Intellectuals* (New York: Doubleday, 1957); Jacob L. Talmon, *History of Totalitarian Democracy* (London: Mercury Books, 1961); Carl J. Friedrich and Zbigniew K. Brzezinski, *Totalitarian Dictatorship and Autocracy* (New York: Praeger, 1967); Hannah Arendt, *The Origins of Totalitarianism* (New York: Schocken Books, 2004); and Karl Popper, *The Open Society and Its Enemies* (London: Routledge, 2011).

14. Festus Omosor, "Biblical Redaction and the Emergence of Absolute Monotheism: Implications for Religious Dialogue and Socio-Political Stability," *KIU Journal of Humanities* 5 (2020): 129–39.

dates us to political engagement?¹⁵ Another issue that requires reflection is the extent of Christian involvement in politics within the framework of Christian principles and convictions. In addition, how should political engagement be defined? Does it mean restricting political engagement to partisan activities, advocating for certain legislative goals, or a more comprehensive involvement in a diverse array of social concerns? Moreover, as Moltmann asks: "If one speaks of 'political theology,' is one not advocating that we return to a situation in which theologians intervene politically, like the mullahs in Iran or the cardinals in the *ancien régime* in France, or even a situation in which one might envisage the establishment of a theocracy?"¹⁶ Han Joon Lee asks pointedly: "Is [public theology] theology that promotes specific government policies? Or is it a theology of a politically motivated group that tries to impose its morality upon the public?"¹⁷

Christians exhibit a range of viewpoints concerning the suitable extent of engagement in political affairs. There are some who support participating actively in the formation of public policies that align with Christian principles, while others prioritize a non-political approach centered on spiritual concerns and personal redemption. Hak Joon Lee, defining public theology, argues that

> The adjective *public* in public theology connotes at least three core intentions: (1) a concern for the well-being of a society, (2) the discovery and communication of the public meaning and import of religious symbols and creeds through dialogue, which is related to (3) a critique of the "private," "sectarian," or "authoritarian" expressions of religion that either reduce religion into individual or parochial matters or refuse to validate its truth and moral claims to its members or outsiders with warrants and evidences.¹⁸

If Lee is correct, then any action related to societal well-being can be considered as Christian political engagement. However, there is a problem. Although certain matters such as abortion or same-sex marriage are commonly regarded as explicitly political-moral concerns among many Christians, other

---

15. See Lorenzo C. Bautista, Aldrin M. Peñamora, Federico G. Villanueva, eds., *Faith and Bayan: Evangelical Christian Engagement in the Philippine Context* (Carlisle: Langham Global Library, 2022), chapters 2 and 7.

16. Moltmann, "European Political Theology," 3.

17. Hak Joon Lee, "Public Theology," in *The Cambridge Companion to Christian Political Theology*, eds. Craig Hovey and Elizabeth Phillips (Cambridge: Cambridge University Press, 2015), 44.

18. Lee, "Public Theology," 44.

issues like poverty alleviation, community development, and social justice may not always be recognized as inherently political, despite their substantial implications for public policy and governance.

Another crucial question, especially among evangelicals, is whether political activism should be in the form of resistance or assistance.[19] Resistance generally entails questioning and opposing established power structures, policies, or behaviors that are seen as unfair or oppressive. These actions may encompass prophetic protests, peaceful acts of civil disobedience, or providing moral guidance to efforts that promote structural reform that address issues of inequality, discrimination, or breaches of human rights.[20] Resistance might mean undermining the existing state of affairs and advocating for substantial societal and political change. Conversely, assistance is centered around furnishing aid, provisions, or amenities to individuals or groups that require help. These initiatives encompass activities such as providing humanitarian help, implementing community development projects, and advocating for legislation that alleviates poverty, improves education, or increases access to public health. Assistance-oriented activism aims to meet urgent needs and enhance the welfare of marginalized or vulnerable groups, typically by operating within established systems to bring about beneficial transformations.

Politics and Theological Education

Given the emergence of political theologies across the globe, along with the emphasis on contextual theological education, it is surprising that political theology has not made it to the curriculum of theological degrees in Asia, particularly in the Philippines. In fact, although the Statement on Contextualization of the Asia Graduate School of Theology, a consortium of Philippine TEIs offering graduate programs, claims that "An AGST education . . . focuses upon shaping message and ministry informed by the contextual needs of the Asian people" and "develops educational forms and structures appropriate to the specific needs of Asia, including its spiritual, socioeconomic, and political

---

19. Steve de Gruchy, "Theological Education and Social Development: Politics, Preferences and Praxis in Curriculum Design," *Missionalia* 31 (2003): 451–66.

20. Agnes Chiu, "A Prophetic Voice in the Wilderness: Church, Political Engagement, and Public Theology," in *Asian Christian Ethics: Evangelical Perspectives*, eds. Aldrin M. Peñamora and Bernard K. Wong (Carlisle: Langham Global Library, 2022), 217–32; Festus Omosor, "The Role of Christian Clerics in Promoting Good Governance and Development in Nigeria: Prophet Amos as a Model," *KIU Journal of Humanities* 4 (2019): 33–46.

situation,"²¹ only its International Graduate School of Leadership (IGSL) offers programs and courses explicitly related to the political arena. Even among the Divinity schools housed within the major Christian universities that are members of the Association of Christian Schools, Colleges and Universities (ACSCU), only Silliman University in Dumaguete City offers programs and courses on politics. Ironically, the seminary not recognized by the government through CHED, Union Theological Seminary in Cavite, is the most vocal and active in political participation.

Renewal of Theological Education

In as early as 1946, Hugh Hartshorne already raised concerns about the nature of theological education. For him, "the pattern of theological education had become what it is today as an unconscious process."²² Paul Sanders's witty observation that "the problem with much of theological education is that it is neither theological nor educational" may be exaggerated, but it conveys a biting truism.²³ What needs to be pursued is not mere repairs, but total reforms.²⁴ At the end of the twentieth century, there is no scarcity of literature expressing dissatisfaction with the nature and methods of theological education, offering criticisms, recommendations, and proposals.²⁵ However, the diversity of proposals about how theological education must proceed only exacerbated the problem, instead of providing workable solutions. Geographical, cultural, denominational, and intellectual biases indubitably influenced the various proposals, each armed with sufficient biblical-theological justification. The confusion is further aggravated by descriptive-analytical writings that have proliferated concerning different models of theological education throughout

---

21. https://www.agstphil.org/philosophy-of-theological-education/.

22. Hugh Hartshorne, "What is Theological Education?" *The Journal of Religion* 26 (1946): 236. See several definitions of theological education in Vhumani Magezi and Walter Madimutsa, "Character Formation and Leadership Development: A Symbiotic Bond for Practice of Theological Education," *Theologia Viatorum* 47 (2023): a206.

23. Paul Sanders, "Evangelical Theological Education in a Globalised World," presentation delivered 17 November 2009, Centre for Theological Education, Belfast, Northern Ireland.

24. Wolfgang Herrmann and Gerd Lautner, *Theologiestudium Entwurf einer Reform* (Munich: Kaiser, 1965), 11.

25. Bernhard Ott, *Beyond Fragmentation: Integrating Mission and Theological Education* (Milton Keynes: Regnum, 2001), 205.

the history of the Christian church, each as valid as the others, whether one prefers to be restorationist or progressivist.[26]

Without a doubt, the renewal or reorientation of theological education is necessary today if it were to be resilient, responsive, and relevant to the needs of the church and society, especially as we are emerging from the COVID-19 pandemic, when socio-political issues such as health inequalities, economic recovery, education crisis, and international relations are at stake. Globally, the United Nations's 17 Sustainable Development Goals for 2030 is nearing its deadline. Nationally, the Philippines's various educational, health, and economic reforms require attention. The Philippine Development Plan 2023–2028 "for deep economic and social transformation to reinvigorate job creation and accelerate poverty reduction," the Universal Health Act (Republic Act 11223) meant to provide health access to every Filipino, and the Second Congressional Commission on Education (EDCOM2) are just a few major socio-political developments that should be within the radar of TEIs in the country.

The much-needed renewal of theological education in the Philippines will be unique. Calls to return to the heart of theological education require the definition of what the heart is. Some say the heart is the church,[27] character formation,[28] theological orthodoxy,[29] the New Testament,[30] leadership development,[31] ministerial preparation,[32] or student-centered learning.[33] Although these proposals are noteworthy, they are all inward-looking. They perceive theological education as "education for discipleship." This cannot be. Theological education for ministerial preparation is "education for apostleship."[34]

---

26. See for instance Robert Bank's various models of theological education (classical, vocation, dialectical, confessional, and missional) in *Reenvisioning Theological Education: Exploring a Missional Alternative to Current Models* (Grand Rapids: Eerdmans, 1999), 155–56. See also Justo L. Gonzalez, *The History of Theological Education* (Nashville: Abingdon, 2015).

27. Gonzalez, *The History of Theological Education*, chap. 15.

28. Magezi and Madimutsa, "Character Formation and Leadership Development."

29. H. Richard Niebuhr, *The Purpose of the Church and its Ministry: Reflections on the Aims of Theological Education* (New York: Harper, 1956).

30. Banks, *Reenvisioning Theological Education*; and Robert W. Ferris, *Renewal in Theological Education: Strategies for Change* (Wheaton: Billy Graham Center, 1990).

31. Magezi and Madimutsa, "Character Formation and Leadership Development."

32. Lebron Fairbanks, "Theological Education for a God-called Ministry," *The Mediator* 5 (2004): 5–19.

33. Berhard Ott, *Understanding and Developing Theological Education* (Carlisle: Langham Global Library, 2016).

34. Daniel Schipani, "The Church and its Theological Education," in *Theological Education on Five Continents*, eds. Nancy R. Heisey and Daniel Schipani (Strasbourg: Mennonite World Conference, 1997), 5–33.

This means that theological education must focus on the personal development of Christian ministers – broadly conceived – whose concerns and engagements involve church *and* society, or church *in* society. The ultimate beneficiary of theological education is not our graduates; it is the world that God so loves.

The Place of Missions in Theological Education

The acknowledgment of the purpose of theological education as "education for apostleship" entails that missions, as Christian engagement beyond the four walls of its sanctuary, must be the center of ministerial training. Missions studies have actually neither been neglected nor marginalized in theological education. TEIs have faithfully followed Friedrich Schleiermacher's scholastic categorization of required components of theological studies, which includes practical theology. Pastoral and missional studies have always been a part of the theological curriculum. But the problem is precisely because missions is considered merely as an aspect of theological education, not its core. Following Schleiermacher's approach means that the purpose of theological education has become equally divided to (1) intellectual acuity, (2) historical perspicacity, and (3) practical pastoral skills. If two-thirds of the curriculum is heavily cognitive and only one-third deals with practical Christian life divided among many other topics, David Rylaarsdam's statement is not surprising: "My acquisition of theological knowledge prepared me for a doctoral program more than it equipped me for the complexity and ambiguity of sin and grace in the everyday life of a congregation."[35]

Martin Kahler's assertion that missions is the mother of theology must be taken seriously. "Just as an unmissionary church is not a church," Christopher Duraisingh argues, "a theology that is not missiological . . . is not theology, certainly not Christian theology."[36] This means that theological education cannot relegate missions studies merely as a component, among many others. Instead, biblical, historical, and theological studies must be approached from a missional perspective, with a focus on connecting Christian faith and interpretation to the present and future concerns of the church and society, not merely gaining

---

35. David Rylaarsdam, "Overhauling the Curriculum," in *Integrating Work in Theological Education*, eds. Kathleen A. Calahan, Edward Foley, and Gordon S. Mikowski (Eugene: Pickwick, 2017).

36. Christopher Duraisingh, "Ministerial Formation for Mission: Implications for Theological Education," *IRM* 81 (1992): 42.

mastery of the past.³⁷ Ott says it succinctly: "The question of the integration of mission into theology and theological education is not merely a pragmatic or structural issue but no less than the theological consequence of the *missio Dei* and the church in mission."³⁸ As articulated in the Lausanne Movement's Cape Town Commitment (2011, II.F.4): "The mission of the Church on earth is to serve the mission of God, and the mission of theological education is to strengthen and accompany the mission of the Church."

In the light of the failures of the past and the challenge of the present, Mark S. Young argues that "theological education for the next evangelicalism must be organized around a vision of the mission of the church." He adds that "its curricular focus must be the spiritual, intellectual, and relational formation of those whose beliefs, virtues, values, and practices embody the gospel in the public square through patient action."³⁹ Missions, of course, naturally involves a wide range of interactions with society, including political activity. TEIs have a responsibility to prepare their students for active political involvement by providing them with spiritual insights as well as the essential tools and convictions to disseminate faith, develop justice, and promote human flourishing. "Theological education, in whatever way it is conceived and practiced," F. Ross Kinsler writes, "is necessary for the training of those who in turn are called to mobilize and equip the people of God for ministry and mission."⁴⁰

Politics in Theological Education

Asian theological education has mostly followed the model of Western theological education institutions.⁴¹ The criticisms about theological education in the West are therefore applicable to TEIs in the Philippines. Sadly, Perry Shaw's admission about seeing "student after student entering college passionate for ministry and leaving passionate for academia, with little idea how to empower the church and often with no genuine desire to do so"⁴² resonates with my own

---

37. David Bosch, *Transforming Missions: Paradigm Shifts in Theology of Mission* (Maryknoll: Orbis Books, 1991), 489–98.

38. Ott, *Beyond Fragmentation*, 210.

39. Mark S. Young, *The Hope of the Gospel: Theological Education and the Next Evangelicalism* (Grand Rapids: Eerdmans, 2022), E-Book, Chapter 15.

40. F. Ross Kinsler, "Equipping God's People for Missions," *IRM* 71 (1982): 133.

41. Allan Harkness, ed., *Tending the Seedbeds: Educational Perspectives on Theological Education in Asia* (Manila: Asia Theological Association, 2010), 264.

42. Perry Shaw, *Transforming Theological Education: A Practical Handbook for Integrative Learning* (Carlisle: Langham Global Library, 2014), vii.

experience. In addition, none of my theological degrees – from undergraduate to post-graduate levels – had equipped me to engage society at large and politics in particular. I take pride in my capability to articulate the Christian faith and demonstrate biblical hermeneutics skills, but when dealing with socio-political issues, I would shrink in absolute silence. Since I left being dean of a TEI in 2021 and have become more engaged in the public sphere, especially in the education sector, I realized my lack of capability in dealing with issues beyond the church. This must not be the case for any minister who has gone through formal ministerial preparation. What follows are opportunities in the country that TEIs must consider in order to equip their students holistically, so that their skills set makes them relevant to the church *ad intra* and *ad extra*.

Mission and Vision Statements

Gone were the days in the Philippines when educational institutions are evaluated with the same prescriptive standards, which placed smaller HEIs such as TEIs at a major disadvantage. In 2012, CHED released CMO 46 to provide policies and standards concerning quality assurance (QA) and outcomes-based education (OBE). One of the changes the CMO introduced is the concept of horizontal typology in QA. All institutions may be identified as either professional institutions, colleges, or universities. In this typology, Bible colleges and seminaries are mostly professional institutions that are meant to "develop graduates with specialized skills" that "lead to professional practice" (Sec 23.1). TEIs must then behave as HEIs that produce graduates with technical skills for a particular sector. The problem is that most TEIs, especially those offering purely graduate programs, behave like universities, which focus primarily on "viable research programs . . . that produce new knowledge" (Sec 23.3).[43] In addition, TEI's have not caught on with the distinction CHED makes between professional degrees and research degrees. Thus, instead of producing professionals that can contribute to "the economic and social development of the country" (Sec 23.1), TEIs have been producing scholars incapable of engaging in socio-political issues as Christian ministers.

CMO 46, S. of 2012 mandates that HEIs must be evaluated based on their individual mission and vision statements (MVS). This is what horizontal typology means. HEIs must not be compared with one another, because each institution has a unique purpose. This has important implications. First, it safeguards the distinct identity and purpose of TEIs, enabling them to uphold their unique

---

43. For graduate programs, see CMO 15, S. of 2019.

theological perspectives, pedagogical methods, and cultural setting without being swayed by external standards. Second, TEIs possess the autonomy to develop curricula that are in accordance with their distinct mission. Third, the assessment of TEIs is not based on standardized criteria of achievement, but rather on their own explicitly stated purposes and objectives, enshrined in their mission and vision statements. This promotes the establishment of attainable objectives by institutions, which align with their principles, priorities, and obligations. Fourth, TEIs possess the authority to establish their own mission and vision, but they are answerable to their stakeholders, who include students, faculty, alumni, accrediting agencies, and denominations.

Sadly, none of the Philippine TEIs has explicitly included "preparing graduates for socio-political engagement" in their mission and vision. Although the MVS of several TEIs mention impacting or transforming society, none is specifically inclined to engage politics. This is obvious in the lack of degree programs and courses that particularly address politics and political issues. Ted Smith is right in saying, "We know what the purpose of theological education needs to be: we need theological education that empowers action for justice. We need theological education that *is* action for justice. We need to put whatever theorizing, theologizing, or talking about telos we do into the service of a politics of resistance and emancipation."[44] To fulfill Smith's important point, TEIs need to revisit and address their institution's "fitness of purpose."[45]

Government and Accreditation Standards

CMO 20, S. of 2013 mandates that all undergraduate programs must contain at least thirty-three units of General Education (GE) courses. Of the eight required GE courses, it is expected from three courses that students would have the knowledge of past and present socio-political currents in the country.[46] In addition to this, all the policies, standards, and guidelines (PSGs) in offering undergraduate and graduate programs in the Philippines since 2017, released in various CMOs, contain prescribed program outcomes that all students must fulfill. Of the five program outcomes common to all undergraduate programs in all types of HEIs, three have patriotic implications and imply contribution

---

44. Ted Smith, "The Politics of Christian Theological Education," in *Theological Education Between the Times: Spotlight on Theological Education* (AAR, 2017), 23.

45. CMO 46, S. of 2012, Sec. 6; Shaw, *Transforming Theological Education*, 19.

46. These three are: (1) Readings in Philippine History, (2) The Contemporary World, and (3) Science, Technology, and Society.

to the socio-political development of the country. This means that all undergraduate programs – professional or research – are expected to equip students with knowledge and skills to appreciate, assess, and address social and political issues. By implication, all baccalaureate degree programs recognized by the government through CHED, include all of the above. However, beyond the three required GE courses that are typically approached independently of each other, theology curricula do not contain additional courses that equip students to engage in the socio-political arena from pastoral and missional perspectives. Also, TEIs appear non-compliant to the extension service requirement of CHED, which expects all HEIs "to develop programs that are relevant to their respective local, regional or national communities/publics."[47]

Interestingly, even Christian accrediting agencies active in the Philippines do not seem to expect training in political engagement as an integral part of undergraduate theology programs.[48] The Asia Theological Association (ATA) only expects graduates of bachelor programs "to function as leaders or ministers."[49] This is too ambiguous (perhaps intentionally, to be inclusive). The Association of Theological Education in South-East Asia (ATESEA), on the other hand, specifies that bachelor programs "prepare students for pastoral leadership in the congregation and other church-related institutions."[50] Although it adds that graduates should "develop a clear understanding of pastoral identity and demonstrate leadership both in the religious and community life,"[51] the "community life" can easily be understood as the church. Thus, in both ATA and ATESEA, no expectation is articulated in relation to social and political engagement. This is quite revealing and saddening.

De-fragmenting the Curriculum

One of the evidences that theological education in the Philippines is largely patterned on the Western approach is the prevalence of theological curriculum containing four-fold categories for learning, which Schleiermacher introduced

---

47. See CMO 46, S. of 2012, Section 5.1.3.7; and CMO 52, S. of 2016.

48. There are three Christian accreditation agencies active in the Philippines: Association of Christian Schools, Colleges, and Universities Accreditation Council Inc. (ACSCU-ACI), Asia Theological Association (ATA), and Association of Theological Education in South-East Asia (ATESEA). However, ACSCU-ACI does not have the instruments to accredit theology degree programs.

49. *ATA Manual for Accreditation* (2021): 72.

50. *ATESEA Handbook* (2014): A.1.1 (page 23).

51. *ATESEA Handbook* (2014): A.1.2 (page 23).

in his *Brief Outline of Theological Studies* in 1811.[52] ATESEA even expects this in its accreditation instrument: "The [Bachelor of Theology and Master of Divinity] curriculum shall demonstrate a balanced distribution of courses that cover the biblical, historical, theological and practical areas of disciplines."[53] Gonzalez argues that this siloed approach ultimately leads to specialization in just one category, which means that students who are mostly interested in biblical studies will most probably take other courses for granted. This canonizes ignorance, Gonzalez argues, because "the pastor is often seen as a specialist in matters of Bible and religion, but as only one among many whom one consults according to different needs – the physician in times of illness, the lawyer in times of litigation, the architect for construction, and so forth." As a result, Gonzalez adds, "since today the cardiologist can declare with impunity not to know the first word about geography or physics, so can today's minister declare not to know about other things than Bible and religion."[54]

In the renewal of theological education, there must be a shift back from "the study of the theological encyclopedia as an aggregate of more or less unrelated subjects" to the "study of theology as a single subject matter."[55] By putting missions as the controlling center, understanding and engagement of social issues and politics will become a dominant part of the curriculum. Gonzalez counsels TEIs: "What ministerial education is to seek is not only that candidates for orders know the Bible and theology but above all that they know how to employ that knowledge in such a way as to encourage dialogue with the rest of human knowledge."[56] This integrative approach is of course much more difficult, but its consequence will be rewarding. Instead of only producing experts in biblical, historical, theological, or pastoral studies, we need to develop professionals competent and confident in relating theological content with the challenges and needs of contemporary society and politics.

Furthermore, Shaw's suggestion that TEIs should "embrace the social sciences and other fields of knowledge" must be taken seriously.[57] TEIs can prepare graduates to engage in socio-political concerns by implementing a

---

52. Ott, *Beyond Fragmentation*, 234–40; See also Edward Farley, *Theologia: The Fragmentation and Unity of Theological Education* (Philadelphia: Fortress, 1983); and Linda Cannell says it well in *Theological Education Matters: Leadership Education for the Church* (Newburgh: EDCOT, 2006).

53. *ATESEA Handbook* (2014): A.1.5 (page 24), and B.1.5 (page 27).

54. Gonzalez, *The History of Theological Education*, 114.

55. Ott, *Beyond Fragmentation*, 235.

56. Gonzalez, *The History of Theological Education*, 121.

57. Shaw, *Transforming Theological Education*, 96.

curriculum that is both multi- and interdisciplinary. Incorporating a range of academic fields, including sociology, political science, economics, and law into the curriculum will equip students with thorough comprehension of the intricate elements that shape socio-political dynamics. This does not mean merely adding courses that are treated independently. Instead, as Shaw suggests, TEIs may cluster courses to form 15-unit multi- and inter-disciplinary courses that are co-taught by several scholars and practitioners.[58] TEIs must not hesitate to invite non-theologians to the planning table, conversation, and training of their graduates. Interdisciplinary approaches foster the development of critical thinking and holistic problem-solving skills, empowering students to examine socio-political issues from multiple angles.

Hidden and Null Curricula

Kathleen Cahalan is right to say that "curriculums rest on philosophical, educational, theological, and pedagogical assumptions about what needs to be learned, in what ways, and toward what purposes."[59] Designing a curriculum involves the question of choice, because although it is possible to teach a wide range of subjects, it is not possible to cover every single one under the sun.[60] Certain subjects will be included in – and excluded from – the curriculum. This is where TEIs need to be mindful of their hidden and null curriculum. The former refers to "the potent sociological and psychological dimensions of education, which are usually caught rather than intentionally taught" while the latter refers to "what is learned through what is not taught – in terms of both the intellectual processes that are promoted or neglected, and the subject areas that are present or absent."[61] What TEIs omit from the curriculum holds equal significance with what is included. Ignorance is not a mere absence of knowledge; it significantly influences the range of choices one can contemplate, the possibilities one can explore, and the viewpoints one can adopt while assessing a situation or addressing difficulties.[62]

The culture and organization of a TEI have a significant impact on the training of ministerial students. The institutional ethos, together with the

---

58. Shaw, Transforming Theological Education,102.

59. Cahalan, "Integrating Dynamics in the Seminary Curriculum," in *Integrating Work in Theological Education*, 75.

60. de Gruchy, "Theological Education and Social Development," 454.

61. Shaw, *Transforming Theological Education*, chap. 5.

62. Elliot W. Eisner, *The Educational Imagination: On Design and Evaluation of School Programs*, 3rd ed. (New York: Macmillan, 1994), 97.

behavior of administrators and faculty members, profoundly influences the values, priorities, and aspirations of students. For example, although a TEI may offer political theology courses as part of its explicit curriculum, the absence of vibrant extension services and faculty members who actively participate in politics will unquestionably reduce the impact of these classes. Students frequently seek direction, inspiration, and practical illustrations from their professors on how to incorporate theological beliefs into real-life situations. If the faculty members are not active in socio-political engagement, students may find it difficult to perceive the significance and urgency of harnessing religious ideas to tackle current social challenges. There are several things TEIs can do. First, TEIs should build a culture that prioritizes social justice, fairness, and empathy by fostering inclusiveness, diversity, and unity inside the school. Second, faculty members and administrators ought to act as exemplars for socio-political involvement. This means that school boards must hire administrators and faculty members – full-time or adjunct – who are deeply engaged in the political spheres. Third, TEIs should develop students' capacity to engage in critical self-reflection regarding their own social position, biases, and advantages, as well as the wider social, political, and economic frameworks that influence their existence. Fourth, TEIs should establish environments that encourage open discourse and courteous contention over socio-political matters. Fifth, TEIs may provide mentorship and assistance to students who want to engage in socio-political activities, which entails connecting students with faculty mentors, alumni networks, and external groups.

Clerkship Model as Practicum

Institutions that offer internships, service-learning experiences, and collaborative research projects with community organizations are more apt to cultivate students' enthusiasm for socio-political involvement. This means that TEIs must intentionally include these in their calendar and operations. Typically, HEIs require practicum or internship in the last year of a student's learning path. Field education is important because it is grounded in the philosophy that adults learn by doing.[63] There are criticisms about the "theory first-practice later" approach, and others have proposed "in-ministry formation"[64] or the

---

63. de Gruchy, "Theological Education and Social Development," 463–65.
64. Banks, *Reenvisioning Theological Education*, 147. Banks refers to this as "learning-in-ministry, learning-for-ministry or learning-alongside-ministry," or "instruction-action-reflection model" (page 243).

sandwich approach.⁶⁵ The proposal of this chapter is not concerned about the timing of the field education, although "in-ministry formation" is preferable. For clergy preparation degree programs, the context or site of "supervised ministry" is typically the church. Although this is logical, it limits the scope of knowledge and skills of upcoming graduates, because they would merely be dealing with intra-church activities.

To increase student engagement in the socio-political sphere, TEIs could consider adopting a model similar to the clerkship program in the Doctor of Medicine (MD) curriculum.⁶⁶ the clerkship program in medical education requires students to complete a minimum of two thousand eighty hours as interns in different hospital departments. (Conversely, field education in clergy training usually consists of only four hundred hours in total.) Medical students engage in rotations in essential areas such as pediatrics, surgery, pathology, ophthalmology, internal medicine, psychiatry, and other fields during their clerkship. This extensive exposure not only equips them with hands-on experience but also cultivates a full comprehension of medical practice and patient care. Following this approach, TEIs need to change, by addition, the learning context of ministerial preparation.⁶⁷ Theological students could greatly profit from internships in local government units, non-governmental organizations, hospitals, jails, indigenous groups, and other agencies actively involved in social action and advocacy. Through their engagement in various environments, students would get direct exposure to tackling social problems, maneuvering intricate community interactions, and championing the rights of oppressed groups. This strategy is in line with the overarching objective of developing versatile professionals who not only possess expertise in their specific domains but also actively contribute to the advancement of society. After all, it is crucial that graduates of TEIs are trained to "enter public debates with sophistication."⁶⁸

Conclusion: Contextualized Theology and Theologized Context

TEIs would readily embrace Marilyn Naidoo's assertion that "for integrative education to become a reality it must first have an educational strategy that is

---

65. Shaw, *Transforming Theological Education*, 102–3.
66. CHED Memorandum Order Series of 2016, Sec. 6.2, p.5; available from https://www.cem-inc.org.ph/nmat/files/upload/CHED_MO_No__18_Doctor_of_Medicine_Program.pdf.
67. Shaw, Transforming Theological Education,97.
68. Dale B. Martin, *Pedagogy of the Bible: An Analysis and Proposal* (Louisville: Westminsters John Knox, 2008), 17.

significantly related to context, including the cultural, social, economic and political contexts, where learning objectives come from the real world."[69] Philippine TEIs were at the forefront in the call for contextualization over the last few decades. Context is given importance in determining hermeneutics, theological formulation, and missiological practice. This emphasis demonstrates a dedication to contextualized theology, which acknowledges the importance of cultural, social, and historical elements in interpreting and applying theological principles. Nevertheless, with the emphasis on contextualization is also the risk that the missional essence of theology might be overshadowed. It is important to understand that theology is fundamentally a dynamic and transformational field of study, capable of influencing and shaping the environment in which it exists. Hence, the present moment offers an opportunity to reassess the equilibrium between context and theology in theological education. In addition to examining the impact of context on theology, theological education should also investigate how theology may actively shape and transform context. TEIs must not only aim for contextualized theology; TEIs must intentionally pursue theologized context.

Ott argues that the context of theological education is not the university, but the church.[70] The society must be added. The church is the immediate context of TE, but the society is the larger context. This means, as Joshva Raja writes, TEIs must "equip students with conceptual tools, spiritual discipline and practical skills which will equip them for a relevant ministry in the church and in society, responding critically to the religio-cultural heritage and socio-political-economic reality."[71] Since engaging in ministerial work within the socio-political sphere is inevitable, it is imperative to provide graduates of TEIs with the necessary competencies to effectively do so. The convergence of theology and socio-political matters is indisputable, since religious communities are expected to play a significant role in tackling citizenship, human rights, electoral engagement, social injustices, welfare, equality, peace and reconciliation, and many others. Theology graduates can demonstrate their comprehension of ethical principles and theological insights to support oppressed communities, confront systematic inequities, and foster social transformation by actively participating in socio-political matters. Confronting socio-political issues is

---

69. Marilyn Naidoo, ed., *Making Connections: Integrative Theological Education in Africa* (Stellenbosch: Sun Media, 2021), 64.

70. Ott, *Beyond Fragmentation*, 222.

71. Joshva Raja, "Relevant and Effective Theological Education in Twenty-first Century India," *Asbury Theological Journal* 60 (2005): 111.

essential to fully accomplish the prophetic and transforming function of the gospel. In the Philippines, religious leaders and ministers still hold considerable sway and moral credibility. Providing them with the necessary skills to navigate the socio-political environment empowers them to effectively interact with policymakers, community leaders, and civil society organizations to promote policies and initiatives that uphold principles of justice, peace, and well-being.

Bibliography

Adogbo, M. P. "Religion as a Strategy for Socio-Political Development in Nigeria." *Abraka Humanities Review* 1 (2005): 1–15.

Alonzo, Antonio Eduardo, ed. *Theological Education Between the Times: Spotlight on Theological Education*. AAR, 2017.

Arendt, Hannah. *The Origins of Totalitarianism*. New York: Schocken Books, 2004.

Aron, Raymond. *The Opium of the Intellectuals*. New York: Doubleday, 1957.

Banks, Robert. *Reenvisioning Theological Education: Exploring a Missional Alternative to Current Models*. Grand Rapids: Eerdmans, 1999.

Bautista, Lorenzo C., Aldrin M. Peñamora, and Federico G. Villanueva, eds. *Faith and Bayan: Evangelical Christian Engagement in the Philippine Context*. Carlisle: Langham Global Library, 2022.

Bosch, David. *Transforming Missions: Paradigm Shifts in Theology of Mission*. Maryknoll: Orbis Books, 1991.

Calahan, Kathleen A., Edward Foley, and Gordon S. Mikowski, eds. *Integrating Work in Theological Education*. Eugene: Pickwick, 2017.

Cannell, Linda. *Theological Education Matters: Leadership Education for the Church*. Newburgh: EDCOT, 2006.

de Gruchy, Steve. "Theological Education and Social Development: Politics, Preferences and Praxis in Curriculum Design." *Missionalia* 31 (2003): 451–66.

Duraisingh, Christopher. "Ministerial Formation for Mission: Implications for Theological Education." *IRM* 81 (1992): 33–45.

Eisner, Elliot W. *The Educational Imagination: On Design and Evaluation of School Programs*. 3rd ed. New York: Macmillan, 1994.

Fairbanks, Lebron. "Theological Education for a God-called Ministry." *The Mediator* 5 (2004): 5–19.

Farley, Edward. *Theologia: The Fragmentation and Unity of Theological Education*. Philadelphia: Fortress, 1983.

Ferris, Robert W. *Renewal in Theological Education: Strategies for Change*. Wheaton: Billy Graham Center, 1990.

Friedrich, Carl J., and Zbigniew K. Brzezinski. *Totalitarian Dictatorship and Autocracy*. New York: Praeger, 1967.

Gearon, Liam. "Paradigm Shift in Religious Education: A Reply to Jackson, or Why Religious Education Goes to War." *Journal of Beliefs and Values* 39 (2018): 358–78.

Gearon, Liam, and Arniika Kuusisto. "Researching Religious Authority in Education: Political Theology, Elite's Theory and the Double Nexus." *Power and Education* 10 (2018): 3–24.

Gonzalez, Justo L. *The History of Theological Education*. Nashville: Abingdon, 2015.

Gray, John. *Black Mass: Apocalyptic Religion and the Death of Utopia*. London: Penguin, 2017.

Harkness, Allan, ed. *Tending the Seedbeds: Educational Perspectives on Theological Education in Asia*. Manila: Asia Theological Association, 2010.

Hartshorne, Hugh. "What is Theological Education?" *The Journal of Religion* 26 (1946): 235–42.

Herrmann, Wolfgang, and Gerd Lautner. *Theologiestudium. Entwurf einer Reform*. Munich: Kaiser, 1965.

Hovey, Craig, and Elizabeth Phillips, eds. *The Cambridge Companion to Christian Political Theology*. Cambridge: Cambridge University Press, 2015.

Kinsler, F. Ross. "Equipping God's People for Missions." *IRM* 71 (1982): 133–44.

Magezi, Vhumani, and Walter Madimutsa. "Character Formation and Leadership Development: A Symbiotic Bond for Practice of Theological Education." *Theologia Viatorum* 47 (2023): a206.

Martin, Dale B. *Pedagogy of the Bible: An Analysis and Proposal*. Louisville: Westminster John Knox, 2008.

Nacpil, Emerito P. *A Spirituality that Secularizes, Vol. 3, The Secularity of the Word*. Manila: Wesleyan College of Manila, 2017.

Naidoo, Marilyn, ed. *Making Connections: Integrative Theological Education in Africa*. Stellenbosch: Sun Media, 2021.

Niebuhr, H. Richard. *The Purpose of the Church and Its Ministry: Reflections on the Aims of Theological Education*. New York: Harper, 1956.

Omosor, Festus. "Biblical Redaction and the Emergence of Absolute Monotheism: Implications for Religious Dialogue and Socio-Political Stability." *KIU Journal of Humanities* 5 (2020): 129–39.

———. "The Role of Christian Clerics in Promoting Good Governance and Development in Nigeria: Prophet Amos as a Model." *KIU Journal of Humanities* 4 (2019): 33–46.

———. "Theological Education and Socio-political Stability in Nigeria: The Role of Religious Leaders." *UNIUYO Journal of Humanities* 22 (2018): 115–31.

Ott, Bernhard. *Beyond Fragmentation: Integrating Mission and Theological Education*. Milton Keynes: Regnum, 2001.

———. *Understanding and Developing Theological Education*. Carlisle: Langham Global Library, 2016.

Peñamora, Aldrin M. "God's *Basileia* in Asia's *Res Publica*: Situating the Sacred in Asia's Public Sphere." In *Asian Christian Theology: Evangelical Perspectives*, edited by Timoteo D. Gener and Stephen T. Pardue, 245–64. Carlisle: Langham Global Library, 2019.

Peñamora, Aldrin M., and Bernard K. Wong, eds. *Asian Christian Ethics: Evangelical Perspectives*. Carlisle: Langham Global Library, 2022.

Popper, Karl. *The Open Society and Its Enemies*. London: Routledge, 2011.

Raja, Joshva. "Relevant and Effective Theological Education in Twenty-First Century India." *Asbury Theological Journal* 60 (2005): 111–23.

Rose, Gillian. *Hegel Contra Sociology*. London: Athlone Press, 1981.

Rowlands, Anna. "Teaching Political Theology as Ministerial Formation." *Political Theology* 13 (2012): 704–16.

Sanders, Paul. "Evangelical Theological Education in a Globalised World." Paper presented at the Centre for Theological Education, Belfast, Northern Ireland, 17 November 2009.

Schipani, Daniel. "The Church and its Theological Education." In *Theological Education on Five Continents*, edited by Nancy R. Heisey and Daniel Schipani, 5–33. Strasbourg: Mennonite World Conference, 1997.

Schmitt, Carl. *Political Theology: Four Chapters on the Concept of Sovereignty*. Translated by G. Schwab. Chicago: University of Chicago Press, 1985.

Scott, Peter, and William T. Cavanaugh, eds. *Blackwell Companion to Political Theology*. Oxford: Blackwell, 2007.

Shaw, Perry. *Transforming Theological Education: A Practical Handbook for Integrative Learning*. Carlisle: Langham Global Library, 2014.

Talmon, Jacob L. *History of Totalitarian Democracy*. London: Mercury Books, 1961.

Young, Mark S. *The Hope of the Gospel: Theological Education and the Next Evangelicalism*. Grand Rapids: Eerdmans, 2022.

17

How Shall the Righteous Elite Govern?

Indigenizing Transformation Politics for Nation-Building and World Peace

David S. Lim

Introduction

How have evangelicals been indigenizing (or localizing) the political theology of Jesus and the New Testament (in the Roman imperial context) in the multiparty democracy of the Republic of the Philippines? A significant minority of Filipino evangelicals have adopted a biblical political theology that has been labeled "transformation politics." In this chapter, I will show what we have done to apply this biblical ideology in the public square of the Philippines for nation-building and world peace. Our undertaking is relevant globally since our world has become a global village mainly through the internet, and since up to today, even developed democracies still struggle with similar issues for sustaining good governance.

The Philippines is a showcase of how hard it is to consolidate democracies.[1] We were experiencing rapid economic gains of 6.3 percent average annual growth under the regime of Benigno "PNoy" Aquino III (2010–2016),

---

1. David Lim, "Consolidating Democracy: Role of Evangelicals in Deepening Democracy in the Philippines from 1986–1998," *Evangelical Christianity and Democracy in Asia*, ed. David H. Lumsdaine (Oxford: Oxford University Press, 2009), 235–84.

with highly praised good governance initiatives especially having high-profile politicians (including three senators) put on trial on corruption charges. He also won an arbitral case from the Hague under the UN Law of the Sea Treaty, against the aggressive incursions of China into our territorial waters in the South China Sea.[2] Aquino remained broadly popular, and left office with a majority approval rating, but with brewing public discontent (not specifically at his governance, but with the edifice of a dysfunctional status quo unbroken), highlighted by a couple of unfortunate events,[3] his well-intentioned reforms resulted in a disastrous twist.

PNoy was succeeded by the populist Rodrigo Duterte, a provincial mayor known for his disciplinary type of governance, which catered to the hopes of the new middle class who long for better "law and order" governance, especially the Overseas Filipino Workers (OFWs) who have been exposed to authoritarian regimes with performance-based legitimacy (in Singapore and the Middle East, for example). As for the lowest 20 percent of the population (living below the poverty line) nothing has changed – still ruled by a few-dozen families and their friends (our corrupt elite).[4] So, in spite of his bad governance, Duterte was able to sustain his high popularity rating during his regime (2016–2022), so that his daughter ranked the highest to succeed him until Bongbong Marcos convinced her to be his running-mate, which gave them both landslide victories. Their rule (2022–2028) did not hold much promise for good governance, although almost anything they did and will do would be an improvement from the previous one.

The mission of transformation politics is based on Jesus's mission: To proclaim good news to the poor, realizing the year of God's favor (Jubilee), starting from his hometown Nazareth (Luke 4:18–20; 7:20–23). His followers are to pray "Thy kingdom come" so that his will shall be done on earth as it is in heaven, and to make it happen – not perfectly but substantially. The mission strategy is similar to what Jesus did and taught his disciples to do: To transform communities by sanctifying each city (*polis*) where they live. World peace (*shalom*) can be attained by disciplining all nations to implement the way of righteousness rooted in the ethic of love (*agape*).

---

2. Richard Javad Heydarian, "The Return of the Marcos Dynasty," *Journal of Democracy* 33, no. 3 (July 2022): 67.

3. These were the slow response to Typhoon Haiyan (November 2013), and the botched Mamasapano counterterror encounter (January 2015).

4. Heydarian, "The Return of the Marcos Dynasty," 68.

Our "compelling vision" of God's kingdom on earth is best depicted in the "Isaiah 65 vision," which is called the New Jerusalem in the New Testament (NT) (Rev 21–22). Isaiah 65:17–25 envisions a "new heavens and new earth" where death, marriage and child-bearing still prevail, yet blessedness or prosperity is passed on for generations (v. 23). Humanity will reach their full potential of "being human" (created in the image of God) through four righteous relationships: political governance (with fellow humans, vv. 17–20, 25), economic justice (with the physical world, vv. 21–22), cultural indigeneity (with ancestral wisdom, v. 23) and secular spirituality (with divine grace, v. 24).[5]

Here then are these four aspects of life where transformation politics will have to be practiced in the Philippines and beyond: political transformation for good governance, economic transformation for poverty eradication, cultural transformation for inter-generational flourishing, and ecclesiological transformation for holistic spirituality.

Political Transformation for Good Governance

Isaiah 65:17–20 describes the "New Jerusalem" as a singular "city of joy" where life is celebrated and God is pleased. Verse 20 tells of people living a long life,[6] which requires good governance for peace and order (cf. 1 Tim 2:1–2), implying that the leaders govern with justice and competence (we call them the "righteous elite"). This regime extends to ecological peace, as verse 25 describes harmony among animals, and of humans with one another.[7] People live in peace as they experience reconciliation with God, self, others, and creation.

The state or government is the most significant sector in building *shalom* in any society. Aspirations for *shalom* can be actualized only through good governance, where righteousness and justice prevail (Ps 89:14; Isa 32:17; cf. Jas 3:17–18).[8] Governance determines the direction and culture of the people for the present and future generations. Hence, engagement with government is

---

5. This follows the Lukan quadrilateral understanding of humanness: body-soul-spirit-in-community – Jesus grew in stature, wisdom, favor with God and with humans (Luke 2:52).

6. Isa 65:20 – "Never again will there be in it an infant who lives but a few days, or an old man who does not live out his years; the one who dies at a hundred will be thought a mere child; the one who fails to reach a hundred will be considered accursed."

7. Isa 65:25 – "The wolf and the lamb will feed together, and the lion will eat straw like the ox, and dust will be the serpent's food. They will neither harm nor destroy on all my holy mountain, . . says the LORD."

8. David Lim, "The Living God in the Structures of Philippine Reality," *Transformation* 5 (April–June 1988), 1–7.

required to realize God's reign on earth. As Pope Francis has affirmed, "Politics is noble; it is one of the highest forms of charity."[9]

We must be grateful for living in a part of the world that is relatively more democratic and just today, mainly because of the many brave people in the past who worked, struggled, and even died for freedom and civil rights. When the United Nations was established in 1947, she had for her motto: "They will beat their swords into plowshares . . . and all nations will not learn war anymore" (Isa 2:4).

The Philippines as one of the founders of the United Nations had a progressive heritage so that even until 1970, we were ranked second in Asia, next to Japan. But as our neighboring countries developed, our experience of Martial Law under the dictatorial rule of Ferdinand Marcos Sr. (1972–1986) with its crony capitalism led to huge economic collapse, making us the basket-case "sick man of Asia."

During the heydays of Martial Law, the highest ranking Roman Catholic cleric Jaime Cardinal Sin used a phrase that appropriately reflects Jesus's transformation politics called "critical collaboration." The political stance is both of cooperation, as well as of prophetic critique. So since 1978 this has been promoted and implemented by a significant number of leaders in the majority Roman Catholic Church and by the National Council of Churches in the Philippines (NCCP),[10] quite consistently up to this day.

Sadly, the Philippines still requires some major political breakthroughs in order to achieve good governance sustainably. We still have to equip and mobilize our constituents to become active members in the civic and development organizations of their localities. There are five items in our political transformation agenda: strengthen the *barangay* structure, fix the electoral system, fight corrupt practices, advocate for the poor, and develop participatory culture.

1. Strengthen The Barangay *(Village) Structure*

To form the "righteous elite," we need above all, to develop servant-leaders from the bottom up through people empowerment. The Preamble of our Constitution clearly provides that "Sovereignty resides in the people, and all

---

9. Pope Francis quoting Pope Paul VI in his encyclical *Fratelli Tutti* (2020).

10. Led by advocates of the Theology of Struggle (Filipino version of Liberation Theology), the NCCP was critical of Martial Law and its abuses from the very start. Robert L. Youngblood, "The Protestant Church in the Philippines' New Society, *Bulletin of Concerned Asian Scholars* 12, no. 3 (1980): 19.

governmental authority emanates from them." Under the Constitution, the real bosses are the people. Its Article 13: Section 16 reinforces this sovereign right of the people when it states: "The right of the people and their organizations to effective and reasonable participation at all levels of social, political and economic decision making shall not be abridged. The State, shall by law, facilitate the establishment of adequate mechanisms to allow this right of the people."

And so the Local Government Code of 1991 fleshes out in statutory form the authority of the people: "as residents of their barangays and acting as Constituent Assemblies of their barangays, to take control of their communities, and in so doing to take control, in a very meaningful and decisive way, of the country itself. . . ." Each *barangay* (our lowest political unit) is a small republic by itself. It can serve as the breeding ground for raising servant-leaders who can grow into national leadership and beyond.

Sociologically, we need to devolve power even lower: into groups of about ten families each, similar to what was proposed to Moses by Jethro, the leader of the Midianites, a nomadic tribe, to appoint qualified leaders of tens, fifties, hundreds, and thousands (Exod 18:21). This zero-budget structure can be run by volunteers and can ensure that every voice is heard and every communal issue is deliberated on by a small group of friends (*purok* or *barkada*) in the neighborhood. They will learn community organizing, organizational development, and social entrepreneurship on-the-job.

A strong *barangay* structure is our best hope to replace the corrupt elite in our land. Having proven to be wise and incorruptible leaders in their locality (and having friendly relations with the officials they had to deal with on a regular basis), our grassroots leaders can be appointed or elected to positions in government.

2. Fix The Electoral System

Since governance posts in democracies are occupied by winners in elections, and electoral results have big consequences, fielding qualified and popular candidates by campaigning as political parties has been key to winning in local elections. Participating in this process is the essential duty of anyone who desires to help in nation-building. It is the democratic way to occupy governance positions required by law. Let gifted leaders form the "righteous elite," like William Wilberforce's Clapham Sect and Abraham Kuyper's Anti-Revolutionary Party.

Many more of our leaders need to find politics and governance as their vocation. Let them join or form political parties that will recruit and campaign for candidates so that the righteous elite can serve in electoral posts in government. They can start serving in the local levels, and those who prove to be effective can then rise to provincial and national levels. Moreover, evangelizing and discipling incumbent leaders to join the righteous elite should be done persistently.

Our country's multi-party system has two main flaws: First, our parties don't have clear governance platforms. Hence our politicians are turncoats (*balimbing*) who move from one party to another after every election, as they flock to the winning party/personality for financial benefits. And second, our parties are led by traditional political (*trapo*) dynasties,[11] who until today have refused to pass the constitutionally-mandated "enabling law" to ban political dynasties.

To fill these two gaps, I consider the best legacy of my political engagement is being one of the founders of the National Council of *Kapatiran* Party (KP, Alliance for the Common Good) in 2003,[12] and serving as its vice-chair up to the present.[13] The party put together our governance platform, which consists mainly of the Catholic Social Teachings,[14] in the form of a booklet entitled *Passport to a New Philippines*, and we also posted it on our website.[15] We envision replacing our nation's corrupt politicians with new servantleaders from the religious, academic, and faith-based development sectors. The rest of this chapter shows what I promoted in this partisan mode of political engagement.[16]

In the May 2022 election, KP allowed me to serve in the *1Sambayan* Coalition which I consider the largest organized movement to endorse and cam-

---

11. *Trapo* has a derogatory meaning: rags.

12. This fulfilled my early call in "Why We Should Form an Evangelical Political Party," *Evangelical Thrust* 13 (August 1986): 12–13; and 14 (September 1986): 14–15, 18–19.

13. We fielded John Carlos "JC" de los Reyes, a councilor in Olongapo City (2007–2010), as our party's presidential candidate in 2010 and senatoriable in 2013, and boycotted the 2016 election.

14. Peter J. Henriot, et al., *Catholic Social Teachings: Our Best Kept Secret* (Maryknoll: Orbis, 1988), 20–22.

15. In 2009, sociologist Randy David recognized KP as one of the only two real political parties in our country with clear governance platforms; the other is the Communist Party of the Philippines (CPP). See our website: https://kapatiranparty.org/wp-content/uploads/2020/11/Passport-to-a-New-Philippines-1.pdf.

16. Providentially, though raised in non-political family and church backgrounds, I got politically involved quite early in life. I won twice for the presidency of the Student Council during the 5th and 6th grades of my elementary education. On the second try, I won by only one vote: I got fifty-one votes, and my two rivals got fifty votes each! Every vote counts.

paign for the righteous elite.[17] Our Leni-Kiko ticket gained fivefold during the campaign period, from 3 percent to 15 percent of the electorate. If we double our votes to 30 percent in 2025, and double it again to 60 percent in 2028, we will surely have a landslide victory in sight. KP has been used to making projections towards achieving success in 2040, given our limited resources.

Moreover, I have been critical of the official position of the Philippine Council of Evangelical Churches (PCEC) to be non-partisan in elections because it self-marginalizes and thus limits our influence and potential impact. The least we could do is to encourage all our constituent individuals and organizations to be partisan during the campaign periods for local and national elections.

As "salt of the earth" (Matt 5:13), we need to preserve the good in our society by highlighting the good practices in governance and honoring those who practice such consistently. When I was dean at the Asian Theological Seminary, our short-lived Asian Center for Transformation Studies (ACTS) gave "Model Public Servant" awards to evangelicals in government (1988–1991).[18] We have to do this more often in our respective associations.

3. Fight Corrupt Practices

Our biggest challenge in governance has always been malversation of funds by the *trapo* dynasties that have made politics their family business. We are still a "pork barrel state" where the oligarchy's main purpose is to use public funds for political patronage to further their personal goals in the public sphere. The pork barrel (public funds dispensed entirely on the personal discretion of power wielders) is at the core of what we denounce as "traditional politics."

The antidote is full transparency and accountability of public funds by legislating a comprehensive "Freedom of Information Act" that will cover all government transactions and operations. "Section 7 of the 1987 Philippine Constitution emphasizes the right of the people to information on matters of public concern. However, thirty years since the first Freedom of Information

---

17. KP planned to field Atty. Alex Lacson to run as vice-president, but decided to let him run for senator in the Leni-Kiko ticket of 1Sambayan.

18. Recipients included Jovito Salonga (1989), Neptali Gonzales (1990) and Leticia Ramos-Shahani (1991). ACTS closed when I left to work at Oxford Centre for Mission Studies (OCMS) in 1992.

(FOI) Bill was filed, the Congress has yet to pass a legislation that promotes access to information."[19]

Leni Robredo, the former vice-president who consistently got the highest audit rating from the Commission on Audit (COA) during Duterte's regime filed the FOI Bill, among others. During her run for the presidency in the 2022 election, she said that when she was still a congresswoman,

> All of . . . the bills I filed were anti-corruption measures. There were measures on transparency, full discretion law, freedom of information law, accountability measures, people empowerment measures . . . because I believed these were the most important so we can eradicate corruption.[20]

She usually said, ". . . [It's not] enough for a public official to be good but there has to be a system that will force him to be good." We missed a great opportunity for good governance when she lost in that fraudulent election.[21]

Moreover, the KP has been advocating to amend our 1955 Bank Secrecy Law. As Bangko Sentral ng Pilipinas (BSP) Governor Amando Tentangco once said, "The Philippines is one of only three remaining countries in the world with ultra secrecy law"; the other two are Lebanon and North Korea.

KP recommended a bill to the Committee on Finance of the House of Representatives (18th Congress). The existing law provides only two exceptions to the secrecy, namely, by waiver of the depositor or by order of the court. This bill proposes an amendment that introduces a third exception, that is, by vesting preliminary inquiry powers on the BSP.

4. Advocate For the Poor

Given the prevailing social conditions in the "only Christian country in Asia," the Roman Catholic Church (almost 80 percent of the population), despite its proclamation of being the "church of the poor," has consistently failed in her

---

19. https://worldjusticeproject.org/sites/default/files/documents/OGP_Philippines_Action-Plan_2019-2021.pdf.

20. Argyle Cyrus Geducos, "Robredo bares anti-corruption efforts; will probe customs, BIR, DPWH," *Manila Bulletin*, 28 February 2022, https://mb.com.ph/2022/02/27/robredo-bares-anti-corruption-efforts-will-probe-customs-bir-dpwh/.

21. This was the finding of the international panel of observers and of private citizens who are challenging the Commission on Elections to randomly open some ballot boxes (which they have refused to comply with).

mission to lead Filipino Christians to live up to the Catholic Social Teachings that emphasize the "preferential option for the poor."[22]

"Those who have less in life should have more in law" was the slogan that defined Ramon Magsaysay's tragedy-shortened presidency.[23] Pro-poor advocacy will remain counter-cultural in almost all contexts; many Christians believe that "the poor will always remain with you." Yet some nations have less poverty and inequality than others, mainly because they have achieved a relatively egalitarian social order (past and present) with better legislation and implementation of social welfare than others.

In the Philippines, our *trapos* have also diminished our nation's democracy. They have redefined the "Party List" concept, an otherwise highly laudable political mechanism to better distribute the power of governance to the poorest sectors. They have bastardized the intent of this system by not requiring that all party list representatives should come from the marginalized sectors. We need to work to restore this system back to its original intent.

At the Constitutional level, KP also hopes that when an opportunity arises, we will campaign for charter change to a parliamentary and federal system, so that the less wealthy can have better chances at winning elections to replace the corrupt elite by just running in the congressional district level.[24]

5. Develop Participatory Culture

In our country we have a multi-party system that has allowed for a variety of opinions and advocacies in the body politic. This should ensure freedom to disagree, oppose, and debate issues that concern the common good. And for society to work in harmony, there is the need for capacity-building for negotiation, consensus, networking, partnership, and collaboration.

Given our current state of affairs, we must also accept the fact that standing for kingdom values often entails being in the opposition and usually as a minority (and in many instances, a tiny minority). Yet we must stay true to our mission amidst criticisms and conflicts (big or small). In fact, in healthy

---

22. Henriot, *Catholic Social Teachings*, 21–22.

23. Aven Piramide, "For the poor only? What about the others?" *The Freeman*, 9 August 2020, https://www.philstar.com/the-freeman/opinion/2020/08/09/2033973/poor-only-what-about-others.

24. Jose Abueva, "Revised Draft Constitution for a Proposed Federal Republic of the Philippines with a Parliamentary Government, Revised 14 February 2005," https://www.kas.de/en/web/philippinen/single-title/-/content/revised-draft-constitution-for-a-proposed-federal-republic-of-the-philippines-with-a-parliamentary-government.

democracies there must always be a true opposition (if possible with its own "shadow government," to develop alternates to the governing majority), mainly to serve as the fiscalizer as a vital function for checks and balance.

The gains of democracy can easily be lost, as Wendell Phillips said, "Eternal vigilance is the price of liberty; power is ever stealing from the many to the few." Hence we must constantly do prophetic critique and improve on our political achievements and policies. We must be "watchdogs" for good governance: to appreciate right (especially pro-poor) policies, and to rebuke corruption and incompetence.

We also need to master different forms of civil disobedience. Many of us have joined prayer rallies, protest marches, boycotts, strikes, and other media-attracting events. In fact we can proudly recall how we modeled how to change corrupt presidents through two peaceful revolutions, the "People Power Revolution" in 1986 and 2001.[25]

While remaining loyal to our Constitution, we must oppose the government when it misuses its power. Though our actions may be misunderstood or not always welcomed, we must be willing to be unpopular and suffer the consequences (even to be persecuted, imprisoned, and risk death) to serve as the conscience of the nation.

Economic Transformation for Poverty Eradication

The second aspect of transformation politics is economic transformation. Nation-building requires transformation of the marketplace. The main cause for the rise of populism in most democracies today is the failure of liberal democracies to deliver economic respite from inflation and inequality, with the wealthy becoming wealthier while the low and middle classes continue to live near the poverty line. Resolving this economic conundrum will be the biggest step forward to stabilize and consolidate democracy.[26]

This calls for three thrusts: Build social and solidarity economy, propagate economic *koinonia* (cooperativism), and advocate a simple lifestyle.

---

25. In both instances, the Supreme Court ruled that each was constitutional. See my "Church and State in the Philippines, 1900–1988," *Transformation* 6.3 (July–September 1989), 27–32; and "Consolidating Democracy," 235–84.

26. Johnstone, "Understanding the state of liberal societies," 1.

1. Build a Social and Solidarity Economy

We must work for an economic system that is truly democratic: for, of, and by the people (poor majority), which integrates the best of capitalism (which excels in production) and socialism (which excels in distribution). In my first book,[27] I already advocated for "social democracy" or "solidarity economy" as the best economic order of God's kingdom on earth. The best models can be found in Europe (especially the Scandinavian countries), Canada, Australia, New Zealand and Japan. These countries have been listed among the top livable and peaceful (and happiest!) nations in the world in the last few decades.

As of 2020, the Philippine Statistics Authority reports that the majority (58.4 percent) of Filipinos still belong to the low-income class, while the middle class comprises around 40 percent of the population. Only 1.4 percent fall in the high-income class.[28] Gladly, in 18 April 2023, our republic joined the vast majority of the United Nations' General Assembly that officially resolved to build the Social and Solidarity Economy (SSE) to help achieve their 17 Sustainable Development Goals (SDGs) by 2030.

2. Propagate Economic Koinonia (Cooperativism)

We can build SSE from the bottom up as we propagate economic *koinonia* (cooperativism) as the "law of the land." This legislation exists globally in the form (with various names) of social democracy or welfare state. It aims for each citizen to enjoy Jubilee "from the cradle to the grave," which for us means reviving *bayanihan* (solidarity) and *walang iwanan* (leave no one behind) in the Filipino way of life.[29]

Isaiah 65:21–22 shows a society where justice prevails, where each one's labor is rewarded accordingly,[30] following the ideal of "each man sitting under

---

27. *Transforming Communities* (Manila: OMF Literature, 1992). But out of stock since 2010.

28. Low-income class includes the poor and those earning less than twice the poverty threshold (less than ₱24,164 per month for a family of 5). Middle-income consists of professionals, entrepreneurs, and skilled workers earning between ₱24,164 and ₱144,984 per month for a family of 5. And the high-income include business tycoons, prominent politicians and other affluent people who earn at least ₱241,640 per month for a family of 5. Philippine Institute for Development Studies, "Understanding Social Classes in the Philippines: Which Class Do You Belong to?" pids.gov.ph (26 April 2022): 1–2.

29. This section is largely taken from my article: David Lim, "Optimizing Discipleship Groups for Fulfilling the Great Commission." *Asian Missions Advance* 85 (Fall 2024): 8.

30. Isaiah 65:21–22 – "They will build houses and dwell in them; they will plant vineyards and eat their fruit. No longer will they build houses and others live in them, or plant and others eat. For as the days of a tree, so will be the days of my people; my chosen ones will long enjoy the work of their hands."

his own vine and fig tree" (Mic 4:4) and the Mosaic laws of gleaning (so none will be poor, Deut 15:1–6) and Jubilee (when every fifty years all lands are returned to the original families, Lev 25). In the NT, the apostolic team of Jesus shared a common fund (Judas was their treasurer), and so did Paul's (Acts 20:33–35), following the practice of the earliest church in Jerusalem (2:42–45; 4:32–37). Paul taught that caring for and sharing with one another for equality manifests in full the mutual love ethic among the Jesus-following communities (2 Cor 8:7–15).

Thus, all Jesus-following churches and organizations should teach their constituents to turn their homes and buildings into community ministry centers and do Matthew 25:31–40 services, implementing the laws of Jubilee to fulfill Jesus's mission (Luke 4:18–21). Those blessed with intelligence, health, talents, and wealth should share their lives and possessions with those with less – because everything we have are God's gracious gifts meant for the common good and not for private use only. Freely we receive, freely we share. We are created in the image of the Triune God eternally sharing generously as equals.

The best (or even the only) structure of Jubilee (modeled in many indigenous cultures) is cooperativism where out of love for neighbors, people contribute towards a common fund that they democratically save, plan, and use in doing business together for the common good. Following the Exodus 18:21 structure mentioned above, each small group of five to ten families (*purok* or *barkada*) can go into business together by saving, planning, working and sharing profits together. Each small group can link with about four other small groups (coordinated by leaders of fifties) to form primary co-ops and organize secondary co-ops (federations led by leaders of hundreds) and tertiary co-ops (confederations led by leaders of thousands).

This structure is being used presently among house church movements (HCMs) in China, India, and the Philippines, too, and a few are starting to "cooperativize."[31] In the country, the original HCM leaders formed an association during its first consultation in 2005, took on the name Star Grass Coalition in 2011, and then it stopped gathering annually since 2015 without registering with the government. Anyone who wants to learn about HCM can connect

---

31. On HCMs, see my "Asia's House Church Movements Today," *Asian Missions Advance* 52 (July 2016): 7–12. Cf. Wolfgang Simson, *Houses That Change the World* (Carlisle: Paternoster, 2001), and Rad Zdero, *The Global House Church Movement* (Pasadena: William Carey Library, 2004).

with any of us and we will find someone to disciple them in person or online, or just refer them to our website: https://stargrass.dalipuga.com/housechurch.[32]

Since 2002, I've co-founded and co-led a faith-based co-op called *Punlad Buhay* Multipurpose Cooperative. It has grown to have its own e-commerce platform called iCanSaveApp.[33] But right after the Lausanne Global Workplace Forum in June 2019, a few colleagues in Lausanne Philippines[34] and Asian School of Development and Cross-cultural Studies (ASDECS)[35] agreed to propagate "Cooperatives as Mission (CAM)." I now serve as board chair of the Asian Transformation Movement (ATM) which is seeking to strengthen co-ops to connect into an eMarket ecosystem for Asia and beyond.

We hope that those in the labor sector would consider transforming their union-organizing (adversarial between labor and management) into cooperative-organizing (empowerment of employees to become entrepreneurs). We also hope that those in the corporate sector will help their employees form worker-owned co-ops, like the PLDT Employees Multipurpose Co-op, the third largest billionaire co-op in the country. This should be our future: Every Filipino a social entrepreneur (and philanthropist).

3. Advocate a Simple Lifestyle

We live in a world that is speeding towards mass extinction caused by people's excessive consumption and irresponsible stewardship of our planet's resources. The annual Conference of the Parties (COP) Climate Change assemblies of the United Nations have been trying to oblige and push all countries, especially the developed ones to contribute towards the planet's survival and humanity's flourishing for generations to come. Unless there's a drastic reduction of carbon emissions, humankind is mass-consuming towards our self-destruction soon. For Jesus-followers, the simplest thing to do is to model the reduction of our

---

32. The preceding paragraphs in this section appear also in Lim, "Optimizing Discipleship Groups," 8–9.

33. iCanSaveApp, "PBMC Profile," *http://icansaveapp.com*.

34. I serve as board chair of Lausanne Philippines Partnership which was formed after we hosted the 6th Asia Lausanne Conference in 2006, and registered with the government to convene national conferences on world evangelization and transformation, which have been held twice in 2007 and 2013.

35. I'm the president emeritus of ASDECS, which specializes in training anyone from any profession in transformational leadership, development management, and community transformation – from certificate to doctoral levels. We have an Asian Institute for Social Entrepreneurship and Enterprise Development (AISEED), which focuses on training in entrepreneurial leadership and business administration.

consumerism, hedonism, and materialism. Sadly, such a call to a simple lifestyle has hardly gained popularity in Christian (and even evangelical) circles.[36]

Cultural Transformation for Inter-generational Flourishing

The third aspect of transformation politics is to ensure the passing on of our flourishing cultural heritage (especially the ancestral wisdom and virtuous customs) to the next generations. Isaiah 65:23 says, "They will not labor in vain, nor will they bear children doomed to misfortune; for they will be a people blessed by the Lord, they and their descendants with them." This eventuality will generate multiple cultures and subcultures even in the borderless harmonious world as envisioned for earth and heaven (Isa 2:1–5; Rev 7:9; 10:11; 21:24–26).

To sustain righteousness in democracies, our goal is to produce an enlightened citizenry who know how to elect servant-leaders that are incorruptible and competent. These righteous elite need to develop righteous character, spiritual virtues, biblical beliefs, and cultural values to overcome temptations of abusing and misusing power. Almost all servant-leaders have organically risen to influence because of their leadership talent and management skill-set that they gained from "being faithful in small things."

The weakest link in producing enlightened electorates have always been our dysfunctional families and neighborhoods, since it takes a village to raise a child. Raising children has been the duty given to parents in all societies even in biblical times (Deut 6:4–9; Eph 6:4). After all, the extended family is the small group in which each person is discipled naturally in intimate relationships and in relation to their neighbors.

Evangelism and disciplemaking are supposed to be the strength of evangelicals in relation to other groups of Christians in our land. We need to be equipping leaders who can evangelize and mentor leaders for the transformation of the culture of their constituencies and beyond.[37]

---

36. My advocacy for simple lifestyle began in my college days, and especially after I promoted Ronald Sider, *Rich Christians in an Age of Hunger* (Nashville: Thomas Nelson, 1978).

37. On the theology and skill-set for leading "Transformational Development" or "Integral Mission," see Bryant Myers, *Walking with the Poor: Principles and Practices of Transformational Development* (Maryknoll: Orbis, 1999), and Samuel and Sugden, *Mission as Transformation*. See also David Lim, "The Doctrine of Creation and Some Implications for Modern Economics," *Transformation* 7, no. 2 (April–June 1990): 28–32; and Vol. 7, no. 3 (July–September): 21–23.

Ecclesiological Transformation for Holistic Spirituality

On the fourth and last aspect: to produce the "righteous elite" to realize societal transformation, we need to transform our ecclesiology and missiology. Perhaps evangelicals can lead in Christianity's rediscovery and implementation of the doctrine of the "priesthood of all believers" where: Every Jesus-follower is a prince or princess and an ambassador of God's kingdom on earth. This is democracy applied in the religious sector, which contrasts with the hierarchicalism and clericalism of our prevalent denominational Christianity today. So far, the church has often ecclesiastically been part of the problem, not the solution.

With all the blessings of political peace, economic justice, and cultural flourishing mentioned above, Isaiah 65:24 depicts a mature spirituality that recognizes that God's grace requires no religiosity. He will pour out his blessings on those who seek him: "Before they call I will answer; while they are still speaking I will hear." What spirituality can put the kingdom's ever-new wine into new wineskins contextually (Mark 2:22), so that holistic transformation would be actualized and renewed sustainably on earth?

Sadly, Filipino Christianity (at least 92 percent of the population) has been more concerned about its religious liturgy and tradition and personal piety than about social justice. Such attitude and behavior have only made our "split-level Christianity"[38] an effective nurturer of hypocrisy among our officials and citizens. Almost all of the corrupt elite are very religious, faithfully going to church and taking communion every Sunday (if not daily), but the rest of the week bribing others and doing all sorts of corrupt deeds. This sad reality has four important implications for transformation politics in our religious sector: simple religiosity, secular spirituality, incarnational ministry, and sociocultural identity.

1. Simple Religiosity

Since "the church is the concrete form in which men experience the history of Christ,"[39] it should represent his kingdom well. All its members can and should enflesh and share God's reign in their historical context and beyond. But sadly, Christendom has been misshapen through the years, having been changed since

---

38. Coined by Jaime Bulatao, "Split-level Christianity," *Philippine Sociological Review* 13, no. 2 (April 1965): 119–21.

39. Jürgen Moltmann, *The Church in the Power of the Spirit* (Minneapolis: Fortress Press, 1993), 35.

Constantine, from the simplicity of an underground social movement into the complexity of an imperial religious institution. Almost all of its resources have been used to building and maintaining its own structures, instead of serving among the poor and sharing life with the poor (Matt 25:31–46).

Jesus taught his disciples to practice three private disciplines: almsgiving, praying, and fasting (Matt 6:1–8, 15–18). Though done in secret, almsgiving will soon be noticed by neighbors, and then the village leaders who will invite the givers to help in solving problems in the community. They become "light of the world" simply through their good works.

Sadly, all too often the church has been rich, powerful, and politically influential, yet unable to be a prophetic presence in society. How poorly have God's people failed to mirror Jesus's self-sacrifice to and for the world. Instead of confirming our transcendence as the community of renewed minds, in cruciform identification with the least and broken of the world, we have been conformed to the world (Rom 12:2), blessing and mirroring its might and triumphalism.

The wealth of Christendom raises the question of how a church that is rich can give testimony to faith in God. When Christians identify with mainstream culture, their political aspirations, their materialism and individualism, and their inability to care for the poor in their neighborhoods must raise questions regarding their ability to relate to Jesus of Nazareth, a poor man. Many churches aspire for alliances with prevailing power structures that guarantee a lack of persecution evidenced by large televangelist ministries and megachurches in the world today.

From the beginning, Jesus chose the power of love rather than the love of power. If God's kingdom is to sanctify the status quo, it must defend that order even against any critique of the word, even at the cost of its integrity. But the critic-from-within-the-establishment will sooner or later be ousted from the corrupt palace. The way in which Christians have become at home with the powers of the wealthy, and the alliance of the older churches with colonialism and capitalism, are both moral failures to faithfully represent Jesus's transformation politics.

In a graft-ridden society, a lack of persecution leads to a lack of meaningful witness to the Jesus whose words and life threatened the power structures of his day. It was through martyrdom that the church triumphed over Rome. Marginalization and suffering should be seen as one of the marks of the church. The only basis for the establishment of the *ekklesia* is found in our willingness to forsake all rights, refuse retaliation, and trust in Christ alone, even in the face of persecution. Blessed are the blessed few who have bravely stood firm and have taken the risks of being red-tagged and worse.

The righteous elite needs to express itself in vulnerability, with a determined avoidance of seeking political power and wealth at any cost. It is commendable that they have the "heavenly vision" to serve God's kingdom in the political arena, given the temptations and corruption that prevail. They are much-needed to represent the values and principles of God's kingdom in legislating and implementing righteousness and justice in public service, but they should never compromise their integrity.

2. Secular Spirituality

The incarnation of Christ was actualized in the servant (diaconal) form of Jesus's life and ministry; it was specifically self-emptying (kenotic) and cross-bearing (cruciform) to sacrificially live and die for the world. "It is not the religious act that makes the Christian, but participation in the sufferings of God in the secular life."[40]

As Jesus-followers practice the first of his three secret disciplines (almsgiving, praying, and fasting) for "every-moment worship" (Matt 6:1–18), doing almsgiving (or "good works" in 5:16; 25:31–40) will naturally lead to doing ministry publicly and secularly in their community. As we obey Micah 6:8, we not only do justice, love mercy, but also walk humbly with God – for Jesus's transformation politics to turn Babylons into the New Jerusalem.[41]

All cultures have seven basic moral values: Help your family, help your group, return favors, be brave, defer to superiors, divide resources fairly, and respect others' property.[42] Without these, societies would not have survived and thrived. Moreover, each religion has some basic beliefs and values that can be used as common ground for inter-religious dialogue, such as for Hinduism: "tolerance and integration," for Buddhism: "negation and objectivity," for Taoism: "nature and environment," for Confucianism: "humanity and society," for Judaism: "covenant faithfulness," and for Islam: "submission and obedience."[43] There is a wide range of "common ground" provided by God's

---

40. Dietrich Bonhoeffer, quoted in Gustavo Gutierrez, ed., *Essential Writings* (Maryknoll: Orbis, 1996), 39.

41. Popularized in my "The City in the Bible," in *Urban Ministry in Asia*, ed. Bong Rin Ro (Taichung: Asia Theological Association, 1989), 20–41.

42. Oliver S. Curry, D. A. Mullins, and Harvey Whitehouse, "Is It Good to Cooperate? Testing the Theory of Morality-as-Cooperation in 60 Societies," *Cultural Anthropology*, Vol. 60, no. 1 (February 2019): 47–69.

43. Daniel J. Kim, "Missional Spirituality in the 21st Century Post-Pandemic Era," *ACTS Theological Journal* 53 (2022): 270.

"common (or prevenient) grace" that we can build on from any religious[44] or secular tradition.

All these traditions can agree with Jesus's teaching in Matthew 25:31–46, that the righteous are those who do social services, not those who do religious services. In the parable of the good Samaritan, Jesus taught that it's not the priest and the levite, but an ordinary trader who is righteous (Luke 10:30–37). Acts of "neighborly love" are of two major kinds: acts of mercy or kindness (to build healthy individuals and families), as well as acts of justice for peace/*shalom* (to build "caring and sharing" distributive communities). Individually, all those who do secular tasks are actually doing God's work; they just need to believe that they are doing these for God (Col 3:23–24). Jesus-followers will be known as people who are the kindest, most friendly, most generous, and most altruistic in society.

Thus we can regard our kingdom communities (KCs) as "flourishing communities" that seek to attain the 17 Sustainable Development Goals of the United Nations, and work with all groups that are aspiring to do the same. God has been working historically through the secularization of society, so that religion functions no longer as a high-profile institutional complex, but as a low-profile spiritual support (yet not peripheral nor absent as prevailing in most secular contexts today) to all the ordinary and special affairs of human life.[45]

3. Incarnational Ministry

Jesus planned his world transformation movement to be simple – through "disciple multiplication movements (DMMs)" by converts in their local contexts. His first twelve were trained to replicate what he did by pairs (Luke 9:1–6), that produced a second batch of seventy-two (10:1–17). They were sent out in pairs to do the same strategy (disciple twelve each) in the villages of Galilee, thereby producing more than five hundred disciples (1 Cor 15:6). At Pentecost, the three thousand converts were baptized immediately, and discipled "from

---

44. Numerous historical instances of "redemptive analogies" are narrated in Don Richardson, *Eternity in their Hearts* (Ventura: Regal, 1981).

45. Dietrich Bonhoeffer called for "holy worldliness" which practices "secret discipline": "The Church is the Church only when it exists for others . . . The church must share in the secular problems of ordinary human life, not dominating, but helping and serving. It must tell men of every calling what it means to live for Christ, to exist for others," in *Letters and Papers from Prison* (London: The Macmillan Press, 1967), 140.

house to house" by five hundred Galilean Jesus-followers, with each pair leading a group of twelve (Acts 2:41–47).[46]

It is simple to multiply disciples in small groups and fellowships incarnationally in all societal structures – hence indigenous and fully decentralized with polycentric leadership. Jesus-followers will lead in the paradigm shift of all societal systems from "hierarchical and centralized" to "flat and decentralized." The Roman Catholic Church has determined to become "church of the poor" and develop "a new way of being church" in the form of Basic Ecclesial Communities (BECs).[47] For Protestants, this has been implemented by the Radical Reformers (Anabaptists) to form KCs (called "societies of friends"), which may be called "cell groups," like the "house churches" in the NT.

Following the doctrine of "the priesthood of all believers," we can affirm the church-hood of every cell and the fellowship (*koinonia*) of all cells as KCs (*ekklesia*) of God's citizens who advocate for justice, peace, and integrity of creation – in their neighborhoods, workplaces, and online in social media – like the zero-budget structure of Exodus 18:21. This structure is achieved from the bottom up as each house church member lives in *koinonia* with two to twelve others in their neighborhood, workplace, and/or circle of influence.

Jesus's incarnational ministry is a social reformation movement that multiplies social reformers who can form informal small groups that lead moral transformation in their neighborhood and workplace. But the question is: How can wealthy churches release their potential for transformation politics? They cannot serve the poor and the common good unless they are willing to divest and to break free from their hierarchical, clergy-centered traditions and the capitalist ecosystem.

By divesting and having no structures to maintain, KCs can use all their resources directly in the community and marketplace, which was what Jesus equipped his disciples to do so that the world can be baptized, discipled, and transformed. He just informally trained them and sent them "with authority" (empowered) to make disciples in and through the house of a "son of peace" (Luke 10:6 KJV, cf. vv. 1–17) in the villages of Galilee. These local persons of

---

46. On DMM, see my "Asian Mission Movements in Asia Today," *Asian Missions Advance* 41 (October 2013): 29–36. Also see my practical articles: "Effective Tentmaking Made Simple," in Ana M. Gamez, *Blessing OFWs to Bless the Nations* (Makati: Church Strengthening Ministry, 2010), 108–13; and "Effective Disciple-making Made Simple," in Dave English et al., *Tentmaking Briefs*, Vol. 1 (September 2012): 61–63.

47. On BECs, see Nicta Lubaale, "Doing Mission at the Margins of Society: Harnessing Resources of Local Visions," and Clemens Mendorca, "Mission According to the Catholic Church in Asia: A New Way of Being Church," both in *Mission Spirituality and Authentic Discipleship*, eds. W. Ma and K. Ross (Oxford: Regnum, 2013), 30–32 and 127–38.

peace will then go "from house to house" (the guests should not, v. 7) to convert their whole village to faith in Jesus, thereby transforming their wolf den into a sheepfold (cf. v. 3) with great success (v. 17).

4. Sociocultural Identity

Lastly, as discussed above, the rich legacy of each culture will be inherited by the next generations. Each culture will be preserved for eternity as each generation builds on their ancestral heritage and contributes to international multi-ethnic and multicultural peace, possibly for "a thousand generations" (Deut 7:9).

The early church multiplied across the empire rapidly with political impact (Acts 17:6), because they used Jesus's incarnational approach. Paul made himself a slave (*doulos*) to become "all things to all men" (1 Cor 9:19–23), and instructed his converts to remain in the vocational, sociocultural, and economic status that they had at the time of their conversion (7:17–24). They could aspire to convert the entire village by winning the community leaders to Christ, "who will then persuade the religious leaders to worship the Creator in Jesus's name." These leaders will seek to transform their existing religious structures into "multi-purpose buildings for good governance there, without constructing another religious structure in the community."[48] This is "zero-budget missions" that set up "zero-budget churches," which follow the contextual "Insider Movement (IM)" approach used in Frontier Missiology.[49]

In the Philippines and Asia, religion, culture, and politics are nearly inseparable, making changing religions a total break from their community. Jesus's concern was the establishment of the kingdom of God, not the founding of a new religion, by inviting people to have faith in him. Often the exact point of transfer from the kingdom of darkness to the kingdom of light cannot be known, but true faith will show in a Christ-like life of "love and good works," set free from all spiritual bondages in Jesus's name. And each HCM will develop their contextual theology by reflecting alone or together on God's Word applied to their life experiences. The existing religion will be gradually (sometimes immediately) transformed – rejecting unbiblical (sinful and demonic) beliefs

---

48. David Lim, "Visions and Strategies of House Church Leaders in Asia," *Asian Mission Advance* 71 (April 2021), 18.

49. On IMs, H. Talman and J. J. Travis, eds., *Understanding Insider Movements: Disciples of Jesus Within Diverse Religious Communities* (Pasadena: William Carey Library, 2015).

and practices, while retaining biblical ones (1 Cor 7:17–24; 1 Tim 4:4–5), as a community *en masse*.

Vast numbers of peoples can be converted and transformed as we allow new converts to retain their sociocultural identity in their community. Fighting the religion-changing battle is the wrong battle. The strategy is that of incarnation or integration, to transform the people with the gospel *from within* their social structures, without setting an alternative religious structure among them. This is vastly different from the "extraction evangelism" paradigm that we have inherited from Christendom's colonial missions that have made Jesus look foreign and irrelevant to our contexts.

We can take advantage of the deconstruction of absolutism and institutionalism that's going to overwhelm our future, with the help of automated and augmented technology. In our postmodern world, we just need to be clear about two absolutes: our Creator God who cares for all his creation and every human being (Heb 11:6), and his clear revelation in Jesus of Nazareth who came to offer his redemption to restore fallen creation and humanity to his kingdom, so that his will (commandments) will be obeyed on earth as it is in heaven. Our mission is simply to share these two absolutes in a relational and friendly way – incarnationally, contextually, servantly – in every context wherever we live and work, by the power of the Holy Spirit.

Conclusion

So, Jesus's understanding and master-plan for the kingdom of God has historically been progressively but incrementally fulfilled by his people, mainly through the few righteous elite among all nations. This transformation politics can be accelerated if we faithfully implement the suggestions in this essay.

What the Philippines and the secularized (mostly nominal Christian) nations need are revivals, which actually have always been simply a return to secular spirituality, where God is part of ordinary conversations and daily life. What the non-Christian countries (which are enjoying humanitarian benefits) need are just simple DMMs that will produce righteous elites. They all need to understand and believe that the roots of the blessings of peace and sustainable development that they now take for granted are based on the biblical worldview that everything good comes from the Creator who loves all and has revealed himself in the life, death, and resurrection of Jesus of Nazareth.

Let's multiply disciplemakers to produce the righteous elite to build *shalom* in all nations. As our world transitions from digital to automated intelligence with supercomputers and smartphones, we can propagate secular spirituality even faster and wider to more networks of friends and partners worldwide online by just working from home. The experience of the COVID-19 pandemic lockdowns has fast-tracked this virtual reality and will soon advance to augmented realities. Such online relationships are genuine, for behind every anonymous blogger or metaverse avatar is a human being. This development makes the possibility of fulfilling transformation politics more diversified, decentralized, and distributed, thus more likely in our generation.

With this transformational political way of multiplying Jesus-followers for nation-building and world peace, let us disciple more servant-leaders whose secular spirituality is not just the "factory reset" of the "better normal" triggered by the recent pandemic, but mainly the "default mode" of the "original normal" that God designed and Jesus implemented to fulfill his redemption plan for fallen humanity and creation to be reconciled to himself through faith in him. Let's empower God's people to disciple all sectors (especially the government sector) in all nations. Let's believe that the best is yet to come. May all Babylons be transformed into the New Jerusalem – not perfectly just yet, but substantially – among all nations through each of us.

"Our Father, your kingdom come, your will be done, on earth as it is in heaven" – in and through the exponential indigenization of flourishing kingdom communities holistically and contextually everywhere – so that the whole earth will experience God's amazing grace as waters cover the sea!

Bibliography

Abueva, Jose. "Revised Draft Constitution for a Proposed Federal Republic of the Philippines with a Parliamentary Government, Revised 14 February 2005," in https://www.kas.de/en/web/philippinen/single-title/-/content/revised-draft-constitution-for-a-proposed-federal-republic-of-the-philippines-with-a-parliamentary-government.

Bonhoeffer, Dietrich. *Letters and Papers from Prison*. London: The Macmillan Press, 1967.

Bulatao, Jaime. "Split-level Christianity," *Philippine Sociological Review* 13, no. 2 (April, 1965): 119–21.

Curry, Oliver S., D. A. Mullins, and Harvey Whitehouse, "Is It Good to Cooperate? Testing the Theory of Morality-as-Cooperation in 60 Societies," *Cultural Anthropology* 60, no. 1 (February 2019): 47–69.

Fukuyama, Francis. *The End of History and the Last Man*. New York: Harper Perennial, 1992.

Geducos, Argyle Cyrus. "Robredo bares anti-corruption efforts; will probe customs, BIR, DPWH," *Manila Bulletin*, 28 February 2022. https://mb.com.ph/2022/02/27/robredo-bares-anti-corruption-efforts-will-probe-customs-bir-dpwh/.

Gutierrez, Gustavo, ed. *Essential Writings*. Maryknoll: Orbis, 1996.

Henriot, Peter J., et al. *Catholic Social Teachings: Our Best Kept Secret*. Maryknoll: Orbis, 1988.

Heydarian, Richard Javad. "The Return of the Marcos Dynasty." *Journal of Democracy* 33, no. 3 (July 2022): 62–76.

iCanSaveApp. "PBMC Profile." http://icansaveapp.com.

Johnstone, Japhet. "Understanding the state of liberal societies: Researchers release open-access dataset to the public." phys.org, 8 July 2024. https://phys.org/news/2024-07-state-liberal-societies-access-dataset.html#google_vignette.

Kim, Daniel J. "Missional Spirituality in the 21st Century Post-Pandemic Era," *ACTS Theological Journal* 53 (2022): 246–90.

Kraft, Charles. *Christianity in Cultures*. Maryknoll: Orbis, 1979.

Lim, David. "Asian Mission Movements in Asia Today." *Asian Missions Advance* 41 (October 2013): 29–36.

———. "Church and State in the Philippines, 1900–1988." *Transformation* 6, no. 3 (July–September 1989): 27–32.

———. "Consolidating Democracy: Role of Evangelicals in Deepening Democracy in the Philippines from 1986–1998." In *Evangelical Christianity and Democracy in Asia*, edited by David H. Lumsdaine, 235–84. Oxford: Oxford University Press, 2009.

———. "Effective Disciple-making Made Simple." *Tentmaking Briefs* 1 (September 2012): 61–63.

———. "Effective Tentmaking Made Simple." In *Blessing OFWs to Bless the Nations*, edited by Ana M. Gamez, 108–13. Makati: Church Strengthening Ministry, 2010.

———. "God's Kingdom as Oikos Church Networks: A Biblical Theology." *International Journal of Frontier Mission* 34, nos. 1–4 (January–December 2017): 25–35.

———. "Optimizing Discipleship Groups for Fulfilling the Great Commission." *Asian Missions Advance* 85 (Fall 2024): 6–11.

———. "The City in the Bible." In *Urban Ministry in Asia*, edited by Bong Rin Ro, 20–41. Taichung: Asia Theological Association, 1989. Also in *Evangelical Review of Theology* 12, no. 2 (April 1988): 138–56.

———. "The Doctrine of Creation and Some Implications for Modern Economics." *Transformation* 7, no. 2 (April–June 1990): 28–32; and *Transformation* 7 no. 3 (July–September): 21–23.

———. "The Living God in the Structures of Philippine Reality," *Transformation* 5 (April–June 1988): 1–7.

———. "The Uniqueness of Christ for Justice and Peace." In *The Uniqueness of Christ*, edited by Bruce Nicholls, 214–30. Carlisle: Paternoster; Grand Rapids: Baker, 1995.

———. *Transforming Communities*. Mandaluyong City: OMF Literature, 1992.

———. "Vision and Strategies of House Church Leaders in Asia." *Asian Mission Advance* 71 (April 2021): 17–20.

———. "Why We Should Form an Evangelical Political Party," *Evangelical Thrust* 13 (August 1986): 12–13; and *Evangelical Thrust* 14 (September 1986): 14–15, 18–19.

Lubaale, Nicta. "Doing Mission at the Margins of Society: Harnessing Resources of Local Visions." In *Mission Spirituality and Authentic Discipleship*, edited by W. Ma and K. Ross, 30–42. Oxford: Regnum, 2013.

Mendorca, Clemens. "Mission According to the Catholic Church in Asia: A New Way of Being Church." In *Mission Spirituality and Authentic Discipleship*, edited by W. Ma and K. Ross, 127–38. Oxford: Regnum, 2013.

Moltmann, Jürgen. *The Church in the Power of the Spirit*. Minneapolis: Fortress Press, 1993.

Myers, Bryant. *Walking with the Poor: Principles and Practices of Transformational Development*. Maryknoll: Orbis, 1999.

Philippine Institute for Development Studies. "Understanding Social Classes in the Philippines: Which Class Do You Belong to?" pids.gov.ph (26 April 2022). https://pids.gov.ph/details/news/in-the-news/understanding-social-classes-in-the-philippines-which-class-do-you-belong-to.

Piramide, Aven. "For the poor only? What about the others?" *The Freeman*, 9 August 2020. https://www.philstar.com/the-freeman/opinion/2020/08/09/2033973/poor-only-what-about-others.

Pope Francis. *Fratelli Tutti* (2020). https://www.vatican.va/content/francesco/en/encyclicals/documents/papa-francesco_20201003_enciclica-fratelli-tutti.html.

Richardson, Don. *Eternity in their Hearts*. Ventura: Regal, 1981.

Samuel, Vinay, and Chris Sugden, eds. *Mission as Transformation*. Oxford: Regnum, 1999.

Sider, Ronald. *Rich Christians in an Age of Hunger*. Nashville: Thomas Nelson, 1978.

Simson, Wolfgang. *Houses that Change the World*. Carlisle: Paternoster, 2001.

Talman, H., and J. J. Travis, eds. *Understanding Insider Movements*. Pasadena: William Carey Library, 2015.

Youngblood, Robert L. "The Protestant Church in the Philippines' New Society." *Bulletin of Concerned Asian Scholars* 12 (1980): 3–29.

Zdero, Rad. *The Global House Church Movement*. Pasadena: William Carey Library, 2004.

List of Authors

Jack Dosejo Alvarez took biblical and theological courses at the Alliance Graduate School and the Asian Theological Seminary. He is the servant-pastor of *Komunidad kay Kristo sa Payatas*, an evangelical, reformational, contextual, and missional church in Quezon City, Philippines. He is currently the chair of the Payatas Evangelical Movement, and along with his fellow pastors in this ministerial organization, he is venturing to bring quality biblical and theological education to the slums of Payatas via *Seminaryo Anawim*. Pastor Alvarez is an active member of *Bawat Isa Mahalaga* (B1M), Human Rights Committee of Justice, Peace and Reconciliation Commission (of PCEC), and *Anawim Misyon sa Mahihirap*, an ecumenical missional movement among the poorest of the poor.

Alvin Ang is a professor of economics at the Ateneo de Manila University. He is also a preaching elder at the Capital City Alliance Church in Quezon City, Philippines. His advocacies are focused on bridging the truth of Scriptures to the realities of everyday economics. He is also regularly consulted by the Philippine Government and Development Agencies on policy matters.

Romel Regalado Bagares has communication and law degrees from the University of the Philippines and an MA (*cum laude*) from the Vrije Universiteit Amsterdam, Netherlands, where he is also working on a doctoral project applying the Dutch Christian philosopher Herman Dooyeweerd's *Encyclopedia of the Science of Law* to international law. He was a visiting lecturer on Christianity, politics, and society at the Asian Theological Seminary. He teaches international law at four Philippine law schools and serves as vice-chair of the Philippine Judicial Academy Department of International Law and Maritime Law. Before turning to law, he worked as a journalist for the *Philippine Star*, an English-language Manila daily. His family attends Pilgrim Community Church in Manila, a confessional Presbyterian congregation of the International Presbyterian Church.

Jayeel S. Cornelio is a sociologist of religion at the Ateneo de Manila University. He has written extensively on religion and public life in the Philippines. Among his books include *People's Christianity: Theological Sense and Sociological Significance* with Jose Mario Francisco (Paulist Press, 2022) and *Discipleship for Today's Filipino* with Federico Villanueva (OMF Lit, 2024), and the

Routledge International Handbook of Religion in Global Society co-edited with François Gauthier, Tuomas Martikainen, Linda Woodhead (Routledge, 2021).

Rei Lemuel Crizaldo serves as the theological commission coordinator of the World Evangelical Alliance and as the theological education network coordinator of Tearfund in East and Southeast Asia. In the Philippines, he teaches at the seminary of the Evangelical Methodist Church in the Philippine Islands. A local author, he writes books in mixed languages, one of which, *Boring ba ang Bible Mo?* (Is your Bible Boring?) – *How Your Story Fits in the Big Story*, won the Filipino Readers Choice Award in 2015. His recent academic publications include chapters written from a decolonial theology perspective in the following volumes: *Missio Dei in a Digital Age* (SCM Press, 2020), *Theologies and Practices of Inclusion* (SCM Press, 2021), and *God's Heart for Children: Practical Theology from Global Perspectives* (Langham Global Library, 2022).

Dick O. Eugenio finished his PhD in theology from the University of Manchester, UK. He served as faculty of theology and dean of the Asia-Pacific Nazarene Theological Seminary for a decade before moving to engage the world through educating the Filipino youth in universities. He served as vice-president for academic affairs of the Wesleyan University Philippines, and now functions as the director of the international affairs and strategic partnerships office of World Citi Colleges. He has published several books and numerous book chapters and journal articles, mostly on matters related to theology and education. He is an eclectic reader, but his primary research interest lies in the intersection between theology and other disciplines.

Marie Joy D. Pring-Faraz serves as the program director of the PhD in transformational development at the Asia-Pacific Nazarene Theological Seminary. A Langham scholar, she also works as an adjunct faculty at several institutions such as the William Carey International University and the Biblical Graduate School of Theology Singapore. Joy was an international research scholar at the Nagel Institute for the Study of World Christianity in Calvin University. She is an advocate for women and at-risk children and has also served as a research consultant for non-profit organizations, such as the International Justice Mission Philippines and ECPAT International New York.

Athena E. Gorospe is vice-president for academic affairs and professor in biblical studies at the Asian Theological Seminary (ATS). She is also the director of the PhD in contextual theology program at ATS. As an Asian scholar, her research interest lies in Scripture's interface with philosophy, culture, and the social context. She is the author of *Judges* for the Asia Bible Commentary Series (Langham Global Library, 2015), and *Narrative and Identity: An Ethical Reading of Exodus 4* (Brill, 2007), as well as author and editor of works that show a dialogue between Scripture and current socio-political realities, including "God's Story of Life: Themes for an Asian Creation Care Ethics," in *Asian Christian Ethics: Evangelical Perspectives* (Langham Global Library, 2022). She has a PhD in theology (Old Testament) from Fuller Seminary, California, USA.

Wilfredo A. Laceda teaches Bible and theology courses at the Penuel School of Theology in Manila, Philippines. He is also a junior fellow at Street Psalms, a global training organization that uses the ideas of René Girard to develop peace theology and incarnational leadership in challenging contexts. He regularly contributes to *Street Psalms' Word from Below* reflections. His publications and research interests focus on the intersection of social theory and theology. He serves as a pulpit minister at a local church in Pasig City.

David S. Lim is the president emeritus and professor in transformational development of the Asian School for Development and Cross-Cultural Studies, which provides formal and non-formal training programs for community transformation. He serves as the board chairman of the Lausanne Philippines Partnership, which has "Cooperatives as Mission" as its flagship program, and an executive council member of the Asia Lausanne Committee. He is also the vice-president of the Asian Society of Missiology, an executive committee member of the Asian Society of Frontier Missions, and the National Council vice-chairman of the *Kapatiran* Party. He earned his ThM (New Testament) from the Asian Center for Theological Studies, and his PhD in theology from Fuller Seminary, California, USA.

Melba Padilla Maggay is a sought-after international speaker and consultant on culture and social development issues, particularly on the interface of religion, culture, and development. As a social anthropologist, she has done research and writing on cross-cultural and development studies at the Nagel Institute for the Study of World Christianity at Calvin University, Yale University under the auspices of the Overseas Ministries Study Center, and at the National Taiwan University on a fellowship grant working on the South China Sea issue. She founded and serves as president of the Institute for Studies in Asian Church and Culture (ISACC). Since 2015, she was president and is now ambassador of Micah Global, a network of about eight hundred faith-based development organizations worldwide. She writes on sociocultural issues for

Rappler and other news media sites, besides serving as editor of PATMOS Online and other publications of ISACC.

Annabel Manzanilla-Manalo, PhD, RPsy, is associate professor and chair of the counseling department at the Asian Theological Seminary. A licensed and certified clinical and counseling psychologist, she earned her PhD in clinical psychology from the Ateneo de Manila University. With over thirty years of experience, she has provided consultancy, training, supervision, and psychotherapy services to NGOs that support marginalized and vulnerable groups. Her work includes developing and implementing mental health and psychosocial support programs for survivors of torture, families affected by enforced disappearances and extrajudicial killings, youth-at-risk, and communities displaced by armed conflicts and natural disasters. She is an advocate for healing and justice among those impacted by state-perpetrated violence and systemic trauma.

Aldrin M. Peñamora holds a PhD in theology in Christian ethics from Fuller Seminary, California, USA. He serves as executive director of the Theological Commission, and the Justice, Peace and Reconciliation Commission of the Philippine Council of Evangelical Churches (PCEC). He is also executive director of the PCEC-affiliated Center for the Study of Christian-Muslim Relations, and the Theological Commission of the Asia Evangelical Alliance. He is co-editor of *Asian Christian Ethics: Evangelical Perspectives* and *Faith* (Langham Global Library, 2022) and *Bayan: Evangelical Christian Engagement in the Philippine Context* (Langham Global Library, 2022). Aldrin also serves as program director of the PhD in peace studies program of the Asia Graduate School of Theology-International Graduate School of Leadership (AGST-IGSL) and is part of the faculty of the PhD/ThM in the theology and church history program of AGST-IGSL.

Nestor M. Ravilas is a public theologian from the Philippines. He and his training community, Penuel School of Theology, are deeply committed to the legacy of the historical Jesus, particularly on his resistance to all forms of oppressive and exploitative power. He has a Master of Divinity in biblical studies from the Asian Theological Seminary and a Master of Theology from the Asian Graduate School of Theology. He is currently doing his PhD in contextual theology at the Asian Theological Seminary.

Emil Jonathan L. Soriano works currently for Tearfund as the theology network and engagement adviser and Reconciled and Peaceful Societies focal lead in Asia. He sits as a board of trustee member for Peacebuilders Community, Inc. He is also part of the PCEC's Commission under Micah Philippines and JPARCOM. He finished his Master of Divinity in cross-cultural missions from the Asian Theological Seminary.

Abigail R. Teh is currently the academic dean and program director for biblical studies at the Alliance Graduate School in Quezon City. She has been teaching the Old Testament for more than two decades. In 2019, she obtained her doctoral degree from the Loyola School of Theology in the same city, writing on "The Pain and Promise of Cultural Trauma: Textual Strategies of Re-symbolization in Ezekiel 40–48" for her dissertation. The phrase *Deus semper major* is her guiding light in teaching. It means "God is always bigger." God is always bigger than our theological systems, bigger than our current experience and understanding of Him. She remains hopeful and open to how God will turn around the situation of the Philippines.

Langham Literature and its imprints are a ministry of Langham Partnership.

Langham Partnership is a global fellowship working in pursuit of the vision God entrusted to its founder John Stott –

> *to facilitate the growth of the church in maturity and Christ-likeness through raising the standards of biblical preaching and teaching.*

Our vision is to see churches in the Majority World equipped for mission and growing to maturity in Christ through the ministry of pastors and leaders who believe, teach and live by the word of God.

Our mission is to strengthen the ministry of the word of God through:
- nurturing national movements for biblical preaching
- fostering the creation and distribution of evangelical literature
- enhancing evangelical theological education

especially in countries where churches are under-resourced.

Our ministry

Langham Preaching partners with national leaders to nurture indigenous biblical preaching movements for pastors and lay preachers all around the world. With the support of a team of trainers from many countries, a multi-level programme of seminars provides practical training, and is followed by a programme for training local facilitators. Local preachers' groups and national and regional networks ensure continuity and ongoing development, seeking to build vigorous movements committed to Bible exposition.

Langham Literature provides Majority World preachers, scholars and seminary libraries with evangelical books and electronic resources through publishing and distribution, grants and discounts. The programme also fosters the creation of indigenous evangelical books in many languages, through writer's grants, strengthening local evangelical publishing houses, and investment in major regional literature projects, such as one volume Bible commentaries like *The Africa Bible Commentary* and *The South Asia Bible Commentary*.

Langham Scholars provides financial support for evangelical doctoral students from the Majority World so that, when they return home, they may train pastors and other Christian leaders with sound, biblical and theological teaching. This programme equips those who equip others. Langham Scholars also works in partnership with Majority World seminaries in strengthening evangelical theological education. A growing number of Langham Scholars study in high quality doctoral programmes in the Majority World itself. As well as teaching the next generation of pastors, graduated Langham Scholars exercise significant influence through their writing and leadership.

To learn more about Langham Partnership and the work we do visit **langham.org**

www.ingramcontent.com/pod-product-compliance
Lightning Source LLC
Chambersburg PA
CBHW050612300426
44112CB00012B/1466

Ana Cristina Araújo
Carlos Moura Martins
Carlota Simões
Fernando Taveira da Fonseca
Fernando B. Figueiredo e António Leal-Duarte
Gustavo Oliveira Ferreira
Pedro Casaleiro

A UNIVERSIDADE POMBALINA

CIÊNCIA, TERRITÓRIO E COLEÇÕES CIENTÍFICAS

ANA CRISTINA ARAÚJO E
FERNANDO TAVEIRA DA FONSECA
(COORD.)

IMPRENSA DA
UNIVERSIDADE
DE COIMBRA
**COIMBRA
UNIVERSITY
PRESS**

SUMÁRIO

Introdução
Ana Cristina Araújo e Fernando Taveira da Fonseca 7

Uma primeira educação do olhar: Universidade
e estudantes de Coimbra na transição reformista
Fernando Taveira da Fonseca 13

Scientiae thesaurus mirabilis: estudantes de origem brasileira
na Universidade de Coimbra (1601-1850)
Fernando Taveira da Fonseca 51

O governo da natureza no pensamento da geração universitária
de finais do século XVIII: os *Estatutos Literários e Económicos
da Sociedade dos Mancebos Patriotas de Coimbra*
Ana Cristina Araújo 87

A ciência como estratégia social: as atividades científicas de
Domingos Vandelli nas redes clientelares de Portugal 1764-1788
Gustavo Oliveira Ferreira 139

A reforma pombalina da Universidade de Coimbra
e a institucionalização das ciências matemáticas e astronómicas
em Portugal
Fernando B. Figueiredo e António Leal-Duarte 191

A aplicação da ciência à política do território na transição
do século XVIII para o século XIX
Carlos Moura Martins 245

Coleções Científicas do Iluminismo na Universidade de Coimbra
Carlota Simões e *Pedro Casaleiro* 313

Bibliografia geral 335

Índice toponímico e antroponímico 353

A UNIVERSIDADE POMBALINA. CIÊNCIA, TERRITÓRIO E COLEÇÕES CIENTÍFICAS

Ana Cristina Araújo
e *Fernando Taveira da Fonseca* (coords.)

Introdução

A inscrição do moderno paradigma científico no quadro estatutário da reforma pombalina de 1772 tem suscitado o interesse de muitos historiadores da cultura, das ciências e das instituições. Valiosas leituras têm vindo a centrar a compreensão dinâmica da relação entre ciência e Universidade em questões de método de ensino e de conteúdos ensinados, tendo por base, numa perspetiva convencional, a institucionalização de um modelo de conhecimento, de matriz racional, experimental e instrumental. Sem prejuízo desta orientação, novos olhares convidam à exploração de diferentes motivos de investigação, a fim de se compreender a extensão da ciência e dos seus campos de aplicação para além do espaço circunscrito em que ela foi praticada e ensinada.

Situada na fronteira entre o transnacional e o local, a Universidade reproduziu e possibilitou a produção de conhecimento do mundo físico e natural, sem qualquer limitação ou restrição de tempo e de lugar, e, por outro lado, forneceu conhecimentos de aplicação imediata, cuja relevância foi testada no plano cultural e ensaiada, no plano político, à escala territorial e local.

Enquanto atividade socialmente organizada, a ciência moderna impôs-se pelo reconhecimento da validade universal das suas observações, procedimentos e demonstrações. Suportada por diversas redes sociais e institucionais, contribuiu, igualmente, para reafirmar a vocação cosmopolita dos seus agentes, acabando por conferir uma clara dimensão emancipatória ao conhecimento técnico-científico.

Deste modo, o domínio das ciências que veio a consolidar-se na Universidade de Coimbra, em finais de setecentos, esteve na origem de novos meios de imposição social do conhecimento e de múltiplas iniciativas de carácter prático e instrumental que, sendo pensadas em benefício das comunidades, assumiram, também, como não poderia deixar de ser, uma dimensão política controlada.

A par das convenções fundantes da credibilidade do discurso científico, às hierarquias universitárias coube a função de alicerçar, na prática, a supremacia do método científico no seio do claustro académico. Fazendo parte de um intrincado sistema de crédito institucional, os cultores da ciência procuraram reforçar, cumulativamente, a sua posição no campo científico através do recurso a mecanismos de poder simbólico, exteriores à lógica da ciência, redefinindo, deste modo, formas de inclusão e de exclusão no seio da comunidade académica.

Inserida nas convenções sociais dominantes, a cultura científica, em processo de enraizamento na Universidade setecentista portuguesa, reflete, em domínios muito sensíveis, a dualidade estratégica dos mentores e/ou executores da reforma académica de 1772. Apesar de serem porta-vozes de novos saberes, os defensores da ciência "oficial" agiram em função da tradição, do sistema de mando e de clientela característico da sociedade de Antigo Regime. Por este motivo, entre outros, as razões sociológicas dos conflitos de representação que depressa se fizeram sentir no campo científico demarcaram, em áreas fundamentais como a Filosofia Natural e a Matemática, as fronteiras de possibilidade dos avanços prometidos pela ciência nos domínios económico, material, cultural e político.

Carreando novos dados para as questões levantadas, coligem-se nesta obra os textos do programa de conferências realizado no âmbito do curso de doutoramento em Altos Estudos em História, na primavera de 2015, na Faculdade de Letras da Universidade de Coimbra, o qual contou com o apoio do Centro de História da Sociedade e da Cultura (FCT). Por iniciativa dos coordenadores deste volume, outros trabalhos de investigação foram agregados ao primeiro conjunto de estudos, permitindo um alargamento de campo historiográfico sobre um tema que comporta um inquérito extenso e exigente, onde cabem outros tópicos de pesquisa igualmente importantes, como sejam: a cronologia e sociologia da população estudantil; a análise de mecanismos de distinção, através de estudos de caso, que revelem o recurso a dispositivos estatutários e simbólicos no processo de reconhecimento social de mestres e discípulos; o levantamento de outras instituições científicas que, a par da universidade, concorreram para a disseminação de programas de melhoramento material e em que se observa o recurso a idêntica formação técnico-científica; e a sinalização de programas desenhados por engenheiros, matemáticos, naturalistas e cosmógrafos que denotam a orientação estatal das políticas de território que despontam em finais de século.

As conclusões a que chegaram os autores desta obra abrem novos horizontes à compreensão da transição institucional iniciada com a reforma universitária de 1772. No capítulo intitulado "Uma primeira educação do olhar: Universidade e estudantes de Coimbra na transição reformista", Fernando Taveira da Fonseca sustenta que a reforma não modificou estruturalmente a Universidade. Reforçou mudanças anteriormente insinuadas no campo da modernização do conhecimento e do crescimento da população estudantil, com o aumento de recrutamento de estudantes de origem brasileira conforme demonstra, de forma pormenorizada, recorrendo a séries sistemáticas de dados estatísticos, em: "*Scientiae thesaurus mirabilis*: estudantes de origem brasileira na Universidade de Coimbra (1601-1850)".

Estes elementos de continuidade articulam-se com a mudança de organização de sistema científico, subjacente à criação das duas novas Faculdades maiores, Matemática e Filosofia, sistema que, longe de se encerrar nos programas dos respectivos cursos, adquiriu uma notória dimensão expansiva, na medida em que os seus fundamentos teóricos iluminam a formação científica obrigatória dos estudantes das restantes Faculdades. Mais do que a dimensão laboratorial da nova ciência ensinada na Universidade, dimensão importantíssima e que contempla, obrigatoriamente, o conjunto de novos espaços em que se organiza a observação, simulação, manipulação e produção de resultados experimentais – que remetem para a criação do Laboratório Químico, Teatro Anatómico, Jardim Botânico, Gabinete de Física e Gabinete de História Natural, Observatório Astronómico – importa realçar o primado epistémico do modelo newtoniano de ciência, marcadamente físico-matemático, no multímodo campo de organização dos saberes universitários. Este traço sistémico é enfatizado por Fernando Figueiredo e António Leal-Duarte em "A reforma pombalina da Universidade de Coimbra e a institucionalização das ciências matemáticas e astronómicas".

Na sequência deste estudo, Carlos Moura Martins debruça-se sobre "A aplicação da ciência à política do território na transição do século XVIII para o século XIX", associando, a cada passo, a política de intervenção no território ao conhecimento técnico-científico ensinado na Universidade pombalina. Neste ponto, em que é notória a convergência de outras iniciativas institucionais de difusão científica, o Estado, assumindo-se como garante e promotor de grandes obras de interesse público, procede, com o concurso de técnicos formados na Universidade, ao lançamento e construção de grandes eixos viários, obras de desassoreamento de zonas costeiras, trabalhos de regularização de cursos fluviais, etc. Em suma, a ciência fornece ferramentas adequadas para racionalização do governo da monarquia, ou melhor, para o governo da população e seus territórios. Semelhante afirmação nada tem de surpreendente, embora se desconheçam, em toda a sua amplitude, as obras ideadas, adiadas e iniciadas em finais do século XVIII. Feita esta ressalva, importa ainda realçar que os objetos e instrumentos científicos se transformaram, definitivamente, em matéria de polícia e de bom governo.

A manifesta implicação prática do conhecimento científico na visão política da *respublica* e a consequente mudança de paradigma social que tal alteração também suscitou compreendem-se nos termos e regras que assinalam o plano de criação de uma sociedade patriótica formada por estudantes e professores, em finais do século XVIII, tema tratado por Ana Cristina Araújo em "O 'governo da natureza' no pensamento da geração universitária de finais de século XVIII. Estatutos literários e económicos da 'sociedade dos mancebos patriotas de Coimbra'".

Assumindo uma feição subalterna e marginal, o associativismo civil ditado pela conveniência dos progressos da ciência colidiu, como se demonstra, com uma outra forma de apropriação e de representação social e política do conhecimento. Tornou-se distintivo entre os mais afamados círculos de sábios, o procedimento de nomeação que permitiu a circulação de objetos de conhecimento com designações derivadas dos nomes de mecenas, patronos e ministros. Estes viram assim a sua identidade consagrada em diversas páginas de livros e compêndios científicos, ou melhor, passaram a ser incluídos na trama do discurso da ciência, embora ignorassem, totalmente, o processo de produção e validação laboratorial dos dados que a ciência observava, descrevia e classificava, conforme ilustra o capítulo escrito por Gustavo Oliveira Ferreira intitulado "A ciência como estratégia social: as atividades científicas de Domingos Vandelli nas redes clientelares em Portugal, 1764-1788)".

Por fim, o último capítulo da obra, de Carlota Simões e Pedro Casaleiro, versa sobre as "Coleções científicas do Iluminismo na

Universidade de Coimbra". Em termos globais, revela uma outra feição do saber experimental e da observação técnico-científica, miniaturizada, classificada e representada em continuidade na narrativa colecionista. Convocando diferentes formas de olhar o mundo físico e o universo natural, os construtores das primeiras coleções científicas de finalidade educativa condicionaram o despertar de uma nova filosofia museológica na Universidade. Neste campo, como assinalam Carlota Simões e Pedro Casaleiro, não abdicaram totalmente da fantasia nem puseram de parte o gosto pelo maravilhoso, pois as coleções ainda se regem pelo primado dos *naturalia et mirabilia*.

No domínio da História Natural, as noções de espécie e género permitiram, em todo o caso, unificar e organizar os saberes sobre a fauna e a flora do novo e do velho mundo, minimizando distâncias e conferindo um carácter patrimonial à arrumação de animais e plantas mortos, rigorosamente conservados para assinalar o êxito de famosas missões expedicionárias e coloniais. Mais, as coleções organizadas no âmbito da Universidade reformada, ao anexarem, como fragmento narrativo da natureza, a tecnologia científica e os utensílios que tornaram possível a exposição plural e diversa da ciência emergente, acabaram por produzir, num gesto de enérgica modernidade, novos patrimónios e com eles novos valores de conservação de uma imagem do mundo em súbita transformação. Enfim, o ato de dar a ver a ciência aliava a comunicação ao espaço onde ela principiava por materializar-se como lição e aprofundar-se como replicação e invenção.

Com esta nota final que remete, insensivelmente, para a função de popularização da ciência na sociedade contemporânea, reafirmamos, também, o desígnio de tornar acessível ao maior número de leitores os avanços e recuos do processo de institucionalização da ciência moderna na Universidade pombalina, chamando a atenção, em particular, para a posição de fronteira desempenhada pela cultura científica na transição do século XVIII para o século XIX.

UMA PRIMEIRA EDUCAÇÃO DO OLHAR: UNIVERSIDADE E ESTUDANTES DE COIMBRA NA TRANSIÇÃO REFORMISTA

Fernando Taveira da Fonseca
Faculdade de Letras da Universidade de Coimbra
Centro de História da Sociedade e da Cultura (FLUC)
fertaveira@gmail.com

Parece não oferecer dúvida que a reforma pombalina da Universidade de Coimbra, formalmente iniciada com a solene entrega dos novos *Estatutos*, em 29 de Setembro de 1772, representou uma decisiva viragem científica e pedagógica só comparável com a que se processara em 1537 e nos anos subsequentes, sob a égide de D. João III. Conforme escrevi em outro momento, para matizar de algum modo uma visão recorrente de contraste estreme entre um 'antes' de trevas e um 'depois' glorioso, a reforma de 1772 "foi necessária e representou um extraordinário progresso, sobretudo porque criou outro tipo de Universidade: mas não terá sido a simples passagem do caos ao cosmos"[1].

Na verdade, não é possível ignorar que a base institucional e económica que se fora consolidando, já a partir da reforma joanina

---

[1] Fonseca 1995: 815. O texto que agora se apresenta resulta da síntese de outros trabalhos do seu autor, devidamente identificados na bibliografia final. Evitar-se-á assim a autorreferenciação, assinalando fundamentalmente, quando pertinente, o contributo de outros autores.

do século XVI, serviu como indispensável suporte da renovação que então se processou; nem esquecer momentos importantes de projeção cultural protagonizados pela universidade no período entre reformas. Importa, por isso, traçar um quadro sintético desse papel cultural e desse processo de consolidação, dando conta de algumas das suas vertentes essenciais. Aceitando-se embora a ideia de que a Reforma de 1772 foi uma "nova fundação", não o foi radicalmente *ex novo*: mesmo o quadro normativo, substancialmente modificado no que diz respeito aos aspetos científicos e pedagógicos, manteve-se quase inalterado noutros domínios. Não se compreenderá cabalmente o 'depois' sem um olhar, crítico mas isento de preconceitos, ao 'antes'.

Entre reformas. Dimensões da consolidação institucional: fixação normativa e paradigma educativo

Uma intensa preocupação normativa percorreu todo o reinado de D. João III, traduzida em modificações pontuais aos estatutos manuelinos, em inúmeras disposições avulsas – algumas com interferência direta no regime dos estudos – e mesmo na promulgação de uns estatutos (1544) cujo texto se perdeu e que também sofreram modificações em alguns dos seus capítulos. Tal preocupação normativa irá continuar depois da morte do Piedoso, e mesmo acentuar-se, e disso é testemunho a promulgação dos estatutos de 1559, elaborados na sequência da visitação de Baltazar de Faria.

Será este o procedimento adotado para futuras remodelações normativas, sinal do cuidado vigilante do poder régio sobre a instituição cuja ortodoxia e fidelidade política importava assegurar: assim é que o visitador D. António Pinheiro está na origem de um texto estatutário – que também se perdeu – destinado a conformar a vida universitária com as disposições do Concílio de Trento; e que, logo em 1583, no início do período da união dinástica, Manuel de Quadros é encarregado de reformar a universidade dando-lhe novos estatutos. As vicissitudes do tempo não permitirão que eles sejam homologados senão em 1591 (e impressos em 1593); logo em 1597 se formulam outros que mantêm a mesma estrutura; e da visitação de D. Francisco de Bragança irão resultar os 162 'artigos da Reformação', anexados em 1612 ao texto estatutário, uma série de modificações pontuais que não mudam nem a estrutura nem o sentido geral desses que se chamariam os "Estatutos Velhos" e que ficariam em vigor até à Reforma Pombalina de 1772[2].

Não, porém, sem que, nesse longo lapso temporal, fosse derrogada uma parcela das suas determinações – essa, sim, substancial –, sinal da cada vez maior interferência do poder régio num dos domínios fundamentais da vida universitária: em 1654 (e depois de anteriores determinações avulsas no mesmo sentido), a pretexto das parcialidades e desordens que se verificavam nos concursos para as cátedras, foi retirada aos estudantes a prerrogativa que os Estatutos lhes conferiam de intervirem – com votos ponderados segundo as pessoas, os cursos e as qualidades – no provimento dos seus professores; como consequência, à Universidade foi retirado o direito de, imediatamente após o escrutínio, dar posse ao candidato escolhido: a decisão ficou a caber a um organismo do governo central, a Mesa da Consciência e Ordens, ao qual eram enviados votos consultivos, individuais, de um júri restrito (Reitor, Cancelário, lentes de Prima e Véspera das quatro faculdades maiores).

Este episódio evidencia que, na sua raiz, a universidade sempre foi um instrumento dos poderes – historicamente coniventes – que governavam a república, e que o exercício da autoridade interna, embora com territórios de autonomia, dependia largamente dos desígnios mais amplos desses mesmos poderes, especialmente do poder régio. É ain-

---

[2] Ampliação desta temática em Gomes 1989: 3-61.

da recorrendo à norma e à sua progressiva evolução que poderemos encontrar os argumentos que sustentam esta afirmação, sobretudo se atentarmos na figura do Reitor e no modo da sua designação.

Autoridade máxima no âmbito universitário, presidente natural de todos os órgãos que constituíam um sistema de governo colegial (Conselho de Conselheiros, Conselho de Deputados, Claustro, Conselho Mor – depois Claustro Pleno), o Reitor não era escolhido de entre o corpo dos professores. Na sua designação, a última palavra cabia sempre ao monarca, quer ele atendesse à lista dupla ou tríplice que lhe chegava da universidade (ou a mandasse reformular), quer procedesse por convite direto, o que aconteceu no início do período aqui considerado e, de forma sistemática, a partir de 1722. O reitor ocupava posição de charneira, entre a universidade e o poder central, e consubstanciava também, na sua pessoa e função, o outro poder, o eclesiástico: de facto, no período entre reformas (e também depois, até ao pleno triunfo do liberalismo) o Reitor pertenceu sempre à ordem clerical (com uma única exceção)[3].

A fixação estatutária de que vimos falando trouxe consigo a definição do paradigma educativo. De facto, o cânon dos estudos – definindo-lhes os conteúdos essenciais – baseia-se em textos que se consideram tesouros de temas, problemas, soluções e autoridades, desde as compilações dos direitos eclesiástico e imperial (e respetivas glosas), à Bíblia e às sumas de Teologia (Pedro Lombardo, Tomás de Aquino), a que se juntam os comentários de alguns autores consagrados (Duns Escoto, Durand de Saint Pourçain, Gabriel Biel), aos escritos dos clássicos médicos como Galeno, Hipócrates, Avicena ou Razi. A temática e a problemática ampliam-se com a atenção às questões suscitadas pela evolução histórica, nomeadamente as decorrentes da expansão europeia e da cisão religiosa, iluminadas, contudo, pelos mesmos princípios doutrinais.

---

[3] Figueiroa 1937; Rodrigues 1990.

Os textos são explorados analiticamente, por via do comentário, transmitido oralmente, nalguns casos sob a forma de ditado (apostila), numa cadência cíclica que colocava o aluno perante matérias diversas ao longo dos seus anos de estudo. O carácter cumulativo desta aprendizagem – para cada faculdade uma única sala de aula reunia todos os estudantes fosse qual fosse o seu tempo de frequência – tinha como consequência que a avaliação dos seus conhecimentos se fizesse apenas na etapa final e privilegiasse a capacidade de memorização e de expressão oral; a pedra de toque, porém, quer da comunicação dos conhecimentos, quer da sua avaliação, parece ter sido o carácter dialético – formalmente dubitativo, mas desaguando necessariamente numa resolução – típico de uma ortodoxia militante.

Um suporte indispensável: património e rendas

A transição para Coimbra havia sido feita de acordo com a perspetiva realista de que nenhum empreendimento intelectual ou educativo pode subsistir se não dispuser de financiamento adequado. A consciência que os poderes tinham – o poder régio que toma a iniciativa e o eclesiástico que a viabiliza – de que o conveniente funcionamento do estudo servia a utilidade comum e se traduzia em proveito geral e particular de todos materializou-se na afetação de fontes de rendimento que a instituição poderia gerir com larga autonomia. Ao património – bens e direitos sobre a produção (dízimos, rações e foros) – que a universidade já possuía em Lisboa foram agregados dois outros grandes núcleos de natureza semelhante que viriam a perfazer o grosso dos rendimentos (cerca de 84% do total). Geograficamente disperso, desde o baixo Mondego ao interior beirão e à região duriense, este património manteve-se praticamente inalterado até à incorporação dos bens que haviam sido dos jesuítas, já em 1774; e, pesem embora períodos menos prósperos, gerou excedentes que permitiram, a partir das décadas iniciais do século XVIII, o investimento em operações de crédito (uma delas em favor do monarca envolvido na Guerra da Sucessão de Espanha, com juro de 5%, regularmente saldado em cada ano) e aumentos salariais de 33%, em 1754.

Tratava-se de um património que transitara de anteriores possuidores, o que gerou situações de conflito que obrigaram a universidade a duros litígios judiciais para defender o que julgava ser sua propriedade. Um deles, sem dúvida o mais longo, com o Mosteiro de Santa Cruz, a propósito de direitos reivindicados por uma e outra das partes relativamente aos bens que haviam transitado do Priorado--Mor, só ficou resolvido mediante intervenção régia, nos inícios do século XVII. Já anteriormente se desenrolara uma outra demanda de contornos semelhantes, com D. Lopo de Almeida: em ambos os casos, por contrato de composição, a Universidade conseguira a posição mais vantajosa de ficar com os bens de raiz a troco do pagamento de uma pensão anual em dinheiro[4]. Mais tarde, contudo, entre 1710 e 1727, litígio semelhante, com os condes da Ericeira, a propósito das rendas do Louriçal, terá desfecho contrário, ficando à Universidade o direito a receber um foro, mas com a outra parte litigante a permanecer na posse da fonte de rendimentos.

O cuidado em preservar e rentabilizar um património essencial à sobrevivência institucional teve reflexos diretos no modo da sua gestão, confiada, em todo este longo período, a uma equipa de professores – um de cada faculdade – dos mais adiantados na carreira (os deputados grandes, proprietários das principais cadeiras), constituindo a Mesa da Fazenda. Para além da gestão corrente e da atualização da memória dos direitos ativos da universidade (através da organização dos registos patrimoniais – tombos e relações das rendas – e contabilísticos) assumiram a administração direta

---

[4] V. Brandão 1990

das rendas – antes confiada a um contratador que, naturalmente, compensava os riscos que assumia com um lucro calculado – assim aumentando notavelmente o fluxo dos ingressos.

Elemento patrimonial nuclear era o edifício onde funcionava o estudo, o palácio régio da acrópole, cedido num momento em que ainda se pensava em construir de raiz instalações próprias. Gorado esse projeto, a universidade consegue adquirir o imóvel em condições vantajosas (1597), conforme nos conta Francisco Carneiro de Figueiroa: "ainda que el Rei D. Filipe [II] não quis fazer à Universidade a mercê que lhe tinha pedido de dar os seus Paços para as Escollas, lhe fez agora a de lhos vender por trinta mil cruzados". Esta venda, contudo, foi acompanhada de duas cláusulas "muito favoráveis": que não poderia ser denunciada, caso se verificasse exiguidade no preço, porque do excesso, se o houvesse, fazia o monarca "pura e irrevogável doação à Universidade"; que os paços, agora das escolas, ficariam conservando "as prerrogativas, preeminências e imunidades dos Paços Reais"[5].

Também neste caso, sobre uma aquisição primordial, se vão implantar novos elementos, não apenas de cariz estético ou funcional, mas correspondendo também a uma intenção cultural e científica: a Porta Férrea (1653), pórtico nobre de elevada simbologia; a renovada Sala Grande dos Atos (1654-1656); os novos Gerais (1698-1702); a Casa da Livraria (1717-1728) destinada a albergar um grandioso espólio bibliográfico que o Reitor Nuno da Silva Teles, em conjunto com toda a universidade – como ele próprio afirma – pretendia adquirir com a finalidade explícita de dotar a instituição de um instrumento de trabalho de que ainda carecia; a Torre (1728) terminada em terraço para nele se poderem colocar instrumentos de observação astronómica[6].

---

[5] Figueiroa 1937: 122.
[6] Borges 1997.

Em linha com a Europa: revolução educativa e projeção científica

Ao tempo em que a fixação normativa se definia – abrangendo, como vimos, não só o paradigma científico e pedagógico mas também organização e o exercício do poder interno e a administração económica – a frequência universitária atingia um dos seus pontos altos: as cinco décadas de 1580 a 1630 – com uma inflexão negativa de que a peste da viragem do século é a principal responsável – correspondem também em Portugal ao que se convencionou chamar, a nível europeu, a "revolução educativa", caracterizada por um incremento quantitativo da procura dos estudos e graus universitários, que implicou uma mutação qualitativa no nível da educação letrada das gerações jovens e nos parâmetros da qualificação necessária para o exercício de funções públicas.

Esta ideia ganha mais consistência se considerarmos que, simultaneamente ao aumento dos contingentes estudantis em Coimbra, um número crescente de estudantes portugueses demandava as universidades de Castela, com a clara predominância de Salamanca: mercê da união dinástica, que anexou politicamente o reino de Portugal à Monarquia Hispânica, sob o cetro de Filipe II, a universidade de Coimbra – que tivera até aí como contraponto apenas a universidade de Évora, no Sul do país – passou a fazer parte de uma rede universitária mais ampla. E se a circulação de professores fora intensa sobretudo no período imediatamente anterior, verifica-se agora uma frequente circulação de estudantes e, mais do que isso, uma ampla irradiação cultural de ressonância europeia, de que mais adiante daremos conta.

O incremento das matrículas, com algumas oscilações cuja explicação podemos procurar nas vicissitudes políticas e bélicas, nos sobressaltos demográficos e nos ciclos económicos, revelar-se-á continuamente ascendente, com patamares bem definidos: médias anuais de 1016 entre 1574 e 1669; de 1639, desde essa data até 1719; de 2766, desde 1719 a 1771. A estes dados acrescentemos que os contingentes salmantinos de portugueses, entre 1579 e 1639, oscilaram entre 25,8% e 53,8%, num valor médio de 41,3% relativamente aos que cursavam em Coimbra[7]. A procura das qualificações académicas revela claramente que elas representavam um capital social indiscutível, um ativo útil e funcional na bagagem de muitos.

Estruturante, neste contexto, foi a rede de colégios universitários de diversa natureza que progressivamente se foi nutrindo de novas fundações. Não só modificaram, se considerarmos a sua dimensão arquitetónica, a face da cidade, como constituíram um instrumento de fixação e de promoção qualitativa da população estudantil.

O colégio, fundação medieval como a própria universidade, era primordialmente uma comunidade de vocação académica, submetida a uma regra de vida comum e formalmente incorporada no grémio universitário[8]. Mas o termo designava também o edifício-morada dessa comunidade dotado de características específicas para a servir. Considerados na primeira aceção, os colégios apresentam um conjunto de elementos comuns que coexistiam com modalidades diversas de realizar a sua vocação académica: comum era o facto de estarem implantados na universidade e em função dos estudos universitários; o de proporcionarem alojamento e alimentação e obviarem a outras despesas dos estudantes que deles faziam parte (o que implicava a existência de uma base económica); e o de, inicialmente, cada um deles constituir uma *societas* autónoma de membros corresponsáveis na gestão, ligados por fortes laços de solidariedade, vivendo uma vida comunitária em que os deveres religiosos assumiam particular importância e uma disciplina rigorosa pautava os comportamentos. As variantes tiveram historicamente origem no objetivo imediato da

---

[7] Marcos de Diós 1976.

[8] Problemática em Maffei e De Ridder-Symoens 1991.

sua fundação (definindo o número e a qualidade dos beneficiários, os critérios de admissão, a afetação de um certo número de bolsas a cada uma das faculdades, o privilegiar determinado tipo de estudos, as exigências relativamente à preparação académica...); ou na dinâmica da sua evolução, gerando respostas diversas ao longo do tempo, à sua finalidade ampla que era a de conceber e dar vida a um instrumento e a um lugar quase ideal orientado para a formação das futuras elites cultas da Igreja e do Estado.

Essa dinâmica evolutiva teve influência direta nas edificações colegiais: a natureza de algumas comunidades – e a complexificação de outras com o desenvolvimento de atividades intelectuais e pedagógicas no próprio espaço colegial – refletem-se na disposição orgânica e na monumentalidade de algumas construções. Em Coimbra, a progressiva implantação dos colégios universitários – com um forte dinamismo, nas décadas imediatas à fixação definitiva da Universidade, o qual, contudo, não esgotou o movimento fundacional – seguiu também estas linhas gerais[9]. Deixando de lado algumas realizações efémeras, a tipologia conimbricense incluía uma maioria de colégios pertencentes às ordens religiosas e às ordens militares. Este conjunto pode considerar-se como a extensão natural da faculdade de Teologia. Em muitos deles se ministrava o ensino das disciplinas preparatórias e o da própria Teologia até níveis de graduação que ultrapassavam a formatura: as numerosas incorporações de religiosos na Universidade, ultrapassada já essa etapa – e na fase preparatória da obtenção dos graus de licenciado e doutor – é disso prova.

Numa fase já adiantada de implantação (1717), quando a Faculdade de Teologia prestou a sua adesão formal e solene à bula *Unigenitus*, quis associar aos seus lentes todos os professores dos colégios incorporados. Apuseram a sua assinatura ao documento, elaborado em Claustro Pleno, 75 religiosos de diversas Ordens, todos eles

---

[9] V. Vasconcelos 1987

se intitulando lentes de Teologia: 5 dominicanos do Colégio de S. Tomás; 10 carmelitas dos Colégios do Carmo e de S. José dos Marianos; 4 Eremitas de S. Agostinho, do Colégio da Graça; 14 franciscanos, dos Colégios de S. Boaventura, S. Pedro, S. António da Pedreira e do Convento de S. Francisco; 13 jesuítas, do Colégio de Jesus; 3 jerónimos, do Colégio de S. Jerónimo; 4 lóios, do Colégio de S. João Evangelista; 6 cistercienses, do Colégio de S. Bernardo; 5 beneditinos, do Colégio de S. Bento; 4 membros do Colégio dos Militares; 3 cónegos regrantes crúzios; 4 religiosos do Colégio da Santíssima Trindade.

Neste contexto, é compreensível a extraordinária preponderância monástica no professorado da Faculdade de Teologia: e se, num primeiro momento, foi mais notória a presença de eclesiásticos seculares, com figuras de primeiro plano como Afonso do Prado, Francisco Monçon, Paio Rodrigues de Vilarinho ou Diogo de Gouveia, ela torna-se depois excecional. Eremitas de Santo Agostinho, Cistercienses, Beneditinos e Jerónimos fornecem os contingentes mais significativos num conjunto onde se devem incluir também Trinitários, Lóios, Carmelitas, religiosos da Ordem de Cristo e Dominicanos. Estes últimos, gozando de uma situação excecional que os fazia transitar diretamente dos seus estudos domésticos para o topo da carreira docente (uma prerrogativa que os fazia quase proprietários das cadeiras de Prima e Véspera de Teologia), viram-se afastados da docência universitária – por intervenção direta do monarca D. João IV – devido a uma divergência doutrinal que os levou a não obedecer à ordem régia de jurar a Imaculada Conceição, então apenas considerada como *pia opinio*.

O segundo tipo colegial conimbricense era constituído pelos colégios reais de S. Pedro e de S. Paulo. Destinados a graduados (preferencialmente doutores), cada um deles tinha efetivamente doze lugares – ou becas – distribuídas pelas diversas faculdades, embora, na realidade, o tempo tivesse levado a que apenas as duas faculdades jurídicas – Cânones e Leis – ficassem com o exclusivo do seu provimento.

Designando-se, em oposição ao tipo anterior, por seculares – uma das condições de admissão era a de o candidato não ter feito voto de entrar em religião – eram comunidades de celibatários (não poderiam mesmo ser desposados por palavras de futuro), reguladas autonomamente por estatutos próprios, governadas pelos colegiais em assembleia geral ou "capela" que elegia anualmente os órgãos diretivos, soberanas nos processos de admissão dos novos membros que era marcada por rigorosos processos de seleção.

Ocupando um terreno académico e institucional idêntico, rivalizavam entre si: nos concursos para as cátedras universitárias, nos jogos de influência para a eleição do Reitor da universidade, nos equilíbrios de poder dentro da mesma universidade. Mas eram, acima de tudo – e porque a condição de colegial era, por natureza, transitória – um poderoso elemento impulsionador da carreira futura dos seus membros, passando por eles uma etapa decisiva, tanto para a docência universitária (coube aos colegiais pedristas e paulistas o quase exclusivo da propriedade das cátedras de Cânones e Leis), como para o acesso aos mais elevados cargos na hierarquia eclesiástica e na administração régia. Ligados por fortes laços de solidariedade forjados no tempo do colégio, os colegiais – e, com eles, os porcionistas, oriundos das famílias da grande nobreza – mantinham essa comunhão afetiva ao longo da sua vida, tornando o colégio a placa giratória de um jogo de influências e de troca de favores mútuos[10].

Um outro colégio escapa às modalidades anteriores e forma uma categoria específica que se poderia assemelhar ao 'collège de plein exercice' da universidade parisiense, constituído essencialmente por uma comunidade pedagógica e vocacionado prioritariamente para

---

[10] V. Oliveira 1996.

o estudo das Humanidades e da Filosofia: trata-se do Colégio das Artes. A sua entrega aos jesuítas, em 1555, não lhe modificou a natureza institucional, continuando em vigor os estatutos elaborados por André de Gouveia, segundo o *modus parisiensis*, e prosseguindo a sua ligação à Universidade, que permaneceu como sede da Faculdade de Artes, para a colação e o registo dos graus. Os estatutos do colégio conimbricense terão desempenhado um papel importante na longa elaboração da *ratio studiorum* jesuítica (cuja redação definitiva é de 1599), desse modo contribuindo para a sistematização de um modelo educativo de raiz humanística, cuja aplicação a uma extensa rede escolar o terá feito responsável pela instauração de uma nova hierarquia dos saberes, conferindo à Retórica e à Literatura a plena cidadania intelectual.

Não terá sido este, contudo, o único – ou mesmo o mais importante – contributo do Colégio das Artes e da Universidade para a cultura e o pensamento europeus. Se o envolvimento dos professores e das autoridades académicas na querela sucessória dera origem à reflexão jurídica – e a uma clara tomada de posição política – a projeção internacional de Coimbra alcançou um ponto alto com a publicação do *Curso Conimbricense* e o magistério universitário de Francisco Suárez.

A União Dinástica não se processara sem algum sobressalto para a Universidade. No período de discussão e definição da legitimidade sucessória (1578-1580), um grupo de professores de Coimbra secundara os procuradores da pretendente D. Catarina de Bragança, escrevendo, em sua defesa, as *Alegações de Direito*, um texto cujo argumentário virá a ser retomado na Restauração. E esta produção intelectual de oposição às pretensões de Filipe II foi secundada institucionalmente: na sequência das cortes de Almeirim, o procurador de Braga, portador de uma provisão dos Governadores do Reino, não conseguiu que os juristas universitários redigissem pareceres corroborando a tendência favorável a Filipe II (o Doutor Luís Correia, canonista, alegou mesmo que todos sabiam que ele era procurador de D. Catarina); por sua vez, o Claustro universitário, tendo notícia da aclamação do Prior do Crato em Santarém, organizou uma procissão de ação de graças e mandou uma delegação dar obediência ao novo rei, reconhecê-lo e fazer-lhe entrega da Protetoria da Universidade. Alguns dos professores que seguiram o partido de D. António pagaram cara – com a privação das cadeiras ou mesmo com a vida – esta sua adesão ao candidato vencido; e os que prestaram obediência a Filipe II, em nome da Universidade, foram o presidente e um dos deputados da Mesa da Consciência e Ordens e não o seu Reitor ou os seus professores. Esta atenção e participação no momento político terá o seu contraponto em 1640, quando o reitor Manuel de Saldanha mandou editar uma coletânea de *Aplausos da Universidade a el Rei Dom João o IV*, o monarca restaurador.

Foi na viragem do século que coincidiram em Coimbra, a publicação do *Curso Conimbricense* e o magistério (1597-1616) de Francisco Suárez. O *Curso Conimbricense* teve por autores alguns mestres jesuítas do Colégio das Artes (Manuel de Góis, o mais prolífico, Baltasar Álvares, Cosme de Magalhães e Sebastião do Couto), cujos tratados, quanto às primeiras edições no nosso país, vieram a lume entre 1592 e 1606. A realização destes tratados (os *Commentarii*), na linha do movimento de restauração da filosofia aristotélico-escolástica em Portugal (de que faz parte igualmente a obra notável e anterior de Pedro da Fonseca) baseou-se, em regra, no aproveitamento das lições manuscritas que constituíam o corpo substancial da doutrina filosófica do Colégio, que aqueles redactores alteraram e ordenaram com o recurso a cortes, aditamentos e variantes.

Os oito *Commentarii Collegii Conimbricensis Societais Jesu* abrangem quase todo o leque dos tópicos filosóficos, tendo por base as diferentes obras de Aristóteles: a *Física*, o tratado sobre *O Céu*, os *Meteoros*, os *Pequenos Naturais*, a *Ética*, o tratado *A Geração e a Corrupção*, o tratado *A Alma* e a *Lógica* (*Universa dialectica*). Falta o comentário à *Metafísica*, mas esta lacuna explica-se pela publicação, que já tinha sido iniciada, da obra de Pedro da Fonseca sobre o mesmo assunto. No seu conjunto, estes comentários obtiveram mais de uma centena de edições, a maior parte no estrangeiro. Já as *Instituições Dialécticas* de Fonseca, publicadas em Lisboa em 1564, viriam a ter pelo menos 53 edições e os *Comentários à Metafísica de Aristóteles* (Roma 1577), do mesmo autor, mais de vinte, sobretudo fora de Portugal.

Tão ampla divulgação – Étienne Gilson encontrou oitenta paralelos textuais na obra de Descartes, no que respeita sobretudo à filosofia natural – ficou a dever-se a diversos fatores: à excelência do método com que o Curso estava organizado, segundo um ideal que privilegiava a ordem e a integração unitária e sistemática dos diferentes ramos do saber filosófico, revelando-se por este motivo em consonância com o espírito renascentista no aspeto pedagógico-didático; à clareza e muitas vezes à elegância da exposição das doutrinas; à rigorosa análise filológica e hermenêutica do texto aristotélico; ao facto de o Curso ir ao encontro de certas exigências intelectuais de uma época que aspirava a recuperar a serenidade do espírito após a Reforma; e talvez sobretudo devido à multiplicidade e à discrepância de doutrinas alternativas à Escolástica medieval, nascidas no seio do Humanismo[11].

O magistério conimbricense de Francisco Suárez estendeu-se de 1597 a 1616: natural de Granada (daí o epíteto de "granatense" pelo qual é conhecido), fez-se jesuíta, estudou no colégio da Companhia em Salamanca e percorreu um périplo magistral que incluiu a mesma Salamanca, Valladolid, Ávila, Segóvia, Roma – onde ocupou a cátedra de Prima de Teologia no Colégio Romano durante oito anos – Alcalá e, finalmente, Coimbra. Os cerca de vinte anos em que foi, aqui também, professor de prima de Teologia terão sido o período

---

[11] V. Coxito 1997.

mais fecundo da sua vida; o conjunto da sua obra (*Opera Omnia*) foi publicado pelo editor parisiense Luis Vives (de 1856 a 1861) em 28 volumes e reparte-se por matérias que abrangem a Teologia, a Metafísica e o Direito.

Do tempo de Coimbra são duas obras capitais para a compreensão do seu pensamento em termos de teoria política, com ramificações tão importantes como a origem do poder e o direito internacional (*De legibus et legislatore Deo*, 1612; *Defensio Fidei*, 1613). O princípio basilar pode enunciar-se desta forma: a sociabilidade natural do homem, cuja expressão fundamental é a família, só se realiza plenamente na sociedade civil que ultrapassa o mero conglomerado das famílias e se funda num pacto pelo qual se promete o auxílio mútuo. *Corpus politicum mysticum*, cuja unidade é moral, a sociedade civil pressupõe a subordinação das pessoas e das famílias a alguém que dirige a comunidade: o poder, contudo, não reside originalmente em quem o exerce, mas na totalidade da comunidade (*in hominum collectione*) que o transfere, mas que pode reavê-lo em casos extraordinários de anarquia social ou tirania; tirano será aquele que ilegitimamente usurpa o poder ou o exerce em contradição com a sua finalidade última, que é a consecução do *commune bonum civitatis* e da *felicitas publica*. O exercício do poder é, deste modo, limitado pelo seu objetivo último, por considerações de ordem moral que podem levar à intervenção da autoridade espiritual, mas também pela coexistência das nações.

Suárez põe o acento na solidariedade que existe entre elas. O seu conjunto seria uma *unitas quasi politica et moralis*, originando um direito específico, o *ius gentium*, conjunto de regras morais e jurídicas que, mais por tradição e costume do que por uma constituição positiva foram introduzidas na sociedade aberta das nações para lhe permitir viver em paz e progredir. Se a guerra é possível, ela é apenas permitida para impedir ou reprimir as injustiças; e vislumbra-se a possibilidade de uma arbitragem internacional quando reconhece ao papa, relativamente aos príncipes cristãos, a capacidade de avocar a si a causa da guerra e proferir sentença, ou quando recomenda ao príncipe que duvida da justeza da sua razão que submeta a sua dúvida ao conselho de homens prudentes. Esta visão ampla, integrada no conjunto mais vasto da teologia moral, teve forte repercussão e difusão e uma inegável influência na formação e desenvolvimento do direito internacional moderno.

O Tempo da Ilustração

Como vimos anteriormente, a empresa da construção da nova casa da livraria, nos inícios do século XVIII (e também, logo depois, da torre da universidade), envolve uma clara intenção de renovação científica que não se limita ao momento da sua realização: para a biblioteca vem grande quantidade de livros de Teologia, Filosofia, História, Direito e Medicina moderna, enviados pelo diplomata D. Luís da Cunha, por ordem do rei, entre 1729 e 1734; uma remessa anterior incluía também instrumentos matemáticos que o P. Carbone encomendara para a Universidade.

O ponto sensível, no quadro de um debate que opunha conservadorismo e modernidade, era a atualização dos estudos de Medicina: consultou-se um exilado ilustre, Jacob de Castro Sarmento, membro da Royal Society de Londres, propôs-se o regresso de António Nunes Ribeiro Sanches, médico dos exércitos imperiais da Rússia; Isaac Samuda foi durante anos ativo intermediário entre a mesma Royal Society e a corte portuguesa; e o monarca pensou mesmo em trazer para Portugal Boerhaave, notável pelo seu magistério inovador em Leida. É ainda Jacob de Castro Sarmento que, em 1731, envia o plano para um jardim botânico destinado a plantas medicinais, dedicando-o aos professores da Universidade de Coimbra.

O auge deste debate situar-se-á, dentro e fora da Universidade, nos anos finais do reinado do Rei Magnânimo: o concurso para a cadeira de Anatomia, em 1739, põe em confronto conceções opostas, com uma forte corrente apologista da 'medicina moderna', de que fazem parte o Reitor e alguns professores da Universidade secundados pelo organismo que superintendia no ensino superior, a Mesa da Consciência e Ordens[12]; Luís António de Verney traça, no *Verdadeiro Método de Estudar* um quadro crítico das conceções filosóficas e pedagógicas vigentes, verberando o tradicionalismo e a autoridade em matéria de ciência. É um tempo em que parece ser mais evidente o que é necessário destruir, sem que os caminhos a percorrer sejam ainda muito claros: alguns anos mais tarde, António Nunes Ribeiro Sanches, médico do Corpo Imperial de Cadetes de S. Petersburgo e sócio correspondente da Academia das Ciências de Paris, irá já desenhar com nitidez um quadro programático para o ensino da Medicina e para a criação de um Colégio Médico[13]. Mesmo aqueles que mais duramente foram criticados pelo seu imobilismo estão envolvidos nesta dialética entre tradição e modernidade. O edital do reitor do Colégio das Artes de 1746, tantas vezes invocado como emblema da posição retrógrada dos Jesuítas – uma vez que nele se proíbe aderir às doutrinas de Descartes, Gassendo ou Newton – terá de entender-se como advertência disciplinadora interna porque, na realidade, os temas da Filosofia Moderna, e particularmente da Filosofia newtoniana, já constituíam objeto de análise nas aulas daquele Colégio, embora não oficialmente[14].

---

[12] V. Santos 1991.
[13] V. Sanches, 1959.
[14] Freitas 2000: 198-199

A "forja dos homens"[15]

Sacudida pelo contraste das ideias, financeiramente desafogada, a Universidade dos anos vinte do século XVIII experimenta a sua maior expansão em termos de matrículas e das consequentes graduações, consolidando-se como a 'forja dos homens' que vão assumir as responsabilidades administrativas, governativas, de direção ideológica, de reprodução de modelos e de produção normativa: mais do que nunca – culminando um processo que enraizara nos séculos anteriores mas se torna mais evidente neste tempo – Coimbra irá ser uma placa giratória, centro fulcral de uma ativa circulação de elites num espaço pluricontinental que incluía o Continente e os domínios ultramarinos.

Uma perspetiva secular que se projete a partir deste momento para captar o papel social e cultural da Universidade de Coimbra terá de ter em conta uma dupla perspetiva: a da exclusividade de que gozou na formação e na concessão de graus em áreas como o Direito (Canónico e Civil) e a Medicina; a das mudanças estruturais que se operaram no curriculum dos saberes, fundamentalmente na Reforma de 1772, acrescentando novidades essenciais que se refletiram na formação final dos graduados e na sua capacidade de intervenção no corpo social.

No período que precede a reforma de 1772, o acento terá de ser colocado na formação jurídica, não só a mais procurada – com cerca de 87% do total das matrículas – como a que proporcionava as melhores oportunidades de carreira. É bem conhecida a ambivalência da formação em Direito Canónico, como qualificação necessária ou preferencial para as administrações eclesiástica e régia. A primeira, fortemente apoiada no sistema de remunerações constituído pelo regime beneficial – a um cargo estava anexada uma dotação cujo

---

[15] V. Almeida 2004

rendimento, não sendo fixo, era na maioria dos casos, apreciável – incluía não apenas os benefícios paroquiais (que faziam dos seus detentores líderes das comunidades locais e elos privilegiados de ligação com as autoridades superiores, tanto eclesiásticas como civis), mas igualmente as posições mais eminentes da hierarquia do clero assim como um sem número de funções ligadas ao aparelho judicial eclesiástico (cúrias e tribunais diocesanos e metropolitanos, o tribunal da Legacia, os tribunais da Inquisição), os canonicatos e as cátedras episcopais.

A Universidade, como instituição, dispunha mesmo da prerrogativa de apresentação nos canonicatos magistrais (destinados a teólogos) e doutorais (para canonistas) na quase totalidade das dioceses do país, assim como em cerca de duas dezenas e meia de benefícios paroquiais: de uns e outros destes benefícios eclesiásticos usufruíram largamente muitos dos que ela própria graduava ou que a serviam como professores.

A administração e a magistratura régias bebiam largamente no contingente dos graduados por Coimbra, dando naturalmente preferência aos legistas (mas não excluindo, como dissemos, os canonistas). Um primeiro nível, constituído pela magistratura periférica ao serviço da Coroa (juízes de fora, corregedores, provedores) tinha como limiar obrigatório um exame de estado (a "leitura"), realizada sob a alçada do Desembargo do Paço. Mas a admissão a este exame dependia do juízo formulado pelo corpo de professores das faculdades jurídicas de Coimbra (as informações da Universidade, transmitidas ao Desembargo do Paço) que classificavam o contingente anual de graduados juristas – do medíocre ao muito bom, passando pelo suficiente e bom. Só eram admitidos à "leitura" os bons ou muito bons.

O nível superior do *cursus honorum* – que, simplificando, poderíamos designar como a carreira dos desembargadores, a elite dos funcionários régios – tinha vias de acesso distintas: só uma minoria era constituída por magistrados que haviam percorrido os graus inferiores da carreira; um número maior acedia à posição por via do parentesco com os anteriores detentores dos cargos (a sua nomeação remunerava os serviços prestados pelos seus familiares); mais frequentemente, contudo (em quase metade dos casos), através de uma faculdade inerente aos direitos de doutor ou lente, com exercício de magistério, da Universidade de Coimbra, nas faculdades de Leis e Cânones. O percurso iniciava-se normalmente no tribunal da Relação do Porto – muitas vezes concomitantemente com o exercício da docência universitária – subindo até ao cargo de desembargador dos agravos da Casa da Suplicação[16]. A carreira docente universitária, já de si prestigiante, era então também a via de acesso a outras carreiras e honras, etapas de percursos sociais ascendentes que muitas vezes conduziam à entrada formal na elite nobiliárquica.

A competência técnica dos juristas ultrapassava, contudo, a judicatura e a docência para se exercer em tarefas tipicamente governativas – no Desembargo do Paço, na Mesa da Consciência, em Conselhos e Juntas – ou diplomáticas, onde se conjugavam o estatuto nobre dos chefes de missão (a quem cabiam sobretudo funções de representação) e a formação universitária jurídica de grande parte dos secretários e negociadores.

Neste contexto, importa mais uma vez pôr em destaque o papel dos colégios seculares de S. Pedro e de S. Paulo, elementos fundamentais de um "complexo protetor"[17] destinado a acolher e promover uma elite intelectual, enquadrando-a e conformando-a normativamente: deles saiu a quase totalidade dos professores das faculdades jurídicas (no período que aqui consideramos); mas os percursos biográficos dos colegiais conjugam maioritariamente

---

[16] V. Subtil 2011.
[17] V. Lario, 1986.

a universidade e os cargos públicos, a universidade e a carreira eclesiástica, ou as três componentes em conjunto. Os porcionistas, por seu lado, poderão fornecer-nos um exemplo de 'consolidação das elites', uma vez que, sendo oriundos da alta nobreza, vêm à universidade adquirir uma qualificação que potencia o seu estatuto originário no acesso aos cargos públicos e sobretudo aos benefícios eclesiásticos. A compreensão da dimensão efetiva desta capacidade criadora e transformadora da formação universitária exige a elaboração de uma prosopografia ampla, apenas em parte elaborada.

Uma aproximação, contudo, pode ser tentada precisamente tendo em conta a origem geográfica dos graduados por Coimbra (aceitando o pressuposto de que a formação universitária terá representado para eles uma aquisição qualitativa que modificou ou, pelo menos, consolidou o seu estatuto social). Neste aspeto, podemos afirmar que a exclusividade de Coimbra se traduziu em captação generalizada em todo o espaço continental – atingindo os centros urbanos e o mundo rural em proporções semelhantes – e tocando significativamente também os espaços insulares e ultramarinos, nomeadamente o Brasil. Como indicadores da generalização da procura universitária poderemos mencionar a estreita correlação – observada no século XVIII – que se verificava entre os contingentes de graduados e a densidade populacional das diferentes regiões do continente, assim como o progressivo alargamento da área de captação, no Brasil, à medida da progressiva ocupação do espaço, com particular destaque para a região de Minas Gerais. A corrente originária da colónia americana, ténue nos inícios de seiscentos, engrossa notavelmente depois da descoberta do ouro. Se tivermos em conta as primeiras entradas nas faculdades jurídicas, o contingente brasileiro atinge uma proporção considerável (7,52% em 1760-1770; 16,5% em 1772--1788). Entre as duas margens do Atlântico gerou-se então uma ativa circulação de quadros (graduados brasileiros que se notabilizam na metrópole, reinícolas que iniciavam a sua carreira de letrados – em alguns casos para 'limpar' uma origem social menos honrada – nos espaços ultramarinos), circulação que se intensificou após a reforma pombalina de 1772.

A "nova fundação" em 1772
Um novo perfil científico-pedagógico

A reforma de 1772 é o exemplo mais evidente de simbiose entre uma ideia de universidade e da sua missão específica – vazada num quadro normativo que renova estruturalmente as dimensões científica e pedagógica – e a criação de infraestruturas e equipamentos suscetíveis de tornarem possível a sua concretização. Como já referimos, o momento fulcral da sua implantação foi a solene outorga, em 29 de Setembro de 1772, dos novos *Estatutos*, elaborados pela Junta de Providência Literária, um organismo comissionado expressamente para os elaborar e cujos elementos eram, na sua quase totalidade, graduados pela universidade que se pretendia reformar: momento charneira no qual culminou um processo longo, de que atrás referimos alguns passos e que não pode ser dissociado da reforma dos estudos médios realizada a partir de 1759 (depois de terem sido expulsos de Portugal os Jesuítas), à qual preside a mesma intenção de reabilitar as Letras Humanas, fundamento essencial sobre que repousa a reabilitação das Ciências, para, desse modo, tornar feliz a Monarquia; mas também momento incoativo da campanha de traduzir em realidades práticas um texto normativo que se entende como regenerador.

Com a Reforma, de facto, implicando uma intervenção direta e exclusiva do poder régio – transferido para um ministro, o Marquês de Pombal, "plenipotenciário e lugar-tenente" do monarca – atinge o seu auge um longo processo de instrumentalização da Universidade, bem expresso na formulação de D. Francisco de Lemos – "não se deve olhar para a Universidade como um Corpo isolado, e concentrado em si mesmo, como ordinariamente se faz; mas sim como hum corpo formado no seio do Estado [...] para animar, e vivificar todos os Ramos da Administração Publica; e para promover a felicidade dos homens"; ou na doutrina expressa nos *Estatutos* de 1772, acerca da importância social dos graus académicos, os quais, afirmam os mesmos *Estatutos*, servem de "regra a ambos os Supremos Poderes, Espiritual e Temporal, para se governarem e regerem por elles no provimento de Dignidades, Benefícios, Ministerios e Empregos [...] sendo esse verdadeiramente o único fim, pelo qual os mesmos Supremos Poderes concederam ás Universidades a faculdade de conferir os dittos Gráos"[18].

Esta alta consciência do serviço do Estado reflete-se no maior rigor dos requisitos de admissão, tendente a selecionar um escol intelectual, na linha do que se chamou o 'malthusianismo ilustrado' que reservava a aprendizagem universitária a um número reduzido de indivíduos a quem deveria ser assegurado o pleno emprego. Em termos científicos, a grande novidade foi a criação das duas novas faculdades de Matemática e Filosofia, assim introduzindo no elenco dos estudos superiores as ciências exatas e as ciências da natureza: conjuntamente com a Medicina, agora também remodelada nos seus fundamentos, passaram a constituir as chamadas faculdades naturais.

Tanto como – ou talvez mais do que – esta inclusão de novos conteúdos, é crucial o carácter propedêutico de que estes saberes se irão revestir também para as faculdades de Direito e de Teologia. Aos estudantes que pretendessem ingressar nestas últimas era exigido que estudassem "privativamente o Primeiro Anno do Curso Mathematico", no qual eram lecionados os Elementos de Geometria (que "são a Lógica, praticada com a maior perfeição que he possível ao entendimento humano") "como subsidio importante

---

[18] Estatutos (1772), liv. I, tít. IV, cap. VI, §2

ao aproveitamento que devem ter nas respetivas faculdades"; para os que pretendessem seguir Direito, era-lhes necessária também a frequência da cadeira de História Natural. Saberes propedêuticos e, como tais, dimensionadores da *forma mentis* que se queria implantar na universidade recriada. A par dos conteúdos, uma profunda revolução no método e no que respeita às funções dos professores.

Quanto ao método, os termos com que explicitamente ele é definido sintetizam-se na expressão 'sintético-compendiário-demonstrativo'. Assim se opunha ao praticado anteriormente, que era textual, analítico, cíclico e cumulativo. Pretendia-se agora introduzir a progressão gradativa do mais simples ao mais complexo (nas matérias e nas cadeiras, rigorosamente escalonadas ao longo dos anos do curso); substituir os antigos textos, a cujas características e funções já nos referimos, por compêndios nos quais se expusessem os fundamentos de uma ciência que progressivamente se iam desvendando e desenvolvendo; abolir a forma tradicional de lecionação por um sistema contínuo e constantemente exploratório dos conhecimentos adquiridos pelos estudantes, de onde derivava um particular cuidado em verificar a sua assiduidade, implicando, pela primeira vez na história da universidade, a possibilidade de retenção no mesmo ano se o nível de aprendizagem não fosse satisfatório; substituir, na avaliação, as disputas, por interrogatórios conduzidos pelo método socrático.

Aos professores, organizados em 'congregações' em cada uma das Faculdades, espécies de academias internas às quais competia não apenas a organização formal das tarefas docentes e de avaliação mas sobretudo a superintendência em tudo o que dizia respeito ao domínio científico, é incumbida a responsabilidade de serem igualmente 'inventores' e, mormente no âmbito das faculdades naturais, irem incorporando nas suas lições os avanços da ciência, próprios ou alheios, e de organizarem para a disciplina de que fossem responsáveis o respetivo compêndio.

O caráter demonstrativo do novo método e o perfil definido para os professores tiveram uma dupla consequência prática. Primeiro, na reformulação do corpo docente: para além dos lentes – os titulares e os substitutos permanentes, na sua grande maioria recrutados propositadamente depois de afastados quase todos os que haviam servido antes da Reforma – vamos encontrar preparadores e demonstradores, os primeiros executando tarefas laboratoriais ou de manipulação e elaboração de peças museológicas, os segundos prestando um auxílio direto nas aulas pela ilustração prática das preleções dos lentes, muitas vezes como primeiro patamar de uma futura carreira docente. Mas, fundamentalmente, as componentes de observação e de experimentação, postulavam a existência de estabelecimentos específicos onde elas pudessem ser eficazmente postas em prática. Assim é que, para os estudos médicos, se determinou a construção do Hospital, do Teatro Anatómico e do Dispensatório Farmacêutico; para a Faculdade de Matemática, a do Observatório Astronómico; para a de Filosofia, a dos Gabinetes de História Natural e de Física Experimental, do Laboratório Químico e do Jardim Botânico.

A renovação científica e pedagógica, alicerçada numa vontade política que proporciona o financiamento e a criação das condições materiais de possibilidade, traduz-se num modelo novo de formação: a do jurista – além da ênfase colocada na racionalidade do direito e nas leis nacionais – adquire tonalidades que lhe orientam a atenção para as realidades da natureza; o médico terá necessariamente que atender a estas mas também aceitar que a cirurgia é parte fundamental da sua bagagem e do seu múnus; o matemático e o naturalista aparecem como vocações autónomas, justificando-se por si próprias. Um novo modelo que terá forte impacto na sociedade, com consequências políticas inegáveis.

Este programa deu origem a uma vasta campanha de obras – tendentes à criação, de raiz, de alguns equipamentos ou à remodelação de espaços já existentes para a implantação de outros – rigorosamente planificadas, orientada a sua execução por um pormenorizado *Regimento* elaborado pelo reitor D. Francisco de Lemos, com data de 10 de Janeiro de 1773 e aprovado pelo Marquês de Pombal a 18 do mesmo mês. O *Regimento* não apenas subordinava todos os procedimentos a uma rígida organização, definindo níveis de responsabilidade, como também promovia a celeridade e rigor da sua execução, estipulando que as remunerações a operários e mestres tivessem em conta os seus níveis de competência e diligência, verificados e anotados semanalmente em três escalões de bom, suficiente e mau, de cujas combinatórias resultaria o estipêndio efetivo a ser pago, ou, em casos de má prestação reiterada, a exclusão.

Quando, em 1777, D. Francisco de Lemos envia à rainha, em defesa da Reforma cujos inimigos ganhavam novo fôlego agora que o Marquês de Pombal caíra em desgraça, a sua *Relação Geral do Estado da Universidade*, anexa-lhe um outro volume no qual dá conta do estado em que se encontravam as obras, juntando as respectivas plantas. Haviam sido gastos já 126 contos de réis; o aproveitamento do antigo complexo jesuítico – incluindo o próprio colégio, a sua igreja agora transformada em catedral, e o Colégio das Artes – tinha permitido instalar o edifício das Ciências Naturais e o Hospital; em terreno adjacente erguera-se de raiz o Laboratório Químico; e os claustros da antiga Sé haviam sido adaptados para instalar a imprensa académica, importante equipamento de apoio, agora que era preciso imprimir novos compêndios e tratados. Todas estas obras estavam já concluídas naquela data. Em curso estavam ainda as obras do observatório astronómico e a remodelação do Paço das Escolas, servindo simultaneamente um projeto de maior dignificação e objetivos pedagógicos de que é exemplo o corredor interno pelo qual o Reitor poderia circular para vigiar o andamento das aulas, sem as perturbar. Muito no início estava a construção do jardim botânico, implantado em terreno inclinado que foi preciso regularizar e cujas obras se prolongaram, entrecortadas pelas invasões francesas de 1807-1810: mesmo antes de concluídas estas, porém, já o jardim – cujo núcleo central se concluiu em 1790 – desempenhava o seu papel de apoio às demonstrações de História Natural

Viagens filosóficas e consciência política

A Reforma de 1772 inaugura, pela própria natureza dos seus objetivos, um período novo de projeção externa da Universidade: intensifica-se a 'circulação das elites', organizam-se viagens de exploração natural – 'viagens filosóficas' – no espaço continental e no Ultramar e implantam-se instituições de ensino e de cultura que se inspiram no modelo e na lição de Coimbra. Por virtude do contacto mais intenso com o Brasil – vista a sua importância económica, o fluxo estudantil intenso a que já fizemos referência e em virtude das vicissitudes políticas que levaram a que, a partir de 1808, a cabeça do império fosse a cidade do Rio de Janeiro – a grande colónia além--Atlântico ganhou um protagonismo ainda maior e lançou as bases da sua independência política. A Reforma Pombalina consolidou um espaço cultural comum, polarizado pela Universidade de Coimbra – e também, a partir de 1779, pela Academia Real das Ciências (que pode considerar-se como *spin-off* da Universidade) – no qual a elite culta da metrópole e da colónia circulava, fazendo na prática as mesmas leituras e recebendo a mesma formação[19].

A implantação de estruturas de ensino e investigação pode exemplificar-se com a criação da Escola de Anatomia e de Cirurgia da Baía (18 de Fevereiro de 1808), o primeiro marco do ensino superior no Brasil, por iniciativa do que já fora professor em Coimbra, José Correia Picanço, e a Escola Anatómica, Cirúrgica e Médica do Rio de Janeiro (5 de Novembro de 1808), as quais se transformaram em

---

[19] V. Silva 1999.

Academias Médico-Cirúrgicas pela reforma de 1813. E como apoio à aprendizagem médica, a organização de jardins botânicos, segundo um modelo que teve como principal mentor Domingos Vandelli – o professor italiano convidado a lecionar no Colégio dos Nobres e depois na Universidade reformada – que punha o acento na utilidade comercial e agrícola das espécies vegetais, para além do gosto de ver juntas as plantas de toda a parte do mundo. O jardim de Belém do Pará (1796), pioneiro, teve como organizador Manuel Joaquim de Sousa Ferraz, médico formado em Montpellier, mas que invocava em seu favor a autoridade de Vandelli e Avelar Brotero – este último, o mais destacado professor de Coimbra no domínio da Botânica; depois, em moldes idênticos, o do Rio de Janeiro (1810), Pernambuco (1811), aos quais se pode juntar o de Caiena (ocupada entre 1809 e 1817) do qual vieram para os outros numerosas espécies.

Ainda no domínio da implantação dos saberes, não pode deixar de ser mencionada a criação da Academia Militar na corte do Rio de Janeiro assim como a Academia dos Guardas Marinhas, ambas em 1810. A finalidade da sua criação, expressa nos *curricula* de uma e outra, ultrapassava os objetivos puramente militares, pois, destinando-se à formação de hábeis oficiais de Artilharia, Engenharia, e ainda mesmo de oficiais da classe de engenheiros, geógrafos e topógrafos, pressupunha que eles se encarregassem também de tarefas respeitantes a minas, caminhos, portos, canais, pontes, fontes e calçadas. Dos sete anos do curso da Academia Militar, quatro eram ocupados com o estudo das ciências exatas (Matemáticas) e das ciências de observação (Física, Química, Mineralogia, Metalurgia e História Natural) – um programa declaradamente universitário. A rica biblioteca da Academia dos Guardas Marinhas – que servia ambas as instituições – continha títulos que englobavam Ciências Naturais, Ciências Matemáticas puras e mistas, Ciências e Artes Navais (o núcleo mais numeroso com 200 obras), Ciências e Artes Militares da Terra; e finalmente 138 obras sobre assuntos diversos (obras gerais, histórias navais, relatos de viagens...) constituindo um apartado que o catálogo denomina Polimatia. No seu conjunto, uma bibliografia com uma razoável atualização para a sua época, maioritariamente constituída por obras estrangeiras, sobretudo em língua francesa[20].

Lugar de implantação dos saberes, o ultramar português é também, neste período, objeto de estudo ou de conhecimento exótico, lugar físico da "viagem filosófica" que era, antes de mais, uma atitude mental, uma curiosidade, tornada agora sistemática e científica, acerca das realidades da Natureza e, ao mesmo tempo, um meio de implantação ou de afirmação de posse e de domínio. Esta empresa – paralela, em muitos aspetos, com o reconhecimento e a reorganização administrativa do espaço continental português – teve como protagonistas um grupo de indivíduos que se foi formando paulatinamente, fruto das transformações relacionadas com as reformas educacionais e pedagógicas deste final de século: a institucionalização da orgânica militar e a reforma da Universidade de Coimbra[21]. Poder-se-á dizer que, seguindo depois vias diversas, eles tinham feito a primeira educação do seu olhar nas aulas coimbrãs. É, a este respeito, eloquente o testemunho do pernambucano Manuel Arruda da Câmara, na dedicatória da sua *Memória sobre a cultura dos algodoeiros*: "Tendo ouvido na Universidade de Coimbra os Mestres comuns da Nação, e na de Montpellier os dois Sabios assaz conhecidos na Republica Litteraria [...] me recolhi ao meu lar, ardendo nos desejos de ser útil à minha Nação pelos conhecimentos que havia adquirido nas Ciências Naturais"[22].

É, com efeito, o já mencionado Domingos Vandelli, que, ao elaborar o "Rol dos instrumentos, Drogas, e mais utensilios pertencentes

---

[20] Silva 1999: 59-71
[21] V. Domingues 1991.
[22] Câmara 1799.

a Historia Natural, Physica, e Chimica que são indispensaveis a hum naturalista que viaja" (1778) nos entreabre a dimensão das incumbências que eram atribuídas a estes cientistas viajantes, de observação, coleção, acondicionamento e conservação, etiquetagem, registo memorial e gráfico[23]; impedido "pelo continuo trabalho da Universidade" de redigir, no mesmo ano, as instruções para os viajantes naturalistas, fá-lo-á no ano seguinte, aprontando um texto que intitulou *Viagens filosóficas, ou Dissertação sobre as importantes regras que o filósofo naturalista, nas suas peregrinações, deve principalmente observar*. É, portanto, sob a orientação científica direta deste professor que estas expedições se farão.

É notável a galeria destes viajantes naturalistas, comissionados oficialmente ou agindo por iniciativa própria, como o Doutor Joaquim Veloso de Miranda, professor substituto de Química e História Natural, o qual, ao solicitar licença para se deslocar a Minas Gerais, sua terra natal, declara querer mostrar-se útil à sua Faculdade de Filosofia, "remetendo várias e escolhidas mostras de produtos naturais até agora pouco conhecidos [...] e fazendo todas as averiguações possíveis [...] para o progresso destes conhecimentos[24]".

Alexandre Rodrigues Ferreira, natural da Baía, doutor em Filosofia por Coimbra, explora a bacia amazónica de 1783 a 1793, numa viagem que coincide, no tempo e no espaço, com a expedição de demarcação da capitania do Rio Negro; ao mesmo tempo, Manuel Galvão da Silva – também baiano e tendo frequentado Filosofia – viaja, com o mesmo intento, para Moçambique, depois de ter passado por Goa; a José da Silva Feijó e Joaquim José da Silva, ambos cariocas, foi confiado o encargo de conduzir expedições com idênticas finalidades em Cabo Verde e Angola, respetivamente. O exemplo mais abrangente será, talvez, o de Francisco José de Lacerda e

---

[23] Cruz 1976: 67-71
[24] Cruz 1976: 66

Almeida, doutorado em Matemática por Coimbra, em 1777: membro da comissão de demarcações de limites das fronteiras do Norte do Brasil e, nessa qualidade (em companhia de António Pires da Silva Pontes, natural de Mariana – e também doutor em Matemática por Coimbra – 1777), procedendo a cuidadosas observações geodésicas, fez numerosas explorações na colónia; veio para a metrópole para exercer o magistério na Real Academia das Guardas Marinhas; terminou o seu percurso em África, na tentativa da travessia do continente, de Moçambique à contracosta de Angola. Morreu nessa expedição, iniciada em Tete, a 30 de Junho de 1798 — a 870 quilómetros (em linha reta) do ponto de partida — vítima de impaludismo[25].

Um dos mais importantes retornos desta empresa de exploração é um assinalável conjunto de relatos escritos – diários, memórias, notícias esparsas – que não só aproveitavam ao imediato conhecimento dos territórios e às finalidades políticas das expedições, mas que, sobretudo, constituíam um acervo científico desde então disponível. E abria-se um amplo espaço para a aquisição de espécimes de que viriam a beneficiar principalmente o Jardim Botânico e o Museu de História Natural de Coimbra.

O impulso inicial destas viagens é retomado no início do século seguinte: em 1 de Abril de 1801 uma carta régia encarrega o Conselho da Faculdade de Filosofia de estabelecer os "planos de viagens e expedições philosophicas pelas diversas provincias do reino [...] e nas possessões ultramarinas", determinação reiterada em 1806, instando para que, "sem demora", se lhes desse início. Chegou mesmo a ser designado o Doutor Luís António da Costa Barradas "para se dirigir ao Brazil, à provincia de Pernambuco, com o fim de colligir productos e plantas com as competentes descripções, e fazer remessas dessas collecções para a Universidade"; e em Congregação de 14 de Janeiro de 1807 tomou-se a resolução

---

[25] V. Pereira 1999; Cruz 1999.

de, "sem perda de tempo" se "fazer uma collecção de todos os productos do reino e colonias"[26]. O período de turbulência que se seguiu (invasões napoleónicas, instabilidade política, revolução liberal e guerra civil) impediu a concretização deste projeto, que, contudo, será retomado em 1840.

Será precisamente a instalação da corte e do governo no Brasil – porventura o único meio eficaz para obstar à intenção dominadora de Napoleão – o fator que irá dar uma maior força à ideia de uma única elite luso-brasileira e, simultaneamente, agudizar a ambiguidade de uma colónia dependente dos interesses da metrópole – e a obrigatoriedade de aqui vir buscar a qualificação proporcionada pelos estudos superiores era um dos sinais mais evidentes dessa dependência – que era, a partir de então, sede do poder e cabeça do império. Essa ambiguidade originara já descontentamento e revolta: a Inconfidência Mineira (1789) – malograda conspiração autonomista de intelectuais que tinha como um dos elementos catalisadores a instalação de uma universidade em Minas Gerais – é interpretada pelo governador, Visconde de Barbacena (ele próprio formado em Filosofia por Coimbra) como inspirada por antigos estudantes de Coimbra: "seja certo ou não o ajuste dos estudantes [...], sempre nesta matéria achei muito arriscados os sentimentos, opiniões e influências dos bacharéis brasileiros que têm voltado à sua pátria, especialmente depois que se julgam instruídos nos direitos públicos e das gentes, nos interesses da Europa e no conhecimento das produções da natureza[27]".

A ambiguidade tornou-se contradição quando as Cortes – o parlamento constituinte resultante da Revolução Liberal de 1820 – exigiram que o príncipe herdeiro abandonasse o Brasil e que na colónia se desmantelasse o aparelho governativo que aí se instalara

---

[26] Carvalho 1872: 44; 50; 85; 92.
[27] Boschi 1991: 142

replicando o de Lisboa: deixaria de existir o reino unido de Portugal e do Brasil (que vigorava desde 1815) para se voltar à política de dependência colonial. A oposição principal a este intento – expressa em vigoroso manifesto – vem de um homem que em si sintetizava uma pluralidade exemplar de matrizes científicas e culturais e uma variada experiência de vida, José Bonifácio de Andrada e Silva: natural de S. Paulo, forma-se em Coimbra em Leis, obtendo também o grau de bacharel em Filosofia (1787), candidata-se à magistratura e é sócio da Academia das Ciências de Lisboa, faz um largo périplo científico pela Europa (França, Alemanha, Itália, Suécia, Bélgica, Holanda, Hungria, Boémia, Turquia) sob patrocínio régio e com a finalidade de adquirir "os conhecimentos mais perfeitos da Mineralogia e mais partes da Filosofia e da História Natural", privando com mestres, escrevendo memórias, visitando sítios naturais e minas, relacionando-se com sociedades científicas; no regresso cria, em Coimbra, a cadeira de Metalurgia e exerce um sem-número de cargos (chegou a exercer simultaneamente onze, dos quais apenas três remunerados), onde conjugava as duas vertentes – jurídica e naturalística – da sua formação; foi tenente coronel do primeiro batalhão académico, em 1809; regressa ao Brasil em 1819, onde irá desempenhar uma missão política de primordial importância no processo de independência[28].

Exemplo ímpar do papel que uma elite letrada, naturalmente vocacionada para o exercício de funções administrativas e judiciais, a diversos níveis da escala do poder, assume em momentos cruciais, José Bonifácio não é o único. Outras trajetórias individuais – tais como a dos irmãos de José Bonifácio, António Carlos e Martim Francisco, a do seu sobrinho José Ricardo da Costa Aguiar de Andrada, as de José Feliciano Fernandes Pinheiro e de José Correia Pacheco e Silva ou a dos também irmãos José e Baltazar

---

[28] Freitas 1959: 153-158.

da Silva Lisboa, a de Hipólito José da Costa Pereira, para apenas citar algumas das mais importantes – apresentam traços comuns, que não apenas a sua formação universitária em Coimbra. Mas esta existe sempre e terá constituído a base e o alicerce de desenvolvimentos culturais posteriores, com influência inegável nos destinos individuais destes e doutros estudantes e na sua ação política, que se exerce, no que toca a estes nascidos no Brasil, tanto nas Cortes constituintes, em Lisboa (1820-1822), como no processo de independência da sua pátria natal.

Perante a ação dos brasileiros graduados por Coimbra, alguns deles marcando decisivamente o período e o processo que conduzem à emancipação do Brasil, poder-se-ia afirmar que eles terão contribuído, pela sua competência científica específica nos domínios das ciências naturais, para a tomada de consciência do corpo físico da grande colónia, dos seus contornos e das suas potencialidades, ponto de partida e alicerce de uma consciência social, moral e política que progressivamente se vai alargando a todo esse vasto corpo. Dessa consciência fazia parte integrante o projeto de instauração do ensino superior. Em 1821, José Bonifácio, o seu irmão Martim Francisco e outro graduado de Coimbra, João Ferreira de Oliveira Bueno, assinam as "Instruções do Governo Provisório de S. Paulo aos deputados da Província às Cortes Portuguesas". Nelas se estabelece um plano de implantação do ensino no Brasil: escolas para as primeiras letras em todas as cidades, vilas e freguesias consideráveis; "um gymnasio ou collegio em que se ensinem as sciencias úteis", em cada província; uma universidade (pelo menos) com uma faculdade filosófica ("composta de três collegios: 1º – de sciencias naturaes, 2º – de mathematicas puras e applicadas, 3º – de philosophia especulativa e boas artes), assim como faculdades de medicina, de jurisprudência e "de economia, fazenda e governo"[29].

---

[29] Freitas 1959: 77-78.

Após a independência manteve-se, a par da continuidade da afluência de estudantes brasileiros em níveis elevados, o dinamismo dos graduados de Coimbra. Apenas dois exemplos: na organização do primeiro curso jurídico em S. Paulo, criado segundo o modelo coimbrão, tal como o de Olinda, pela lei de 11 de Agosto de 1827, quando a Secretaria de Negócios do Império era ocupada pelo já mencionado José Feliciano Fernandes Pinheiro, Visconde de S. Leopoldo, teve papel preponderante um outro graduado em Direito por Coimbra, José Arouche de Toledo Rendon, o primeiro que o dirigiu, um advogado que se dedicou depois à carreira das armas e participou ativamente na vida política; mais tarde, em 1838, o elenco dos 27 fundadores do Instituto Histórico e Geográfico Brasileiro conta com cerca de um terço de nascidos em Portugal (tendo-se deslocado, eles ou os seus parentes, para o Brasil com a família real): 16 haviam feito a sua formação académica na antiga metrópole, 12 deles na Universidade de Coimbra[30].

Era, assim, notória a continuidade da matriz formativa da Universidade reformada a par de outras instituições de ensino que bebiam da mesma inspiração. Deste modo se explica que a primeira grande leitura da história do Brasil, a *História Geral do Brasil* (1854-1857) de Francisco Adolfo Varnhagen – um engenheiro que passara pelo Colégio da Luz, pela Academia Real da Marinha e a Academia Real de Fortificação, depois pela Academia das Ciências, e que privara com românticos portugueses como Herculano e Garrett – transmitisse a imagem de uma nação civilizada do Novo Mundo, moldada pela colonização portuguesa, esta consequentemente encarada como "tarefa civilizadora". Não é inocente esta perspetiva, que contradizia uma outra enraizada no nativismo, mas ela dá conta da força de que então ainda gozava uma liderança intelectual e política que bebera em fontes do

---

[30] V. Guimarães, 1991.

outro lado do Atlântico, com um claro predomínio da metrópole portuguesa e da Universidade de Coimbra.

A força da liberdade

Atentos à trajetória do Brasil colónia para o Brasil nação independente que se esboçou a traços largos, não podemos esquecer que na Universidade se refletiu a conjuntura turbulenta das três primeiras décadas do século XIX. Desde logo as invasões francesas (1807-1811) que obrigaram à interrupção das aulas (1810- 1811). Na resistência à primeira invasão teve o corpo universitário papel de relevo: organizou-se um batalhão académico – formado por lentes, opositores e estudantes – que obteve importantes sucessos contra as tropas francesas de Junot; o vice-reitor Manuel Pais de Aragão Trigoso foi governador de Coimbra, incentivando os seus cidadãos à luta contra o invasor; o lente de Química, Tomé Rodrigues Sobral, coadjuvado por outros colegas e por estudantes, fabricava pólvora no Laboratório Químico[31]. Mais tarde (1826), e em apoio ao ideário liberal, são os estudantes que espontaneamente se organizam em novo batalhão, atitude que repetem em 1828, tempo de revolta malograda contra o absolutismo de D. Miguel e prenúncio da guerra civil.

Terá sido este período em que se estremava a oposição entre fações – absolutistas e liberais – aquele em que, com mais nitidez, o corpo estudantil assume consciência política. Estudantes como Almeida Garrett, o poeta romântico que cursava ainda em Coimbra quando se deu a Revolução Liberal (1820) – de que foi paladino e depois colaborador ativo – ou graduados com um contributo incontornável para a nova ordem finalmente vitoriosa em 1834, como Joaquim António de Aguiar, que fora colegial de S. Pedro e lente de

---

[31] V. Araújo 2009.

Direito Pátrio, e José Xavier Mouzinho da Silveira (este seguindo, depois de formado em Leis, uma carreira na advocacia e depois na administração), serão apenas os exemplos mais notáveis daqueles que em 1823 pediam às Cortes legislativas licença para se armarem contra os inimigos da liberdade.

A Universidade não deixou de sentir a crítica que lhe advinha de ser uma instituição secular, instrumento de um poder absoluto que agora era contestado e sendo financiada por um regime senhorial que se desmantelava nos seus principais fundamentos. Fora, além disso, nos últimos anos (a partir de 1794), o organismo que superintendia nos níveis inferiores do ensino: a Junta da Diretoria Geral dos Estudos e Escolas do Reino tinha a sua sede em Coimbra, sendo o seu presidente o Reitor e os seus deputados e secretário membros do corpo docente, o que, num contexto em que proliferavam as propostas de reforma educativa, a tornava alvo de contestação. Em causa estavam sobretudo as faculdades chamadas positivas – Direito e Teologia, cujos professores efetivamente seguiam em geral posições mais conservadoras – e opiniões mais radicais propunham não apenas a sua remodelação mas a sua extinção. A Universidade de Coimbra, porém, irá subsistir e os estudos de Direito continuarão a ser maioritários: o modelo da reforma de 1772 criara um alicerce sólido que permanecerá até ao século XX.

SCIENTIAE THESAURUS MIRABILIS: ESTUDANTES DE ORIGEM BRASILEIRA NA UNIVERSIDADE DE COIMBRA (1601-1850)*

Fernando Taveira da Fonseca
Faculdade de Letras da Universidade de Coimbra
Centro de História da Sociedade e da Cultura (FLUC)
fertaveira@gmail.com

Já em outro lugar tivemos ocasião de referir o notável afluxo de estudantes de origem brasileira à universidade de Coimbra no período de 1700 a 1771. Os dados então apurados colocavam alguns dos agregados populacionais do Brasil — com grande destaque para a Baía e para o Rio de Janeiro — a par de outros continentais, nas posições cimeiras da hierarquia dos lugares que mais graduados haviam tido entre os seus naturais, durante aquele período[1]. Foi ainda possível dar conta do regime especial que, a partir de 1719, regulava a contagem do tempo da sua frequência, sendo-lhes comutados em um ano de mercê os dois períodos de quinze dias que eram concedidos aos reinícolas para fazerem as suas viagens de ida para a universidade e de regresso a suas casas[2]; de algumas peculiaridades relativamente à sua origem social[3]; ou da preferência

---
* Este trabalho reproduz, com modificações pontuais, Fonseca 1999.
[1] Fonseca, 1995: 170-171.
[2] Fonseca, 1995: 74.
[3] Fonseca,1995: 255; 306-307.

acentuada que, de acordo com o padrão geral da frequência universitária coimbrã, manifestaram pelos estudos canonísticos, seguidos, a grande distância, pelos de Leis e de Medicina[4].

Em outro estudo[5] tivemos ocasião de nos debruçar sobre o papel desempenhado pelos estudantes e graduados ultramarinos, no continente ou em outros espaços, com especial destaque para os originários do Brasil.

O presente trabalho, alargando o período cronológico sob observação, procurará, sem pretensões de novidade, pormenorizar alguns aspectos no que diz respeito ao ritmo das matrículas e à origem geográfica dos estudantes brasileiros que cursaram na universidade de Coimbra[6]. A data escolhida como limite inicial — 1601 — marca o ponto em que começa a observar-se alguma regularidade nas vindas de além-Atlântico; no outro extremo — 1850 (o ano lectivo de 1849--1850) — pretendeu-se ultrapassar com alguma margem o momento da independência no sentido de verificar quais as consequências induzidas por esse acontecimento a curto e a médio prazo.

---

[4] Dos 808 estudantes que se graduaram entre aquelas duas datas, 74,5% (602) eram canonistas, 19,8% (160) haviam cursado Leis e 5,7% (46) Medicina.

[5] Fonseca, 1997.

[6] Utilizei como fonte de informação o elenco elaborado por Francisco Morais. "Estudantes da universidade de Coimbra nascidos no Brasil". *Brasília*, suplemento ao vol. IV, Coimbra, 1949. Com base nesta e em outras fontes elaborou Walter Cardoso "Estudantes da universidade de Coimbra nascidos no Brasil (1701-1822): procedências e graus obtidos". In *Universidade(s). História, Memórias, Perspectivas. Actas do Congresso História da Universidade*. Coimbra, 1991, 166-179. Uma outra relação, também resultante da compilação de Francisco Morais, *Estudantes brasileiros na universidade de Coimbra (1772-1872)*. Rio de Janeiro: Imprensa Nacional, 1943, não foi publicada pelo seu compilador e tem data de edição anterior à do suplemento da Brasília. O cotejo das duas relações revela discrepâncias notáveis nos anos imediatos à Reforma de 1772. Trata-se, contudo de um diferente arranjo na colocação de alguns estudantes que haviam começado os seus cursos antes da Reforma e os prosseguiram a seguir a ela: o organizador da edição de 1943 colocou-os em 1772 ou depois; Francisco Morais, que assina as palavras introdutórias à relação publicada em 1949, assinalou a sua primeira matrícula, anterior à Reforma. É óbvio que nos conformámos com este último critério.

1. O ritmo das matrículas

O ponto de partida para a análise que nos propomos efetuar pode ser a observação do quadro 1 e do gráfico 1, onde estão assinaladas as entradas anuais (primeira matrícula) de estudantes originários do Brasil na universidade de Coimbra, durante dois séculos e meio. Antes de 1601, estas vindas não têm significado estatístico — são assinaladas treze entre 1577 e 1599, com vários anos em que nenhuma teve lugar. Não deixa, contudo de merecer reparo o facto de, muito pouco tempo depois de os registos universitários de matrículas se tornarem regulares[7], neles figurarem estudantes brasileiros, o que deixa supor que já anteriormente alguns teriam iniciado os seus estudos em Coimbra[8]

Os dados expressos e a curva desenhada pelas novas entradas de estudantes vindos do Brasil apresentam um perfil onde se destaca de imediato o grande salto positivo iniciado em 1720, que se prolonga, de forma sustentada, até à Reforma de 1772 (com um novo surto nos anos imediatamente anteriores a esta). Já antes, a partir dos meados da década de 1670 o crescimento se esboçara, para se esbater — à semelhança do que se passou com a curva geral da matrícula coimbrã — nos inícios do século XVIII[9].

---

[7] O mais antigo livro de matrículas é de 1573-1574. (Vasconcelos, 1941: 2, 116.) Para o período que medeia entre 1537 e aquela data podem apenas colher-se elementos dispersos ou fazer estimativas a partir de outros dados (Fonseca, 1997: 533-535; Oliveira, 1971-1972: vol. II, apêndice, gráfico 94).

[8] Ao relatar os inícios da então província de Pernambuco, o autor da *Corografia Brazilica* refere que, em 1554, por morte de Duarte Coelho Pereira que obtivera a capitania do mesmo nome em 1534, ficou o seu governo entregue à consorte, D. Brites de Albuquerque, "athé à chegada de seu filho herdeiro, Duarte Coelho d'Albuquerque, que se achava no Reino estudando." (Corografia Brazilica, 1817: 153-154.)

[9] Para a comparação com o ritmo geral das matrículas em Coimbra, vide Fonseca, 1995: 30-37; Fonseca, 1997: 534-537. Tendo em consideração que a frequência das faculdades jurídicas representou uma proporção média de 87,31%, para todo o período anterior à Reforma Pombalina, tomaram-se as matrículas em Instituta — corrigidas por um índice de 1,127 — como estimativa do total de novas entradas durante esse período. O cômputo das primeiras entradas depois da Reforma de 1772, até

Quadro 1 — Estudantes brasileiros que se matricularam em Coimbra (1601-1850)

(Valores quinquenais)

Quinquénios	Número	Média anual	Quinquénios	Número	Média anual
1601-1605	2	0,4	1731-1735	119	23,8
1606-1610	5	1,0	1736-1740	82	16,4
1611-1615	9	1,8	1741-1745	120	24,0
1616-1620	11	2,2	1746-1750	99	19,8
1621-1625	3	0,6	1751-1755	119	23,8
1626-1630	13	2,6	1756-1760	92	18,4
1631-1635	10	2,0	1761-1765	92	18,4
1636-1640	4	0,8	1766-1770	196	39,2
1641-1645	10	2,0	1772-1775	98	24,5
1646-1650	14	2,8	1776-1780	86	17,2
1651-1655	19	3,8	1781-1785	87	17,4
1656-1660	8	1,6	1786-1790	94	18,8
1661-1665	10	2,0	1791-1795	80	16,0
1666-1670	11	2,2	1796-1800	55	11,0
1671-1675	29	5,8	1801-1805	65	13,0
1676-1680	32	6,4	1806-1810	20	4,0
1681-1685	31	6,2	1811-1815	57	11,4
1686-1690	32	6,4	1816-1820	142	28,4
1691-1695	65	13,0	1821-1825	121	24,2
1696-1700	50	10,0	1826-1830	86	17,2
1701-1705	18	3,6	1831-1835	11	2,2
1706-1710	38	7,6	1836-1840	42	8,4
1711-1715	13	2,6	1841-1845	46	9,2
1716-1720	38	7,6	1846-1850	36	7,2
1721-1725	113	22,6			
1726-1730	128	25,6	TOTAL	2761	11,1

1820, foi feito por Manuel Alberto Carvalho Prata (Prata, 1989: 57-74). Este autor tem o cuidado de apresentar separadamente os valores para os alunos ordinários de Matemática e Filosofia, os únicos que verdadeiramente se podem contabilizar como primeiras entradas nestas duas faculdades. Para o período posterior, utilizei as contagens de António de Vasconcelos (Vasconcelos, 1941: 124-136). Neste último caso, os valores para Matemática e Filosofia, foram os referidos para o 4.º ano (no qual, em princípio, só existiriam alunos ordinários).

Gráfico 1 — Estudantes originários do Brasil matriculados na Universidade de Coimbra (1600-1850)

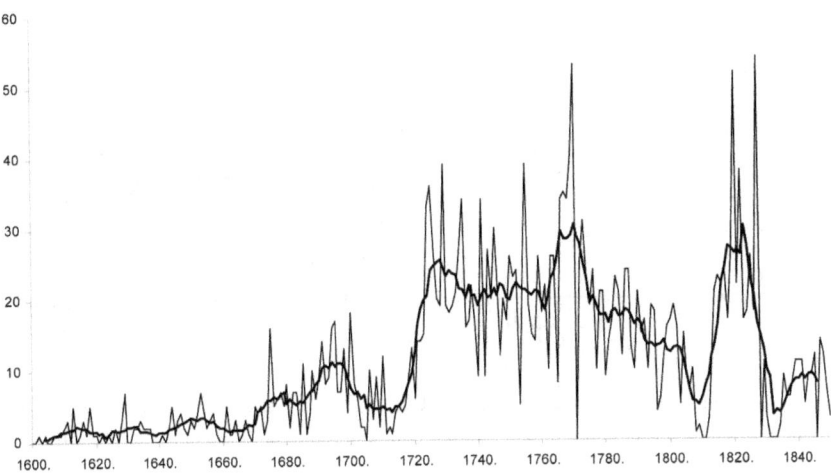

Esta semelhança com o ritmo global de novas entradas na universidade de Coimbra, visível no gráfico 2, no qual as duas curvas se encontram projetadas comparativamente — é caracterizada, contudo, por uma particularidade no que respeita à amplitude do movimento: o dos estudantes brasileiros é muito mais vigoroso. Por um lado, em termos absolutos, a média anual de ingressos mais que triplica relativamente à vintena de anos anterior, para se manter elevada nas décadas seguintes. Por outro, e mais significativo ainda — adoptando sempre como referência as inscrições em Instituta (corrigidas, de acordo com o critério enunciado na nota 9) como indicador global das primeiras entradas na universidade — podemos dar-nos conta que a percentagem que cabe aos brasileiros no cômputo geral dessas primeiras entradas se modifica substancialmente (quadro 2).

Gráfico 2 — Entradas de brasileiros comparadas com o total de primeiras matrículas

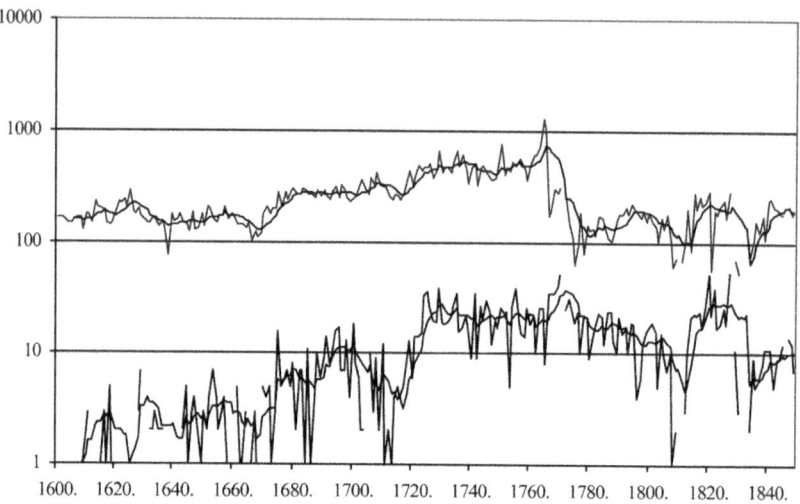

Quadro 2 — Primeiras matrículas: proporção de brasileiros no conjunto da população estudantil de Coimbra

Período	%	% (corrigida)	Coef. de variação (%)
1600 -1639		0,80	118
1640 -1679		1,66	77,9
1680 -1699		2,97	58,6
1700 -1719		1,88	87,7
1720 -1739		4,56	31,4
1740 -1759		4,61	41,9
1760 -1770		7,52	86,0
1772 -1789	15,6		48,7
1790 -1809	7,4		45,0
1810 -1829	11,6		81,7
1830 -1849	4,3		67,8

A partir de então e até à Reforma de 1772 — sempre no contexto de um crescimento continuado do conjunto da população estudantil coimbrã — a proporção dos originários do Brasil não cessa de aumentar. E é precisamente nos anos que imediatamente a antecedem e a seguem que são atingidos os valores máximos. Será preciso notar, contudo, que o período imediatamente antecedente é marcado por uma grande irregularidade no que diz respeito às novas matrículas: ao excesso de entradas dos anos de 1764-65 e 1765-66[10] sucedeu-se um quinquénio em que elas baixaram para níveis bastante inferiores. Deste modo, se naqueles dois anos a percentagem de brasileiros desce para 2,04% e 0,77%, respectivamente, já nos cinco seguintes é, em média, de 16,2%: na totalidade destes sete anos antes da Reforma, a proporção dos brasileiros é de 12%, correspondendo ao maior contingente que até então tinha demandado a universidade (com uma média anual de 39 novas entradas).

Mas é no quinquénio posterior a 1772 que melhor se nota o efeito deste acrescido contingente que acorre à universidade. Ao manter-se em níveis elevados — contrastando com a forte quebra que sofrem as matrículas dos continentais — vai traduzir-se em reforço da proporção de brasileiros: para todo o período de 1772 a 1789, esta sobe para 15,6% em média, embora chegue pontualmente aos 30,2% (em 1775). A evolução das duas curvas do gráfico 2 faz-se, a partir dessa altura, em sentido divergente — diminuem em termos absolutos e relativamente às matrículas totais, as dos originários do Brasil — até que, a partir de 1813, uma nova aproximação se regista, num crescendo que só o encerramento da universidade, em 1828-29, vem interromper. O retomar dos trabalhos universitá-

---

[10] Já tivemos ocasião de referir que na origem deste fenómeno esteve a legislação sobre recrutamento militar, então promulgada, a qual isentava das sortes "os Estudantes que nos Collegios e Universidades se applicão às artes e sciencias." Fonseca, 1995: 122.

rios foi fugaz: quando se reatam, depois de nova interrupção (de 1831-32 a 1833-34) e passada a guerra civil, é débil o contingente dos que iniciam os seus estudos universitários (pouco mais de sete dezenas, ao todo) e deles apenas 2 brasileiros: a proporção destes baixa significativamente para valores muito semelhantes aos do primeiro arranque (a partir 1720), mas bastante inferiores aos dessa época em termos absolutos, aproximando-se mais dos que a haviam precedido.

Em termos gerais, poderemos afirmar que o movimento longo de entradas de brasileiros na universidade de Coimbra que se inicia na terceira década do século XVIII, com um forte contingente, é marcado depois por uma lenta erosão, pouco sensível até meados dos anos sessenta, mais acentuada no período que começa uma década depois, mas cortada por dois ciclos de duração média que contrariam vigorosamente aquela tendência: o primeiro situa-se à volta da Reforma de 1772; o segundo toma balanço imediatamente a seguir à instalação da Corte portuguesa no Brasil como consequência das invasões francesas, e tem o seu máximo para lá de 1822 — em 1827 — só então iniciando a fase descendente.

Antes de tentarmos explorar o significado destes movimentos, teremos de dar-nos conta de outra característica que parece crucial para a sua compreensão. Refiro-me à origem geográfica destes estudantes que demandam a universidade de Coimbra: no contexto de um espaço que progressivamente se alarga, é imprescindível atentar neste aspecto.

2. A origem geográfica dos estudantes brasileiros

Ao abordarmos este outro momento de análise não poderemos deixar totalmente de lado a dimensão diacrónica que até aqui nos havia orientado. A razão fundamental já atrás ficou expressa: ao longo de grande parte do período que nos ocupa, o território brasileiro está em construção[11]. Daí a necessidade de captar, também na frequência universitária, as implicações desse facto. O estabelecimento de marcos temporais teve por base a própria curva dos efetivos de primeiras matrículas: há indubitavelmente um antes e um depois de 1720, assim como é incontornável a Reforma de 1772 com o seu ciclo específico, como atrás assinalámos; conviria igualmente colocar uma cesura numa data próxima da ida da Corte para o Brasil, a partir da qual se inicia a fase ascendente de outro ciclo médio. Com base nestas referências, fez-se uma divisão por períodos mais ou menos regulares. Os dados assim organizados foram reunidos no quadro A.1. (em apêndice), e sintetizados no quadro 3.

É necessário, antes de mais, explicitar os critérios que conduziram à arrumação dos topónimos da forma que é apresentada. Uma das dificuldades encontradas foi a frequente utilização, na indicação da naturalidade dos estudantes, de nomes designando áreas vastas (capitanias, províncias, comarcas...) que são, muitas vezes, coincidentes com a designação do seu agregado populacional mais importante, o que torna difícil determinar qual das duas referências escolher. Em contrapartida, essa indicação mais genérica revelou-se de grande utilidade quando acompanhava a dos outros topónimos, permitindo assim uma mais fácil identificação e localização destes. Deste modo, no quadro geral, apresentado em apêndice, mantiveram-se todas as

---

[11] Magalhães, 1998: 28 e ss. O autor reproduz um mapa de Fréderic Mauro no qual se assinalam os limites de Brasil em 1650, 1750 e 1800. É visível que, até àquela primeira data, o território ocupado se limitava a uma extensa faixa litoral apenas mais profunda na altura de Rio de Janeiro e de S. Paulo, sendo notável ainda a extensão das zonas insubmissas em 1800.

Quadro 3 — Origem geográfica dos estudantes brasileiros que frequentaram a universidade de Coimbra (1600-1850)

Designação	1600-1720 N.º	1600-1720 %	1721-1771 N.º	1721-1771 %	1772-1810 N.º	1772-1810 %	1811-1850 N.º	1811-1850 %	1600-1850 N.º	1600-1850 %
BRASIL	16	3,4	3	0,3			1	0,2	20	0,7
BAÍA	244	51,6	398	34,5	103	17,6	145	26,9	890	32,3
Outros lugares			23	2,0	20	3,4	43	8,0	86	3,1
Total	244	51,6	421	36,5	123	21,0	188	34,9	976	35,5
C.ª SACRAMENTO			15	1,3	5	0,9		0,0	20	0,7
GOIÁS			6	0,5	10	1,7	4	0,7	20	0,7
MARANHÃO			3	0,3	30	5,1	76	14,1	109	4,0
MINAS GERAIS			36	3,1	17	2,9	2	0,4	55	2,0
Mariana			44	3,8	10	1,7	3	0,6	57	2,1
S. João d'El Rei	4	0,8	7	0,6	21	3,6	3	0,6	35	1,3
Sabará			22	1,9	13	2,2	5	0,9	40	1,5
Vila Rica			47	4,1	20	3,4	6	1,1	73	2,7
Outros lugares			69	6,0	44	7,5	14	2,6	127	4,6
Total	4	0,8	225	19,5	125	21,3	33	6,1	387	14,1

PARÁ	2	0,4	9	0,8	17	2,9	16	3,0	44	1,6
PERNAMBUCO	89	18,8	75	6,5	74	12,6	43	8,0	281	10,2
Outros lugares	4	0,8	9	0,8	9	1,5	11	2,0	33	1,2
Total	93	19,7	84	7,3	83	14,2	54	10,0	314	11,4
RIO DE JANEIRO	99	20,9	307	26,6	125	21,3	103	19,1	634	23,0
Outros lugares	1	0,2	14	1,2	23	3,9	23	4,3	61	2,2
Total	100	21,1	321	27,8	148	25,3	126	23,4	695	25,3
S. PAULO	4	0,8	25	2,2	19	3,2	9	1,7	57	2,1
Santos	5	1,1	24	2,1	7	1,2	1	0,2	37	1,3
Outros lugares			2	0,2	1	0,2	6	1,1	9	0,3
Total	9	1,9	51	4,4	27	4,6	16	3,0	103	3,7
OUTROS	3	0,6	11	1,0	16	2,7	23	4,3	53	1,9
Não identificados	2	0,4	5	0,4	2	0,3	2	0,4	11	0,4
TOTAL	473	100,0	1154	100,0	586	100,0	539	100,0	2752	100,0

designações encontradas (depois de reduzidas a uma só as variantes que indicavam um mesmo agregado[12]) subordinando-as à área mais ampla em que se enquadravam, umas vezes por referência explícita da fonte de informação, outras como resultado da sua identificação e localização. No quadro-síntese (quadro 3) reduziu-se a multiplicidade das designações, mantendo explícitas as que se referiam a espaços mais vastos ou aos seus agregados principais (em termos de frequência universitária) e agrupando as restantes sob a rubrica de "outros lugares"[13].

Na representação cartográfica (mapas 1 a 4) seguiu-se um critério semelhante, agregando numa mesma superfície circular sombreada, centrada no seu agregado mais importante, a totalidade dos contributos de uma área, e assinalando com outro sombreado os de outras localidades que se revelassem quantitativamente significativos[14].

---

[12] Em alguns casos (por exemplo Rio das Mortes e S. João d´el Rei ou Mariana e Ribeirão do Carmo) mantiveram-se os diferentes nomes por um se ter sucedido a outro na designação do mesmo agregado.

[13] O principal instrumento utilizado para a identificação e localização dos topónimos foi a *Corografia Brazilica ou Relação Historico-Geografica do Reino do Brazil composta e dedicada a Sua magestade fidelissima por hum presbitero secular do Gram Priorado do Crato*. 2 tomos, Rio de Janeiro: Na Impressão Regia, 1817. Para uma localização contemporânea foram utilizados vários atlas, nomeadamente o *Atlas 2000. A nova cartografia do mundo*. Lisboa: Círculo de Leitores, s.d.

[14] Quer as áreas sombreadas, quer as mais escuras que aparecem no interior ou na proximidade daquelas são proporcionais ao número de estudantes originários da região em que são colocadas. Será importante referir que as mais escuras são apenas explicitações ou desmembramentos da área geral sombreada, não podendo, por isso acumular-se àquelas. A proporcionalidade adoptada é de carácter exponencial (com base na fórmula da superfície do círculo).

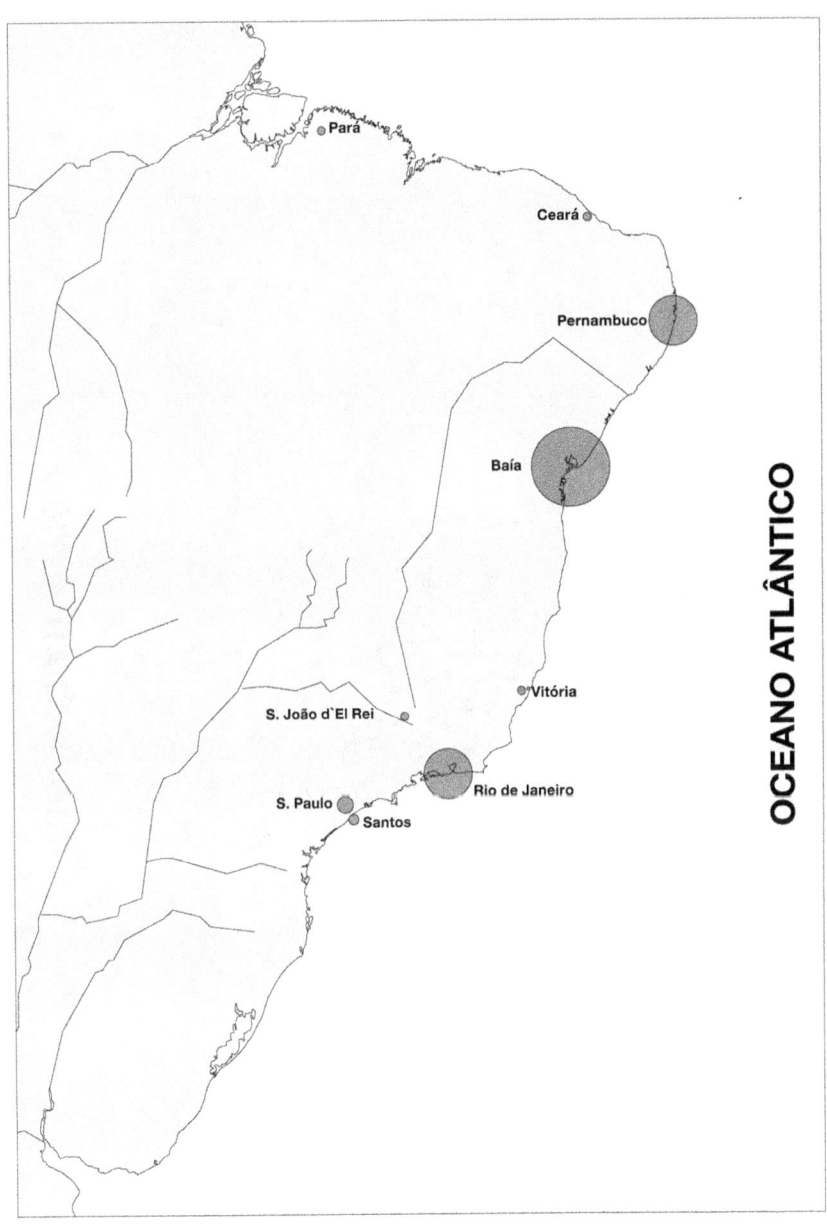

Mapa 1 – Origem geográfica dos estudantes brasileiros (1600-1720)

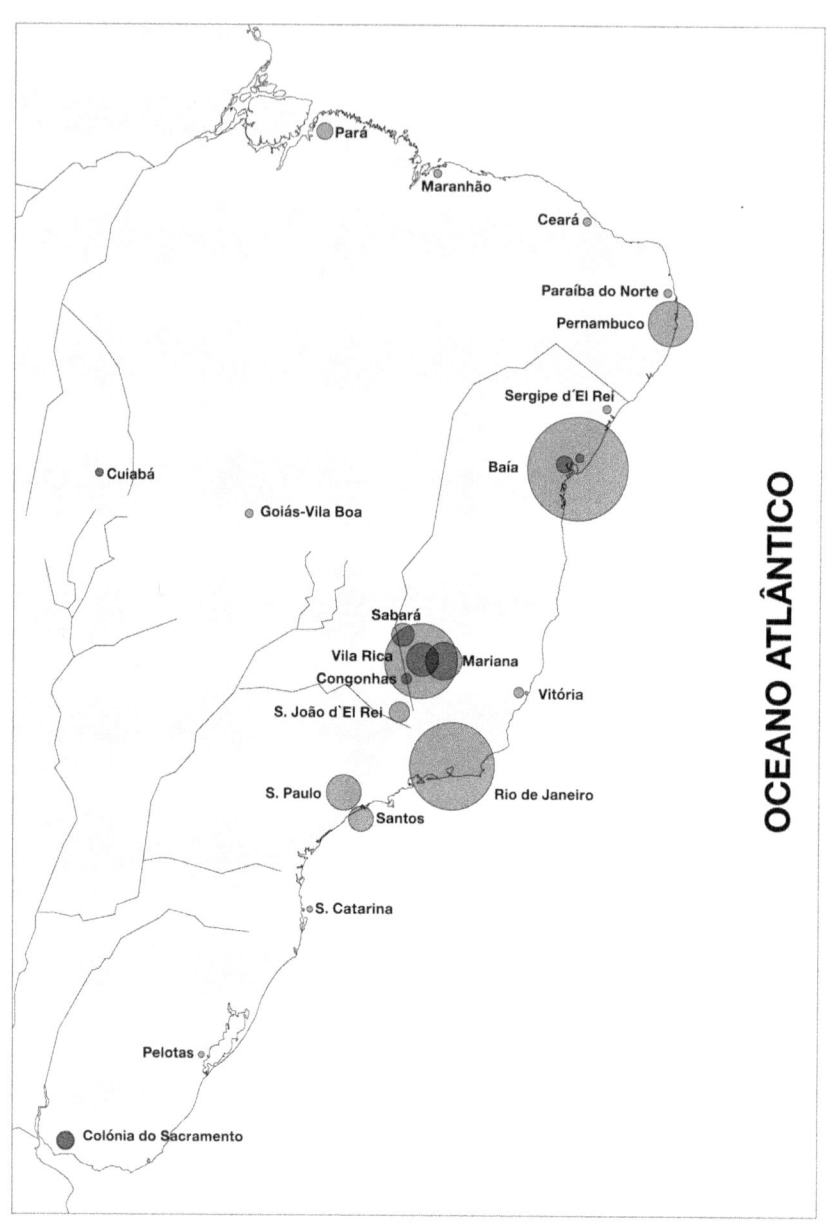

Mapa 2 – Origem geográfica dos estudantes brasileiros (1721-1771)

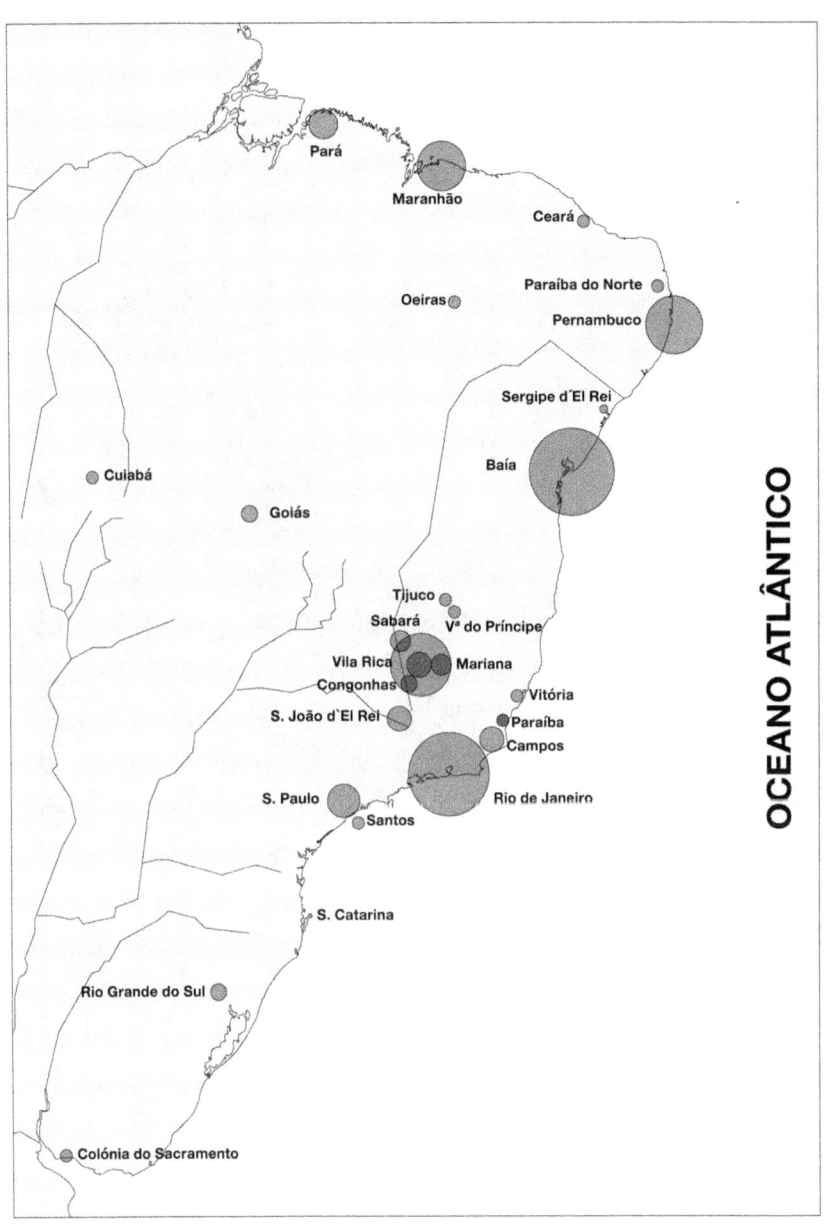

Mapa 3 – Origem geográfica dos estudantes brasileiros (1772-1850)

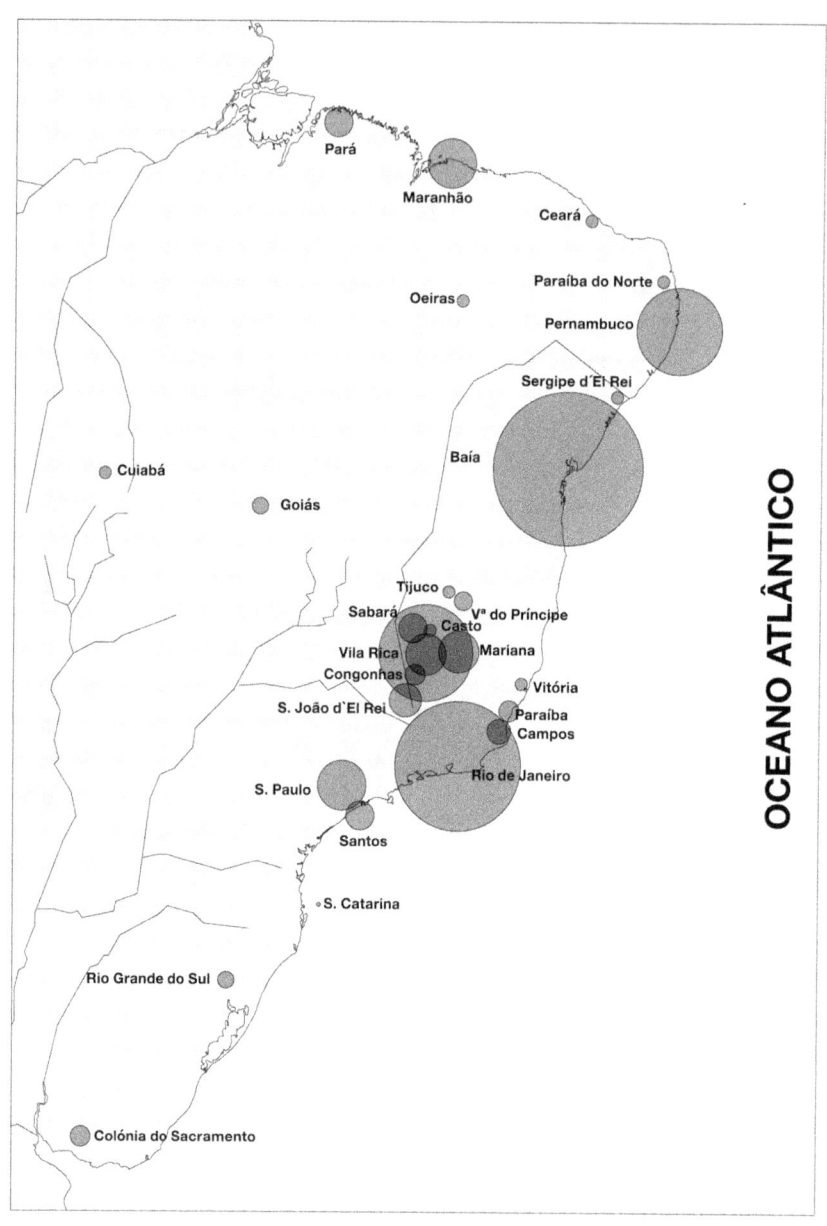

Mapa 4 – Origem geográfica dos estudantes brasileiros (1600-1850)

A conjugação dos dados numéricos com a representação cartográfica permite algumas observações interessantes. Antes de mais, a grande concentração — em termos de designação, mas presumivelmente também em termos reais — em alguns agregados populacionais dos diversos espaços considerados[15]. Este fenómeno tem a sua tradução nas baixas percentagens de estudantes originários de "outros lugares", no quadro 3. No primeiro grande intervalo cronológico (1600-1720), são pouquíssimas as designações toponímicas (todas cartografadas no mapa 1[16]), desde logo constituindo uma estrutura que se irá manter como dominante, sobretudo nos seus três grandes centros de captação de estudantes universitários — Baía, Rio de Janeiro e Pernambuco — com o conjunto S.Paulo-Santos com alguma representatividade, mas a bastante distância daqueles. A grande novidade do período seguinte — 1721-1771 — é a entrada em força da região mineira. Não se trata, realmente, apenas de uma nova designação, derivada da criação da província de Minas Gerais, em 1720, mas da inclusão de um novo espaço, neste caso com vários agregados — Mariana, Vila Rica de Ouro Preto, Sabará, S. João d'El Rei e mesmo Congonhas — repartindo entre si contributos interessantes para a população estudantil de Coimbra. Na hierarquização das áreas de captação universitária, este facto significa o relegar de

---

[15] Haja em vista que é a designação de alguns deles que depois se estende, por um processo de ampliação, a espaços maiores. Podemos exemplificar com o caso de Pernambuco: "Este nome *Pernambuco*, derivado ou corrupção de *Paranânbuca*, com que os Cahetés designavam o porto, onde hoje [1817] surgem as embarcações menores, comprehende vulgarmente duas Povoações distinctas, a Cidade d´Ollinda, e a Praça ou Villa do Recife, com o intervallo de huma legua, e comunicadas por uma restinga de area estreita, e baixa de N. a S. e também por um braço de mar" (*Corografia Brazilica*, II, 170-171). No momento da recolha das informações, verificámos que eram raras as referências ao Recife e a Olinda (22 em 314), o que se deve evidentemente ao facto de ser mais comum a designação de Pernambuco englobando aquelas duas localidades e depois a capitania.

[16] Embora a província de Minas Gerais tenha sido criada apenas em 1720, nos quadros toponímicos ficou sempre nela incluída a vila de S. João d'El Rei, que passa a ter esta designação a partir de 1712, mas que pertencia, até àquela primeira data, a S. Paulo. (*Corografia Brazilica*, I, 356 e 377.)

Pernambuco — que perde também em termos absolutos — para uma posição mais modesta (7,3% do total, quando, no período anterior, detinha 19,7%) e uma significativa perda na dominância da Baía (de 51,6% para 34,5%) que, mesmo assim, conserva o primeiro lugar; pelo contrário, o Rio de Janeiro vê o seu peso relativo aumentado (de 20,9% para 26,6%), o mesmo acontecendo com S. Paulo. Quer dizer que o grande impulso que a frequência universitária de originários do Brasil regista a partir de 1720 se deve ao dinamismo de uma grande área que engloba um conjunto de espaços contíguos: Rio de Janeiro, Minas Gerais e S. Paulo; ao mesmo tempo, a Baía, embora perca proporcionalmente, regista também um aumento notável, em termos absolutos: comparado com o crescimento global de 144%, o da Baía foi menor (72,5%) mas o do Rio de Janeiro ultrapassou-o largamente (221%[17]) .

O retrocesso relativo da Baía acentuou-se no período de 1772--1810, com uma drástica diminuição em números absolutos: para um decréscimo global de 49,2%, o desta área foi muito mais acentuado — 71%. Mas o movimento ascendente de matrículas que se inicia imediatamente a seguir marca também uma nítida recuperação, em termos relativos, desta área: em contrapartida, a de Minas Gerais sofre uma diminuição acentuada (de 74%, muito maior que a dos efetivos globais, que foi de apenas 8%), perdendo assim muitos pontos da sua cota proporcional. Mas o dado que mais importa assinalar é a emergência, a partir de 1772, de zonas que antes tinham uma diminuta representatividade, nomeadamente o Maranhão, cujo peso proporcional está em aumento até ao final

---

[17] É evidente que estas percentagens têm de ser ponderadas a partir da proporção que cabe a cada um destes espaços. Por isso, carece de significado apresentar a percentagem de crescimento de S. Paulo (466,7%) uma vez que se refere a um aumento de 9 para 51 estudantes, em números absolutos, assim como referir igual indicador para Minas Gerais, área que praticamente aparece de novo.

do período observado, alcançando, no último intervalo temporal (1811-1850), uma proporção significativa (14,1%).

Esta análise das variações relativas não pode deixar de lado aquela que parece ser a característica mais saliente da origem geográfica dos universitários brasileiros, já atrás assinalada: uma notável continuidade dos centros que primitivamente fornecem estudantes, aos quais se vão agregando outros. Na escala dos contributos, só o de Minas Gerais alcança uma amplitude semelhante à daqueles. O cômputo global para toda a duração secular — visível nas últimas colunas do quadro 3 e no mapa 4 — vem confirmar esta afirmação: a Baía — no lugar cimeiro — com o Rio de Janeiro, Pernambuco e S. Paulo-Santos (que em 1600-1720 perfaziam 94,3% do total de matriculados[18]) tomam à sua conta 74,7% do total. As Minas Gerais fazem subir esta proporção para 88,8%. E o conjunto de Maranhão e Pará que, no intervalo de 1811 a 1850 chega a atingir 17,1% de todos os matriculados, quando encarado na perspectiva mais ampla dos dois séculos e meio sob observação, mostra uma contribuição bem mais modesta de 5,6%.

3. Os tesouros das minas e o tesouro da ciência

Da análise que temos vindo a efetuar até este momento destaca-se o grande aumento que, como já referimos, se regista no número de novas entradas na universidade de estudantes brasileiros, a partir de 1720. A verificação de que um impulso semelhante percorre a frequência universitária, considerada globalmente, leva a concluir

---

[18] Durante este período é ainda de assinalar a percentagem (3,38%) dos que declaram como sua naturalidade apenas o Brasil. Não seria demasiada ousadia pensar que se trataria de naturais de algum daqueles lugares, o que nos permitiria dizer que a quase totalidade de brasileiros é deles originária.

que para um e outro terão contribuído idênticas condições de possibilidade e idênticas motivações[19].

Mesmo tendo sempre em mente a especificidade da sociedade brasileira, é certo que, em muitos aspectos, se transplantaram para a colónia formas de organização e valores dominantes na sociedade continental. Referindo-se à organização administrativa do Brasil, afirma Joaquim Romero Magalhães que "a construção do império atlântico, pela proximidade de Lisboa e pela relativa facilidade de transportes, não exigiu a montagem no Brasil de um dispositivo de governo delegado, como o que existia no Oriente. [...] As vilas e cidades que entretanto iam sendo criadas eram administradas segundo o modelo normal que vigorava no reino. [...] A justiça era exercida por juízes ordinários que se encontravam à frente das câmaras"[20]. Por sua vez, Caio Boschi acentua o papel do sistema paroquial como base do trabalho missionário e da administração eclesiástica, tendo sido em função da existência de paróquias "(desde os anos 30 do século XVI) e, sobretudo, da importância do seu trabalho que, dentre outras razões, se decidiu, em 1551 pela criação da diocese de Salvador, na Bahia"[21]. E não podemos esquecer que os horizontes dos que demandavam Coimbra, vindos de além-Atlântico, não se confinavam ao exercício das qualificações universitárias nos espaços da sua naturalidade: estava-lhes aberto todo o império, assim como o acesso aos cargos da administração central do reino[22].

Observámos, contudo, que o impulso ascendente referido é, no que toca aos originários do Brasil, de muito maior amplitude que o da matrícula geral. Devido a dois factores principais: o apareci-

---

[19] Tivemos ocasião de referir em outro lugar as condições do crescimento da frequência universitária, a partir da terceira década do século XVIII. (Fonseca, 1995: 112-117.)

[20] Magalhães, 1998: 28.

[21] Boschi, 1998: 2, 419.

[22] Fonseca, 1997: 1030-1032

mento de um novo espaço — Minas Gerais — e o incremento que anteriores zonas de captação universitária (nomeadamente o Rio de Janeiro) experimentaram.

Não será nunca demasiado salientar o papel catalisador que a descoberta das jazidas de ouro e diamantes teve na fixação de uma nova geografia do Brasil e na dinamização da economia brasileira. A colorida descrição de André João Antonil, impressa em 1711, dá--nos conta da poderosa atração que elas exerceram:

> "A sêde insaciável do ouro estimulou a tantos a deixarem suas terras, e a meterem-se por caminhos tão asperos, como são os das minas, que difficultosamente se poderá dar conta do numero das pessoas, que actualmente lá estão. Comtudo os que assistirão nellas nestes ultimos annos por largo tempo, e as corrêrão todas, dizem, que mais de trinta mil almas se occupão, humas em catar, outras em mandar catar nos ribeiros do ouro; e outras em negociar, vendendo, e comprando o que se ha mister não só para a vida, mas para o regalo, mais que nos portos do mar"[23]

A animação do comércio era motivada pela carência de tudo o que era necessário á subsistência — "sendo a terra que dá ouro esterilissima de tudo o que se ha mister para a vida humana e não menos esteril a maior parte dos caminhos das minas" — e também pela abundância e qualidade dos meios de pagamento:

> "...tanto que se vio a abundancia do ouro, que se tirava, e a largueza, com que se pagava tudo o que la hia; logo se fizerão estalagens, e logo começárão os mercadortes a mandar às minas o melhor que chega nos navios do reino, e de outras partes, assim de mantimentos, como de regalo, e de pomposo para se

---

[23] Antonil, 1922: 213.

vestirem, além de mil bugiarias de França, que lá tambem foram dar. E a este respeito, de todas as partes do Brazil se começou a inviar tudo o que dá a terra, com lucro não somente grande mas excessivo. E não havendo nas minas outra moeda mais que ouro em pó; o menos que se podia, e dava por qualquer cousa, erão oitavas. Daqui se seguiu mandarem-se às Minas Geraes as boiadas de Paranaguá, e às do Rio das Velhas, as boiadas dos campos da Bahia, e tudo o mais que os moradores imaginavão poderia apetecer-se, de qualquer genero de cousas naturaes, e industriaes, adventicias, e proprias"[24]

Importa atentar em dois aspectos: por um lado, a fixação de gente, dando origem a arraiais de exploração que depois se ampliam em agregados populacionais que atingem notoriedade e vão sendo dotados de armadura administrativa[25]; por outro, a circulação de víveres — nomeadamente o gado vivo — e mercadorias, através de rotas e caminhos, alguns já conhecidos e percorridos, outros explorados agora. Assume particular importância, neste contexto, o "caminho novo", aberto, em 1704-1705 por Garcia Rodrigues Pais (mas ficando a passagem em boas condições só por volta de 1725), ligando a região mineira ao Rio de Janeiro. Encurtava-se de trinta

---

[24] Antonil, 1922: 217.

[25] O arraial de Ouro Preto foi fundado em 1697, por António Dias de Oliveira. Em 1711 é elevado à categoria de vila, com o nome de Vila Rica; Mariana fora também arraial do Carmo, até que, na mesma data, D. João V a tornara Vila Leal do Carmo, elevando-a à categoria de cidade episcopal em 1745 e dando-lhe o nome da sua consorte; só em 1712 foram também criadas as vilas de S. João d´El Rei (antes Rio das Mortes) e Vila Real do Sabará e, em 1714, a Vila do Príncipe. Outros exemplos poderiam ser aduzidos, mas importa ainda referir que, nas proximidades destes centros se formaram numerosos arraiais, muitos dos quais depois deram origem a paróquias (Piranga, Catas Altas, Arraial de António Pereira, Santa Bárbara, Cocais, S. Romão, Barra do Rio das Velhas, S. António do Tijuco...) de alguns dos quais vieram também estudantes para Coimbra. Assinale-se outra forma de implantação como era a construção de capelas, necessárias para a assistência religiosa às populações, de que há numerosíssimos exemplos na região mineira. Cfr. *Corografia Brazilica*, 363-402.

para doze dias o tempo necessário para vencer aquela distância[26]. Consequentemente, o Rio de Janeiro "o mais próximo ancoradouro de ligação de Minas à Europa e também à África fornecedora de escravos, cresce e ganha uma importância no todo do território que até então não tivera. Por aí também se canalizava obrigatoriamente o ouro dos quintos devido à Fazenda real. [...] Ao Rio de Janeiro passa agora a caber a função de servir como "boca das Minas" sobretudo pela sua posição marítima"[27].

Reorganiza-se, deste modo, o espaço brasileiro, não sem desequilíbrios, uma vez que a afluência de gente e de escravos à zona das Minas desguarnece sobretudo a área de produção açucareira do Nordeste, e que a carestia de vida—e também a da mão-de-obra que era preciso adquirir[28] — vai a par com e radica na própria extração do minério. Não será de estranhar que esses mesmos desequilíbrios se tenham reflectido no número de candidatos à frequência universitária, levando, como já verificámos à perda da importância relativa da Baía e, sobretudo, de Pernambuco.

Não se trata, contudo, de subversão. O caso do Rio de Janeiro é típico e exemplar. Aí convergem duas ordens de razões que vão explicar o extraordinário aumento verificado: o novo dinamismo económico e a existência de uma infraestrutura de ensino que terá sido a principal responsável pela afluência de brasileiros à universidade no período anterior (1600-1720). Sem que se possa dar um peso exclusivo a este factor —basta lembrar a importância da Baía

---

[26] Viana, 1949: 114-115

[27] Magalhães, 1998: 23-24.

[28] É, a este propósito, muito elucidativa a relação dos preços (referidos a 1703) que Antonil insere na sua *Cultura e opulencia do Brazil*, pp. 218-220, no fim da qual acrescenta o seu comentário: "E estes preços tão altos, e tão correntes nas minas, forão causa de subirem tanto os preços de todas as cousas, como se experimenta nos portos das cidades e villas do Brazil, e ficarem desfornecidos muitos engenhos de assucar das peças necessarias; e de padecerem os moradores grande carestia de mantimentos, por se levarem quasi todos, aonde vendidos hão de dar maior lucro" (p. 220).

como capital administrativa — ele terá constituído a ossatura básica geradora de uma apetência intelectual que, uma vez enraizada, permanece e se amplia.

No conjunto da rede de ensino pré-universitário, os três colégios jesuíticos da Baía, do Rio de Janeiro e de Pernambuco, estavam, juntamente com alguns outros do continente (Lisboa, Porto, Braga e Santarém — a partir de 1716 — e, naturalmente, Évora) e o dos oratorianos de Lisboa (só a partir de 1708), em posição privilegiada, pois o primeiro ano dos estudos filosóficos que neles fosse concluído era contabilizado como se tivesse sido cursado nas faculdades jurídicas de Coimbra. Pelo *Catalogo dos P.P. e Irmãos da Provincia do Brasil em Janeiro de 600*[29], temos notícia de que, nesse ano, o colégio da Baía tinha um lente de Teologia, um outro de Casos de Consciência, um mestre do curso de Artes, assim como outros três de Gramática (um da primeira classe e dois da segunda, um destes também mestre de ler e escrever).

Um século depois, dos 157 jesuítas que o Colégio alimenta (118 vivendo no próprio edifício, 33 nas aldeias e residências a ele anexas), dois ensinam Teologia Especulativa, um Teologia Moral, um Filosofia, dois Humanidades e outros dois Gramática e um, primeiras letras[30]. O edifício do colégio é descrito como "satis extensum" e localizado na parte melhor da cidade, com uma biblioteca ampla e abundante, contendo cerca de três mil volumes de todo o género de escritores que se pudesse desejar, seis grandes aulas rodeando o pátio — havia pouco circundado de pórticos para proteger os estudantes do sol e da chuva —, uma sala de maiores dimensões destinada às disputas públicas, aos atos literários e também aos exercícios dos escolares da ordem.

---

[29] Leite, 1938: 578 e ss.
[30] Leite, 1945: 588 e ss.

Em 1757, o corpo docente do Colégio aparece reforçado com um especialista em Sagrada Escritura ("explanator Sacrae Scripturae") provavelmente apenas para os da casa, porque a relação dos mestres das classes superiores inclui um prefeito máximo, três professores de Teologia (de Prima, de Véspera — segundo a nomenclatura universitária — e de Teologia Moral), um professor de Matemática (da "faculdade de Matemática", como refere o Catálogo que vimos seguindo), um prefeito das classes menores, encarregado da biblioteca, e um mestre de Filosofia com o seu substituto; nas classes inferiores, um professor de Retórica, três de Gramática (da primeira, segunda e terceira classes) e um professor da escola elementar de meninos que era também diretor da sua confraria[31]. A descrição que da cidade do Salvador nos dá a Corografia Brazilica de 1817 refere que, nessa altura, há na cidade oito cadeiras régias: de Filosofia, de Retórica, de Matemática, de Grego e quatro de Gramática Latina, para além de "uma Biblioteca Pública na Salla do Collegio ex-Jezuitico, que servia do mesmo mister no tempo dos fundadores[32].

O exemplo da Baía — e não aduzimos outros de cariz semelhante para não alongar inutilmente esta exposição — é significativo daquela continuidade que a implantação de uma estrutura de ensino é susceptível de gerar. Os jesuítas criaram e desenvolveram um sistema que, á semelhança do que aconteceu no reino, gerou as condições da sua pronta substituição pela abertura que sempre teve ao exterior. Ao traçar, no tomo VI da sua História da Companhia de Jesus no Brasil, o percurso do Colégio do Rio de Janeiro, Serafim Leite chama a atenção para a evolução física do edifício e para a ampliação das disciplinas lecionadas, que o colocavam, nessa altura, a par do da Baía. Mas observa igualmente que oito dos onze professores que formavam o corpo docente desse mesmo Colégio eram naturais

---

[31] Leite, 1949: 435 e ss.
[32] *Corografia Brazilica*, II, 120.

do Brasil: "três paulistas, dois pernambucanos, um alagoano, um do Rio, um da Baía". E acrescenta: "prepondera Santos, donde são naturais todos aquêles paulistas, contemporâneos de Alexandre e Bartolomeu de Gusmão, que, por sua vez, foram alunos dos Padres, e o segundo mais que aluno, porque foi noviço"[33].

O *Catalogus brevis* de 1757 fornece-nos sinteticamente o panorama da implantação dos jesuítas na província do Brasil nas vésperas da sua expulsão. Eram, ao todo, 476 sócios, em diversas casas de diferente dimensão e finalidade: os colégios e, na sua dependência, residências, aldeias, missões. Para a finalidade que aqui diretamente nos ocupa, interessa, sobretudo dar conta dos colégios e instituições afins: o Colégio da Baía, cuja composição já observámos; aí ainda, uma casa de provação e dois seminários (o de Belém, fundado pelo P. Alexandre de Gusmão, e o novo); o Colégio do Rio de Janeiro com professores de Teologia (3), de Filosofia (1 com o seu substituto), dois professores de Gramática, um de Retórica, um da escola elementar e dois prefeitos dos estudos; o Colégio de Paranaguá com um mestre de Gramática; o do Espírito Santo (Vitória), com um mestre de Gramática e um padre encarregado da resolução de casos de consciência; o Colégio de S. Paulo com um mestre de Teologia Moral, outro de Gramática e um da escola elementar; o Colégio de S. Miguel, em Santos, com prefeito dos estudos ao qual estava também confiado o encargo de resolver os casos de consciência, um professor de Gramática e outro da escola elementar; o Colégio de Olinda com um professor de Filosofia que era também prefeito dos estudos, um substituto deste, um mestre de Gramática e um professor da escola elementar de meninos; o Colégio do Recife, com um professor de Teologia Moral que era igualmente prefeito dos estudos, mestres da 1ª e 2ª classes de Gramática e um da escola elementar; o Colégio e seminário de Paraíba com um diretor do seminário que era também

---

[33] Leite, 1938-1950: tomo VI, 7.

prefeito dos estudos, um professor de Gramática e outro da escola elementar; o Real Hospício do Ceará, em Aquirás, também com um professor de Gramática que tinha a seu cargo a biblioteca.

Na vice-província do Maranhão, o Colégio de Nossa Senhora da Luz, que atingira o estatuto de *colégio máximo*, em 1709, depois que, aos estudos de Latim, Humanidades e Retórica se haviam acrescentado os de Filosofia e de Teologia Especulativa e Moral[34]; dele dependiam outras casas nas quais se ministrava o ensino do Latim (na própria cidade de S. Luís, na missão de Guanaré e na Parnaíba); uma estrutura semelhante se criou no Pará — o Colégio de Santo Alexandre, que apenas não teve permanentemente estudos de Teologia dogmática; a ele anexo a casa da Vigia, com ensino de primeiras letras e Latim e o seminário de Nossa Senhora das Missões, onde funcionou também o curso de Filosofia. As bibliotecas destas casas — a do Colégio de S. Luís, com cinco mil volumes, com mais de dois mil a do Colégio de Santo Alexandre, e a da casa da Vigia com mais de mil — somariam, com outras de menores dimensões, um total de doze mil, em 1760[35].

É visível a diferente graduação destes colégios, alguns apenas com o ensino elementar e da Gramática, outros com estudos de nível superior, embora, nalguns casos, com dificuldades de implantação e intermitências. Mas importa salientar a intenção sistemática de fazer acompanhar a missionação da difusão do saber — ou de considerar esta como forma privilegiada de acção pastoral.

Quando elabora a sua *Corografia Brazilica*, já diversas vezes aqui citada, o P. Manuel Aires do Casal tem o cuidado de assinalar esta que fora a presença dos jesuítas, dando conta do destino de muitos dos edifícios que eles tinham construído e utilizado no seu labor, a maior parte deles transformados em residências de governadores,

---

[34] Leite, 1938-1950: tomo IV, 262-265.
[35] Leite, 1938-1950: tomo IV, 287-290.

hospitais ou palácios episcopais. O aspecto mais interessante para nós, contudo, é a atenção que ele presta às estruturas de ensino — nomeadamente as cadeiras régias — que vai encontrando nos diversos agregados populacionais que descreve[36]. Assinala dezanove localidades onde há aulas régias de Gramática Latina, e outras dezassete, nas quais a estas se juntam as primeiras letras. Cuiabá (Mato Grosso) e Vila Rica (Minas) têm, além disso, professor régio de Filosofia. Os centros mais dotados são, contudo, aqueles onde, desde mais longa data, se enraizara o estudo. S. Paulo tem professores desde as primeiras letras à Gramática, Retórica e Filosofia; mas a cidade está dotada também com uma cadeira régia de Teologia Dogmática e uma outra de Teologia Moral financiada pela mitra[37]. Na Baía, para além das cadeiras já atrás mencionadas e da biblioteca pública, o antigo edifício do colégio jesuítico alberga o hospital da tropa, onde há Aula de Cirurgia. Impressivo é também o caso de Pernambuco, onde o Recife conta com três professores régios de Latim, um de Filosofia e outro de Eloquência e Poética, mas onde Olinda, cidade episcopal desde 1676 e "uma bella habitação para estudiosos, convalescentes e melancolicos, que aborrecem os tumultos" tem um seminário no colégio ex-jesuítico com aulas e professores de Latim, Grego, Francês, Geografia, Retórica, Historia Universal,

---

[36] Uma atenção que parece constante, a julgar pelo comentário que ele faz a propósito da então província do Piauí: "O Subsídio Litterario, imposto no gado desta provincia, he assaz importante: mas em oitocentos e oito ainda não havia nella uma cadeira de Primeiras Letras, nem de Latim: sem duvida por não terem sido pedidas; pois que d´humas, e outras se vêm em algumas aldêas d´outras provincias" (*Corografia Brazilica*: II, 250).

[37] Um dos aspectos curiosos desta obra é o comentário prospectivo que, por vezes, complementa a descrição da realidade coeva. Acerca de S. Paulo, afirma: "A salubridade, e temperamento do clima, a abundancia, e barateza de viveres fazem julgar que se lhe dará preferencia para a premeditada fundação da Universidade, que lhe dará crescimento, lustre, commercio, e celebridade. Os corpos tem aqui mais vigor para a applicação; e os insectos damnificam menos as Bibliotecas" (tomo I, 236). A cidade tinha então "huns quatro mil e vinte vizinhos com vinte e tres mil setecentos e sessenta habitantes" (tomo I, 235).

Filosofia, Desenho, História Eclesiástica, Teologia Dogmática e Moral. No Norte, tanto S. Luís do Maranhão como Belém do Pará têm professores de Latim, Retórica e Filosofia. Por fim, o Rio de Janeiro, sede da Corte desde 1807, com dois seminários e o antigo colégio dos jesuítas transformado em Hospital Real Militar dotado de Aulas de Cirurgia[38], uma Academia da Marinha, várias aulas de primeiras letras, três de Latim, uma de Grego, assim como de Retórica, de Filosofia, de Comércio, de Desenho, e algumas de línguas vivas. A biblioteca real, com mais de sessenta mil volumes, estava franqueada ao público.

Não se implantara ainda, apesar da "inversão brasileira" que a ida da Corte motivara, o estudo do Direito, permanecendo Coimbra — e outras universidades europeias, tais como Montpellier e as de Inglaterra e da Alemanha[39] — como etapa necessária daqueles que queriam prosseguir estudos superiores nestes domínios ou nos das Ciências Exatas e Naturais. O ciclo ascendente que se iniciou logo após a ida da Corte para o Rio de Janeiro marcou também uma reformulação do equilíbrio relativo dos lugares de origem dos estudantes brasileiros, uma vez que a Baía — agora com um conjunto de lugares menores que de perto a circundavam — retomava a posição hegemónica, em contraste com uma diminuição muito acentuada de Minas Gerais.

No cômputo global, os efeitos dos tesouros das Minas e a semente de cultura lançada e longamente sazonada — o inestimável tesouro da ciência — não podem ser dissociados, e aparecem-nos como elementos fundamentais para a compreensão da procura acrescida de qualificações académicas dos estudantes originários do Brasil.

---

[38] O curso de Cirurgia durava cinco anos com um currículo que incluía a Anatomia, a Química, a Farmacêutica, a Fisiologia, A Higiene, a Etiologia, a Patologia, a Terapêutica, a Obstetrícia, Instituições Cirúrgicas, e a prática da Medicina. Aos que, concluído o 5º ano, voltassem a repetir o quarto e quinto anos, era-lhes concedida a graduação de fomados em Cirurgia. *Corografia Brazilica*: tomo II, 29.

[39] Vargues, 1999: XVI.

Quadro A. 1. – Origem geográfica dos estudantes brasileiros

DESIGNAÇÃO	1600-1640	1641-1680	1681-1700	1701-1720	Total	1721-1740	1741-1760	1761-1771	Total	1772-1790	1791-1810	Total	1811-1830	1831-1850	Total	TOTAL
Brasil	14	2			16	2	1	1	3				1		1	20
Baía	11	84	92	57	244	190	114	94	398	62	41	103	129	16	145	890
Baía – Cachoeira						2	5	3	10	6		6	8		8	24
Baía – Cairu											1	1	1		1	2
Baía – Cotinguiba											1	1				1
Baía – Iguape													1		1	1
Baía – Itapagipe													1		1	1
Baía – Itapicuru														1	1	1
Baía – Jacobina							1		1	1		1	2		2	4
Baía – Jaguaripe													1		1	1
Baía – Maragogipe								2	2		2	2	1		1	5
Baía – Monforte						1	2		3							3
Baía – Muritiba							1		1	1		1				2
Baía – Nazaré										1		1				1
Baía – Rio das Contas								1	1	2		2	2		2	5
Baía – Rio das Contas (Minas do)							1		1							1
Baía – Rio Fundo										2		2	1		1	3
Baía – S. António de Vila Nova											1	1				1
Baía – S. Domingos de Sabará													1		1	1
Baía – S. Félix										1		1				1
Baía – S. Francisco						1			1				2		2	2
Baía – Santa Ana do Camisão																
Baía – Santo Amaro						1			1				1		1	1
Baía – Santo Amaro da Purificação						1			1		1	1	16	1	17	19
Baía – Valença													1		1	3
Baía – Vila Nova de Boipeba													1		1	1
Total					244				421			123			188	976
Capitania do Espírito Santo							4		4	1	1	2				6
Capitania do Espírito Santo – Vitória			1		1					2		2				3
Total					1				4			4				9

DESIGNAÇÃO	*1600-1640*	*1641-1680*	*1681-1700*	*1701-1720*	**Total**	*1721-1740*	*1741-1760*	*1761-1771*	**Total**	*1772-1790*	*1791-1810*	**Total**	*1811-1830*	*1831-1850*	**Total**	***TOTAL***
Ceará				1	**1**			1	**1**				1		**1**	***3***
Ceará – Aracati											1	**1**	1		**1**	***2***
Ceará – Januária														1	**1**	***1***
Total					**1**				**1**			**1**			**3**	***6***
Colónia do Sacramento							10	5	**15**	4	1	**5**				***20***
Goiás													3		**3**	***3***
Gioás – Meia Ponte de (Goiases)							1		**1**	5		**5**				***6***
Goiases								1	**1**							***1***
Goiases – Minas de Goiases								1	**1**		1	**1**				***2***
Goiases – Minas de Goiases – Santa Ana							1		**1**							***1***
Goiases – Vila Boa							2		**2**	2	2	**4**	1		**1**	***7***
Total									**6**			**10**			**4**	***20***
Maranhão										3	15	**18**	32	16	**48**	***66***
Maranhão – Alcântara											6	**6**	7	6	**13**	***19***
Maranhão – Campo Maior											1	**1**	1		**1**	***2***
Maranhão – Caxias													1	2	**3**	***3***
Maranhão – Peagim								1	**1**							***1***
Maranhão – S. Luís						2			**2**	3	2	**5**	3	6	**9**	***16***
Maranhão – Viana													1		**1**	***1***
Total									**3**			**30**			**75**	***108***
Mato Grosso – Cuiabá										1	2	**3**	1		**1**	***4***
Mato Grosso – Cuiabá – Minas do Bom Jesus										1		**1**				***1***
Mato Grosso – Santo António							1		**1**							***1***
Total									**1**			**4**			**1**	***6***
Minas Gerais						12	18	6	**36**	14	3	**17**	1	1	**2**	***55***
Minas Gerais – Borda do Campo								1	**1**	1		**1**				***2***
Minas Gerais – Caeté – Vila Nova da Rainha							2	2	**4**	2		**2**	1		**1**	***7***
Minas Gerais – Carijós								1	**1**							***1***
Minas Gerais – Catas Altas								1	**1**	2		**2**				***3***
Minas Gerais – Congonhas do Campo								2	**2**	4	1	**5**	5		**5**	***12***
Minas Gerais – Congonhas do Sabará							3		**3**	1		**1**				***4***
Minas Gerais – Jacuí													1		**1**	***1***
Minas Gerais – Lançções							1		**1**							***1***

DESIGNAÇÃO	1600-1640	1641-1680	1681-1706	1701-1720	Total	1721-1740	1741-1760	1761-1771	Total	1772-1790	1791-1810	Total	1811-1830	1831-1850	Total	TOTAL
Minas Gerais – Mariana						4	32	12	44	7	3	10	3		3	57
Minas Gerais – Ribeirão do Carmo						4	4		8							8
Minas Gerais – Mariana-Arraial de Antônio Pereira										1		1				1
Minas Gerais – Mariana – Campanha de Rio Verde										2		2				2
Minas Gerais – Mariana – Casa Branca							1		1							1
Minas Gerais – Inficionados							1	2	3							3
Minas Gerais – Mariana – Monsus							1		1							1
Minas Gerais – Mariana – S.Bartolomeu							1		1							1
Minas Gerais – Mariana – Salcelas								1	1							1
Minas Gerais – Mariana – Vila do Príncipe										1		1				1
Minas Gerais – Minas Novas dos Fanados										3		3				3
Minas Gerais – N.ª Sr.ª da Natividade										1		1				2
Minas Gerais – Ouro Branco										2		2	2		2	5
Minas Gerais – Paracatu							2	2		1		1	1		1	4
Minas Gerais – Pitangui											1	1				1
Minas Gerais – Pouso Alto						1	8	1	10	3		3				13
Minas Gerais – Rio das Mortes							1		1		1	1				2
Minas Gerais – Rio das Mortes – Prados (Arraial)						1		1	2	1		1				3
Minas Gerais – Rio das Mortes – S. José								2	2							2
Minas Gerais – Rio das Mortes – S. Ant. da Casa Branca	1		2	1	4		5	2	7	18	3	21	3		3	35
Minas Gerais – S. João d'El Rei													1		1	1
Minas Gerais – S. Pedro do Fanado						3	13	6	22	6	7	13	4	1	5	40
Minas Gerais – Sabará										1		1				1
Minas Gerais – Sabará – N.ª Sr.ª da Encarnação													1		1	1
Minas Gerais – Sabará – S. Miguel de Piracicaba							1		1							1
Minas Gerais – Sabará – Santa Rita							2	2	4							4
Minas Gerais – Santa Bárbara								1	1	2	2	2				3
Minas Gerais – Santa Luzia							4	5	9	2	2	4				13
Minas Gerais – Serro Frio											2	2				2
Minas Gerais – Serro Frio – Vila do Príncipe							1		1							1
Minas Gerais – Sumidoiro										7	2	9				9
Minas Gerais – Tejuco (Arraial de)								1	1							1
Minas Gerais – Vila Boa																
Minas Gerais – Vila Rica de Ouro Preto						7	32	8	47	13	7	20	6		6	73

DESIGNAÇÃO	1600-1640	1641-1680	1681-1700	1701-1720	Total	1721-1740	1741-1760	1761-1771	Total	1772-1790	1791-1810	Total	1811-1830	1831-1850	Total	TOTAL
Minas Gerais – Vila Rica – Guaripiranga							3		3	2		2	1		1	5
Minas Gerais – Vila Rica – Itaberaba																1
Total					4				225			128			32	389
Pará		2			2	3	1	2	3	7	7	14	6	4	10	29
Pará – Belém							2	1	6	1	1	2	5		5	13
Pará – Cachoeira do Rio Arari											1	1	1		1	1
Pará – Monte Alegre					2				9			17			16	44
Paraíba do Norte							1		1	2		2	1		1	4
Paraíba do Norte – Vº Real do Brejo da Areia									1				1		1	4
Total	25	25	26	13	89	36	27	12	75	44	30	74	24	19	43	281
Pernambuco – Alagoa				1	1					1	1	2				3
Pernambuco – Bananeiras													1		1	1
Pernambuco – Barra do Rio Grande													1		1	1
Pernambuco – Campo Largo							1		1	1		1	1		1	3
Pernambuco – Goiana			2	1	3	4			4	1		1	1		1	9
Pernambuco – Olinda							3	1	4	3	1	4	5		5	13
Pernambuco – Recife										1		1	1		1	1
Pernambuco – Serinhém																
Pernambuco – Sertão de					93				84	1	1	83			54	314
Total										1	1	2	1		1	3
Piauí – Oeiras													1		1	1
Piauí – Pernaguá					1							2			2	4
Total													1		1	1
Porto Seguro – Vila Verde do Prado	2	19	50	28	99	143	84	80	307	81	44	125	62	41	103	634
Rio de Janeiro								2	2				2			2
Rio de Janeiro – Cabo Frio											2	2	2	1	3	5
Rio de Janeiro – Campos											4	4	10	7	17	21
Rio de Janeiro – Campos de Goitacazes											1	1				1
Rio de Janeiro – Ilha do Catalão						1			1							1
Rio de Janeiro – Ilha Grande				1	1	2	4	1	7	8	1	9				17
Rio de Janeiro – Paraíba										1		1				1
Rio de Janeiro – Inhomerim																

DESIGNAÇÃO	1600-1640	1641-1680	1681-1700	1701-1720	Total	1721-1740	1741-1760	1761-1771	Total	1772-1790	1791-1810	Total	1811-1830	1831-1850	Total	TOTAL
Rio de Janeiro – Laguna								1	1	1		1				2
Rio de Janeiro – N.ª Sr.ª da Conceição								1	1							1
Rio de Janeiro – Parati											1	1	2		2	3
Rio de Janeiro – Parati – N.ª Sr.ª dos Remédios								1	1							1
Rio de Janeiro – Magé										1	1	2				2
Rio de Janeiro – S. Maria de Maricá										1	1	1	1		1	2
Rio de Janeiro – Vila do Campo								1	1		1	1				2
Total					100				321			148			126	695
Rio Grande do Norte													1		1	1
Rio Grande do Sul									1		1	1	7	2	9	10
Rio Grande do Sul – Pelotas						1								1	1	1
Rio Grande do Sul – Porto Alegre													1		1	1
Rio Grande do Sul – Viamão											1	1				1
Rio Grande do Sul – Vila do Rio Pardo													1		1	1
Total							1		1		1	2		11	11	14
Santa Catarina							1		1		1	1				2
S. Paulo		2	1	1	4	8	10	7	25	15	4	19	6	3	9	57
S. Paulo – Iguaçu						1			1					1	1	1
S. Paulo – Itu											1	1	2		2	3
S. Paulo – Mogimirim														1	1	1
S. Paulo – Paranaguá						1			1				1		1	1
S. Paulo – Santos	1	2	1	1	5	9	8	7	24	1	6	7		1	1	37
S. Paulo – Vila Bela da Princesa													1		1	1
S. Paulo – Vila Nova do Príncipe													1		1	1
Total					9				51			27		16	16	102
Sergipe d'El Rei							1		1				1	2	3	4
Sergipe d'El Rei – Santa Luzia								1	1							1
Total					2				2			2		3	3	5
Não identificados					2				5			2		2	2	11
TOTAL					472				1153			589		538	538	2752

O GOVERNO DA NATUREZA NO PENSAMENTO DA GERAÇÃO UNIVERSITÁRIA DE FINAIS DO SÉCULO XVIII: OS *ESTATUTOS LITERÁRIOS E ECONÓMICOS DA SOCIEDADE DOS MANCEBOS PATRIOTAS DE COIMBRA*[1]

Ana Cristina Araújo
Faculdade de Letras da Universidade de Coimbra
Centro de História da Sociedade e da Cultura (FLUC)
araujo.anacris@sapo.pt

Em nome do bem público

Do espaço indefinido e sem fronteiras linguísticas, religiosas e territoriais da "República das Letras", concebida, no século XVIII, como uma espécie de "Jerusalém Filosófica", brota um novo espírito de cidadania que liga os homens de letras à pátria comum do saber e da filosofia. Na sua vocação apolítica, o patriotismo filosófico das Luzes aprofunda os vínculos de igualdade e de fraternidade no seio das comunidades letradas e académicas. Por força da razão, o *topos* cosmopolita, assimilado ao ideal de cidadania da "República das Letras", dá sentido à fraternidade intelectual, à partilha de conhecimentos e à corresponsabilização de todos na construção do

---

[1] Este trabalho é uma versão revista e aumentada, com apêndice documental, de Araújo 2015.

bem público. É na base de tais princípios que os cultores das letras, os publicistas e os propagadores de conhecimentos úteis pugnam pela aplicação dos progressos realizados no campo das ciências e das artes[2].

Em sentido amplo, o papel do filósofo, comprometido com as questões do seu tempo, é inseparável da crença no poder do conhecimento. O seu quadro de atuação não se dissocia da dimensão secularizadora atribuída à educação, nem tão-pouco do ideal de "felicidade do Estado", segundo as palavras da época. No essencial, o homem de letras do século XVIII alia o imperativo ético da filosofia ao superior interesse do público. O trabalho do filósofo é, portanto, concebido como procura desinteressada da verdade em prol da sociedade, respeitando o carácter cosmopolita do conhecimento e articulando a sua divulgação com o benefício específico do Estado. É na base destes princípios que surgem projetos de carácter utópico como o das sociedades de amigos do bem público, constituídas para a circulação de ideias económicas, divulgação de novas técnicas e realização de obras públicas. Estas associações, forjadas por homens de letras, estimulam a criação de uma espécie de "banco europeu da cultura", composto por repertórios enciclopédicos, catálogos de bibliotecas escolhidas, memórias e periódicos destinados à divulgação popular do conhecimento. Para satisfazer o desígnio de propagação de conhecimentos úteis, surgem os chamados "jornais-biblioteca" que, periodicamente, disponibilizam informação bibliográfica sobre letras, artes, ciências e ofícios. Obedecem a um modelo internacional, circulam por toda a Europa em versões adaptadas ao mercado editorial de cada país, são lidos em várias línguas e dão a conhecer obras e autores de referência. Em Portugal, para além da *Gazeta Literaria*

---

[2] Simões, Ana, Carneiro, Ana, Diogo, Maria Paula 1999: 1-40; Araújo, Ana Cristina 2003. Para uma visão de conjunto, vejam-se, especialmente, Bots, Hans e Waquet, François 1987; Goodman, Dena 1994; Roche, Daniel 1988; Frijhoff, W. 1999: 31-40.

ou *noticia exacta dos principaes escriptos, que modernamente se vão publicando na Europa* (1761-1762) e do *Jornal Enciclopédico dedicado á Rainha Nossa Senhora, e destinado para instrucção geral com a notícia dos novos descobrimentos em todas as Sciencias, e Artes* (1779-1793), várias coletâneas transportam para o espaço público um conjunto amplo de novidades científicas e literárias. Incluem-se neste segmento de leitura, entre outros, a *Miscellanea Curioza e Proveitoza ou compilação tirada das melhores obras das nações estrangeiras* (1779-1785), a *Bibliotheca das Sciencias e Artes* (1793), as *Novidades Literárias, Filosóficas, Scientificas, Poeticas e Mercantis* (1801) e a *Bibliotheca Universal* (1803)[3].

Tais projetos, associados a outros meios de apropriação e vulgarização do conhecimento científico, permitiram que, progressivamente, a perceção do tempo regular e imutável da natureza se inscrevesse na experiência moderna de aceleração da vida social e política e, reciprocamente, que a esperança e o sentido de devir, de matriz cristã, ganhasse foros de evidência empírica, no quadro de uma conceção secularizada e progressiva do tempo e da História[4].

Admitindo que o cosmopolitismo das Luzes não opera, forçosamente, uma disjunção entre o mundo terreno e o mundo da transcendência, Eisenstadt reforça aquela ideia ao colocar a exploração racional das leis 'naturais' no eixo do programa cultural da modernidade, programa, sob muitos aspetos, identificado com a divisa de emancipação do género humano através do conhecimento[5]. Numa perspetiva conjugada, pode dizer-se que a "visão promissória da modernidade" comporta a ilusão de uma prognose redentora da filosofia e da ciência aplicada à ideia eurocêntrica

---

[3] Nunes, Maria de Fátima 2001: 56-71.
[4] Koselleck, Reinhart 2003.
[5] Eisenstadt, S. N. 2007: 25.

de civilização e á crença universal no progresso da humanidade[6]. Neste quadro, o cosmopolitismo setecentista remete para uma ordem física do mundo através da qual se manifesta, idealmente, o espírito da razão universal.

Em termos práticos, o domínio gradual das ciências da natureza foi paulatinamente alterando a forma de pensar a sociedade. A decifração da ordem necessária e imutável da natureza, a observação rigorosa dos seres vivos e das coisas que rodeiam o indivíduo que passa elaborar e a controlar, de forma metódica, procedimentos de organização, exploração, produção e reprodução do mundo físico, contribuíram, decisivamente, para elevar a cotação do trabalho do naturalista na sociedade setecentista. Em Portugal, pela primeira vez, a atividade do naturalista é equiparada a uma profissão distinta, digna de formação superior, nos *Estatutos da Universidade de Coimbra* de 1772[7].

Em geral, os procedimentos, passíveis de replicação, utilizados pelos cultores das ciências da natureza, eram confirmados pela experiência, facto que, em parte, contribuiu para a projeção pública alcançada pela História Natural, tanto nos meios académicos como entre curiosos, colecionadores e letrados. Progressivamente, foi-se impondo a ideia de que o estudo da natureza recreava o espírito e era útil à sociedade, porque a aplicação dos conhecimentos científicos gerava novos recursos económicos e mais riqueza. Deste modo, a História Natural passa a fornecer respostas concretas para os problemas sociais e políticos ligados à produção e à subsistência das populações, contribuindo, ao mesmo tempo, para a recriação de velhos sonhos de abundância. À semelhança de outros conhecimentos instrumentais ligados à exploração do mundo físico, a História

---

[6] Arnason, J. P., Eisenstadt, S. N. e Wittrock, B. 2005.

[7] Os estatutos consagram que a filosofia ensinada na Universidade seja "dividida em três profissões: a saber: na de Naturalistas: na de Medicos: e na de Mathematicos", *Estatutos da Universidade de Coimbra* 1772: Livro III, I, Introdução, 7, 4.

Natural dissemina-se nas sociedades educadas, policiadas e bem governadas. Bem vistas as coisas, estas sociedades aperfeiçoam-se a partir do olhar do naturalista, porque o estádio de desenvolvimento e de civilização passa a ser determinado pelo poder de multiplicação dos seres vivos e de transformação dos recursos naturais, em prol do bem estar coletivo e da felicidade do género humano.

Ministros e conselheiros régios recorrem ao saber dos naturalistas, com vista à apropriação científica do mundo natural e à exploração integrada, à escala intercontinental, dos recursos da terra. Assim o fizeram, de forma consistente, o ministro Martinho de Melo e Castro (1716-1795) e o seu sucessor na pasta da Marinha e Domínios Ultramarinos, D. Rodrigo de Sousa Coutinho (1755-1812). Correlativamente, "a *expertise* relativa ao mundo natural constitui condição de acesso a lugares proeminentes de aconselhamento político"[8] e de ação governativa, conforme comprovam, entre outros exemplos, a nomeação de Domingos Vandelli, professor jubilado da Universidade de Coimbra, para os cargos de diretor do Real Jardim Botânico da Ajuda e de deputado da Real Junta do Comércio, e a designação de outro professor jubilado da Faculdade de Filosofia, José Bonifácio de Andrada e Silva, para a Intendência Geral de Minas e Metais do Reino e direção do Laboratório Químico da Casa da Moeda, em Lisboa.

Em suma, o trabalho dos naturalistas no século XVIII, marcado pela preocupação de controlo do mundo natural, ajuda a conformar a ideia moderna de estado de civilização[9], ao mesmo tempo que fomenta uma atitude de auto-compreensão dos agentes sociais perante o conhecimento que eles próprios produzem ou divulgam, porque, como explicita Emma Spary, "natural historical knowledge was considered a valuable means of sef-improvement because its

---

[8] Cardoso, José Luís 2003:15 e Fonseca, Fernando Taveira da 1997: 1017-1040.
[9] Kury, Lorelay 2001: 24.

very acquisition repeated the steps of self-development judged necessary for the enlightened individual [...] the trajectory of individual confronted with nature mirrored that conceptual shift".[10]

Porém, no plano prático, os valores das Luzes funcionam como fator de distinção, demarcam, em diferentes regiões e latitudes, o modo de pensar do sábio do de outros homens, incapazes de interpretarem, na perspetiva dos filósofos do século, as aspirações de progresso dos povos e os sinais de caducidade histórica da sociedade e do Estado. Assim sendo, e com o objetivo de aproximar a visão do homem e da sociedade da perspetiva utilitária da ciência, o Iluminismo cosmopolita tende a acentuar o sentimento de pertença igualitária a um estado de natureza comum, em que todos os indivíduos nascem livres e iguais entre si. Um tal horizonte de referência cria expectativas de justiça e de realização coletiva nunca antes antevistas, abrindo, em concreto, novas vias de renovação, reforma ou mesmo mudança social. A coberto das doutrinas jus-racionalistas que desaguarão, tarde ou cedo, na aceitação revolucionária dos princípios de liberdade, igualdade e fraternidade, fortalecem-se os argumentos que alimentam o patriotismo cívico moderno, de cariz jurídico-político. Logo, a nova expressão identitária do todo social e político, sendo sucedânea do patriotismo literário e filosófico das Luzes, supunha a adesão voluntária a um universo de valores e aspirações comuns. No respeito por essa renovada matriz racional de enunciar a ligação do indivíduo à comunidade, o sentimento de pertença à pátria cívica passa a assentar em três grandes pilares: a observância da lei, a prática da virtude e o exercício da liberdade, primeiro no estado natural e depois na sociedade civil – ideias primaciais desenvolvidas, mais tarde, do ponto de vista político

---

[10] Spary, Emma C. 1999: 295.

e constitucional, na sociedade portuguesa oitocentista, conforme salientou Fernando Catroga em estudo fundamental sobre o tema[11].

De todo o modo, em finais do século XVIII, já coexistem no léxico corrente duas aceções diferentes de pátria, uma de referente antigo, que remete, literalmente, para a terra de naturalidade dos pais ou dos antepassados, e outra de referente moderno que, recuperando a noção de *patria civitatis* de Cícero, sacraliza, com base nos ideais filosóficos das Luzes, a união de todos e a exemplaridade de cada um, forjando um sentimento de pertença coletivo, de lastro simultaneamente afetivo, voluntário e racional, que clama por liberdade, em nome do interesse público e do bem comum.

Na prática, como veremos a propósito de alguns aspetos relacionados com a vocação expansiva das elites ilustradas portuguesas, o limiar filosófico da modernidade conjugado com o emergente espírito de patriotismo cívico, de base filosófica, acentuou, no plano ideológico, a desconstrução do universo político que tornara possível e credível a aspiração cosmopolita das Luzes, desconstrução que foi ganhando terreno por força de iniciativas públicas promovidas por indivíduos ou associações que, no respeito pelos ideias filantrópicos e patrióticos do século, procuravam interpretar o chamado interesse geral dos povos.

Uma dessas iniciativas públicas que aqui analisamos, desponta, em Portugal, no meio académico, na década de oitenta do século XVIII. Falamos da criação da *Sociedade dos Mancebos Patriotas Estabelecida em Coimbra,* cujos estatutos literários e económicos, mantidos inéditos até aos nossos dias, formam um caderno manuscrito de trinta páginas, cuja folha de rosto apresenta o desenho do emblema da sociedade, envolvido num círculo[12]. Este notável documento corporiza

---

[11] Catroga, Fernando 2013.

[12] ANTT – Real Mesa Censória, n.º 702, *Estatutos Literarios e Economicos da Sociedade de Mancebos Patriotas Estabelecida em Coimbra no anno de 1780 debaixo da Real Protecção de sua Alteza o Serenissimo Senhor Principe do Brazil.* Em anexo

a intencionalidade social e política da primeira leva de estudantes formados na Universidade pombalina, nos cursos de Filosofia e Leis, e reflete, em todos os domínios do conhecimento, o espírito cosmopolita das Luzes.

Como é sabido, no campo jurídico, a reforma Pombalina operou a transposição da "Weltbürger" germânica para o ensino do "Direito natural, público e universal e de Direito das gentes", comum às Faculdades Jurídicas de Leis e Cânones. Esta inovação teórico--doutrinal teve consequências práticas conhecidas, pois é com base na doutrina produzida no âmbito desses cursos que, como salientou António Manuel Hespanha, "se formaram as categorias com que o direito irá lidar até bem depois da revolução liberal"[13]. Paralelamente, a reforma pombalina da Universidade institucionalizou o ensino da ciência moderna, de matriz newtoniana e de carácter experimental, promoveu uma conceção integrada do conhecimento científico e abriu novos horizontes à intervenção cívica, patriótica e política de estudantes e professores.

Ciência e História Natural

Fixemos, então, os traços fortes da cultura pública que emerge do ensino superior das ciências na Universidade de Coimbra, depois de 1772. Em primeiro lugar, saliente-se que as mudanças introduzidas pelos novos estatutos não dizem apenas respeito aos três cursos

---

encontra-se a *Copia de hum memorial entregue ao Illmo S.or Principe do Brazil em Queluz*, sem data. O texto dos *Estatutos* contém poucas anotações, em diferente traço caligráfico, e apresenta, no frontispício, um desenho, para possível gravação do selo/emblema da sociedade, representando uma colina com duas águias em sobrevoo envoltas num círculo. A divisa "sic itur ad astra" (Virgílio, *Eneida,* liv IX, v. 64) inscreve-se, por entre raios solares, nesta representação circular. Saliente-se que a data do documento se encontra rasurada. Na mesma inscrição sobrepõem-se os anos de 1780 e 1786.

[13] Hespanha, António Manuel 2004: 33.

científicos, designados por curso Médico, curso Matemático e curso Filosófico, aos quais correspondiam três Faculdades maiores. O ensino científico e experimental generaliza-se com a lecionação obrigatória da cadeira de Filosofia Natural aos restantes cursos (Leis e Cânones e Teologia). As novas gerações formadas na Universidade teriam assim de habilitar-se, com rigor e método, na *Estrada Real da Experiência*, segundo as palavras do legislador. A pioneira institucionalização do ensino matemático na Universidade de Coimbra, com a criação de uma Faculdade autónoma, iniciativa sem paralelo em outras universidades europeias da época, comportava ainda uma novidade de monta, a exigência estatutária de integração do ensino preparatório da Geometria no sistema de formação de teólogos, juristas e médicos.

À semelhança do que acontecia com o curso de Geometria, frequentado por estudantes *ordinários, voluntários* e *obrigados* – estes últimos com matrícula em outra Faculdade –, também os cursos de História Natural, Física Experimental e Química eram obrigatórios para os estudantes de Medicina, tal como o eram os de Filosofia Natural e Moral para os estudantes de Teologia, Leis e Cânones. E o motivo deste cruzamento de saberes justificava-se, uma vez que, segundo a letra dos estatutos da nova Faculdade, "a Filosofia he a Sciencia Geral do homem, que abraça, e compreende todos os conhecimentos, que a luz da Razão tem alcançado e ha de alcançar em Deos, no Homem e na Natureza"[14].

Como se depreende, a complementaridade científica dos modernos ramos do conhecimento ministrados na Universidade comportava uma mudança de paradigma no método dos estudos, acarretando, também, alterações profundas na conceção dos edifícios das Faculdades, nos equipamentos laboratoriais, na atitude de compromisso à causa pública por parte de professores e estudantes e no

---

[14] *Estatutos da Universidade de Coimbra* 1772, Livro III, I, Introdução, 3, 2.

livre exercício da crítica, despoletada pela assimilação de doutrinas e ideias ensinadas e vulgarizadas no interior do claustro académico[15].

Poucos anos volvidos sobre o lançamento da reforma dos estudos, os estudantes faziam bom uso da crítica, recusando a persistência de costumes académicos obsoletos, a tendência para o ensino de doutrinas enfadonhas e, sobretudo, a falta de liberdade e de tolerância no quotidiano da academia. No prólogo ao poema herói-cómico *O Reino da Estupidez* que circulou, anonimamente, em diferentes versões manuscritas, no início da década de oitenta, salva-se, em parte, a imagem da Faculdade de Filosofia. Aí se afirma que "a reforma trouxe à Universidade as sciencias naturaes, que na verdade tiverão e tem ainda alguns mestres dignos de tal nome; mas que estes ficão tão submergidos pela materialidade dos companheiros, que fazem a maior porção, que para os distinguir he preciso ter a vista bem perspicaz"[16].

Correlativamente, no extenso exame sobre as falhas e as potencialidades do novo modelo de ensino superior público, o reitor reformador, D. Francisco de Lemos, assinala a reduzida frequência dos novos cursos. Declara que, cinco anos volvidos sobre o lançamento da reforma da Universidade, a Faculdade de Filosofia funcionava apenas com quatro alunos ordinários e a Faculdade de Matemática com cinco alunos, também ordinários[17]. A par deste reduzido escol de naturalistas e matemáticos em formação, os alunos obrigados, oriundos de outras Faculdades, constituíam o núcleo estudantil alargado que assistia às aulas e às demonstrações laboratoriais. Esta situação irá persistir, pontualmente agravada, durante o período das

---

[15] Araújo, Ana Cristina 2014.
[16] Albuquerque, Luís de 1975: 76.
[17] Lemos, Francisco de 1980: 85.

Invasões Francesas (1807-1811), pois até 1820 a Faculdade de Filosofia apresenta, em média, 15 matrículas ordinárias por ano[18].

Para colmatar o problema da baixa procura de formação graduada em Filosofia e tornar mais atrativas as escolhas e as saídas profissionais dos filósofos com carta de curso, o reitor reformador, D. Francisco de Lemos, propõe, logo em 1777, que "ninguem possa ser empregado nos empregos para a direcção dos quaes esta Faculdade subministra os princípios e regras, sem ter nella o seu curso, e recebido o grau de bacharel formado. Estes empregos são as Intendências de Agricultura, das Fábricas e Manufacturas; do Ouro e Minas, as Provedorias das Cazas da Moeda, e outros muito similhantes, os quaes todos dependem dos princípios solidos d'esta sciencia"[19].

A par da questão das saídas profissionais, da crítica estudantil e dos programas ensinados na Faculdade de Filosofia, importa ressaltar o alcance prático atribuído ao magistério dos estudos naturalistas e a matriz sistémica que passou a vigorar no ensino da Filosofia e da História Natural, saberes indispensáveis, como veremos, para a formação dos membros da futura sociedade patriótica de Coimbra.

Na linha de Carl von Lineu, Domingos Vandelli, que fora o grande mentor do ensino de Filosofia Natural na Universidade de Coimbra[20], sustentava que "a força e a prosperidade das nações

---

[18] O decréscimo global de população estudantil que se observa na Universidade, entre 1772-1820 afetou, de forma desigual, todas as Faculdades. É de notar também o elevado número de desistências e reprovações, especialmente no curso filosófico. Nesse período, dos "7117 alunos (ordinários e obrigados) apenas 432 conseguiram o grau de bacharel, 108 o de bacharel formado e 32 o de licenciado", Prata, Manuel Alberto Carvalho 1991: 201-202.

[19] Lemos, Francisco de 1980: 106.

[20] Domingos Vandelli (1735-1816), lente de Medicina e Filosofia pela Universidade de Pádua, chegou a Lisboa no ano 1764, para lecionar no recém-fundado Colégio dos Nobres – não havendo qualquer evidência de que o tenha feito. Participou na instalação e organização do Gabinete e Jardim Botânico da Ajuda, para onde regressou como diretor em 1791, cargo que então acumulou com o de deputado da Junta do Comércio, Agricultura, Fábricas e Navegação. De 1772-1791 foi professor de História Natural e Química na Universidade de Coimbra, assegurando também a Intendência do *Laboratório Chimico*, oficina cometida por inerência ao professor da disciplina,

sempre dependeram da ciência da natureza, que ensina os homens a utilidade de cada produção da terra, e que vivifica o comércio e a agricultura, duas fontes de vida dos Estados. Esta ciência anima e promove a indústria; prepara e franqueia novos benefícios; afasta os espíritos dessa funesta turbulência política, dessa ambição fatal, que forja cadeias para os reis e para os povos"[21].

Para Vandelli, tal como para Lineu, a regulação das matérias económicas dependia da acumulação de conhecimento científico. Para ambos, como afirma José Luís Cardoso, a "ideia básica a reter é, por conseguinte, o carácter prático e aplicado do conhecimento alcançado nos diversos ramos da história natural. Daqui decorre a íntima relação entre a ordem natural e a ordem económica, o que conduz à conclusão de que uma não subsiste sem a outra. Isto é, a história natural ficará estéril e inconsequente se não for perspectivada em função das suas aplicações económicas; a economia não logrará atingir estatuto científico se não alicerçada no conhecimento consolidado pela história natural"[22].

Vandelli, que foi correspondente de Carl von Lineu, adotou o sistema de classificação botânica do naturalista sueco e, numa estratégia de valorização científica e de afirmação do seu prestígio pessoal, procurou alargar o leque da nomenclatura lineana, com o inventário e descrição sistemática de novas espécies, conforme atestam as suas obras. Fez escola, foi pioneiro em vários empreendimentos na Corte e na Universidade, lançou as viagens filosóficas ultramarinas e tornou-se um autor de referência no campo da História Natural, em Portugal e no Brasil. No que concerne à Química, cujo curso regeu durante a sua passagem por Coimbra, o seu magistério teve menos

---

a instalação e direção do *Jardim Botânico*, a formação e a organização do grande *Theatro da Natureza*, ou seja, do *Museu* ou *Gabinete de História Natural*.

[21] Vandelli, Domingos 2003: 98.

[22] Vandelli, Domingos 2003: 16. Cardoso, José Luís 2003 e Serrão, José Vicente 1994:13-36.

influência. A sua atuação como diretor do *Laboratorio Chimico* motivou, desde logo, a renúncia do mestre de oficina, Manuel Joaquim Henriques de Paiva[23] e suscitou críticas abertas ou veladas de brilhantes alunos, tais como Vicente José Coelho da Silva Teles, futuro lente da Faculdade e autor dos famosos *Elementos de Chimica* [24] e Gregório José de Seixas que cultivou o enciclopedismo, traduziu as *Tábuas sinópticas da Química* de Fourcroy e se destacou, mais tarde, como intrépido defensor da causa liberal [25].

[23] Manuel Henriques de Paiva reclama ser o autor da "primeira obra chimica que em nossa lingoagem sahe a luz", Prólogo aos *Elementos de Chimica e Farmácia*, Lisboa, Impressão da Real Academia das Sciencias, 1783. Este naturalista e médico, com vasta obra publicada, foi bacharel em Filosofia (1775) e doutor em Medicina (1781). Exerceu a função de mestre de oficina do laboratório químico (1775-1783). Integrou a sociedade de homens de letras que lançou o primeiro *Jornal Enciclopédico* (1779-1791) e foi um dos seus principais redatores. Exerceu o cargo de médico da Real Câmara, deputado da Real Junta do Proto-Medicato e censor Régio da Mesa do Desembargo do Paço. Foi membro da Academia Real das Ciências, de que se afastou em 1787, da Real Academia de Ciências de Estocolmo, da Academia Real de Medicina de Madrid, e da Sociedade Económica de Haarlem. No decurso das Invasões Francesas, foi condenado pela Junta da Inconfidência, em juízo de 24.3.1809, vindo a ser reintegrado nas suas honras e prerrogativas por decreto de D. João, em 1818. Em 1824 ainda ensinava no Colégio Médico-Cirúrgico da Baía.

[24] Vicente José Coelho Seabra da Silva Teles, em anotação crítica ao curso de Química de Vandelli apontou a "maledicência" daqueles que "querem saber tudo, e de tudo querem julgar, mas nada se atrevem a escrever: são muitos os maldizentes, e poucos os críticos", *Elementos de Chimica*,1788: XII. Concluiu o curso de Filosofia em 1786 tendo-se doutorado em 1791, no mesmo ano em que obteve a formatura em Medicina. Foi membro da Academia Real das Ciências de Lisboa e participou nas suas Memórias. Publicou, entre outras obras, os *Elementos de Química; oferecidos à Sociedade Literária do Rio de Janeiro para uso do seu curso de Química*. Coimbra,1788-1790; *Dissertação sobre o calor; oferecido ao Sr. José Bonifácio de Andrada e Silva*. Coimbra,1788; *Memória sobre os prejuízos causados pelas sepulturas dos cadáveres nos templos e métodos de os prevenir*. Lisboa, 1800; *Nomenclatura química portuguesa, francesa e latina; a que se ajusta o sistema de caracteres químicos adoptados a esta nomenclatura por Hassen, Graetz e Adet*. Lisboa, 1801.

[25] Gregório José de Seixas, bacharel em Filosofia (1790) e Medicina (1794) pela Universidade de Coimbra, exerceu a função de demonstrador da cadeira de Metalurgia, instituída na Universidade de Coimbra, em 1801, e regida por José Bonifácio de Andrada e Silva. Nessa qualidade foi destacado ajudante do doutor João António Monteiro no Laboratório Químico da Casa da Moeda, em Lisboa (1803--1822). Durante primeira Invasão Francesa foi implicado no grupo conspirativo que se manifestou a favor de uma outorga constitucional de Napoleão a Portugal. Em 1822 é nomeado provedor da Casa de Moeda. Militou nas hostes liberais e lançou, entre outras obras, um projeto editorial, de pendor enciclopedista, *A Tecnologia do*

Na fase inaugural do lançamento do curso filosófico, as relações do regente da cadeira de Química com o *"operário e demonstrador do Laboratorio Chimico"* não foram as melhores. Sabe-se que Henriques de Paiva acabou por abandonar aquela função, vindo a estabelecer-se em Lisboa, depois de ter sido denunciado à Inquisição de Coimbra em 1779. Mas outras razões terão ditado a formação de dois grupos influentes no seio da Faculdade de Filosofia, o dos seguidores de Vandelli e o grupo dos estudantes e opositores reunidos em torno de Manuel Henriques de Paiva. Importa aqui considerar algumas dessas divergências, pois julgamos que elas estão relacionadas com o aparecimento da sociedade literária e económica, cujo nascimento pretendemos contextualizar e analisar.

A mais remota notícia de um projeto talvez próximo do programa da *Sociedade dos Mancebos Patriotas Estabelecida em Coimbra* surge logo no ano de 1776. De modo lacunar, sinaliza-se, então, a existência de um grupo de estudantes organizado com o objetivo de suportar a edição de uma obra de divulgação científica. Concretizando, a 4 de março de 1776, sob a presidência do doutor José Monteiro da Rocha, a Congregação da Faculdade de Filosofia desaprova e rejeita "huma dissertação sobre a utilidade da Chimica feita por huma sociedade literária pela qual se pedia a aprovação para se imprimir, tendo os censores a que se mandou examinar a dita obra se assentou [sic] uniformemente que não merecia a aprovação da Faculdade por varias cauzas que se exposerão sobre a matéria nesta Congregação"[26].

Após o malogro de 1776 e de acordo com as provas que coligimos, a ideia da constituição de uma sociedade literária e científica volta a dar que falar em 1780. Neste curto intervalo de tempo, foi-

---

Doutor Beckmann, para servir de prelúdio ao Dicionário de Artes e Ofícios, como resumo dos seus respectivos tratados, Lisboa, 1813.

[26] *Actas das Congregações da Faculdade de Filosofia* 1772-1780. 1978: 8.

-se tornando evidente a resistência de Vandelli, tanto a iniciativas de carácter estudantil desligadas da tutela de direção da escola, como a políticas normalizadoras do Estado em relação à sua função intendencial no Laboratório, no Jardim Botânico e no Museu de História Natural.

Desde logo, o lente do curso de Filosofia recusa dar cumprimento a uma ordem régia de 1778, que previa a articulação estreita entre o laboratório e as fábricas nacionais e mandava que na oficina universitária se realizassem "preparações chimicas em grande", ou seja, manipulações de elementos fornecidos pelas indústrias e com interesse comercial[27].

A par do problema apontado, outras questões de fundo subsistem a respeito do funcionamento do *Laboratorio Chimico*[28], cuja ausência de regimento preocupa o reitor reformador, D. Francisco de Lemos, que lamenta a inexistência de regras de funcionamento do laboratório na relação que apresentou ao governo de D. Maria I sobre o Estado Geral da Universidade, em 1777[29].

Entretanto, avança-se na preparação e aprovação das viagens filosóficas no reino e no ultramar. Embora estas não estivessem expressamente previstas nos Estatutos da Faculdade de Filosofia, cabia estatutariamente ao lente do curso filosófico "dar por si mesmo aos seus discípulos exemplo do trabalho, e constancia, que se requerem no Observatório da Natureza"[30].

---

[27] Acrescente-se que a Universidade também rejeitou a reativação, a partir do seu laboratório, de uma fábrica de loiça num edifício que a Universidade possuía junto ao rio Mondego, onde se fizera telha para os novos edifícios. Sobre o assunto, veja-se: Costa, A. M. Amorim da 1987: 353-371.

[28] O *Regimento do Laboratorio e o Regimento do Operario Chymico e Demonstrador* só foram aprovados em Congregação das Faculdades de Filosofia e Medicina, em 1783. Cf. Costa, A. M. Amorim da 2000: 205-207.

[29] Lemos, Francisco de 1980: 146-147.

[30] *Estatutos da Universidade de Coimbra* (1772). Liv. III, P. III, Tit. 3, cap. 4, 254.

Decorrendo daquele princípio, as primeiras expedições universitárias foram aprovadas em Congregação da Faculdade de Filosofia e Matemática, a 2 de junho de 1779. O Conselho de lentes, reconhecendo a vantagem das viagens a realizar por doutores e estudantes, encarregou Vandelli e Dalla Bella de redigirem os respectivos programas e instruções. Ao mesmo tempo, foram nomeados os doutores Joaquim Veloso de Miranda e António José Figueiredo, aos quais se associou, depois, José Álvares Maciel, para dirigirem duas viagens de estudo e exploração às serras da Estrela e do Gerês[31].

Parece ter havido, nesta matéria, convergência de pontos de vista dos membros da Congregação de Faculdade que projetam as viagens filosóficas em estreita articulação com a recém-criada Academia Real das Ciências de Lisboa (1779). Num primeiro momento, a orientação do grupo de Domingos Vandelli e dos seus interlocutores ministeriais centra-se na elaboração de diários dos três reinos da natureza no espaço ultramarino[32].

Vários textos, nomeadamente as *Viagens Filosoficas ou Dissertação Sobre as importantes regras que o Filosofo Naturalista, nas suas peregrinações deve principalmente observar* (1779) de Vandelli, *O Methodo de Fazer Observações* (c.1783) do estudante Agostinho Martins Vidigal e as *Breves Instruções aos Correspondentes da*

---

[31] *Actas das Congregações da Faculdade de Filosofia* (1772-1780). 1978:16. Esta expedição, comunicada por Vandelli a Correia da Serra, vice-presidente da Academia Real das Ciências, é reveladora dos objetivos estratégicos comuns das duas instituições. Curiosamente, *a Gazeta de Lisboa* de 1 de Fevereiro informava o público de que "Os objectos em que a nova Academia deve ocupar-se, são, as Sciencias Fysicas e Mathematicas, e sobre tudo a aplicação destas á Agricultura, ás Artes, e á Industria popular (...) para o que dará principio a huma Bibliotheca e Museo nacional".

[32] Na correspondência trocada com o Visconde de Barbacena e nas missivas aos ministros de D. Maria I, Vandelli defende a colocação dos seus discípulos em missões de exploração de cariz político-geográfico, dirigidas ao espaço colonial português. Sobre o assunto, e com mais remissões bibliográficas, veja-se Brigola, João Carlos (2003). Para uma melhor compreensão do problema, importa também atender ao peso específico dos estudantes universitários brasileiros neste período. Sobre o assunto veja-se o estudo fundamental de Fonseca, Fernando Taveira da 1999: 527-559.

Academia das Sciencias de Lisboa sobre as remessas dos produtos, e notícias pertencentes a Historia da Naturteza, para formar um Museo Nacional, vindas a lume sem autoria, em 1781[33], atestam a rápida propagação da cultura técnico-científica ensinada na Universidade. Portanto, a disponibilidade da teoria para uso político, e a consequente exploração dos recursos da terra com vista à musealização das produções naturais, estava assegurada[34].

A *Gazeta de Lisboa* e, a partir dos anos oitenta, o *Jornal Enciclopédico*, na sua secção denominada "Economia Civil e Rústica", muito contribuíram para conformar os contributos técnicos científicos da cultura académica com as exigências concretas da vida quotidiana e com o crescente interesse pela valorização da produção económica. Esta via de imposição prática do bom governo da natureza remete para a emergência, na esfera pública, de uma corrente de pensamento de pendor enciclopedista, centrada na expansão do campo literário e científico e na captação de novos leitores e destinatários para as notícias, informes, instruções, memórias e traduções de compêndios que se iam publicando[35]. Neste contexto, a afirmação do patriotismo em iniciativas da sociedade civil "ecoa em muitos textos, particularmente naqueles que apresentam propostas de criar sociedades para instrução popular"[36]. Entre outras tomadas de posição, refiram-se os *Discursos Políticos ou Conversação dos Amigos da Pátria*, oferecidos à rainha, e dirigidos a seus ministros e demais homens instruídos a quem se pede "que produzam obras dignas do amor da Pátria"[37].

---

[33] Brigola, João Carlos 2003:177 e ss..

[34] Com enfoque nas missões científicas à escala do império português, Simon, J. William 1983, Domingues, Ângela 1991 e 2012, Raminelli, Ronald 2001: 968-992.

[35] Araújo, Ana Cristina 2003: 51 e ss..

[36] Vaz, Francisco António 2002: 193.

[37] BACL, Série Vermelha, ms. 129.

A ideação do *Estado Polícia*

Em termos doutrinais, os textos científicos e económicos vindos a público e outros que permaneceram inéditos, a maioria dos quais, de estudantes e professores da Universidade e de membros da Academia das Ciências[38], participam do espírito de abertura cosmopolita das Luzes, dando a conhecer o pensamento de autores estrangeiros e nacionais e os resultados de descobertas e de experiências bem sucedidas em outros países europeus. Em termos funcionais, a ação do naturalista tende a confundir-se, cada vez mais, com a do administrador/filósofo. Ambos reclamam a construção do *Estado Polícia*.

O alargamento do campo intelectual às questões emergentes da filosofia que mais diretamente se relacionavam com a *economia da natureza* (Lineu) acabou também por deslocar para a sociedade civil o debate sobre um conjunto diverso de iniciativas e propostas reformistas que pressupunham a tradução de compêndios e livros ligados à corrente cameralista germânica, o mapeamento do território, a elaboração de cadastros, a discussão de projetos de obras públicas que requeriam o apoio do Estado[39] e o lançamento de programas de assistência à pobreza e à mendicidade integrados ou não na ação das poucas sociedades patrióticas que se instituíram em Portugal na segunda metade século XVIII[40].

De facto, o debate de ideias aponta, inequivocamente, nesta direção. Senão vejamos: o modelo do *Compendio de Observaçoens que formão o plano de Viagem Politica e Filosofica que se deve fazer dentro da Patria* (1783) do jurista José António de Sá (1756-1819)[41]

---

[38] *Memórias...*:1987 e 1990/91.

[39] Martins, Carlos Henriques de Moura Rodrigues 2014.

[40] Vaz, Francisco António 2002: 221 e ss..

[41] José António de Sá doutorou-se em leis, em 1782, foi opositor às cadeiras da sua Faculdade e sócio da Academia Real das Ciências (1781). Exerceu a magistratura, tendo ocupado, sucessivamente, os cargos de juiz de fora e corregedor da comarca

– que, como os demais colegas que ingressaram no curso de Leis depois de 1772, frequentara cadeiras de Filosofia – sem pôr em causa a matriz lineana da escola de Coimbra, confere à viagem filosófica a função de harmonização do governo do território, seguindo uma lógica em que o pleno domínio político-administrativo do Estado se articula com o conhecimento técnico-científico dos recursos naturais, demográficos, corográficos e históricos da nação. Por isso, José António de Sá reclama ter sido "o primeiro, entre os portugueses, que apresenta um projeto de viagem, para utilidade da pátria"[42], coligindo observações filosóficas e políticas indispensáveis ao bom governo do reino e ao bem público.

Parte do princípio de que "todo o país que pretende reformar-se deve ser viajado". E defende que o "Estado conheça exactamente o número, forças, natureza, génio, índole dos cidadãos de cada Provincia, para delles poder melhor usar em pública utilidade" e "que saiba quaes são as leis particulares dos povos" para que "possa melhor formar hum perfeito Codigo de Jurisprudencia; pois os costumes, foraes, e privilégios próprios de cada povo constituem huma jurisprudência particular, que limita as leis geraes, e faz huma parte essencial do Codigo Patrio"[43]. Afirma que a "Economia é a sciência que praticamente aplica os produtos naturaes para uso da vida"[44] e apela "ao estudo do governo" para a "dedução dos fieis planos" de reforma da sociedade.

---

de Moncorvo e de desembargador da Relação do Porto. No início do século XIX, foi nomeado Superintendente Geral das Décimas da Corte do Reino e conselheiro da Fazenda, cargos que acumulou com os de juiz conservador da Real Companhia do novo estabelecimento para a criação e torcidos das sedas e de diretor da Fábrica das Sedas e Águas Livres.

[42] Sá, José António de 1783: 5 sn..

[43] Sá, José António de 1783: 3-5 sn..

[44] Sá, José António de 1783: 27. O mesmo autor acrescenta: "A Economia he sempre objecto de adiantamento. Os homens vão cada vez mais achando novas descobertas, com que se augmentão as comodidades da vida" 1783: 28.

É claro que José António de Sá se inspira na ação e na teoria político-administrativa do prussiano Johann Heinrich Gottlob von Justi, cuja obra, *Grundsätze der Polizey-Wissenschaft* (1756), cita a partir de uma tradução francesa. Ao pensamento deste autor associa alguns apontamentos retirados da *Cameralisten Bibliothek* (1752) de Georg Heinrich Zincke. Aliás a ideia de que a lição dos livros devia ser completada com a escola do mundo e com a observação da natureza é retirada de Zincke que afirmava também ser dever do homem político viajar.

A ciência cameral, que na Alemanha constituía um ramo específico de estudo e era ensinada nas Universidades, não apontava apenas para um sistema racional de travejamento jurídico-político do Estado, requeria igualmente, o *"habitus"* do praticante e a racionalidade do decisor. Desta exigência prática decorria, como sublinhou Paolo Napoli, a capacidade política de apreciar circunstâncias, minimizar particularismos e harmonizar diferenças na administração do território e no ordenamento jurídico[45]. O alargamento da esfera de ação da polícia é, portanto, acompanhada por uma mudança fundamental na conceção do exercício do poder político. Neste campo, Foucault ajudou a precisar o lugar central e a alteração de paradigma do modelo policial, mostrando que a polícia contribuiu para a formação de um "saber de Estado", ou seja, para precisar a norma e desenvolver uma tecnologia de poder. A ideia de "governabilidade", correlata deste alargamento da esfera policial, centra-se em aspetos essenciais da vida das populações, contribuindo para a formação de instrumentos concretos de intervenção pública sobre espaços, pessoas e coisas banais[46].

---

[45] Napoli, Paolo 2003: 260-261.

[46] Michel Foucault alarga o seu campo de reflexão, partindo de *Surveiller et Punir* (1975), nos cursos ministrados no Collège de France nos anos de 1976-1980. Trabalha então o conceito de "governabilidade". Cf. Foucault, Michel 1994, 2004 e 2012. Com revisão do tema e mais bibliografia: Denis, Vincent 2013/14: 60-4/4,139-155.

Em suma, a ideia de bem público, lida à luz das preocupações jurídico-administrativas e técnico-filosóficas das Luzes, abre caminho à aceitação da doutrina cameralista de matriz germânica, de que von Justi foi um dos mais influentes teorizadores[47]. Logo, a necessidade de sistematizar, conceptualmente, um conjunto de profissões técnicas essenciais ao fortalecimento do *Estado Polícia* leva à integração social e política das mesmas e ao aperfeiçoamento das leis e dos próprios organismos de governo. De acordo com esta linha de pensamento, José António de Sá publicará, mais tarde, as *Instrucções Geraes para se formar o Cadastro ou mappa arithmetico politico do reino* (1801). Com esta obra demonstrava a necessidade que o homem público tinha de dominar a técnica da administração e, em particular, a estatística, considerada um instrumento indispensável para a boa gestão dos recursos do Estado[48].

Neste movimento, a revisão e codificação das leis gerais do Estado acompanha a diferenciação das funções acometidas ao poder central. A "boa polícia" perde o significado de regime político para se tornar sinónimo de racionalidade e diferenciação funcional do Estado, que investe em novos dispositivos legais e administrativos tendo em vista a ordem pública. Enfim, o conceito de polícia ganha maior complexidade porque o Estado chama a si questões como o bem-estar social, a racionalidade urbanística, a diminuição da pobreza, o aumento da população, a supressão da mendicidade, a segurança pública a normalização fiscal e a saúde pública. Neste quadro, as questões relacionadas com a filantropia e a felicidade dos povos ocupam um lugar central no conjunto de meios criados para assegurar a administração eficiente da justiça e o aumento da riqueza do Estado.

---

[47] Guerrero, Omar 1986.
[48] Sousa, Fernando de 1995: 92.

Entroncam também nesta linha programática, as primeiras diligências tomadas no sentido da uniformização e codificação geral das leis do reino, que datam de 1778, ano em que é constituída uma Junta de ministros incumbida de apresentar o projeto do *Novo Código de Direito Público* (segundo o modelo adotado na Prússia, Áustria e Sardenha). Os resultados alcançados ficaram muito aquém do que fora projetado, ainda que, no plano administrativo, tenham sido tomadas medidas concretas no sentido da redefinição das funções da Intendência Geral de Polícia da Corte e do Reino, criada em 1760, a par de outras iniciativas de reforma do sistema penitenciário e de alargamento da esfera assistencial do Estado, com a criação da Casa Pia, mudanças que ocorrem a partir de 1780 e que coincidem com a nomeação de Pina Manique para o cargo de Intendente Geral da Polícia[49]. As expectativas criadas pelo novo figurino administrativo, legal e disciplinar da Polícia, imposto pelo governo de D. Maria I, desencadeiam, entretanto, outras linhas de intervenção, menos conhecidas mas particularmente interessantes, da parte da sociedade civil.

Assim, a 15 de maio de 1787, a *Gazeta de Lisboa* noticiava a publicação dos *Elementos da Policia Geral de Hum Estado* (1786-1787), traduzidos e adaptados por João Rosado de Vilalobos e Vasconcelos, professor de Retórica em Évora[50]. A obra, segundo aquele jornal, continha "varias notas historicas, e criticas do traductor, adequadas às leis, e costumes de Portugal, obra util a todos os magistrados, ministros, e negociantes, e a todas as pessoas que

---

[49] Abreu, Laurinda 2013: 105 e ss.. Sobre o debate acerca das funções da Polícia que, na mesma altura, ocorre em vários países europeus, veja-se: Denys, Catherine, Marin Brigitte e Milliot, Vincent 2009.

[50] ANTT-Ministério do Reino, livro 550 fl. 2. O assento de João Rosado de Vilalobos e Vasconcelos como professor de Retórica em Évora abrange os anos 1774 a 1785. A menção da profissão do autor consta da folha de rosto da sua última obra publicada postumamente: *Elementos da Policia Geral de hum Estado* 1786-1787.

tiverem algum emprego publico, ou particular, em qualquer genero de administração"⁵¹.

Surgindo na sequência da edição do *Dictionnaire Universel de Police* (1786) de Des Essarts, os *Elementos da Policia Geral de Hum Estado* retomam a ideia de que a "polícia é a ciência de governar os homens e de os tornar sociáveis e felizes". A reflexão proposta nasce da necessidade de um plano de governo assente na simplificação, racionalização e uniformização da legislação, "na ligação das leis de polícia com o tesouro público", na promoção da ordem e da prosperidade pública, tendo em vista a conservação e o aumento da população.

Para "habituar o povo a pensar com espírito patriótico", o obreiro desta "tradução popular" – as palavras são suas – alega ter lido muitos livros sobre o assunto que o convenceram de que "não ha meio mais fácil, do que as instrucções da Policia" "para adoçar o espírito marcial da nação, e temperar o entusiasmo da nobreza, com que se erigio, sustentou e accrescentou a monarchia, para animar a agricultura, e a industria, a navegação, e o comercio, sustentar a paz interior do reino, e fazer mais commoda, e polida a vida dos homens. Destes conhecimentos procedem depois todos os outros, que são populares, e sensíveis, que são úteis e interessantes à sociedade. Eles gerão as idéas patrióticas, crião o espírito nacional em beneficio da utilidade, e honra da pátria [...] e produzem por muitos modos, e meios a felicidade publica de hum Estado"⁵².

Para melhor substanciar a sua reflexão, Vilalobos e Vasconcelos acolhe, entusiasticamente, *La Scienza della Legislazione* (1780-1785) de Filangieri, discute a modernidade política do *Espírito das Leis* (1748)

---

⁵¹ *Gazeta de Lisboa*, n.º XX, 15 de maio de 1787.
⁵² Vasconcelos, João Rosado de Vilalobos e 1786: 1, 9-10 sn.

de Montesquieu[53], aprecia as "circunstâncias de governo" do país e adopta como texto matricial os *Grundsätze der Policey-Wissenschaft* (1756) de Johan Heinrich Gottlob von Justi, que explicita uma filosofia sistemática da ação do Estado, de natureza cameral, assente em dispositivos legais de boa polícia (Staatswissenschaften). Embora não ignore a primeira tradução francesa de 1769, trabalha sobre uma versão posterior, reduzida e adaptada por Fortunato Bartolomeo Felice, *Elements de la Police Général d'un Etat* (1781)[54]. No essencial, acomoda o pensamento de Gottlob von Justi à realidade social portuguesa e sobre ela discorre.

O programa da sociedade económica e de instrução

Deixando de lado outros aspetos de conteúdo muito interessantes desenvolvidos nos dois volumes dos *Elementos da Policia Geral de Hum Estado*, merece aqui reparo a forma como é tratada a questão patriótica. O princípio geral enuncia-se assim:

> "Em qualquer estado que hum homem seja nascido, se elle morre sem ter feito nada para a Sociedade que o protege, elle morre devedor à Patria"[55].

---

[53] "Este ensaio de Policia [...] estava já na imprensa, e muito adiantado, quando me veio á mão huma parte de hum excelente livro, cuja continuação devem todos desejar que apareça com brevidade: he a *Sciencia da Legislação* do cavaleiro Caetano Filangieri [...]. O celebre Montesquieu indagou o espírito das leis, que se tem feito: o filosofo napolitano mostra as razões e as regras daquellas que se deveriam fazer", e prossegue revelando o conteúdo dos dois volumes da obra de Filangieri. Vasconcelos, João Rosado de Vilalobos e 1787: 2, 10 e ss..

[54] Cunha, Alexandre Mendes 2010: vol. 8-1, 1-11.

[55] Vasconcelos, João Rosado de Vilalobos e 1786: 1, 290.

O fim da vida passa a ter um significado adicional para aqueles que ficam, porque a morte acrescenta valor ao cidadão exemplar. A virtude civil sendo sinónimo de mérito individual aplica-se ao cidadão que age em conformidade "com leis boas e justas" e que trabalha "para o bem geral do Estado"[56]. Ora, como "a educação é o meio mais poderoso para fazer bons cidadãos", atribui-se ao Estado a tutela da escola e à lei a função de conformar a união de todas as partes do corpo social, de modo a "acender no coração" de cada homem "as chamas do amor da Patria; fazendo-lhe conhecer em que consiste a verdadeira gloria, e que a sua própria conveniência consiste e he inseparável do bem geral." A tónica identitária e emocional funciona, portanto, como um espelho onde se projeta "o amor racionável [...] e bem dirigido" de cada indivíduo e cujo reflexo, percecionado coletivamente, é considerado o "principio ativo, e a origem fecunda de todas as virtudes sociais"[57].

Segundo este duplo registo, a ação patriótica carece de três caminhos de afirmação conjunta: o primeiro decorre da relação que cada cidadão virtuoso estabelece com o Estado; o segundo revela-se nas obrigações que os cidadãos contraem recíproca e mutuamente, sendo filantropos, responsáveis e solidários; e o último inscreve-se no espírito individual do cidadão, "nas virtudes e obrigações para consigo mesmo"[58], que preparam o seu ânimo para o trabalho e para todo o tipo de sacrifícios cívicos.

Assim formulada, a expressão identitária do patriotismo de Vilalobos e Vasconcelos, desenvolvida na obra que temos vindo a analisar, aflora também em *O Perfeito Pedagogo na Arte de Educar a Mocidade* (1782) e na tradução adaptada do tratado filantrópico

---

[56] Vasconcelos, João Rosado de Vilalobos e 1787: 2, 118.
[57] Vasconcelos, João Rosado de Vilalobos e 1787: 2, 90, 117.
[58] Vasconcelos, João Rosado de Vilalobos e 1787: 2, 119.

de Bernard Ward que o autor português intitulou: *Plano de uma obra pia, geralmente util ao Reino de Portugal, para serviço da Igreja e do Estado* (1782). Tratando-se de uma matéria recorrente nos escritos de Vilalobos e Vasconcelos emerge como assunto central de outro livro que o autor diz ter escrito mas que não chegou a publicar, intitulado: *O Patriotismo Portuguez, explicado nos officios do bom cidadão, para saber excitar os verdadeiros interesses da sua Patria*[59]. A remissão surge no tomo segundo dos *Elementos da Policia Geral de Hum Estado*, que veio a lume, dois anos depois da morte Vilalobos e Vasconcelos[60]. Na verdade, os dois tomos do livro saíram postumamente e o borrão da obra anunciada, que em vão procurámos, nunca chegou a ver a luz do dia. Ao longo da pesquisa fomos percebendo que Vilalobos e Vasconcelos enfrentou vários pareceres de reprovação da censura[61]; beneficiou de uma complexa rede de contactos na Corte, no estrangeiro e no meio livreiro; manteve relações de proximidade com importantes figuras públicas, como Frei Manuel do Cenáculo Vilas Boas, e com outros protagonistas influentes, nem sempre de fácil identificação. Apesar das boas alianças institucionais que cultivou, nem por isso viu concretizado o plano que ideara para o estabelecimento de uma *Sociedade Patriótica* em Évora, cujos estatutos redigiu[62].

---

[59] Vasconcelos, João Rosado de Vilalobos e 1787: 2, 117, nota.

[60] Arquivo Distrital de Évora – *Testamento de João Rosado de VilaLobos e Vasconcelos*, Cx.41, n.º 8. O testamento foi redigido em 23 de Outubro de 1785 e o averbamento que acompanha o seu termo de abertura data de 26 de Outubro de 1785.

[61] A primeira versão do *Perfeito Pedagogo*, com o título *Educação Nacional em que se dão as regras da polícia e urbanidade christam proporcionados aos usos e costumes de Portugal* foi apresentada à Real Mesa Censória, em 1777. De acordo com o parecer dos censores, a obra foi suprimida a 25 de setembro desse ano, ANTT-Real Mesa Censória, caixa. 10, nº 85; para as censuras das obras publicadas em 1782, Real Mesa Censória, caixa 12, nºs 9, 44. Retenha-se a não existência de censura, nos documentos conservados no fundo da Real Mesa Censória, para o livro intitulado: *Elementos da Policia Geral de hum Estado*.

[62] "Em cada capital poderia haver uma Sociedade [...]. Estou tão persuadido deste meio, que propuz a Sua Magestade em 1781 hum Plano desta Sociedade em

A este respeito, retenha-se que a ideia de criação de sociedades patrióticas em todas as províncias do país parece decorrer do modelo espanhol das sociedades económicas "de los amigos del país". Este movimento, que se expandiu a partir do País Basco, com a Sociedade Vascongada (1764), contou com o apoio do ministro Campomanes. Entre outros textos deste ilustrado espanhol que tiveram eco em Portugal, o *Discurso sobre el fomento de la industria popular*[63] define, com clareza, a vocação de tais agremiações, fundadas para a instrução popular, a assistência pública, a difusão de novas técnicas e a promoção das atividades económicas regionais. Com significativo atraso em relação ao que se passava em Espanha, não surpreende que a primeira concretização de um plano congénere para Portugal, como demonstram os Estatutos da *Sociedade Económica dos Bons Compatriotas, Amigos do Bem Publico* de Ponte de Lima (1780), apresente similitudes estatutárias com os objetivos das sociedades "de los amigos del país".

Porém, outras iniciativas europeias associadas à ideia de instrução popular das gentes rurais e ao papel das associações mutualistas na dinamização do tecido produtivo nacional, surgiram na imprensa

---

Evora, e foi approvado a 29 de Janeiro do dito anno, e mandando fazer os seus Estatutos, os fiz, e lhe forão consultados a 17 de Junho do dito anno". Vasconcelos, João Rosado de Vilalobos e 1787: 2, 192, nota. Mais à frente, acrescenta: "Além da Sociedade Patriotica Eborense, que tenho promovido, e que já se acha aprovada por S. Magestade desde 29 de Janeiro de 1782, tenho traduzido alguns livros patrióticos e composto outros relativos a este assunto", 1787: 2, 314. Outras fontes confirmam que a aprovação do plano da Sociedade Patriótica eborense ocorreu na última data mencionada pelo autor, embora não se conheçam todos os seus signatários. Vaz, Francisco António Lourenço 2002: 221-222. Após várias tentativas para localizar os referidos estatutos, acabei por encontrar, sem qualquer notícia prévia, os *Estatutos Literários e Económicos da Sociedade dos Mancebos Patriotas Estabelecida em Coimbra no ano de 1780 debaixo da Real Protecção de sua Alteza o Serenissimo Senhor Principe do Brazil*. Para a pesquisa inicial no Arquivo da Torre do Tombo, contei com a ajuda do Dr. Paulo Tremoceiro, a quem muito agradeço.

[63] Cremos tratar-se da obra que lhe é atribuída: *Discurso sobre el fomento de la industria popular*, Madrid, Imprenta de Antonio Sancha, 1774. Sobre as questões de autoria do texto e os seus ecos em Portugal, veja-se Nunes, Maria de Fátima 2001: 172-173.

portuguesa, vindo a substanciar, do ponto de vista doutrinal, programas de fomento e instrução mais exigentes. Neste capítulo, merecem destaque os textos didáticos e as memórias instrutivas que remetem para a *Sociedade Económica de Berna*, criada em 1766, textos que circularam em Portugal na década de oitenta do século XVIII, como demonstram as traduções e artigos publicados na *Miscellanea Curioza e Proveitoza*, entre 1781 e 1785; as remissões feitas ao sistema associativo e filantrópico de Berna por José António de Sá e Vilalobos e Vasconcelos; o próprio modelo estatutário da *Sociedade dos Mancebos Patriotas Estabelecida em Coimbra no ano de 1780 debaixo da Real Protecção de sua Alteza o Serenissimo Senhor Principe do Brazil*[64]; e a tradução de Francisco Xavier do Rego Aranha dos *Elementos de Agricultura fundados sobre os mais sólidos princípios da razão, e da experiência, para uso das pessoas do campo, que mereceram o premio da Sociedade Economica de Berne em 1774 por Mr. Bertrand*, dada ao prelo, em Lisboa, em 1788.

A conceção deste livro remonta ao tempo de fundação e/ou refundação da *Sociedade dos Mancebos Patriotas de Coimbra*, aceitando como balizas do ciclo de vida desta agremiação a data de 1780 e a rasura de 1786 que constam do texto manuscrito dos seus Estatutos. Conforme explica na dedicatória e na advertência a esta edição Manuel Henrique de Paiva, que dá ao prelo a obra, a tradução daquela memória, cujo autor era pastor protestante e membro da Sociedade de Berna, fora realizada pelo "bacharel F. X. Aranha [...] no tempo, em que estudava jurisprudencia e historia natural na Universidade de Coimbra: e havendo-ma entregado para della fazer o que entendesse,

---

[64] Além das normas estatutárias que respeitam a organização e funcionamento da Sociedade, pretende-se que: "Para maior adiantamento [...] se tenha uma exacta licção de todos os papéis periódicos de Economia que sahirem, por exemplo os que publica a Sociedade de Berne e sahem em Estocolmo", ANTT- Real Mesa Censória, nº 702, *Estatutos Literários e Económicos da Sociedade ...*, fl. 27.

assentei comigo que faria grande utilidade ao Publico, publicando-a com algumas notas, que aclarassem a matéria".

Na verdade, havendo total concordância de objetivos, verifica-se que no centro das duas iniciativas está Manuel Henriques de Paiva, o bacharel formado em Filosofia que, como atrás referimos, se incompatibilizou com o lente Domingos Vandelli. No tempo em que aquele exercia o cargo de demonstrador do Laboratório Químico e, cumulativamente, cursava Medicina, promoveu em sua casa algumas reuniões de estudantes e académicos com o intuito de fundar uma sociedade promotora do bem público, que ficou conhecida como a *Sociedade dos Mancebos Patriotas*. As traves mestras da ação do grupo passavam pela divulgação da ciência, por meio de memórias redigidas pelos sócios e traduções, e pela instrução técnica das chamadas classes industriosas.

Em 1779, o grupo inicial de sócios é conhecido e denunciado à Inquisição no processo instaurado a Manuel Henriques de Paiva, acusado de "libertino" e de dirigir um "conciliábulo" de jovens estudantes de Leis, Medicina, Filosofa e Matemática de "depravados costumes" e de "erróneas" doutrinas[65]. Do grupo de estudantes denunciados faziam parte: Vicente Júlio Fernandes, António Caetano de Freitas, Francisco José de Almeida, os irmãos Diogo e Justiniano de Morais Calado e Nuno de Freitas. Nele também se incluíam, com grande probabilidade, alunos matriculados na Universidade de Coimbra naturais do Brasil como António de Moraes Silva, Alexandre Rodrigues Ferreira, António Pereira de Sousa Caldas, Miguel de Alvarenga Braga e Francisco de Melo Franco. Muitos destes jovens conseguem escapar à primeira leva de denúncias, em 1779, outros

---

[65] ANTT – Inquisição de Lisboa, Processo nº 13369. Parece não merecer dúvida que estamos perante um grupo estudantes bem diferente daquele que Vandelli procurava atrair e conquistar para os seus projetos, conforme revela em carta dirigida ao Visconde de Barbacena, datada de 22 de Outubro de 1781, cit. in Aires, Cristóvão 1927: 200.

acabaram julgados e sentenciados, em agosto de 1781, acusados de serem "hereges, naturalistas, deístas e blasfemos"[66].

Em 1781, a *Gazeta de Lisboa* dava também conta do afã e do redobrado trabalho voluntário de alguns membros da Academia, publicando esta breve notícia: "He de admirar que huns sujeitos carregados com o trabalho da Universidade se privem dos recreios, furtem o tempo ao sono e cheguem a empregar os mesmos dias, que justamente são dados para a refeição do corpo, em tão continuas applicações, chegando a contribuir com as próprias mezadas para as despezas da Sociedade"[67].

A esta possível identificação do núcleo dirigente da *Sociedade dos Mancebos Patriotas*, acrescem outros nomes conhecidos como: Francisco Xavier do Rego Aranha, António Rodrigues de Oliveira e Francisco Rodrigues de Oliveira, distinguidos por Manuel Henriques de Paiva, como bons patriotas[68]. Finalmente, não excluímos que uns poucos opositores e professores da Universidade tenham aderido ao projeto da Sociedade, nomeadamente o professor Miguel Franzini, lente da Faculdade de Matemática e mestre do príncipe D. José e do infante D. João desde 1777[69]. A mediação entre os homens da Academia, em Coimbra, e o príncipe, na Corte, parece ter sido assegurada por Miguel Franzini.

No memorial que acompanha os *Estatutos Literários e Económicos da Sociedade*, refere-se que, sob a direção do mesmo mestre, Miguel Franzini, todos são condiscípulos, o príncipe iluminado e protetor e os "mancebos estudiosos, filhos da Universidade, aplicados às Sciencias da Natureza, e que para o futuro jurarão prestar à Pátria

---

[66] Ramos, Luís Oliveira 2001: 311-326.
[67] *Gazeta de Lisboa*, 21 de Abril de 1781.
[68] Dedicatória à obra de Aranha, Francisco Xavier do Rego 1788.
[69] Ferro, João Pedro 1989: 63.

os esforços de todos os seus talentos"[70]. A divisa inscrita no selo da sociedade, extraída de Vergílio (*Eneida,* liv IX, v. 64) – "sic itur ad astra" –, repete aquela ideia ao conferir a todos os patriotas, sem distinção, o direito à imortalidade terrena.

Em síntese, pretendia-se que a Sociedade fosse "uma Escola Económica", conforme afirmam os seus promotores[71], capaz de suprir, com o ensino da disciplina, cultivada e praticada em articulação com a História Natural, uma falha curricular patente nos Estatutos da Universidade de 1772. Nessa medida ela seria um elemento de mobilização dos estudantes universitários, um instrumento de progresso local e um meio de governo esclarecido do povo. Em nome da causa pública, o papel atribuído à instrução popular e o apelo lançado a todos os possíveis benfeitores apontavam para uma sociedade civil mais igualitária, responsável e livre que, tarde ou cedo, acabaria por clamar por mudanças efetivas no conceito de cidadania e na forma de conceber a governação política.

---

[70] ANTT – Real Mesa Censória, n.º 702, *Copia do hum memorial entregue ao Sereníssimo Senhor Príncipe do Brazil em Queluz*, fl. 2 sn.

[71] ANTT – Real Mesa Censória, n.º 702, *Estatutos Literários e Económicos da Sociedade ...*, fl. 13.

ANEXOS DOCUMENTAIS[72]

ANEXO I

ESTATUTOS LITERARIOS E ECONOMICOS
Da Sociedade dos Mancebos Patriotas estabelecida em Coimbra no anno de *1780* [1786] *debaixo da Real Protecção de Sua Alteza o Serenissimo Senhor Principe do Brazil.*

[desenho circular com a inscrição: *Sic itur Ad Astra. Conimbricae* 1780 (1786)]

Lisboa, na Real Officina Typographca MDCCLXXX(VI)

Ao Muito Alto e Muito Poderoso Principe O Senhor D. José. Pela Sagrada obrigação de Vassalos, Pela uniformidade de zelo e amor da Patria, Pela felicissima razão dos mesmos Estudos e Mestre, Recorrem e suplicão a Sua Real Protecção.
Os sócios da Sociedade dos Mancebos Patriotas.

(a) Eu vos prometto filha que vejais
Esquecerem-se os Gregos e os Romanos
Pelos illustres feitos que esta gente
Hade fazer (b) em tenra mocidade
Em quem[73] o pais * (c) conhece (d) seu traslado

---

[72] Os dois documentos que reproduzimos foram localizados em ANTT – Real Mesa Censória, n° 702. Na transcrição dos documentos originais respeitámos a grafia, desdobrámos as abreviaturas e mantivemos a pontuação.

[73] *Alude à Real Academia das Sciencias de Lisboa
(a) Camões *Lusiadas* canto 2 – 44; (b) canto 3 – 27; (c) canto 3 – 49; (d) canto 3 – 27.

Que do Mundo os mais fortes igualava
Que de tal pais tal filho se esperava

Estatutos Literarios e Economicos dos Mancebos Patriotas
Sic itur ad Astra

1

Os Estados e as Nações todas sendo, como he evidente, nutridas pela Industria, Artes e Sciencias, devem reconhecer que o estudo destas lhes he tão indispensavel, como o são as mesmas suas producções quanto alimentão: desta verdade excitados alguns estudiosos bons cidadãos, a quem o amor da Patria deve o maior disvelo, procurão e determinão enterter em Coimbra esta sociedade, pelo meio da qual todos os seus socios enriquecendo a propria instrucção, promovão o adiantamento das Sciencias Naturaes e da Industria. Estes fins lhe derão o nome de Sociedade dos Mancebos Patriotas.

2

Mas sendo a Natureza nos seus trez Reinos o vastissimo campo e objecto das mesmas Sciencias, Artes e Industria e sendo a repetida experiencia polida por uma prudente e exacta observação a chave unica que [Fl.2] pode abrir as portas da mesma Natureza as mais recônditas, e a obriga a declarar as verdades e produzir os fructos que por si não quer sempre dar, serão Observações e Experiências as fieis guias que encaminhem a esta Sociedade para as suas descobertas.

3

Sobre por que a Natureza em geral envolve Sciencias tão vastas e dilatadas que não podem dignamente cultivar-se senão forem repartidas em differentes classes, destinando para cada uma dellas outras corporações que se empreguem com mais seria applicação no seu respectivo e particular fim, será o objecto geral dos trabalhos da Sociedade, dividida em quarto classes ou divisões: a primeira de Historia Natural em que entra a Chimica, a segunda de Agricultura, (a) terceira a das Manufacturas e (a) quarta de Economia e Comercio.

4

Logo serão tãobem os seus socios divididos em quatro corporações: a primeira de Naturalistas, a segunda de Agricultores, a terceira de Artistas, a quarta de Comercio [Fl.3] compreendendo cada huma sete socios effectivos assistentes em Coimbra, dos quais serão quatro practicos hum para cada classe. O practico da Historia Natural será desenhador.

5

Os socios Naturalistas destinados a indagar todas as producções da Natureza, ainda as mais triviaes pertencentes aos trez Reinos: Mineral, Vegetal e Animal em que ela se divide e que fazem o objecto da Historia Natural, reduzirão todo o seu cuidado e attenção:

1.º A estudar e aprofundar quanto lhes for possível, sem se obcecarem com a auctoridade de algum sistema a História Natural em geral e a Chimica em particular, para poderem entrar no Mundo sensivel pelo grande livro da mesma Natureza que consiste nas verdades de facto havidas pela certa e verdadeira observação junta com as experiencias tiradas da Sciencia da Chimica, e depois disto

2.º A examinar o sitio e altura dos lugares, as direcções, depressões, aberturas, conexões e alturas dos montes que existem na superfície da terra: [Fl.4] a investigar a índole dos bancos ou camadas que firmão os mesmos montes, o que constitui a Topographia do lugar.

3.º A medir as direcções, angulos, comprimentos, alturas das veias Metallicas e dos bancos, as concavidades, fundo, caminhos e bocas de minas que constitui a Geometria subterranea.

4.º A indicar os differentes meios e machinas ategora inventadas, tanto de agua como de ar para arrancar e separar as pedras e as minas do monte, o que faz a Metallurgia Mechanica.

5.º A descrever e delinear a Architectura das casas e habitações dos povos, seus costumes, os seus vestidos, os ritos particulares, as inscripções antigas e modernas, que se acharem, as sepulturas, as ruinas e tudo quanto houver de notavel.

6.º A recolher todas as minas de Portugal e suas conquistas, e sobre ellas fazer os ensaios convenientes para se saber a natureza e quantidade do metal que contem: e despois examinarem os socios das outras classes se será ou não conveniente [Fl.5] a sua extracção e todo o exame se faça no Laboratorio da Sociedade e o cuidado delle pertencerá a esta classe e especialmente ao Director com subordinação a toda a Sociedade.

7.º A recolher, preparar e embalçamar qualquer producção pertencente aos trez Reinos da Natureza, para se guardar no Gabinete da Sociedade, e colocar nelle os productos pella ordem que ella julgar mais adequada; estando o cuidado e asseio delle, como se disse, do Laboratorio, ao cargo dos naturalistas e Director.

8.º A descrever finalmente todas as producções naturaes que se acharem ou nas Províncias de Portugal ou nas suas conquistas, notando o lugar de sua habitação, o nome trivial, e mostrando as propriedades observadas em todas as referidas producções, advertindo porem que se a producção estiver já descrita por algum Naturalista, bastará notar o sitio donde se colligio, o seu nome trivial, e uso que della fazem.

6

Os socios Agricultores destinados a promover [Fl.6] a cultura das terras, e força-las para nos subministrar todas as delicias e riquezas de que ella for capaz, cuidarão:

1.º Em instruir-se profundamente na sciencia geral da Agricultura e na arte Veterinaria ou Medicina dos Animaes para poderem entrar na Agricultura particular de Portugal.

2.º Examinarão o estado della, a causa dos seus progressos, ou da sua decadencia, os obstaculos assim fysicos como moraes que podem retarda-la, e os meios que ha para remedia-los.

3.º Examinarão os instrumentos de que usão os nossos Agricultores nas diversas comarcas, e compararão o efeito delles com o de outras Nações, para conhecerem as vantagens de huns sobre outros.

4.º Como tao bem os generos de terras que se achão em cada Provincia fazendo experiencias sobre a maneira de as tornar ferteis já com a mistura de outras terras, já dos estrumes.

5.º Saberão dos mesmos lavradores o modo, o tempo e como elles colhem, guardão, semêão, [Fl.7] plantão e recolhem as suas producções.

6.º Compararão este methodo com o de outros paizes e sobre ambos farão experiencias para se conhecerem as avantagens de hum e outro.

7.º Cuidarão em promover e propagar a cultura de algumas producções que espontaneamente nascem entre nós como, por exemplo, a resina dos tintureiros, o lirio, o anil, o [?], a cochonilha etc. e que pela arte se podem obter com mais facilidade e elegancia.

8.º Multiplicarão entre nós algumas outras producções estrangeiras de que a Nação pode obter utilidade e que facilmente se criam nas diferentes Províncias de Portugal, inculcando o parallelismo do clima e do terreno, donde e para onde serão transplantadas.

9.º Terão em vista a grande utilidade que tira o Estado da cultura das matas, já para a construção dos navios, já para a dos edifícios, procurando examinar os terrenos próprios para sua plantação ou conservação e o comodo para a condução das madeiras.

[Fl.8] 10.º Indagarão as doenças a que são sogeitos os gados no nosso Reino, as suas causas e os remédios que empiricamente lhes aplicam e o effeito que delles reste.

11.º Cuidarão em descrever medicamente as sobreditas doenças com os seus signaes caractheristicos, e examinando as causas indicarão os meios com que se previnem e curam semelhantes enfermidades naquelas Nações em que deveras se cuida neste objecto: para o que he necessario que hum ou dois socios Agricultores sejam Medicos.

12.º Terão outrosim em vista a grande necessidade que ha de promover a construção dos prados artificiaes e naturaes, como tãobem dos pastos, sem a qual não se pode augmentar a Agricultura Pecoaria, e indicarão todos os meios de multiplicar os gados de maneira que as sua producções sejam as mais elegantes, e finalmente sobre todos estes objectos se farão Memorias, que a Sociedade publicará.

7

Os socios Artistas destinados a tractar das [Fl.9] diversas artes sobre objectos pertencentes aos trez reinos da Natureza reduzirão a sua atenção:

1.º A instruir-se nas Artes em geral, em particular daquellas, que mais influem no sistema Economico e que preparão as materias de primeira necessidade.

2.º Averiguarão as diversas Artes e Manufacturas que em todos os tempos tem havido em Portugal e suas conquistas, e as que se forem estabelecendo cuidando muito em saber como e quando se fundarão e os progressos que fizerão.

3.º Indagarão as causas fysicas e moraes porque humas se augmentaram e augmentam e outras descahiram, ou não subsistem, indicando os meios de remover os obstaculos que tem impedido fazerem maior progresso.

4.º Examinarão as Manufacturas e Artes de que mais a Nação carece, e as comarcas que são mais próprias para ellas, indicando para isso as que se devem estabelecer nesta ou naquella comarca [FL.10] os meios de funda-las ou promove-las, descrevendo as machinas conducentes para simplificar o trabalho das Manufacturas em que se poupa hum grande numero de operarios.

5.º Farão experiencias em cada huma dellas a fim de facilitar a sua practica ou adoptar a de outras Nações, ou no Laboratorio da Sociedade, ou na casa destinada ao trabalho deste genero.

6.º Farão em cada huma dellas Memorias que a Sociedade deve publicar.

8

Os sócios Comerciantes não devem empregar-se em dar Leis á escripturação Mercantil, ou qualquer outra practica do comercio, mas sim a aplicar o fomento á industria do povo, porque descobrindo já novos géneros, já arguindo-o da sua indolência, possão criar nelle o espirito traficante do presente seculo: para o que

1.º Deverão instruir-se nas Leys da Economia e nas do Comercio.

[Fl.11] 2.º Por si mesmos farão exames, quanto for possível exactos, do trafico de cada Provincia ou de cada povo, procurando saber das Alfandegas os generos importados e exportados, quer estas sejão dos portos, quer estejão nas raias.

3.º Com a maior applicação procurarão saber todas as causas da ruina do nosso comercio interno e nacional e reduzir a Memorias os seus passos retrogados, por exemplo a causa porque as Feiras de Portugal tem hido sensivelmente a cahir já em menor concorrencia, já em pobreza de generos: e juntamente da diminuição das bestas de frete para o transporte; se talvez os maus caminhos, se outras razões poderão oppor-se a que não continuassem ao menos na sua conservação.

4.º Procurarão calcular o numero dos navios com a sua tripolação e carga e o das pequenas embarcações como hiates e ainda os barcos de pescaria.

5.º Daqui vem a necessidade de observar e reduzir a compendio as causas da decadência da nossa navegação em certos portos como no de Vianna do Minho, etc.

[Fl.12] 6.º Os motivos porque sendo a situação deste Reino a mais propria para a pesca he ella desanimada, *v. g.* porque a Companhia do pescado do Algarve não tirou as consequências/ vantagens que justamente esperava.

7.º Deverão reduzir a cálculos e taboas os exames que os socios das outras faculdades houverem concluido, mostrando com a evidencia de que he capaz a Arithmetica as vantagens que tira a Nação deste ou daquelle estabelecimento; seja da Agricultura ou Fabricas; e dissolver as dificuldades que se offerecem ao principio, quando em concorrência com as fazendas e producções estrangeiras, as nossa são ou menos elegantes ou mais caras.

8.º E finalmente farão papeis volantes e periodicos sobre este ou aquele objecto, até que se possão hum dia juntar todos, e construir hum sistema completo dos interesses dos Portuguezes, e taboas Economicas igualmente exactas que utilíssimas.

9

Ainda que os socios sejão repartidos em diferentes corporações, e que cada huma dellas deva empregar-se com maior [Fl.13] attenção no seu respectivo objecto, não ficarão por isso excluidos de trabalharem noutros, antes será muito louvável que elles estendão as suas vistas a mais, contanto que não fiquem por isso mesmo com superficiaes conhecimentos de todas as materias, e de nenhuma profundas: portanto todos os socios effectivos devem cada anno dar huma Memoria, escolhida a seu arbítrio, nas materias que a Sociedade examina e trabalha.

10

E porque esta Sociedade he ao mesmo tempo huma Escola Economica aonde os Socios ensinão-se mutuamente e cuja licção he para o futuro do maior enteresse, a Sociedade admettirá de novo somente estudantes das seis Faculdades, e só aquelles em que alem das virtudes moraes necessárias a toda a Congregação, concorra o conhecimento de qualquer das materias do objecto da sociedade, acompanhado de genio, disposição e gosto para os estudos, exceptuando, como ficou dito, os quatro sócios practicos, que ordinariamente não serão estudantes. Mas porque pode haver alguma pessoa de letras, que ainda que não siga os estudos da Universidade, conhecendo a suma utilidade das assembleias, conferencias, licções procure entrar no numero dos socios, haverá quatro lugares, hum em cada [Fl.14] classe para esta sorte de sogeitos que com tão louvável zelo procurarão alistar-se à sociedade. Todos são effectivos e são como todos iguaes.

11

E serão admittidos como socios honorarios aquellas pessoas cujas qualidades e empregos as embaracem a trabalhar nos estudos já ditos; mas que levados do amor da Patria queirão concorrer para a subsistencia desta Sociedade com as contribuições que lhes parecer, ou ainda voluntariamente queirão facilitar algumas composições em qualquer genero de doutrinas. O numero he indeterminado.

12

E até a Sociedade admittirá ás suas assembleias alguns estudantes que pelo seu procedimento e zelo pelas Sciencias derem esperança de grandes progressos; porem que pelas actuaes occupações ou falta de maiores conhecimentos não possão applicar-se ao trabalho destribuido pela sociedade. Estes serão até ao numero de oito e deverão cursar ao menos a aula de Historia Natural. Não serão obrigados a contribuir com pensões em dinheiro, e serão chamados sócios extranumerários, que passarão a effectivos, quando em concorrência de quaisquer outros que o não tiverem sido, se lhes reconhecerem iguais [Fl.15] conhecimentos ou estudos superiores, contudo no segundo anno farão huma Memoria no ponto que cada hum escolher, contanto que entre nos que a Sociedade trate.

13

E porque a ordem das corporações pede que haja para a sua subsistência, hum chefe ou cabeça que os reja, haverá em cada huma das sobreditas classes hum Director que terá a seu cargo:

1.º Procurar com a maior vigilância e cuidado os progressos da sua respectiva classe.

2.º Dirigir e ensinar a cada hum dos Socios da sua repartição os meios mais faceis de alcançar o fim a que se propoem.

3.º Requerer na mesma Sociedade tudo aquillo que for util para o melhoramento della em particular o da classe que lhe pertencer.

4.º Referir nas assembleias ou por escripto todas as noticias literarias que tiver adquirido por meio do seu estudo e reflexão, as que poderem contribuir para o bem e progresso da Sociedade.

[Fl.16] 5.º Cuidar com muito zelo em que os estatutos se observem exactamente e arguir contra a falta da sua observancia perante toda a Sociedade.

14

O Director será sempre hum dos socios effectivos mais sabio da sua respectiva classe, e que tenha dado a conhecer o seu bom gosto no estudo da sua repartição por meio do bom uso que nella houver feito. A tudo isto, alem da constancia de animo e promptidão de espirito ajuntará hum juízo maduro e solido.

15

Sendo manifesto que nas corporações literarias ocorrem cada dia cousas que se devem notar, escrever e conservar, haverá na Sociedade hum Secretario e hum Vice-secretario, o qual primeiro, e nas suas faltas o segundo, será obrigado:

1.º A escrever substancialmente tudo o que se propozer agitar, examinar e resolver na Sociedade.

2.º A registar os escriptos ou Memorias que se lerem no dia da assembleia pela ordem da leitura.

[Fl.17] 3.º A expedir todos os papeis, ordens ou cartas que pela Sociedade forem mandadas expedir.

4.º A comunicar aos socios qualquer resolução escripta ou Memoria que estiver na sua mão e de que o dito socio tenha necessidade.

5.º A guardar todos e quaisquer papeis, Memorias que se lerem na assembleia e copiar os manuscriptos que os socios correspondentes remetterem à Sociedade, facilitando só a copia, ou manda-la fazer do dinheiro do cofre.

6.º A dar no fim de cada anno hum extracto de tudo o que se passou nas assembleias, e do que tiver no seu registo, ou huma historia sucinta em que estejão resumidos e substanciados os factos e providencias que forem de alguma importancia, e notado fiel e exactamente o estado actual da Sociedade e do seu estabelecimento.

16

O Secretario deverá ser hum socio de qualquer das classes dos mais sábios e eruditos, e que escreva com pureza, elegância e expedição na lingua portugueza.

17

[Fl.18] E porque a Sociedade hade fazer algumas despezas, estas as fará ou do dinheiro havido dos socios adiante declarados, ou de algum outro que ella adquirir, e que deve estar guardado; haverá na sociedade hum cofre com trez chaves, das quais huma guardará o presidente, outra o Secretario, e a terceira hum socio que for o depositário, este terá a seu cargo:

1.º Receber dos socios as contribuições ordinarias, ou outro qualquer dinheiro que entrar para a Sociedade e estas carregar em hum livro.

2.º Fazer as despezas necessárias, e que a Sociedade determinar, as quais notará no livro proprio das sahidas.

3.º Dar conta de trez em trez mezes do dinheiro que tiver em seu poder, e da despezas que houver feito.

4.º Tomar entrega e guardar todos os livros scientificos que a Sociedade possuir e os aparelhos e simplices que no Laboratório houver.

18

O depositario deverá ser hum socio das classes dos mais desocupados e que assista todo o anno em Coimbra, e tenha conhecimento bastante do modo de arrumar os livros mercantis, a que chamam partidas dobradas, a isto [Fl.19] ajuntará alem da verdade e abonação hum sufficiente conhecimento dos preços dos generos.

19

Como por huma parte a mesma Sociedade se propoem a examinar o estado particular das cousas em cada Provincia ou Comarca para haver de lhe applicar os remedios, e porque por outra parte os socios effectivos de cada classe se demorão a maior parte do anno em Coimbra, e consequentemente não podem examinar de perto e com a devida exacção o que lhes parecer necessario, haverá na Sociedade os socios correspondentes assistentes na diversas Comarcas e Provincias de Portugal e suas conquistas, os quais terão ao seu cuidado:

1.º Examinar o estado particular da Agricultura, Artes e Comercio das terras de sua residencia

2.º Comunicar ao Director da respectiva classe o que tiver observado para este o propor á Sociedade

3.º Recolher, preparar, embalsamar e remetter á Sociedade todas as produções ou da Natureza ou da Arte que houver na sua residência

4.º Remeter huma cópia de algum manuscripto [Fl.20] interessante ou facilita-lo ao secretário

20

E porque a Sociedade além dos Directores particulares necessita de hum Intendente Geral, a quem pertença a direcção de todas as corporações, haverá nella um Prezidente o qual terá o primeiro lugar e voto, e em sua falta julgarão os Directores, e além das obrigações a que estes estão sogeitos terá demais a seu cuidado:

1.º Vigiar perpetua e incessantemente sobre a observancia dos Estatutos, e procurar cada vez mais o estudo da sociedade em geral.

2.º Fazer cessar todos e quaisquer abusos e relaxações que tenham começado a introduzir-se contra a disposição dos mesmos Estatutos.

3.º Vigiar exactamente que nas occasiões em que alguns dos socios forem de opiniões encontradas não empreguem algum termo de desprezo, ou seja nos discursos, ou seja nos escriptos, e que quando combaterem os sentimentos de alguns sabios, o fação sempre com respeito para o que não [Fl.21] se procederá já a votos sobre qualquer matéria sem que o dito Presidente o mande, ou seja resolução de toda a Sociedade ou advertência oferecida por algum socio.

4.º Enterter algum comercio literario com os diversos sabios estrangeiros afim de ser promptamente informado do que houver de curioso relativamente aos objectos da Sociedade.

21

O Presidente deverá sempre ser hum dos socios de qualquer das classes que alem de possuir as qualidades dos Directores tenha conhecimentos mais amplos em quasi todas as classes.

22

Logo a Sociedade se comporá de vinte oito socios de honorários, oito extraordinarios, e correspondentes. Dos primeiros se escolherão o Presidente, os Directores, hum Secretario, hum Vice-secretario, hum Depositario cuja eleição será abaixo declarada, n.º 24.

23

O Presidente, Secretario e Directores conferirão [Fl.22] mutuamente o merecimento de algum que quiserem eleger para socio, despois propo-lo-hão em huma assembleia sem dizer mais que o nome, para que todos os socios se informem das suas qualidades. Na seguinte proceder-se-ha por escrutinio no voto de todos os socios presentes, bastando cinco em contrario para a sua insufficiencia e não tornara a propor-se nesse anno. O mesmo se fará com os extranumerarios e correspondentes com a excepção de que a respeito destes bastará huma honrosa informação de algum socio effectivo que delle tiver particular conhecimento que afiance o seu credito, para merecer que os votos lhe sejão favoraveis.

24

Porquanto todos os cargos devem ser annuais, e quando muito permittir-se-há a sua reeleição até o terceiro anno, quando a Sociedade entender que tanto lhe enteressa, na penultima sessão de Maio em que se devem eleger dous socios effectivos aquelles que no anno seguinte se hão-de encarregar dos empregos da Sociedade, o Secretario dará a cada hum dos socios os nomes de todos, e correndo-se o escrutinio, cada [Fl.23] um delles lançará o nome que lhe parecer, decidindo a pluralidade dos votos daquele a quem se deve confiar o emprego.

25

O novo socio será avizado em carta pelo Secretario da sua eleição, e sem outra resposta na primeira assembleia fará huma brevissima oração em prova da aceitação e agradecimento á Sociedade: e o Secretario lhe entregara um diploma em titulo de ser Membro della. Os correspondentes que morarem fora de Coimbra o farão por carta.

26

As assembleias reunirão precisamente o tempo que for necessário, e não se tratará nellas cousa que não pertença á Sociedade. O seu objecto he a conferencia das materias Scientificas e Economicas, o lerem-se as Memorias, e proporem-se pontos para ellas, posto que qualquer socio possa trabalhar á sua escolha e arbítrio.

27

E por fim as assembleias nunca serão de menos de duas horas, sempre principiarão com a leitura de [Fl.24] algum livro antes escolhido, que trate da materia que á sessão pertencer. Porquanto na primeira sessão do mez o Director da Historia Natural, na segunda o de Agricultura, na terceira o das Artes e em fim na quarta a do Comercio fará na sobredita materia huma prelecção ao menos de meia hora. E quando qualquer dos Directores estiver legitimamente impedido, em seu lugar fará a prelecção o Presidente podendo ser, ou hum socio da sua respectiva classe, que se escolher.

28

No principio e fim de cada anno e fim de cada trimestre em huma assembleia particular, a que assistirão o Presidente, Secretario, Directores e os Socios que quizerem, o Depositario dará contas e se tratará também dos gastos e economia de todo o referido tempo.

29

As assembleias devem sempre constar do Presidente, Secretario e ao menos dous Directores, os quais assignarão todos os termos. O numero dos socios effectivos é para o valimento das assembleias indeterminado, [Fl.25] contanto que haja hum de cada classe, e nessa conferencia se não trate materia de importancia, como exames de Memorias e eleicções de socios. Mas se o Presidente estiver legitimamente impedido julgarão os Directores e Secretario.

30

As assembleias se farão ás quintas feiras de tarde e sendo feriado, ou no primeiro dia desocupado da semana, e á maneira dos anos lectivos da Universidade principiarão na primeira semana de Novembro, e será a ultima na primeira de Junho. A abertura se fará com huma breve falla do Presidente e a ultima sessão com outra semelhante do Secretario.

31

O Presidente sentar-se-há á direita do Secretario entre os quatro Directores. Os mais sócios, quer effectivos, honorarios, extranumerarios e correspondentes o farão simultaneamente sem diferença de artistas, practicos de qualquer qualidade.

32

[Fl.26] As Memorias serão sempre precisamente extractos e redacções do que se achar nos melhores autores: as traducções tãobem devem passar com semelhante nome.

33

Alem disto quando qualquer dos socios compuzer alguma peça que despois de examinada pelos Directores e Presidente pareça digna de se publicar, a tornará a receber o seu Autor para a retocar conforme as notas que lhe fizeram a respeito do methodo, estilo e substancia e consentindo na impressão, far-se-há logo e espalhar-se--há sem espera de outra alguma; por quanto não comvem a demora, que será inevitável para se fazer hum volume. E com a Memoria que se remeter a cada socio se lhe mandará outra, para que elle a dê a alguma pessoa, que julgar hábil e digna.

34

Huma Sociedade que nasceo sobre os votos de bons cidadãos mais que nenhuma outra deve recomendar a união, a simplicidade no comportamento, a sinceridade nas consultas e conferencias, que ou se practiquem nas [Fl.27] assembleias ou se fação particulares.

35

E sendo porventura em semelhantes corporações huma decente liberdade a mais vigilante e inculpável espia contra os abusos, a cada hum dos socios será permittido advertir nas conferencias qualquer ponto que entender necessário. E o Presidente mandará precisamente votar sobre a proposta para se seguir ou regeitar-se pela pluralidade.

36

Quando qualquer socio houver de expor algum prejuízo que esteja arreigado no povo ou que seja apoiado em alguma lei, o fará com todo o respeito e sinceridade sem palavras vehementes.

37

Para maior adiantamento he necessario que com o dinheiro da Sociedade se tenha huma exacta licção de todos os papeis periodicos de Economia, que sahirem, por exemplo, os que publica a Sociedade de Berne e saem em Estocolmo. Os Directores farão extractos destas materias para os ler nas [Fl.28] sessões competentes. Para diante cuidar-se-ha em comprar as obras maiores, fundamentaes de semelhantes Sciencias. E quando alguma obra da Sociedade se imprimir, vender-se-ha pelo preço tal que não exceda o gasto da impressão.

38

Far-se-ha todos os anos as viagens que poder ser. A eleição do socio que a executar fica á escolha da Sociedade em corpo e ella mesmo lhe dirá por escripto as observações que devem fazer-se sem fallencia, alem das que o viajante procurar por si. E o genero das observações fará ver de qual das classes sahira o viajante, este dará conta da viagem em huma ou mais Memorias. O Depositario lhe dará do cofre o dinheiro para os gastos que a Sociedade determinar e estará pelos que o Socio lhe der, em huma só parcella, por escripto.

39

A Sociedade dará todos os annos huma medalha de prata a quatro socios, dos quais cada hum na sua classe tiver escripto alguma Memoria util e com [Fl.29] superioridade aos outros. O Presidente e os Directores não terão medalhas.

40

Dará tãobem annualmente seis premios a seis pessoas aprendizes que se distinguirem nas suas artes, quatro homens e duas mulheres.

Advertindo que o collegio de Pereira que sem duvida as mereceria pelo adiantamento com que nelle se promovem as manufacturas, não ganhará outro premio alem do que se lhe destinou annualmente.

41

Todos os annos recitará hum Socio que se eleger huma Oração no felicissimo dia de anniversario de Nossa Soberana, e outro para o elogio ao Augustissimo Rei, o Senhor D. José de saudosa memoria no dia do seu fallecimento.

42

Cada um dos socios effectivos contribuirá com seis mil reis por anno.

43

Finalmente a Sociedade roga a todos os seus sócios [Fl.30] de qualquer das quatro Divisões, que por distinctivo do seu zelo e amor da Pátria e pela sua mesma instituição gastem, quanto lhes for possível, unicamente das fazendas produzidas e manufacturadas no Reino.

Armas da Sociedade

Dentro em hum circulo se vê sobre o horizonte, o qual he feito por huma linha que o divide em dous segmentos, hum monte baixo: distante delle se vê voando ao alto huma Aguia pequena que acompanha outra maior já próxima ao Sol, que está pouco declinado do Zenith, entre estas palavras: SIC ITUR AD ASTRA. No segmento inferior estão as letras CONIMBRICAE 1780.

ANEXO II

Copia de hum Memorial entregue ao Serenissimo Senhor Principe do Brazil em Queluz

Serenissimo Senhor

Os Principes tanto conhecem a necessidade das Academias, que ou presidem á grande obra das suas creações, ou as enriquecem despois com remunerações Reaes. Estão justamente persuadidos que as Sciencias ensinão ao povo até a obedecer aos Soberanos, e que ellas sejão objecto de semelhantes corporações ninguém o pode negar.

Neste seculo, Senhor, em que a razão parece que mais copiosamente brilha, e que se tem apoderado cada vez mais do espirito dos homens, vê-se que em muitos Reinos as Academias contão-se pelas cidades, e as Nações que se não applicavão até agora a esta sorte de estabelecimento cuidão hoje muito diligentes em firmá-los entre o povo. A providencia com que para grandes bens de Portugal, as Sociedades Literarias, neste sabio governo applicão ás suas vistas para exame e indagação, até então impossíveis, he já conhecida de todos. Era contudo necessario que no centro das Escolas os Mancebos Portuguezes bebessem este leite que tanto esforça os espíritos e lhes imprime aquelle [Fl.2] sagrado zelo pelos Reis e pela Patria, sem o qual he debalde o intentar a emenda e adiantamento de huma Nação. A reforma da Universidade deo quanto é licito dezejar acerca das Sciencias, e habilita os estudantes para serem sabios; mas faltava o estudo da Economia e o practicar os principios colhidos nas aulas. Possuidos desta verdade alguns dos grandes genios que Portugal muito frequentemente produz, supportando o demaseado pezo das obrigações da Universidade se offerecem a trabalhar para a Patria, e criarão em Coimbra esta Sociedade. O campo he muito largo e coberto de espinhos. Os reis são os unicos para quem não há impossiveis, e que vivem sem amparo por si mesmos, obrão quanto emprendem: todos os mais homens são dependentes, todos necessitam de hum patrono.

Assim, Serenissimo Senhor com a creação deste ~~Sociedade~~ Corpo nasceu a necessidade de huma protecção debaixo de cujo respeitavel Nome possa elle respirar livremente. Huma obra publica, huma acção que se derrama pelo Reino inteiro pertence por direito ao Soberano que abraça a Nação inteira.

Mancebos estudiosos filhos da Universidade applicados ás Sciencias da Natureza, e que para o futuro jurão prestar á Patria os esforços de todos os seus talentos, facilmente se [Fl.3] persuadirão de uniforme consentimento que a V. Alteza deviam correr, e reverentes protestar-lhe que elles acreditão como hum vehementissimo principio de segurança para o patrocinio dezejado, o ter V. Alteza, posto que em grao eminente, estudos da mesma especifica sciencia, que eles frequentão: ter honrado a Universidade sua mãe com a escolha de hum Mestre que tãobem o foi e he delles, permitindo-lhes por isso o titulo de Condiscipulos: e aprender finalmente de mais perto da Augustissima e Sapientissima Soberana o mesmo ardentíssimo zelo, admirando nella, aprendem e procurão inspirar aos Portugueses. Debaixo da Real Protecção de V. Alteza promettem cumprir com o muito que lhes prescrevem os seus Estatutos: e se por ventura o não poderem de todo practicar, basta que estudem semelhantes materias, e que adquirão a louvavel paixão pelo bem da Patria que arde de continuo nos peitos dos verdadeiros Cidadãos e basta á mesma Patria que se ensinem mutuamente. Assim principiarão na Europa Sociedades que hoje sustentão o credito das Letras Nacionaes. Se o Mundo para o diante respeitar os Sabios de Portugal, e se V. Alteza, vir ao redor do Augustissimo Trono, que ha-de felizmente [Fl.4] occupar, Ministros habeis creados á sua sombra e animados com a sua Augustissima Protecção, como he razão de esperar, Senhor que gloria para V. Alteza, o distribuir ordens a vassalos eruditos para que V. Alteza sendo Principe os amparou, quando a maior gloria dos Reis, he governar povos disciplinados por eles mesmos já sentados no Trono. Portanto Serenissimo Senhor, esta Sociedade ainda nascente supplica a V. Alteza, queira dignar-se o permettir-lhe pôr o seu Augustissimo Nome na frente dos estatutos em signal da sua Real Protecção do mesmo modo que a Fidelíssima Rainha Mãe de V. Alteza o concedeo á de Ponte de Lima e á Real Academia de Lisboa. A Nação agradecerá a V. Alteza e os soccessos farão bem lograda esta beneficiencia e a Sociedade se fará digna, se tanto é licito escrever, de hum tão alto Protector.

A CIÊNCIA COMO ESTRATÉGIA SOCIAL: AS ATIVIDADES CIENTÍFICAS DE DOMINGOS VANDELLI NAS REDES CLIENTELARES DE PORTUGAL 1764-1788

Gustavo Oliveira Ferreira
Centro de História da Sociedade e da Cultura (FLUC)
gustavococvelozo@gmail.com

1. Introdução

O Doutor Domingos Vandelli, italiano de nascimento, é conhecido entre os naturalistas por causa de alguns escritos, mas especialmente em virtude das suas relações com Lineu. Deve ter sido na sua juventude um homem dinâmico, que fez muito e tinha ambição de se tornar famoso. Seu professor de Botânica foi Pontedera. Sob Pombal foi chamado com outro Italiano, Dalla Bella, e veio para Lisboa na qualidade de intendente principal do museu real do Jardim Botânico. Tornou-se, além disso, vogal da Aula de Comércio e, através de muitas voltas, conseguiu um salário anual superior a 800 cruzados[1].

---

[1] *apud* Brigola 2010:73.

Poucos viajantes que passaram por Portugal no final do século XVIII deram informações tão precisas sobre a vida do naturalista Domingos Vandelli (1735-1816) como o prússio Henrich Friderich Link (1767-1851), em viagem a Portugal, onde se encontrou com o próprio Vandelli e outros naturalistas lusos da época, como Félix de Avelar Brotero (1744-1828), com quem trocou informações sobre a história natural portuguesa e seus "profissionais". O relato de Link nos dá uma síntese muito reveladora sobre Vandelli chamando a atenção na direção de pontos importantes para a inteligibilidade da trajetória desse naturalista em Portugal, designadamente no que diz respeito à sua sociabilidade.

Ao usar a expressão "através de muitas voltas", o naturalista evidencia que Vandelli era um homem bem relacionado junto ao poder régio e que, através dessas relações, obteve um salário anual elevado. Essa afirmativa nos levou a analisar a atuação de Domingos Vandelli no universo científico português da segunda metade do século XVIII, sob a ótica da nova história social das ciências, procurando compreender as atividades deste homem de ciências em seu meio social.

Parte dos trabalhos hoje desenvolvidos no âmbito da nova historiografia das ciências tem verificado que os produtores do conhecimento certificado são indivíduos dotados de versatilidade, atuando e interagindo, simultaneamente, em círculos científicos, políticos e culturais. Tal perspectiva tem como base a premissa de que a prática científica é uma atividade social e historicamente situada, e deve ser entendida em relação com o contexto em que é desenvolvida[2]. Outro ponto importante dessa historiografia é a noção de que sucessos e fracassos científicos são resultados de negociações estabelecidas em determinados contextos socioculturais pelos "praticantes" das ciências. Tal ponto de vista tem reabilitando carac-

---

[2] Shapin 2000: 26.

terísticas importantes na construção e validação do conhecimento, como os embates, querelas e estratégias socioprofissionais, nuances inerentes a esse processo, anteriormente percebidos como questões secundárias ou mesmo desvios no desenvolvimento das ciências[3].

À luz da nova historiografia, o nosso objetivo, no presente trabalho, tem como foco a atuação de Domingos Vandelli em Portugal na segunda metade do século XVIII e as influências do universo social na sua prática científica. Intentamos demonstrar que a atividade científica no referido período pode ser considerada como um dispositivo social, cumprindo muitas vezes funções locais, como a manutenção de laços sociais e o reconhecimento de relações de proteção, subordinação e homenagem. E que tal característica na ciência praticada por Vandelli foi uma estratégia decisiva nos espaços sociais que atuou, como a Corte Josefina, a Universidade de Coimbra e a Academia Real de Ciências de Lisboa.

2. Os italianos e a reforma educacional

A historiografia sobre o século XVIII português é enfática no que se refere às transformações ocorridas nas mentalidades decorrentes do desenvolvimento da racionalidade das Luzes. Dentro dessas alterações, que Hernâni Cidade (1929) chamou de "crise mental" estava presente o desejo de uma renovação cultural à luz do conhecimento racional da época. No bojo desse desejo de renovação, estava a valorização do conhecimento teórico e prático e dos novos métodos, que na opinião da época, dotariam o homem de

---

[3] A historiografia das ciências externalista, influenciada pelos trabalhos do sociólogo Robert K. Merton, sempre se mostrou mais preocupada no estudo das forças que possibilitavam os sucessos científicos. Tal ponto de vista só veio a ser alterado com as contribuições de investigadores como David Bloor 1980, Steven Shapin 1985 e Simon Schaffer 1985.

esclarecimento, possibilitando o progresso do Estado e promovendo a felicidade e o bem público. Em Portugal a valorização desse tipo de conhecimento significou o incentivo do Estado na educação e na promoção do conhecimento racional. Ainda na primeira metade do século XVIII, no reinado de D. João V (1707-1750), o monarca já demonstrava interesse no desenvolvimento dessa nova mentalidade; um bom exemplo, foi a autorização régia dada aos Oratorianos para a abertura do Colégio de Nossa Senhora das Necessidades em 1745, onde vigorava um ensino voltado para o conhecimento empírico e para o experimentalismo[4]. Embora algumas iniciativas de renovação da educação tenham sido feitas no reinado de D. João V, ao longo dos anos persistia a ideia de alguns homens de letras como Luis Antonio Verney (1713-1792) e Teodoro de Almeida (1722-1804) entre outros, de que a renovação da educação deveria ser ampla e em todas as instituições de ensino portuguesas complementando disciplinas e práticas pedagógicas.

Embora a reforma educacional fosse um dos tópicos de discussão ainda na primeira metade do século, a grande reforma da educação só veio a ocorrer no reinado de D. José I (1750-1777), mais propriamente durante o período ministerial de Sebastião José de Carvalho e Melo, Conde de Oeiras (1699-1782). Foi durante esse período, diferente das percepções do reinado de D. João V, que a educação foi encarada como um dever público, destinando-se a manutenção de uma crença da ordem universal de valores que compatibilizassem o progresso humano de matriz cristã, com a finalidade técnica decorrente da utilidade social da ciência[5]. Para este fim, o Conde de Oeiras organizou uma junta composta por homens de letras de sua inteira confiança, consonante com as aspirações regalistas da sua política educativa.

---

[4] Carneiro, Diogo e Simões 2000:73.
[5] Araújo 2000: 9-10.

É neste contexto que surge, depois de um longo debate sobre o tema, a primeira instituição secularizada dedicada à educação da melhor juventude do reino, o Colégio dos Nobres em Lisboa. Seria nessa instituição que os meninos da nobreza receberiam as primeiras aulas de disciplinas, até então fora da grade curricular oficial, como a física e a matemática, servindo este modelo de parâmetro para outras instituições que se dedicavam ao ensino de habilitação à Universidade. Para o funcionamento do Colégio dos Nobres eram necessários mestres capazes de ministrar aulas das novas disciplinas, não existindo em Portugal, naquele momento, número suficiente de professores que se dedicassem ao estudo das ciências modernas e aptos para as lecionarem. A solução que se apresentava para sanar esse quadro deficitário, foi a da contratação de profissionais estrangeiros para que se completasse o quadro de professores da nova instituição. Tradicionalmente, Portugal já possuía estreitos laços com os reinos da península itálica como Nápoles, Veneza e Piemonte, possuindo nessas regiões representantes diplomáticos atuantes e que normalmente mediavam contratações de profissionais para a Coroa portuguesa. Dos diversos profissionais que atuaram em Portugal durante o século XVIII, provenientes dessas regiões, podemos citar: o músico Domingos Scarlatti (1685-1757) professor de música da infanta Maria Bárbara (1711-1758), o arquiteto Filipe Juvarra (1658-1736), responsável pelas obras do convento de Mafra, e os matemáticos Miguel António Ciera (fl.-1770) e João Ângelo Brunelli (1722-1804) que dirigiram os trabalhos matemáticos e cartográficos da Comissão demarcadora de limites no norte do Brasil, entre 1753-1761.

Desses profissionais destacamos o papel de Miguel António Ciera, que após término das atividades na colônia e retorno a Portugal, foi designado pelo Conde de Oeiras como colaborador na obra de fundação do Colégio dos Nobres. O papel de Ciera na organização institucional do Colégio e reforma do ensino português foi relevante, já que, juntamente com o ministro de D. José, entrou em contato com Jacob Facciolati (1682-1769), reitor da Universidade de Pádua, solicitando sugestões para as alterações curriculares do ensino em Portugal[6]. Além de pedir sugestões, Ciera e o ministro chegaram a propor a contratação do reitor e a sua consequente deslocação para Lisboa, a fim de acompanhar de perto o lançamento do Colégio dos Nobres. Adicionalmente, solicitaram-lhe um exemplar dos estatutos da Universidade de Pádua, para serem usados como modelo na reforma que o ministro tinha *in animo* para Coimbra[7]. Facciolati declinou do convite, mas atendeu aos pedidos sobre as sugestões e enviou os referidos estatutos.

Por intermédio do cônsul de Portugal em Génova, Nicolau Piaggio(?), foram contratados na "Itália" os novos professores do Colégio dos Nobres indicados por Facciolati: Luís António Dalla Bela (1730-1823) e Miguel Franzini (?-1810) para assegurarem as disciplinas de matemática, álgebra e cálculo. Naquela época, havia, em Portugal, necessidade de incremento do ensino da matemática pois a contratação de matemáticos pela Coroa portuguesa revelava-se difícil dentro do reino. Os matemáticos atuavam como cosmógrafos e cartógrafos nas missões demarcadoras, possuindo um papel ativo no exército e na marinha, existindo um cuidado especial por parte da Coroa portuguesa ao escolher esses profissionais que demarcavam os limites dos domínios entre os impérios coloniais da época. Era importante que estes profissionais não fossem de impérios percebidos como concorrentes, Espanha, França, Inglaterra ou Holanda. Daí a política de realizar contratações em reinos tidos como neutros, sem interesses territoriais na América, como eram os estados e principados da península itálica ou do império germânico[8].

---

[6] Ferreira 2011:4.

[7] Brigola 2008:41.

[8] Durante boa parte do século XVIII, a Coroa portuguesa diligenciou a contratação de matemáticos; a primeira contratação destes profissionais ocorreu durante o reinado de D. João V, em 1720, para atualização das cartas geográficas da colónia

Embora com forte preocupação com as disciplinas de cálculo, foi contratado também Domingos Vandelli, médico, naturalista, especialista reconhecido no campo da química, história natural e do colecionismo, membro da Academia de Ciências de Pádua, correspondente do naturalista sueco Carlos Lineu (1739-1778).

3. Redes de Sociabilidade

Durante o período moderno era importante que os indivíduos que pretendessem cargos nas mais diferentes cortes da Europa estivessem inseridos dentro de redes de sociabilidade que possibilitassem o acesso a variados cargos e serviços demandados por nobres e monarcas. Em larga medida, a historiografia hoje produzida e que trata do período moderno, é enfática no que se refere ao estudo das sociabilidades e estabelecimento de uma cultura mecenática que funcionava de acordo com regras das relações clientelares. O mecenato e a clientela são estudados como uma forma fundamental de vinculação social e de organização hierárquica entre indivíduos socialmente diferentes, sendo frequentemente compreendido como relação de patrocínio e proteção, estabelecida entre profissionais prestigiados (cliente), mobilizados por indivíduos detentores de poder político (patrono) que por sua vez estavam ligados a uma fonte de poder maior (mecenas)[9].

As lógicas sociais do mecenato da Europa moderna, funcionavam de acordo com as normas associativas das relações clientelares, ou seja, pressupondo uma relação de trocas e dependências recíprocas.

---

portuguesa na América. Segundo Ferreira, em 1750, no contexto do tratado de Madrid, a carência em Portugal desses profissionais ainda se mantinha levando a Coroa a buscar outros matemáticos em Bolonha e Viena. Para mais detalhes ver Ferreira 2011: 3.

[9] Ago 1990: 58.

Os bens envolvidos nessas relações não possuíam, muitas vezes, um valor econômico definido, o que torna difícil de constatar qual o real valor da "troca", tendo em vista que o capital envolvido, muitas vezes era algo simbólico, podendo-se configurar em alianças políticas duradouras. As denominadas relações clientelares são compreendidas como relações sociais informais, onde existem agentes capazes de arregimentar um número significativo de indivíduos (clientes) e intermediar com estâncias superiores interesses mútuos, como entre um músico e um cardeal, um matemático e um príncipe, e, no presente caso, um homem de ciências e um soberano.

Participar de tais redes de clientela não pode ser compreendido como algo opcional, se tivermos em conta que este tipo de sociabilidade fazia parte da sociedade europeia, há séculos, não se restringindo a temporalidades e espaços estanques. No período moderno estar fora desse tipo de relação pode ser considerado como um "suicídio" social, pois era através dessas relações que eram viabilizadas certas mobilidades sociais, bem como a celebração de laços de sangue com famílias abastadas e prestigiadas. Também não pode ser compreendido como mero conjunto de estratégias e de relações racionais que visavam benesses exclusivamente econômicas, pois se acabaria por acreditar que os clientes eram indivíduos totalmente racionais e, no presente caso, empenhados numa espécie de programa de investigação, em função do qual tentavam manipular esse sistema. Em síntese, compreende-se tal forma de sociabilidade como parte integrante da cultura do Antigo Regime, incorporada na etiqueta, norma, educação e controlo de práticas sociais correntes[10].

Dentro dessa instituição sem paredes, legitimada pelo costume, existiam deveres bem definidos para todas as partes envolvidas nesse tipo de relação social – dar, receber, restituir. Embora fossem atos considerados voluntários, eram realizados sob fortes imperati-

---

[10] Biagiolli 2003:17-19 e Xavier; Hespanha 2008: 339-349.

vos sociais. Caso uma qualquer obrigação decorrente de um desses compromissos de honra não fosse cumprida, pesados constrangimentos sociais recaíam sobre as partes implicadas na troca de favores[11]. Esse tipo de sociabilidade fixava e constituía escalas sociais e reforçava hierarquias e estatutos numa sociedade normativa e fortemente verticalizada. Dentro dessas relações sociais, normalmente entre indivíduos socialmente diferentes, merece destaque o papel exercido pelo patrono como a figura de intermediação. Um cliente mais modesto não poderia abordar diretamente um mecenas mais poderoso; por exemplo, Vandelli não poderia abordar diretamente a rainha da Rússia, para conquista de um cargo na corte de São Petersburgo; então solicitava ao naturalista sueco Carlos Lineu, seu patrono científico, sua intervenção para que pudesse alcançar tal posto naquele reino[12].

Para que um cliente se candidatasse ao patrocínio era necessário que possuísse boa reputação, honra, e determinado prestígio pelas suas funções. Essas "qualidades" seriam abonadas pelo patrono junto ao mecenas e ambos garantiam ao cliente estabilidade social e proteção no exercício de suas funções. Em contrapartida, o cliente possuía o dever da gratidão, que deveria ser manifestada e evidenciada de forma pública. No presente caso, no universo científico, o oferecimento de uma obra era algo costumeiro ou, ainda, a nomeação dos resultados com o nome que referenciava o patrono e o mecenas da "descoberta científica". O cumprimento dessas regras

---

[11] A quebra das obrigações sociais, dar, receber, restituir, poderia configurar como uma quebra de relações implicando em constrangimento das partes envolvidas. No caso de um cliente pouco agradecido, implicava em perda do patrono, e não reinserção em nova rede de influências. No caso de falta por parte patrono consubstanciava como perda de poder político e simbólico e a desarticulação da rede. Para mais detalhes ver: Gellner, Waterbury 1977; Pitt-Rivers 1963.

[12] As cartas trocadas entre Domingos Vandelli e Carlos Lineu entre 1759-1779 estão transcritas por Sílvia Moura 2008.

confirmava a ligação entre as partes e consolidava a relação entre indivíduos socialmente diferentes.

Na segunda metade do século XVIII, essas normas, herdadas do passado, regiam ainda as relações de sociabilidade entre homens de letras e ministros em quase toda a Europa, interligando diferentes grupos sociais e indivíduos com funções diferentes na sociedade. Nessas redes de sociabilidade é comum perceber as ligações de negociantes, arquitetos, músicos, escultores, pintores e outros profissionais a serviço do alto escalão político e religioso da época.

Homem de ciências de seu tempo, Vandelli também participou de tais redes de sociabilidade, como demonstram as cartas que trocou com Lineu a partir 1759, no período em que residiu em Pádua. Nessas missivas é possível perceber o desejo de Vandelli em ser contratado por alguma corte europeia, por via da intercessão do prestigiado naturalista sueco. Embora suas solicitações junto a Lineu não tenham resultado, presumimos que a sua contratação em Portugal esteja ligada ao empenho pessoal de Miguel Ciera junto ao Conde de Oeiras. Acreditamos que o empenho de Ciera na contratação do naturalista está relacionado aos resultados "secundários" da comissão demarcadora de limites, em que havia participado anos antes. Um de seus companheiros nessa missão, João Ângelo Brunelli, de retorno a Portugal, publicou na Academia de Ciências de Bolonha, importantes memórias sobre a natureza do Brasil, tendo como temas o fenómeno da Pororoca (1767), os usos da Mandioca (1767) e o rio Amazonas(1791)[13]. A persistência de Ciera na contratação de um

---

[13] Assim como Miguel Ciera, João Ângelo Brunelli teve um papel importante no contexto português da segunda metade do século XVIII. De retorno a Portugal publicou as memórias, *De Mandioca* 1767, *De Pororoca* 1767 e *De Flumine Amazonum*, 1791 nos periódicos da Acadêmia de Ciências de Bolonha. Além da escrita das memórias sobre a história natural da américa portuguesa é de sua autoria a tradução para o português da obra "*Elementos de Euclides dos seis primeiros livros e undécimo, e duodécimo da versão latina de Frederico Commandino adicionados e ilustrados por Robert Simson... e traduzidos em português para uso do Real Colegio dos Nobres 1768*", adotados nas aulas do Colégio dos Nobres, onde

naturalista pode ainda ser observada na carta de Nicolau Piaggio ao Conde de Oeiras enviada de Génova, a 16 de Maio de 1764:

> O apresentador desta será (....) o Dr. físico Domingos Vandelli, que vem ai aos pés de Vossa Ex.ª, em vigor das ordens que da esse Dr. Miguel Ciera [sic] por parte de Vossa Ex.ª lhe foram dadas, para ter a honra de se empregar por um dos professores nesse Real Colégio, à teor das cartas do dito Dr. Ciera, que me apresentou. Como o referido Dr. Vandelli alem de ser pessoa muito civil, filho do celebre Francisco Vandelli professor na universidade de Pádua, é muito erudito, e capaz, estas suas prerrogativas, me fez tomar à Confiança de suplicar à Vossa Ex.ª de lhe acordar á sua alta proteção[14].

Com o sucesso dos esforços de Ciera, Vandelli viajou para Lisboa, onde o ministro se tornou seu principal patrono, garantindo a sua proteção e a continuidade dos seus trabalhos em Portugal.

Após chegar à capital portuguesa, Vandelli retomou o contato com Lineu, enviando uma remessa substancial de amostras de géneros naturais lusos para Suécia. Em resposta, o naturalista, que revela alguma animosidade em relação a outro correspondente que tinha em Portugal, espera receber de Vandelli mais informações sobre a história natural lusa. Segundo Lineu, "depois que a Europa inteira foi calcada pelos pés dos botânicos, resta agora somente Portugal, terra próspera que merece a alcunha de Índia da Europa"[15].

Na correspondência entre os naturalistas, eram constantes as trocas de amostras da história natural, de informações científicas

---

também lecionou ao lado de Ciera, Dalla Bella e Franzinni. Para maiores detalhes ver: Papavero et al 2010: 493-533.

[14] ANTT, Ministério dos Negócios Eclesiásticos e Justiça, Caixa 66, Maço 77, 1.º
[15] Moura 2008: 58-59.

e também de favores. Embora boa parte dos trabalhos sobre as relações entre homens de ciências tenham ressaltado a troca de amostras como cortesia entre os membros da República das Letras, em nossa perspectiva essas trocas obedeciam também às regras de clientela da época – dar, receber, restituir. Essa movimentação pode ser observada no conteúdo das cartas trocadas entre Vandelli e vários de seus contatos. No caso da correspondência com Lineu tal prática fica ainda mais evidente: um diamante bruto do Brasil enviado por Vandelli era motivo de solicitação de algumas lâminas confeccionadas em Uppsala. Um espécime botânico raro, não classificado, proveniente das ilhas portuguesas no Atlântico rendeu a Vandelli maior prestígio junto do seu patrono científico, que, no diapasão das relações de clientela, demonstrava a sua gratidão homenageando o seu cliente, no batismo de um novo espécime, com o nome *Dracaena Vandelli*, o reconhecido *Dragoeiro*[16]. A par desta relação, o naturalista manteve-se membro da rede de clientela de Lineu, dado que esse tinha interesse em continuar recebendo as amostras oriundas de Portugal e das colônias portuguesas e, por outro lado, Vandelli precisava de Lineu para lhe garantir prestígio internacional, além de outros favores[17].

Fazer parte de uma de rede clientelar não quer dizer que o cliente ou patrono participassem de um único circulo, ambos poderiam participar de vários círculos ao mesmo tempo, contanto que tal não representasse constrangimento a nenhuma das partes. Cada elo desse emaranhado social deve ser observado como um indivíduo capilar, capaz de fazer múltiplas ligações, o que garantia a cada membro um maior trânsito social e, principalmente, segurança, no caso do desaparecimento de um centro poder, o que acontecia com regularidade no período. Como se percebe Vandelli passou a articular-se com

---

[16] Moura 2008: 88-89.
[17] Moura 2008: 69-70.

duas redes de clientela, uma científica onde Lineu era o patrono, e outra política, onde o Conde de Oeiras era seu protetor, em nome do mecenas D. José I. Como cliente de duas redes distintas, Vandelli devia obediência simultânea aos dois patronos. Boa parte de seus trabalhos e publicações exemplifica os compromissos de fidelidade e obediência que contraíra.

4. A divulgação da História Natural na Corte Josefina

Tendo chegado a Portugal em 1764 sem um cargo formal definido, já que o seu nome não constava sequer na lista dos professores do Colégio dos Nobres, é de crer que, num primeiro momento, Vandelli se tenha empenhado na divulgação da história natural na Corte Josefina. O naturalista foi-se aproximando da nobreza da época e da alta burguesia, cujos membros, por interesse ou diletantismo, cultivavam a história natural e conheciam a sua utilidade, como Pedro José de Noronha Camões de Albuquerque Moniz e Sousa (1716-1788), Marquês de Angeja, Luís Pinto de Sousa Coutinho (1735-1804), e Gerard de Visme (1725-1797), entre outros personagens importantes do universo político e cultural da época. Durante os primeiros anos em Portugal, Vandelli atuou como um divulgador da história natural na Corte, justificando a utilidade do campo para a economia e demais artes, tónica sempre presente em seus escritos.

Embora Vandelli tenha encontrado alguns nobres afeitos e receptivos à história natural, de maneira geral a sociedade portuguesa da época não estava convencida das vantagens do desenvolvimento da nova área de conhecimento. Em Portugal, assim como em toda a Europa, no referido período, a história natural não possuía o reconhecimento unânime de sua utilidade, sendo alvo de significativas críticas, quando não era reputada como um entretenimento cortesão inútil. Sobre essa atmosfera em Portugal comentava Vandelli, em carta a Lineu:

> A RAINHA aprecia a história natural. Grande administrador deste reino, nosso colega, de Oeiras, reconhece sua utilidade e grandeza. Mas o vulgo daqui considera a história natural mera curiosidade, e quase todos julgam o estudo adequado apenas para que horas sejam gastas e que hajam algum deleite para alma, não creem que a utilidade percebida por esse estudo possa ser grande a ponto de ele dever cultivado por muitos[18].

Esse tipo de visão da história natural como sendo ridícula ou inútil era um lugar-comum no século XVIII, e, por mais estranho que pareça, até mesmo Lineu sofreu duras críticas sobre a utilidade dos seus estudos, o que levou o seu discípulo Christopher Gedner a justificar:

> Uma pergunta sempre é feita, uma objeção é sempre colocada a aqueles que se mostram curiosos acerca da Natureza. Essas pessoas perguntam muitas vezes, com riso trocista: "para que serve?"... elas pensam que a filosofia natural tem que ver somente com uma satisfação da curiosidade ou apenas uma distração para passar o tempo de pessoas preguiçosas e desmioladas[19].

Embora na segunda metade do século XVIII os museus e jardins fossem vistos pelos especialistas como instituições vocacionadas para o estudo sistemático da natureza, para a maioria dos seus utilizadores estes lugares, que enquadravam o convívio cortesão, satisfaziam, acima de tudo, o deleite e a curiosidade dos cultores do mundo

---

[18] Moura 2008: 69-70.
[19] *apud*. Outran 1972: 84.

natural. Esta linha de sensibilidade, sendo dominante, influenciou a visão de muitos membros da sociedade, acabando por matizar o juízo produzido sobre aqueles que praticavam a história natural. Neste contexto, a "contratação" e a permanência de Vandelli em Portugal podem ser consideradas no âmbito das inicitivas da política ministerial portuguesa, tendentes à reforma das instituições de ensino. Era importante que, mesmo sem uma função ou local social definida, o naturalista permanecesse em Lisboa, à disposição da Coroa e do ministro de D. José. Vandelli atuava assim como consultor de assuntos científicos e como divulgador da história natural no interior da sociedade, colocando Lisboa nas principais redes de conhecimento científico da época. Embora, numa primeira fase, não tivesse um cargo atribuído ou mesmo uma função definida, o naturalista não descurou de seus estudos, iniciando a inventariação da história natural de Portugal, em conformidade com a classificação sistemática lineana.

A consulta da correspondência que trocou com Lineu revela bem o empenho de Vandelli na construção de uma história natural portuguesa, desígnio que Lineu louvava, já que pouco se sabia da natureza lusa, faltando livros sobre o tema; os poucos existentes eram considerados ultrapassados e obscuros[20].

Somente em 1768 Vandelli celebrou o primeiro contrato formal com a Coroa portuguesa, recebendo a incumbência da construção de um jardim botânico anexo ao estabelecimento de um museu de história natural no Palácio de Ajuda, residência oficial de D. José I. Tal fato é relevante e pode ser considerado como o primeiro passo para o início do reconhecimento da legitimidade cognitiva da história natural e sua utilidade em Portugal. Com essa ação a Coroa tornava patente o compromisso de incentivar os conhecimentos úteis,

---

[20] Moura 2008: 58.

construindo no palácio real espaços dedicados ao estudo sistemático das ciências.

Com a ajuda de outro "italiano", Júlio Mattiazzi, contratado pela Coroa portuguesa por solicitação de Vandelli, foi iniciada a construção do espaço museológico e botânico no Palácio de Ajuda. Para o efeito, Vandelli reuniu as mais variadas produções para exposição no Real Museu e no Jardim Botânico, oriundas da Europa e das colônias portuguesas, mostra grandiosa que chegou a ter cerca de 5 mil espécies diferentes e oriundas de variadas regiões do mundo[21]. A organização desses espaços demandava uma atuação mais ampla e uma maior articulação entre Vandelli e outros indivíduos, tais como administradores coloniais, capitães de navios e demais pessoas que poderiam possibilitar a aquisição de exemplares dos três reinos da natureza. Resultado dessa articulação é a ligação que Vandelli estabeleceu com Luís Pinto de Sousa Coutinho, naquela altura governador da Capitania de Mato Grosso no Brasil, com o qual se correspondia. As cartas recebidas por Vandelli mostram a deferência com que o Capitão General do Mato Grosso tratava o naturalista e lhe solicitava alguns favores, como, por exemplo, usar de sua influência junto ao Mordomo Mor de D. José I, Marquês de Angeja, requisitando o seu regresso ao reino por não gozar de boa saúde nos trópicos[22]. Normalmente tais pedidos vinham acompanhados por grandes remessas de géneros naturais, plantas secas e vivas, sementes, animais conservados em cachaça e algumas produções dos indígenas daquela região do Brasil, destinados ao Real Museu e ao Jardim Botânico, sendo expedidas sempre ao cuidado de Vandelli. Ainda nessa documentação se atesta que o naturalista possuía um ótimo trânsito no Palácio Real e um acesso significativo a muitos nobres em cargos de relevo.

---

[21] Cardoso 2003: 51-58.

[22] AHMB, CN/B-93 Carta de Luís Pinto de Sousa Coutinho a Vandelli.

Transitar no alto escalão das Cortes não era algo simples, principalmente quando se tratava de um filósofo ou homem de ciências. De maneira geral as Cortes europeias do período moderno são consideradas como uma formação social na qual estão definidas maneiras específicas das relações entre os sujeitos sociais que constituíam esses espaços. Era nas Cortes principescas que as dependências recíprocas eram legitimadas engendrando códigos de conduta e de comportamentos específicos a serem seguidos pelos membros dessa sociedade[23]. Dentro da Corte a vida coletiva era ritualizada pela etiqueta, delimitando as áreas de atuação de seus membros e reforçando hierarquias sociais e poderes simbólicos. Nesse universo, cada membro desempenhava o seu papel de acordo com a etiqueta pertencente ao seu estamento, diferenciando marqueses, condes e viscondes, o que tornava a Corte um ambiente restrito a nobres, aristocratas, fidalgos e o alto clero[24]. Não era comum o acesso de homens de ciências nas Cortes, ou reconhecidamente com este "título", normalmente os sábios/filósofos eram contratados para funções específicas em espaços delimitados, como o ensino aos jovens príncipes ou para alguma apresentação de inovações técnicas, configurando uma espécie de entretenimento cortesão. Para que o acesso permanente fosse concedido era necessário que o filósofo tivesse o domínio rigoroso da etiqueta cortesã e seu cerimonial que o permitisse fazer "antecâmaras" com os nobres de primeira Grandeza.

Segundo tal etiqueta, normatizada por vários moralistas como Baltazar Gracián (1601-1668) em seu livro *Agudeza y Arte de Ingenio* de 1644, existiam formas adequadas de falar, pensar e agir no

---

[23] Elias 2011:10.

[24] Embora a Corte seja considerada um espaço social fechado, frequentado por nobres, fidalgos e clérigos, havia também um grande número de criados responsáveis pelas várias tarefas do Palácio. Estes funcionários subdivididos em categorias, também obedeciam a normas rígidas circulando em espaços delimitados do palácio. O livre acesso, ou *Libré* no caso da Corte francesa, era um benefício específico, concedido apenas à guarda pessoal do monarca. Ibidem:143.

ambiente de Corte, estabelecendo que o cortesão deveria ser prudente, agudo e discreto em suas palavras e gestos. Outro moralista que tratava das maneiras na Corte, principalmente no que diz respeito aos filósofos e homens de ciências, é Matteo Pellegrini (1595-1652), autor de *Che al Savio è convenevole il Corteggiare libri IIII* de 1624. Neste livro dedicou um capitulo ao tratamento do comportamento do filósofo em ambiente de Corte, intitulado "As Qualidades do Sábio que são inconvenientes para o Cortesão". No texto, Pellegrini dizia que os filósofos teriam poucas possibilidades de obter favores dos príncipes se mantivessem as "maneiras rígidas e aparência rude". Sublinhando que o filósofo "pouco acostumado em apreciar o prazer, evita-o e, ao fazê-lo, aborrece aqueles[príncipes] que pelo contrário o procuram." Pellegrini aconselhava o filósofo que aspirava frequentar a corte a não aborrecer o príncipe com questões sofísticas e fastidiosas sobre assuntos de Estado[25]. O filósofo cortesão deveria ser dotado de sensibilidade, falar, agir e atuar dentro dessa etiqueta, e seus trabalhos deveriam refletir as normas de aceitação da Corte, diluindo a aridez das questões investigadas aos formatos típicos da "literatura" do Antigo Regime.

Cremos que Domingos Vandelli conhecia bem esse padrão de etiqueta. Embora a sua família não possuísse títulos nobiliárquicos, alguns dos seus familiares mantinham ligações estreitas com prestigiadas famílias da "Itália", o que nos faz crer que o médico naturalista foi educado dentro das regras impostas pelo convívio social da nobreza. Vandelli era, portanto, um homem de ciência, cortesão versátil, próximo da nobreza portuguesa e bem relacionado com comerciantes importantes, como o inglês Gerard de Visme. Para além do mais, mantinha ativa correspondência com muitos naturalistas internacionais, como Lineu e Joseph Banks (1743-1820).

---

[25] Biagiolli 2003: 126.

Na sua primeira publicação científica em Portugal, resultante de suas atividades como Intendente do Real Museu e Jardim Botânico de Ajuda, é possível anotar os primeiros sinais do compromisso cortesão estabelecido por Vandelli na Corte de Lisboa. O trabalho em referência, produzido nos alvores da sua estadia em Portugal, veio à luz do dia com o título *Fasciculus Plantarum, cum novis generibus et speciebus*, tendo sido impresso na tipografia Régia, em 1771.

Neste pequeno livro, merecem destaque os novos géneros botânicos classificados, descritos e nomeados por Vandelli, nomeadamente: *Bragantia, Pombalia Ipecacuanha, Angeja* e *Balsamona Pinto*. Essas nomenclaturas são homenagens muito claras a pessoas importantes do xadrez social em que se movia Vandelli. Teve ainda o cuidado de apresentar os novos géneros botânicos respeitando na atribuição da respectiva nomenclatura a posição relativa de cada indivíduo da Corte portuguesa. O primeiro novo género descrito, nomeado e apresentado na publicação, é o *Bragantia*, em homenagem a casa real de Bragança e, portanto, em homenagem ao Rei D. José I[26]. Na sequência, é apresentado o género *Pombalia Ipecacuanha* que representa, sem dúvida, uma homenagem e um louvor ao ministro Marquês de Pombal, e que mencionado a seguir à casa real[27]. Depois é apresentado o género botânico *Angeja*, em homenagem ao Marquês de Angeja[28]. Por último, é apresentado o género *Balsamona Pinto*, em louvor de Luís Pinto de Sousa Coutinho[29].

Vandelli foi muito cuidadoso na apresentação e na nomenclatura dos novos géneros botânicos, cumprindo as regras sociais da época e agradecendo ao Rei e ao ministro a sua contratação, e ainda

---

[26] Vandelli 1771: 6.
[27] Ibidem:7.
[28] Ibidem:13.
[29] Ibidem:15.

referendando colaboradores de peso, como é Luís Pinto. Além de obedecer às regras sociais, Vandelli também usou de maneira consciente as normas da produção intelectual da época, pois a apresentação deste volume foi arquitetada conforme as normas que regulavam as "Artes"[30], ou seja, usando recursos retóricos como o engenho e a agudeza, no sentido de agradar ao leitor cortesão.

O uso de recursos retóricos por homens de ciências que atuaram dentro das lógicas do mecenato, embora pouco explorado, parece ter sido corrente, como recentemente destacou Mario Biagiolli, a respeito de Galileu Galilei (1564-1642). Boa parte dos textos científicos, apresentações e missivas do pensador italiano foram elaborados no rspeito pelas melhores regras da retórica. Segundo Biagiolli, Galileu percebia que sua produção científica era algo nobre, não uma arte mecânica ou menor, como era percebida até ao seu tempo. O uso de artifícios retóricos como o engenho e a agudeza na escrita científica, distinguia o homem de ciência na corte, pois elevava o debate e era considerado um recurso elegante[31].

Vandelli na corte portuguesa não foi diferente, utilizando todo o repertório cerimonial na apresentação e deitando mãos aos recursos retóricos na construção de seu pequeno livro. Das normas retóricas utilizadas por Vandelli destacamos o da agudeza, característica de pessoas de alto grau de erudição e logo de elevada condição social. A agudeza é definida por João Adolfo Hansen como "metáfora resultante da faculdade intelectual do engenho, que produz como o "belo eficaz" ou efeito inesperado de maravilha que espanta, agrada e

---

[30] No referido período, o conceito de Arte é definido por Rafael Bluteau como "regras, e methodo, com cuja observação se fazem muitas obras uteis, aggradaveis, e necessarias à Republica". Sendo subdividida em dois tipos, Artes Liberais e Mecânicas. Das Artes Liberais faziam parte a Gramática, a Retórica, Lógica, Aritmética, Música, Arquitetura e a Astronomia. As Artes Mecânicas, eram compreendidas como artes menores, mas não menos úteis: Agricultura, Caça, Guerra, ofícios fabris em geral e a Cirurgia. Bluteau 1728: 573.

[31] Biagiolli 2003: 123.

persuade" – e subdividida em: "A) agudeza de "conceito", que supõe a "sutileza do pensar", ou, especificamente, o ato do entendimento que descobre correspondências inesperadas entre coisas; B) agudeza de "palavra" ou "verbal", que consiste nas correspondências inesperadas estabelecidas entre as representações gráficas, sonoras e conceituais; C) agudeza de "ação", relativa a sentidos agudos produzidos por gestos engenhosos[32]."

Lançando mão da agudeza de conceito, Vandelli faz a comparação entre planta e o personagem homenageado, numa clara demonstração de que a planta e o indivíduo partilham qualidades semelhantes. O caso da *Pombalia Ipecacuanha,* com a qual Vandelli homenageou Pombal, pode ser considerado o caso mais evidente.

A Ipecacuanha era um género botânico muito procurado por suas propriedades medicinais. Embora a planta tenha sido descrita ainda no século XVII, pelo "naturalista" flamengo Willem Piso (1611-1678) e pelo alemão Georg Marcgraf (1610-1644), na época da dominação neerlandesa no Nordeste da colônia portuguesa na América (1630--1654), ainda não se sabia, ao certo, qual era, de facto, a planta que fornecia a raiz medicinal[33]. A Ipecacuanha era usada nas boticas da Europa como remédio para várias moléstias e, sobretudo, no controle de febres, sendo produto muito comercializado. Vandelli ao observar tais qualidades medicinais da planta, que julgava ser a Ipecacuanha, de forma muito aguda, comparou tais propriedades com a política do Marquês de Pombal. Dessa forma, fica-nos a consideração do naturalista de que o remédio dos males de Portugal era a política pombalina.

Evidentemente esse tipo de recurso retórico pressupunha um leitor capacitado para perceber toda a versatilidade, perspicácia e agudeza de quem propõe o efeito. Neste caso, Vandelli dirigiu expressamente o seu livro ao universo cortesão, nele envolvendo,

---

[32] Hansen 2000: 317-342.
[33] Lopes, 1879: 32.

como destinatários, nobres, fidalgos e naturalistas. A sua estratégia foi bem sucedida, pois em carta datada de 1 de julho de 1772, Lineu felicitava Vandelli pela publicação do livro, com as seguintes palavras: "Recebi tua carta com plantas raras e o *Fasciculus Plantarum*, por ambos rendo-te os maiores agradecimentos. Este seu fascículo agradou-me, não apenas pelas plantas raras, mas sobretudo pelas perspicazes descrições."[34]

Embora o impresso tenha saído em pequeno formato, Vandelli procurou produzir uma obra mais volumosa, compilando um número significativo de espécies inventariadas entre 1765 e 1771, desejo que não chegou a concretizar, apesar de reconhecer que o ministro de D. José I aguardava também pela publicação de uma obra mais ampla e completa[35].

O *Fasciculus Plantarum* tinha uma dupla função, divulgar a história natural em Portugal e, principalmente, no exterior, recolocando Lisboa no mapa da ciência da época, não só como fornecedora de amostras da história natural, mas também como centro produtor de conhecimento científico moderno, garantindo, deste modo, o autor reconhecimento junto da Corte portuguesa pela publicação da referida obra.

Como não poderia deixar de ser, o livro gerou algumas reações no universo científico europeu da época. Tenha-se em vista o citado género da Ipecacuanha, até então não identificado de forma cabal, o que acarretou uma certa disputa por parte dos naturalistas que disputaram aquela classificação e nomenclatura. O naturalista Daniel Wickman (1741-1803), sob a orientação de Lineu, promoveu uma revisão dos estudos realizados até àquele momento sobre a planta, e acabou por concluir que a Ipecacuanha fazia parte do género *Viola*. No trabalho de Wickman, datado de 1774, a identificação de

---

[34] Moura 2008:105.
[35] Idem Ibidem: 63.

Vandelli é constantemente citada, sendo mesmo considerada importante no seu estudo a localização da espécie descrita por Piso.[36] Ressalte-se que o trabalho de Wickman e Lineu também foi revisto por outros botânicos ao longo do século XIX, visando corrigir as diversas observações e as classificações sobre a planta. Embora o táxon *Pombalia* tenha sido substituído oficialmente, permanece até hoje como sinônimo da Ipecacuanha branca[37].

À medida que a consolidação dos espaços no palácio de Ajuda avançava, Vandelli, com o prestígio em alta na Corte, vai participar, em 1772, de outro projeto da Coroa portuguesa, sem deixar o cargo que ocupava na direção do Museu e Jardim Botânico de Ajuda, sendo destacado pelo ministro de D. José I para auxiliar na reforma da Universidade de Coimbra.

5. A Universidade de Coimbra e as oportunas propostas

No período ministerial de Sebastião José de Carvalho e Melo, são observadas, nas várias instituições de Portugal, alterações significativas. Na linha do despotismo esclarecido adotado pelo ministro, o fortalecimento do poder real foi sentido nas instituições que até aquele momento possuíam alguma autonomia. Importante instituição no contexto cultural português, a Universidade de Coimbra também sentiu de maneira significativa a política ministerial e a interferência do poder da Coroa na sua administração interna. Como já foi referido, o Marquês de Pombal planejava uma reformulação de todo o sistema de educação português. Os primeiros passos dessa reforma visaram a reformulação do ensino secundário e reflectiram-se,

---

[36] Wickiman 1774: 8.

[37] Para maiores detalhes verificar *Pombalia Ipecacuanha Vand.* nos sites das bases de dados, Tropicos.org (*Missori Botanical Garden*) e theplantlist.org (*Kew Gardens*) último acesso em 23/03/2016.

depois, na criação do Colégio do Nobres. Esta trajetória sinaliza--se ainda melhor se levarmos em conta o pedido dos estatutos da Universidade de Pádua a Faciolatti, em 1760, e a redação da *Dedução Cronológica e Analítica*, em 1768.

Para execução desses levantamentos e andamento das reformas educacionais e institucionais, o ministro contava com colaboradores da sua inteira confiança e que faziam valer seus interesses. As primeiras iniciativas concretas tomadas por Carvalho e Melo no que se refere à Universidade de Coimbra foram a nomeação de Francisco de Lemos de Faria Pereira Coutinho (1735-1822) para o cargo de reitor, em 1770. Tal nomeação deve ser vista como um passo importante para a execução da reforma universitária, e deve ser percebida como primeira abertura da universidade às redes de clientela do Marquês de Pombal, que a partir daquele momento tinha um representante com mandato de reformador no principal cargo da instituição. Desse modo, a Universidade deve ser vista como mais uma ferramenta de Estado. A partir daquele momento o Reitor da Universidade de Coimbra, era um agente com dupla função, representava os interesses da Universidade junto a Coroa e, simultaneamente, os interesses do Estado dentro da instituição. A partir da reforma pombalina houve uma reformaulação no conceito de Universidade, como observa Francisco de Lemos, a instituição não era mais percebida como um organismo fechado em si mesmo, mas parte integrante do Corpo do Estado[38].

Além da nomeação para o cargo de Reitor, D. Francisco de Lemos também foi convocado para compor a Junta da Providência Literária, conselho criado para avaliar o estado do ensino praticado na Universidade de Coimbra e que recebeu também o encargo de

---

[38] Essa visão expressa pelo Reitor Reformador reitera a subordinação da corporação académica ao poder político e a tutela do Estado, como ja salientado por Araújo, Ana Cristina 2000: 37-38

redigir os novos estatutos da instituição. Dessa junta faziam parte, D. João Cosme da Cunha, Frei Manuel do Cenáculo Vilas Boas, José Ricalde Pereira de Castro, José de Seabra da Silva, Francisco António Marques Giraldes, Francisco de Lemos, Manuel Pereira da Silva, João Pereira Ramos de Azeredo Coutinho além do próprio Marquês de Pombal. Embora oficialmente composta por estes homens de letras e de poder, a Junta recebeu auxílio de outros indivíduos, não nomeados oficialmente, como José Monteiro da Rocha (1734-1819) e Domingos Vandelli, cuja colaboração foi fundamental para a elaboração do tomo III, dedicado às duas faculdades Maiores recém criadas na Universidade, Matemática e Filosofia[39].

A reforma da Universidade de Coimbra tem sido considerada pela historiografia luso-brasileira como momento inaugural da institucionalização da ciência moderna em Portugal, pois é a partir de 1772 que as ciências físico-matemáticas de base experimental passam a compor, oficialmente, a malha curricular daquela instituição. Configura, igualmente, o reconhecimento sociocognitivo da história natural como campo de conhecimento legítimo e digno de ser lecionado na Universidade de Coimbra e impõe a validação social do conhecimento que produz, consignando estatutariamente as profissões de matemático e naturalista[40].

Nos compêndios dos estatutos, foi apresentado um renovado programa de instruções, pautado pelas modernas concepções de humanidades e ciências em voga na Europa setecentista. As quatro áreas de formação pré-existentes foram reestruturadas: a esfera de atuação da Teologia foi redefinida, dela se separando a Filosofia e a Moral; a Jurisprudência Civil e Canônica foram atualizadas. No que

---

[39] Brigola 2004: 41.

[40] Embora a Coroa portuguesa contratasse matemáticos, internamente não havia documento que reconhecia oficialmente essa como profissão. O reconhecimento profissional do matemático só veio a partir de 1772 na letra dos novos estatutos da Universidade de Coimbra. *Estatutos* 1772: T.III, 1772: 7.

se refere o ensino das ciências foram criadas duas novas faculdades, a de Filosofia, abrangendo a Filosofia Racional e Moral e a Filosofia Natural, e a faculdade de Matemática. Além da criação das novas faculdades e cursos, os novos estatutos determinavam a construção de novos espaços destinados às aulas práticas, um observatório astronómico na Faculdade de Matemática, um Gabinete de História Natural, um Jardim Botânico, um Gabinete de Física Experimental e um Laboratório Químico na Faculdade de Filosofia. Além desses espaços, os estatutos ainda mencionam a fundação de uma associação de homens de ciências, a Congregação Geral das Ciências, no intuito de se discutir os avanços científicos e sua implementação na Universidade de Coimbra[41].

Nas novas faculdades foram alocados os professores, João António Dalla Bella, Miguel Franzini e José Monteiro da Rocha, responsáveis pelas disciplinas de matemática e física, e Domingos Vandelli para as cadeiras que compunham Filosofia Natural: história natural, zoologia, botânica, mineralogia e química. Em conformidade com os novos estatutos universitários, Vandelli iniciou as aulas nas disciplinas adotando sempre os livros e procedimentos de Lineu, já que os estatutos delegavam ao lente dessas cadeiras a eleição dos autores mais indicados para o ensino das novas ciências[42]. Vandelli possuía uma significativa liberdade dentro da universidade, era próximo do reitor e de importantes figuras políticas da época, possuindo o título de Lente proprietário das disciplinas que lecionava, nelas lecionando os Filósofos que julgava ser os mais adequados e propondo atividades de campo aos alunos da instituição com o aval do reitor.

Além das aulas, Vandelli se engajou na construção dos novos espaços destinados às aulas práticas. Em 1773, juntamente com Dalla Bella, projetou o Jardim Botânico da Universidade, projeto este que

---

[41] *Estatutos* 1772: T. III, 1772: 8.
[42] *Estatutos* 1772: T. III, 1772: 352.

foi rejeitado pelo Marquês de Pombal, por o considerar excessivo e dispendioso[43]. Aos cuidados de Vandelli também foi confiado a adequação da cozinha e refeitório do antigo Colégio dos Jesuítas para as aulas de Química e a preparação dos espaços onde seria instalado o Museu de História Natural, onde toda a comunidade académica poderia apreciar as amostras dos três reinos da natureza, além de produções humanas dignas de exposição. No caso do museu, Vandelli tem um papel fundamental na formação do acervo inicial. Ainda em Pádua, o naturalista possuía uma coleção com amostras dos três reinos da natureza, algumas antiguidades e um autómato na forma de um centauro, podendo ser considerado como típico *Studiolo*, mesclando amostras naturais e produções humanas de variados períodos históricos[44]. Ao deslocar-se para Portugal manteve o seu acervo em sua terra natal, mas, no contexto das reformas institucionais, Vandelli propõe vender a sua coleção à Universidade de Coimbra. Durante as negociações de venda, o naturalista ainda ofertou à Universidade uma segunda parte, amealhada em Portugal desde sua chegada, em 1764, até aquela data. Somada às duas coleções foi também incorporado o acervo pertencente ao Capitão José Rollem Van-Deck, possibilitando assim a abertura do Gabinete de História Natural da Universidade de Coimbra[45].

A universidade de Coimbra, durante os primeiros tempos da reforma, foi um lugar aparentemente homogéneo, sem grandes querelas ou embates obedecendo às diretrizes reformistas do Marquês de

---

[43] Costa 2004: 179.

[44] O *Studiolo* é um espaço tipicamente encontrado na península itálica, considerado precursor do conceito de museu, sendo compreendido como lugar privado dedicado aos estudos e ao saber, buscando deslumbrar o visitante pelo espetáculo de peças notáveis destinadas ao aprofundamento das pesquisas científicas, sendo motivo de orgulho nacional. Esse tipo de espaço contrapõe os conceitos germânicos de *Wunderkammer*, Câmara das Maravilhas e *Kunstkammer*, Câmara das Artes, espaços destinados maioritariamente ao deleite cortesão e o espetáculo do poder. Camargo-Moro 2004: 1922.

[45] Brigola 2004: 45.

Pombal que acompanhava de perto as transformações na instituição. Nestes primeiros anos Vandelli aproximou-se de muitos alunos, com destaque para os luso-brasileiros, como é caso de Joaquim Veloso de Miranda (1736-1817), Alexandre Rodrigues Ferreira (1756-1815), Joaquim José da Silva (?), João da Silva Feijó (1766-1824), entre outros portugueses, como Luís António Furtado de Castro do Rio de Mendonça e Faro (1754- 1830) e Francisco José Simões da Serra ((?)--1785), sendo possível perceber nos estudos já realizados, uma rede de influência entre o professor e os alunos[46]. É notória a simpatia de Vandelli por alguns alguns alunos, que, por sua indicação, após o término dos cursos obtiveram o grau de Doutor e, em seguida, foram aproveitados como demonstradores nas disciplinas de História Natural como foi o caso de Joaquim Veloso de Miranda[47] e de vários outros indicados pelo professor em cargos na Universidade.

No decorrer dos anos, o cenário político começou a alterar-se. No ano de 1777, em fevereiro, morreu o rei D. José I, subindo ao trono D. Maria I, o que veio alterar a política interna do reino. O Marquês de Pombal foi destituído do cargo e boa parte da política passou a ser reorganizada pela rainha. A queda de Pombal significou o desaparecimento de um centro de poder que garantia a muitos a estabilidade no exercício de suas funções, ficando comprometida a rede de influências articulada pelo ministro. Receando revezes na reforma universitária, o reitor Francisco de Lemos saiu em defesa da

---

[46] Boa parte da historiografia luso-brasileira que trata da atuação dos egressos da Universidade de Coimbra nas colônias portuguesas deixam entrever uma rede de informações e influências na qual Domingos Vandelli funcionava como um articulador relevante. É reconhecido o desvelo com que o naturalista dirimia questões de alguns de seus alunos como Joaquim Veloso de Miranda e Alexandre Rodrigues Ferreira. Em outros casos, a ausência de empenho do professor chegava a ser cobrada por ex-alunos, como foi o caso de João da Silva Feijó naturalista enviado para Cabo Verde, onde se envolveu em disputas locais recebendo duras críticas de D. Martinho de Melo e Castro. Para maiores detalhes ver: Pataca 2004; Boschi 2012, Cruz 2004, Pereira 2002.

[47] Boschi 2012:14.

Universidade de Coimbra, retirando-se em Lisboa para redação de um detalhado relatório dirigido à rainha, dando conta dos progressos da reforma universitária, e que ficou conhecido pela designação de "Relação Geral do Estado da Universidade de Coimbra 1777". Tal iniciativa do reitor surtiu um efeito positivo. A reforma universitária prosseguiu sem alterações significativas, ficando quase incólume o seu corpo docente e administrativo. Vandelli continuou com os mesmos cargos que acumulava, lente proprietário das disciplinas de História Natural, intendente do *Laboratorio Chimico*, do Museu de História Natural e do Jardim Botânico.

Em 15 março de 1777, menos de um mês depois do falecimento de D. José I, Vandelli iniciou a redação de um detalhado inventário do Museu de História Natural da Universidade de Coimbra, dando conta de seus trabalhos naquele espaço, e segundo o naturalista, corria bem[48]. Ainda em 1777, no contexto do tratado de Santo Ildefonso entre Portugal e Espanha, sobre a questão da partilha setentrional do Brasil na América, Vandelli apresentou ao Marquês de Angeja a proposta de envio de uma comitiva de naturalistas formados na Universidade de Coimbra a agregar à comissão demarcadora de limites[49]. Tal proposta tinha em vista o levantamento de uma vasta série de informações sobre a colônia e visava inventariar as potencialidades da natureza no norte do Brasil. No referido período, outros impérios coloniais como os de França, Inglaterra e Holanda, promoviam viagens de reconhecimento nas suas colónias e delas obtinham resultados consideráveis, não só no campo científico, mas também econômico. Esta constatação aflorava na carta que Vandelli dirigia ao Marquês de Angeja em abono do sucesso da expedição sugerida.

---

[48] AUC-IV-1D-9-2-372, Processo do Professor Domingos Vandelli, rol dos itens do Museu de História Natural da Universidade de Coimbra, 15 de março de 1777. Manuscrito s/n.

[49] Carta de Domingos Vandelli ao Marquês de Angeja. Transcrito in: *Jornal de Coimbra* 1818: XVIII, parte I: 47-48)

As viagens filosóficas, como eram chamadas, são compreendidas como mais um passo para a institucionalização da história natural, configurando o início da profissionalização da área, já que para tais empreendimentos eram necessários homens treinados e capazes de indagar sobre a utilidade e relevância das amostras e produtos a serem recolhidos. A proposta de Vandelli foi bem recebida pelo Marquês de Angeja que por sua vez, escreveu a Tomás Xavier de Lima Nogueira Vasconcelos Telles da Silva (1727-1800), Visconde de Vila Nova de Cerveira, no intuito de persuadir as Coroas, portuguesa e espanhola, signatárias do tratado, dos benefícios de uma tal expedição[50]. A proposta também foi bem recebida pela Coroa portuguesa e Vandelli logo iniciou os preparativos para a grande viagem Filosófica, da qual seria responsável Alexandre Rodrigues Ferreira, seu antigo aluno. No decorrer dos preparativos da viagem e por motivos pouco claros, a partida dos naturalistas em direção ao Brasil sofreu atrasos e alterações. A grande comitiva foi desmembrada e os naturalistas foram enviados também para as colónias em África, seguindo um pequeno grupo para o Brasil em 1783. Entretanto, anos antes do início das viagens, Vandelli adiantava-se e, em 1779, despachava outro antigo aluno para uma viagem filosófica ao interior do Brasil, o Doutor Joaquim Veloso de Miranda.

Embora lente substituto na Universidade, o Doutor Veloso de Miranda decidiu pedir licença da instituição e retornar à capitania de Minas Gerais, no Brasil, a pretexto de cuidar de negócios de sua casa. A licença de Veloso Miranda foi concedida, ficando o mesmo obrigado a manter correspondência regular com a Universidade de Coimbra, ou seja, dando "notícias" da ciência que praticava

---

[50] Carta do Marquês de Angeja ao Visconde de Vila Nova de Cerveira transcrita in: *Jornal de Coimbra* 1818 XVIII, parte I, p 48-50.

na colônia[51]. Tal condição nunca veio a ocorrer conforme a letra da licença. Veloso de Miranda despachava os resultados de suas investigações aos cuidados de Vandelli e não da Universidade de Coimbra, boa parte do material enviado da capitania de Minas Gerais nunca chegou de facto à instituição.

Entre 1777 e 1779, Vandelli era considerado importante membro da comunidade académica. D. Francisco de Lemos solicitava ao mestre naturalista e ao Visconde de Barbacena parecer sobre a fundação da Congregação Geral das Ciências. Sobre este assunto, o Visconde respondia ao reitor com cepticismo, opinião partilhada também por Vandelli que julgava a Universidade de Coimbra "dominada pela inércia e conformismo"[52]. Embora o naturalista tenha criticado o corpo docente, fora justamente nesse período que passou a enfrentar algumas resistências e contestações no interior da Universidade. A atuação de Vandelli nas disciplinas não era de aprovação unânime, sofrendo oposição de um grupo de alunos reunidos em torno de Manuel Joaquim Henriques de Paiva (1752-1829). Na perspectiva de Ana Cristina Araújo (2015) tais divergências estão relacionadas com as movimentações de fundação de uma sociedade literária e económica, nomeadamente a *Sociedade dos Mancebos Patriotas estabelecida em Coimbra* em 1786[53]. As principais críticas desses opositores estão relacionadas com a atuação de Vandelli nas aulas e na condução do laboratório de Química, do qual era intendente. Ressalte-se que o naturalista possuía o título de Lente Proprietário das disciplinas que lecionava, o que lhe dava uma grande autonomia de decisão sobre vários aspectos das aulas práticas e teóricas. Embora contestado por alguns alunos, Vandelli continuou no exercício de suas funções com o "suporte" e a confiança de Francisco de Lemos. Entretanto, já

---

[51] Boschi 2012:101.
[52] BACL, série azul, ms. 24, carta n.º 3 e ms.1944 n.º 1.
[53] Araújo 2015: 336.

em 1779, a reitoria da Universidade passara a ser tutelada por José Francisco Rafael Miguel António de Mendonça (1725-1808) o que para Vandelli significou a perda do seu principal aliado na instituição. A partir da mudança do Reitor delineou-se na Universidade uma nova conjuntura, em larga medida correlacionada com as movimentações que ocorriam na Corte, na sequência da desarticulação da rede de influências do Marquês Pombal. Após a troca de reitor, o corpo docente da Universidade passou a movimentar-se de forma mais expressiva, os professores dos cursos de Cânones e Teologia reclamavam equiparação salarial e solicitavam alterações em alguns compêndios adotados. Segundo Virgínia Valadares (2004) alguns cursos da universidade ficaram acéfalos após a reforma de 1772 como foi o caso da Teologia, e outros como a Medicina funcionando sem um número adequado de lentes; tal quadro preocupava a direção da instituição e a Coroa portuguesa que intervinha diretamente na Universidade[54].

Com estas movimentações na Universidade, Vandelli passou a estar mais ausente da instituição, iniciando um período de sucessivas licenças na Corte. Admitimos que essas licenças tenham sido articuladas entre o próprio naturalista e o Visconde de Vila Nova de Cerveira, que naquele momento ocupava o cargo de secretário da rainha, em substituição do Marquês de Angeja. Em carta datada de 7 de novembro de 1780, o Visconde requeria ao reitor D. Francisco de Mendonça licença para que Vandelli se ausentasse de Coimbra para desenvolver atividade em Lisboa[55], relacionada, provavelmente, com as viagens filosóficas e com a supervisão do Jardim e Museu de Ajuda, entretanto decaído devido à ausência do seu Intendente du-

---

[54] Valadares 2004:178.

[55] AUC-IV-1D-9-2-372, Processo do Professor Domingos Vandelli, carta de 07 novembro de 1780 do Visconde de Vila Nova de Cerveira ao reitor reformador Principal Mendonça.

rante 8 anos consecutivos[56]. Durante os períodos de afastamento do naturalista das atividades na universidade, este era substituído por antigos alunos já formados e por ele indicados. Embora em regime de licença, Vandelli, como era da praxe, continuou a receber os seus honorários, como é possível perceber na correspondência dirigida ao reitor pelo Visconde de Vila Nova de Cerveira, recomendando o pagamento dos salários dos meses não lecionados[57].

Com mais tempo em Lisboa, Vandelli foi redimensionando as suas relações sociais, delimitando novamente a sua influência no interior da Corte, uma vez que a conjuntura política era bem diferente de 1764. O naturalista tentou aproximar-se de ministros e conselheiros da rainha, nomeadamente do Visconde de Vila Nova de Cerveira e do próprio príncipe D. João, tendo ainda alguma proximidade com D. Martinho de Melo e Castro. Tal estratégia de Vandelli garantiu-lhe alguma estabilidade e até o reconhecimento de um certo protagonismo na condução de projetos científicos da Coroa na América portuguesa.

6. A fundação da Academia de Real de Ciências de Lisboa: novos patronos e antigos clientes

Durante os primeiros anos do reinado de D. Maria I houve um esforço por parte da rainha em conciliar os "órfãos" de Pombal com os grupos políticos que retornaram ao poder. Muitos indivíduos alocados em postos da administração, pessoas de confiança do

---

[56] Durante os períodos em que Vandelli se dedicava às aulas na Universidade de Coimbra, a condução do jardim e do Museu ficava a cargo de Júlio Matiazzi, sempre retomando as funções nas épocas de férias universitárias.

[57] AUC-IV-1D-9-2-372, Processo do Professor Domingos Vandelli, carta de 14 de julho de 1787 do Visconde de Vila Nova de Cerveira ao reitor reformador principal Castro.

Marquês, foram destituídos de seus cargos, outros, muito provavelmente, viram-se ameaçados e para outros ainda houve uma redução significativa de influência política. Durante este período, as redes de influências foram redimensionadas em torno a homens considerados proeminentes na Corte, dada a proximidade que mantinham com a rainha. Nesse contexto de reorganização, muitos nobres e homens de ciências residentes no exterior retornaram a Portugal, alterando dinâmicas de poder e redes de sociabilidade. Nessa conjuntura destacamos o retorno a Portugal de D. João Carlos de Bragança de Sousa Ligne Tavares Mascarenhas da Silva (1719-1806), Duque de Lafões, após mais de vinte anos de residência em outros países europeus, Inglaterra, Áustria e França, países em que pôde aceder a priveligiados espaços de convívio filosófico e a academias de ciência[58].

No mesmo período, regista-se o retorno do Abade José Francisco Correia da Serra (1751-1823) ao reino. Nascido em Porugal, o abade residiu 26 anos em Itália nas cidades de Nápoles e Roma. Nos anos de residência em Roma, estudou botânica no *Collegio della Sapienza*, onde estabeleceu contatos com Francesco Maratti[59] e João Jacob Ferber[60], iniciando nesse período troca de correspondência com Lineu[61], sendo reconhecido como importante representante português na República das Letras.

---

[58] Carvalho 1986:141-171.

[59] Francesco Maratti professor de botânica no *Collegio della Sapienzza* era reconhecido opositor do sistema sexual de classificação lineana. Maratti era adepto do sistema de classificação Tournefort que privilegiava a comparação entre as partes das partes das plantas buscando suas semelhanças e afinidades. Simões, Diogo, Carneiro. 2006: 23.

[60] É atribuída ao sueco João Jacob Ferber a intermediação dos contatos entre Correia da Serra e Carlos Lineu. Resultado dessa troca de correspondência entre Correia da Serra e Lineu foi a movimentação promovida pelo Abade junto ao Cardeal Francesco Saverio Zelada em 1774, na defesa do sistema de classificação lineana e sua adoção na Universidade Romana, pois até aquele momento a metodologia era considerada herética. Simões, Diogo, Carneiro. 2006: 25.

[61] Simões, Diogo, Carneiro. 2006: 20-32.

De retorno a Portugal, em passagem por Serpa no Alentejo, sua terra natal, Correia da Serra seguiu para Beja em visita a Frei Manuel do Cenáculo, então prelado daquela localidade. Durante todo o reinado de D. José I, frei Manuel Cenáculo era considerado um importante homem de letras e um braço de ferro do Marquês de Pombal nas esferas educativa e religiosa, possuindo uma importante rede de contatos em Portugal e no exterior, que, em parte, manteve no reinado de D. Maria I. Na ocasião do encontro entre Cenáculo e o Abade esteve também presente o Duque de Lafões, e acreditamos que foi nesse encontro que foram delineados novos projetos científicos e um novo núcleo de sociabilidade em torno do Duque de Lafões[62].

Após esse encontro, já em Lisboa, o Duque iniciou, em 1779, negociações tendentes à fundação de uma instituição dedicada ao debate e à divulgação das ciências praticadas em Portugal, visando a continuidade do desenvolvimento científico, teórico e prático. A instituição almejada era uma Academia ou Sociedade de Ciências, embora em Portugal, nos anos anteriores, já houvesse iniciativas de grupos que se reuniam no intuito de discutir novas ideias e postulados, essas eram agremiações não institucionais, funcionando com reuniões esporádicas[63]. A pretensão do Duque de Lafões, e de outros ilustrados da época, era a abertura de uma instituição permanente como havia em outros países. Era nas academias e sociedades que homens de ciências de diferentes orientações políticas e culturais discutiam sobre a pertinência e validade do conhecimento produzido, avaliando os procedimentos e resultados segundo preceitos metodológicos, éticos e normativos. Célebres homens de ciências, atuaram nessas instituições como Robert Boyle (1627-1691) e Isaac Newton (1643-1727) na *Royal Society* na Inglaterra, e Galileu Galilei

---

[62] Simões, Diogo, Carneiro. 2006: 35.
[63] Simões, Diogo, Carneiro. 2006: 35.

na *Accademia del Cimento* na Itália, no século XVII. Em boa parte da Europa já existiam agremiações científicas destinadas ao debate das ciências e das humanidades, como as de Pádua, a Real Academia de Upsala na Suécia, a *Accademia dei Lincei* em Roma, a *Académie des Sciences* de Paris e a Academia de Ciências de São Petersburgo, na Rússia, para só referir algumas das mais conhecidas.

As academias, que incorparavam as regras de tratro social, possuíam uma estrutura fortemente hierarquizada. Por vezes, a eleição de um novo sócio estava condicionada pela sua influência política e pelos privilégios que poderiam ser auferidos com a admissão de um novo sócio poderoso e prestigiado, o que acontecia, com frequência, em países de monarquia absoluta que patrocinavam e intervinham diretamente no funcionamento institucional dessas agremiações de sábios e eruditos. Similar às academias, as sociedades de ciências, embora criadas com idênticos fins, apresentavam diferenças. As sociedades normalmente eram instituições mais horizontalizadas, não possuíam uma hierarquia social rígida, a escolha de novos sócios não estava essencialmente condicionada a privilégios. Embora o Estado também patrocinasse as sociedades, não havia uma intervenção direta em seu funcionamento, mantendo estas umas certa autonomia institucional. Geralmente as sociedades mantinham-se financeiramente com fundos próprios e com doações efetuadas por filantropos[64].

Em Portugal, a ideia de criar uma instituição que privilegiasse o debate científico acompanha os trabalhos preparatórios da reforma da Universidade de 1772. D. Francisco de Lemos sugere a necessidade de um regimento para a "Congregação geral das Ciências", sendo a mesma mencionada nos novos estatutos da Universidade de Coimbra[65]. Ignoramos se houve ou não um debate sobre o modelo

---

[64] Silva 2015: 10-11.

[65] Na *Redação geral do estado da universidade de Coimbra 1777*, Francisco de Lemos informa que já havia trabalhado nos estatutos de uma instituição ou congregação a ser fundada em Coimbra, destinada ao debate dos avanços das novas

a adoptar nesta fundação mas, por motivos políticos, uma academia que viesse a funcionar nos moldes da existente em Paris parecia mais adequada aos anseios da Coroa portuguesa. Um dos seus grandes impulsionadores, o Duque de Lafões, contou com apoio de homens de ciência que residiam em Portugal, como sócios honorários, e com a colaboração de sábios residentes no estrangeiro, como sócios correspondentes, ficando o abade Correia da Serra, o Visconde de Barbacena e Vandelli responsáveis pela redação dos respectivos estatutos.

Na articulação deste grupo é notório o clima de tensão entre Vandelli e Correia da Serra sobre alguns assuntos, como foi o caso da aprovação do funcionamento da instituição, em 1780, sem um espaço próprio para as reuniões. Em carta, o abade criticava o naturalista reputando-o como "mesquinho". Evitando maiores constrangimentos, o Duque de Lafões, em negociações pessoais com a Rainha, conseguiu garantir para instalação da instituição a cedência de algumas salas do Palácio das Necessidades[66]. Já em relação ao Visconde de Barbacena, é de crer que Vandelli cultivasse uma relação mais harmoniosa. Vandelli e Barbacena defendiam a criação de uma junta voltada para o desenvolvimento económico e industrial de Portugal, tendo por base a exploração racional dos recursos naturais do reino e das colónias. A Comissão da Indústria, como foi chamada, foi incorporada nos estatutos da Academia Real das Ciências de Lisboa com caráter de *in perpetuum*. Seria composta por oito sócios, eleitos, em períodos de três anos, sendo responsável

---

ciências. Segundo Francisco de Lemos tal texto seria o livro IV dos novos Estatutos universitários que não foram publicados dada a pressa do Marquês de Pombal em lançar a reforma em 1772. Tendo em vista tal informação, concordamos com José Luis Cardoso quando afirma que a ideia de fundação de uma Academia de Ciências em Portugal tem suas origens ligadas à redação dos estatutos da Universidade de Coimbra em 1772. Para mais detalhes ver Lemos, 1777 fl. 119-123, *fac símile* 1980: 107-110 e Cardoso 1989: 30.

[66] Silva 2015: 48.

pela articulação de uma extensa rede que difundiria as ciências a todos os recônditos do reino[67]. Além do conteúdo programático da instituição, fora também ideado pelos fundadores da Academia um plano de divulgação das ciências, por meio de periódicos que abarcassem todas as áreas de conhecimento.

Em 1780, nas suas sessões inaugurais, a Academia Real das Ciências de Lisboa apresentava um corpo de sócios, divididos por classe de conhecimento, presidida pelos primeiros membros da respectiva classe. Para a classe de Ciências de Observação: Domingos Vandelli, Abade José Correia da Serra, João Faustino (1736-1820), Bartolomeu da Costa (1732-1801), Visconde de Barbacena, António José Pereira (?-1792), António Soares Barbosa (1734-1801), Vicente Ferrer da Rocha (1727-1814). Para a classe de Ciências de Cálculo: D. António Rolim de Almeida Tavares [Conde de Azambuja] (1709--1782), Teodoro de Almeida (1722-1804), D. João de Almeida Portugal [Marquês de Alorna], José Joaquim Soares de Barros (1721-1793), José Monteiro da Rocha, João António Dalla Bella e Miguel Franzini. Para a classe das Belas Letras: Duque de Lafões, Miguel Lúcio de Portugal e Castro, Joaquim de Foios (?), Fernando Telles da Silva [Conde de Tarouca] (1754-1818), Pedro José da Fonseca (1737-1816), Principal Mascarenhas (1752-1791), Gonçalo Xavier de Alcáçova Carneiro (1712--1785) e António Pereira de Figueiredo (1725-1797).

A organização da instituição tentou conciliar diferentes sensibilidades e pontos de vista como as que eram representadas pelos oratorianos Teodoro de Almeida, Joaquim de Foios e João Faustino e o ex-jesuíta José Monteiro da Rocha[68]. Tentou conciliar, também,

---

[67] Silva 2015: 236.

[68] A partir da fundação do colégio dirigido pela Congregação do Oratório, que, em 1750, passou a funcionar no Convento das Necessidades, intensificaram-se as críticas aos colégios da Companhia Jesus. Eram diferentes os métodos e conteúdos ensinados nas instituições escolares das duas congregações, conforme salientou Dias, J. S. da Silva 1953: 196 e ss. Tais divergências ganharam expressão pública

antigos colaboradores do Marquês de Pombal como Vandelli, e inimigos do antigo ministro como o Marquês de Alorna. Digna de nota é a ausência de Francisco de Lemos e frei Manuel do Cenáculo do núcleo fundador da instituição. A falta de Cenáculo era lamentada pelo Abade Correia de Serra, que antevia, sem ele, um "naufrágio" para a academia[69]. Tais ausências talvez sejam o resultado da prudência política do Duque, uma vez que a presença dos dois letrados poderia ser tomada como tentativa de reorganização da Junta da Providência Literária, da qual tinham feito parte.

Antes da abertura da Academia de Real das Ciências de Lisboa, os seus sócios fundadores tendiam a polarizar-se entre "Marianos" e "Pombalinos". Essa tensão tornou-se patente na sessão inaugural da instituição, quando Teodoro de Almeida, na oração de abertura, comparou o estádio de desenvolvimento das ciências de Portugal ao do Marrocos. As suas palavras foram percepcionadas como um libelo anti-pombalino e geraram uma polémica que ultrapassou a própria instituição[70].

Embora os membros da Academia Real das Ciências de Lisboa articulassem propostas que privilegiavam o adiantamento das ciências em Portugal, esses projetos passavam por caminhos e concepções diferentes, em certa medida alimentadas por interesses políticos e pessoais distintos. De facto, a Academia Real das Ciências de Lisboa não pode ser percebida como uma instituição una, com um corpo de sócios coeso ou mesmo homogéneo e menos ainda como uma agremiação exclusivamente científica, já que a instituição era composta por homens de poder e de alto prestígio na Corte e no exterior, possuindo ligações diretas com o poder régio que patrocinava as suas actividades.

---

nas páginas de periódicos da época, como o *Mercúrio Philosóphico*. Simões, Diogo, Carneiro. 2002: 73.

[69] Simões, Diogo, Carneiro. 2006: 53.
[70] Silva 2015: 39.

Muitos dos sócios da Academia Real das Ciências de Lisboa cultivam entre si laços de amizade mais antigos e relações sociais pautadas por motivos diversos. Vandelli era próximo de José Monteiro da Rocha, Miguel Franzini, António Soares Barbosa, António José Pereira e João António Dalla Bella, professores da Universidade de Coimbra, mantendo também relações próximas com o Visconde de Barbacena, secretário da Academia. Tal grupo pode ser considerado o núcleo "Pombalino" da Academia de Ciências, tendo sido boa parte desses homens colaboradores diretos de Pombal ou identificados com a política do antigo ministro. Do outro lado, o grupo Mariano, composto pelos Oratorianos como Teodoro de Almeida, Joaquim de Foios, João Faustino, e nobres como o Marquês de Alorna e, ainda, outros sócios correspondentes e supranumerários. Embora os sócios possuíssem diferentes pontos de vista, organizando-se em "facções políticas", os possíveis embates delas decorrentes não inviabilizavam o funcionamento da instituição. O Duque de Lafões e o abade Correia da Serra conseguiram, num primeiro momento, aglutinar os membros da academia, minimizando os embates decorrentes do confronto de diferentes sensibilidades políticas e ideológicas.

7. Novas flores para um novo patrono

A fundação da Academia Real de Ciências de Lisboa foi um passo importante para os homens de ciência da época. Criou espaço e condições de segurança para a discussão de ideias e de resultados de pesquisa. Após avaliação e validação pelos académicos, novas experiências ou específicas aplicações da ciência eram objeto de publicação e divulgação, de acordo com o que a instituição propunha. Nesse sentido, cada sócio apresentava um trabalho, destinado a ser apreciado e debatido pelos membros da instituição. Na altura, Vandelli já recebia de seus antigos alunos dispersos nas colônias um grande volume de amostras da história natural, ainda não estudadas nem catalogadas. Da capitania de Minas Gerais no Brasil, recebeu do Doutor Joaquim Veloso de Miranda, em 1781, uma remessa de amostras acompanhada de desenhos de flores daquela região. Embora Veloso de Miranda possuísse o título de Doutor e de sócio correspondente da Academia Real das Ciências de Lisboa[71], era praxe confiar a um naturalista mais experiente a análise dos elementos coligidos e a nomeação dos géneros botânicos. Ao fazer esse trabalho, Vandelli decidiu nomear as plantas da mesma forma do *Fasciculus Plantarum* de 1771, ou seja, dando às flores nomes em homenagem a pessoas de suas relações sociais. O *Herbário* do Dr. Veloso, com as correções de Vandelli, é composto por oito páginas, cinco das quais preenchidas com desenhos botânicos e outras três com a descrição lineana, com o título *Fasciculus plantarum Brasiliensium*, apresentado à Academia, em 1787, com a seguinte proposta de nomenclaturas:

Fasciculus Plantarum Brasiliensium[72]

Género	Referência à pessoa ou casa ilustre
Lavradia	Casa dos Marqueses de Lavradio
Galvania	Casa dos Condes de Galveias
Fereiria	Vicente Ferrer
Barbacenia	Casa dos Viscondes de Barbacena
Quelusia	Palácio de Queluz.
Davilla	Casa dos Viscondes de Vila Nova de Cerveira
Lemia	Francisco de Lemos
Marialva	Casa dos Marqueses de Marialva
Correia	Abade Correia da Serra

---

[71] Pouco depois de sua partida para o Brasil, Joaquim Veloso de Miranda foi admitido na recém-fundada Academia Real das Ciências de Lisboa como sócio correspondente. Sua admissão é atribuída à indicação de Vandelli seu antigo professor e aceite pelo visconde Barbacena. Boschi 2012:125.

[72] Aqui colocamos somente os nomes das plantas que conseguimos localizar homenagem correspondente faltando ainda os géneros Botânicos: *Amomun, Vochia, Callisia, Contarenia, Urceola, Tapanhuacanca.*

Vellosia	Joaquim Veloso de Miranda
Lafoensia	Duque de Lafões
Paliavana	Quinta da Palhavã
Limia	Casa dos Marqueses da Ponte de Lima
Mella	Martinho de Melo Castro
Orobanchia	Arraial do Ouro Branco, Minas Gerais, Brasil
Mendoncia	Luís António Furtado de Castro do Rio de Mendonça e Faro
Vismia	Gerard de Visme
Bragantia	Bragantia – Casa de Bragança

De maneira geral, Vandelli homenageou boa parte da nobreza dirigente de Portugal do final do século XVIII, indivíduos importantes e das suas relações sociais. Com a espécie *Galvania* Vandelli fez uma homenagem à casa dos Condes de Galveias; ressalte-se que tal homenagem estava relacionada diretamente com o ministro D. Martinho Melo e Castro (1716-1795), que, embora não tivesse esse título, era neto de D. André de Melo e Castro (1668-1753), quarto Conde de Galveias[73]. E, ainda, em homenagem ao mesmo ministro, Vandelli criou a taxonomia *Mella*. O mesmo aconteceu com o género *Marialva*, numa menção a D. Rodrigo José de Meneses (1750-1807) membro da casa dos Marqueses de Marialva, que ocupava o cargo de governador da capitania de Minas Gerais no ano 1781, ano do envio da remessa[74]. Outra figura proeminente que Vandelli também homenageou foi o Marquês de Lavradio, Luís de Almeida Portugal Soares de Alarcão d'Eça e Melo Silva Mascarenhas (1729-1790), Vice-Rei do Brasil entre 1769-1778, com o espécime *Lavradia*.

Da Universidade de Coimbra, Vandelli homenageou o reitor reformador D. Francisco de Lemos Pereira de Faria Coutinho com o género *Lemia* e os discípulos Joaquim Veloso de Miranda e o Visconde de Barbacena, ao atribuir os nomes *Vellozia* e *Barbacenia*, respec-

---

[73] Gayo 1938: 138.
[74] Gayo 1938: 97.

tivamente. Além de homenagear Veloso de Miranda, Vandelli ainda deu a uma planta o nome do local onde o naturalista residia naquele momento, o arraial de Ouro Branco, com o espécime *Orobanchia*. Além de indivíduos, o naturalista teve a preocupação de dar às plantas os nomes de locais que julgava importantes para as ciências em Portugal, como por exemplo, a taxonomia *Paliavana*, que referencia uma quinta nos arredores de Lisboa, denominada Palhavã, cuja propriedade pertencia à D. Henrique de Meneses (1727-1787), Marquês do Louriçal e Conde da Ericeira. O Conde da Ericeira teve um papel importante na divulgação e debate das Luzes na primeira metade do século XVIII. Outra flor que designa um local é o género *Queluzia* por meio da qual o naturalista fazia referência ao Palácio Real de Queluz, residência de verão da rainha D. Maria I.

Da Academia de Real das Ciências, Vandelli teve o cuidado de homenagear alguns membros honorários como o presidente e fundador da instituição, o Duque de Lafões com o género *Lafoensia*, Vicente Ferrer com o género *Fereiria*. No caso do abade Correa da Serra, segundo secretário da Academia, o próprio Vandelli comunicou o batismo da flor com o nome do naturalista, em missiva datada de 12 julho de 1782: "Eu continuo a fazer abrir os novos géneros do nosso Veloso, que acabei de examinar o seu herbário e a um deles lhe ponho o nome *Corrêa*"[75].

O espécime *Vismia*, representou uma homenagem a um importante negociante inglês residente em Portugal, Gerard de Visme. Visme era amigo próximo de Joseph Banks e é possível que a proximidade entre o prestigiado naturalista inglês e Vandelli tenha sido promovida por este negociante. Tal aproximação pode ter ocorrido entre 1764 e 1771 já que nas notas de abertura do *Fasciculus Plantarum* de 1771 há um poema dedicado a Banks escrito por Vandelli[76]. Ressalte-se que os desenhos originais das plantas feitos por Veloso de Miranda

---

[75] Pataca 2006: 309.
[76] Luckhurst 2011: 127-160.

foram enviados a Londres, aos cuidados de Banks, podendo ser consultados ainda hoje no Arquivo do Jardim Botânico de Kew[77]. Embora alguns dos nomes que constam na lista não fossem membros honorários da Academia ou diretamente ligados ao campo científico, de alguma forma contribuiram para o desenvolvimento das ciências em Portugal. É o caso de Tomás Xavier de Lima, Marquês da Ponte de Lima e Visconde de Vila Nova de Cerveira, ministro do Exterior e Guerra, que foi homenageado duas vezes com os géneros *Davilla* e *Limia*. A dedicação que lhe mereceu esta personalidade espelha a complexa teia de contrapartidas geradas pelas práticas científicas setecentistas. Vandelli precisava do apoio do ministro de D. Maria I e conseguiu obter o imprescindível auxílio do exército na implementação das Viagens Filosóficas no norte do Brasil. As expedições militares asseguraram o transporte de géneros naturais, desbravaram território e colaboraram com os exploradores científicos, em terra ou no mar[78]. Por outro lado, Vandelli devia manifestar a sua gratidão ao Visconde de Vila Nova de Cerveira que o protegia, dirimindo questões na Universidade de Coimbra relacionadas com o programa das viagens filosóficas. Portanto, aquela homenagem confirmava o papel de patrono assumido pelo Visconde de Vila Nova de Cerveira em relação a Vandelli e vinha compensar o parcial isolamento político criado com a queda do Marquês de Pombal.

Como se percebe, Vandelli usou os mesmos recursos retóricos de agraciemento ao nomear as plantas apresentadas à Academia Real das Ciências de Lisboa, chegando em alguns casos a homenagear duas vezes a mesma pessoa e referenciando locais que julgava importantes na difusão das ciências. De acordo com as lógicas do mecenato, da clientela e do decoro cortesão, a nomenclatura do *Fasciculus Plantarum*

---

[77] Arquivo Kew Gardens, Londres, Joaquin Velloso de Miranda (1785). Autograph letter to Sir J. Banks, consisting of descriptions, with water colour drawings of genera of Plants collected. Foll. 84.°, Minas Geraes.

[78] Domingues 2001: 823-838.

Brasiliensium reunia condições para ser louvada pelos membros da Academia Real das Ciências de Lisboa. Boa parte dos nomes eram membros dessa instituição e faziam parte das relações sociais de Vandelli. No entanto, tal nomenclatura também causou certo mal-estar na agremiação. Um dos sócios, João de Loureiro (1710-1791), recém--aceite, acusou Vandelli "de adulador e de falta de rigor científico".

8. Nomes contra os princípios da ética

É importante observar de perto o naturalista que acusa Vandelli. Trata-se do ex-jesuíta João de Loureiro. Como já referimos, personalidades antes postas à margem do processo político e cultural pelo Marquês de Pombal retornaram, durante o reinado de D. Maria I, ao país. Como os jesuítas haviam sido expulsos de Portugal, seria de esperar que João Loureiro tivesse alguma dificuldade em voltar ao reino, após um longo período de permanência no Oriente. Porém, a avançada idade daquele congregado e o facto de ter dedicado parte da sua vida ao estudo da História Natural tornaram irrelevante a sua atuação como membro da Companhia de Jesus. Na verdade, Loureiro era um botânico de renome internacional e mantinha boas relações com alguns políticos ilustrados portugueses. A sua indicação como membro da Academia Real das Ciências de Lisboa partiu de Luís Pinto de Sousa Coutinho[79], como demonstra este passo de uma carta do Visconde de Barbacena a Vandelli:

> Chegou a Portugal um Ex Jesuíta português da Conchinchina chamado Frei Loureiro, que a Academia já tinha há muitos meses

---

[79] Luís Pinto de Sousa Coutinho, reconhecido político da época, só vai obter a confirmação do título de Visconde de Balsemão em decreto de 14 de agosto de 1801; entretanto, como se observa na carta do Visconde de Barbacena anos antes da confirmação, já era tratado por Balsemão. Zuqueti 1984:386.

eleito membro correspondente(...) Dizem- me que é grande Botânico e muito observador, e por tal tinha sido lembrado e recomendado pelo Balsemão, que nos deu a conhecer[80].

Como se percebe, Loureiro chegou a Portugal e reatou contactos com nobres ilustrados e com alguns membros da Academia Real de Ciências de Lisboa. No interior da instituição, Loureiro ter-se-á aproximado do abade Correia da Serra. Ressalte-se que, embora o abade tivesse sido homenageado por Vandelli, a convivência entre ambos nunca foi pacífica. Nas cartas trocadas com outros naturalistas e políticos da época, Correia da Serra demonstrava descontentamento pela ciência praticada por Vandelli, qualificando-o de péssimo botânico[81]. Bem relacionado com os membros da Academia e sem temer retaliações, Loureiro contestou o herbário apresentado por Vandelli.

Da polêmica ocorrida entre Vandelli e Loureiro, a propósito da questão do herbário, não conseguimos localizar a maior parte dos documentos que possam ter existido. No entanto, conhece-se o manuscrito anónimo, com o título *Notas sobre o Fasciculus plantas do Brasil de Joaquim Velloso de Miranda*, que hoje se encontra na Biblioteca do *Muséum d'Histoire Naturelle*, em Paris, atribuído ao próprio João de Loureiro, onde se pode ler:

> Tendo-se lido em uma assembleia da Academia este Fasciculus Plantarum Brasiliensium do Senhor Veloso, se notou, que aos novos generos desta estimável coleção botânica se tinham posto pela maior parte os nomes das famílias ilustres de Portugal, sem motivo, ou fundamento algum Botânico: e que isso em outras Nações poderia ser julgado por adulação. A mim pareceu-me, que

---

[80] apud Brigola 2003:12.
[81] ANTT, Arquivo da casa de Linhares. Mç. 63, n.º 112. Carta de Correia da Serra a Rodrigo de Sousa Coutinho. Londres, 28 de julho de 1800.

os nomes Bragantia, Barbacenia, e Correana se poderiam conservar sem aquele receio, pelo motivo, que em seu lugar se declara. Todos os outros em que não milita semelhante razão (ou eu a ignoro) vão trocados como melhor me ocorreu. O Senhor Vandelli poderá conserva-los ou muda-los, conforme julgar: e assim também as notas, que sendo mandado fiz sobre a dita coleção de plantas: o que tudo sujeito ingenuamente a sua correção e da Academia[82].

Os nomes listados para serem trocados por Vandelli eram: *Galvanea, Fereiria, Queluzia, Correia, Vellosia, Lafoensia, Barbacenia, Davillia, Lemia, Marialva, Paliavana* e *Mendoncia*. O autor do documento ainda ressaltava que, "saindo a luz estas plantas em nome do Sr. Veloso, é contra os princípios da ética, que ele ponha o seu nome a alguma delas"[83].

É possível observar na escrita do documento que algumas ponderações foram feitas pelo autor com o intuito de não desagradar a pessoas ilustres, como é o caso da planta batizada com a designação de *Bragantia*, em homenagem à casa real de Bragança. Mesmo tendo sido publicada em 1771, no tempo de D. José I, Vandelli tenta republicar a mesma nomenclatura, provavelmente para chamar a atenção da rainha. As flores com os nomes que homenageavam o Abade Correia da Serra e o Visconde de Barbacena, secretários da Academia de Ciências naquele momento, segundo o autor, também poderiam continuar, pois estes eram naturalistas. Na avaliação do autor do documento é perceptível que a posição social não deixara de ser um critério na nomeação das plantas, apesar das exclusões propostas. Sugeria-se assim que Vandelli modificasse não todos mas apenas alguns nomes dos gêneros identificados,

---

[82] MHNP, Mss. 2445 Notas sobre o Fasciculus plantas do Brasil de Joaquim Velloso de Miranda.

[83] MHNP, Mss. 2445 Notas sobre o Fasciculus plantas do Brasil de Joaquim Velloso de Miranda.

para publicação no primeiro tomo das *Memórias da Academia Real das Ciências de Lisboa*.

A avaliação negativa da atitude de Vandelli em relação ao nomes não significa que Loureiro não tenha compreendido a estratégia do naturalista. Os sócios perceberam o efeito desejado por Vandelli, ao chamar a atenção dos homenageados e, principalmente, a fim de manter laços sociais duradouros, o que segundo as lógicas cortesãs ainda vigentes no período, traria mais prestígio e favores ao proponente. Esse tipo de homenagem era comum no meio científico da época. O próprio Vandelli foi homenageado por Lineu, alguns anos antes. E, em Minas Gerais, José Vieira Couto (1752-1827) nomeou uma região, Nova Lorena Diamantina em homenagem ao governador da capitania, Bernardo José de Lorena (1756-1818), e uma colina, Monte Rodrigo em homenagem ao ministro D. Rodrigo de Sousa Coutinho (1755-1812), sem grande escândalo[84]. Estamos assim em crer que a censura feita a Vandelli pelos membros da Academia foi uma tentativa de comprometer velhos laços de fidelidade, contendo-se, deste modo, o seu papel de adulador de ministros e a sua proeminência na Corte.

No que diz respeito à falta de rigor científico e demais críticas feitas por outros homens de ciência, como o abade Correia da Serra, à sua actuação como botânico, elas derivam, provavelmente, da percepção de que as descrições botânicas deveriam ser claras, objetivas e não "obscuras" ou agudas, como ainda era habitual em algumas academias e sociedades. Em finais do século XVIII, a comunidade científica já se movimentava no sentido de uma universalização das

---

[84] No período moderno esse tipo de homenagens sempre foi comum. No caso de José Vieira Couto, assim como Vandelli, a intenção era usar essa estratégia para chamar a atenção do Ministro D. Rodrigo Sousa Coutinho e do Governador de Minas na época, Bernardo José de Lorena, no intuito de angariar apoio nas dificuldades enfrentadas pela família Vieira Couto com o intendente do distrito Diamantino, João Inácio do Amaral Silveira. Para maiores detalhes ver: Silva. 2002:65.

práticas metodológicas, o que só foi ocorrer de fato no século XIX[85]. Parte desses esforços eram pautados pela noção de que a história natural viria a tornar-se um campo de conhecimento autónomo, autojustificado e universal. Logo, a sua metodologia deveria estar de acordo com as lógicas internas de justificação da ciência.

Como se percebe, procedimentos e valores até então aceites passaram a ser problemáticos, sendo evocados princípios éticos na fundamentação da crítica da nomenclatura botânica proposta. Naquele momento, a honra e o prestígio social do homem de ciência davam lugar à capacidade de produção de conhecimento válido e certificado por uma coletividade específica. As Cortes deixaram de ser espaços de validação do conhecimento científico, embora muitos homens de ciências tenham exercido funções no seu interior, esses atuavam também nas sociedades de ciências. Embora a Academia Real de Ciências de Lisboa possuísse um número elevado de sócios de extração nobre, aquele não era um espaço cortesão propriamente dito. Ao contrário da sociabilidade horizontal que a academia pretendia impor, Vandelli agiu como se estivesse no ambiente palaciano, obedecendo às lógicas sociais daquele espaço. De qualquer modo, embora Vandelli tenha sido muito criticado na sua forma de fazer ciência, a metodologia lineana que adoptou não estava em causa; o que era contestado era sua postura profissional, usando a ciência *ad homimem* e para fins pessoais.

Em contrapartida, a *Flora Cochinchinensis* de Loureiro, publicada em 1789, não apresenta qualquer evidência de que o naturalista fizesse uso de técnicas retóricas na apresentação de seus resultados. A obra de Loureiro ficou mundialmente conhecida sendo mencionada em várias academias de ciências da Europa[86]. Em discurso proferido na

---

[85] Kury 2011: 5.

[86] A obra de João de Loureiro, *Flora Cochinchinensis* foi muito bem-recebida na comunidade científica internacional. Em carta enviada ao abade Correia da Serra, José Bonifácio de Andrada e Silva noticiava o sucesso da obra de Loureiro e

Academia Real das Ciências de Lisboa no dia 12 de maio 1792, "Elogio ao Sr. Loureiro", por ocasião de sua morte, o Abade Correia da Serra deixa muito clara a qualidade da ciência praticada pelo botânico:

> Que abundância de descobrimentos, que multidão de observações, e sobretudo que originalidade junta a elegância, se mostra em huma obra composta tão longe de onde taes obras se compõem. Os botânicos verão em alguns poucos lugares della vestigios da incomoda situação em que foi compos[ta] mas que o são ao mesmo tempo do demasiado escrúpulo e atenção do autor, mas a *viveza das descrições a clareza da exposição, e do methodo* encantão, e é tudo seu[87].

Neste contexto, percebe-se que o prestígio de Domingos Vandelli tenha declinado drasticamente, podendo a perda de reputação científica de sua pessoa ser compreendida como momento crucial para a compreensão de seu papel nos anos que se seguiram. Em finais de século, Vandelli envolveu-se em outras querelas, com o naturalista Félix Avelar Brotero (1744-1828) e, novamente, com Manoel Joaquim Henriques de Paiva, além de desavenças com seu auxiliar nos jardins do palácio de Ajuda, Júlio Mattiazzi. Na maioria dos casos, Vandelli obteve sucesso em sua defesa, pois estava muito bem escudado junto do príncipe D. João e de outros nobres com funções de relevo, como o Visconde de Vila Nova de Cerveira.

Como Vandelli não alterou nenhum dos nomes por si propostos para as plantas que constavam do seu herbário, teve de enfrentar a supressão do mesmo no primeiro tomo das *Memórias da Academia das Ciências de Lisboa*, saído em 1797. No interior desse tomo, na

---

os constantes pedidos de aquisição por outros homens de ciência. Simões, Diogo, Carneiro. 2006:57.

[87] ANTT, Arquivos Particulares, Abade Correia da Serra, Caixa 2B, A 42. 4 f... (sublinhado nosso).

página 37, ainda é possível ler a apresentação na qual consta o nome do Doutor Joaquim Veloso de Miranda como autor dos desenhos, à data da apresentação do trabalho à Academia das Ciências de Lisboa, em abril de 1787. No entanto, nas folhas seguintes, não consta nenhuma das flores anunciadas, saltando da página 37 à 40[88].

No que se refere ao Dr. Joaquim Veloso de Miranda, conhecem-se sanções imediatas: o seu nome deixou de constar da lista de sócios correspondentes da Academia das Ciências de Lisboa[89].

Embora a comunidade científica portuguesa tenha dado ganho de causa a Loureiro, Vandelli não se deu por vencido. Os nomes "científicos" das polémicas flores vieram à luz numa publicação da Tipografia Académico-Régia de Coimbra, em 1788, intitulada *"Florae Lusitanicae et Brasiliensis Specimen [...] et Epistolae ab Eruditis viris Carolo A Linné, Antonio de Haen ad Dominicum Vandelli scriptae"*. Mais uma vez, é possível observar que tal publicação não agradou a muitos homens de ciência, como relata o abade Correia da Serra em carta dirigida ao inglês James Edward Smith, datada de outubro de 1788:

> As novidades que posso lhe dar sobre História Natural são poucas. O Professor Vandelli acabou de publicar o Dicionário Português de História Natural, pobre rapsódia, assim como a Specimen Flora Luzitanicae et Brasiliensis, cheias de géneros que batizou com o nome de quem não conhece uma palavra de botânica, mas que ele quer lisonjear, em virtude da sua importância ou posição[90].

---

[88] *Memorias da Academia Real das Sciencias de Lisboa* 1797: 37.
[89] Boschi 2012: 123.
[90] *apud* Simões, Diogo, Carneiro. 2006: 53.

9. Conclusão

Como é possível observar, a atuação de Domingos Vandelli em Portugal foi marcada por uma intensa atividade social, que se reflectiu em boa parte de sua produção científica. A sua proeminência e atuação nos vários projetos científicos da Coroa portuguesa requeria a manutenção de laços sociais com importantes membros da política da época. Para esse fim, ajustou a estratégia a "capitalização" da sua produção científica aos valores simbólicos do Antigo Regime, o que lhe possibilitou fazer valer a sua posição de conveniência no interior da Corte Portuguesa.

Mas à medida que a história natural se foi transformando num campo epistemologicamente autojustificado, esses valores foram-se tornando problemáticos no interior da comunidade científica. O prestígio embora contribuísse para credibilidade do homem de ciência, já não legitimava, por si mesmo, o conhecimento produzido, e também não dispensava a avaliação colectiva. Neste processo a honra foi deixando de ser valor indispensável para a prática científica dando lugar à credibilidade e à capacidade de produção de conhecimento válido, o que deixa entrever uma mudança crucial do sistema social das ciências e o início das transformações deontológicas na prática científica em Portugal.

Vandelli atuou num mundo em transformação, tendo sido criticado por alguns contemporâneos mais jovens que tinham outra percepção da "difícil arte de fazer ciência", nas palavras do abade Correia da Serra. É no quadro dessas transformações e desses debates inerentes ao processo de desenvolvimento do conhecimento científico que a história natural foi se firmando em Portugal, num contexto de renovação política, cultural e, principalmente, mental.

A REFORMA POMBALINA DA UNIVERSIDADE DE COIMBRA E A INSTITUCIONALIZAÇÃO DAS CIÊNCIAS MATEMÁTICAS E ASTRONÓMICAS EM PORTUGAL

Fernando B. Figueiredo
CITEUC/CMUC, Departamento de Matemática da Universidade de Coimbra
bandeira@mat.uc.pt

António Leal-Duarte
CMUC, Departamento de Matemática da Universidade de Coimbra
leal@mat.uc.pt

Introdução

No século XVIII, particularmente na segunda metade, a astronomia desenvolve-se em torno do chamado programa newtoniano. Um programa que se caracteriza por uma íntima relação entre a astronomia observacional (astrometria), fortemente impulsionada pela precisão instrumental atingida, e os avanços da astronomia teórica (mecânica celeste) permitidos pelos trabalhos de astrónomos e matemáticos, como D'Alembert (1717-1783), Euler (1707-1783), Clairaut (1713-65), Lagrange (1736-1813) ou Laplace (1749-1827). O programa científico dos principais observatórios astronómicos europeus dos finais do século XVIII e inícios do XIX, como por exemplo o de Greenwich, Paris, ou Berlim, caracteriza-se por uma demanda constante de observações e medições precisas da posição dos corpos do sistema solar e estrelas, na tentativa de melhoria da mecânica newtoniana e das ferramentas matemáticas envolvidas, nomeadamente das tabelas astronómicas. Laplace é esclarecedor:

> "*L'astronomie, considérée de la manière la plus générale, est un grand problème de Mécanique, dont les éléments des mouvements célestes sont les arbitraires; sa solution dépend à la fois de l'exactitude des observations et de la perfection de l'analyse, et il importe extrêmement d'en bannir tout empirisme et de la réduire à n'emprunter de l'observation que les données indispensables*"
> (Laplace 1878-82: i)

Neste processo contínuo de desenvolvimento de métodos instrumentais, de redução dos dados observacionais e refinamento da teoria, a prática astronómica ocorre principalmente em torno da medida angular das ascensões e declinações dos astros que atravessam os meridianos dos observatórios. Um programa que Jim Bennett intitula de '*international meridian program consensus*':

> "*Thus programs of meridian measurement came to be pursued in all the active observatories of Europe [...] they [observational data] were accumulated by the activity that became the sine qua non of an astronomical observatory.*" (Bennett 1992)

Em Portugal só depois da Reforma Pombalina, e particularmente com a entrada em funcionamento em 1799 do Real Observatório Astronómico da Universidade de Coimbra, é que o país se sintoniza verdadeira e consequentemente com este programa astronómico internacional. De facto, esta Reforma do ensino universitário português inicia um processo de institucionalização da ciência moderna em Portugal, nomeadamente da matemática e astronomia. Não estamos com isto a afirmar que antes não houve atividade astronómica alguma no país; bem pelo contrário[1]. O que sustentamos é que foi a partir da Reforma que o ensino e a atividade astronómica portuguesa se organizou e estabeleceu em moldes formais semelhantes aos que se já haviam estabelecido em muitos países da Europa Iluminista. No entanto podemos recuar aos anos 20-30 da primeira metade do século XVIII para assistir a uma emergente atividade astronómica no país, e que teve inclusive alguns ecos além-fronteiras. Muita dessa atividade está intimamente ligada à ação científica e educacional dos Jesuítas e dos Oratorianos.

A astronomia portuguesa até à primeira metade do século XVIII

Até muito recentemente a historiografia portuguesa caracterizou o período de aproximadamente 200 anos que vai de Pedro Nunes (1502-1578) às reformas Pombalinas como um período de quase absoluta estagnação da educação científica em Portugal, cabendo em grande parte aos jesuítas a responsabilidade por tal[2]. Faz já algum tempo que vários e importantes estudos começaram a derrubar essa *'narrativa convencional'*[3].

Em Portugal, desde a fundação da nacionalidade que certamente alguns estudos de astrologia/astronomia existiriam nas escolas dos principais mosteiros (p. ex. Santa Cruz de Coimbra ou Alcobaça).

---

[1] Veja-se por exemplo Carvalho 1985.

[2] Os jesuítas instalaram-se em Portugal em 1540 e em duzentos anos estabelecem uma ampla rede de escolas para a educação da juventude. Em 1759, ano em que foram expulsos, tinham mais de 40 colégios (e a Universidade de Évora), oferecendo ensino gratuito a cerca de 20.000 alunos (estima-se em cerca de 3 milhões a população de Portugal nesta altura). A Universidade de Coimbra embora não lhes pertencesse era muito influenciada pelo Colégio das Artes, uma faculdade dedicada à preparação dos estudos universitários que lhes pertencia.

[3] Veja-se, por exemplo, Baldini 2004 e Leitão 2007.

É sabido que em 1431 o Infante D. Henrique, o Navegador (1394--1460), doou uma série de casas à Universidades com o propósito de nelas se estabelecerem o ensino das *Sete Artes Liberais* onde se incluía a "*astrologia*".

Com as sucessivas viagens de descoberta e exploração da costa africana o interesse pela astronomia e cartografia intensifica-se, o *Tractatus de Sphera* de Sacrobosco (c. 1195-c. 1256) é amplamente estudado e comentado. Em 1496 Abraão Zacuto (1450-1522) imprime em Leiria o *Almanach Perpetuum*, fornecendo várias tabelas com as posições dos astros (efemérides); a '*quinta táboa*' permitia calcular a declinação do sol, coordenada fundamental para o cálculo da latitude. No reinado de D. Manuel I (1469-1521), em 1518, é criada na Universidade a cadeira de Astronomia. Pedro Nunes, nomeado em 1544 por D. João III (1502-1557) professor da cadeira de Matemática e Cosmógrafo-Mor, alargará o estudo da astronomia a um nível científico, muito além da base empírica da astronomia náutica do século anterior[4]. Nos séculos seguintes (XVI e XVII) a matemática seria estudada na Universidade de Coimbra e nos colégios Jesuítas, principalmente em Lisboa, na *Aula da Esfera*, como era conhecido entre 1590 e 1759 o curso de matemática do Colégio Jesuíta de Santo Antão. Durante este período os estudos de matemática e astronomia na Universidade passam por uma fase de enfraquecimento, sendo na prática o ensino e treino dos pilotos, até meados do século XVIII, baseado essencialmente em duas estruturas, o *Cosmógrafo-Mor* e a já referida *Aula da Esfera*.

De acordo com o '*Regimento do Cosmógrafo-Mor*' do ano 1592, era dever deste dar uma aula de matemática aos pilotos, timoneiros e pessoas nobres que quisessem servir a marinha. Era também sua

---

[4] Pedro Nunes é considerado um dos maiores matemáticos da história portuguesa. Foi professor de matemática e astronomia na Universidade de Coimbra entre 1544 e 1557 e *Cosmógrafo-mor* do reino. Sobre a sua vida e obra veja-se (Leitão 2002); especialmente sobre os seus contributos na astronomia (teórica) veja-se Almeida, no prelo.

obrigação examinar todos os que desejassem publicar cartas de marear e fabricar instrumentos náuticos; bem como servir de juiz em disputas sobre demarcação de terras e mares. A jesuítica *Aula da Esfera*, surge no contexto de uma sistematização e institucionalização do ensino da náutica portuguesa do século XVI e do seu desenvolvimento ao longo do seguinte[5]. O seu principal objetivo era proporcionar conhecimentos matemáticos e astronómicos não só aos estudantes jesuítas, mas também aos membros da nobreza e outros estudantes leigos, especialmente aqueles que se relacionavam com a vida marítima, como os pilotos, os cartógrafos ou fabricantes de instrumentos náuticos. A partir de 1540 e até 1759 será não só o centro de estudo da ciência náutica em Portugal, mas também uma das principais instituições educacionais e de prática científica do país. Nesta *Aula* era ensinada geometria, aritmética, rudimentos de álgebra, trigonometria esférica e sua aplicação à ciência náutica, ótica, astronomia e cosmografia, bem como arquitetura militar e marítima.

Embora, e ao contrário do que se passava em outros países europeus, a tendência do ensino jesuíta português fosse forte e assumidamente avessa às novas teorias científicas (até porque o número de jesuítas dedicados à ciência era diminuto), não é menos verdade que dentro da Companhia havia alguns homens, que a estudando, estavam cientes das ideias mais progressistas do seu tempo. Muitos dos professores da *Aula da Esfera* são um bom exemplo disso. O problema estava em alguma cristalização e rigidez de pensamento e de falta de abertura da Assistência portuguesa como um todo às ideias de Bacon (1561-1626), Descartes (1596-1650), Galileu (1564-1642), Pascal (1623-1662), Huygens (1629-1695) e Newton (1643--1727). Neste aspeto os Jesuítas perderam muito para os seus rivais do Oratório. Em geral estes eram mais abertos e recetivos às *'novas ciências'* incorporando-as no sistema de educação e pedagógico das

---

[5] Sobre a *Aula da Esfera* veja-se Albuquerque 1972 e Leitão 2008.

suas escolas[6]. Na primeira metade do século XVIII, no entanto, o Colégio de Santo Antão, o Colégio das Artes e a Universidade de Évora, a par do Colégio Oratoriano das Necessidades, desenvolveram uma importante atividade pedagógica e científica no domínio das ciências físico-matemáticas. Também no Colégio jesuíta brasileiro de São Salvador da Baía o ensino das matérias científicas era de bom nível; foi aí que José Monteiro da Rocha (1734-1819), que mais tarde desempenhará um importantíssimo papel na Reforma da Universidade, fez grande parte dos seus estudos[7].

Durante o reinado de D. João V (1689-1750) uma nova atitude cultural começa a despontar, em boa parte devido a uma melhoria da situação económica permitida pela enorme quantidade de ouro vindo do Brasil. Durante este período, a divulgação e consolidação em Portugal das novas ideias científicas são em grande parte devidas aos *estrangeirados*, uma espécie de rede informal de portugueses, principalmente diletantes e polímatas, que estavam em contacto com os círculos culturais e intelectuais europeus (muitos deles foram enviados pelo próprio rei para estabelecer contactos diplomáticos e científicos com outros países e instituições). Esta elite iluminada de *estrangeirados* foi a principal responsável na primeira metade do século XVIII pela tradução para português de alguns marcos das novas ciências[8]. D. João V deu uma particular atenção e interesse

---

[6] Veja-se Martins 1997.

[7] José Monteiro da Rocha foi uma das principais figuras da institucionalização da ciência matemática e astronómica iniciada com a Reforma Pombalina da Universidade. Primeiro, como responsável pela conceção do programa curricular da nova Faculdade de Matemática, e depois pelo papel que desempenhará em toda a subsequente atividade letiva, científica e administrativa da Universidade. Será professor das cadeiras de Foronomia (1772-83) e Astronomia (1783-1804) Diretor do Observatório Astronómico (1795-1819) e Vice-Reitor da Universidade (1786-1804). Para mais, veja-se Figueiredo 2011 e Figueiredo 2013.

[8] *"That given their heterogeneous social origins, backgrounds and careers, they should not be seen as a homogeneous group. Rather, they were part of a fluid network, although they did not consider themselves as such. What they definitely shared was a common scientific culture"*. Carneiro 2000.

à astronomia[9]. Em 1722, com o objetivo de fazer um levantamento dos territórios portugueses na América do Sul, o rei contrata dois astrónomos jesuítas italianos, Giovanni Baptista Carbone (1694-1750) e Domenico Capassi (1694-1736). Carbone, que acabará por ficar em Lisboa, fundará o observatório astronómico do Palácio Real (1722--1755) e o observatório astronómico do Colégio de Santo Antão (1723-1759), sendo os instrumentos provenientes principalmente de França e Inglaterra[10]. Carbonne será o primeiro em Portugal a fazer uma observação astronómica (o eclipse lunar de 11 de janeiro de 1724) num local expressamente destinado a esse efeito. Durante cerca de oito anos (1724-1732) será muito ativo em observações astronómicas, trocando regular correspondência com alguns astrónomos europeus, principalmente com Delisle (1688-1768). Será eleito membro da Royal Society inglesa (1729), publicando algumas das suas observações nas *Philosophical Transactions*[11].

A década de 1750 é de grande atividade astronómica em Portugal, sendo relevantes os trabalhos de João Chevalier (1722-1801), na Casa das Necessidades da Congregação do Oratório (1750-1768)[12], de Miguel Pedegache (1730? -1794), de Manuel Campos (1681-1758) e de Soares de Barros (1721-1793)[13].

Durante o reinado do rei D. José I (1714-1777), e antes da expulsão dos jesuítas em 1759, é de destacar a atividade astronómica de Eusébio da Veiga (1718-1798), o último professor da *Aula da Esfera*

---

[9] Veja-se Simões 1999 e Tirapicos, no prelo.
[10] Veja-se Carvalho 1985 e Tirapicos 2010.
[11] Veja-se Carvalho 1955-56 e Fiolhais 2011.
[12] João Chevalier chegou a ser membro da Academia Real das Ciências de Paris. Uma memória sobre as suas observações de 4 de maio de 1759 do cometa Halley foi lida em sessão académica.
[13] Joaquim José Soares de Barros estudou e trabalhou com Delisle no observatório do Hotel de Cluny. Foi eleito membro correspondente da Academia Real das Ciências de Paris e da Academia das Ciências e Belas Artes de Berlim. As suas observações do trânsito de Mercúrio de 6 de maio de 1753 foram apresentadas à academia parisiense.

(1753-1759), que em 1758 publica o *Planetário Lusitano*. Com o objetivo expresso de *"ajudar a navegação Portuguesa"*, fornecia dados astronómicos para os anos de 1758, 1759 e 1760. O *Planetário Lusitano*, calculado (sob o paradigma do modelo Tychoniano) para o meridiano do observatório de Santo Antão, consistia em 3 folhas mensais com as efemérides em tempo verdadeiro do sol (I), da lua (II) e dos planetas Mercúrio, Vénus, Marte, Júpiter e Saturno. É surpreendente verificar que o único método referido para determinar a longitude é o método dos satélites de Júpiter. Um bom método para utilização em terra, mas de todo impróprio para a determinação a bordo no alto mar, pois era dificílimo encontrar e manter os satélites no campo de visão dos telescópios. Eusébio da Veiga não faz qualquer reflexão sobre o problema da determinação da longitude a bordo, nem nada diz sobre os métodos de distâncias lunares que por esta altura se tornavam uma questão central da ciência astronómica e da náutica internacional.

O problema das longitudes

O conhecimento adquirido pela maior parte dos marinheiros e pilotos daqueles tempos estava longe de os transformar em especialistas em ciências astronómicas. Neste aspeto, o seu ensino e treino consistia em não muito mais do que memorizar algumas regras e obter a posição do navio fazendo uso de tabelas e de dispositivos para observação das estrelas.

Até à primeira metade do século XVIII, o cálculo da latitude e da longitude tinham abordagens e soluções de tipo diferente[14].

---

[14] A latitude define-se como sendo o ângulo ao centro da Terra (supondo-a esférica) entre um ponto do equador terrestre (círculo máximo que serve de referência) e outro ponto situado num determinado paralelo. A longitude define-se como o arco do equador compreendido entre dois meridianos (círculos máximos que passam pelos

A questão da determinação da latitude era assunto que já antes do século XV estava encerrado, a partir das observações da estrela Polar ou do Sol com o astrolábio, quadrante ou balestilha, e mais tarde com o octante. Já o problema da determinação precisa da longitude no mar foi até aos finais do século XVIII um dos maiores problemas técnico-científicos enfrentados pelos astrónomos e matemáticos[15]. Mesmo em terra, apesar da questão ser mais simples devido ao método dos satélites de Júpiter, muitos dos mapas apresentavam ainda nesta altura enormes erros e imprecisões. Por exemplo, o astrónomo e explorador francês J.-B. Chappe d'Auteroche (1722-1769) na sua viagem à Baixa Califórnia, em 1769, detetou nos mapas daquela região erros de mais de 5 graus nos valores da longitude. Até essa data a determinação da longitude era essencialmente feita por estima, recorrendo-se à barquinha (que os ingleses denominavam por 'lock'), ou através da declinação magnética. Este método, que havia sido sugerido por João de Lisboa (? -1525) no seu *Tratado da Agulha de Marear* (1514), baseava-se no facto da declinação magnética (ângulo entre o pólo magnético e o geográfico) parecer variar na superfície da Terra regularmente com a longitude. Durante muitos anos pensou-se, erradamente, que havia uma lei para a declinação magnética, o que permitiria assim saber qual a verdadeira direção do norte geográfico e consequentemente a longitude de um lugar.

Nas décadas de 1750 e 1760 o debate sobre a solução para o problema de determinar a longitude no mar está no auge. As duas soluções – a mecânica (o relógio) e a astronómica (baseada no movimento da Lua) –, sugeridas nas primeiras décadas do sécu-

---

pólos), o de referência (que a partir de 1884 passou a ser o de Greenwich) e o do lugar. Esta diferença angular pode ser facilmente relacionada com uma diferença de tempo, visto a Terra dar uma volta sobre si mesma em 24h ($360°/24h=15°/h$); assim, dois observadores que registem 1h de diferença na passagem do Sol pelo zénite do respetivo meridiano, têm entre si uma diferença de longitude de $15°$.

[15] A bibliografia sobre o problema da determinação das longitudes é vastíssima; por exemplo veja-se Andrewes 1996, Dunn 2014 e Gazeta de Matemática 2014.

lo XVI estão agora, graças aos avanços técnicos da construção de instrumentos e teóricos, com a elaboração de tabelas lunares e solares muito fiáveis, capazes de resolver satisfatoriamente a questão. A todos estes progressos não é alheio o prémio de £20.000 que o *Longitud Act* (1714) inglês estabeleceu para quem solucionasse o problema da determinação da longitude no mar com uma precisão inferior a meio grau. Em 1760 John Harrison (1693-1776) conseguiu construir uma maravilha técnica, o seu relógio marítimo H4 (1760). Testado pela primeira vez numa viagem à Jamaica, tendo partido de Inglaterra no dia 18 novembro de 1761, chegou ao destino no dia 27 de janeiro de 1762 com um atraso apenas de 5 segundos. Do lado astronómico Lacaille (1713-1762) propõe em finais da década de 1750 um protocolo de observação e de cálculo rigoroso para aplicação e observação do método das distâncias lunares (Lacaille 1759). Lacaille propunha que se calculasse um almanaque náutico, em que se tabelassem, de 3 em 3 horas, as distâncias da Lua a determinadas estrelas para todos os dias do ano. O piloto deveria fazer as observações necessárias para a regulação do seu relógio (i.e., determinação da hora local pela altura do Sol ou das estrelas), observar a distância da Lua às estrelas do almanaque, e reduzir essa distância observada à verdadeira. Seguidamente, consultando nas efemérides do almanaque os valores das distâncias lunares tabeladas determinava a hora no meridiano de referência, e consequentemente pela diferença horária a longitude do navio. Uma das dificuldades que se colocava era na redução das observações dos efeitos da refração e paralaxe para determinar a distância lunar 'verdadeira'. Tal exigia proceder a uma série de cálculos fastidiosos e complicados envolvendo o uso de várias tabelas auxiliares, de métodos gráficos e trigonometria esférica, o que para a maior parte dos pilotos estava para além das suas fracas competências matemáticas e astronómicas. Assim, apesar da proposta de Lacaille ter sido adotada por Maskelyne (1732-1811) em 1766 para o *Nautical Almanac (NA)*, e que Lalande

(1732-1807) copiará em 1772 para o *Connaissance des Temps (CDT)*, serão precisos ainda alguns anos até à sua introdução e aplicação prática e efetiva a bordo. O que só se verificará a partir da década de 1780, depois de J.-C. de Borda (1733-1799) ver publicado em 1779 por Lévêque (1746-1814) um protocolo por si estabelecido relativamente simples para a redução das observações.

Em Portugal Monteiro da Rocha está ciente de toda esta problemática e num manuscrito escrito por volta de 1765-66 faz uma análise crítica da questão[16]. Neste trabalho, mostrando-se completamente a par de toda a discussão técnico-científica, propõe uma modificação do método das distâncias lunares de Lacaille. O seu conhecimento não é só teórico é também prático, adquirido com o exame que faz das técnicas observacionais por si mesmo realizadas *"várias vezes no mar, e na terra"*. Embora a intenção fosse fornecer aos pilotos portugueses técnicas observacionais e métodos astronómicos para a determinação da longitude no mar, contribuindo assim para a *"utilidade pública da Navegação Portuguesa"* que *"faz a maior parte dos interesses públicos, e fará sempre glorioso o nome dos Portugueses"*, por serem *"os primeiros, que abrirão o caminho das ondas até as ultimas balizas do mundo"*[17], o trabalho de Monteiro da Rocha não é de todo um texto didático. Trata-se antes do mais de um trabalho técnico-científico sobre um dos problemas mais gritantes da astronomia da época. É o primeiro trabalho sobre a questão das longitudes, escrito no contexto do debate internacional que se trava na década de 1760, por um português[18]. Parece-nos óbvio

---

[16] Methodo de achar a Longitude Geográfica no mar y na terra Pelas observações y cálculos da Lua Para o uso da Navegação Portugueza. Biblioteca Nacional de Portugal – Manuscritos Reservados, PBA Ms. 511.

[17] BNP, Ms. 511, fls.3 e 17v.

[18] Neste sentido, o manuscrito é bastante singular, tanto no panorama nacional como no panorama internacional. Num artigo em que trabalhamos (em coautoria com Guy Boistel da Universidade de Nantes, França), com o título provisório, *'José Monteiro da Rocha (1734-1819) and the international debate in the 1760's on the*

que Monteiro da Rocha vê a ciência e a matemática não só como instrumentos para a resolução de problemas, mas sobretudo como saberes fundamentais para a edificação de um conhecimento útil e necessário ao estado. Esta visão utilitária da ciência, que abraça durante toda a sua futura vida científica e académica, norteia toda a dimensão reformista da Universidade de Coimbra da qual virá a ser um dos principais responsáveis.

Na realidade a questão da longitude estava muito para além de um grande problema científico ou náutico. Era uma questão de poder político e comercial, de domínio dos mares e da terra. A questão era vital para um país como Portugal. Ainda para mais na segunda metade do século XVIII, uma época em que Portugal já havia perdido a sua predominância dos mares para as potências marítimas inglesa e francesa. Portugal, um país com séculos de vocação marítima, era proprietário de um vasto império ultramarino que se estendia de África ao Brasil e Ásia. A importância do comércio com a colónia brasileira era capital para a economia nacional. E Monteiro da Rocha está bem ciente disso. Por isso está fortemente empenhado em publicar o trabalho[19]. Dedica-o ao *"Ilustríssimo e Exmo. Senhor Conde de Oeiras, Ministro e Secretário dos Negócios do Reino"*, isto é a Sebastião José de Carvalho e Melo (1699-1782), o futuro Marquês de Pombal[20], a quem pede apoio para a sua publicação. Infelizmente o manuscrito não é publicado. Várias poderão ser as razões, o caso de Monteiro da Rocha não ser conhecido, ser um ex-jesuíta, e também o facto de que na altura

---

astronomical methods to find the longitude at sea: its proposals and criticisms of the method of lunar distances of Lacaille', estas questões são estudadas. Porém, o manuscrito já foi alvo de alguns estudos. Pereira 2008, Figueiredo 2011: 418-439.

[19] *"A navegação faz a maior parte dos interesses públicos, e fará sempre glorioso o nome dos Portugueses, a cujas empresas deve a mesma navegação o seu princípio, e deverá a última perfeição"*. BNP, Ms. 511, fl. 3.

[20] Sebastião José só recebeu o título de Marquês de Pombal em 1769; o título de Conde de Oeiras data de 6 de junho de 1759.

muito poucos estariam capazes de alcançar a verdadeira natureza e profundidade do trabalho. Note-se também que a adoção a bordo dos métodos que propunha seria muito difícil devido à baixa formação dos marinheiros. Monteiro da Rocha mostra-se muito preocupado com esta questão das possíveis dificuldades que os pilotos teriam com as técnicas observacionais e matemáticas que propõe, *"não deixo de ficar com o receio, que a oficialidade ma marinha, a quem se dirige, receba com indiferença o resultado dos meus cálculos, e experiências"*. Por isso são constantes os apelos que faz contra o preconceito dos marinheiros em *"se fiar na longitude calculada pelas observações"* e aconselha que continuem com a sua prática habitual mas de espírito aberto a experimentarem os métodos propostos *"até que a experiência lhes mostre, quanto poderão fiar-se do método, que propomos"*.

Na realidade na década de 1760 o estado do conhecimento dos pilotos portugueses estava longe de satisfazer as necessidades. Portugal vê-se sem qualquer formação técnica ou científica para seus pilotos. O ensino de matérias de matemática e astronomia, e, consequentemente, da náutica tinha sido na prática suspenso com a expulsão dos jesuítas e o fim das aulas do cosmógrafo-mor. A situação é tal que em 1761 os comerciantes de Porto apresentam uma petição ao rei para a criação de uma 'Aula de Náutica' para a instrução dos pilotos para duas fragatas que se pretendiam construir a fim de proteger a frota mercante que cruzava o Atlântico partindo daquela cidade para o Brasil. Em novembro de 1764 iniciam-se as aulas. O ensino ministrado era essencialmente prático, complementado com várias viagens marítimas, principalmente ao Brasil e Mar Báltico (Pinto 2012: 27-30). Apenas em 1772 com a criação da Faculdade de Matemática na Universidade de Coimbra, e, principalmente com a criação, alguns anos mais tarde da Academia Real da Marinha (1779) e da Academia Real dos Guardas-Marinhas (1782), é que as necessidades de uma formação técnica e científica sólida dos futuros pilotos e oficiais da marinha portuguesa (tanto militar como e comercial) são de facto satisfeitas. Será também no âmbito da Reforma Pombalina da Universidade que a ciência astronómica, depois de um período de cerca de 15 anos onde todas as atividades astronómicas praticamente cessaram[21], sofrerá um impulso como nunca tinha sofrido no passado.

A reforma universitária de Pombal (1772): a criação da Faculdade de Matemática e do Real Observatório Astronómico

As reformas do sistema educativo foram uma das características da política interna do rei D. José I e do seu ministro Marquês de Pombal (1699-1782). A Reforma da Universidade de Coimbra (1772) então levada a cabo pretendia ser a concretização de um projeto que tinha por finalidade sintonizar Portugal com as ideias iluminadas da Europa e encaminhá-lo na direção do progresso e das ciências. A Reforma queria fazer da Universidade não apenas um centro de ensino atualizado, mas um centro de produção de conhecimento útil para servir as necessidades técnicas, científicas, administrativas e religiosas do país. A ideia e visão de conhecimento e ciência, nomeadamente das ciências matemáticas, que se expressam nos Estatutos está em perfeita sintonia com as ideias do Iluminismo europeu, particularmente com a sua expressão francesa[22]. A influência de D'Alembert é manifesta. Muitas das ideias que o filósofo e matemático francês expressa por exemplo no *Essai sur*

---

[21] Com exceção de algumas observações feitas por António Miguel Ciera (1726--82), entre os anos 1761 e 1764, e por Soares de Barros. Algumas das observações de Ciera seriam mais tarde publicadas por Custódio Villas-Boas nas Memórias da Academia das Ciências de Lisboa. Villas-Boas 1797.

[22] O 3.º volume dos *Estatutos* diz respeito aos *'cursos das sciencias naturaes e Filosoficas'*, i.e., às faculdades de Medicina, Matemática e Filosofia Natural.

les Éléments de Philosophie (1759) ou na *Encyclopèdie* (1750-72), um dos projetos editoriais mais importantes do Iluminismo, perpassam os novos Estatutos (Carvalho 2008; Figueiredo 2011: 57-91). Entre as grandes inovações desta Reforma universitária destaca-se a criação dos *Cursos das Sciencias Naturaes e Filosoficas*, com a reforma total da Faculdade de Medicina e a fundação das novas Faculdades de Matemática e Filosofia. São também reformadas as Faculdades de Teologia e de Cânones e Leis, assentes num novo programa de humanidades, filosofia e ciências pautado por conceções modernas, e onde nenhum dos antigos professores teve lugar.

O estabelecimento da educação científica na Universidade de Coimbra foi de facto um dos aspetos mais importantes. E uma das realizações mais significativas foi a criação da Faculdade de Matemática e do Observatório Astronómico. A criação da Faculdade de Matemática (primeira no mundo) pode ser vista como o resultado do desenvolvimento que a própria disciplina toma no quadro mais amplo do desenvolvimento científico e técnico europeu do século XVIII. A matemática é reconhecida pública e assumidamente como uma disciplina fundamental e estruturante do pensamento:

> *"[ilumina] superiormente os entendimentos no estudo de qualquer outras disciplinas: mostrando-lhe praticado o exemplo mais perfeito de tratar uma matéria com ordem, precisão, solidez, e encadeamento fechado, e unido de umas verdades com outras: inspirando-lhes o gosto, e discernimento necessário para distinguir o sólido, do frívolo; o real, do aparente; a demonstração, do paralogismo: e participando-lhe uma exatidão, conforme ao Espírito Geométrico; qualidade rara, e precisa, sem a qual não podem conservar-se, nem fazer progresso algum os conhecimentos naturais do Homem em qualquer objeto que seja."* (Estatutos 1772: (3)141-142)

Por isso a cadeira de Geometria, lecionada na Faculdade de Matemática, é obrigatória a todos os alunos universitários, sejam eles de Teologia, dos cursos jurídicos ou de 'Sciencias'

> *"porque os Elementos de Geometria, que no primeiro ano do dito Curso [de matemática] se ensinam, são a Lógica, praticada com a maior perfeição, que é possível ao entendimento do homem; cujo exemplo é mais instrutivo, do que todas as regras, e preceitos, que se podem imaginar, para dirigir e encaminhar o discurso: Ei por bem, e Sou servido ordenar, que todos os estudantes, destinados aos Cursos, Teológico e Jurídico, sejam também obrigados a estudar privativamente o primeiro ano do Curso Matemático, como subsídio importante ao aproveitamento, que devem ter no estudo das suas respetivas Faculdades."* (Estatutos 1772: (3)152)

A formação técnico-científica de quadros que dessem sustentação aos interesses económico-administrativos do país é um dos principais objetivos dos reformadores. E as ciências matemáticas são reconhecidas como de capital importância para uma série de profissões, e lugares no funcionalismo público, ao serviço do progresso e bem-estar do Estado e da Sociedade. Legisla-se que todos os que se formassem em Matemática e

> *"[...] quiserem entrar no meu serviço, serão admitidos a servir na Marinha, sem preceder outro algum exame; e na Engenharia, sem preceder exame de Matemática, mas tão-somente do Ataque, e Defesa das Praças. E havendo concurso dos Postos de Engenharia dos Matemáticos da Universidade com os Aulistas das Escolas Militares, que Eu for servido criar: Ordeno, que de uns, e outros se Me consultem sempre em igual número de sujeitos; e que se despachem com a mesma igualdade. Porque assim é Minha vontade; e assim convém ao Meu serviço, por ser de grande vantagem, que*

entre os Engenheiros Práticos haja sempre um grande número, que possua fundamentalmente as Ciências Matemáticas, que são a base de todas as operações militares. Da mesma sorte Ordeno, que os ofícios de Arquiteto da cidade de Lisboa, e das outras cidades do Reino; e que os ofícios de Medidores dos Conselhos em todos os Meus Reinos, e Domínios, não possam ser daqui por diante providos em sujeitos curiosos, e meros práticos; havendo Matemáticos, que tenham cursado na Universidade, e os queiram servir. E concorrendo eles a requerer os ditos ofícios, será o provimento, que em qualquer outra pessoa se fizer, nulo, e de nenhum efeito."
(Estatutos 1772, (3)150)

Porém, e apesar de se assegurarem em letra de lei saídas profissionais a verdade é que a questão dos alunos (ou melhor a falta deles) será uma questão marcante na vida da Faculdade ao longo do século XIX (Figueiredo 2011: 161-195). Júlio Dinis (1839-1871) retrata bem o pouco prestígio social do matemático no Portugal de meados de Oitocentos quando estão em causa os estudos que o menino Tomás deveria seguir em Coimbra. O conselho familiar era unânime em reconhecer que a Faculdade de Matemática não merecia entrar em linha de conta: *"no nosso país, um matemático [...] não tem uma posição segura e definida. Os nossos governos encomendam as estradas aos enxurros, e as pontes fazem-se quando os ventos derrubam os troncos das árvores através das correntes dos ribeiros"* (Dinis 1979: 5-6), dizia o doutor, com concordância do médico e do abade.

Apesar desta imagem, a verdade é que será a Faculdade de Matemática, direta e indiretamente, a responsável pela formação de muitos dos quadros técnico-científicos no Portugal de finais do século XVIII e inícios do XIX. A maioria dos futuros engenheiros que serão formados nas academias militares terão como professores gente por sua vez formada nas Faculdades de Matemática e Filosofia

Natural da Universidade de Coimbra. E como muito bem João Brigola assinala será essa frequência estudantil, de prevalência militar, que irá democratizar o acesso à cultura matemática na sua dimensão operativa – arquitetura militar, engenharia naval e civil, pilotagem, cartografia, estatística, geodesia e meteorologia (Brigola 2003). Será destas Faculdades que sairão os homens que encabeçarão as grandes expedições científico-militares dos finais de Setecentos às fronteiras do Brasil e que inventariarão os recursos naturais da colónia e das possessões ultramarinas de África e da Ásia.

Nas décadas de 1790 e 1800 os cursos *Mathematico* e *Filosofico* sofrerão reformas curriculares numa nítida tentativa de darem uma resposta mais capaz às necessidades técnico-científicas do país e do império. Em 1791 é criada na Faculdade de Filosofia a cadeira de Botânica e Agricultura e dez anos depois, em 1801, a de Metalurgia. Também neste ano serão criadas duas novas cadeiras na Faculdade de Matemática, a de Hidráulica e de Astronomia Prática. O surgimento destas cadeiras no panorama letivo da Matemática decorre da necessidade de encontrar novas respostas cientificamente atualizadas, indispensáveis para a atividade do Observatório Astronómico recentemente inaugurado (1799), assim como para a realização de uma série de obras públicas de engenharia hidráulica em que o país se via envolvido (encanamento do rio Mondego e barra de Aveiro e barra do Douro).

O *'Curso Mathematico'*

O plano de estudos do *'Curso Mathematico'* distribuía-se inicialmente por 8 cadeiras (5 da Faculdade de Matemática e 3 da Faculdade de Filosofia). As cadeiras de matemática pura eram lecionadas nos dois primeiros anos e as matemáticas mistas ou aplicadas nos 3.º e 4.os anos: 1.º ano, Geometria; 2.º ano, Álgebra; 3.º ano, Foronomia (ou física-matemática); 4.º ano, Astronomia. Havia ainda uma cadeira anexa de Desenho e Arquitetura a ser frequentada no 3.º ou no 4.º ano[23]. Na verdade, qualquer aluno da Universidade a podia frequentar, contudo só os alunos das ciências eram especialmente incentivados à sua frequência (p. ex. no caso dos futuros médicos, *"por lhes ser o Desenho muito útil, para poderem, quando necessário, executar por si mesmos as Estampas Botânicas, e Anatómicas"*). O seu estudo compreendia as noções fundamentais de perspetiva, bem como noções para o desenho de seres vivos e da natureza. Na parte do desenho arquitetónico (civil e militar), o objetivo era fornecer aos alunos os rudimentos do desenho e leituras de plantas e alçados, assim como dos diferentes tipos de edificações de fortificação militar. Por fim ainda se contemplavam ensinamentos sobre a *"praxe do risco das cartas geográficas, e topográficas"*. Infelizmente o seu provimento revelou-se bastante difícil. Nos primeiros anos terá sido Miguel Ciera, professor de Astronomia (1772-1779), que terá assegurado aos alunos os conhecimentos e prática da disciplina (Mendes 1965). Mas depois, e durante muitos anos, a cadeira de desenho não é lecionada de forma regular (só em 1840 é que passou a ter um professor próprio[24]). Segundo Carlos Martins, a ausência de sólida formação dos matemáticos em desenho poderá ser uma explicação para que os militares, nomeadamente do Real Corpo de Engenheiros, acabem por ser preferidos para a produção projetual e prática de obra do vasto programa de obras públicas que se estabelece nos finais do século XVIII e inícios do seguinte,

---

[23] *"Haverá mais extraordinariamente uma Cadeira de Desenho, e Arquitectura, tanto Civil, como Militar [...] subordinad[a] à Congregação de Matemática, a qual proverá nesta Cadeira, como em tudo o mais, que pertence à sua Profissão"*. Estatutos 1772 (3): 167.

[24] Pinto 1882-83.

ocupando assim uma série de lugares inicialmente pensados para os matemáticos[25].

Do curso constavam mais três cadeiras obrigatórias ministradas na Faculdade de Filosofia: Filosofia Racional e Moral, História Natural e Física Experimental. A importância destas cadeiras no curso era valorizada no sentido da complementaridade científica e pedagógica das duas faculdades. A ideia era que pela experiência induziam-se as leis fundamentais que depois se generalizavam com a matemática, sistematizando-as em leis seguras e verdadeiras das quais se deduziriam depois todas e quaisquer particularidades. Precisamente neste sentido também os alunos do 'Curso Filosófico' eram obrigados a fazer as cadeiras de Geometria e Álgebra[26]. Por isso não é difícil encontrar gente formada em Coimbra com bacharelatos, ou licenciaturas em Matemática e Filosofia, ou até mesmo em Medicina (do currículo médico constavam 3 cadeiras de Matemática e outras tantas de Filosofia).

De todas as disciplinas matemáticas a Álgebra, *"a arte de representar por símbolos gerais todas ideias, que se podem formar no nosso espírito, relativamente às quantidades"*, é considerada a mais importante, todavia devido à maior dificuldade e abstração que exigia era lecionada após o estudo da aritmética, geometria e trigonometria (cadeira de Geometria). A cadeira de Álgebra compreendia para além da álgebra propriamente dita (expressões algébricas, equações, séries, secções cónicas e *"tudo o mais que constitui um curso de álgebra elementar perfeito, e completo"* com as suas aplicações à geometria e à aritmética), o cálculo infinitesimal. Assinale-se que é a primeira vez que o cálculo diferencial e integral, base da matemática e da física do século XVIII, é enquadrado no quadro de um

---

[25] Ver texto de Carlos M. Martins neste volume.

[26] Sobre a complementaridade científica e pedagógica das Faculdades de Matemática e de Filosofia Natural veja-se Martins 2000; e sobre o ensino das ciências naturais veja-se Costa 2000.

programa curricular estruturado e institucionalizado e é ensinado e estudado em Portugal[27].

Depois de bem instruídos nestas matérias os alunos passariam a estudar nos últimos dois anos do curso *"a ciência completa do movimento, tanto dos sólidos como dos fluidos [e] todos os ramos subalternos das ciências físico-matemáticas"*. No 3.º ano, na cadeira de Foronomia estudava-se estática, dinâmica, mecânica (máquinas simples), balística, hidráulica, ótica, acústica. No capítulo da dinâmica, *"a teórica do movimento dos corpos solicitados por quaisquer forças; tanto sendo eles livres; como sendo sujeitos a mover-se; ou por planos inclinados; ou por quaisquer linhas curvas"*, eram também estudadas as forças centrais, preâmbulo para a cadeira de Astronomia a ser estudada no ano seguinte:

> *"Com muito particular cuidado se tratará do movimento por linhas curvas em virtude das forças centrais: para que os discípulos, ajudados da explicação elementar desta doutrina, possam no seguinte ano entrar com facilidade na inteligência das aplicações, que dela felizmente se tem feito, ao movimento dos corpos planetários."* (*Estatutos* 1772: (3)185)

A Astronomia embora fosse considerada um ramo da física-matemática *"aplicada ao movimento dos astros"*, ocupava todo o 4.º ano como disciplina autónoma; isto era justificado pela vastidão do seu objeto e pela sua própria importância dentro do ramo das ciências matemáticas que a obrigava a *"ocupar separada, e constituir inteiramente o objeto do trabalho, e cuidado de um professor."* O estudo incluía história da astronomia, trigonometria esférica, o

---

[27] Também o ensino da álgebra literal (pós Descartes) e da geometria analítica seriam até então incipientes; por exemplo Inácio Monteiro (1724-1812) no Compendio dos Elementos de Mathematica, Coimbra, 1754-56, não vai além das equações do 1.º grau.

estudo da chamada *'astronomia física'* (mecânica celeste), que incluía os movimentos planetários, o problema dos três corpos e *'teórica da Lua'*, os movimentos dos cometas, os eclipses do sol e da lua, e os trânsitos de Vénus e Mercúrio. Esperava-se que os estudantes adquirissem prática e habilidade no uso dos instrumentos de observação e um conhecimento sólido em cálculos astronómicos, pois *"no decorrer deste curso a teoria e a prática devem sempre estar juntos"*. Para tal os Estatutos previam a criação de um Observatório Astronómico não só para as aulas práticas dos alunos, mas também destinado ao trabalho e à investigação dos professores. Esta tónica dada à observação, à experimentação e à aplicabilidade dos conhecimentos teóricos é um dos pontos inovadores que se estabelece na Reforma da Universidade. Para tal são criados vários estabelecimentos científicos em dependência das respetivas Faculdades, no sentido de instituir uma efetiva prática pedagógica de cariz empírico-experimental. Sob a responsabilidade da Faculdade de Matemática ficava o Observatório Astronómico, a Faculdade de Medicina tutelava o Teatro Anatómico e o Hospital, partilhando com a Faculdade de Filosofia a direção do Gabinete de História Natural, o Gabinete de Física Experimental, o Laboratório Químico e o Jardim Botânico.

No que diz respeito aos manuais a escolha deveria obedecer essencialmente a dois princípios: a atualidade – *"pois nelas [nas lições de matemática] se aperfeiçoam cada dia muitas coisas e se inventam outras"* – e a clareza de método. São assim adotados e traduzidos alguns dos autores franceses à época mais atuais (com exceção dos *'Elementos de Euclides'* para o ensino da geometria, o único que expressamente os Estatutos impõem[28]). São livros que

---

[28] Inicialmente adotaram-se nove, sendo que sete foram traduzidos para português. No que diz respeito aos Elementos de Euclides, os Estatutos mandavam que se estudassem apenas os livros de geometria elementar; será adotada a tradução que Giovanni Angelo Brunelli (1722-1804) havia feito em 1768 para o Colégio dos Nobres.

se inserem na tradição francesa da época de *'livres élémentaires'*, destinados a ensinar os fundamentos das ciências (Schubring 1997). Étienne Bézout (1730-1783), o principal autor adotado, organiza os seus compêndios numa maneira simples e clara para que o aluno possa acompanhar com facilidade os conteúdos, recorrendo sempre a exemplos concretos para elucidar passos teóricos. Esta preocupação com a clareza e explanação dos conceitos era totalmente defendida por D'Alembert, um dos ideólogos do ensino da matemática na França do século XVIII.

Para os dois primeiros anos do curso traduziram-se os volumes referentes à aritmética, à trigonometria plana, à álgebra e ao cálculo infinitesimal do *Cours de Mathématiques à l'usage des Gardes du Pavillon et de la Marine* (Paris, 1764-69), de Bézout. Na década de 1760, o duque de Choiseul (1719-1785), ministro de Louis XV (1710--1774), empreende uma reforma do ensino na marinha francesa, confiando a Bézout, nomeado em 1764 examinador dos *Gardes de la Marine*, a missão de redigir um curso completo de matemática para os alunos. Nos 5 anos que se seguem redige o famoso *Cours de Mathématiques*, composto por 6 volumes[29]. Mais tarde, entre 1770 e 1772, Bézout escreverá um outro, especialmente destinado para ensino da escola de artilharia: *Cours de Mathématiques à l'usage du Corps Royal de l'Artillerie* (4 volumes)[30]. Fortemente baseado no da marinha, os 2 primeiros volumes são na prática uma versão

---

[29] Éléments d'Arithmétique (1764), Élémens de Géométrie, la Trigonométrie rectiligne, & la Trigonométrie sphérique (1765), Algèbre & l'application de cette Science à l'Arithmétique & à la Géométrie (1766), Les Principes généraux de la Mécanique, précèdes des Principes de Calcul qui servent d'introductions aux Sciences Physico-Mathématiques (1767), Contenant l'application des Principes généraux de la Mécanique, à différents cas de Mouvement & d'Équilibre (1767) e o Traité de Navigation (1769).

[30] Arithmétique, Géométrie et Trigonométrie rectiligne (1770), Algèbre et applications de l'Algèbre à la Géométrie (1770), Principes généraux de la Mécanique et de l'Hydrostatique précédés des principes de calcul qui servent d'introduction aux Sciences Physico-Mathématiques (1772) e Application des principes généraux de la Mécanique à différents cas de Mouvement et d'Équilibre (1772).

simplificada dos 3 primeiros volumes do curso da marinha, onde a trigonometria esférica é suprimida. A maior diferença está nos 3º e 4º volumes dedicados à mecânica, neles Bézout desenvolve com mais profundidade temas que aborda superficialmente (ou não aborda de todo) no primeiro curso (p. ex., o movimento dos projéteis). O 6.º volume (*Traité de Navigation*) é suprimido por nele serem ensinadas matérias específicas à marinha e que não faziam sentido num curso de artilharia. Em Portugal os livros de Bézout foram adotados não só na nova Faculdade de Matemática, como também o serão nas Academias Militares que, entretanto, serão criadas.

Apesar de Bézout dedicar dois volumes aos '*Principes généraux de la Méchanique*' nenhum deles foi adotado para a cadeira do 3.º ano. Para a cadeira de Foronomia e Astronomia foram escolhidos 4 outros autores: Marie (1738-1801) para o estudo da mecânica dos corpos rígidos, com a tradução para português do seu *Traité de Méchanique* (1774); Bossut (1730-1814) para o estudo da mecânica dos fluidos, com a tradução do seu *Traité Élémentaire d'Hydrodynamique* (2 vols., 1771); e Lacaille, com 2 obras: uma para o estudo da ótica, *Leçons Élémentaires d'Optique* (1750), e outra para o ensino da Astronomia, *Leçons Élémentaires d'Astronomie Géometrique et Physique* (1746). Para esta última cadeira também seria adotado o *Astronomie*, de Lalande, cuja 1ª edição data de 1764. Todas as traduções (os livros de Lacaille e Lalande não foram traduzidos) seriam impressas entre os anos de 1773 e 1775 com a chancela da Imprensa da Universidade, que desde 1773 detinha o privilégio exclusivo (outrora pertença do Colégio dos Nobres) da impressão dos livros das ciências matemáticas.

Em 1801 com a entrada no currículo da cadeira de Astronomia Prática são introduzidos novos livros, o *Traité élémentaire d'astronomie physique* (1805), de Biot (1774-1862) e o *Traité de Mécanique Céleste* (5 vols., 1799-1825), de Laplace. Este último não se pode de maneira alguma considerar um livro de texto: embora tenha alguns traços em comum, é vincadamente um livro científico de referência e de coletânea de artigos. A sua introdução no panorama letivo evidencia uma atualidade no ensino da Astronomia e da própria atividade do Observatório. Já o mesmo não se verifica nos livros destinados às outras matérias, pois embora a sua escolha tivesse um carácter provisório para suprir as necessidades imediatas de uma Faculdade que se criava de raiz, a verdade é que o provisório se tornou mais ou menos definitivo e durante cerca de 50 anos foram esses os compêndios que serviram ano após ano para as aulas. Curiosamente seria gente da Academia da Marinha, alguns professores e formados na Faculdade de Matemática, como Manuel Jacinto Nogueira da Gama (1765-1847), ou Manoel Ferreira de Araújo Guimarães (1777-1838), professor de Astronomia na Academia Real Militar do Rio de Janeiro, entre outros, que iriam empreender uma série de traduções de livros de texto (franceses) mais atuais para o ensino das ciências matemáticas (Carolino 2012), (Saraiva 2014). Na Universidade a partir de 1838 novos compêndios são introduzidos, as matérias das duas primeiras cadeiras passam a usar o *Curso Completo de Mathematicas Puras* (1838-39), de Francouer (1773–1849), tradução de Rodrigo Ribeiro de Sousa Pinto (1811-1893) e Francisco de Castro Freire (1809-1884)[31].

O Real Observatório Astronómico da Universidade de Coimbra (OAUC)

> *"As vantagens, que resultam de se cultivar eficazmente a Astronomia, com todas as mais partes da Matemática, de que ela depende, são de tão grande ponderação, e de consequências tão importantes ao adiantamento geral dos conhecimentos humanos; e à perfeição particular da Geografia, e da Navegação; que*

---

[31] Sobre a produção e adoção compendiaria nos anos 1830 veja-se Freire 1872.

tem merecido em toda a parte a atenção dos Soberanos, fazendo edificar Observatórios magníficos, destinados ao progresso da Astronomia, como Ciência necessária para se conseguir o conhecimento do Globo terrestre; e se terem nas mãos as chaves do Universo." (*Estatutos* 1772: (3)213)

A criação do Observatório Astronómico da Universidade de Coimbra (OAUC), fundamental para a institucionalização da ciência astronómica em Portugal, decorreu como já referimos durante um período (últimas décadas do século XVIII) em que a astronomia, sustentada pelos grandes avanços teóricos da mecânica celeste e da matemática aplicada, dentro do programa newtoniano, vinha enfrentando questões práticas ligadas aos problemas de navegação, geodesia e cartografia, e outras mais teóricas como a determinação de órbitas de planetas, cometas e medições astrométricas. Estas, à semelhança de outros observatórios europeus, estão na base da criação e planificação do futuro Observatório de Coimbra – que embora ligado à Universidade, será o primeiro observatório astronómico do país com profundas características de observatório nacional.

A ideia de um observatório astronómico como local próprio contendo telescópios e outros instrumentos de observação onde os astrónomos se dedicam ao estudo do Universo é hoje mais ou menos corrente. Porém, o mesmo não se pode dizer acerca do observatório do século XVIII. Neste século o desenvolvimento da astronomia dependia muito de observadores privados que tinham os seus próprios observatórios, a maior parte das vezes com poucos instrumentos, e em geral instalados em locais não necessariamente fixos ou permanentes (uma torre, uma ala de um palácio, uma simples janela). Também no que diz respeito aos programas de investigação os observatórios setecentistas apresentavam uma vasta gama de interesses. Não há uma linha de investigação bem definida, nem uma direção eficaz no que se pretende investigar. São várias as frentes de atividade astronómica que dependem quase em absoluto dos interesses privados dos seus astrónomos e diretores. O astrónomo profissional ainda não é uma realidade fora dos grandes observatórios nacionais. Não existe ainda, no sentido catual, uma comunidade astronómica internacional, os astrónomos trabalham mais ou menos isolados deparando-se com grandes dificuldades na troca de informações e observações entre si. Uma realidade que nos finais do século se começa a transformar graças aos esforços de Lalande e de von Zach (1754-1832), que como responsáveis pelas publicações do *Connaissance des Temps* (Paris), das *Allgemeine Geographische Ephemeriden* (Gotha) e do *Monatliche Correspondenz* (Gotha) muito fizeram por publicar e difundir artigos astronómicos e notícias científicas dos vários pontos da Europa. Para além deste grupo privado de observatórios existem outros dois tipos, a que chamaremos observatórios nacionais e observatórios universitários/escolares. Estes são custeados por dinheiros provenientes dos impostos coletados pelos diversos governos, ao contrário dos privados cujo financiamento é evidentemente particular. Os observatórios nacionais, em geral bem equipados, são criados com uma função utilitária bem específica, a de servirem as necessidades do Estado especialmente no que diz respeito aos problemas astronómicos requeridos pela navegação – determinação das longitudes – e determinação da hora, sendo os observatórios de Greenwich, Paris, Berlim e Palermo exemplos paradigmáticos. São dirigidos por um diretor, que para além de um estatuto particular goza de grande reconhecimento social; aí sob proteção Real dirige um programa de trabalhos de observação sistemática dos movimentos dos corpos do sistema solar e das posições das estrelas fixas com vista ao melhoramento das tabelas astronómicas que suportam a elaboração das efemérides astronómicas. O Observatório de Greenwich foi fundado por Carlos II (1630-85), em 1675, com o propósito específico da *'retificação das tabelas dos movimentos dos céus e dos lugares das estrelas fixas, de forma a encontrar a tão desejada longitude no mar, a fim de aperfeiçoar a arte da navegação e da astronomia'*. As mesmas questões estão também subjacentes à criação do Observatório de Paris, no reinado de Luís XIV (1638-1715). Na verdade, o cálculo das efemérides é o principal objetivo da atividade astronómica dos grandes observatórios nacionais até às décadas de 1820 e 1830. Já os observatórios escolares têm por objetivo principal a formação e o ensino. São criados em ligação estreita às universidades e às escolas das quais são dependentes e em que o financiamento, embora 'público', é feito sob um orçamento relativamente restrito e negociado com estas. São geralmente dirigidos por um professor cujo principal papel é a atividade letiva, embora também esteja presente alguma atividade de investigação. Também a sua localização é específica, próxima da universidade, o que a maior parte das vezes acaba por comprometer o próprio progresso dos trabalhos.

O papel e a prática astronómica que se requeriam para o futuro Observatório Astronómico da Universidade de Coimbra (traçados desde logo nos *Estatutos* de 1772), prendem-no a uma dicotomia muito própria. Por um lado, como observatório universitário, nomeadamente na investigação científica dos seus professores e no papel pedagógico como estabelecimento para as aulas de astronomia e, por outro, como observatório nacional, envolvendo-o na elaboração das efemérides astronómicas *"para uso da Navegação Portuguesa"* e desenvolvimento da ciência astronómica. Através dele Portugal sintonizar-se-ia com a Europa científica e astronómica do seu tempo. De facto, após a sua entrada em funcionamento em 1799, será o primeiro observatório português com a missão específica de fazer observações sistemáticas e elaborar/desenvolver e calcular efemérides astronómicas

> *"Para o meridiano do Observatório, e para uso dele (assim como se pratica nos mais célebres da Europa) se calculará a*

Efeméride Astronómica, a qual igualmente possa servir para uso da navegação Portuguesa. Esta Efeméride não será reduzida e copiada do Almanaque do Observatório de Greenwich, nem de outro algum, mas calculada imediatamente sobre as Taboas Astronómicas. E para sair sempre com a antecipação conveniente, para ser transportada aos países mais distantes, começar-se-á logo pelo trabalho da que há-de servir no ano de 1804 e depois dela nas dos seguintes." (§.7 do Regulamento do Observatório)[32]

No Regulamento de 1799 a atividade letiva fica de algum modo subalternizada, pois recomendava-se expressamente não deixar as aulas e a prática letiva interferir com as observações e práticas astronómicas quotidianas do observatório (§.9 do Regulamento).

A construção do Observatório esteve planeada inicialmente para o sítio do Castelo da cidade. A obra, planeada por Guilherme Elsden (?-1779), apesar de iniciada logo em finais de 1772, não se viria a concretizar devido ao seu elevado custo. Para em 1775 quando o edifício projetado pouco vai além do rés-do-chão[33]. Entretanto para suprir as necessidades letivas foi edificado um pequeno observatório interino no terreiro do Paço das Escolas – viria a funcionar provisoriamente durante cerca de 15 anos!

O problema da efetiva falta de um verdadeiro observatório astronómico na Universidade exige uma solução que se começa a desenhar em finais da década de 1780. O pequeno observatório provisório não possuía as necessárias condições de acomodação dos instrumentos que se estavam a adquirir em Londres, nem as condições mínimas de trabalho a uma efetiva atividade astronómica e cálculo de efemérides. Para mais a Academia Real das Ciências de

---

[32] Carta Régia de 4 de dezembro de 1799.

[33] Sobre as vicissitudes da construção do observatório veja-se (Martins 2008) e mais detalhadamente Figueiredo 2014.

Lisboa inaugura em janeiro de 1787 o seu observatório astronómico do Castelo de São Jorge, com a finalidade de dar sequência a um projeto interno de publicar umas efemérides *"para utilidade da navegação portuguesa"*, colidindo diretamente com os interesses da Universidade e com um dos principais objetivos do seu pretendido observatório. Parece-nos bastante provável que o Aviso Régio de 1 de outubro de 1787 (Almeida 1979: 177-178) seja uma consequência direta de sucessivas interpelações da Universidade (leia-se José Monteiro da Rocha, que para além de professor da cadeira de Astronomia é também vice-reitor desde 31 de julho de 1786) face à inexistência de um verdadeiro observatório astronómico na Universidade capaz de trabalhar no *'adiantamento da astronomia'*.

Será através da estreita colaboração entre Monteiro da Rocha e o arquiteto Manuel Alves Macomboa (? -1815), com o impulso político do 2.º governo mariano liderado por José Seabra da Silva (1732-
-1813), que surgirá o projeto definitivo para este estabelecimento. O projeto é aprovado pela Universidade em 5 de fevereiro de 1791 e em 1799 o edifício, composto de um corpo horizontal (41m de frente por 11m de lado) com um telhado plano e uma torre central de três andares (altura de 24m), está concluído e pronto para iniciar a sua atividade.

A atividade científica do OAUC

A prática astronómica de um observatório está, obviamente, ligada ao acervo instrumental que este possui, ou, para sermos mais precisos, devemos afirmar que é o acervo instrumental de um observatório que dita o seu programa observacional, ou seja, a sua real e efetiva prática astronómica. Por exemplo, a brevidade do fenómeno condiciona o uso dos instrumentos, tal é o caso, por exemplo, dos trânsitos dos planetas Mercúrio e Vénus sobre o disco solar. A preocupação com o apetrechamento instrumental do futuro observatório, bem como dos vários estabelecimentos científicos da Universidade, foi desde logo uma preocupação dos reformadores:

> "*E será logo provido de uma coleção de bons instrumentos: procurando-se um Mural, feito por algum dos melhores artífices da Europa; e um bom sortimento de Quadrantes; de Sextantes de diferentes grandezas; de Micrómetros; de Instrumentos de Passagens; de Máquinas Paraláticas; de Telescópios; de Níveis; de Pêndulos; e de tudo o mais necessário a um Observatório, em que se há-de trabalhar eficaz, e constantemente no exercício das observações, e progresso da Astronomia.*" (Estatutos 1772: (3)214)

Estes são efetivamente os principais instrumentos que no século XVIII constituem o cerne instrumental para se estabelecer um efetivo *'international meridian program'*. Serão também estes que se vêem localizados e especificados na planta de 1792 do projeto aprovado para o futuro *'Observatorio Conimbricense'*: um quadrante – *'Fundamentum Quadranti Murali destinatum ubi interim Quadrans mobilis tripedalis, opus Troughtoni absolutissimum'*; um instrumento de passagens – *'Fundamentum pro Telescopio Meridiano acromatico Cel. Dollondi'* – uma luneta paralática – *'Podium australe, ubi Columna pro Instr. Parallat. cl. W. Cary'*; um sector – *'Ichnographia plani superioris, ubi Sector G. Adams decempedalis, quem ternae columnae limbo ortu respiciente, ad occidentem verso, ternae aliae sustinent'*; bem como três pêndulas e ainda pequenos telescópios – *'speculae minores'* [34]. Em 1808 o geógrafo italiano Adrien Balbi (1782-1848) visita o Observatório, escrevendo que *"il était aussi*

---

[34] Observatório Astronómico da Universidade de Coimbra, Fundo Antigo da Biblioteca e Arquivo, G-006.

trés-bien fourni d'instrumens", colocando-o a par dos bons observatórios europeus da época (Balbi 1822: (2)95). Também Lalande se lhes refere: *"Nous avons reçu encore une description de l'Observatoire de Coimbre, par laquelle on voit qu'il y a des instruments considérables; un secteur de dix pieds, une lunette méridienne de cinq pieds, un quart-de-cercle de trois pieds et demi, divisé à Londres par Troughton"* (Lalande 1803: 871-872).

O trabalho astronómico de qualidade faz-se não só com bons instrumentos, mas também com acesso a livros e a obras de referência. Através dos inventários de 1810 e de 1824 é possível perceber que a *'casa de livraria'* foi sendo bem fornecida, articulando-se com as orientações de investigação astronómica e matemática que se delineou para o Observatório[35]. Nela podiam-se encontrar os autores mais atuais. Não faltavam as obras dos grandes matemáticos e astrónomos da época, como D'Alembert, Euler, Clairaut, Bézout, Lagrange, Lacroix ou Laplace. No que diz respeito a efemérides e tabelas astronómicas o OAUC possuía as mais representativas: *Connaissance des Temps, Ephémérides des Mouvements Célestes; Nautical Almanak; Berliner Astronomische Jahrbuch; Ephemeridi Astronomiche di Milano; Allgemeine geographische Ephemeriden; Almanaque náutico y efemérides astronómicas do Observatório Real de Cádiz*. No que diz respeito a tabelas astronómicas constavam as de Halley (1656-1742) e de Mayer (1723-62); as *Tables astronomiques pour servir a la troisième édition de l'Astronomie* (1792), de Lalande; as *Tables Astronomiques du Bureau des Longitudes* (1806), de Delambre e Bürg (1766-1835); as *Tables Astronomiques de Jupiter, de Saturne et d'Uranus* (1821) de Bouvard (1767-1843), entre outras. Também não faltam as famosas publicações de observações

---

[35] *"Catálogo i enventario no observatorio da universidade [1810]"*, e *"Inventario dos instrument. livros e moveis do Observator. R. da Universidade de Coimbra em 1824"*, Observatório Astronómico da Universidade de Coimbra, Fundo Antigo da Biblioteca e Arquivo.

do Observatório de Greenwich, publicadas pelos astrónomos reais, James Bradley (1693-1762), Maskelyne e John Pond (1767-1836); nem o *Monatliche Correspondenz* que von Zach publicou a partir de 1800. No que diz respeito aos livros de astronomia e de instrumentos estão presentes os autores mais representativos como: Lacaille, Lalande, Delambre, Pingré, Bailly, Bouguer, Borda, Laplace, Bird, Berthoud, entre outros. Também se regista a existência de várias cartas celestes e mapas cartográficos de várias regiões do gobo, em especial da América do Sul e Brasil.

O Regulamento de 1799 pretende estabelecer o OAUC como um verdadeiro estabelecimento científico, reforçando-lhe as características de observatório nacional que já se esboçam nos Estatutos de 1772. Monteiro da Rocha, desde 1795 Diretor do Observatório (Carta Régia de 4 de abril de 1795), foi incumbido de redigir o referido regulamento que deveria organizar e regular a futura atividade do Observatório (Carta Régia de 4 de dezembro de 1799). Nada foi deixado ao acaso, desde a organização dos vários espaços, com salas destinadas a funções específicas para observação e aulas, redução das observações e cálculo astronómico das efemérides. Em termos de pessoal o Regulamento estabelece *"um Diretor, dois Astrónomos, quatro Ajudantes, um Guarda, um Praticante de Guarda e um Porteiro"*, aumentando assim consideravelmente o quadro de pessoal que de duas (segundo os Estatutos) passa a dez pessoas. Todos seriam nomeados pelo Governo por proposta do Reitor, com exceção dos dois Astrónomos que seriam professores da Faculdade de Matemática (o titular e o substituto da cadeira de Astronomia), e por isso mesmo indicados pela Congregação de Matemática aquando da distribuição do serviço docente. Dois anos depois, em 1801, aquando da reforma curricular da cadeira de Astronomia, o lugar de 1.º Astrónomo ficará atribuído ao professor de Astronomia Prática, ficando o professor da cadeira de Astronomia Teórica sem lugar e estatuto no OAUC. Esta situação algo problemática será resolvida pela Carta Régia de 5 de março de 1805 com a criação da figura de 3.º Astrónomo.

Quanto ao cargo de Diretor, seria ocupado por *"um Lente Jubilado, de cujo zelo, atividade e conhecimentos se possa bem confiar o progresso deste importante estabelecimento"*, não se impondo que fosse da Faculdade de Matemática. O facto de os cargos de Diretor, dos Ajudantes (doutores ou bacharéis formados em Matemática) e do pessoal menor serem de nomeação Real, sem que a Congregação da Faculdade fosse tida ou achada, é mais um reflexo do carácter de nacional que se pretendia para o OAUC. Cabia ao Diretor dirigir e planear as observações e o trabalho teórico de cálculo das efemérides. As observações diárias compreendiam *"as passagens dos Planetas e das Estrelas pelo Meridiano, e as suas alturas; [...]; todos os Eclipses do Sol, da Lua, dos Satélites, ocultações das Estrelas, e todos os fenómenos dos movimentos celestes"*. Ou seja, o Regulamento de 1799 indica de modo preciso o programa observacional que os Estatutos em 1772 já haviam estipulado: o de *"fazer todas as observações [mais apuradas e exatas], que são necessárias para se fixarem as Longitudes Geográficas; e retificarem os Elementos fundamentais da mesma Astronomia"* (Estatutos 1772: (3)213). Todas as observações efetuadas seriam registadas e depois de coligidas e reduzidas (i.e., depois de calculadas as refrações, paralaxes e erros instrumentais) seriam difundidas nas *"Coleções Gerais das Observações"*. A publicação destas Coleções nunca viria a ser feita.

Um aspeto que merece destaque no Regulamento (§. 13 e 14) é a determinação da realização de viagens científicas, com carácter periódico (de 10 em 10 anos), para estabelecimento de intercâmbios científicos, a instituições científicas estrangeiras e observatórios astronómicos, *"onde a arte de observar estiver na maior perfeição, para tomar conhecimento do modo, com que neles se pratica, da qualidade dos seus instrumentos, e de tudo o mais, que convier."* Esta disposição não se restringia apenas à Astronomia, contemplava também outras áreas científicas *"estabelecidas na mesma Universidade"*. Manuel Pedro de Melo (1765-1833), doutorado em matemática (1795) e à data professor na Academia Real da Marinha, é nomeado em 1801 professor da cadeira de Hidráulica na Universidade e enviado para a Europa numa destas viagens (Carta Régia de Outubro de 1801). Nas instruções que leva, redigidas por Monteiro da Rocha, para além de assuntos específicos à organização da nova cadeira de Hidráulica, também é contemplada a Astronomia; recomendava-se-lhe que diligenciasse em

> *"adquirir notícias, multímodas, acerca dos Observatórios de Greenwich, de Paris, de M. Zach; e fosse proposta a correspondência deles com o de Coimbra, [...] Emprega[sse] todas as diligências para experimentar os telescópios de Herschel, e fazer juízo, se seria conveniente dar uma grande soma por um instrumento desses; conferenciar com Lenoir, que em Paris começava a ter grande reputação de construtor de instrumentos astronómicos, sobre o preço, condições e formas de um círculo pequeno, portátil, como o que serviu a Méchain nos triângulos de Dunquerque, e de outro maior, como o que se fizera para o Observatório de Paris."* (Ribeiro 1871-1914: (5)55-56)

Em Paris irá colaborar com Delambre, publicando em 1808 naquela cidade, *Mémoires sur l'Astronomie Practique* (Paris, Courcier, 1808), onde traduz algumas memórias de Monteiro da Rocha publicadas nas *Ephemerides Astronómicas* do Observatório de Coimbra.

As '*Ephemerides Astronomicas*' do OAUC

A Carta Régia de 1799 (§.7) expressa claramente que toda a atividade do OAUC se deve focar nas tarefas essenciais para a preparação das *'Ephemerides Astronomicas'* (EAOAUC) para o ano de 1804 e seguintes (EAOAUC 1803: VIII). Monteiro da Rocha como responsável científico dos métodos matemáticos e astronómicos, algoritmos e tabelas subjacentes ao cálculo começa desde logo a trabalhar. Em dezembro de 1802, em carta para o reitor, confessa-se bastante assoberbado com os cálculos da futura publicação, que *"diferentes de todas as outras Efemérides em muitos pontos essenciais, interessa o crédito da Nação, da Universidade e o meu"*[36]. Em 1803 é então publicado, pela Imprensa da Universidade de Coimbra, o primeiro volume com os dados astronómicos para 1804,

> *"Ephemerides // Astronomicas // calculadas // para o meridiano do Observatório Real da Universidade // de Coimbra: // para uso do mesmo Observatório, e para o da navegação // Portugueza // volume I // para o anno de 1804. // [estampa do OAUC] // Coimbra // na Real Imprensa da Universidade, // 1803 // Por Ordem do Principe Regente Nosso Senhor"*

As EAOAUC serão publicadas ininterruptamente até 1827 (volume 19 com as efemérides para 1828), sendo depois suspensas[37]. As perseguições do governo Miguelista, a guerra civil (1828-1834) e os anos conturbados que se lhes seguiram refletem-se também durante na vida da Universidade, com forte impacto no quadro de pessoal do OAUC (Freire 1872: 61-64, 97). A publicação será retomada em 1840 com um volume duplo para os anos de 1841 e 1842[38]. É interessante

---

[36] "Cartas do Dr. José Monteiro da Rocha a D. Francisco de Lemos de Faria Pereira Coutinho", O Instituto, vol. XXXVII (1889-90), p. 476.

[37] Durante este período houve alguns volumes duplos com a publicação de efemérides para dois anos consecutivos: *EAOAUC* para 1808 e 1809 (1807); *EAOAUC* para 1815 e 1816 (1814); *EAOAUC* para 1817 e 1818 (1815); *EAOAUC* para 1819 e 1820 (1816); *EAOAUC* para 1821 e 1822 (1818) e *EAOAUC* para 1823 e 1824 (1821).

[38] *EAOAUC* para os anos 1841 e 1842 (1840). As *EAOAUC* foram desde então, e sem interrupção, publicadas até inícios do século XXI.

notar algumas mudanças no título que as *'Ephemerides Astronomicas'* sofrem ao longo da 1.ª série, refletindo as mudanças no panorama político nacional e a própria importância do Observatório no quadro das instituições do Estado. A partir do volume 13 (1816) passam a ser impressas por *"Ordem de Sua Majestade El-Rei Nosso Senhor"*, a partir do volume 15 (1821) por *"Ordem de Sua Majestade"* e no volume 17 (1825) já vem, por *"Ordem de sua Majestade Imperial e Real"*. Também há mudanças na designação do Observatório que passa de *"Observatório Real"* para *"Observatório Imp[erial] e R[eal] da Universidade de Coimbra"* e no começo da 2.ª série passa a *"Observatório Nacional da Universidade de Coimbra"*.

Ao longo dos volumes que constituem a 1ª série (1803-1827) as EOAUC seguiram com alterações mínimas a organização delineada logo no 1º volume. Forneciam 10 *'Folhas Mensais'*, com as efemérides correspondentes a cada um dos meses do ano, precedidas de duas páginas com informação vária, sobre as *'épocas principais do ano'* (festas móveis religiosas e civis), as datas históricas significativas (p. ex. da primeira Olimpíada, da fundação de Roma, da fundação da Nacionalidade Portuguesa, da Reforma da Universidade de Coimbra, entre outras); com os *'sinais e abreviaturas'* usadas ao longo do texto; e ainda os eclipses (solares e lunares) que se verificarão no respetivo ano (os eclipses visíveis em Coimbra eram devidamente assinalados com um asterisco); forneciam também um *'Catálogo das estrelas principais'* e a *'Explicação e uso dos Artigos principais destas Ephemerides'*.

As 10 *'folhas mensais'* das EAOAUC, á semelhança do *Connaissance des Temps* ou do *Nautical Almanac*, providenciavam os dados astronómicos convencionais do Sol, da Lua e planetas e das distâncias lunares. A *folha I* fornecia as efemérides do Sol (longitude, ascensão reta, declinação, equação do tempo, semidiâmetro, tempo de passagem pelo meridiano, movimento horário e paralaxe horizontal); a *folha II*, a ascensão reta do meridiano do OAUC e os fenómenos astronómicos do mês; a *folha III* as efemérides dos planetas (Mercúrio, Vénus, Marte, Júpiter, Saturno e Úrano); as *folhas IV-VII* eram todas dedicadas às efemérides da Lua (longitude, latitude, declinação e ascensão reta (0h e 12h), paralaxe horizontal, semidiâmetro, fases da Lua); as *folhas VIII-IX* as distâncias lunares ao sol, às estrelas e planetas; e a *folha X* fornecia informação sobre os eclipses dos satélites de Júpiter. A única mudança significativa que ocorre na 1.ª série é a inclusão nos últimos 3 volumes de um *'Calendário Náutico'*[39]. Introduzido por Joaquim Maria de Andrade (1768-1830), diretor interino à época do OAUC, com a finalidade de facilitar aos pilotos e marinheiros o uso das distâncias lunares, fornecia a declinação do sol e a sua ascensão reta em tempo verdadeiro e as distâncias lunares tabeladas a cada 3 horas. Nos volumes anteriores as distâncias lunares eram apresentadas de 12 em 12 horas o que implicava cálculos difíceis para interpolar distâncias para instantes não tabelados. No *'calendário náutico'*, como as distâncias lunares eram apresentadas de 3 em 3 horas era possível o uso da regra de três simples, o que facilitava enormemente os cálculos a todos os que não dominavam o uso avançado das interpolações, como era o caso dos pilotos.

As *'Ephemerides Astronomicas'* apresentaram também desde o início outras particularidades. Ao contrário das congéneres estrangeiras que usavam o tempo verdadeiro ou aparente, as de Coimbra eram calculadas para o tempo médio do meridiano do observatório, usavam ainda a medida dos 360° e não a amplamente utilizada unidade de signo, e forneciam as distâncias da Lua aos planetas. Mas a principal particularidade estava no cálculo das posições da Lua. Ao contrário das outras efemérides estrangeiras que calculavam as posições do nosso satélite, tanto para o meio-dia como para a meia-noite, diretamente a partir das tábuas astronómicas,

---

[39] *EAOAUC* para 1826 (1825); *EAOAUC* para 1827 (1826) e *EAOAUC* para 1828 (1827).

as de Coimbra calculavam apenas o lugar do meio-dia diretamente das tábuas, sendo o lugar da meia-noite calculado por interpolação segundo um método concebido por Monteiro da Rocha (Figueiredo 2014). Estas inovações seriam alvo de críticas positivas por parte de alguns dos principais astrónomos da época, por exemplo de Delambre e do 6º astrónomo real inglês John Pond, que as incorporariam mais tarde nas publicações que dirigiam,

> *"The attention of the Committee was, in the first instance, directed to a subject of general importance, as affecting almost all the results in the Nautical Almanac; viz., whether the quantities therein inserted should in future be given for apparent time (as heretofore), or for mean solar time. Considering that the latter is the most convenient, not only for every purpose of Astronomy, but also (from the best information they have been able to obtain) for all the purposes of Navigation; at the same time that it is less laborious to the computer, and has already been introduced with good effect into the national Ephemerides of Coimbra and Berlin, the Committee recommend the abolition of the apparent time in all the computations of the Nautical Almanac; excepting only the place, &c of the sun at the time of its transit over the meridian."*
> (*Nautical Almanac* 1833: XII)

A propósito das singularidades das EAOAUC escreveria mais tarde Filipe Folque (1800-74),

> *"Contudo não devemos ocultar para crédito, e glória do nome Português, que só a Efeméride de Coimbra foi a única, que, não se servindo de elemento algum calculado nas Efemérides estrangeiras, teve logo desde o seu inicio maior cópia de elementos astronómicos, onde se viram muitas novidades, grandes aperfeiçoamentos, suma perfeição, e donde as Efemérides estrangeiras tem tirado alguns*

dos seus melhoramentos [...] não posso deixar de me encher de um nobre orgulho, e de tributar com maior entusiasmo, e respeito as devidas homenagens a seu Diretor o Sábio Astrónomo Português o senhor Doutor José Monteiro da Rocha, cujo zelo, e luzes tanto contribuíram para os progressos das Ciências em Portugal." (Folque 1832: iii-iv)[40]

Também à semelhança das suas congéneres as EAOAUC publicaram (principalmente nos volumes de 1803 a 1813) vários artigos de astronomia teórica e de prática instrumental e diversas tabelas astronómicas. Estes, da autoria de Monteiro da Rocha, estão relacionados de uma maneira ou de outra com o próprio cálculo, elaboração e uso das EAOAUC. Alguns seriam traduzidos para francês por Manuel Pedro de Melo e mereceriam boas recensões por Delambre[41].

As efemérides astronómicas são calculadas a partir de tabelas astronómicas e a construção destas últimas depende da íntima conjugação das previsões teóricas com os dados observacionais, dos quais depende a identificação das irregularidades dos movimentos dos astros que a própria teoria prevê. Nos finais do século XVIII as tabelas astronómicas mais precisas haviam sido publicadas por Lalande em 1792, na 3.ª edição do seu *Astronomie*. As primeiras EAOAUC

---

[40] Também o matemático e geógrafo José António Madeira (1896-1976) um século mais tarde se sintoniza com Folque, *"A sua concepção [das EAOAUC] foi tão originalmente prática e as suas explanações tão preciosas e claras, sob o ponto de vista matemático, que rapidamente adquiriram grande fama, sendo largamente usadas na navegação. E desta forma as Efemérides conquistaram para o Real Observatório Astronómico de Coimbra, a justa consideração e nomeada que tem perdurado até aos nossos dias."* Madeira 1933: 59.

[41] «*Le traducteur, M. de Mello, a pensé, avec beaucoup de raison, que ces Mémoires méritaient d'être répandus encore davantage, et il les présente réunis dans une langue plus universellement connue [...]. Les Mémoires que nous annonçons, ont paru dans les Éphémérides de Coimbra, et nous avons déjà parlé du plus considérable, dont nous avons donné un extrait détaillé dans la Connaissance des Tems de l'an 1809 ; mais nous n'avons pu rapporter que les formules les plus importantes, et nos lecteurs seront sans doute curieux d'en connaitre les démonstrations [CDT pour l'an 1810]*». CDT 1808: 471.

são calculadas usando precisamente as *'Tables Astronomiques'* que Lalande aí apresenta; com exceção das posições de Marte que são calculadas usando tabelas elaboradas pelo próprio Monteiro da Rocha[42]. Em 1806 o *Bureau des Longitudes* francês publica umas tabelas do Sol e da Lua da autoria de Delambre e de Bürg e que serão usadas nas EAOAUC (as posições dos outros corpos continuam a ser calculadas pelas tabelas de Lalande). Monteiro da Rocha acrescenta-as e adapta-as ao meridiano de Coimbra, publicando em 1813 as *'Taboas Astronómicas ordenadas a facilitar o Calculo das Ephemerides da Universidade de Coimbra'*, que passam a partir do volume 11 (1814) a constituir a base de cálculo das posições do Sol, da Lua e dos planetas,

> "*Os lugares do Sol e da Lua, tanto para o ano de 1815 e 1816, foram já calculados pelas novas Tábuas Astronómicas, reduzidas ao meridiano do Observatório pelo seu Diretor, o qual, conservando-lhes toda a exatidão, as dispôs e ordenou de uma forma engenhosa, e admirável, que as torna muito cómodas para os calculadores; e por isso muito recomendáveis. Os lugares dos Planetas para o ano de 1815 foram calculados pelas antigas Taboas, em razão de não estarem impressas ainda as novas, que lhes eram relativas; não é assim para 1816, em que já todas vão calculadas pelas Novas*" (EAOAUC 1814: advertência)

Aquando do recomeço da 2.ª série, os lugares do Sol e da Lua continuam a ser calculados pelas tabelas de Monteiro da Rocha, mas para os planetas passam a ser usadas as de Damoiseau de Monfort (Júpiter) e as de Bouvard (Saturno e Úrano).

---

[42] "Taboas de Marte para o Meridiano do Observatório Real da Universidade de Coimbra". EAOAUC 1803: I-XV.

Devido às suas características as *Ephemerides Astronomicas* de Coimbra foram sempre mais astronómicas que náuticas. Isto é, mais vocacionadas e orientadas para a atividade dos astrónomos e seus observatórios do que para os marinheiros no alto mar. Os pilotos, especialmente da marinha mercante, preferiam usar as *Efemérides Nauticas ou Diario Astronomico* (ENACL), copiadas do NA inglês para o meridiano de Lisboa, que a Academia das Ciências de Lisboa publicava desde 1788. Eram mais abreviadas e apresentavam as distâncias lunares tabeladas a cada 3 horas, sendo por isso mais amigáveis para o uso a bordo. O *Calendario Nautico* foi uma tentativa frustrada do OAUC dar eco às necessidades mais imediatas da marinha.

A criação da Academia Real das Ciências de Lisboa e da Academia Real da Marinha

Após a morte de D. José I, e o afastamento de Pombal, os primeiros anos do reinado de D. Maria (1734-1816) foram tempos algo conturbados. A Universidade reformada, um dos símbolos maiores do regime Pombalino, enfrenta alguns ataques por parte das forças mais conservadoras da sociedade[43]. Contudo, o esforço de modernização do país assente na formação de quadros prossegue e fortalece-se. Durante o período mariano-joanino[44] as políticas

---

[43] Em 1777 a Inquisição entra em força na Universidade e prende José Anastácio da Cunha (1744-87), professor de Geometria, que se vê afastado para sempre de Coimbra em consequência do processo que lhe foi movido. São também vários textos reagindo, criticando e gozando o retrocesso conservantista do ambiente académico que se viverá então, um exemplo paradigmático é o poema satírico *Reino da Estupidez* de 1784. Albuquerque 1975.

[44] Este período historiográfico abrange dois reinados, o de D. Maria I (1777--1816) e o de D. João VI (1816-26). Em 1792 D. Maria I fica mentalmente instável começando o Príncipe D. João (1767-1826) a assinar em seu nome. Em 1799 a rainha é declarada incapaz de gerir o reino, assumindo o Príncipe a regência. Como rei, D. João VI reinará entre 1816 e 1826.

de ensino continuam de certa maneira a orientar-se pelo modelo pombalino. As reformas estendem-se ao ensino técnico, com a criação de várias instituições com uma matriz semelhante à dos cursos científicos da Universidade – Academia da Marinha (1779), Academia dos Guardas-Marinhas (1782), Academia de Fortificação, Artilharia e Desenho (1790), Real Corpo de Engenheiros (1790-3), Academia da Marinha e Comércio da cidade do Porto (1803). Dá-se a especialização profissional e científica dos matemáticos, astrónomos, engenheiros, botânicos, químicos e mineralogistas, com a Academia Real das Ciências de Lisboa a desempenhar um importante papel no pensar o país e suas políticas de fomento[45].

A Academia Real das Ciências de Lisboa (ACL) foi criada em 24 de dezembro de 1779 por um grupo de homens encabeçados pelo Duque de Lafões (1719-1806), entre os quais se encontra Vandelli (1735-1816) professor de Química e História Natural da Faculdade de Filosofia, e o Abade Correia da Serra (1750-1823), preocupados com o desenvolvimento do país. Influenciados pelos valores do Iluminismo pretendiam fomentar o desenvolvimento da ciência e da técnica em Portugal e assim contribuir utilmente para o desenvolvimento económico e social do país. *"As Colunas, em que se estriba a nossa Academia, são a ciência e a indústria livres de afetação e prejuízos, tendo por objeto o bem da Pátria."*, escrevia José António de Sá (? -1819) para Luís António Furtado, Visconde de Barbacena (1754-1830)[46]. Nesse sentido e à semelhança das suas congéneres estrangeiras, como a de Paris, Berlim ou S. Petersburgo, a ACL promoverá a publicação de trabalhos científicos dos seus sócios e de concursos científicos nas várias classes, com atribuição de uma medalha de ouro de 50$ reis às memórias premiadas. Os temas a

---

[45] Ver neste volume texto de Carlos M. Martins. Para um aprofundamento veja-se a sua tese de doutoramento, Martins 2014: 569-775.

[46] Carta de 5 de fevereiro de 1781 transcrita em Aires 1927: 161-163.

concurso são estabelecidos com cerca de 3 anos de antecedência, abordando temas diversos das ciências aplicadas, agricultura e indústria, mas também em literatura, direito e história portuguesa. No período de 1780 a 1820 a Academia lançará 253 concursos, sendo 178 relativos às ciências da observação e 75 às ciências exatas (matemática, astronomia e navegação), numa média anual de temas nas *'Ciências de Observação'* mais do dobro do das *'Ciências de Cálculo'* (5,23/ano e 2,21/ano, respetivamente) (Saraiva 2013). A preocupação com o conhecimento do território nacional, a estatística dos seus recursos naturais e humanos para uma melhor intervenção no território e um melhor entendimento do potencial económico do país, bem como das suas regiões ultramarinas na Ásia, África e América do Sul estava na linha da frente das necessidades do governo e das preocupações dos académicos. E os temas a concurso refletem bem esta necessidade. Durante este período houve temas que tanto pela sua importância, como pela falta de respostas satisfatórias, foram recorrentes ao longo dos anos: é o caso da *"Descrição Física e Económica de alguma Comarca, ou território considerável do Reino ou Domínios Ultramarinos, com observações uteis á Agricultura e Industria Nacional"*; ou de *"Um plano de canal para aproveitar as aguas de algum rio de Portugal na irrigação dos campos, com todas as nivelações, e cálculos necessários"*; ou ainda de *"Uma derrota, em que o uso das observações astronómicas seja o mais frequente, principalmente as das distâncias da lua ao sol, ou às estrelas sendo estas calculadas segundo métodos e tabuadas que a Academia tem indicado e continua a indicar em as Efemérides Náuticas, que para uso dos nossos pilotos tem mandado calcular todos os anos"*. No que diz respeito aos temas propostos em astronomia estavam na maior parte dos casos diretamente ligados a questões de ciência e prática náutica, como é o caso deste tema da *'derrota'*, pretendendo respostas ao problema da determinação da longitude no mar e pesquisa de outros protocolos para as distâncias lunares alternativos ao método de

Borda. Há também temas sobre instrumentos náuticos, sua utilização e construção. O desenvolvimento económico Português assentava fortemente no seu comércio ultramarino, muito dependente de boa preparação da marinha mercante e militar. A criação e publicação a partir de 1788 das *Ephemerides Nauticas ou Diario Astronomico* por parte da ACL com participação de alguns académicos e professores da Academia Real da Marinha são mais uma resposta a essa necessidade.

A criação em Lisboa da Academia Real da Marinha (ARM) em 1779, e três anos mais tarde, em 1782, da Academia Real dos Guarda--Marinhas (ARGM), inicia o período de institucionalização em linhas modernas e sintonizado com instituições europeias similares do ensino da ciência náutica em Portugal (Ferreira 2014). Estas duas academias são criadas como estabelecimentos de ensino teórico--prático dos futuros pilotos e oficiais da marinha mercante e de marinha guerra, respetivamente. A estrutura curricular de ambas as instituições foi em parte inspirada na da Faculdade de Matemática, porém com conteúdos e matérias menos exigentes. O curso da Academia da Marinha era composto por diversas disciplinas teóricas e práticas distribuídas por 3 anos. O ensino da matemática incluía a aritmética, geometria e trigonometria plana, álgebra e cálculo infinitesimal; as ciências físico-matemáticas compreendiam o estudo da estática, dinâmica, hidrostática, hidráulica e ótica. O terceiro ano incluía o ensino da astronomia esférica, e os fundamentos da navegação teórica e prática e o uso de instrumentos. A componente prática era feita a bordo, sendo necessária a quem desejasse ascender ao posto de tenente a experiência de dois anos no mar, que devia incluir uma viagem à Índia ou ao Brasil. O programa da Academia dos Guardas-Marinhas era idêntico, destacando-se a especial atenção dada à formação no desenho técnico, nas manobras náuticas e de artilharia. Em 1791 Francisco António Ciera (1763-1814), professor de Navegação, propõe a construção de um observatório astronómico para as aulas práticas. O Observatório Real da Marinha seria inaugurado em 1798 (o seu regulamento data de 23 de julho de 1799), assumindo a partir daí a responsabilidade formal pela elaboração das *'Ephemerides Nauticas'*, que desde o primeiro volume estavam sob a responsabilidade do observatório da ACL[47].

As *'Ephemerides Nauticas, ou Diario Astronomico'* (ENACL)

A intenção por parte da ACL de elaborar e publicar umas efemérides data do ano de 1781, tendo para isso sido consultado expressamente Monteiro da Rocha. Monteiro da Rocha considera boa ideia a elaboração de um almanaque se o seu uso não se restringir apenas à marinha nacional, mas que *"fosse também procurado dos estrangeiros"*[48]. Porém, não considera o projeto viável por faltar gente capaz de proceder aos cálculos necessários à sua elaboração. Todavia, acrescenta que se poderia quando muito fazer *"o que fizeram os Franceses, que é copiá-las fielmente, mudando-lhes somente os tempos conforme a diferença dos meridianos"*. Esta hipótese exigia um relativo pequeno esforço de cálculo quando comparada com o cálculo de raiz das efemérides pelas tabelas astronómicas, pois bastava apenas ter em conta a diferença de longitude entre os meridianos de Greenwich e Lisboa. Mesmo assim Monteiro da Rocha recomendava ainda dois revisores para examinarem cuidadosamente todos os cálculos com os dados fornecidos pelo CDT e NA. Apesar de considerar exequível um almanaque náutico deste género, Monteiro da Rocha não o considerava uma mais-valia pois na verdade não

---

[47] A edificação começa em 1785, sendo inaugurado em 9 de janeiro de 1787.

[48] Em 7 de Outubro de 1781 José Monteiro da Rocha escreve ao Visconde de Barbacena, secretário da ACL, manifestando-lhe o que pensava acerca do projeto de um *"Almanach Astronómico"* ou um *"Almanach próprio para a Marinha"*. Figueiredo 2011: 365-371.

passaria de uma cópia (recalculada) de publicações já existentes. O que seria efetivamente desejável e *"empresa digna do zelo da Academia"* escreve, é que as distâncias lunares fossem calculadas diretamente de outras tábuas astronómicas *"que não fossem as de Mayer, nas quais são fundados os cálculos do Nautical Almanac, e a cópia deles que vem no Conhecimento dos Tempos"*. Ou seja, o que Monteiro acaba por sugerir é que as efemérides eventualmente a publicar pela Academia das Ciências fossem calculadas por *"outras tábuas de crédito como as de Clairaut ou de Euler"* e aí sim, um *"Almanach desta sorte seria interessante em toda a Europa marítima, e glorioso à Corte de Portugal, assim é à da Inglaterra o outro, até agora único, fundado nas Taboas de Mayer."* Infelizmente, tal não era possível por não haver pessoas em número suficiente que as soubessem e pudessem calcular, concluindo assim que tal projeto teria que se adiar *"para quando se puder executar"*.

Na verdade, este plano de calcular umas efemérides que não fossem reduzidas ou copiadas *"do Almanach do Observatório de Greenwich, nem de outro algum, mas calculada[s] imediatamente sobre as Tábuas Astronómicas"*, viria a ser por si concretizado cerca de 20 anos mais tarde no Observatório Real Astronómico da Universidade de Coimbra, com as *'Ephemerides Astronomicas'*. Seja como for, a verdade é que durante a década de 1780 vai-se reunindo capacidade por parte de alguns académicos, professores da ARM e formados na Faculdade de Matemática, para levar avante a ideia de um almanaque náutico copiado do inglês. O projeto seria formalmente discutido em sessão académica a 5 de dezembro de 1787, ficando assente a sua publicação paro o ano seguinte[49]. Custódio Gomes Villas-Boas (1744-1808), diretor do observatório da Academia

---

[49] *"Determina a Academia que se imprima à sua custa, e debaixo do seu privilégio as Ephemerides Náuticas para o ano de 1789 calculadas para o meridiano de Lisboa [José Correia da Serra, Secretário da Academia, Sessão de 13 de março de 1788]."* ENACL 1788.

das Ciências, ficou responsável pelos cálculos de uma equipa também composta por Francisco António Ciera[50] e Francisco Garção Stockler (1759-1829). Em 1788 é então publicado o primeiro volume das *"Ephemerides Nauticas, Ou Diario Astronomico"* (ENACL)[51],

> *"Com estes subsídios é de esperar que os Navegantes Portugueses não cederão aos mais destros Pilotos das outras nações, muito mais se se lembrarem que eles de nós aprenderam a navegar ousadamente por mares desconhecidos, para os quais os nossos lhe abriram o caminho [ENACL para o ano de 1789]"* (*ENACL* 1788: prólogo)

Custódio Gomes dirigirá a publicação entre os anos de 1788 e 1795. Segue-se-lhe, entre 1796 a 1798, José Maria Dantas Pereira (1772-1836), a quem sucede o *émigré* Charles Marie Damoiseau de Monfort (1768-1846), que as dirigirá entre 1799 a 1806[52]. Serão suspensas em 1808. A transferência da Academia Real da Marinha para

---

[50] Ciera e Custódio Gomes traduzirão e publicarão em 1804 o famoso catálogo estelar *Atlas Coelestis* (1729) de Flamsteed. Villas-Boas 1804.

[51] *"Ephemerides Nauticas, Ou Diario Astronomico [...] que contém todos os elementos necessários para determinar a latitude no mar, não só pela altura meridiana do Sol; mas também pela da Lua, pela dos Planetas superiores, e pela das Estrelas fixas, com as distâncias da Lua ao Sol, e às Estrelas para determinar a Longitude do navio a qualquer hora, e o método de a deduzir. Calculado para o meridiano de Lisboa e publicado por ordem da Academia Real das Sciencias para utilidade da Navegação Portugueza, e aumento da Astronomia"* [ENACL]. No prólogo do 1.º volume, assinado por Custódio Gomes Villas-Boas, informa-se que o volume foi concluído em 25 de setembro de 1788.

[52] Damoiseau de Monfort, matemático e oficial francês, havia-se exilado em Portugal aquando da Revolução Francesa. Durante a sua estada em Portugal (1795--1807?) faz parte do exército e da marinha portuguesa, chegando ao posto de Capitão-Tenente da Real Marinha, será eleito sócio da Academia Real das Ciências de Lisboa e da Sociedade Real Marítima, Militar e Geográfica. Depois de regressar a França desenvolverá extenso trabalho sobre as tabelas da Lua, sendo eleito membro da *Académie des Sciences/Institut de France* e do *Bureau des Longitudes*. Com a morte de Burckhardt (1773-1825) Damoiseau assumirá o cargo de diretor do observatório da École Militaire. Em 1831 receberá a Medalha de Ouro da Royal Astronomical Society. Em 1836 publicará as *Table écliptiques des satéllites de Jupiter* (Paris, 1836), que serão usadas para o cálculo das posições dos satélites de Júpiter do CDT até ao ano de 1914.

o Brasil (1807), com o embarque da maior parte dos instrumentos e dos livros do observatório da marinha que fica bastante empobrecido, bem como o regresso de Damoiseau de Monfort a França são fatores determinantes. Em 1820 a publicação das ENACL é reiniciada, cessando definitivamente em 1863.

Como escrevemos anteriormente as ENACL eram mais fáceis de usar pelos marinheiros. O serem calculadas em tempo verdadeiro para o meridiano de Lisboa, cidade onde se situava o porto mais importante do país, e de disporem as distâncias lunares tabeladas de 3 em 3 horas facilitava enormemente os cálculos acessórios à determinação das longitudes. As ENACL forneciam os dados astronómicos em 8 folhas mensais[53]. Para além das efemérides mensais eram também publicadas tabelas e artigos de interesse para a marinha. Por exemplo logo no 1.º volume foram publicados 2 artigos de especial interesse: *"Método para determinar o tempo verdadeiro pela altura das estrelas"* e *"Método do cavalheiro Borda para o cálculo das longitudes no mar, determinadas pelas distâncias da Lua ao Sol, ou às Estrelas"*, bem como 14 tabelas auxiliares para redução das observações (*ENACL* 1788: 102-142, 166-167, 170-181).

Os trabalhos cartográficos em Portugal e no Brasil

O interesse das efemérides astronómicas não se restringe de todo às questões de determinação da longitude no mar. As efemérides fornecem dados astronómicos essenciais para as triangulações e operações topográficas. Os grandes avanços técnicos na precisão

---

[53] Folha I, declinação do Sol e da Lua; a folha II fornecia informação sobre o nascimento e ocaso, passagem pelo meridiano e paralaxe horizontal da Lua; a folha III, as posições dos planetas Marte, Júpiter e Saturno; a folha IV prestava informação sobre os eventos astronómicos para o mês em questão; e as folhas V a VII forneciam as distâncias lunares.

dos instrumentos portáteis e nas efemérides astronómicas vão permitir nas últimas décadas do século XVIII avanços extraordinários à cartografia 'científica'. O correto conhecimento e mapeamento das regiões do interior, das costas e portos dos territórios metropolitanos e coloniais para definição de fronteiras, uma melhor exploração dos recursos, e uma eficaz administração civil desses territórios é uma questão de estado para todos os países europeus da época[54]. Portugal não é exceção (Moreira 2012).

Como já havíamos escrito, a chegada nos anos de 1720 dos italianos Carbone e Capassi está relacionada com a necessidade das demarcações dos territórios portugueses e espanhóis na Colónia de Sacramento e do Rio da Prata[55]. Como resultado do Tratado de Madrid, assinado entre os dois países em 1750, o italiano Miguel Ciera (c. 1726-1782) foi contratado como matemático, astrónomo e geógrafo para integrar a equipa que deveria estabelecer os limites do sul do Brasil. Durante três anos, entre 1752 e 1756, esta chamada de *Terceira Partida de Limites* subiu o rio Paraguai até chegar à nascente do rio Jauru, onde colocou uma marca como símbolo da demarcação das terras portuguesas e espanholas (Costa 2009). Ciera será o primeiro professor de Astronomia da nova Faculdade de Matemática (1772-78) e mais tarde professor de trigonometria esférica e Navegação na Academia Real da Marinha (1779-82).

---

[54] Em França, o primeiro levantamento cartográfico moderno é realizado entre 1756-89 ('Carta Cassini') e serviria de modelo para as futuras campanhas cartográficas em outros países.

[55] O célebre explorador francês Louis Antoine de Bougainville (1729-1811), que em 1767 passa pela região, descreve bem a situação, *"Avant la dernière guerre il se faisait ici une contrebande énorme avec la colonie du Saint-Sacrement, place que les Portugais possèdent sur la rive gauche du fleuve, presque en face de Buenos Aires; mais cette place est aujourd'hui tellement resserré par le nouveaux ouvrages dont les Espagnols l'ont enceinte que la contrebande avec elle est impossible s'il n'y a connivence; les Portugais même qui l'habitent sont obligés de tirer par mer leur subsistance du Brésil. Enfin ce poste est ici à l'Espagne, à l'égard des Portugais, ce que lui est en Europe Gibraltar à l'égard des Anglais."* Bougainville 1889: 30-31.

Em 1777, outra campanha é enviada para a mesma região para empreender novas demarcações impostas pelo Tratado de Santo Ildefonso (o Tratado de Madrid fora revogado em 1761). Esta equipa é liderada por António Pires da Silva Pontes (1750-1805) e Francisco José de Lacerda e Almeida (1750-1798), ambos doutorados em matemática e ex-alunos de Ciera e Monteiro da Rocha. Pela primeira vez temos uma missão científica cartográfica comandada por cientistas e técnicos portugueses formados em Portugal (Curado 2014). Várias informações sobre a longitude de muitos lugares do interior do Brasil e do Peru, resultantes desta missão cartográfica, serão publicados nas EAOAUC de 1805 e 1815. Mas não era só no Brasil que as questões de mapeamento eram importantes. A não existência de bons mapas do Portugal metropolitano também era um facto. Na década de 1720 Manuel de Azevedo Fortes (1660-1749) propusera, no quadro da Academia Real da História Portuguesa, um rigoroso levantamento cartográfico do reino, porém o projeto frustrou-se por falta de vontades e meios (Moreira 2012: 77-80). Assim até 1790 ano em se começam os trabalhos cartográficos da *Carta do Reino* os mapas utilizados eram em geral adaptações de mapas estrangeiros[56].

O projeto para se fazer o levantamento cartográfico científico de Portugal continental começa a ser discutido na Academia das Ciências de Lisboa em finais de 1788. Na opinião de Custódio Gomes Villas-Boas o projeto devia ser coordenado por Monteiro da Rocha, a quem reconhecia a maior capacidade científica. Tal não vem a acontecer. Quem ficará à frente dos trabalhos será Francisco António Ciera, professor na Academia Real da Marinha. Francisco Ciera era filho de Miguel Ciera e tinha feito os seus estudos na Faculdade de

---

[56] Dos mapas de Portugal publicados entre 1750 e 1812 só 14% deles são-no em Portugal Moreira 2012: 230. Neste período dois mapas de Portugal são particularmente importantes, um da autoria de Thomas Jefferys (c.1710-1771), *'Mappa ou Carta Geographica dos Reinos de Portugal e Algarve'* (1762), e outro de Tomás López (1730-1802), *'Mapa General del Reyno de Portugal'* (1778).

Matemática onde se doutorara. Mas Monteiro da Rocha acaba por se ver diretamente envolvido no projeto: a ele se deve a invenção e fabrico das réguas que serão usadas nas medições das principais bases da rede de triangulação[57]. Em 1804 os trabalhos são interrompidos, serão retomados apenas em 1835 com Pedro Folque (1744-1848), e seu filho Filipe Folque (1800-1874), ele próprio também doutorado em matemática por Coimbra. Só em 1865 se concretizaria o tão ambicionado mapa científico do território nacional. Contudo durante a primeira metade do século XIX foram feitos diversos levantamentos de diferentes partes e regiões do território, na maior parte das regiões costeiras e dos portos marítimos principais. Esses trabalhos foram projetados segundo a matriz de rede de Ciera[58]. Ao mesmo tempo, alguns procedimentos de normalização de escalas foram implementados. Um exemplo ilustrativo é o mapa da *Província de Entre Douro e Minho* feita por Custódio Gomes Villas-Boas em 1794--95, mas só publicado após 1805[59].

Nestas atividades de mapeamento e cartografia devemos destacar duas instituições: a Academia Real das Ciências de Lisboa e a Sociedade Real Marítima, Militar e Geográfica para o Desenho, Gravura e Impressão das Cartas Hidrográficas, Geográficas e Militares. Esta foi criada em 1798 pelo Ministro da Marinha, Rodrigo de

---

[57] *"Em Portugal ninguém pode me ajudar melhor do que o Dr. José Monteiro da Rocha, que foi meu professor em Coimbra. Este homem de gênio raro, que sem dúvida pode ser inscrito no grande grupo matemáticos europeus, pode contribuir muito nesta expedição."*, Francisco Ciera (c.1790), citado em Mendes 1965.

[58] Em 1801 foi feita uma lei específica, conhecida por *'Lei dos Cosmógrafos'* (9--6-1801), que pretendia criar em cada distrito a profissão de cosmógrafo (para um matemático formado pela Universidade de Coimbra), cujo principal trabalho seria fazer um levantamento topográfico da região de acordo com as regras estabelecidas na *Carta do Reino*, e *"intender sobre todas as obras públicas"*. Esta lei, cuja redação é de Monteiro da Rocha, pretende introduzir uma grande reforma administrativa, transferindo para os novos funcionários da administração central um conjunto de competências anteriormente reservado aos magistrados. Segundo Balbi esta lei havia sido inspirada no modelo francês. Balbi 1822: (2) cvj.

[59] Para os levantamentos cartográficos realizados em Portugal entre 1790 e 1807 veja-se Dias 2007.

Sousa Coutinho (1745-1812), com o objetivo explícito de elaborar e publicar cartas hidrográficas e militares de Portugal. Entre os seus membros contam-se entre outros, alguns professores da Academia Real da Marinha e da Academia Real de Fortificação, Artilharia e Desenho, bem como dois professores da Universidade de Coimbra, sendo Monteiro da Rocha um deles. Embora a Sociedade tivesse tido uma vida curta, cessou em 1807, a sua atividade foi relevante. São várias as memórias sobre questões técnicas suscitadas pelo conjunto de catividades científicas que a Sociedade tinha por objeto. São vários os trabalhos sobre longitudes donde se destaca a *Taboada Nautica para o calculo das Longitudes* apresentada por Monteiro da Rocha em 1799.

Conclusão

As modernas ideias científicas e tecnológicas europeias transpõem fronteiras e institucionalizam-se em Portugal com a denominada Reforma Pombalina da Universidade de Coimbra (1770-72), que faz uma aposta clara nas ciências matemáticas, físicas e naturais, bem como num ensino experimental/laboratorial. Anos mais tarde, nos reinados de D. Maria I e de seu filho D. João VI, surgem projetos educativos e científicos análogos noutras instituições, como é o caso da Academia Real da Marinha (1779) e da Academia Real das Ciências (1779), que prosseguem as transformações iniciadas no reinado de D. José. A Universidade e estas escolas superiores serão de facto responsáveis pela formação de quadros nas mais diversas áreas técnico-científicas (matemática, astronomia, arquitetura militar, engenharia naval e civil, pilotagem, cartografia, estatística, geodesia e meteorologia) todos eles dotados de formação matemática e astronómica, e de uma maneira geral pela presença de uma certa cultura matemática que se verifica na sociedade portuguesa de finais de Setecentos.

A criação de estudos científicos pela Reforma da Universidade de 1772 marcam, sem dúvida, o início de uma nova era para a ciência portuguesa. É evidente que esta Reforma se destina a ajustar o país ao novo paradigma científico que havia surgido com a revolução científica dos séculos XVII e XVIII, colocando Portugal ao lado dos países do Iluminismo europeu. No que diz respeito à astronomia, o *Curso Mathematico* formaliza em absoluto o ensino da astronomia newtoniana e mecânica celeste em Portugal. A criação do *Real Observatório Astronómico da Universidade de Coimbra*, um verdadeiro observatório astronómico de cariz nacional, promoverá o progressivo estabelecimento de uma futura comunidade astronómica portuguesa.

A atividade astronómica pensada para o OAUC, e efetivamente realizada, coloca-o a par das principais instituições astronómicas europeias da época, como os observatórios de Paris ou Greenwich. Na história da astronomia portuguesa nunca havia existido algo similar. Os primitivos espaços astronómicos fundados pelos jesuítas no reinado de D. João V, tanto em Santo Antão como no Palácio da Ribeira, não podem em qualquer aspeto ser comparados. Nem em tamanho, e nem, principalmente, no que diz respeito aos seus programas astronómicos.

Desde a sua criação e ao longo da sua história, o OAUC tentou seguir, e contribuir para as tendências contemporâneas da pesquisa astronómica internacional. Fê-lo inicialmente no campo da mecânica celeste e suas aplicações, que até aos meados do século XIX foi o eixo principal da sua atividade, e continuou a fazê-lo após as décadas de 1850 e 1860, quando se abriu às novas aventuras sugeridas pela astrofísica, e em particular aos estudos da astronomia solar.

A APLICAÇÃO DA CIÊNCIA À POLÍTICA DO TERRITÓRIO NA TRANSIÇÃO DO SÉCULO XVIII PARA O SÉCULO XIX

Carlos Moura Martins
Faculdade de Ciências e Tecnologia da Universidade de Coimbra
Departamento de Arquitetura
mouramartins@gmail.com

O desenvolvimento da cultura técnico-científica e as políticas de fomento do território; continuidades e mudanças

Os conceitos iluministas do valor da instrução e dos melhoramentos materiais, enquanto índices de desenvolvimento económico e social, repercutiram-se nas políticas dos Estados europeus para a ciência e para o território. Reflectiram-se, nomeadamente, nos modelos de ensino, vocacionados para a aplicação prática do conhecimento, associando ensino e investigação, e no modo de apreender o território que se procurava medir, ordenar e transformar com bases planificadas[1].

Em Portugal, similarmente, o desenvolvimento da cultura técnico-científica esteve intimamente relacionado com a produção de políticas de fomento para o território. No final do século XVIII, as instituições científicas portuguesas foram objecto de reformas

---

[1] Para o exemplo francês, o mais influente e precoce na Europa, ver Picon, 1992.

continuadas, envolvendo a modernização das instituições existentes e a fundação de novos estabelecimentos. Em simultâneo com o processo de reformas, foi definido progressivamente o quadro das políticas de intervenção territorial. Na interligação entre ciência e território, a formação de competências nos vários ramos do conhecimento constituiu a base de uma futura política estatal de fomento económico de longo prazo.

No tema em questão, podem definir-se três tempos distintos: o período final da governação pombalina (1770-1777), tempo de preparação e de organização, donde se destaca a formação de conhecimento; o período do primeiro governo de D. Maria I (1777-1788), tempo de diagnóstico e reflexão, onde a ênfase é colocada na produção de conhecimento; e o período do segundo governo de D. Maria I e primeiros governos do príncipe regente D. João (1789-1807), tempo de planeamento e acção, onde o esforço é colocado na aplicação prática do conhecimento. Nesta sequência, prevalece a ideia de continuidade mas com mudanças significativas que emanam da própria evolução do processo reformista[2].

O primeiro tempo é marcado pela reforma da Universidade de Coimbra. Constituiu um momento decisivo para a modernização do ensino superior e para a institucionalização da investigação científica em Portugal. As faculdades de Matemática e de Filosofia Natural (ciências físicas e naturais) são criadas de raiz e a faculdade de Medicina é integralmente reformada. As instalações universitárias são reestruturadas e os diversos cursos equipados com laboratórios modernos e apetrechados com colecções, bibliotecas e instrumentos científicos actualizados.

Os novos *Estatutos* da Universidade (1772), documento essencial para a compreensão do projecto político pombalino, encaravam a

---

[2] Ver "Anexo 1 Governos do reinado de D. Maria I e da regência do príncipe D. João, 1777-1810", Martins, 2014: 950-959.

ciência como a disciplina chave para a modernização e mudança de mentalidades do país[3]. Para além das componentes orgânica e pedagógica, os *Estatutos* continham intenções políticas para a administração do território. Previam a incorporação de técnicos formados nas faculdades de Matemática e de Filosofia em cargos da administração pública, como alternativa aos magistrados e aos engenheiros militares[4]. O objectivo não era apenas a saída profissional dos estudantes formados nestas faculdades mas a renovação do pessoal técnico, vontade determinada pelo excessivo peso dos magistrados na administração do território e pela desconfiança do poder político relativamente à capacidade técnica dos engenheiros portugueses[5].

O segundo tempo, sensivelmente correspondente à década de oitenta, deu continuidade ao objectivo pombalino de desenvolvimento do ensino técnico-científico, introduzindo, todavia, alterações significativas. Da mesma forma que já o tinham feito vários estados europeus (ex.: França e Espanha), o ensino científico foi em parte canalizado para as instituições militares, procedendo-se à descentralização dos estudos superiores. Em Lisboa, são criadas a Academia Real da Marinha (1779) e a Academia Real dos Guardas-Marinhas (1782) e, no Porto, a Aula de Debuxo e Desenho (1779), associada à cadeira de Náutica. A prioridade dada à Marinha teve como consequência o adiamento do estabelecimento de uma escola de engenharia para o Exército, assegurando a Academia da Marinha o funcionamento provisório dos cursos de Engenharia Militar e Civil e as ciências de Artilharia e Minas.

A fundação da Academia Real da Marinha, instituição já pensada nos *Estatutos* pombalinos, encerrou a tradição das aulas régias e

---

[3] Ver Araújo, 2000: 9-40.
[4] Ver *Estatutos da Universidade de Coimbra,* 1772. Ver Lemos, 1980: 86-97; 105-107.
[5] Ver, como exemplo desta desconfiança, Lemos, 1980: 94.

regimentais, dando início à fase das Academias – escolas superiores de ensino regular, equiparadas à Universidade de Coimbra – com estatutos, regulamentos, planos de estudos e quadro de professores próprios. O prestigiado e exigente curso de matemática da Academia da Marinha teve por base o curso da faculdade de Matemática da Universidade de Coimbra, onde se formaram grande parte dos seus professores. Nesta altura, não foi necessário recorrer a académicos estrangeiros, como aconteceu aquando da criação do Colégio dos Nobres ou da reforma da Universidade. A Academia da Marinha veio dar suporte a um ensino profissional, facultando novas competências técnico-científicas para os quadros da Marinha e do Exército.

Em dezembro de 1779 é fundada a Academia Real das Ciências, tendo igualmente como referência os *Estatutos* pombalinos e como modelo as academias científicas europeias, em particular a francesa. Algumas das figuras fundamentais na concepção da Academia das Ciências estavam ligadas à Universidade de Coimbra: Domingos Vandelli (1735-1816), professor na faculdade de Filosofia, e José Monteiro da Rocha (1734-1819), professor na faculdade de Matemática, e Luís António Furtado de Mendonça, visconde de Barbacena, (1754--1830), o primeiro doutorado em Filosofia e o primeiro secretário da Academia[6]. Desde a sua fundação, a Academia foi pensada como a "articulação necessária entre a Universidade pombalina e as exigências da investigação e do fomento económico", como refere Óscar Lopes[7]. Durante este período, a Academia das Ciências funcionou como um instituto de investigação, tendo produzido uma intensa actividade em torno do conhecimento do território. O conhecimento dos recursos naturais do país e do seu potencial era, para as elites ilustradas, uma das chaves para o desenvolvimento económico.

---

[6] Consultar a correspondência sobre a fundação da Academia das Ciências publicada por Aires, 1927.

[7] Óscar Lopes, "Academias", in Serrão, 1985, 1: 14-15.

A constituição de novas instituições como a Academia das Ciências e a Academia da Marinha, sete anos depois da reforma da Universidade, revela que a formação de competências nas áreas científicas era um facto. Vários exemplos confirmam a concretização deste propósito: as expedições de demarcação de fronteiras ao Brasil, em 1780, após o tratado de Santo Ildefonso (1777), onde participaram vários astrónomos doutorados em Matemática (José Joaquim Vitorino da Costa, José Simões de Carvalho, António Pires da Silva Pontes Leme e Francisco José de Lacerda e Almeida), ao contrário das expedições após o Tratado de Madrid (1750), maioritariamente integradas por astrónomos estrangeiros, entre os quais o eminente cartógrafo e matemático Miguel António Ciera (?-1782); as expedições científicas às colónias, em 1783, de que são exemplo a viagem de Alexandre Rodrigues Ferreira (1756-1815) ao interior da Amazónia e a Mato Grosso, e a viagem de João da Silva Feijó (1760-1824) ao arquipélago de Cabo Verde; e a ocupação de cargos políticos no espaço do Império por quadros formados na faculdade de Filosofia, como foi o caso dos naturalistas Manuel Galvão da Silva, secretário do governo de Moçambique (1783-1793), e Joaquim José da Silva, secretário do governo de Angola (1783-1803)[8].

Neste segundo tempo, tomaram-se as primeiras medidas concretas de fomento económico para o território continental. O objectivo principal do primeiro governo de D. Maria I foi o do desenvolvimento da agricultura. O mau estado das vias de circulação constituía um dos maiores obstáculos a este desenvolvimento, ao dificultar a comunicação entre os centros de produção e os núcleos urbanos consumidores e exportadores. A medida mais urgente a tomar, para facilitar o escoamento dos produtos do interior e para estimular o mercado interno, era a modernização das vias terrestres e fluviais,

---

[8] Cf. Simon, 1983.

como referiu insistentemente Domingos Vandelli[9]. As opções iniciais privilegiaram, assim, duas das regiões agrícolas mais produtivas do país, funcionando as respectivas intervenções como projectos-piloto: a Norte, o distrito vinhateiro do Alto Douro, em articulação com a cidade do Porto (1779), e, a Sul, os férteis campos baixos do Ribatejo, em articulação com a cidade de Lisboa (1782). No caso do Douro, o objectivo foi a ampliação da região demarcada dos vinhos ao Douro Superior, demolindo o Cachão da Valeira e estendendo a navegação fluvial até Barca de Alva[10]. No Ribatejo, o objectivo prioritário foi o aumento da produção cerealífera, com a construção de canais de rega e de navegação e com a modernização das estradas e caminhos, melhorando as condições de abastecimento à cidade de Lisboa e tornando-a menos dependente do mercado de importação[11]. É possível apreender nestas opções de política económica, por parte do primeiro governo mariano, um indício de que o pensamento fisiocrático poderia ser preponderante na secretaria de Estado do Reino; pensamento já muito influente na reformada Universidade de Coimbra, tornando-se mesmo dominante com a criação da Academia Real das Ciências.

O terceiro tempo, que essencialmente corresponde à década de noventa, representa um momento de viragem nas políticas públicas. Com a reformulação governativa de 15 de dezembro de 1788 e a chegada ao poder de José de Seabra da Silva (1732-1813) e de Luís Pinto de Sousa (1735-1804), respectivamente ministros do Reino e dos Negócios Estrangeiros e da Guerra, a orientação principal do papel do Estado passou a ser a concretização de políticas de fomento para o território. A mobilização de inúmeros técnicos, tanto

---

[9] Ver "Plano de uma Lei Agrária", ca. 1788-1789, Vandelli, 1994: 109-130.

[10] Ver Fonseca, 1996. Ver Martins, 2014: 785-787; 802-805.

[11] Sobre as políticas de fomento do primeiro governo de D. Maria I, em particular no Ribatejo, ver o estudo pioneiro de Vasconcelos, 1970. Ver, ainda, Pato, 1999.

para as tarefas de concepção e direcção como de administração e fiscalização dos diversos trabalhos a empreender, implicou um novo impulso ao objectivo pombalino de desenvolvimento do ensino técnico-científico. Esta insistência na formação técnico-científica deve--se, em parte, a que no final da década de oitenta do século XVIII existiam poucos quadros formados em Matemática e Filosofia na Universidade de Coimbra[12]. O campo de acção na formação de competências desenvolveu-se, sobretudo, através da criação de novos estabelecimentos ou organismos com carácter técnico e científico: a Academia de Fortificação, Artilharia e Desenho (1790), o Real Corpo de Engenheiros (1790), o Observatório Astronómico da Universidade de Coimbra (1790), o Observatório Astronómico da Academia da Marinha (1798), a Sociedade Real Marítima, Militar e Geográfica (1798), o Laboratório Químico da Casa da Moeda (1801), o Arquivo Militar (1802) e a Academia da Marinha e Comércio do Porto (1803). Paralelamente, envolveram-se as instituições científicas e de ensino superior existentes, como a Academia das Ciências, a Universidade de Coimbra ou a Academia da Marinha. Desta cooperação, realçam-se as medidas tomadas para a Universidade de Coimbra. As iniciativas envolveram a modernização dos cursos de Matemática e Filosofia, pela criação de novas cadeiras; a organização de viagens científicas, pelo envio de bolseiros para a Europa, elegendo os melhores alunos e professores para as expedições científicas; a conclusão de equipamentos científicos iniciados no período da reforma pombalina da universidade; e o estabelecimento de carreiras na administração pública para os quadros formados nestes cursos.

Neste terceiro tempo, a intervenção no território saiu do plano experimental e do debate teórico e tornou-se um objectivo político

---

[12] Ver Lemos, 1980: 85-107; ver, também, de Domingos Vandelli, "Memória sobre a Faculdade de Filosofia da Universidade de Coimbra", ca. 1789-1790, Vandelli, 1994: 101-106.

concreto. Os dois novos ministros vão dar um sentido estratégico e unitário às políticas públicas promovidas pelo primeiro governo mariano e aos programas de fomento discutidos na Academia das Ciências. Começarão por proceder à clarificação dos programas prioritários e à definição dos métodos e meios para os pôr em prática. Os principais programas de fomento, lançados pelo novo ministério, decorreram entre 1789 e 1792, intenso período de decisões políticas e legislativas. As reformas projectadas confluem para uma centralização das decisões no núcleo governativo e integram-se numa estratégia de racionalidade do exercício do poder, associado a uma ideia de unidade política, administrativa e territorial. A forma de actuação e o processo de decisão estavam subjacentes a um modelo de intervenção previamente planeado. O planeamento por parte do Estado era ancorado no domínio da legislação existente, das capacidades e limitações financeiras e técnicas e das condições no terreno. Revestido de um carácter pragmático, o planeamento traduzia-se em propostas cuja validade era determinada pelo conceito de utilidade geral. Neste modelo de actuação, sobressai o papel do desenho enquanto instrumento prioritário de concepção técnica e de decisão política para a intervenção no espaço territorial e urbano. Incluía-se nesta estratégia a nomeação de quadros para os cargos de direcção, fiscalização e gestão dos diversos trabalhos, baseada na competência técnica e não na confiança pessoal; uma mudança de paradigma relativamente à administração pombalina.

Os programas de fomento de âmbito nacional, com carácter estruturante e de longo prazo, foram fundamentalmente três: a construção de um novo mapa geográfico e militar de Portugal, cujos trabalhos de triangulação geodésica, de observações astronómicas e de medição de um grau do meridiano constituem o início do conhecimento científico do território continental (1790); o reordenamento jurídico-administrativo do espaço do Reino, no qual se procurava desenhar uma nova demarcação das comarcas, concebidas como unidades administrativas uniformes (1790); e a realização de um programa de obras públicas para o desenvolvimento dos transportes e comunicações (1791). A estas iniciativas do Estado, juntou-se, uma década depois, o programa mineiro, metalúrgico e florestal (1801). Os vínculos entre cartografia, reforma administrativa das comarcas e organização do espaço territorial e urbano são estreitos e visavam, respectivamente, o conhecimento, ordenamento e transformação do território. Estes programas de fomento não corresponderam a respostas circunstanciais a problemas de conjuntura ou a iniciativas casuísticas e sem continuidade mas constituíram políticas estruturantes, de longo prazo, através das quais se procurava dar sentido estratégico ao papel do Estado como orientador e interveniente decisivo no desenvolvimento do território. Pensados de forma global e unitária, estes programas não tinham precedente mariano, pombalino ou outro anterior. Pela sua complementaridade e intencionalidade marcam um tempo novo em que as políticas do Estado se concentraram no fomento do território.

Iniciadas num período de paz e de prosperidade económica da Europa e lançadas praticamente em simultâneo, estas políticas tinham como objectivo o desenvolvimento económico e social e estavam focadas no espaço do Reino e não propriamente no espaço do Império. Procurava-se aumentar a capacidade produtiva do país, tendo como orientação fundamental o crescimento da actividade agrícola, considerado o principal factor para a dinamização do mercado interno. Procurava-se, igualmente, promover o aumento da população, melhorando as condições sociais de vida e de saúde pública, através da qualificação do território e dos espaços urbanos. O papel das vias de circulação, dentro desta complementaridade de políticas de fomento, era encarado não apenas do ponto de vista económico, enquanto dinamizador das trocas, mas também como factor estruturante da organização e desenvolvimento da sociedade, acompanhando os sucessivos progressos da humanidade.

O envolvimento da Academia das Ciências na construção das políticas de fomento do Estado; da antecipação à colaboração

A Academia das Ciências teve um papel antecipador na construção das políticas de fomento que se implementaram a partir de 1789. Durante a década de oitenta, através de concursos, inquéritos e viagens científicas e da apresentação de memórias nas suas sessões públicas, a Academia produziu inúmeros trabalhos. A sua produção envolveu o conhecimento e a descrição dos recursos naturais, assim como o diagnóstico das carências económicas e dos entraves ao desenvolvimento. Envolveu igualmente a elaboração de propostas de conteúdo reformista que vieram a tornar-se relevantes no campo programático e metodológico[13]. O esforço da Academia na caracterização dos obstáculos ao desenvolvimento e na formulação de programas de intervenção para o território, culminaram com a publicação das *Memórias Económicas*, cujo primeiro ciclo editorial, organizado por José Correia da Serra (1750-1823), decorreu entre 1789 e 1791[14].

Os concursos da Academia para o conhecimento e transformação do território; a antecipação das políticas de fomento (1780)

Dentro da definição de programas de intervenção para o território tiveram um importante significado os concursos promovidos pela

---

[13] Ver a importante síntese de José Correia da Serra, "Coup d'œil sur l'état des sciences et des lettres parmi les Portugais pendant la seconde moitié du siècle dernier", publicada pela primeira vez em 1804 e reeditada em 1822 por Balbi, 1822, 2: cccxxxiij-ccclviij.

[14] Ver *Memórias Económicas da Academia Real das Ciências de Lisboa (1789--1815)*. (1990/91); *Memorias da Academia Real das Sciencias de Lisboa,* 1797; ver, ainda, *Memórias Económicas Inéditas 1780-1808* (1987).

Academia, lançados no seu primeiro ano de actividade (1780)[15]. No *Programma* dos concursos, a Academia definiu com clareza o método a utilizar nos trabalhos: "a observação e a experiencia confirmada ou generalizada pelo cálculo, são a base e a forma dos discursos sobre a Natureza". Retira-se do discurso da Academia que o conhecimento do real, baseado na explicação dos fenómenos através da observação e da experiência, apoiado pela análise quantitativa e comparativa, constituía o quadro de partida para o processo reformista.

Um dos concursos, a concretizar no ano seguinte, tinha como programa a elaboração de "Hum Plano calculado para fazer navegavel algum dos rios de Portugal". O concurso fazia parte da classe das Ciências Exactas, no ramo da Hidráulica, enquadrando-se, portanto, na área da Matemática. A Academia pretendia que os concorrentes ao prémio apresentassem o plano para o encanamento de um rio com o objectivo de melhorar a circulação e o comércio interno. O plano deveria ser representado em desenho, suportado pelo levantamento do terreno de intervenção e acompanhado da memória da proposta. A memória explicaria os obstáculos à navegação e a maneira de os remover, demonstraria a utilidade da obra para as populações e incluiria o nivelamento das águas e cálculo do seu volume e a estimativa do custo da obra. O conjunto destes elementos devia assentar em bases rigorosas de forma a poder avaliar-se o custo/benefício da obra.

Outro dos concursos, a concretizar em 1782, tinha como programa "Huma Descripção Fysica e Economica de alguma Comarca ou território considerável deste Reino, com observações úteis á Agricultura e á Industria". O concurso fazia parte da classe das Ciências Naturais, no ramo da Física, enquadrando-se, portanto, na área da Filosofia. A Academia pretendia obter um conhecimento

---

[15] Ver da Academia Real das Sciencias (1780). Programma. Lisboa: Na Regia Officina Typografica.

preciso e individualizado da realidade do país, tendo a comarca como referência territorial. Com exactidão e clareza de exposição, as memórias deviam descrever o território segundo o sistema de Lineu, tratando o reino mineral, vegetal e animal. Da maior importância era a descrição económica: as observações sobre o estado da povoação, da agricultura, das artes mecânicas, da indústria e do comércio interno e externo. A partir da análise geográfica, económica e social, as memórias incluiriam propostas para melhorar as condições de vida e a economia dos territórios observados. Ainda neste concurso, a Academia dava preferência às memórias que estivessem ilustradas com mapas e desenhos e que contivessem amostras das produções naturais a que fizessem referência.

Estes dois concursos que a Academia promoveu tornaram-se fixos para todos os anos, mantendo-se por mais de três décadas, embora com algumas alterações. O plano de navegabilidade passou a incorporar também canais e, em 1790, veio a transformar-se num plano de canal de derivação das águas de um rio para irrigação dos campos[16]. O plano de descrição física e económica sofreu ligeiras alterações; a partir de 1788 passou a incorporar, além do espaço da metrópole, o espaço do império. Estes dois concursos, distintos no programa e no tipo de trabalho – um de projecto, outro de análise descritiva – pela forma como foram concebidos, dirigiam-se, acima de tudo, aos bacharéis formados nas faculdades de Matemática e de Filosofia da Universidade de Coimbra.

Um exemplo é o da memória premiada pela Academia na assembleia pública de 27 de julho de 1783 que tem como tema a descrição física e económica da cidade de Coimbra e seus arredores[17]. O concorrente, Manuel Dias Baptista, formado em Filosofia

---

[16] Ver da Academia Real das Sciencias (1790). *Programma*. Lisboa: Na Officina da Academia Real das Sciencias.

[17] Ver Baptista, Manoel Dias (1789). "Ensaio de huma descripção, física, e economica de Coimbra, e seus arredores", in *Memorias Economicas...*, 1789, 1: 254-298.

e Medicina pela Universidade de Coimbra, seguiu com rigor o modelo definido pela Academia, fazendo acompanhar a memória de amostras recolhidas na região. Outro exemplo é o da memória premiada pela Academia na assembleia pública de 13 de maio de 1789 que tinha como tema a descrição física e económica da comarca dos Ilhéus, no Brasil[18]. O concorrente, Manuel Ferreira da Câmara (1762-1835), nascido em Minas Gerais, era recém-formado em Leis e Filosofia pela Universidade de Coimbra (1787). Estas duas memórias vieram a fazer parte da primeira série das *Memórias Económicas*, publicada em 1789.

O mesmo não aconteceu com o projecto para o encanamento de um rio. As propostas a concurso foram rejeitadas por não responderem ao modelo estabelecido pela Academia. Uma proposta que não foi aceite a concurso foi o projecto para o melhoramento da navegação do Lima, entre Ponte de Lima e Ponte da Barca, apresentado por volta de 1782 por José Fernando da Silva, juiz de Fora e dos Órfãos da vila de Ponte da Barca[19]. Embora revele conhecimento das dificuldades associadas à navegação fluvial, apresente propostas pertinentes, aborde a questão do custo da obra e seus benefícios e inclua um desenho esquemático, José Fernando da Silva não responde às exigências técnicas do concurso, de elaboração de um projecto com desenhos rigorosos e cálculo do nivelamento das águas.

---

[18] Ver Camara, Manoel Ferreira da (1789). "Ensaio de Descrição Física, e Econômica da Comarca dos Ilhéus na América", in *Memorias Economicas...*, 1789, 1: 304-350.

[19] Ver o manuscrito de José Fernando da Silva (ca. 1782). Projecto Economico sobre a navegação do Rio Lima, no estado que actualmente banha as Villas da Barca, e Ponte de Lima. Offerecido Academia Real das Sciencias para entrar no 1.º Concurso, BNRJ, [Real Biblioteca], Ms. 04-01-17.

O projecto de Valleré de navegabilidade do rio Sorraia; a definição de um modelo e de um método para a intervenção no território (1785)

Fig. 1 – Guilherme Luís António Valleré, *Project d'un Canal de navigation et en partie d'arrosage au Nord de la Province de Alemtejo*, esquisso, [ca. 1785], AHM, DIV-3-20-1-11.

O concurso para o plano de navegabilidade de um rio concretizou-se, pela primeira e única vez em 1785, com a atribuição do prémio ao projecto de Guilherme Luís António de Valleré (1727-1796), oficial de Engenharia e Artilharia do Exército e sócio da Academia desde 1780. De origem francesa e naturalizado português, Valleré formou-se em Paris, em arquitectura, com Blondel

(1705-1774) e, em engenharia, com Perronet (1708-1794) de quem foi um dos primeiros alunos. Era exímio nas ciências da engenharia e da artilharia, utilizando com a mesma facilidade o cálculo, através do uso da geometria e da matemática, tal como o desenho, que dominava com mestria. Ingressou no Exército português em 1757 e, desde 1762, comandou o Regimento de Artilharia de Estremoz (deslocado posteriormente para Elvas), onde dirigiu uma importante escola de ensino militar, conhecida pela sólida formação dos seus oficiais em ciências exactas.

Valleré tinha um conhecimento profundo do Alentejo e via enormes vantagens para o desenvolvimento da região se fossem reunidas as várias linhas de água existentes e aproveitadas para a navegação fluvial e para a rega. Elegeu para o plano de navegabilidade o rio Sorraia que percorre o alto Alentejo de nascente para poente e desagua no Tejo, recebendo ao longo do seu curso e em ambas as margens muitas ribeiras (ex.: Seda, Alcôrrego, Tera, Sor e Divor, entre outros). A presença de população e de actividade agrícola e comercial era um factor fundamental para o funcionamento da actividade fluvial, condições que o Sorraia reunia, existindo vários núcleos urbanos situados junto às suas águas ou nas proximidades (ex.: Monforte, Fronteira, Ervedal, Avis, Mora, Couço, Erra, Coruche, Benavente e Samora Correia).

O projecto consistia na construção de um canal artificial na margem esquerda do rio, com a extensão 155 km, desde Monforte até Benavente, local onde teria um porto de marés. A diferença de nível entre o ponto mais baixo, em Benavente, e o ponto mais elevado, próximo a Monforte, determinada por Valleré em 330 m, seria vencida através de sistemas de açudes com eclusas ao longo do curso do rio e de pontes-canais na travessia de ribeiras. Através das albufeiras e do canal de navegação seriam construídos canais de derivação para a rega dos campos. Para a realização das obras de arte de açudes com comportas e de pontes-aquedutos (Fig. 1),

Valleré remete para as obras de Perronet[20], quanto ao canal de Borgonha, e de Lalande[21], quanto ao canal de Languedoque. O plano que Valleré apresentou à Academia continha ainda uma segunda parte que consistia na ligação do Sorraia ao Guadiana, perfurando a serra do Bispo em 15 km. Com uma extensão total de cerca de 180 km de navegação fluvial, o canal proposto por Valleré estabelecia, assim, a comunicação entre o Tejo e o Guadiana[22].

A Academia das Ciências, na sua sessão pública de 17 de janeiro de 1785, premiou a primeira parte do projecto de Valleré, não se pronunciando sobre a segunda parte. O projecto de Valleré correspondia aos objectivos da Academia: a definição de um modelo de intervenção previamente planeado, compreendendo elementos desenhados e escritos, cálculo do movimento de terras e orçamento das obras, assim como a definição dos terrenos aproveitáveis para regadio; um tipo de resposta que a maioria dos concorrentes não estava habilitada a dar. Mesmo os matemáticos da Universidade de Coimbra teriam muita dificuldade em dar resposta ao enunciado deste concurso por não terem o ensino do desenho na sua formação. Prevista nos *Estatutos* pombalinos, a cadeira de Desenho não foi implementada, tendo sido Miguel António Ciera, durante o seu magistério na faculdade de Matemática (1772-1780), quem assegurou a prática do desenho no ensino universitário[23]. O insucesso deste

---

[20] Ver Perronet, Jean-Rodolphe (1782). Description des projets et de la construction des ponts de Neuilli, de Mantes, d'Orléans, de Louis XVI, etc. On y a ajouté le projet du canal de Bourgogne, pour la communication des deux mers par Dijon; et de celui de la conduite des eaux de l'Yvette et de la Biévre à Paris. Paris: Imprimerie Royale.

[21] Ver Lalande, Joseph (1778). Des Canaux de navigation et spécialement du Canal du Languedoc. Paris: Veuve Desaint.

[22] O projecto original perdeu-se. Ver alguns elementos preparatórios do projeto em AHM, DIV-3-20-1-11. Ver, ainda, de Guilherme Luís António de Valleré (ca. 1790). "Memorial dos Serviços do Tenente General Inspector Geral de Artilharia, Fortificação e Real Corpo de Engenheiros, Guilherme Luiz Antonio Valleré...", transcrito e publicado por Sepúlveda, 1929, 16: 154-169.

[23] Ver Mendes, 1965, 3: 11-25.

concurso, à excepção do projecto de Valleré, demonstra que os engenheiros militares estavam mais bem preparados que os matemáticos e naturalistas para responder a este tipo de obras públicas, uma realidade que se tornará evidente poucos anos depois.

Pela realização deste concurso e em particular deste projecto, percebe-se o importante significado que a Academia dava ao fomento das vias de transporte, nomeadamente à navegação fluvial. Para além da definição programática, a Academia propunha um método de intervenção suportado pelo planeamento prévio, e um modelo de projecto em que o desenho e o cálculo tinham um papel fundamental.

Os debates em torno da construção de um novo Mapa de Portugal; da antecipação à colaboração (1787-1790)

Ainda dentro da definição de programas de intervenção para o território, teve um papel igualmente relevante o debate em torno da construção de um novo Mapa de Portugal, ocorrido em 1787 na secção de Ciências da Academia. No debate terao participado vários sócios, nomeadamente militares e professores da Academia Real da Marinha. A proposta de construção de cartografia rigorosa de Portugal surgiu da necessidade de uma carta geográfica do território continental, de cartas topográficas das províncias e comarcas e de cartas hidrográficas dos portos e da costa marítima. Os mapas existentes eram demasiado imprecisos, contendo erros graves na configuração do território, em particular da linha de costa desde o cabo da Roca até ao rio Minho, na representação da orografia e hidrografia, na localização dos lugares e sua toponímia e no itinerário das estradas e caminhos. Nos mapas de Rizzi Zannoni e de Thomas Jefferys, de 1762, e no mapa de Tomás Lopez, de 1778, estes erros são recorrentes. No entanto, o *Mappa General del Reyno de Portugal*, da autoria de Tomás Lopez (1730-1802), era o mapa do território continental mais desenvolvido e utilizado na época, tanto pela Administração central e local como pelo Exército, diplomatas e viajantes[24]. Os sócios da Academia envolvidos no debate consideravam que a construção de uma nova Carta Geográfica do Reino, segundo bases científicas modernas, era indispensável para a administração civil e militar e para o desenvolvimento de políticas de fomento do território e de planos de defesa militar. Segundo as palavras de Francisco de Borja Garção Stockler (1759-1829), a Carta deveria ser construída numa escala suficientemente grande "para sobre ella se formarem, e se discutirem quaesquer projectos economicos, ou militares, que podessem concorrer para a segurança, fertilidade, e commercio interior d'este paiz"[25]. Foi um debate que não se traduziu em concursos ou memórias da Academia, tendo no entanto consequências como programa de fomento integrado nas políticas públicas do segundo governo de D. Maria I.

Seguiu-se ao período de antecipação das políticas de fomento, protagonizado pela Academia das Ciências, um período de colaboração entre a Academia e o novo governo, formado em dezembro de 1788. A partir de 1789, o debate em torno de um novo mapa de Portugal deixou de ser centralizado na Academia e passou por uma fase de diálogo no qual teve um papel decisivo o ministro Luís Pinto de Sousa. Desta colaboração, abriram-se duas frentes em simultâneo: por um lado, iniciou-se um debate sobre o modelo e os métodos a adoptar para a realização da Carta Geográfica e Militar de Portugal; por outro lado, elegeu-se uma zona piloto para proceder aos trabalhos cartográficos e estatísticos – a comarca de Setúbal.

No debate ocorrido entre 1789 e 1790, terão participado, para além de Luís Pinto de Sousa, o secretário da Academia, José Correia

---

[24] Sobre os mapas de Portugal elaborados por Tomás Lopez e sobre a produção cartográfica relativa a Portugal publicada nesta época, ver Moreira, 2012.

[25] Stockler, 1813: 13-18.

da Serra, e os sócios, Miguel Franzini (ca. 1730-1810), Francisco António Ciera (1763-1814), Custódio Gomes de Vilas Boas (1741--1809) e Francisco de Borja Garção Stockler. O que estava nos objectivos dos políticos e dos académicos e cientistas era o levantamento do conjunto do território continental e não levantamentos parciais, como o iniciado experimentalmente para a comarca de Setúbal. Enquanto tarefa nova, exigia a tomada de inúmeras decisões prévias, quer quanto aos métodos, aos instrumentos, às escalas e aos processos de trabalho a adoptar, quer quanto aos meios financeiros e humanos de suporte a um trabalho de longa duração, árduo, exigente e oneroso.

Francisco António Ciera, matemático e astrónomo formado na Universidade de Coimbra, e Custódio Gomes de Vilas Boas, astrónomo e oficial de Artilharia, ambos professores da Academia da Marinha, apresentaram propostas concretas para a elaboração do mapa de Portugal. As propostas têm um aspecto comum: a divisão dos trabalhos em duas tarefas distintas. A primeira compreendia a construção do esqueleto da carta, a mais exigente das tarefas, a partir de triangulações e de medições de latitudes e longitudes realizadas por matemáticos e astrónomos; a segunda, feita a partir do esqueleto da carta, consistia na elaboração das cartas topográficas parciais, com toda a informação necessária para o conhecimento do território, realizada por engenheiros militares. O que distinguia as propostas eram os métodos e os processos de construção do esqueleto da carta, embora as cartas topográficas parciais também fossem objecto de discussão, nomeadamente, quanto à sua ordenação por comarcas (quarenta e quatro), provedorias (vinte e três) ou províncias (seis). A falta de técnicos treinados nos exercícios práticos de geodesia, tanto de matemáticos e astrónomos como de engenheiros geógrafos, era uma condicionante apontada nos planos. Outra condicionante era a falta de instrumentos geodésicos e astronómicos e a necessidade de adquirir várias colecções de instrumentos actualizados para os distribuir pelas equipas no terreno, algo de muito custoso e demorado a obter[26].

Ciera, que tinha testado no Observatório Astronómico da Academia das Ciências todos os métodos que propunha, sugeriu dirigir todo o trabalho de construção da triangulação primária empreendendo uma viagem pelo Reino para a determinação dos pontos de observação mais adequados à definição de uma rede geodésica. A escolha dos pontos seria determinada não por centros urbanos, como sugeriu Custódio Gomes de Vilas Boas, mas pelos lugares mais elevados dos cumes das serras. À imagem de outras nações europeias (ex.: França, Espanha e Grã-Bretanha), Ciera associou à construção da triangulação do Reino um objectivo "puramente científico" em que pretendia medir um grau de meridiano, utilizando um arco de superfície entre o cabo Ortegal, na Galiza, e o cabo de São Vicente, no Algarve. Este objectivo de Ciera associava-se aos trabalhos de triangulação entre Paris e Greenwich, realizados em 1787 por engenheiros, matemáticos e astrónomos britânicos e franceses (William Roy, Legendre, Méchain e Cassini IV), tendo como objectivo aprofundar a "descrição geométrica da Europa", inserindo, assim, os trabalhos portugueses no contexto da activa colaboração científica internacional[27].

Em 1790, depois das propostas e debates sobre a Carta do Reino e no final da experiência da carta da comarca de Setúbal, Luís Pinto de Sousa escolheu Francisco António Ciera para dirigir os trabalhos de construção do novo mapa de Portugal e, para seus colaboradores directos, os engenheiros militares Carlos Frederico Bernardo de Caula (1766-1835) e Pedro Folque (1757?-1848). O nome de Ciera impôs-se "por mérito próprio" e teve o significado de levar a car-

---

[26] Para uma leitura mais detalhada das propostas de Ciera e de Vilas Boas, ver Martins, 2014: 77-86.

[27] Ver Mendes, 1965, 3: 11-25.

tografia portuguesa em direcção à prática científica moderna. Aos poucos, vieram juntar-se aos trabalhos desta equipa jovens formados na Academia de Fortificação, Artilharia e Desenho que participaram nesta autêntica escola de formação e estágio de engenheiros geógrafos. O Estado assegurou por inteiro a realização do novo mapa de Portugal, ficando de fora a Academia das Ciências e a Universidade de Coimbra, instituições propostas por Vilas Boas para integrarem os trabalhos geodésicos. José Monteiro da Rocha, mestre de Ciera e homem de engenho raro, deu um contributo decisivo aos trabalhos cartográficos com a idealização e construção das réguas para a medição das bases geodésicas (quatro réguas, cada uma com 3 braças de comprimento, ca. 6,60 m). Vilas Boas e Stockler não incorporaram os trabalhos da Carta do Reino, provavelmente por ser essencial que apenas uma pessoa dirigisse todo o processo de forma coerente e metódica. Os trabalhos correspondiam a uma tarefa única, complexa e especializada, sendo difícil de conciliar com o programa de descrição das comarcas proposto por Vilas Boas. A ênfase não era na descrição mas no conhecimento da forma do território, apoiado em bases científicas modernas. Contudo, o programa de descrição de uma comarca não foi rejeitado, tendo sido redireccionado pelo ministro José de Seabra da Silva para a reforma administrativa das comarcas do Reino.

A experiência piloto da comarca de Setúbal; base da Carta do Reino e da reforma administrativa das Comarcas (1789-1790)

A comarca de Setúbal foi eleita como zona piloto para os trabalhos de reconhecimento do território. Este trabalho experimental envolveu o levantamento geodésico e topográfico do território e o conhecimento económico, social e estatístico da comarca, um programa que a Academia das Ciências apoiava desde o início da sua actividade. Com estes elementos procurava-se a elaboração de um cadastro que estabelecesse princípios estatísticos considerados necessários para a administração económica e militar. A metodologia utilizada agrupava os trabalhos cartográficos e as descrições económicas das comarcas, como processo de aproximação à realidade interna do país.

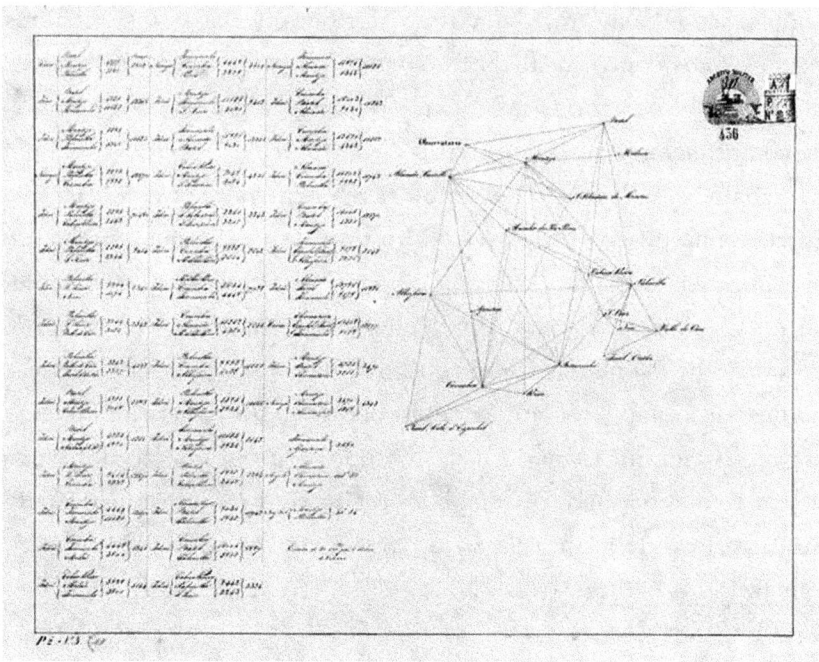

Fig. 2 – Francisco António Ciera, Conrado Henrique de Niemeyer, *Esquema de triangulação de parte da Península de Setúbal*, [ca. 1790], GEAEM/DIE, 3872/I-1-2-2 (cópia posterior a 1818).

Os trabalhos desenvolveram-se durante os anos de 1789 e 1790, e a equipa nomeada integrava oficiais de engenharia do Estado e sócios da Academia das Ciências. Para a realização da carta topográfica foram nomeados os oficiais militares, Jacob Chrysostomus Praetorius (1730-1798), pela Academia das Ciências, e Conrado Henrique

Niemeyer (1756-1806), pelo ministro dos Negócios Estrangeiros e da Guerra. Para a descrição económica e física da comarca de Setúbal foram nomeados, pela Academia das Ciências, Tomás António de Vila Nova Portugal (1775-1839) e Joaquim Pedro Gomes de Oliveira (1762-1833), ambos magistrados e futuros ministros de D. João VI. O modelo adoptado compreendia uma divisão de tarefas associando dois trabalhos distintos mas complementares: os trabalhos cartográficos pertenciam aos engenheiros; e os trabalhos económicos e estatísticos, aos magistrados.

Os trabalhos pouco ultrapassaram as questões metodológicas mas foram percursores no tipo de equipas criadas e nos modelos de trabalho adoptados. Nos trabalhos da Carta da comarca de Setúbal, Henrique Niemeyer encarregou-se sobretudo das tarefas de triangulação e de medição de uma base (Fig. 2) e dos trabalhos topográficos parciais (Fig. 3), fazendo parte da sua equipa os engenheiros militares, Maximiano José da Serra (ca. 1750-1834), Pedro Celestino Soares, João Manuel da Silva (ca. 1770-1849) e Joaquim Peito de Carvalho (17?-1820)[28]. Neste processo de colaboração entre o governo e a Academia, Conrado Henrique Niemeyer leu um relatório sobre a actividade desenvolvida no levantamento da carta de Setúbal, na sessão pública de 13 de outubro de 1790, onde discutiu questões de método associadas aos trabalhos geodésicos. Contudo, o trabalho cartográfico não se chegou a completar, em parte, por desentendimentos entre a Academia e Jacob Praetorius.

A Academia viria a publicar três memórias relativas à descrição da comarca de Setúbal, em 1791[29]. Uma das memórias, as *Observações sobre o Mapa da Povoação do termo da Vila de Azeitão*, da autoria de Vila Nova Portugal, é extremamente rica em informação pela análise comparativa dos dados recolhidos, onde utiliza fórmulas de

---

[28] Cf. Mendes, 1978, 26: 199-234.

[29] Ver *Memorias Economicas...*, 1791, 3.

cálculo estabelecidas por vários autores europeus. A análise incide sobre a evolução da população, dos trabalhadores sazonais e das profissões, sobre a produção das terras e do consumo *per capita*, ou sobre o crescimento e decadência das freguesias. Uma das conclusões mais evidentes dos dados estatísticos é o elevado número de artífices e operários, superior à população agrícola; um sintoma de decadência da agricultura, do qual se queixavam os *memorialistas* da Academia, em particular, Domingos Vandelli.

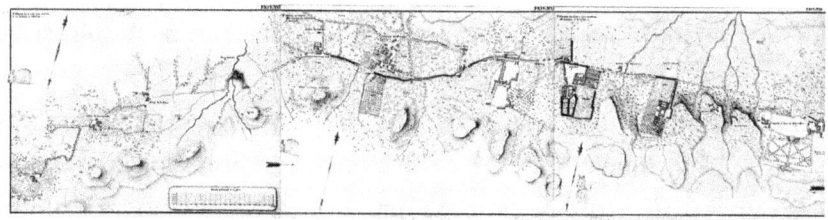

Fig. 3 – Conrado Henrique Niemeyer, Maximiano José da Serra, *Planta da carta que contem as aldêas d'Azeitão*, [1790], GEAEM/DIE, 3104/I-2A-25-35 a 3104/III-2A-25-35 (o desenho não se encontra completo).

Os textos de Vila Nova Portugal são acima de tudo propostas de objectivos e de métodos para a realização da descrição económica de uma comarca. Constituíram, a partir de então, o modelo adoptado pela Academia das Ciências para o seu concurso anual. Segundo o plano de Tomás António de Vila Nova Portugal, esta descrição económica dizia respeito essencialmente ao estado actual dos territórios em análise, embora incluísse o conhecimento da sua história, matéria essencial para averiguação da evolução local. A descrição devia abarcar o censo da população, o estado da agricultura, do comércio e da indústria e os modelos de arrecadação dos impostos, para que fossem elaborados cálculos estatísticos e fossem tiradas conclusões com base em dados quantitativos; devia ainda incluir a descrição física do território, complemento essencial para a leitura da carta topográfica.

Desta colaboração entre governo e Academia das Ciências fica o modelo de equipas a implantar no terreno e os métodos cartográficos e descritivos desenvolvidos pelos engenheiros e magistrados, modelo e métodos que seriam influentes na implementação das políticas de fomento.

O termo da colaboração entre a Academia das Ciências e o governo (1790-1791)

A proximidade entre governo e Academia foi também visível, em 1790, com a preparação da viagem pela Europa de três bolseiros designados pelo Estado, tendo como objectivo o estudo de minas e mineralogia. Os bolseiros, Manuel Ferreira da Câmara, Joaquim Pedro Fragoso de Sequeira e José Bonifácio de Andrade e Silva, recém-formados em Filosofia na Universidade de Coimbra, tinham ingressado há pouco tempo na Academia Real das Ciências de Lisboa. Ainda antes de partirem para a expedição científica, publicaram vários trabalhos nos primeiros dois volumes das *Memórias Económicas* (1789 e 1790).

O mesmo espírito de colaboração entre a Academia e o novo governo esteve presente aquando da publicação, em 1791, das memórias para o encanamento do rio Mondego de Domingos Vandelli[30] e de Estêvão Dias Cabral (1734-1811)[31]. O processo teve início um ano antes (1790-06-14), quando José de Seabra da Silva designou Estêvão Cabral para a elaboração de um plano de regularização do rio Mondego, desde Coimbra até à Figueira. A discussão pública e

---

[30] Domingos Vandelli apresentou a "Memória sobre o encanamento do Rio Mondego" na sessão da Academia das Ciências de 27 de outubro de 1790; ver *Memorias Economicas...*, 1791, 3: 13-19.

[31] Estêvão Dias Cabral apresentou a "Memória sobre os danos do Mondego no campo de Coimbra, e seu remédio" na sessão da Academia das Ciências de 14 de dezembro de 1790; ver *Memorias Economicas...*, 1791, 3: 141-165.

a publicação destas duas memórias representam um interesse e um envolvimento da Academia das Ciências nos trabalhos do governo para o fomento da agricultura e dos transportes, para além de constituírem um contributo significativo ao desenvolvimento dos conhecimentos empíricos e das técnicas de hidráulica fluvial.

O ciclo decorrido durante a década de oitenta na Academia das Ciências foi intenso e profícuo para futuro, com a discussão de políticas de fomento e a construção de instrumentos no campo programático e metodológico, mas encerrava-se com esta fase de colaboração institucional. Com o segundo governo mariano, as políticas de fomento transitaram dos gabinetes para o terreno. As grandes obras públicas começaram a ser concretizadas em 1789 e tiveram início no espaço de influência da cidade do Porto, com as obras de estradas e caminhos do Alto Douro, de navegabilidade do Douro desde o Cachão da Valeira até Barca de Alva, da barra e porto marítimo do Douro e da estrada Porto-Guimarães, articulando, assim, vias terrestres, fluviais e marítimas. O conhecimento físico do território, após a experiência pioneira em Setúbal, avançou para a totalidade do território continental, com os trabalhos geodésicos para a realização da Carta do Reino a terem início em 1790. O quadro legislativo para a reforma administrativa das Comarcas foi promulgado em 1790 e 1792, repetindo-se, nesta nova tarefa, o modelo utilizado na experiência piloto da comarca de Setúbal, de separação entre o reconhecimento cartográfico e a descrição física e económica. O conhecimento do território, que tinha por base modelos definidos na Academia das Ciências, estava agora integrado em propostas com um sentido operativo concreto. O conhecimento era assim dirigido para políticas de fomento que envolviam o ordenamento e a transformação do território, em simultaneidade e paralelismo de acções[32].

---

[32] Ver um ponto de vista diferente por Ana Cristina Nogueira da Silva e António Manuel Hespanha, "O quadro espacial", in Mattoso, 1998, 4: 35-41.

A fundação da Academia de Fortificação, Artilharia e Desenho e a institucionalização do Corpo de Engenheiros; uma reforma comum

Luís Pinto de Sousa deu um forte impulso na formação e profissionalização do Exército, procedendo a uma série de reformas que envolveram a sua reorganização e modernização[33]. O Exército encontrava-se praticamente paralisado, em parte devido à ausência de guerra na Europa. Após a guerra *Fantástica* (1762), uma parte significativa das reformas propostas pelo conde de Lippe (Wilhelm zu Schaumburg-Lippe, 1724-1777) não foi posta em prática. Luís Pinto de Sousa introduziu de imediato alterações na estrutura militar, preenchendo o vazio nos quadros do Exército, pela promoção dos oficiais mais competentes. Por sua vez, reforçou a componente profissional dos militares, valorizando as suas capacidades técnicas e científicas e o seu saber especializado. A profissionalização da função militar foi acompanhada do reconhecimento do seu papel social. O mérito passou a ser o factor de progressão na carreira militar, em detrimento da antiguidade no posto ou da condição social de origem, equiparando todos os oficiais e todas as armas. Com estas medidas, em que eram limitados os privilégios e pretensões de alguns sectores do Exército, em particular da aristocracia, o ministro criou as condições para a autonomização e valorização da arma de Engenharia.

Em simultâneo, Luís Pinto de Sousa foi nomeando oficiais de engenharia para as diferentes partes do território continental, normalmente com comissões de serviço associadas: obras públicas de estradas, rios e portos, abastecimento de água pública às cidades e

---

[33] As políticas de Luís Pinto de Sousa para a reorganização do Exército encontram-se por estudar. Ver brevíssimas sínteses em Amaral, 2010, 1: 9-11; Amaral, 2011, 2: 7-50.

vilas, construção e modernização de quartéis, fortificações e equipamentos militares, exploração mineira, cartografia militar, topográfica e hidrográfica, e trabalhos geodésicos de construção do novo mapa de Portugal[34].

Os engenheiros militares estavam maioritariamente integrados no corpo de infantaria, não formando um corpo próprio dentro do Exército; tão pouco existia uma escola superior de engenharia a funcionar de forma regular. Em resposta a estas carências e debilidades e com o objectivo de fornecer aos oficiais engenheiros uma uniformidade na formação e perspectivar-lhes uma carreira definida, Luís Pinto de Sousa tomou duas iniciativas produtivas e duradouras: a fundação da Academia Real de Fortificação, Artilharia e Desenho e a institucionalização do Real Corpo de Engenheiros[35]. Dentro das reformas do Exército, estas acções do ministro da Guerra estavam relacionadas com as políticas de fomento em curso que exigiam quadros com conhecimentos teóricos e práticos, científicos e técnicos, e domínio do desenho, enquanto instrumento prioritário de conhecimento, concepção e comunicação.

Uma escola de base técnico-científica destinada ao ensino superior (1790)

A Academia de Fortificação, Artilharia e Desenho foi criada a 2 de janeiro de 1790 e abriu as suas aulas no dia 20 do mesmo mês e ano[36]. Estabelecia-se, pela primeira vez, uma escola de base técnico-científica destinada ao ensino superior do Exército, ficando

---

[34] Ver inúmeras medidas tomadas por Luís Pinto de Sousa para os oficiais engenheiros em AHM, Fundo Geral 5, Livros de Registo Antigos.

[35] Sobre este tema, ver Caixaria, 2006: 52-59.

[36] Ver o decreto de fundação da Academia Real de Fortificação, Artilharia e Desenho, Silva, 1828: 578-582.

equiparada à Academia Real da Marinha e à Universidade de Coimbra. Berço do ensino moderno da engenharia em Portugal, onde coexistiram as formações científica, técnica e artística, a nova Academia vinha preencher a precaridade existente no ensino e recrutamento de oficiais militares e ultrapassar o habitual recurso à contratação de técnicos estrangeiros, largamente difundido pelo marquês de Pombal. Não deixarão de ser contratados alguns técnicos estrangeiros para comissões específicas em áreas em que eram especializados, como são exemplo, os franceses José Auffdiener (ca. 1760-1811) e Luís André Dupuis (17?-1807) e os piemonteses Carlos António Napion (1756-1814) e José Teresio Michelotti (1762-1819), quadros técnicos que vieram para Portugal entre 1789 e 1802.

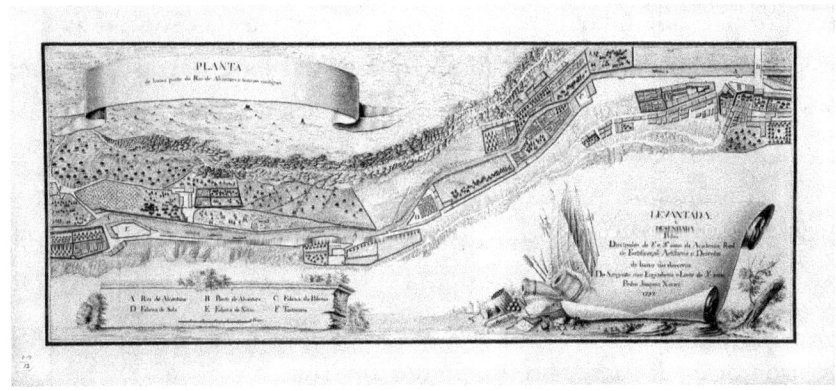

Fig. 4 – *Planta de huma parte do Rio Alcântara, e termo contíguo levantada e desenhada pellos Discípulos do 2.º, e 3.º anno da Academia Real de Fortificação, Artilharia, e Desenho de baixo das direçoens do Sargento mor Engenheiro, e lente do 2.º anno Pedro Joaquim Xavier,* 1797, BPMP, C-M&A, 19(12).

A nova escola militar tinha como missão formar oficiais para os quatro ramos do Exército de Terra: Infantaria, Cavalaria, Artilharia e Engenharia. No acesso às bolsas que se destinavam aos alunos da Academia, tinham prioridade os cursos de Engenharia e de Artilharia, as duas Armas de maior pendor técnico-científico que o ministro da Guerra procurava promover. O curso de Engenharia, tal como o de Artilharia, tinha quatro anos e os candidatos eram obrigados a frequentar os dois primeiros anos da Academia da Marinha, além de prestar provas de francês, a língua franca da época. Esta formação, que passava pelas duas academias, estabeleceria uma ligação muito forte entre os seus professores e alunos. Serão estas duas instituições, na sua interdependência, que irão criar a Escola Politécnica de Lisboa e a Escola do Exército, durante as reformas dos estabelecimentos de ensino, após a revolução liberal de 1833-1834[37].

A Academia de Fortificação facultava uma formação simultaneamente militar e civil. As matérias mais presentes eram a fortificação, a artilharia e a hidráulica. A cadeira de Hidráulica era da maior importância por ser uma disciplina necessária em muitas áreas do território e por lidar com problemas complexos e especializados: assoreamento da costa marítima, dos estuários e barras dos rios; zonas pantanosas e pouco salubres próximas de áreas urbanas; falta de abastecimento de água nos centros urbanos e intenso uso de energia hidráulica para as actividades agrícolas e fabris. A aula de desenho tinha uma presença dominante ao ser transversal a todo o curso e era de frequência diária nos três primeiros anos, constituindo o momento de reunião dos estudantes da escola (Fig. 4). A promoção do desenho, enquanto instrumento essencial para o exercício da profissão, foi uma preocupação constante de Luís Pinto de Sousa, manifestando-se na escolha cuidada dos professores e substitutos da cadeira, assim como se revelou com a fundação da Academia de Artilharia, Fortificação e Desenho (1792), no Rio de Janeiro, e mais tarde, com a fundação da Academia da Marinha e Comércio do Porto (1803). Além da formação teórico-prática, o plano

---

[37] Ver o importante texto de Alexandre Herculano, "Da Escola Politécnica e do Colégio dos Nobres", publicado em 1841 e reeditado em Herculano, 1984, 3: 45-81.

de estudos da Academia dava particular importância aos exercícios de campo realizados pelos alunos e professores[38]. Os exercícios práticos consistiam na realização de levantamentos topográficos e hidrográficos, no uso dos instrumentos geodésicos, na configuração do território através do desenho a *golpe de vista*, no exercício de projecto de estruturas fortificadas (baterias e redutos) e a sua concretização parcial no terreno, e ainda, nos exercícios sobre a resistência dos materiais, alcance das peças de fogo, potência das bombas, manuseamento da pólvora e de minas.

Vários quadros do Exército vão realizar compêndios ou traduzir obras, para uso da escola. José António da Rosa (1745-1830), chamado para dar a cadeira de 3.º ano de Artilharia, publicou o livro *Compêndio das Minas* em 1791. António Teixeira Rebelo (1750--1825), embora não fosse professor, publicou a tradução do *Tratado de Artilharia*, de John Muller, em 1793. António José Moreira (ca. 1751-ca. 1794), professor da cadeira de Desenho, publicou, também em 1793, as *Regras de Desenho* sendo a obra acompanhada de trinta estampas[39]. Vários dos professores traduziram os seis volumes do *Tratado de Arquitectura Militar*, de Antoni. A estes compêndios associavam-se uma ampla biblioteca, cujo acervo continha as obras mais modernas das ciências e cultura europeias. Luís Pinto de Sousa, através dos embaixadores portugueses, fará uma série de encomendas para a permanente actualização desta biblioteca[40].

O acesso à Academia de Fortificação foi alargado aos alunos que tivessem frequentado as aulas militares estabelecidas nos regimentos das províncias, podendo aceder directamente à escola

---

[38] Ver o manuscrito de Pedro Joaquim Xavier e António José Moreira (ca. 1791--1793). Memoria sobre os exercícios práticos que anualmente costumam executar os lentes e os discípulos da Academia Real de Fortificação, Artilharia e Desenho, AHM, DIV-4-1-6-20.

[39] Ver Moreira, 1793.

[40] Ver Carvalho, 1995, 61: 95-185.

depois de realizarem exames na Academia da Marinha. Luís Pinto de Sousa procurou, conjuntamente, reforçar a formação superior em ciências exactas estimulando os alunos dos regimentos e da Academia de Fortificação a frequentarem a faculdade de Matemática da Universidade de Coimbra[41], de que são exemplo, Baltazar de Azevedo Coutinho (ca. 1766-18?), do regimento de Lagos, e Luís Máximo Jorge de Bellegarde (1773-1811), aluno da Academia de Fortificação. Com estas medidas, o ministro motivava a uma articulação entre as várias instituições e, em particular, entre as duas academias de Lisboa e a Universidade de Coimbra. Estabelecer-se-ia uma relação intermitente mas duradoura entre estas instituições com intercâmbio de estudantes e de professores, de que são exemplo, entre outros, Francisco de Paula Travassos (1765-1833), Manuel Pedro de Melo (1765-1833) e Tristão Álvares da Costa Silveira (1768-1811).

A construção do corpo de engenharia; a formação de uma nova elite (1790-1792)

A constituição do Corpo de Engenheiros resulta da criação da Academia de Fortificação e é parte de uma mesma reforma. A autonomização dos oficiais de engenharia e a sua organização no quadro do Exército, como uma nova Arma, estava subjacente à formação desta escola militar. Enquanto organismo autónomo, o Corpo de Engenheiros português surge do âmago da estrutura do Exército, tornando-se independente das Armas de Infantaria, Artilharia e Cavalaria.

A reunião dos oficiais engenheiros num corpo próprio foi sucessivamente adiada em Portugal, desde o início do século XVIII, altura em que o mesmo foi criado em França e em Espanha. O conde de Lippe já tinha proposto a sua criação nas *Observações Militares*

---

[41] Ver BPMP, Reservados, Ms. 435.

dirigidas ao Conde de Oeiras (1764), sugerindo a formação de duas classes: a dos engenheiros propriamente ditos e a dos engenheiros geógrafos[42]. Do ponto de vista militar, a importância do Corpo de Engenheiros tinha-se manifestado de forma decisiva na Guerra dos Sete Anos (1757-1763), guerra em que o conde de Lippe participou pela Casa de Hanôver e onde os engenheiros geógrafos tiveram um papel determinante no lugar de *quartel-mestre general*. Luís Pinto de Sousa, porém, não procederá a esta divisão, privilegiando a unidade do corpo e a formação multidisciplinar.

A institucionalização do Real Corpo de Engenheiros, nome pelo qual veio a ser designado o corpo de oficiais de engenharia, processou-se de forma gradual, balizada entre a fundação da escola, no início de 1790, e a conclusão do curso pelos primeiros alunos, no final de 1792. Neste intervalo de tempo, Luís Pinto de Sousa procedeu à organização do topo da hierarquia do Exército, nomeando o duque de Lafões, D. João Carlos de Bragança (1719-1806), para o cargo de comandante do Exército e das quatro armas (Infantaria, Cavalaria, Artilharia e Corpo de Engenheiros) e o tenente-general Guilherme Luís António de Valleré para o cargo de inspector-geral de Artilharia, Fortificações e Corpo de Engenheiros. É desconhecida a actividade de Valleré à frente do Corpo de Engenheiros. No entanto, a sua influência na formação dos jovens oficiais foi significativa, no que concerne à actualização dos sistemas de fortificação, nomeadamente pela adopção do sistema de *fortificação perpendicular* de Montalembert e pelo abandono do sistema de *fortificação abaluartado* de Vauban[43]. Em novembro de 1792, Luís Pinto de Sousa criou os postos de Segundo--Tenente e Primeiro-Tenente, para acesso à carreira de Engenharia, e terminou com o lugar de Ajudante, que correspondia ao início de

---

[42] Manuel Amaral (2001-2009). "Arquivo Militar". Disponível em http://www.arqnet.pt/exercito/arquivo.html; consultado em 2015-10-21.

[43] Sobre as mudanças nos sistemas de fortificação e sua expressão em Portugal, ver Martins, 2014: 153-160; ver Prazeres, 2016.

carreira[44]. Em dezembro do mesmo ano, igualou os ordenados dos oficiais efectivos de Engenharia aos dos outros oficiais do Exército, entrando a lei em vigor no ano imediato. Com esta norma, Luís Pinto de Sousa encerrou o processo de organização e de autonomização do Corpo de Engenheiros como nova arma do Exército[45].

Ao organizar, pela primeira vez em Portugal, o Corpo de Engenheiros, o ministro Luís Pinto de Sousa adoptou como modelo institucional a associação do corpo de oficiais a uma escola de formação e recrutamento, à imagem das escolas francesas de *Ponts et Chaussées* e de *Mézières*, não seguindo, no entanto, o modelo francês de divisão do Corpo de Engenheiros em civil e militar[46], nem uma estrutura hierarquizada de âmbito nacional, subdividida por províncias ou comarcas do Reino, com funções de controlo, gestão e desenho do território, à semelhança do *Département des Ponts et Chaussées*, em França.

Os engenheiros do Exército, cujo levantamento do quadro de oficiais no activo foi feito aquando da criação da Academia de Fortificação[47], transitaram para o Real Corpo de Engenheiros. No Corpo de Engenharia reuniram-se, assim, várias gerações com formações distintas: a geração formada durante a década de setenta na Aula Militar da Corte e nas *Aulas Regimentais*; a geração formada durante a década de oitenta na Academia da Marinha; e a geração formada na nova escola de engenharia; todos usufruindo de uma saída profissional directa como ambicionavam os matemáticos e naturalistas da Universidade de Coimbra.

---

[44] Ver, do príncipe D. João, decreto de 3 de novembro de 1792, Silva, 1828a: 83.

[45] Ver, do príncipe D. João, decreto de 17 de dezembro de 1792, Silva, 1828a: 89-90.

[46] Ver Picon, 1992: 139-145; 221-223.

[47] Ver a relação dos "Offeciaes de Infantaria com exercício de Engenheiros (...)", Almanaque para o anno de 1789, Lisboa: Na Off. da Academia Real das Sciencias, 105-107; comparar com a "Relação Alphabetica de todos os Offesiaes Inginheiros (...)", 1790, Sepúlveda, 1928, 15: 187-191.

Fig. 5 – Manuel Joaquim Brandão de Sousa, *Mappa de Campo do terreno em que estão acampados os regimentos portuguezes e hespanhoes, em que vão notadas as trincheiras, redutos e postos avançados: compondo tudo a parte da linha e exercito da Catalunha nas immediaçoens da villa de Figueiras no anno de 1794*. Feito em Julho de 1794 no Quartel General de Figueiras, na Catalunha, por Manoel Joaquim Brandão e Souza, Primeiro Tenente do Real Corpo de Engenheiros do Exercito Portuguez Auxiliar à Hespanha, 1794, GEAEM/DIE, 4509-3-41-56.

Desde o início, o Real Corpo de Engenheiros foi direccionado tanto para os trabalhos de defesa militar e de apoio aos movimentos do Exército, quanto para a intervenção no ordenamento do território e dos centros urbanos. O modelo de organização do Corpo de Engenheiros, na sua dupla componente militar e civil, conferiu-lhe uma grande heterogeneidade, permitindo o ingresso de técnicos sem formação militar, como José Auffdiener, formado na *École des Ponts et Chaussées* de França, ou Carlos Amarante (1748--1815), arquitecto e engenheiro de formação autodidacta. O Corpo integrou discípulos das faculdades de Matemática e de Filosofia da Universidade de Coimbra, como Francisco de Paula Travassos, Manuel Pedro de Melo ou António José Vaz Velho (1771-1860) e recebeu por transferência quadros da Armada, como Manuel do Espírito Santo Limpo (1755-1809), Manuel Jacinto Nogueira da Gama (1765-1847), Eusébio Cândido Cordeiro Pinheiro Furtado (1777-1861) ou Marino Miguel Franzini (1779-1861), entre outros.

Em janeiro de 1793, começaram a ser chamados os primeiros engenheiros da nova escola para "comissões activas" do Estado, encerrando-se a política pombalina de permanente recurso a oficiais estrangeiros. Da primeira geração nomeada para comissões régias, Luís Gomes de Carvalho (1771-1826) foi colocado na obra da barra do Douro, como colaborador de Reinaldo Oudinot (1744-1807); Manuel Joaquim Brandão de Sousa (1757?-1833?) fez parte da brigada de engenheiros enviada para a guerra do Rossilhão, na Catalunha (Fig. 5); e seis engenheiros, Segundos Tenentes, foram nomeados para a reforma administrativa do Reino, para trabalharem em conjunto com os juízes *demarcantes* dos Limites das Comarcas, entre os quais se destaca Custódio José Gomes de Vilas Boas (1771-1809), na província do Minho.

As nomeações referidas constituem um acto inaugural. A partir desta data, os primeiros quadros formados na nova escola começaram a ingressar na arma de Engenharia do Exército dando-se início, na prática, ao funcionamento do Real Corpo de Engenheiros[48]. Estas

---

[48] Ver os relatórios dos professores da Academia de Fortificação: Matias José Dias Azedo (ca. agosto a novembro de 1792). Memória sobre os alunos da Academia

nomeações demonstram que o dispositivo institucional criado começava a dar frutos e a ter efeitos concretos e são reveladoras de uma nova competência do Estado central. Em apenas quatro anos, Luís Pinto de Sousa pôs a funcionar um corpo de engenheiros, formado numa academia portuguesa, capaz de dar respostas técnicas às diversas necessidades públicas, civis e militares, nas diferentes partes do território. No sistema político-administrativo desta época, os engenheiros ao serviço da administração do Estado vão adquirir um novo papel, anteriormente reservado, quase em exclusivo, aos magistrados, enquanto representantes das políticas régias. Esta mudança configura o lento mas inexorável processo de perda para os magistrados e a ascensão de um grupo que progressivamente se afirmaria na sociedade, alcançando o pleno poder durante a segunda metade do século XIX.

Os membros do Corpo de Engenheiros tiveram uma acção determinante na implementação e concretização das políticas de fomento do Estado, tendo sido chamados para a concepção e direcção de obras públicas, para os trabalhos geodésicos de construção do mapa de Portugal e para a nova demarcação de comarcas. Enquanto técnicos que dominavam os instrumentos de desenho e projecto, estenderam a sua área de intervenção às transformações operadas nos centros urbanos, à construção de equipamentos públicos (principalmente câmaras e quartéis), ao abastecimento de água a vilas e cidades e aos trabalhos cadastrais e estatísticos. O Real Corpo de Engenheiros foi a instituição que centralizou em si a capacidade técnica e científica de intervenção no território; e o Arquivo Militar, verdadeira escola de profissionalização em desenho e topografia, em articulação com o Corpo de Engenheiros, constituiu o centro de reunião

---

de Fortificação, Artilharia e Desenho, seguido de Projecto de Alvará, AHM, DIV-1--11-21-13; Matias José Dias Azedo, António José Moreira (15 de outubro de 1792). Relações de merecimento de alunos da Real Academia de Fortificação, Artilharia e Desenho, AHM, DIV-3-6-3-24.

da produção de cartografia topográfica e militar e dos projectos de obras públicas do Estado[49]. O Real Corpo de Engenheiros teve uma intensa actividade produtiva, o que lhe permitiu uma aquisição de experiência e um desenvolvimento ímpares na sua longa vigência. Os seus membros foram adquirindo um lugar crescente na definição e condução das políticas públicas, tendo um papel relevante no processo de afirmação do Estado central[50].

A mobilização das instituições e dos técnicos; o papel da Universidade de Coimbra

> "Os Filosofos, e os Mathematicos da nossa Universidade seria a unica classe de homens, que em Portugal se podia destinar para este emprego [conservador das estradas, comércio, fábricas e agricultura por comarca], pois que ás suas Faculdades, estabelecidas neste Reino por hum plano sabio, formado, sobre o das Naçoens mais civilizadas, pelas luzes, e trabalho do Ministério do Senhor Rei D. Jozé, pertence privativamente os conhecimentos anunciados [História Natural, Hidráulica, Geometria e Mecânica]."
>
> José Diogo Mascarenhas Neto
> *Methodo para Construir as Estradas em Portugal*, 1790[51]

As políticas públicas para o desenvolvimento do ensino técnico-científico na Universidade de Coimbra, após a reforma pombalina, tiveram a sua maior expressão na década de noventa do século XVIII, pela acção de José de Seabra da Silva, ministro do Reino, e nos

---

[49] Sobre o Arquivo Militar, ver a obra de Caixaria, 2006.

[50] Sobre a actuação do corpo de engenharia na segunda metade de oitocentos, ver Macedo, 2009.

[51] Neto, 1790: 92. José Diogo Mascarenhas Neto era nesta altura corregedor de Guimarães e inspector da estrada Porto-Guimarães.

primeiros anos do século XIX, pela actividade de D. Rodrigo de Sousa Coutinho (1755-1812), ministro da Fazenda. Por parte da Universidade, couberam aos reitores, D. Francisco Rafael de Castro (1750-1816) e D. Francisco de Lemos (1735-1822), propor ou pôr em prática as políticas públicas para o ensino universitário[52]. O matemático e astrónomo José Monteiro da Rocha (1734-1819), director da faculdade de Matemática e vice-reitor da Universidade, teve um papel preponderante em várias destas iniciativas.

A preocupação com o reforço da formação técnica e científica foi impulsora das reformas neste período. A intenção de que os técnicos formados nas faculdades de Filosofia e Matemática participassem na administração do território e na concretização das políticas de fomento esteve na base das iniciativas dos governos, visando a valorização destes cursos e dos seus quadros. As medidas tomadas tentaram abranger o processo de formação, especialização e profissionalização dos estudantes e professores. Como medidas mais significativas, realçam-se a construção do Observatório Astronómico (1789-1799), as reformas dos planos de estudos das faculdades de Filosofia e Matemática (1791 e 1801), o programa de envio de bolseiros para a Europa (1790) e a implementação de carreiras na administração pública para os quadros formados em ciências (1801).

O Observatório Astronómico da Universidade de Coimbra; de um monumento simbólico a um equipamento público para o ensino e a investigação (1772-1799)

A ideia de construir um observatório astronómico para a faculdade de Matemática ficou consagrada nos *Estatutos* da reforma

---

[52] Ver o texto de José Correia da Serra, de 1804, reeditado por Balbi, 1822, 2: CCCXXXIIJ-CCCLVIIJ.

pombalina. Pretendia-se um estabelecimento para o ensino e investigação, onde os estudantes tivessem aulas de astronomia prática e os professores se dedicassem às observações para se fixarem as longitudes geográficas e rectificarem os elementos fundamentais da astronomia.

Fig. 6 – [Guilherme Elsden], Teodoro Marques Pereira da Silva, *Alçado da Frente Principal do Observatorio Astronomico da Universidade de Coimbra*, s.d. [ca. 1773], OAUC, D-026.

É com base neste programa que Guilherme Elsden (?-1779), o arquitecto e engenheiro militar escolhido pelo marquês de Pombal para dirigir as Obras da Universidade de Coimbra, desenvolveu o projecto do observatório. A decisão sobre o local e o programa de intervenção envolveu os professores da nova faculdade de Matemática, Miguel António Ciera, José Monteiro da Rocha e Miguel Franzini[53].

---

[53] Ver, de Guilherme Elsden, "Jornal das Obras Públicas da Universidade de Coimbra desde o dia 25 de julho do presente anno de 1773", publicado por Viterbo, 1922, 3: 293-294.

O edifício situava-se na vertente da Alta de Coimbra, oposta ao Paço das Escolas, e abria-se ao extenso território que se desenvolvia a Norte e a Nascente. Em confronto com o colégio de São Jerónimo, o observatório foi implantado no sítio ocupado pelo castelo medieval (actual largo de D. Dinis), local onde afluía uma das mais importantes vias de acesso à Alta. A monumentalidade da proposta de Guilherme Elsden advém do carácter simbólico atribuído a este equipamento (Fig. 6). O Observatório Astronómico constituía a síntese do programa pombalino expresso nos *Estatutos* que encaravam a ciência como a base para o desenvolvimento do país e a astronomia como a disciplina "necessaria para se conseguir o conhecimento do Globo terrestre; e se terem nas mãos as chaves do Universo"[54].

Em 1773 inicia-se a construção deste vasto equipamento, com a demolição do castelo medieval e a regularização do terreno, e em 1775 estava realizado o essencial do piso térreo. O elevado custo dos trabalhos conduziu a Universidade a interromper o projecto, estando por realizar parte significativa da obra. Um sintoma da possível desproporção entre a vontade régia e as reais capacidades da Universidade.

D. Francisco de Lemos, reitor da Universidade, consciente do tempo que levaria a construir o edifício, mandou fazer provisoriamente um observatório interino. Foi, assim, construído de imediato (ca. 1775) um pequeno edifício em madeira, no terreno do Paço das Escolas. O local dispunha de um amplo espaço aberto sobre o vale do Mondego, distante dos acessos à Alta e mais recatado para o exercício de um trabalho que exigia longo isolamento. Este conjunto de condições explicará, talvez, a posterior escolha deste mesmo sítio para o definitivo observatório da Universidade.

O governo formado após a subida ao poder da rainha D. Maria I, em 1777, não contribuiu para dar um novo impulso às obras da

---

[54] *Estatutos da Universidade de Coimbra*, 1772: 213.

Universidade de Coimbra, pela lentidão e dificuldade em levar as reformas e projectos até ao fim; uma situação a que o segundo governo mariano procurou pôr cobro. José de Seabra da Silva, assim que chegou ao governo, deu um impulso decisivo à obra do Observatório Astronómico. No seu programa de acção incluía-se a conclusão de projectos que não tinham sido materializados e de obras pendentes como o Tribunal da Relação e o Hospital de Santo António, no Porto, ou os faróis do Cabo Carvoeiro e do Cabo Espichel. Com o regresso à questão do Observatório Astronómico, o ministro pretendia concluir o plano pombalino de apetrechar a Universidade de infra-estruturas e equipamentos modernos.

Do primeiro corpo de professores da faculdade de Matemática restava apenas José Monteiro da Rocha. O projecto definitivo para o observatório surgiu da estreita colaboração entre Monteiro da Rocha e o arquitecto das Obras da Universidade, Manuel Alves Macomboa (17?-1815). A nova solução envolveu a localização do edifício, transferida para o topo Sul do Paço das Escolas (fronteiro à rua da Trindade), e incluiu uma redução drástica do programa de instalações. Foram realizados vários projectos, entre 1788 e 1790, tendo como temas comuns o programa de instalações e a amarração do edifício ao muro do terreiro do Paço. Variavam na forma e na disposição volumétrica. O projecto definitivo foi aprovado em 1791, iniciando-se de imediato a obra que ficou concluída em 1799 (Fig. 7).

A carga simbólica e a função urbana iniciais deram lugar à criação de um simples estabelecimento astronómico, de acordo com o espírito utilitário e pragmático da época. Este edifício é exemplo do desfasamento entre as ambições da reforma pombalina e a nova realidade. O observatório astronómico, pensado por José Monteiro da Rocha, seu director, e desenhado por Manuel Alves Macamboa, criou as condições necessárias para o ensino e investigação da astronomia prática. Foi o início de um instituto científico altamente qualificado, cuja actividade lhe conferiu, desde o seu início, o carácter de observatório nacional[55].

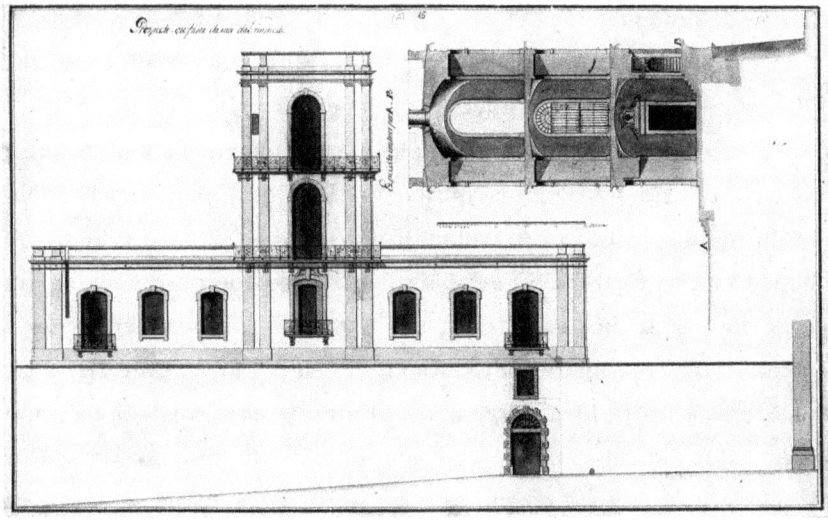

Fig. 7 – [Manuel Alves Macomboa], *Prospecto ou fasia da rua da Trindade e Expecato emtrior por A B*, s.d. [1791], BGUC, Ms. 3179, 15.

As reformas pós-pombalinas dos planos de estudos da Universidade de Coimbra; as novas disciplinas de carácter fisiocrático (1791-1801)

As principais mudanças introduzidas nos planos de estudos dos cursos de Filosofia e de Matemática compreenderam a inserção de novas cadeiras que vieram reforçar o ensino de índole fisiocrática e o carácter científico, técnico e prático da Universidade. As novas disciplinas de Botânica e Agricultura, Zoologia e Mineralogia,

---

[55] Sobre a actividade científica de José Monteiro da Rocha e sobre o processo de construção e funcionamento do Observatório da Universidade, ver Figueiredo, 2011: 214-300; ver, ainda, Martins, Figueiredo, 2008, 21: 57-61.

Metalurgia, Hidráulica e Astronomia Prática são a expressão de uma especialização crescente nas áreas técnico-científicas, consequência do desenvolvimento contínuo das ciências físico-matemáticas ao longo do século XVIII.

O plano de estudos da faculdade de Filosofia foi alterado, em 1791, com o objectivo de uma aproximação à prática da agricultura e da mineralogia. Foi criada a cadeira de Botânica e Agricultura, por extinção da cadeira de Filosofia Racional e Moral; para a sua regência, foi nomeado Félix de Avelar Brotero (1744-1828), recentemente chegado a Portugal (1790) depois de doze anos de permanência em Paris, onde se dedicou à investigação botânica. Foi igualmente criada a cadeira de Zoologia e Mineralogia, em substituição da cadeira de História Natural[56]. Esta reforma do programa curricular da faculdade de Filosofia relaciona-se com as políticas de fomento do sector agrícola e surge após o envio de bolseiros para a Europa onde se especializariam em minas e mineralogia, áreas que se encontravam em grande evolução técnica e científica.

Uma década depois, em 1801, foram alterados os planos de estudos das faculdades de Matemática e Filosofia, reforma motivada pela necessidade de desmultiplicação das cadeiras dos dois cursos perante a ampliação e especialização das matérias desde a criação das duas faculdades.

Na faculdade de Filosofia foi criada a cadeira de Metalurgia, para a qual foi nomeado regente José Bonifácio de Andrade e Silva após a sua viagem pela Europa como bolseiro do Estado[57]. Seguiu-se a nomeação de José Bonifácio para Intendente Geral das Minas e Metais do Reino e para a direcção do Laboratório Químico da Casa da Moeda, como conhecedor de toda a estrutura deste tipo

---

[56] Ver Abreu, 1851: 39. Ver Carvalho, 1872.

[57] Ver Abreu, 1851: 54. Ver Carvalho, 1872; Cruz: 1979, 20: 215-276.

de estabelecimentos, desde a lavra até à administração[58]. A reforma curricular da faculdade de Filosofia esteve, assim, directamente relacionada com a implementação do programa de fomento mineiro, metalúrgico e florestal em Portugal, plano empreendido por D. Rodrigo de Sousa Coutinho[59]. É no âmbito desta reforma que a faculdade de Filosofia foi encarregada da organização de planos de viagem e expedições naturalistas pelas províncias do Reino, associando as expedições científicas ao interior do país às viagens internacionais.

Na faculdade de Matemática foram criadas as cadeiras de Hidráulica e de Astronomia Prática[60]. A instituição da cadeira de Hidráulica pode ter tido o impulso de D. Rodrigo de Sousa Coutinho que conheceu de perto a produção científica em hidráulica na Universidade de Turim e manifestou, em vários textos, a importância desta disciplina para o desenvolvimento económico do país[61]. Terão contribuído também, o grave assoreamento da costa marítima na zona centro, nomeadamente na barra de Aveiro, as dificuldades com a obra de encanamento do rio Mondego, obra sobre a qual a faculdade de Matemática estava a elaborar um relatório pedido pelo governo[62], e as várias obras hidráulicas discutidas ou em actividade nesta altura. A parte teórica da cadeira de Hidráulica compreendia a hidrostática, hidrodinâmica, resistência de fluidos e teoria das máquinas para a elevação e condução das águas. A parte prática tinha como objectivo

---

[58] Ver Carta Régia, de 18 de maio de 1801, Silva, 1828a: 702-703. Ver Carvalho, 1872: 302-309.

[59] Encontra-se por estudar a actividade mineira, metalúrgica e florestal em Portugal durante o período da regência e do reinado de D. João VI. Também se encontra por estudar a actividade profissional de José Bonifácio durante o período em que trabalhou em Portugal, que vai de 1800 a 1819, altura em que partiu para a sua terra natal, o Brasil. Ver uma breve síntese em Martins, 2014: 305-313; 409-420.

[60] Ver Abreu, 1851: 55. Ver Freire, 1872.

[61] Sobre o plano hidráulico de D. Rodrigo de Sousa Coutinho, ver Martins, 2014: 592-598.

[62] Sobre o relatório da faculdade de Matemática, ver Martins, 2014: 331-335.

a explicação em detalhe dos sistemas construtivos de obras e máquinas hidráulicas, com demonstrações através de modelos e estampas. A instituição desta cadeira tinha em vista a formação de quadros técnicos com competências em todo o tipo de obras hidráulicas, como encanamento de rios, abertura de barras, construção de diques, aquedutos e canais de navegação e de rega, aproveitamento e direcção de correntes para mover engenhos fabris, drenar pântanos, etc. Correspondia no fundo à formação de engenheiros civis por contraponto à formação militar dos engenheiros na Academia de Fortificação, Artilharia e Desenho. Manuel Pedro de Melo, professor na Academia da Marinha desde 1798 e activo membro da Sociedade Marítima, Militar e Geográfica, foi nomeado para reger a cadeira de Hidráulica. Matemático e astrónomo brilhante, formado e estimado na Universidade de Coimbra, Manuel Pedro de Melo era bacharel em Filosofia (1792) e em Medicina (1797) e doutorado em Matemática (1795), tendo sido aí *opositor*[63]. Após a sua nomeação, por decisão entre a Universidade e o governo, Manuel Pedro de Melo foi designado para uma viagem científica pela Europa, para a observação de obras de hidráulica e o estudo aprofundado desta ciência. Dava-se, assim, continuidade ao programa de bolseiros, iniciado em 1790.

A cadeira de Astronomia Prática deve a sua criação à laboração em pleno do Observatório Astronómico da Universidade. Assim que se concluíram as obras do novo edifício, foi promulgado o *Regulamento do Observatório Real da Universidade de Coimbra*[64] que teve o importante significado de transformar o que era uma escola de ensino da astronomia, a funcionar em instalações provisórias desde 1775, num verdadeiro estabelecimento astronómico nacional, com objectivos claros no campo do ensino e no campo da investigação e produção científicas. O novo estabelecimento tinha como missão

---

[63] Ver Freire, 1872: 50-51; 81-82.

[64] Ver Carta Régia, 4 de dezembro de 1799, em Abreu, 1851: 49-54.

trabalhar continuadamente nas observações para a verificação e rectificação das tábuas astronómicas e promover os conhecimentos de geodesia e de náutica. As novas condições de trabalho permitiram e exigiram a reestruturação da cadeira de Astronomia que se dividiu em Teórica e Prática. A cadeira de Astronomia Prática ficou agregada ao Observatório, associando a actividade pedagógica e a produção científica de forma continuada e regular. Foi instituído um corpo de astrónomos responsável pelo Observatório (um director, dois astrónomos e quatro ajudantes) que empreendeu de imediato a publicação anual das *Efemérides Astronómicas*. Concebida e dirigida por José Monteiro da Rocha, a obra teve um lugar de relevo na produção científica portuguesa e alcançou expressão europeia, pelos métodos inovadores utilizados.

As reformas curriculares de 1791 e de 1801 reflectem o esforço de actualização da Universidade face à especialização disciplinar das ciências físico-matemáticas e aos avanços científicos europeus; reflectem, também, a preocupação com a componente técnica e prática do ensino superior.

As viagens de bolseiros para a Europa; a formação de uma elite para a modernização do aparelho administrativo do Estado

No âmbito das reformas curriculares, foram enviados bolseiros para a Europa em viagens científicas. As mais importantes expedições foram elaboradas em parceria entre o governo e a Universidade e envolveram jovens formados e professores. Esta orientação constituiu um importante complemento à profissionalização de quadros das áreas técnico-científicas e um meio de ultrapassar o isolamento português em relação às inovações tecnológicas e avanços científicos europeus. Nestes domínios, as culturas francesa, inglesa e alemã foram as mais influentes. As bolsas permitiram o uso das novas práticas metodológicas que privilegiavam o trabalho de campo e o contacto directo com o objecto de estudo, tendo um papel relevante a observação e a experiência. Associava-se à dimensão científica da viagem, a dimensão política. O apoio governativo a estas expedições visava, a prazo, o processo de modernização do Estado português, pela formação de funcionários com habilitações específicas e a sua nomeação futura para cargos públicos estratégicos[65].

A primeira missão científica organizada pelo governo compreendia os estudos de minas e mineralogia e tinha, como principal objectivo, a futura recuperação do sector mineiro, metalúrgico e florestal, um tema profusamente tratado nas *Memórias Económicas* da Academia das Ciências. Havia a intenção de activar a exploração mineira e de desenvolver políticas florestais para ultrapassar as carências em combustíveis, nomeadamente devido à falta de lenhas, e reiniciar a exploração e transformação do ferro para as necessidades crescentes deste metal, dentro do processo de industrialização.

A expedição científica foi programada para ter início em 1790 e foram eleitos três jovens formados na faculdade de Filosofia, os naturalistas, Joaquim Pedro Fragoso de Sequeira (1760-1833), Manuel Ferreira da Câmara Bettencourt e Sá (1762-1835) e José Bonifácio de Andrade e Silva (1763-1838). A viagem, que se previa longa, foi organizada pelo ministro dos Negócios Estrangeiros e da Guerra, Luís Pinto de Sousa. O ministro criou as condições para o financiamento da expedição, a cargo do Erário Régio, e tomou todas as diligências para o apoio logístico aos bolseiros nas deslocações e permanência nos diferentes destinos, através das embaixadas portuguesas na Europa. Elaborou detalhadas e ambiciosas instruções para a viagem. O documento discrimina o roteiro europeu e o tipo

---

[65] Cf. Varela, 2006: 223-260.

de estudos teóricos e práticos a aprofundar[66]. Os bolseiros tinham como missão estudar, praticar e recolher informação nas áreas da química, mineralogia, geologia, exploração mineira e metalúrgica. O primeiro destino era Paris, onde os bolseiros deveriam frequentar os cursos de Química e de Mineralogia. Seguidamente dirigir-se--iam a Freiburg, o centro mais avançado da Europa em mineração, e tirariam o curso completo de Minas. Para além da formação académica, deveriam visitar as minas da Saxónia, Boémia, Áustria, Rússia, Suécia, Noruega, Escócia, País de Gales e, por fim, Biscaia, em Espanha.

Luís Pinto de Sousa associou à viagem uma missão paralela, não inscrita nas instruções mas significativa dos propósitos do governo na formação técnica dos jovens saídos da Universidade de Coimbra: os bolseiros estavam encarregados de visitar as grandes obras públicas que se estavam a realizar na Europa. Em Paris, o director da *Ecole des Ponts et Chaussées*, Jean-Rodolphe Perronet, por intermediação de Valleré, ofereceu as condições para os bolseiros poderem cumprir essa missão, sugerindo assistirem à descofragem da ponte Luís XVI, sobre o rio Sena[67]. Esta vertente paralela e não oficial da expedição é significativa, correspondendo à expectativa futura de que os estudantes das áreas de ciências da Universidade pudessem dirigir obras públicas, o que se veio a concretizar, embora excepcionalmente.

A expedição prolongou-se por toda a década, tendo os três bolseiros visitado as principais regiões mineiras e unidades metalúrgicas da Europa central e setentrional. Em Paris, em pleno ambiente re-

---

[66] Ver, de Luís Pinto de Sousa, "Instrução para a realização da viagem de aperfeiçoamento técnico através da Europa", 31 de maio de 1790, publicada por Mendonça, 1933: 25-27.

[67] Ver "Resposta de M. Perronet a huma carta do tenente general De Valleré, na qual este lhe recomenda três membros da Academia Real das Sciencias de Lisboa, mandados a viajar", Paris, 28 de agosto de 1790, carta publicada em Stockler, 1808: 202-206.

volucionário, assistiram às aulas de Fourcroy e de Duhamel e, em Freiburg, frequentaram o conceituado e influente curso de Werner. Durante a expedição, os bolseiros divulgaram os seus estudos, publicando artigos em revistas científicas internacionais. Ferreira da Câmara e Fragoso de Sequeira regressariam a Portugal em 1798 e José Bonifácio em 1800.

Esta intensa viagem pela Europa foi extremamente fecunda e teve repercussões posteriores, primeiro em Portugal e depois no Brasil. Câmara e Bonifácio, ambos nascidos no Brasil, seriam convocados por D. Rodrigo de Sousa Coutinho para importantes papéis dentro da administração central do império português com vista a concretizar, com técnicas modernas e com estruturas administrativas reformadas, a exploração mineira e metalúrgica e a produção florestal[68]. Durante os anos em que trabalhou em Portugal (1800-1819), José Bonifácio utilizou os conhecimentos adquiridos enquanto bolseiro por via das instruções paralelas: foi chamado por António de Araújo de Azevedo (ministro dos Negócios Estrangeiros e da Guerra e interinamente do Reino), em 1807, para dirigir a obra de encanamento do rio Mondego, suspensa desde 1800, e para a concepção de uma ponte em ferro sobre o rio de Sacavém, entre outras obras públicas civis e militares que concebeu.

A segunda expedição, organizada em 1801 e iniciada nos princípios de 1802, foi proposta ao governo pelo reitor D. Francisco de Lemos e surgiu no âmbito da criação da cadeira de Hidráulica e da nomeação de Manuel Pedro de Melo. Esta expedição teve como objectivo principal a preparação desta nova cadeira, de modo a conferir-lhe um conteúdo não apenas teórico mas também técnico e prático. Manuel Pedro de Melo tinha conhecimentos teóricos

---

[68] Sobre a questão mineira, metalúrgica e florestal, ver os cinco discursos (1798--1803) pronunciados na abertura anual dos trabalhos da Sociedade Real Marítima, Militar e Geográfica por Coutinho, 1993, 2: 179-212.

em hidráulica, tendo estudado os principais autores europeus do século XVIII (Bernoulli, d'Alembert, Bossut, Bélidor, Perronet, Guglielmini, Fabre, entre outros). A principal fundamentação desta expedição científica era a aquisição de conhecimentos na componente prática da disciplina. Tratava-se de observar algumas das principais obras hidráulicas europeias, tendo contacto directo com distintos lugares de intervenção e com diferentes soluções, analisando o benefício ou insucesso das obras.

A comissão de Manuel Pedro de Melo foi objecto de duas instruções distintas: uma, relativa aos assuntos hidráulicos e, outra, mais vasta, de teor científico e pedagógico. As "Instruções para huma viagem hydraulica", concebidas, muito provavelmente, por José Monteiro da Rocha, são constituídas por um conjunto de onze artigos de carácter técnico onde são descritos os assuntos fundamentais que deviam ser objecto da expedição em matéria de hidráulica[69]. Estão muito presentes nestas instruções os problemas dos rios portugueses e de forma especial o Mondego e a barra de Aveiro. Os propósitos da viagem continham a visita a obras hidráulicas, sendo referidas em particular as obras do rio Pó, da foz do rio Loire e do rio Elba, junto aos campos de Magdeburgo. Pretendia-se a observação das obras de melhoramento da navegação fluvial, de desassoreamento dos rios e barras e de conservação dos campos agrícolas; a análise dos sistemas de canais de navegação e de rega e dos métodos construtivos usados; e o conhecimento das máquinas hidráulicas utilizadas para comportas, aquedutos, fábricas e engenhos. Fazia, ainda, parte das instruções para a viagem hidráulica a aquisição de estampas e de modelos de máquinas e instrumentos significativos para a Universidade de Coimbra. As segundas instruções, os "apontamentos para a viagem de Manuel Pedro", foram redigidas pouco tempo antes da sua partida e revelam que os propósitos da

---

[69] Ver AUC, Processos dos Professores, Cx. 164.

viagem foram ampliados por José Monteiro da Rocha, não se limitando ao objecto da sua cadeira[70]. Grande parte dos catorze pontos dos apontamentos invoca a formação de Manuel Pedro de Melo em Matemática, Filosofia e Medicina. O professor e bolseiro tinha como principais missões científicas e pedagógicas: visitar as instituições de ensino dos vários ramos das ciências, recolhendo informação regulamentar e curricular e os compêndios em uso; visitar os gabinetes de História Natural, tendo como objectivo a troca de informação e de materiais da Europa e do Médio Oriente por "produtos privativos das nossas colónias"; visitar os observatórios astronómicos de Greenwich, Paris e Gotha e tomar conhecimento dos regulamentos e dos instrumentos e métodos de observação utilizados, procurando criar condições para a elaboração de observações astronómicas combinadas de modo a produzirem-se análises comparadas. Devia, ainda, entre outras missões mais específicas – como, por exemplo, experimentar o telescópio de Herschel –, promover o estabelecimento de correspondências entre as várias instituições visitadas e os estabelecimentos congéneres da Universidade de Coimbra. Estes requisitos para a expedição científica manifestam a importância crescente das trocas científicas entre os centros de produção de conhecimento, no contexto europeu, e os interesses e necessidades da Universidade nas áreas da ciência e da técnica, no dealbar do novo século.

No âmbito da preparação da viagem, Manuel Pedro de Melo foi nomeado major do Real Corpo de Engenheiros, transitando da Marinha[71] para o Exército. Esta nomeação espelha o empenho da Universidade no acesso dos seus alunos à carreira de engenharia do Exército, para além de mostrar a importância crescente do estatuto

---

[70] Ver "Apontamentos sobre a viagem litteraria do doutor Manuel Pedro de Mello", 20 de dezembro de 1801, Rocha, 1890, 37: 268-271.

[71] Manuel Pedro de Melo deixou a Universidade de Coimbra e foi dar aulas de Matemática para a Academia da Marinha em 1798. Nessa altura, obteve a patente de capitão-tenente da Armada.

de engenheiro no quadro internacional. Representa a execução de um dos pontos dos *Estatutos* da reforma pombalina relativo aos matemáticos e ao corpo de engenharia que D. Francisco de Lemos chama a atenção na *Relação Geral do Estado da Universidade* (1777): que "entre os Engenheiros haja Mathematicos de Profissão, que saibam estas Sciencias ao fundo. Estes devem ser a alma da Engenharia"[72].

Manuel Pedro de Melo partiu no início de 1802 na companhia do embaixador António de Araújo de Azevedo (1754-1817) que se dirigia para a Holanda. Percorreu a Holanda, Bélgica, Inglaterra, Itália e França, visitando inúmeros estabelecimentos científicos e obras públicas. Durante a sua longa estadia em Paris, trabalhou activamente como ajudante de Jean-Baptiste Delambre (1749-1822), conceituado astrónomo francês que em 1804 passou a dirigir o Observatório de Paris. Publicou em língua francesa um dos seus mestres, José Monteiro da Rocha, e recolheu imenso material que deixou à Universidade de Coimbra. Adquiriu cartografia, estampas e livros para o Observatório Astronómico, estampas para a cadeira de Botânica e instrumentos e máquinas para as cadeiras de Física e Hidráulica[73]. Depois de uma intensa actividade científica e literária internacional, o bolseiro regressou a Portugal em 1815, após o fim da guerra na Europa, iniciando a regência da cadeira de Hidráulica. Pela sua formação especializada em Hidráulica, veio a ser consultado pela regência do Reino para várias obras públicas portuárias e de encanamento de rios[74].

---

[72] Cf. Lemos, 1777: 94.

[73] Ver Carta de Manuel Pedro de Melo, *Jornal de Coimbra*, Lisboa, Na Impressão Régia, 1817, vol. 11, parte 2, pp. 59-61.

[74] Não se encontrou nenhum estudo sobre esta expedição científica nem tão pouco sobre este importante matemático e astrónomo português. Silvestre Pinheiro Ferreira (1769-1846) tentou, em vão, que Manuel Pedro de Melo publicasse os seus manuscritos; ver uma breve descrição da expedição em "Viagem do sr. Manuel Pedro de Mello a differentes paizes da Europa", Freire, 1872: 81-82.

A lei dos Cosmógrafos e a participação dos matemáticos no aparelho do Estado; uma promessa malograda (1801)

A questão colocada pelos *Estatutos* da reforma pombalina da saída profissional dos estudantes formados nas faculdades de Matemática e Filosofia mantinha-se sem resolução passadas quase três décadas, explicando em boa parte a pouca frequência de alunos ordinários nestes cursos. Em 1777, D. Francisco de Lemos desenvolveu as medidas propostas em 1772 para a atribuição de funções públicas aos estudantes formados nas áreas de ciências. A mais importante de todas as medidas era a criação do lugar de Cosmógrafo por comarca, cargo que devia ser ocupado exclusivamente por matemáticos graduados[75]. D. Francisco de Lemos, de novo reitor, a partir de 1799, e José Monteiro da Rocha, director da faculdade de Matemática e do Observatório Astronómico, retomam a questão, tendo o apoio do ministro D. Rodrigo de Sousa Coutinho[76].

O objectivo da Universidade foi concretizado em junho de 1801 com a promulgação da lei dos Cosmógrafos, uma medida que tornava efectiva a participação dos matemáticos no aparelho administrativo do Estado[77]. Seguramente redigida por José Monteiro da Rocha, a lei criava um Corpo de Cosmógrafos, instituindo em cada uma das comarcas do país (ao todo 44) um matemático com o título de Cosmógrafo, cujo cargo era equiparado ao de Provedor. O alvará preconizava uma profunda reforma na administração do território, ao transferir para os novos funcionários do Estado central um conjunto de incumbências dos corregedores e provedores das comarcas. As competências relativas a intendências e inspecções de obras públicas – encanamento de rios, abertura de barras, estradas e pontes, artes

---

[75] Lemos, 1980: 86-97; 105-107.
[76] Ver Rocha, 1889, 36: 663.
[77] Ver Alvará de 9 de junho de 1801, Silva, 1828a: 707-710.

fabris e mecânicas e condução de águas – passavam a pertencer exclusivamente aos cosmógrafos. Competia-lhes, ainda, decidir sobre limites de terrenos, servidões, logradouros e bens dos concelhos. A lei dos Cosmógrafos dava particular importância aos trabalhos topográficos e cadastrais, cruzando-se, portanto, com os trabalhos da Carta do Reino e com os trabalhos de demarcação das Comarcas[78]. Os cosmógrafos tinham como primeira função elaborar uma carta topográfica da comarca, em coordenação com Francisco António Ciera, director dos trabalhos geodésicos. A comarca era a unidade territorial de referência, na passagem dos trabalhos geodésicos para os trabalhos topográficos, aos quais se seguiam dois níveis de registo topográfico progressivamente mais detalhados: o do concelho e o da propriedade urbana e rural. Os cosmógrafos deviam, ainda, elaborar um Registo Geral com todos os títulos dos bens imóveis. Demonstrando ter ideias próprias sobre o modelo de organização do levantamento cartográfico nacional, Monteiro da Rocha veio a definir para a carta das comarcas a escala 1:80.000, para a carta dos concelhos a escala 1:8.000 e para a carta dos prédios rústicos e urbanos a escala 1:800[79]. O levantamento, a várias escalas, do território das comarcas e o registo geral da propriedade integravam a preparação do Cadastro do Reino. Este instrumento seria fundamental para uma acção mais concreta do Estado, nos vários domínios da administração e das finanças (com relevo para o imposto das Sisas), estando a ser coordenado, no plano jurídico e administrativo, pelo magistrado José António de Sá (1756-1819)[80].

Segundo o alvará, os levantamentos cartográficos e os projectos de obras públicas seriam efectuados por engenheiros militares sob

---

[78] Ver Balbi, 1822, 2: ciij-civ.

[79] Ver Rocha, 1890, 37: 478-479.

[80] Ver, de José António de Sá, "Instrucções Geraes para se formar o Cadastro, ou o Mappa Arithmetico-Politico do Reino (...)", de 1801, publicadas por Instituto Nacional de Estatística, 1945, 1.

a inspecção dos cosmógrafos. Ou seja, os engenheiros passariam a ter por intendentes matemáticos, ou homens das ciências, em detrimento dos magistrados, ou homens de leis. Nesta transferência e redistribuição de competências entre cientistas, engenheiros e magistrados, os engenheiros militares continuavam a ter a responsabilidade da direcção de obras públicas, assim como a responsabilidade do levantamento e desenho de trabalhos cartográficos; quanto à administração do território, os magistrados viam reduzidas as suas vastíssimas atribuições, consagradas nas *Ordenações do Reino*. Para além de colocar os engenheiros militares sob tutela dos matemáticos, a lei dos Cosmógrafos fixava que no Corpo de Engenheiros existissem, em igual número, membros formados na Universidade e nas academias militares, reforçando o acesso dos matemáticos à estrutura militar do Estado. A divisão de tarefas entre matemáticos e engenheiros presente na lei dos Cosmógrafos deixa transparecer uma realidade na formação científica da Universidade: o afastamento da disciplina do desenho, enquanto instrumento essencial para o conhecimento e transformação do território. Caberia principalmente às academias de Lisboa e do Porto a continuidade de uma cultura de desenho que ficou ausente do ensino na Universidade desde a saída de Miguel Ciera para a Academia da Marinha.

A sobreposição entre funções atribuídas aos corregedores e provedores pelas *Ordenações do Reino* e as novas disposições para os cosmógrafos exigia um regulamento eficaz que não se veio a realizar, apesar da insistência e disponibilidade de José Monteiro da Rocha para a sua execução. Embora tenham sido nomeados alguns cosmógrafos, a lei não chegou a ser totalmente implementada nem obedeceu exactamente aos seus princípios. Os poucos cosmógrafos nomeados tinham a dupla formação em Filosofia e Leis, dado revelador da dificuldade em implantar a nova carreira na administração pública sem uma formação em Direito: António José Vaz Velho foi empossado no cargo de Cosmógrafo da comarca de Tavira e Filipe

Neri da Silva Coutinho foi provido no lugar de Provedor Cosmógrafo da comarca de Évora; o primeiro viria a ingressar no corpo de engenharia e o segundo seguiu a carreira da magistratura.

O insucesso desta importante reforma foi múltiplo, reflectindo-se na Universidade de Coimbra. A intenção de promover os estudos nas áreas científicas da Universidade e de integrar os jovens graduados no processo de modernização do Estado não se concretizou de forma eficiente, tarefa em que se empenharam, durante os seus magistérios, José Monteiro da Rocha para a faculdade de Matemática e Domingos Vandelli para a faculdade de Filosofia. Também não se conseguiu ultrapassar o excessivo peso dos magistrados no funcionalismo público. As dificuldades políticas e financeiras que antecederam as invasões francesas, a desestruturação institucional e social provocada pela transferência da capital de Lisboa para o Rio de Janeiro e agravada pela guerra e a posterior retracção económica e demográfica impediram a implantação de uma reforma que exigia tempo e continuidade.

Para ultrapassar o problema da saída profissional, a opção que tomaram muitos alunos, como o matemático Alberto Carlos de Meneses e o naturalista José Bonifácio de Andrade e Silva, foi o de se formarem simultaneamente nas áreas de ciências e de leis. A saída profissional por via da formação em Direito permitia aceder aos cargos da administração pública, como intendentes, inspectores, corregedores, provedores e juízes de fora, onde os conhecimentos nas áreas das ciências se tornaram cada vez mais importantes.

Apesar da pouca frequência de alunos nas faculdades de Matemática e de Filosofia, a Universidade manteve uma prestigiada formação científica em parte pela eleição dos estudantes mais qualificados para a renovação do quadro de professores[81]. Alguns

---

[81] Ver a lei que definiu os procedimentos para o preenchimento do quadro de docentes, de José de Seabra da Silva, "Artigos Decididos sobre a economia das aulas,

dos jovens formados leccionaram nas Academias da Marinha e de Fortificação, em Lisboa, e da Marinha e Comércio, no Porto, ou trabalharam em institutos de investigação, como o laboratório químico da Casa da Moeda. Outros integraram a administração pública do espaço do Império ou seguiram a carreira militar e política. A prática de transferência de quadros da Universidade para o Corpo de Engenheiros manter-se-ia ao longo do século XIX. Um exemplo significativo é o de Filipe Folque (1800-1874), filho de Pedro Folque que foi membro do Real Corpo de Engenheiros desde a sua constituição e colaborador de Ciera na Carta Geográfica do Reino. Filipe Folque doutorou-se em Matemática na Universidade de Coimbra, em 1826. Aluno brilhante, foi ajudante do director das obras de encanamento do rio Mondego e ajudante do Observatório Astronómico, obtendo conhecimentos especializados em hidráulica e em astronomia e geodesia. Foi professor na Academia da Marinha e na Escola Politécnica de Lisboa. Ingressou no Exército, vindo a ser comandante do Real Corpo de Engenheiros e director dos trabalhos geodésicos e cartográficos do Reino.

Ciência e território; a colocação em prática das políticas de fomento

Os esforços realizados para o desenvolvimento do ensino técnico-científico e para a mobilização das instituições e dos técnicos adquiriram um novo impulso e um outro enquadramento a partir de 1789 pois passaram a ser simultâneos com as medidas tomadas para a aplicação no terreno das políticas de fomento.

---

actos, e acções academicas, mandados observar pela Carta Regia de 28 de Janeiro de 1790", publicada em Abreu, 1851: 33-38.

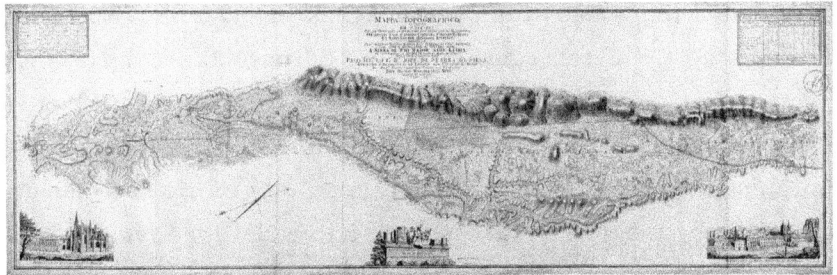

Fig. 8 – Luís Cândido Cordeiro Pinheiro Furtado, Conrado Henrique Niemeyer, Carlos Luís Ferreira da Cruz Amarante, *Mappa topographico levantado em MDCCXCI (...) para servir de delineamento da estrada desde a Serra de Rio-Maior athe Leiria, na conformidade do Alvara de XXVIII de Março do mesmo anno e das instrucçoens dadas pelo Illustrissimo e Excelentíssimo Senhor Joze de Seabra da Silva Ministro e Secretario de Estado dos Negocios do Reino ao Dezembargador Superintendente Geral das Estradas Joze Diogo Mascarenhas Neto.* Quartel de Condexa, 16 de agosto de 1793, IGP, CA-436.

As políticas do Estado para o fomento do território tiveram como principais programas a construção do novo mapa de Portugal, a reforma administrativa do território e o melhoramento das vias de circulação do país, terrestres, fluviais e marítimas. Para a implementação destes programas requeria-se uma vontade política continuada pois seriam precisos muitos anos, na maior parte dos casos décadas, até à plena concretização destes projectos. Contudo, colocavam-se diferenças significativas quanto à concretização dos vários programas de fomento, com reflexos nos modelos operativos e na organização das equipas e, portanto, no recrutamento de quadros com formação científica.

O novo mapa de Portugal constituía a base das políticas de fomento que o governo procurava implementar. Era um instrumento essencial para a elaboração de planos administrativos, económicos ou militares e para um funcionamento mais eficaz da administração pública, central, regional ou local. Constituindo um programa nacional autónomo, de puro conhecimento e levantamento, o seu empreendimento não tinha implicações directas no território. A Comissão Geodésica, uma estrutura desburocratizada sob inspecção directa da secretaria de Estado dos Negócios Estrangeiros e da Guerra e subvencionada pelo Erário Régio, era constituída por uma pequena equipa, única para todo o território continental, dirigida por um matemático com o apoio de dois engenheiros militares, auxiliada durante as expedições por soldados do Exército. Esta equipa, que correspondeu ao modelo subjacente aos *Estatutos* pombalinos consagrado na lei dos Cosmógrafos, constituiu um caso raro mas profícuo de colaboração entre matemáticos e engenheiros.

A reorganização do mapa jurídico-administrativo das comarcas do Reino tinha como objectivo a uniformização das unidades políticas e administrativas, integrando todas as terras na administração do Estado e eliminando os encravamentos gerados por descontinuidades das próprias comarcas ou pela existência de territórios com administração autónoma. Constituindo uma profunda reforma política, com consequências futuras no ordenamento do território, este programa de fomento estava muito condicionado pelo sistema de forais. Foram organizadas seis equipas, uma por província, cada uma formada por um magistrado[82] e um engenheiro[83]. Estas equipas mínimas, sob alçada da secretaria de Estado do Reino e do Desembargo do Paço e subvencionadas pelo Erário Régio, não tinham uma máquina administrativa própria, tendo por suporte de

---

[82] Os magistrados nomeados foram: Francisco António de Faria (Minho); Columbano Ribeiro de Castro (Trás-os-Montes); João Bernardo da Costa Falcão e Mendonça (Beira); José de Abreu Bacelar Chichorro (Estremadura); Joaquim José Torres Salgueiro (Alentejo); João António Barahona Fragoso (Algarve); ver Silva, 1998: 395-397.

[83] Os engenheiros nomeados foram: Custódio José Gomes de Vilas Boas (Minho); José Joaquim de Freitas Coelho (Trás-os-Montes); António Sebastião A. Silva Negrão (Beira); Francisco Assis Blanc (Estremadura); Eusébio de Sousa Soares (Alentejo); Sebastião Rodrigues (Algarve); ver, de Luís Pinto de Sousa, Aviso Régio, 6 de abril de 1793, AHM, FG-5, Livro 1709, fls. 214-215.

trabalho a legislação promulgada entre 1790 e 1793[84]. Os métodos de trabalho e o modelo de distribuição de tarefas entre magistrados e engenheiros tinham por base a experiência-piloto da comarca de Setúbal[85]. A orgânica das equipas privilegiava os magistrados e os engenheiros em detrimento dos matemáticos e naturalistas, embora José Manuel Carvalho Negreiros (1751-1815), membro do Real Corpo de Engenheiros, criticasse a subordinação dos engenheiros aos magistrados[86]. A opção de privilegiar os magistrados e engenheiros deve-se ao tipo de reforma que exigia, por um lado, conhecimentos jurídicos e domínio da legislação e, por outro lado, técnicos treinados no desenho para a realização dos levantamentos topográficos das seis províncias e dos mapas com os antigos e novos limites das comarcas. Neste programa de fomento, os matemáticos e naturalistas da Universidade de Coimbra não tinham espaço de intervenção.

O programa de obras públicas revestia-se de uma complexidade que não era comparável aos outros programas de fomento. As iniciativas tinham implicações directas no território e nas populações e desmultiplicavam-se em vários tipos de obras, com escalas e exigências muito variadas. A colocação em prática das obras de estradas e pontes, de encanamento de rios e de melhoramento dos portos compreendeu: a criação de legislação nacional para as obras públicas, inexistente até então no código legislativo português; a reformulação do modelo de recrutamento de mão-de-obra operária, extinguindo a prática da *corveia* e impondo o trabalho assalariado; o estabelecimento de instituições administrativas regulares, com

---

[84] Como legislação mais significativa refere-se: Lei de 19 de julho de 1790, Alvará de 7 de janeiro de 1792 e Provisão do Desembargo do Paço de 17 de janeiro de 1793.

[85] Ver a acta da reunião dos magistrados, de 4 de fevereiro de 1793, publicada por Silva, 1998: 398-399.

[86] Ver, de José Manuel de Carvalho Negreiros (1797). Reprezentação que serve de introdução para se projectar hum Regulamento para o Real Corpo dos Engenheiros Civiz, e todas as suas dependências, BNP, Ms. 6, fls. 12v-17.

competências próprias, providas de regulamentos para todo o pessoal interveniente, desde o intendente ao operário; e a montagem de um modelo planeado de intervenção no território, com propostas programadas no tempo e balizadas no território. O planeamento envolveu principalmente a concepção de projectos, fundamentados em desenhos e memórias justificativas, acompanhados de trabalhos de reconhecimento topográfico e hidrográfico e de recolha de informação estatística, financeira e legislativa. Pelo facto de algumas das obras abrangerem várias províncias e múltiplas comarcas, como as Estradas e Caminhos do Alto Douro ou a Estrada Lisboa-Porto (Fig. 8), a infra-estruturação do território não obedeceu a uma lógica de distribuição uniforme das equipas de trabalho por unidades administrativas e compreendeu a construção de um modelo operativo determinado pela articulação em rede entre os diferentes modos de circulação (terrestre, fluvial e marítimo). Por um lado, foi criada uma instituição a nível nacional, a Superintendência Geral das Estradas do Reino (1791), para a qual foi nomeado José Diogo Mascarenhas Neto (1752-1826), magistrado e autor do primeiro manual de estradas de Portugal (1790)[87], e para seu ajudante foi nomeado Alberto Carlos de Meneses (1761-183?), formado em Matemática e em Leis, assim como foram designadas duas equipas de engenheiros[88]. Por outro lado, foram sendo formadas equipas técnicas e reformados ou criados organismos (intendências e inspecções), concebidos de acordo com o local de intervenção e o tipo de obra. Neste modelo operativo, cabia aos engenheiros a concepção e direcção das

---

[87] Neto, 1790. O *Methodo para Construir as Estradas em Portugal* foi realizado na sequência da sua experiência de obra na estrada Porto-Guimarães, iniciada em 1789, em que trabalhou sucessivamente com dois engenheiros militares: José Champalimaud de Nussane (1730-1799) e Joaquim de Oliveira (1743?-1816). Em 1791 seria nomeado superintendente das Estradas do Reino.

[88] A equipa com o tramo da estrada de Rio Maior a Leiria era constituída por Luís Cândido Cordeiro Pinheiro Furtado, Conrado Henrique Niemeyer e Carlos Luís Ferreira da Cruz Amarante; a equipa com o tramo de Leiria a Coimbra era constituída por Joaquim de Oliveira, João Manuel da Silva e Inácio José Leão.

obras e aos magistrados a gestão administrativa e financeira. Aos engenheiros competia a elaboração dos planos, quer de levantamento quer de projecto, fundamentados em desenho e em relatórios; competia-lhes, ainda, a montagem dos estaleiros, a construção de máquinas para os inúmeros trabalhos a executar, a condução das obras e a direção do pessoal operário que podia atingir as centenas e, por vezes, milhares de homens. Aos magistrados competia a adjudicação e inspecção dos trabalhos, a contratação de empreiteiros ou de mão-de-obra operária, a gestão das receitas e despesas, as negociações relativas a avaliações e expropriações de terrenos e a resolução dos diferendos litigiosos. Nesta lógica de atribuição de competências, os engenheiros, enquanto autores dos projectos e directores das obras, e os responsáveis pelas opções de transformação do território, sobrepunham-se aos magistrados, limitados a funções que, embora fossem decisivas (e hierarquicamente superiores), eram essencialmente logísticas e auxiliares. Não era fácil, neste modelo de divisão de tarefas entre engenheiros e magistrados, encontrar lugar para os matemáticos e naturalistas quando estes não dominavam o desenho, instrumento fundamental para o levantamento do território e para o projecto, e não tinham alçada nos assuntos do direito público, com a importante excepção dos bacharéis formados simultaneamente em ciências e em leis. Mais do que a tradição usada nas obras régias ou a falta de quadros formados na Universidade de Coimbra, o que explicava esta opção política eram as competências específicas dos técnicos. Juntava-se a esta opção, o facto de o bom andamento dos trabalhos, muito propensos à suspeição das populações e à conflitualidade interna entre pessoal, depender, em certa medida, da presença da autoridade do magistrado com a sua beca e do engenheiro com a sua farda militar[89].

---

[89] Ver, como exemplo, a contestação das populações da comarca de Aveiro à superintendência e direcção da obra de abertura da barra, Martins, 2014: 402-409.

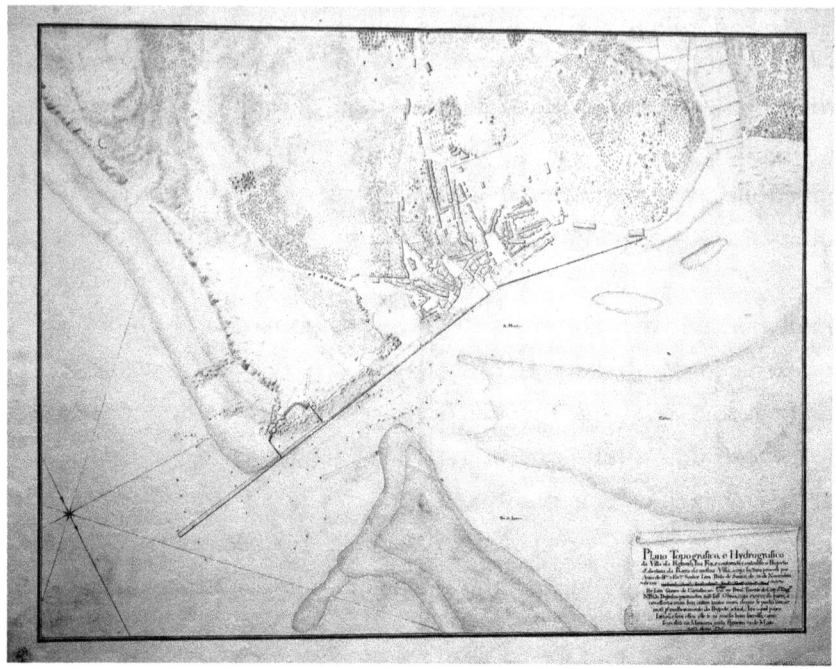

Fig. 9 – Luís Gomes de Carvalho, *Plano Topografico, e Hydrografico da Villa da Figueira, sua Foz, e contornos; contendo o Projecto d'abertura da Barra da mesma Villa, a cuja factura procedi por Avizo, do Ill.mo e Ex.mo Senhor Luiz Pinto de Souza, de 26 de Novembro de 1794, por Luiz Gomes de Carvalho, Primeiro Tenente do Corpo d'Engenheiros*, 26 de maio de 1795, BPMP, C-M&A, 18(11).

Conclusão

O investimento na formação técnico-científica, iniciado com a reforma pombalina da Universidade de Coimbra, foi um objectivo aprofundado pelos governos marianos e joaninos. A fundação das academias de ensino superior para o Exército e para a Marinha permitiu diversificar e ampliar a formação de quadros, ultrapassando a dúvida quanto à capacidade técnica dos engenheiros portugueses. Com a ampliação das instituições de ensino, a base de recrutamento e selecção de cientistas e de técnicos para as novas instituições e tarefas do Estado deixou de depender da importação de quadros estrangeiros. A política de envio de bolseiros para a Europa permitiu, ainda, a aquisição de formação especializada e de prática profissional actualizada nos campos da ciência e da técnica, na tentativa de ultrapassar o isolamento português relativamente à cultura e ciência moderna europeias. Por sua vez, a institucionalização do Corpo de Engenheiros garantiu a existência de um organismo técnico qualificado e estável capaz de assegurar todo o tipo de intervenções do Estado no território e no espaço urbano. A vontade política de incorporação no aparelho administrativo do Estado dos matemáticos e naturalistas formados na Universidade de Coimbra, apesar das inúmeras iniciativas, não teve o alcance desejado. O insucesso da lei dos Cosmógrafos impediu que estes quadros da Universidade fossem uma alternativa aos magistrados e a ausência da disciplina de Desenho na sua formação constituiu um obstáculo a serem uma alternativa aos engenheiros militares.

Na inter-relação entre ciência e território, a reforma das instituições científicas e a formação de quadros precederam e acompanharam a aplicação da ciência ao território. A mudança política ocorrida com a formação do segundo governo mariano foi decisiva para a sistematização de políticas de fomento do território estruturantes e de longo prazo. A grande transformação deve-se à definição de um novo papel para a acção do Estado no dealbar da nossa contemporaneidade. Com este ideário político, a insistência na formação de técnicos qualificados passou a ser dirigida para um objectivo concreto: a colocação em prática das políticas de fomento. Os novos quadros eram directamente mobilizados para o exercício profissional permitindo a aquisição de experiência e fomentando o aprofundamento contínuo e tendencialmente especializado do seu saber técnico e científico. Como exemplo, os engenheiros Luís Gomes de Carvalho (Fig. 9), Custódio José Gomes de Vilas Boas e Manuel

Joaquim Brandão de Sousa, todos pertencentes à primeira geração de alunos que entraram para a Academia de Fortificação, Artilharia e Desenho, em 1790.

Os engenheiros militares serão os principais obreiros das políticas de fomento governamentais. Constituem excepções a este quadro, naturalistas como José Bonifácio de Andrade e Silva, António Vaz Velho e Gregório José de Seixas (1763-1830) ou matemáticos como Francisco António Ciera e Alberto Carlos de Meneses. Neste âmbito, José Bonifácio representa um caso excepcional. Enquanto estudante de ciências e de leis, bolseiro do Estado para a Europa, professor da Universidade de Coimbra, intendente de Minas e Metais, fundador e director do laboratório químico da Casa da Moeda e, simultaneamente, intendente e director da obra de encanamento do rio Mondego, José Bonifácio espelha uma capacidade que foi obtida pela continuada promoção do ensino técnico-científico e da investigação aplicada e pelas constantes políticas de fomento.

As políticas de fomento empreendidas por José de Seabra da Silva e Luís Pinto de Sousa marcaram a acção dos governos do final do antigo regime e tiveram uma influência decisiva nas políticas públicas ao longo do século XIX. Quer do ponto de vista dos programas eleitos, quer do ponto de vista legislativo, técnico e administrativo, estas políticas constituíram o corpo de ideias para a intervenção no território. Os modelos e métodos utilizados viveram da complementaridade entre reformas administrativas introduzidas pelos políticos e capacidade técnica desenvolvida pelos engenheiros militares. Com a revolução liberal (1833-1834), seria implementada a reforma administrativa do território, já tentada depois da revolução de 1820 mas só concretizada após a abolição dos Forais (1832). Os vários programas de fomento, iniciados em 1789, ficarão unificados com Fontes Pereira de Melo (1819-1887), uma vez criado o ministério das Obras Públicas (1852). Os múltiplos programas para o território (reordenamento administrativo do território, mapa de Portugal, obras públicas, recenseamentos da população, elaboração do cadastro e exploração mineira e florestal) passarão a ser liderados pelo Corpo de Engenheiros, com o ministério das Obras Públicas como centro político agregador. Às obras públicas foi associado o caminho-de-ferro, e aos trabalhos cartográficos foi associada a carta geológica, mapa essencial para a implantação do novo meio de transporte e para a exploração mineira. Este período corresponde a uma nova etapa das políticas de fomento, onde a coordenação dos projectos, à escala nacional, e a presença de um vasto corpo de quadros técnicos se reflectirá na construção de uma rede integrada de vias de circulação e na concretização do novo mapa de Portugal. Os trabalhos do período do *fontismo* serão coordenados pelos engenheiros do Estado, formados principalmente nas academias da Marinha e de Fortificação (ou nas escolas que lhes sucederam – escola do Exército e escolas Politécnicas de Lisboa e do Porto) e na Universidade de Coimbra. Luís da Silva Mouzinho de Albuquerque (1792-1846), Filipe Folque, João Crisóstomo de Abreu e Sousa (1811-1895) ou Fontes Pereira de Melo, são exemplo de técnicos e políticos que acumularam o conhecimento adquirido pelos oficiais engenheiros desde o final do século XVIII. Os magistrados deixarão de ter um papel activo neste processo de continuidade de um saber colectivo, transmitido de geração para geração, através do corpo de engenharia e através das instituições de ensino e dos seus professores. Os engenheiros, ao longo do século XIX, não só assegurarão a direcção dos trabalhos públicos, como exercerão as funções de administração e fiscalização anteriormente pertencentes aos magistrados, vindo a ter o domínio completo da intervenção no território. Este grupo social, depois de uma contínua evolução na administração pública, subirá ao poder na segunda metade do século XIX e concretizará as políticas de fomento que se iniciaram sessenta anos antes.

"Tenho a consolação de sigurar a V. Ex.ª; que a pratica das obras das estradas nem oprime, nem descontenta os Povos, e que a sua construção se dirige com solidez, e boa ordem: tudo isto se deve por huma parte ao zelo, e inteligencia dos officiaes Engenheiros, que V. Ex.ª destinou para meus camaradas, por outra ao sistema de escolher para Administradores rapazes instruidos nas sciencias naturaes, e livres do genio, e ideias forenses, que não combinão com a prosperidade e economia publica. A Armonia entre os Engenheiros e Administradores satisfas me infinitamente, e athe respeito as conferencias, que eles fazem comunicando as suas ideias reciprocamente para melhor progresso das suas respectivas comiçoens".

José Diogo Mascarenhas Neto
Superintendente das Estradas do Reino
24 de novembro de 1792[90].

---

[90] Carta de José Diogo Mascarenhas Neto para Luís Pinto de Sousa, Condeixa, 24 de novembro de 1792; ver, ainda, carta do mesmo para José de Seabra da Silva, com idêntica data; AHM, DIV-1-11-7-22.

COLEÇÕES CIENTÍFICAS DO ILUMINISMO NA UNIVERSIDADE DE COIMBRA[1]

Carlota Simões
Museu da Ciência
Departamento de Matemática da Faculdade de Ciências e Tecnologia
e Centro de Física da Universidade de Coimbra

Pedro Casaleiro
Museu da Ciência
e Centro de Estudos Interdisciplinares do Século XX
da Universidade de Coimbra

Resumo

Grande parte das coleções científicas da Universidade de Coimbra são hoje geridas pelo Museu da Ciência, inaugurado em Dezembro de 2006. A sua sede está instalada num edifício neoclássico magnificamente recuperado, o *Laboratorio Chimico*, contemporâneo do nascimento da química moderna, construído entre 1773 e 1777 a mando do Marquês de Pombal e o mais antigo edifício laboratório químico do mundo que manteve esta função quase até aos nossos dias. Os primeiros objetos das coleções do Museu da Ciência datam igualmente, na sua maioria, do Século das Luzes. Muito contribuíram para a riqueza do espólio as *Viagens Philosophicas* de Alexandre Rodrigues Ferreira, mas também a transferência para Coimbra da

---

[1] Este trabalho é uma versão revista e aumentada do texto (Simões et al. 2013).

coleção de física experimental do Colégio dos Nobres em Lisboa. Parte do acervo do Museu da Ciência pode ainda hoje ser visitado nas salas originais do século XVIII, no Colégio de Jesus, mais um edifício do complexo jesuítico transformado pelo Marquês de Pombal com o objetivo de promover em Coimbra o ensino experimental das ciências.

O *Laboratorio Chimico* e o Colégio de Jesus

O Museu da Ciência da Universidade de Coimbra distribui-se por dois edifícios: o *Laboratorio Chimico*, recuperado já durante o século XXI, e o Colégio de Jesus, que alberga grande parte das coleções científicas da Universidade de Coimbra (Pires e Pereira 2010). Os dois edifícios foram desenhados pela Casa do Risco, sob orientação do engenheiro militar e tenente-coronel William Elsden, que se salientou como diretor das Obras da Reforma da Universidade de Coimbra levada a cabo pelo Marquês de Pombal (Araújo 2000).

Elsden foi fundamental na criação e remodelação dos edifícios da Universidade iluminista, mas foi com o Bispo D. Francisco de Lemos (1735-1822), nomeado Reitor da Universidade de Coimbra em 1770 e Reformador da mesma Universidade em 1772, que a nova mentalidade iluminista se instalou (Franco 1983). Os novos Estatutos da Universidade (Estatutos 1772) foram publicados logo em 1772 e nenhum lente em exercício antes dessa data viu reconduzidas as suas funções. Para lecionar na nova universidade, Pombal trouxe para Coimbra Domenico Vandelli (1730-1816), Doutor em Medicina pela Universidade de Pádua, nomeado Lente de História Natural e Química em 1772; o Padre Monteiro da Rocha (1734-1819), nomeado Lente de Matemática em 1772 e de Astronomia em 1773; Giovanni Antonio Dalla Bella (1730-c.1823), da Universidade de Pádua, nomeado Lente de Física Experimental em 1772; Michele Antonio Ciera, engenheiro de Piemonte, nomeado Lente de Astronomia em 1772.

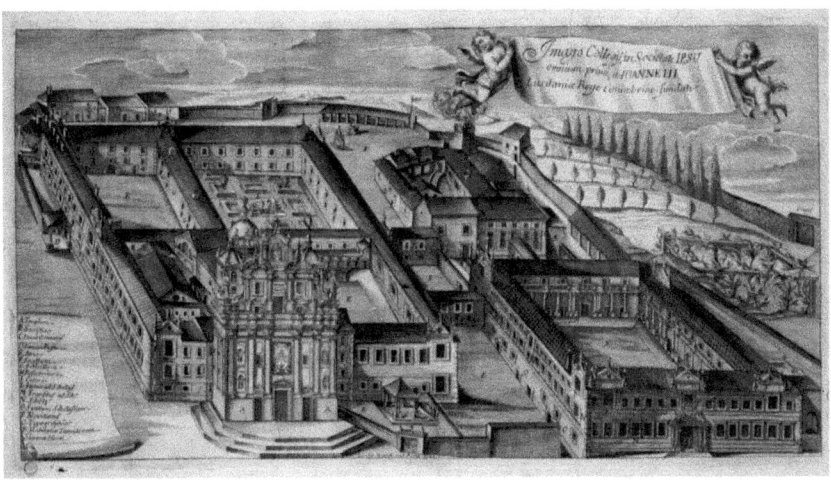

Fig. 1 – O complexo jesuítico no século XVIII, antes da intervenção Pombalina. À esquerda o Colégio de Jesus, à direita o Colégio das Artes. O refeitório é o edifício em segundo plano, à direita, e tem ligação direta aos dois colégios (gravura de Carlo Grandi, 1732, Biblioteca Nacional de Portugal).

O *Laboratorio Chimico* foi construído para o ensino da Química, entre 1773 e 1777, materializando a ideologia iluminista do ensino experimental da ciência (Pires 2006). Domenico Vandelli foi o seu primeiro Diretor (Costa 1986). Tomé Rodrigues Sobral (1759-1829), que sucedeu a Vandelli, alargou as potencialidades do Laboratório quando o adaptou temporariamente ao fabrico de pólvora para as tropas defensoras da cidade, na sequência da ocupação e saque de Coimbra pelas tropas napoleónicas em 1 de Outubro de 1810, ficando conhecido como o "mestre da pólvora".

No decurso das obras de adaptação do *Laboratorio Chimico* a Museu, os trabalhos arqueológicos revelaram que o edifício do século XVIII fora construído a partir da sala do refeitório que servia o complexo dos colégios jesuítas do século XVI, composto pelo

Colégio de Jesus e pelo Colégio das Artes. A intervenção trouxe à luz, intactas, algumas provas da utilização do edifício pela Companhia de Jesus: várias janelas e um púlpito, bem como as fundações das cozinhas. Os elementos encontrados foram integrados na recuperação do edifício: o púlpito, uma janela conservada com a cantaria original, duas janelas no fundo da sala e o vigamento do teto, do qual se manteve o desenho e os tirantes originais (Casaleiro et al. 2006: 58).

Fig. 2 – Parede interior do *Laboratorio Chimico* onde se identifica o púlpito e uma janela do refeitório jesuíta (fotografia de Emanuel Brás).

O projeto de arquitetura que consistiu na requalificação e adaptação do *Laboratorio Chimico* à função museológica, da responsabilidade dos arquitetos João Mendes Ribeiro, Carlos Antunes e Desirée Pedro, viu reconhecida a sua qualidade com a atribuição dos Prémios de Arquitetura Diogo de Castilho em 2007 e ENOR em 2009. O Museu da Ciência foi o vencedor do Prémio Micheletti 2008, que distingue o melhor e mais inovador museu europeu do ano em ciência, técnica e indústria (MCUC 2017). Quanto à exposição permanente Segredos da Luz e da Matéria que inaugurou em simultâneo com o edifício, é hoje uma mostra interdisciplinar de exemplares das várias coleções científicas da Universidade de Coimbra (Van Praët et al. 2006: 24).

Fig. 3 – O *Laboratorio Chimico*, depois da intervenção do século XXI (fotografia de Emanuel Brás).

O Colégio de Jesus, face a face com o *Laboratorio Chimico*, alberga hoje as coleções de física, zoologia, geologia, mineralogia e paleontologia (Ruivo 1997), (Ribeiro 2000), (Pinto e Marques 1999). O edifício que chegou aos nossos dias é a reconstrução do antigo Colégio de Jesus, estabelecido em 1542 pela Companhia de Jesus. A intervenção pombalina entre 1773 e 1775 adaptou o colégio, criando uma nova fachada principal virada a nascente de modo a tornar-se um edifício universitário, que passou a albergar os equipamentos destinados ao ensino experimental das ciências em magníficas instalações (Brigola 2003: 146).

Fig. 4 – O Colégio de Jesus (fotografia de Gilberto Pereira).

Com este espírito foram criados no edifício o Gabinete de História Natural e o Gabinete de Física Experimental, no quadro da Faculdade de Filosofia então criada (Estatutos 1772), preservados no Colégio de Jesus até aos nossos dias, e ainda o Hospital e o Dispensatório Farmacêutico, no quadro da Faculdade de Medicina.

Fig. 5 – O Gabinete de História Natural (fotografia de Gilberto Pereira).

Fig. 6 – O Gabinete de Física (fotografia de Gilberto Pereira).

A reforma criou também o Jardim Botânico, ainda hoje um dos tesouros da cidade de Coimbra e um Observatório Astronómico, que viria a publicar regularmente efemérides astronómicas.

Antes da Reforma Pombalina, a Botânica era sobretudo ensinada na Faculdade de Medicina; com a criação do Jardim Botânico incrementou-se o seu crescimento enquanto disciplina independente, embora nesta altura ainda fosse ensinada na cátedra de História Natural, juntamente com a Zoologia e a Mineralogia, por um único professor, Domenico Vandelli (Cruz 1976: 5), (Amaral R. 2011: 40).

Do Observatório Astronómico pombalino nada resta: projetado para ser construído na Praça D. Dinis sobre o castelo medieval, viu abandonada a construção ainda no final do século XVIII sem sequer estar terminado o seu piso térreo, acabando por ser demolido nos anos 40 do século XX (Figueiredo 2013a).

Fig. 7 – Projeto do Observatório Astronómico Pombalino, Elsden, c. 1773 (Museu Nacional Machado de Castro, Inv. 2945/DA 23).

Ainda no século XVIII, seria construído um edifício mais modesto no topo sul do Paço das Escolas, junto à Biblioteca Joanina, projeto da autoria de Manuel Alves Macomboa, que em 1782 passara a ser o arquiteto responsável pelas obras universitárias (Craveiro 1990), mas também este edifício acabaria por ser demolido durante as obras de requalificação da Universidade por ordem expressa de Salazar:

'A Alta é já de si, por obra dos nossos antepassados, uma grandiosa cidade universitária, só bastando para dar-lhe realce e valor libertá-la de incrustados, malfazejos e indignos das construções fundamentais, e completá-la com instalações apropriadas às exigências dos novos estudos. Isolar a colina sagrada, só cativa para o estudo na doce e calma atmosfera coimbrã; integrar no conjunto o edifício do Governo Civil, os Grilos, possivelmente S. Bento; fazer sobressair as imponentes massas de construções, hoje afogadas, que são o edifício central da Universidade, a Biblioteca, a Farmácia, a Faculdade de Letras, os Hospitais, a Associação Académica, a Sé Nova, o Museu; e – Deus me perdoe! – além de muitas outras coisas feias, *deitar abaixo aquela excrescência do Observatório Astronómico para deixar intacto aos olhos encantados o panorama maravilhoso do Mondego, das Lágrimas, da quinta das Canas, do Seminário, das encostas de tristes oliveiras, com a serra no horizonte longínquo* - é obra sem dúvida cara, mas realizável e útil e que só por si dará a Coimbra um lugar excecional entre todas as universidades do mundo.' (Salazar 1937)

Fig. 8 – O Observatório Astronómico (Figueiredo 2013a).

O Gabinete de Física

A coleção de instrumentos científicos e didáticos de Física da Universidade de Coimbra é, decerto, uma das mais notáveis e raras da Europa. Estabelecida inicialmente no Colégio dos Nobres em Lisboa por Dalla Bella, foi transferida para Coimbra para fundar o Gabinete de Física associado à disciplina de Física Experimental entretanto criada pelos Estatutos Pombalinos de 1772 (Martins 2013: 72). Dalla Bella, que entretanto tinha regressado a Pádua, foi convidado a voltar a Portugal, desta vez para Coimbra, tendo sido um dos responsáveis pela transferência da coleção de Lisboa para Coimbra (Carvalho 1978).

Fig. 9 – Um exemplar emblemático transferido do Colégio dos Nobres em exposição no Gabinete de Física é o equilibrista (MCUC|FIS.0021), um instrumento de demonstração do centro de gravidade de um corpo, na forma de um equilibrista trajado à época
(fotografia de José Meneses).

Ao Gabinete chegaram, ao longo de mais de dois séculos, máquinas, aparelhos e instrumentos que o foram enriquecendo, acompanhando o desenvolvimento da física experimental (Antunes e Pires 2010). O que resta do Gabinete de Física do século XVIII é hoje um conjunto de verdadeiras obras de arte, valorizadas pela riqueza dos materiais e pela perfeição na execução, que ainda ocupam as salas e o mobiliário originais. A coleção conta com mais de três mil objetos e cerca de quinhentos livros antigos.

O Gabinete de História Natural

> 'Para recolher os produtos naturais, que por qualquer via adquirir a Universidade, haverá uma Sala com a capacidade que requer um Museu, ou Gabinete digno da mesma Universidade.'
> (Estatutos 1772, Livro III: 265)

De acordo com os Estatutos da Universidade, o Gabinete de História Natural da Universidade de Coimbra deveria englobar não só coleções particulares, mas sobretudo coleções resultantes de colheitas efetuadas ou coordenadas pelos professores da Faculdade de Filosofia (Baptista 2010: 52). Deste modo se deu o progressivo enriquecimento do espólio do Gabinete de História Natural, iniciado com a incorporação de uma coleção privada de Domenico Vandelli, proveniente de um museu que este tinha iniciado em Pádua e que constituía o seu gabinete particular, a que se juntaram as produções recolhidas por Vandelli durante a sua estadia em Lisboa; um terceiro lote de material foi doado à Universidade pelo Capitão José Rollem Van-Deck (Brigola 2003: 161). Com a extinção do Real Museu da Ajuda em 1836, podemos hoje afirmar que a Universidade de Coimbra tem à sua guarda o mais antigo museu de Portugal. O espólio foi entretanto enriquecido com as remessas enviadas do Brasil ao longo de anos por Alexandre Rodrigues Ferreira (1756 – 1815), recolhidas no âmbito da sua Viagem Philosophica (1783-1792) à Amazónia (Areia et al. 1991), mas para um estudo aprofundado do tema das ligações culturais e científicas entre Portugal e Brasil no século XVIII e início do século XIX, recomendamos (Felismino 2014) e (Lourenço 2016).

No final de 2010, no âmbito de um levantamento das coleções científicas pertencentes à Universidade de Coimbra, foram encontrados 68 exemplares do século XVIII de peixes do Brasil, de diferentes espécies, conservados em seco e montados sobre cartão segundo a técnica de herbário. Pelas suas características únicas foram atribuídos à coleção do Real Museu da Ajuda e tudo leva a crer que em grande parte se podem tratar de exemplares das recolhas efetuadas por Alexandre Rodrigues Ferreira (Casaleiro et al. 2011). No arquivo do antigo Museu Bocage, hoje Museu Nacional de História Natural e da Ciência da Universidade de Lisboa (MUHNAC), encontram-se os documentos relativos à remessa do Real Museu recebida em Coimbra em 1806 (Felismino 2014: 47). Em Portugal conhecem-se mais alguns exemplares de peixes conservados através desta técnica, que pertencem à coleção da Academia das Ciências de Lisboa. Muitos dos exemplares do Real Museu foram transferidos para Paris por ocasião das invasões francesas, fazendo hoje parte do acervo do Museu de História Natural de Paris.

Fig. 10 – Um exemplar de peixe conservado com a técnica de herbário (MCUC|ZOO.000018) (fotografia de José Meneses)

As coleções

Tanto Vandelli como Avelar Brotero (1744-1828) foram diretores do Jardim Botânico da Universidade de Coimbra, mas é em Lisboa, no Museu Nacional de História Natural e da Ciência, que se encontram os herbários que eles organizaram, já que ambos dirigiram também o Real Museu e o Jardim Botânico da Ajuda. O herbário da Universidade de Coimbra – que hoje tem mais de 800 000 exemplares – foi iniciado por Júlio Henriques em 1879. As restantes coleções científicas da Universidade de Coimbra compreendem cerca

Fig. 11 – O magnete chinês (MCUC | FIS.0290) é um dos objetos emblemáticos do Gabinete de Física e a sua história antecede o Colégio dos Nobres. O instrumento possui uma magnetite oculta numa armação que representa a coroa real. A magnetite foi um presente do Imperador da China a João V, Rei de Portugal em 1722 e o instrumento foi armado por William Dugood (1715-1767), membro da Royal Society que viveu em Portugal (fotografia de José Meneses).

de 550 000 objetos distribuídos por quatro categorias principais – História Natural, Etnografia, Instrumentos Científicos, Modelos – e ainda mais de duas mil obras em papel que incluem livro antigo, cartografia, painéis pedagógicos e arquivos. Cerca de 90% destes objetos são exemplares de História Natural da área da Zoologia. Os instrumentos e objetos de astronomia, física, química, história natural e medicina do século XVIII documentam de forma exemplar o ideal iluminista da busca pelo conhecimento científico.

Zoologia

A coleção zoológica é a mais numerosa, atingindo cerca de 500 mil exemplares. Contém o maior exemplar animal em museus portugueses, um esqueleto montado de uma baleia-comum (*balaenoptera physalus*, Linnaeus, 1758) de 20 metros de comprimento, em exposição permanente na Galeria de História Natural do Museu da Ciência. A coleção de vertebrados representa 5% do total e é composta por peles de espécimes de mamíferos, aves e peixes conservadas em seco e montadas através da taxidermia para exposição; espécimes completos de répteis e anfíbios conservados em líquido; e uma coleção osteológica de esqueletos montados e crânios. Entre os mamíferos encontram-se exemplares únicos a nível nacional, nomeadamente um exemplar de urso e um casal de cabras do Gerês, ambos extintos em Portugal. Os invertebrados representam o resto da coleção, dos quais 75% são insetos. As coleções mais importantes são as de escaravelhos, borboletas e conchas.

Botânica

O espólio de botânica é composto por uma coleção de mais de três mil exemplares de frutos, sementes e ramos conservados em seco ou em líquido e uma série de produtos vegetais como resinas, gomas, fibras, cascas e madeiras do Brasil e países africanos de expressão portuguesa. Existe uma coleção importante de cerca de quinhentos modelos de flores e frutos, em cera e papier-maché, produzidos pelas mais famosas casas de modelos na Europa de finais do século XIX: Auzoux, Brendel, Jauch-Stein, Les Fils d'Émile Deyrolle entre outros (Amaral R. 2011: 85). O acervo de espécimes vegetais é complementado por uma valiosa coleção de fósseis de plantas, de instrumentos como microscópios e lupas, e ainda uma série de artefactos produzidos com materiais vegetais.

Mineralogia e Geologia

No último quartel do século XIX, o Museu de História Natural foi dividido em secções, de acordo com as grandes áreas das Ciências Naturais, sendo então criado o Museu Mineralógico e Geológico, que hoje integra a Galeria de Mineralogia do Museu da Ciência. As coleções de mineralogia, geologia e paleontologia estimam-se em mais de vinte mil exemplares com origem nas coleções criadas no fim do século XVIII, resultado de recolhas em Portugal e países de expressão portuguesa. A coleção paleontológica, de cerca de dez mil fósseis, é a mais numerosa (Callapez et al. 2010: 66). Entre 1890 e 1913 foram adquiridas coleções mineralógicas e paleontológicas a importantes casas europeias, como a Krantz (Schem-Gregory & Henriques 2013), (Callapez et al. 2014).

O acervo mineralógico constitui uma coleção de minerais portugueses e estrangeiros com cerca de cinco mil espécimes, assim como um conjunto de modelos cristalográficos. As coleções de rochas de Portugal e estrangeiras contêm mais de seis mil amostras.

Fig. 12 – O mineral Andradite (MCUC | MIN.SIL.001143)
(fotografia de José Meneses)

Da coleção de mineralogia faz parte o mineral *Andradite*, assim nomeado em 1868, em homenagem ao mineralogista José Bonifácio de Andrada e Silva (1763-1838), professor de Metalurgia da Universidade de Coimbra no início do século XIX (Ferreira 1998), e que também lutou pela liberdade e independência dos povos. Prova da luta que desenvolveu toda a sua vida é o facto de Andrada e Silva ter participado na resistência durante as invasões francesas em Portugal e ter sido em seguida figura central do processo de independência no Brasil. No entanto, a primeira publicação sobre metalurgia em Portugal é a obra *Metallurgiae Elementa* (Barjona 1798) da autoria de Manuel José Barjona (1760-1831), lente substituto na Universidade de Coimbra em 1791 e professor catedrático de 1801 a 1828, quando foi preso na cadeia da Universidade por ter aderido à causa liberal. Já depois de libertado, foi-lhe aplicada pena de demissão, acabando por terminar a sua vida na miséria.

Antropologia

A coleção antropológica é um acervo de cerca de catorze mil objetos constituído por coleções etnográficas e de osteologia humana, tendo como núcleo inicial a coleção recolhida por Alexandre Rodrigues Ferreira, na sua *Viagem Philosophica* à Amazónia no século XVIII (Ferrão e Soares org. 2005). Durante a sua viagem, descreveu a aparência, vestuário, adereços, armas, tatuagens e costumes das comunidades índias. Apenas a título de exemplo, Alexandre Rodrigues Ferreira recolheu junto dos índios Jurupixuna várias máscaras usadas em danças de agradecimento ou celebração que remeteu para o Real Museu da Ajuda e que foram integradas na Universidade de Coimbra em 1806, em conjunto com todo o material recolhido durante a viagem. A tribo Jurupixuna já não existe, nem deixou quaisquer máscaras como estas no Brasil, sendo hoje um conjunto de máscaras raríssimo e de valor incalculável. Faz parte do acervo da Real Academia das Ciências de Lisboa, um conjunto similar de objetos que completa esta coleção.

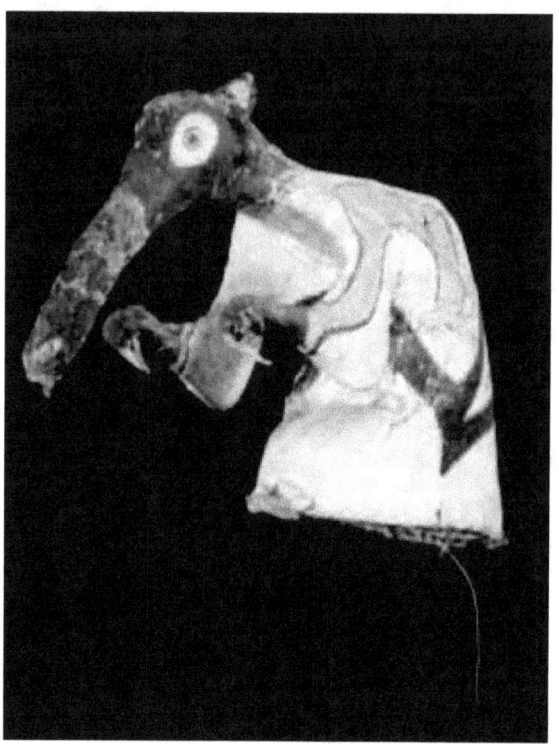

Fig. 13 – Máscara zoomorfa usada pelos índios Jurupixuna, que representa um papa-formigas (MCUC | ANT.Br.137). Foi recolhida por Alexandre Rodrigues Ferreira durante a sua *Viagem Philosophica* ao Brasil, no século XVIII (fotografia de Carlos Barata)

As coleções etnográficas, recolhidas em missões, por aquisição, oferta ou doação, na sua maioria durante o século XIX, representam Portugal e os países de língua portuguesa: Brasil, Angola, Moçambique, S. Tomé, Guiné, Macau, Timor e Goa entre outros (Amaral, A. R. et al. 2013). Do acervo antropológico faz também parte uma coleção notável de modelos de frenologia adquiridos em Paris e legados pelo Comendador Gama Pereira.

Química

A coleção de química tem o seu início associado às atividades de ensino e de investigação implementadas no *Laboratorio Chimico* em 1772. Destaca-se pela sua raridade uma coleção de fornos cerâmicos de reverbero fabricados no próprio laboratório, assim como um conjunto de sete potes de botica em faiança do fim do século XVIII, atribuídos a Domenico Vandelli. A coleção no seu conjunto reúne, para além das raridades da química do século XVIII, mais de mil peças maioritariamente datadas do século XIX e XX. Deste núcleo faz parte um conjunto de mobiliário químico de bancadas e nichos de evaporação, e um grande número de balanças, retortas, frascos e estufas (Costa 1986).

Astronomia

O núcleo mais antigo da coleção de astronomia está associado à atividade científica do Observatório Astronómico fundado no século XVIII, que incidia no estudo da astronomia e da matemática para a geografia e para a navegação (Alves org. 2004). O Padre Monteiro da Rocha, matemático e astrónomo, foi nomeado diretor do Observatório Astronómico em 1795, equipando-o com instrumentos vindos do Colégio dos Nobres de Lisboa e com encomendas ao construtor João Jacinto Magalhães em Londres. Fazem parte da coleção uma dezena de instrumentos da autoria de um dos mais importantes construtores de instrumentos científicos do século XVIII, o inglês George Adams.

Fig. 14 – Esfera armilar com planetário (MCUC | AST.I.006), construída por George Adams, século XVIII. Trata-se de um modelo da Terra, do Universo e do Sistema Solar. A esfera possui, no seu interior, um planetário com o Sol no centro rodeado pelos planetas conhecidos na época (fotografia de José Meneses)

A coleção de astronomia foi saqueada pelas tropas napoleónicas durante as invasões francesas em Coimbra, em 1810. Da coleção faz hoje parte uma pêndula de compensação de Berthoud, um instrumento utilizado para a determinação da hora de observações astronómicas, que caiu durante o saque partindo-se uma roda dentada, tendo o oficial encarregado desistido dele.

Fig. 15 – Pêndula de Berthoud (MCUC | AST.I.023)
(fotografia de João Armando Ribeiro)

A coleção atual é constituída por cerca de mil objetos incluindo mais de 200 instrumentos de observação, complementados por um conjunto de acessórios e ferramentas. Existe ainda uma coleção de desenhos, mapas e cartas celestes assim como um núcleo de livro antigo.

Conclusão

Ao longo de mais de dois séculos, foram muitos os que contribuíram para a coleção de Coimbra, adquirindo, produzindo ou sugerindo a inclusão de novos objetos. O Marquês de Pombal, Vandelli, o Padre Monteiro da Rocha, Alexandre Rodrigues Ferreira, bem como outros homens dos séculos XVIII e XIX foram fundamentais para a construção e preservação deste verdadeiro tesouro científico e patrimonial. Coimbra foi atacada e espoliada no início do século IX, mas mesmo assim, a coleção continuou vasta e valiosa. O século XX iria destruir o Observatório Astronómico e o Gabinete de Física Experimental esteve prestes a ser diminuído, não fosse a intervenção providencial de Mário Silva (1901-1977) (Nobre, 1997). Apesar de todos os contratempos, uma boa parte da coleção do Século das Luzes conseguiu chegar intacta ao século XXI. O Museu da Ciência é um projeto de grande fôlego da Universidade de Coimbra, que visa a preservação, a divulgação e o estudo deste valioso património do iluminismo nacional.

A Universidade de Coimbra foi classificada como Património Mundial pela UNESCO em 2013 e faz parte da Associação de Cidades e Entidades do Iluminismo desde Outubro de 2015. Já o Gabinete de Física, porque permanece no seu espaço de origem mantendo as suas características desde o tempo da sua fundação e porque a sua coleção de instrumentos científicos é uma representação notável da evolução da Física nos Séculos XVIII e XIX, foi recentemente classificado como Sítio Histórico pela Sociedade Europeia de Física. Passaram 727 anos desde a assinatura do documento fundador da Universidade de Coimbra, *Scientiae thesaurus mirabilis*: graças ao Rei D. Dinis, o documento fundador da Universidade de Coimbra já continha em si a palavra *ciência*.

BIBLIOGRAFIA

Abreviaturas

ADE – Arquivo Distrital de Évora
AHMB – Arquivo Histórico do Museu Bocage
AHU – Arquivo Histórico Ultramarino
AKG – Arquivo Kew Garden de Londres
ANTT – Arquivo Nacional da Torre do Tombo
AUC – Arquivo da Universidade de Coimbra
BACL – Biblioteca da Academia de Ciências de Lisboa
BNP – Biblioteca Nacional de Portugal
BNRJ – Biblioteca Nacional do Rio de Janeiro
MCUL – Museu da Ciência da Universidade de Lisboa
MHNP – Muséum d'Histoire Naturelle Paris

Fontes manuscritas

ADE – Cx. 41, n.º 8, Testamento de João Rosado de Vilalobos e Vasconcelos.

AHMB – CN/B-93, Carta de Luís Pinto de Sousa Coutinho a Vandelli.

AHU – Reino, Maço 2701, "Jardim Botânico", Relação dos productos naturaes, e do que se quer para o Rial Gabinete d'Ajuda dos Continente de Goa, Macao, e das Ilhas de Timor [1789].

ANTT – Arquivos Particulares, Abade Correia da Serra, Caixa 2B, A 42. 4 f.

ANTT – Arquivo da Casa de Linhares, Mç. 63, n.º 112. Carta de Correia de Serra a Rodrigo de Sousa Coutinho. Londres, 28 de julho de 1800.

ANTT – Inquisição de Lisboa, Processo n.º 13369.

ANTT – Ministério dos Negócios Eclesiásticos e Justiça, Caixa 66, Maço 77, 1.º

ANTT – Real Mesa Censória, n.º 702, "Estatutos Literarios e Economicos da Sociedade de Mancebos Patriotas Estabelecida em Coimbra no anno de 1780 debaixo da Real Protecção de sua Alteza o Serenissimo Senhor Principe do Brazil".

ANTT – Ministério do Reino, livro 550 fl. 2.

ANTT – Ministério do Reino, Maço 444, Domingos Vandelli, Relação da origem, e estado prezente do Real Jardim Botanico, Laboratorio Chymico, Museo de Historia Natural, e Caza do Risco, s/d. [1795].

ANTT – Ministério do Reino, Maço 444, Cx. 555 (1821-1833), Ofício de Félix de Avelar Brotero ao ministro Joaquim Pedro Gomes de Oliveira (22 de Setembro de 1823),

ANTT – Ministério do Reino, Maço 444, Cx. 555 (1821-1833), Ofícios do Escrivão da Fazenda do Real Museu ao Conde de Basto (7 de Setembro de 1830 e 2 de Março de 1832).

ANTT – Ministério do Reino, Maço 444, Cx. 555 (1821-1833), Resposta de Félix de Avelar Brotero a uma portaria do ministro Filipe Ferreira de Araújo e Castro (16 de Novembro de 1822),

Arquivo Kew Gardens, Londres, Joaquin Velloso de Miranda (1785). Autograph letter to Sir J. Banks, consisting of descriptions, with water colour drawings of genera of Plants collected. Foll. 84.°, Minas Geraes, 1785.

AUC-IV-1ªD-9-2-372 – Processo do Professor Domingos Vandelli: carta de 07 novembro de 1780 do Visconde de Vila Nova de Cerveira ao reitor reformador principal Mendonça; carta de 14 de julho de 1787 do Visconde de Vila Nova de Cerveira ao reitor reformador principal de Castro; rol dos itens do Museu de História Natural da Universidade de Coimbra, 15 de março de 1777. Manuscrito s/n

BACL, série azul, ms. 24, carta n.° 3 e ms. 1944 n.° 1.

BACL, Série Vermelha, Ms. 129.

BNP – Manuscritos Reservados, PBA Ms. 511, Methodo de achar a Longitude Geográfica no mar y na terra Pelas observaçõens y cálculos da Lua Para o uso da Navegação Portugueza. Pelo P. Jozé Monteiro da Rocha.

BNP – Códice n.° 3750, Hortus Olisiponensis Exhibens Plantas Exoticas Horti Regii specimenque Historie Naturalis Lusitanie Cum novis Generibus et Speciebus.

BNRJ – Divisão de Manuscritos, I-21, 10/49-8-13, Alexandre Rodrigues Ferreira, Inventário Geral e Particular de todos os Productos Naturáes, e Artificiáes, Instrumentos, Livros, Utensiz e Moveis pertencentes ao Real Gabinete de História Natural, Jardim Botânico, e suas Cazas annexas (...) Tudo como nelle se declara (8 de Novembro de 1794).

MCUL – Inv. n.° 55, Livro De Registo dos Decretos, Portarias, Avisos, e outras Regias Determinaçoens, que baixão ao Real Jardim Botanico, Laboratorio Chimico, Musêo, e Casa do Risco.

MHNP, Mss. 2445, Notas sobre o Fasciculas plantas do Brasil de Joaquim Velloso de Miranda.

Fontes impressas

Abreu, José M. de (1851), *Legislação Académica desde os estatutos de 1772 até ao fim do anno de 1850*. Coimbra: Imprensa da Universidade.

Actas das Congregações da Faculdade de Filosofia (1772-1780) (1978). Coimbra: Universidade de Coimbra.

Almeida, Manuel Lopes de (1979), *Documentos da Reforma Pombalina*. Coimbra: Imprensa da Universidade. 2 vols.

Antonil, André João (1922) – *Cultura e opulencia do Brazil por suas drogas e minas. Com um estudo bio-bibliographico por Affonso de E. Taunay*. S. Paulo: Companhia de Melhoramentos de S. Paulo.

Aranha, Francisco Xavier do Rego (1788). *Elementos de Agricultura Fundados sobre os mais sólidos princípios da razão, e da experiência, para uso das pessoas do campo, que mereceram o premio da Sociedade Economica de Berne em 1774 por Mr. Bertrand, cura da igreja d'Orbe, e membro da Sociedade Economica de Berne*. Lisboa: Officina de Filippe da Silva Azevedo.

Barjona, Manuel José (1798). *Metallurgiae Elementa*. Coimbra: Typis Academicis.

Bougainville, L. A. (1889), *Voyage de Bougainville autour du monde [...] en 1766, 1767, 1768 et 1769, raconté par lui-même*, Lille: Société Sainte Augustin, 1889.

Bluteau, Raphael (1728). *Vocabulario Portuguez & Latino*, Coimbra: Colégio das Artes da Compania de Jesus. (Dicionarios.bbm.usp.br. Último acesso 23/03/2016).

Câmara, Manuel Arruda da (1799). *Memória sobre a cultura dos algodoeiros*. Lisboa: Officina da Casa Litteraria do Arco do Cego.

Campomanes, Pedro Rodríguez (1774). *Discurso sobre el fomento de la industria popular*. Madrid: Imprenta de Antonio Sancha.

Catalogus Brevis Provinciae Brasiliensis an. 1757, apud Leite, Serafim (1949). *História da Companhia de Jesus no Brasil*, tomo VII.

Catalogus rerum temporalium, 1701. *Status habitualis provinciae brasilicae*, apud Leite, Serafim (1945). História da Companhia de Jesus no Brasil, tomo V, Apêndice E, pp. 588 e ss.

[CDT] *Connaissance des Tems, ou des Mouvemens Célestes, à l'usage des Astronomes et des Navigateurs pour l'an 1808 (1810)*. Paris: Imprimerie Impériale.

Corografia Brazilica ou Relação Historico- Geographica do Reino do Brazil composta [...] por hum presbítero secular do Gram Priorado do Crato (1817). Rio de Janeiro: Na Impressão Regia.

Coutinho, D. Rodrigo de Sousa (1993). *Textos políticos, económicos e financeiros (1783-1811)*. Lisboa: Banco de Portugal, 2 vols.

Couto, José Vieira (1806). *Memória sobre as salitreiras naturaes de Monte Rodrigo: maneira de as auxiliar por meio das artificiaes, refinaria do nitrato de potassa ou salitre, escrita no anno de 1803*. Rio de Janeiro: Imprensa Régia (archive.org. Último acesso 22/03/2016).

[EAOAUC] *Ephemerides Astronomicas calculadas para o Meridiano do Observatorio da Universidade de Coimbra para o uso do mesmo Observatorio, e para o da navegação Portugueza, para o anno de 1804*, volume I (1803). Coimbra: Real Imprensa da Universidade.

[ENACL] *Ephemerides náuticas, Ou Diário Astronómico para o ano de 1789* (1788). Lisboa: Academia Real das Sciencias de Lisboa.

Estatutos da Universidade de Coimbra (1772), II Centenário da Reforma Pombalina. Por Ordem da Universidade de Coimbra, 3 volumes (1972). Coimbra: Universidade de Coimbra.

Gazeta de Lisboa, 21 de Abril de 1781.

Instituto Nacional de Estatística (1945). *"Cadastro do Reino, 1801-1812", Subsídios para a História da Estatística em Portugal*, 1.

Lacaille, N. L. (1765). "Mémoire sur l'observation des longitudes en mer par le moyen de la Lune", in *Memoires de l'Académie Royale des Sciences de Paris* Année DCCLIX, Avec les Mémoires de Mathématique & de Physique, pour la même Année.

Lalande, Jérôme (1771/1781). *Astronomie*, 4 vols. [3 vols. em 1771 e o 4.º vol. em 1781]. Paris: Veuve Desain.

Lalande, Jérôme (1803). *Bibliographie Astronomique, avec l'Histoire de l'Astronomie depuis 1781 jusqu'à 1802*. Paris: L'Imprimerie de la Republique, An XI [1803].

Laplace, Pierre Simon (1878/1882). *Mécanique Céleste. Oeuvres complètes de Laplace*. Paris: Gautiher-Villars.

Lemos, Francisco de (1980). *Relação Geral do Estado da Universidade (1777)*. Prefácio de Luís de Albuquerque. Coimbra: Universidade de Coimbra.

Lopes, José Carlos (1879). *A Ipecacuanha acções Physiologicas e aplicações Therapeuticas*. Porto: Tipografia ocidental.

Loureiro, João de (1790). *Flora Cochinchinensis: sistens plantas regno Cochinchina nascentes*. Tomo I, Lisboa: Tipografia da Academia de Ciências (biodiversitylibrary.org. Acesso em 23/03/2016).

Memórias da Academia Real das Sciencias de Lisboa desde 1780 até 1788 (1797), Tomo I. Tipografia da Academia. (archive.org último acesso 22/03/2016).

Memórias Económicas da Academia Real das Sciencias de Lisboa, para o Adiantamento da Agricultura, das artes e da Indústria em Portugal, e suas conquistas (1789-1815). Lisboa: Na Officina da mesma Academia.

Memórias Económicas da Academia Real das Ciências de Lisboa, para o Adiantamento da Agricultura, das artes e da Indústria em Portugal, e suas conquistas (1789-1815). (1990/91). Ed. e dir. José Luís Cardoso, 5 vols. Lisboa: Banco de Portugal.

Memórias Económicas Inéditas 1780-1808 (1987). Pref. Manuel Jacinto Nunes, introd. e notas José Luís Cardoso. Lisboa: Academia das Ciências.

Neto, Jozé Diogo Mascarenhas (1790). *Methodo para Construir as Estradas em Portugal, dedicado ao Senhor Dom Joao Principe do Brazil*. Porto: Antonio Alvarez Ribeiro.

[NA] *Nautical Almanac and Astronomical Ephemeris for the year 1834, published by the Lords Commissioners of the Admiralty* (1833). London: William Clowes.

O Reino da Estupidez (1975). Edição, introdução e notas de Luís de Albuquerque. Coimbra: Atlântida.

Rocha, José Monteiro da (1889-1890). "Cartas do Dr. José Monteiro da Rocha a D. Francisco de Lemos de Faria Pereira Coutinho", *O Instituto*, 36-37.

Sá, José António de (1783). *Compendio de Observaçoens que formão o plano de Viagem Politica e Filosofica que se deve fazer dentro da Patria*. Dedicado a sua

Alteza Real o Serenissimo Principe do Brasil. Lisboa: Offic. de Francisco Borges de Sousa.

Silva, António Delgado da (1828). *Collecção da Legislação Portugueza. Legislação de 1775 a 1790*. Lisboa: Typografia Maigrense.

Silva, António Delgado da (1828). *Collecção da Legislação Portugueza. Legislação de 1791 a 1801*. Lisboa: Typografia Maigrense.

Stockler, Francisco de Borja Garção (1808). *Elogio Historico de Guilherme Luiz Antonio de Valleré, recitado na sessão pública da Academia Real das Sciencias de Lisboa*, de 20 de Janeiro de 1798. Paris: Firmin Didot.

Stockler, Francisco de Borja Garção (1813). *Cartas ao autor da Historia geral da invazaõ dos Francezes em Portugal e da restauração deste reino*. Lisboa: Na Impressão Regia.

Vandelli, Domingos (1771). *Fasciculum Plantarum cum novis generibus, et speciebus*. Lisboa: Tiphographia Régia.

Vandelli, Domingos (1994). *Aritmética Política, Economia e Finanças*. Introdução José Vicente Serrão. Lisboa: Banco de Portugal.

Vandelli, Domingos (2003). *Memórias de História Natural*. Edição e introdução de José Luís Cardoso, Porto: Porto Editora.

Vasconcelos, João Rosado de Vilalobos e (1782). *O Perfeito Pedagogo na arte de educar a mocidade, em que se dão as regras de polícia e urbanidade christã, conforme os usos e costumes de Portugal*. Lisboa: Tipografia Rolandiana.

Vasconcelos, João Rosado de Vilalobos e (1786/87). *Elementos da Policia Geral de hum Estado*. Lisboa: Offic. Patr. de Francisco Luiz Ameno, 2 tomos.

Wickiman, Daniel (1774) *Dissertatio Botanico-medica de viola ipecacuanha*. Upsaliae: Typis Edmannianis (Bayriche Staats Bibliothek Digital. Último acesso 22/03/2016)

Referências bibliográficas

Abreu, Laurinda (2013). *Pina Manique, um reformador das Luzes*. Lisboa: Gradiva.

Ago, Renata (1990). *Carriere e clientela nella Roma barroca*. Bari: Laterza.

Aires, Cristóvão (1927). *Para a História da Academia das Ciências de Lisboa*. Coimbra: Imprensa da Universidade.

Albuquerque, Luís de (1972). "A 'Aula da Esfera' do Colégio de Santo Antão no Século XVII", *Anais da Academia Portuguesa de História*, 21, 2.ª série, 337-391.

Almaça, Carlos (1996). *A natural history museum of the 18th century: the royal museum and botanical garden of Ajuda*. Lisboa: Museu Nacional de História Natural.

Almeida, Joana Estorninho de (2004). *A forja dos homens: estudos jurídicos e lugares de poder no século XVII*. Lisboa: Imprensa de Ciências Sociais.

Almeida, Bruno (no prelo). "For the Sake of Cosmography: Notes on Pedro Nunes' Contributions to Astronomy", *Cahiers François Viète* (numéro spécial sur l'Histoire de l'Astronomie au Portugal), Série II, n.º 8-9.

Alves, Artur Soares et al. (org.) (2004), *Laboratório do Mundo: Idéias e Saberes do século XVIII. Catálogo de exposição*. São Paulo: Pinacoteca do Estado de São Paulo.

Amaral, Ana Rita; Martins, Maria do Rosário; Miranda, Maria Arminda (2013). "O contexto museológico da Antropologia na Universidade de Coimbra: uma síntese histórica (1772-1933)", in Fiolhais et al., *História da Ciência na Universidade de Coimbra 1772-1933*. Coimbra: Imprensa da Universidade de Coimbra, 129-166.

Amaral, Manuel (2010-2011). *A luta política em Portugal nos finais do Antigo Regime*. Parede: Tribuna da História, 3 vols.

Amaral, Raquel (2011). *Modelos Didáticos na Museologia e Ensino da Botânica na Universidade de Coimbra*. Dissertação de Mestrado. Coimbra: Faculdade de Letras da Universidade de Coimbra.

Andrade, António Alberto Banha de Andrade (1981-1984). *A reforma pombalina dos estudos secundários (1759-1771). Contribuição para a história da pedagogia em Portugal*. Coimbra: Universidade de Coimbra.

Andrewes William J. H. ed. (1998). *The quest for longitude: the proceedings of the Longitude Symposium*, Harvard University, Cambridge, Massachusetts, November 4-6, 1993. Collection of Historical Scientific Instruments. Cambridge, MA: Harvard University.

Antunes, Ermelinda; Pires, Catarina (2010). "O Gabinete de Física da Universidade de Coimbra", in Marcus Granato e Marta C. Lourenço (eds.) *Coleções Científicas Luso-Brasileiras: Património a ser descoberto*. Rio de Janeiro: MAST/MCT, 159-184.

Araújo, Ana Cristina (coord.) (2000). *O Marquês de Pombal e a Universidade*. Coimbra: Imprensa da Universidade.

Araújo, Ana Cristina (2000a). "Dirigismo cultural e formação das elites no pombalismo", in Ana Cristina Araújo (coord.). *O Marquês de Pombal e a Universidade*. Coimbra: Imprensa da Universidade, 9-40.

Araújo, Ana Cristina (2003). *A Cultura das Luzes em Portugal. Temas e problemas*. Lisboa: Livros Horizonte.

Araújo, Ana Cristina (2009). "A participação do batalhão académico de Coimbra na derrota dos franceses no Porto", in *O porto e as invasões francesas. 1809-2009*, Porto: Público-Câmara Municipal do Porto, vol. 2, 275-308.

Araújo, Ana Cristina (coord.) (2012). *O Marquês de Pombal e a Universidade*. 2.ª ed. Coimbra: Imprensa da Universidade.

Araújo, Ana Cristina (2015). Cosmopolitismo e patriotismo: A propósito dos "Estatutos Literários e Económicos da Sociedade dos Mancebos Patriotas de Coimbra", in *Tempo e História, Ideias e Políticas, Estudos para Fernando Catroga*. Coimbra: Almedina.

Areia, M. L. R.; Miranda, M. A.; Hartmann, T. (1991). *Memória da Amazónia. Alexandre Rodrigues Ferreira e a Viagem Philosophica pelas Capitanias do Grão-Pará, Rio*

Negro, Mato Grosso e Cuyabá. *1783-1792*. Coimbra: Museu e Laboratório Antropológico da Universidade.

Arnason, J. P.; Eisenstadt S. N.; Wittrock, B. (2005). *Axial Civilizations and World History*. Leiden/Boston: Brill.

Balbi, A. (1822), *Essai Statistique sur le Royaume de Portugal et d'Algarve comparé aux autres États de l'Europe*. 2 vols. Paris: Rey et Gravier Libraires.

Balbi, Adrien (2004). *Essai statistique sur le Royaume de Portugal et d'Algarve, comparé aux autres États de l'Europe*. Edição fac-similada. 2 vols. Lisboa: Imprensa Nacional-Casa da Moeda.

Baldini, Ugo (2004). "The teaching of mathematics in the Jesuit colleges of Portugal from 1640 to Pombal", in Saraiva, L. and Leitão, H. (eds.), *The Practice of Mathematics in Portugal. Papers from the International Meeting organized by the Portuguese Mathematical Society*, Óbidos, 16-18 November, 2000. Coimbra: Imprensa da Universidade.

Baptista, Maria Teresa A. M. (2010). "O Gabinete de História Natural da Universidade de Coimbra", in Brandão, José M.; Callapez, Pedro M.; Mateus, Octávio; Castro, Paulo (eds.), *Colecções e Museus de Geologia: Missão e Gestão*. Coimbra: Fundação para a Ciência e a Tecnologia, Ministério da Ciência e do Ensino Superior, 51-60.

Bennett, J. A. (1992). "The English Quadrant in Europe: Instruments and the growth of consensus in practical astronomy", *Journal for History of Astronomy* 23, 1-14.

Biagiolli, Mário (2004). *Galileu, Cortesão: a prática da ciência na cultura do absolutismo*. Porto: Porto Editora.

Borges, Nelson Correia (1997). "Instalações da Universidade de Coimbra (II)", in *História da Universidade em Portugal*. Coimbra-Lisboa: Universidade de Coimbra--Fundação Calouste Gulbenkian, 423-439.

Boschi, Caio (1991). "A Universidade de Coimbra e a formação das elites mineiras coloniais", in *Universidade(s). História, Memória, Perspectivas*. Actas. Coimbra: Comissão Organizadora do Congresso 'História da Universidade', 133-150.

Boschi, Caio Cesar (2012). *Exercícios de Pesquisa Histórica*. Belo Horizonte: PUC Minas.

Bots, Hans; Waquet, François (1997). *La République des Letttres*. Paris: Ed. Belin.

Brandão, Mário (1990). *D. Lopo de Almeida e a Universidade*. Coimbra: Universidade de Coimbra.

Brigola, João Carlos (2008). "Domingos Vandelli um naturalista a serviço de Portugal e Brasil", in *O Gabinete de curiosidades de Domenico Vandelli*. Rio de Janeiro: Dantes Editora

Brigola, João Carlos (2013). *Colecções, Gabinetes e Museus em Portugal no século XVIII*. Lisboa: Fundação Calouste Gulbenkian/ Ministério da Educação e Ciência.

Caixaria, Eduardo (2006). *O Real Archivo Militar. Cronologia Histórica e Documental, 1802-1821*. Lisboa: Direcção de Infra-Estruturas, Gabinete de Estudos Arqueológicos de Engenharia Militar.

Callapez, Pedro M.; Marques, Júlio F.; Paredes, Ricardo; Rocha, Carla (2010) "Retrospectiva histórica das colecções de paleontologia do museu mineralógico e geológico da Universidade de Coimbra", in Brandão, José M.; Callapez, Pedro M.; Mateus, Octávio; Paulo, Castro (eds.). *Colecções e Museus de Geologia: Missão e Gestão*, Coimbra: Fundação para a Ciência e a Tecnologia, Ministério da Ciência e do Ensino Superior, 61-68.

Callapez, Pedro; Brandão, José Manuel; Paredes, Ricardo; Barroso-Barcenilla, Fernando; Santos, Vanda Faria dos; Segura, Manuel (2014). "The Krantz collections of palaeontology held at the University of Coimbra (Portugal): a century of teaching and museum activities", in *Historical Biology an International Journal of Paleobiology*, Taylor & Francis.

Camargo-Moro, Fernanda (2008). "Câmaras das Maravilhas, studiolo e Gabinetes de Curiosidades: Vandelli e sua circunstância", in *O Gabinete de Curiosidades de Domingos Vandelli*. Rio de Janeiro: Dantes Editora.

Cardoso, José Luís (2003). "From natural history to political economy: the enlightened mission of Domenico Vandelli in late eighteenth-century Portugal", *Studies in History and Philosophy of Science*, 34, 781- 803.

Cardoso, Walter, "Estudantes da universidade de Coimbra nascidos no Brasil (1701--1822): procedências e graus obtidos", in *Universidade(s). História, Memórias, Perspectivas*. Actas do Congresso História da Universidade. Coimbra, 1991.

Carneiro A.; Simões A.; Diogo M. P. (2000). "Enlightenment Science in Portugal: The Estrangeirados and Their Communication Networks", *Social Studies of Science* 30:4, 591-619

Carolino, L. Miguel (2012). "Manoel Ferreira de Araújo Guimarães, a Academia Real Militar do Rio de Janeiro e a definição de um gênero científico no Brasil em inícios do século XIX", *Revista Brasileira de História*. São Paulo, 32:64, 251-278.

Carvalho, Flávio Rey de (2008). *Um Iluminismo Português? A reforma da Universidade de Coimbra (1772)*. São Paulo: Annablume.

Carvalho, Joaquim Augusto Simões de (1872). *Memoria Historica da Faculdade de Philosophia*. Coimbra: Imprensa da Universidade.

Carvalho, Manuel Jorge Pereira de (1995). "Objectivos na criação da Academia Real, de Fortificação Artilharia e Desenho, 1790". *Boletim do Arquivo Histórico Militar*, 61, 95-185.

Carvalho, Rómulo de (1955; 1956). "Portugal nas 'Philosophical Transactions', nos séculos XVII e XVIII". *Revista Filosófica* 15, 231-260; 16, 94-120.

Carvalho, Rómulo de (1978). *História do Gabinete de Física da Universidade de Coimbra desde a sua fundação (1772) até ao jubileu do professor italiano Giovanni António Dalla Bella (1790)*. Coimbra: Biblioteca Geral da Universidade de Coimbra.

Carvalho, Rómulo de (1985), *A Astronomia em Portugal no Século XVIII*. Lisboa: Biblioteca Breve.

Casaleiro, Pedro; Pires, Catarina; Filipe, Sónia; Morgado, Paulo (2006), "Memória do Laboratorio Chimico", in Mota, Paulo Gama (coord.). *Museu da Ciência Luz e Matéria. Catálogo de exposição*. Coimbra: Universidade de Coimbra, 38-61.

Casaleiro, Pedro; Rufino, Ana Cristina; Heitor, Filipa; Mota, Paulo (2011). "Redescoberta da colecção ictiológica do Século XVIII no Museu da Ciência, Universidade de Coimbra", in Fiolhais et al. (coord.), *Livro de Actas do Congresso Luso-Brasileiro de História das Ciências*, Universidade de Coimbra, 26 a 29 de Outubro de 2011. Coimbra: Imprensa da Universidade de Coimbra, 1006-1017.

Catroga, Fernando (2013). *A Geografia dos Afectos Pátrios. As Reformas Político--Administrativas (Sécs. XIX-XX)*. Coimbra: Almedina.

Cidade, Hernâni (1929). *Ensaio sobre a crise mental do século XVIII*. Coimbra: Imprensa da Universidade de Coimbra.

Costa, A. M. Amorim da (1986). "Domingos Vandelli (1730-1816) e a cerâmica Portuguesa", in *História e Desenvolvimento da Ciência em Portugal*. Lisboa: Academia das Ciências de Lisboa, 1, 353-371.

Costa, António Marinho Amorim da (1986). "A Universidade de Coimbra na Vanguarda da Química do Oxigénio", in *História e Desenvolvimento da Ciência em Portugal*. Lisboa: Academia das Ciências de Lisboa, 403-416.

Costa, A. M. Amorim da (2012). "As ciências naturais na Reforma Pombalina da Universidade. 'Estudo de rapazes não ostentação de príncipes'", in Araújo, Ana Cristina (coord.). *O Marquês de Pombal e a Universidade*, 2.ª ed., Coimbra: Imprensa da Universidade.

Costa, Maria de Fátima (2009). "Miguel Ciera: um demarcador de limites no interior sul-americano (1750-1760)", *Anais do Museu Paulista*, 17:2, 189-214.

Coxito, Amândio (1997). "A Filosofia", in *História da Universidade em Portugal*. Coimbra-Lisboa: Universidade de Coimbra-Fundação Calouste Gulbenkian, 735-761.

Craveiro, Maria de Lurdes (1990). *Manuel Alves Macomboa: arquitecto da reforma Pombalina da Universidade de Coimbra*. Coimbra: Instituto de História de Arte da Faculdade de Letras da Universidade de Coimbra.

Cruz, Guilherme Braga da (1979). "Coimbra e José Bonifácio de Andrada e Silva". *Memórias da Academia de Ciências de Lisboa*, Classe de Letras, 20, 215-276.

Cruz, Ana Lúcia Rocha Barbalho da (1999). *As viagens philosophicas como textos de auto-etnografia*. Projeto de investigação para doutoramento.

Cruz, Ana Lúcia R.Barbalho da (2004). *Verdades por mim vistas e observadas Oxalá foram fábulas sonhadas: cientistas brasileiros do setecentos, uma leitura auto--etnográfica*. Tese de doutoramento da Universidade Federal do Paraná. Curitiba: UFPR .http://hdl.handle.net/1884/10388

Cruz, Lígia (1976). "Domingos Vandelli. Alguns aspectos da sua actividade em Coimbra", *Boletim do Arquivo da Universidade de Coimbra*, 2, 67-71.

Cunha, Alexandre Mendes (2010) "Police Science and Cameralism in Portuguese Enlightened Reformism: economic ideas and the administration of the state during the second half of the 18th century", *e-Journal of Portuguese History*, 8, n.º 1, 1-11.

Curado, Silvino da Cruz (2014). "Os primeiros matemáticos formados em Coimbra e o Brasil", *Conferência Plenária Inaugural, 7.º Encontro Luso-Brasileiro de História da Matemática*, Óbidos, 15 a 19 de Outubro de 2014.

Denis, Vincent (2013/14). "L'Histoire de la police après Foucault. Un parcours historien", *Revue d'Histoire Moderne et Contemporaine*, 60-4/4 bis, 139-155.

Denys, Catherine; Marin, Brigitte; Milliot, Vincent (2009). *Réformer la police. Les mémoires policiers en Europe au XVIIIe siècle*. Rennes: Presses Universitaires de Rennes.

Dias, José Sebastião da Silva (1953). "Portugal e a Cultura Europeia: sec.s XVI a XVIII", *Biblos. Revista da Faculdade de Letras*, 28.

Dias, Maria Helena (2003). "As explorações geográficas dos finais de Setecentos e a grande aventura da Carta Geral do Reino de Portugal", *Revista da Faculdade de Letras – Geografia*, 19, 383-396.

Dias, Maria Helena (ed.) (2007). *Portugal em vésperas das Invasões Francesas. Conhecimento Geográfico & Configurações*. Lisboa: Instituto Geográfico do Exército.

Dinis, Júlio (1979). *Serões da Província*, Lisboa: Círculo de Leitores.

Domingues, Ângela (1991). *Viagens de Exploração Geográfica na Amazónia em Finais do Século XVIII: Política, Ciência e Aventura*. Funchal: Secretaria Regional do Turismo, Cultura e Emigração do Funchal.

Domingues, Ângela (2001). "Para um Melhor conhecimento dos domínios coloniais: a constituição de redes de Informação no Império português em finais de setecentos", *Revista História, Ciências, Saúde Manguinhos*, vol. VIII (suplemento), Rio de Janeiro.

Domingues, Ângela (2012). *Monarcas, ministros e cientistas: mecanismos de poder, governação e informação no Brasil Colonial*. Lisboa: Centro de História de Além-Mar.

Dunn, Richard; Higgit Rebeka (2014), *Finding Longitude: How ships, clocks and stars helped solve the longitude problem*. Greenwich: National Maritime Museum.

Eisenstadt, S. N. (2007). *Múltiplas Modernidades. Ensaios*. Lisboa: Livros Horizonte.

Elias, Norbert (2011). *A Sociedade de Corte*. Rio de Janeiro: Editora Zahar.

Felismino, David (coord.) (2014). *Saberes, Natureza e Poder. Colecções científicas da antiga Casa Real Portuguesa*. Lisboa: Museus da Universidade de Lisboa.

Ferrão, Cristina; Soares, José Paulo Monteiro (org.) (2005). *Viagem ao Brasil de Alexandre Rodrigues Ferreira – Colecção Etnográfica*. 3 Volumes. Petrópolis: Kapa Editorial.

Ferreira, Mário Clemente (2011). "Os demarcadores do Tratado de Madrid (1750) e as reformas pombalinas do ensino", *Anais do IV Simpósio Luso-Brasileiro de Cartografia Histórica Porto*, 9 a 12 de Novembro de 2011. (eventos.letras.up.pt. Acesso em 20/07/2015).

Ferreira, Martim Portugal (1998). *200 anos de Mineralogia e arte de Minas: desde a Faculdade de Filosofia (1772) até à Faculdade de Ciências e Tecnologia (1972)*. Coimbra: Faculdade de Ciências e Tecnologia da Universidade de Coimbra.

Ferreira, N. (2014). *A institucionalização do ensino da náutica em Portugal (1779--1807)*. Tese de doutoramento, Universidade de Lisboa. http://repositorio.ul.pt/handle/10451/10963

Ferro, João Pedro (1989). *Um príncipe iluminado português: D. José (1756-1788)*. Lisboa: Lúcifer Edições.

Figueiredo, Fernando B. (2011). *José Monteiro da Rocha e a actividade científica da 'Faculdade de Mathematica' e do 'Real Observatório da Universidade de Coimbra': 1772-1820*. Tese de doutoramento, Universidade de Coimbra. http://hdl.handle.net/10316/17927

Figueiredo, Fernando B. (2011a). "A Faculdade de Mathematica da Universidade de Coimbra (1772-1820): um ensaio estatístico", *Suplemento do Boletim da Sociedade Portuguesa de Matemática*, 65, 15-18

Figueiredo, Fernando B. (2013). "José Monteiro da Rocha (1734-1819)". In Zilhão, I.; Macedo, M.; Raposo, P. (eds.), *Biografias de Cientistas e Engenheiros Portugueses*. CIUHCT. http://ciuhct.org/pt/jose-monteiro-da-rocha

Figueiredo, Fernando B. (2013a). "O Observatório Astronómico (1772-1911)", in Fiolhais et al., *História da Ciência na Universidade de Coimbra 1772-1933*, Coimbra: Imprensa da Universidade de Coimbra, 43-64.

Figueiredo, Fernando B. (2014) "O método de interpolação usado nas Ephemerides Astronomicas do Observatório Astronómico da Universidade de Coimbra", in Nobre, Sergio; Bertato, F; Saraiva, L. (eds.), *Actas do 6.º Encontro Luso-Brasileiro de História da Matemática*. Natal: RN (SBHMat), 415-433.

Figueiredo, Fernando B. (2015). "From Paper to Erected Walls: The Astronomical Observatory of Coimbra: 1772–1799", in Pisano, R. (ed.). *A Bridge between Conceptual Frameworks, Sciences, Society and Technology Studies, History of Mechanism and Machine Science* 27. Dordrecht: Springer,155-178.

Figueiroa, Francisco Carneiro de (1937). *Memórias da Universidade de Coimbra*. Coimbra: Universidade de Coimbra.

Fiolhais, Carlos (2011). *Membros Portugueses da Royal Society / Portuguese Fellows of the Royal Society*. Coimbra: Imprensa da Universidade.

Folque, Filipe (1832). *Ephemerides das distancias do centro do Sol, e planetas Vénus, Marte, Júpiter e Saturno, ao centro da Lua, e dos lugares heliocêntricos, e geocêntricos destes astros para 1833*, Lisboa: Impressão Régia.

Fonseca, Álvaro Baltazar Moreira da (1996). *As demarcações marianas no Douro vinhateiro*. Porto: Instituto do Vinho do Porto (obra póstuma).

Fonseca, Fernando Taveira da (1995). *A Universidade de Coimbra (1700-1771). Estudo social e económico*. Coimbra: Por Ordem da Universidade.

Fonseca, Fernando Taveira da (1997). "Os corpos académicos e os servidores", in *História da Universidade em Portugal*. Coimbra-Lisboa: Universidade de Coimbra--Fundação Calouste Gulbenkian, 499-616.

Fonseca, Fernando Taveira da (1997) "As finanças (Universidade de Coimbra)", in *História da Universidade em Portugal*. Coimbra-Lisboa: Universidade de Coimbra--Fundação Calouste Gulbenkian, 445-485.

Fonseca, Fernando Taveira da (1997). "O saber universitário e os universitários no Ultramar", in *História da Universidade em Portugal*. Coimbra-Lisboa: Universidade de Coimbra-Fundação Calouste Gulbenkian, 1017-1040.

Fonseca, Fernando Taveira da (1999). "*Scientiae thesaurus mirabilis*: estudantes de origem brasileira na universidade de Coimbra (1601-1850)", *Revista Portuguesa de História*, 33, 527-559.

Fonseca, Fernando Taveira da (2000). "A dimensão pedagógica da Reforma de 1772. Alguns aspectos", in Ana Cristina Araújo (coord.). *O Marquês de Pombal e a Universidade*. Coimbra: Imprensa da Universidade, 43-68.

Fonseca, Fernando Taveira da (2001). "A Reforma Pombalina da Universidade: antecedentes e realizações", in *Congresso O Marquês de Pombal e a sua época*

– *Colóquio O Século XVIII e o Marquês de Pombal*, Actas. Oeiras – Pombal: Câmara Municipal de Oeiras – Câmara Municipal de Pombal, 369-379.

Fonseca, Fernando Taveira da (2007). "The social and cultural roles of the university of Coimbra (1537-1820). Some considerations", *e-Journal of Portuguese History*, vol. 5, 1.

Foucault, Michel (1994). *Dits et écrits (1954-1988)*. Paris: Gallimard.

Foucault, Michel (2004). *Sécurité, territoire, population: cours au Collège de France (1977-1978)*. Édition établie sous la direction de François Ewald et Alessandro Fontana par Michel Sennellart. Paris: Gallimard-Seuil-EHESS.

Foucault, Michel (2012). *Du gouvernement des vivants: cours au Collège de France (1979-1980)*. Paris: Gallimard-Seuil-EHESS.

Franco, Matilde Pessoa de Figueiredo Sousa (1983). *Riscos das Obras da Universidade de Coimbra, o valioso álbum da Reforma Pombalina*. Coimbra: Museu Nacional Machado de Castro.

Freire, Francisco de Castro (1872). *Memoria Historica da Faculdade de Mathematica nos cem annos decorridos desde a Reforma da Universidade em 1772 até o presente*. Coimbra: Imprensa da Universidade.

Freitas, Décio Ruivo (2000). "As ciências Físico-Matemáticas em Portugal e a Reforma Pombalina", in Ana Cristina Araújo (coord.). *O Marquês de Pombal e a Universidade*. Coimbra: Imprensa da Universidade, 193-262.

Freitas, Divaldo Gaspar de (1959). *Paulistas na Universidade de Coimbra*. Coimbra: Universidade de Coimbra.

Frijhoff, W. (1999). "Cosmopolitisme", in Vicenzo Ferrone e Daniel Roche (ed.) *Le Monde des Lumières*. Paris: Fayard, 31-40.

Gayo, Felgueiras (1938). *Nobiliário de famílias de Portugal*. Braga: Oficinas Gráficas.

Gellner, Ernest; Waterbury, John (1977). *Patrons and Clients in mediterranean Societies*. Londres: Duckworth.

Gomes, Joaquim Ferreira (1989). "Os vários Estatutos por que se regeu a Universidade Portuguesa ao longo da sua história", *Revista Portuguesa de Pedagogia*. Nova Série, 20, 3-61.

Goodman, Dena (1994). *The Republic of Letters. A Cultural History of French Enlightenment*. Ithaca: Cornell Universty.

Guerrero, Omar (1986). *Las Sciencias de la Administación en el Estado Absolutista*. Mexico: Fontamara.

Guimarães, Manuel Luiz Lima Salgado (1991). "A civilização nos trópicos: intelectuais e história do Brasil na primeira metade do século XIX", in *Universidade(s). História, Memória, Perspectivas*. Actas. Coimbra, 161-175.

Hamy, E.-T. (1908). "La mission de Geoffroy Saint-Hilaire en Espagne et en Portugal (1808). Histoire et documents", *Nouvelles Archives du Museum National d'Histoire Naturelle*, 4.ª série, t. X, 1-66.

Hansen, João Adolfo (2000). "Retórica da Agudeza", *Revista Letras Clássicas*, n.º 4, São Paulo: USP.

Herculano, Alexandre (1984). "Da Escola Politécnica e do Colégio dos Nobres". *Opúsculos*. Porto: Editorial Presença, 3, 45-81.

Hespanha, António Manuel (2004). *Guiando a Mão Invisível. Direitos, Estado e Lei no Liberalismo Monárquico Português*. Coimbra: Almedina.

Koselleck, Reinhart (2003). *Aceleración, prognosis y secularización*. Traducción, introducción y notas de Faustino Oncina Coves. Valencia: Pre-Textos.

Kury, Lorelay (2001). *Histoire naturelle et voyages scientifiques (1780-1830)*. Paris: L'Harmattan.

Kury, Lorelai (2011). "As viagens Luso-Americanas e as práticas científicas do século das Luzes", *Anais do XXVI Simpósio Nacional de História* – ANPUH. Julho de 2011, São Paulo.

Lario, Damaso de (1986). "Mécénat des Collèges Majeurs dans la formation de la bureaucratie espagnole (XIVe-XVIIe siècle)", *Revue Historique*, 558, 307-342.

Leitão, H. (2008). *A Ciência na Aula da Esfera do Colégio de Santo Antão, 1590--1759*, Lisboa: Comissariado Geral das Comemorações do V Centenário do Nascimento de S. Francisco Xavier.

Leitão, H., (2007) "Azulejos que testemunham uma tradição de ensino científico", in *Azulejos que ensinam. Catálogo da Exposição*. Coimbra: Museu Nacional Machado de Castro, Centro de Matemática da Universidade de Coimbra,16-33.

Leitão, H. (2002). "Introdução", in *Pedro Nunes, 1502-1578: Novas terras, novos mares e o que mays he: novo ceo e novas estrelas. Catálogo bibliográfico sobre Pedro Nunes*. Lisboa: Biblioteca Nacional, 15-28.

Leite, Serafim (1938-1950). *História da Companhia de Jesus no Brasil*, 10 vols. Lisboa-Rio de Janeiro: Livraria Portugália-Civilização Brasileira.

"Longitud Act – 300 anos" (2014), *Gazeta de Matemática*, 173, ano LXXV, Lisboa: Sociedade Portuguesa de Matemática.

Lourenço, Marta (coord.) (2016). *A Universidade de Lisboa: Museus, Coleções e Património*. Lisboa: Imprensa da Universidade de Lisboa

Luckhurst, Gerald, (2011). "Gerard de Visme and the introduction of the English landscape garden to Portugal (1782- 1793), *Revista de Estudos Anglo-portugueses*, 20, 127-160.

Macedo, Marta Coelho de (2009). *Projectar e Construir a Nação: engenheiros e território em Portugal (1837-1893)*. Coimbra: tese de doutoramento, Universidade de Coimbra. http://hdl.handle.net/10316/14554

Madeira, J. A. (1933). *Missão de estudo nos observatórios astronómicos de Greenwich e Paris: relatório apresentado à Junta de Educação Nacional*. Coimbra: Faculdade de Ciências da Universidade de Coimbra.

Maffei, Domenico; De Ridder-Symoens, Hilde (coord.) (1991). *I collegi universitari in Europa fra il XIV e il XVIII secolo*. Milão: Giuffrè Editore.

Magalhães, Joaquim Romero (1998). "A construção do espaço brasileiro", in *História da expansão portuguesa*. Dir. de Francisco Bethencourt e Kirti Chauduri. Lisboa: Círculo de Leitores, vol. II, 28-64.

Marcos de Diós, Angel (1976). "Proyección cultural de la universidade de Salamanca en Portugal durante el reinado de los Felipes", *Arquivos do Centro Cultural Português*, X, 135-169.

Martins, Carlos Moura; Figueiredo, Fernando B. (2008). "O Observatório Astronómico da Universidade de Coimbra, 1772-1799", *Rua Larga*, Universidade de Coimbra, 21, 57-61.

Martins, Carlos Henriques de Moura Rodrigues (2014). *O Programa de Obras Públicas para o Território de Portugal Continental, 1789-1809. Intenção Política e Razão Técnica – O Porto do Douro e a Cidade do Porto*, 2 vols. Tese de Doutoramento, Universidade de Coimbra.

Martins, Décio R. (1992). *Aspectos da Cultura Científica Portuguesa até 1772*. Tese de doutoramento. Universidade de Coimbra, 1992.

Martins, Décio R. (2000). "As Ciências Físico-Matemáticas em Portugal e a Reforma Pombalina", in Araújo, Ana Cristina (ed.). *O Marquês de Pombal e a Universidade*. Coimbra: Imprensa da Universidade, 193-262.

Martins, Décio Ruivo (2013), "A Faculdade de Filosofia Natural (1772-1911)", in Fiolhais et al., *História da Ciência na Universidade de Coimbra 1772-1933*. Coimbra: Imprensa da Universidade de Coimbra, 65-116.

Mattoso, José (dir.) (1998). História de Portugal. *O Antigo Regime* (coord. A. M. Hespanha), vol. 4. Lisboa: Editorial Estampa.

Mendes, Humberto G. (1965). "Francisco António de Ciera, renovador da cartografia portuguesa". *Geographica – Revista da Sociedade de Geografia de Lisboa*, 3, 11--25.

Mendes, Humberto Gabriel (1978). "A abertura e exploração da Mina de Azougue de Coina, no final do século XVIII, em duas plantas da Mapoteca do Instituto Geográfico e Cadastral. Um engenheiro alemão, Conrado Henrique Niemeyer ao serviço de Portugal", *Revista da Universidade de Coimbra*, 26, 199-234.

Mendonça, Marcos Carneiro de (1933). *O Intendente Camara. Manoel Ferreira da Camara Bethencourt e Sá, Intendente Geral das Minas e dos Diamantes, 1764--1835*. Rio de Janeiro: Imprensa Nacional.

Morais, Francisco (1949). "Estudantes da universidade de Coimbra nascidos no Brasil", *Brasília*, suplemento ao vol. *IV*, Coimbra, 1949.

Moreira, Luís Miguel (2012). *Cartografia, Geografia e Poder: o processo de construção da imagem cartográfica de Portugal, na segunda metade do século XVIII*. Tese de doutoramento. Braga: Universidade do Minho. http://hdl.handle.net/1822/24567

Moura, Sílvia (2008). *De Vandelli para Lineu. De Lineu para Vandelli. Correspondência entre Naturalistas*. Rio de Janeiro: Dantes Editora.

Museu da Ciência da Universidade de Coimbra – sítio da internet (2017): http://www.museudaciencia.org/ (acedido a 26 de Fevereiro de 2017).

Napoli, Paolo (2003). *Naissance de la police moderne. Pouvoir, normes, société*. Paris: Éditions la Découverte.

Nobre, João Paulo da Silva Gil (1997). *Prof. Dr. Mário Augusto da Silva – biografia*. Coimbra: http://nautilus.fis.uc.pt/museu/msilva/biografia.html (acedido a 15 de fevereiro de 2016).

Nunes, Maria de Fátima (2001). *Imprensa Periódica Científica (1772-1852). Leituras de "Sciencia Agricola" em Portugal*. Lisboa: Estar Editora.

Oliveira, António de (1971-1972). *A vida económica e social de Coimbra*. Coimbra: Instituto de Estudos Históricos Doutor António de Vasconcelos.

Oliveira, Cristóvão José Pinto Correia (1996). *O saber e o poder: O Colégio Real de S. Pedro da Universidade de Coimbra (1700-1834)*. Dissertação de Mestrado. Coimbra: Faculdade de Letras.

Outran, Dourinda (1999). *O iluminismo*. Lisboa: Temas e Debates.

Papavero, Nelson et al. (2010). "Os Escritos de Giovanni Angelo Brunelli, astrônomo da Comissão Demarcadora de Limites portuguesa (1753-1761), sobre a Amazônia brasileira", *Boletim do Museu Paraense Emilio Goeldi*, V. 5, Belém, 493-533 (Scielo. br: último acesso 23/03/2016).

Pataca, Ermelinda Moutinho (2006). *Terra, Água e Ar nas Viagens Científicas Portuguesas (1755-1808)*. Tese de doutoramento. Campinas: UNICAMP (Instituto de Geociências).

Pato, António Vaz (1999). "A primeira sinalização rodoviária moderna em Portugal: os Marcos do Conde de Valadares (1788). Um património a preservar", in *1.º Encontro de Estradas e Arqueologia: actas*. Lisboa: Junta Autónoma de Estradas, Direcção de Serviços de Projectos, 63-76.

Pereira, J. M. Malhão (2007). "Um manuscrito de cerca de 1767, do P. José Monteiro da Rocha, S.J. com uma solução matemática para a obtenção da longitude pelas distâncias lunares", *Cuadernos de Estudios Borjanos*, L-LI (2007-08) 339-94.

Pereira, Magnus Roberto de Mello (1999). "Brasileiros ao serviço do império. A África vista por naturais do Brasil, no século XVIII", *Revista Portuguesa de História*, 33, 153-190.

Pereira, Magnus R. de Mello (2002). "Um jovem naturalista num ninho de cobras: a trajetória de João da Silva Feijó em Cabo Verde, em finais do século XVIII". *Revista História. Questões & Debates*, 36, Curitiba/UFPR, 29-60.

Picon, Antoine (1992). *L'invention de l'Ingénieur Moderne. L'École des Ponts et Chaussées, 1747-1851*. Paris: Presses de L'École Nationale des Ponts et Chaussées.

Pinna, Giovanni (1997). *Fondamenti teorici per un museo di storia naturale*. Milão: Jaka Book.

Pinto, Abílio Augusto da Fonseca (1882-83). "Discurso [por Manuel da Fonseca Pinto]", *O Instituto: jornal scientifico e litterario*. XXX, 376-384

Pinto, H. (2012). *A Matemática na Academia Politécnica do Porto*. Tese de doutoramento. Universidade de Lisboa.

Pinto, José Manuel Soares; Marques, Júlio (1999). *Catálogo da Galeria de Minerais José Bonifácio d'Andrade e Silva*. Coimbra: Museu Mineralógico e Geológico, Faculdade de Ciências e Tecnologia da Universidade de Coimbra.

Pires, Catarina Pereira, (2006). *Laboratório Chimico da Universidade de Coimbra: interpretação histórica de um espaço de ensino e divulgação da ciência*. Dissertação de Mestrado. Aveiro: Universidade de Aveiro.

Pires, Catarina; Pereira, Gilberto (2010). "O Museu da Ciência da Universidade de Coimbra: Valorização de um património científico secular", in Marcus Granato e Marta C. Lourenço (ed.). *Coleções Científicas Luso-Brasileiras: Património a ser descoberto*. Rio de Janeiro: MAST/MCT, 185-210.

Pitt-Rivers, John (1963). *Mediterranean Countrymen*. Paris: Mouton.

Prata, Manuel Alberto Carvalho (1989). *Ciência e Sociedade. A Faculdade de Filosofia no período pombalino e pós-pombalino (1772-1820)*. Dissertação de mestrado, Guarda.

Prata, Manuel Alberto Carvalho (1991). "Ciência e Sociedade. A Faculdade de Filosofia no período Pombalino e pós-Pombalino (1772-1780)", in *Universidade(s). História. Memória. Perspectivas, Actas do Congresso "História da Universidade"*. Coimbra, 1, 195-214

Prazeres, Tiago Miguel Castanho (2016). *O Forte de Nossa Senhora da Graça. Arte e Regra do Desenho*. Dissertação de Mestrado Integrado em Arquitectura, FCTUC. Coimbra.

Raminelli, Ronald (2001). "Do Conhecimento Físico e Moral dos Povos", *História, Ciências, Saúde – Manguinhos*. Rio de Janeiro, VIII, 968-992.

Ramos, Luís Oliveira (2001). "Sobre os ilustrados da Academia de Coimbra", in *Estudos de Homenagem a João Francisco Marques*. Porto: Universidade do Porto, 2001, 2, 311-326.

Ribeiro, José Silvestre (1871-1914), *Historia dos estabelecimentos scientificos litterarios e artisticos de Portugal nos successsivos reinados da monarchia*, 19 volumes. Lisboa: Academia Real das Sciências.

Ribeiro, Rui. coord. (2000). *Gabinete de História Natural – Revivências*. Coimbra: Museu de História Natural, Faculdade de Ciências e Tecnologia da Universidade de Coimbra.

Roche, Daniel (1988). *Les Républicains des Lettres. Gens de culture et Lumières au XVIIIe siècle*. Paris: Fayard.

Rodrigues, Manuel Augusto (1990). *A Universidade de Coimbra e os seus Reitores. Para uma história da instituição*. Coimbra: Arquivo da Universidade.

Ruivo, Conceição (introd.) (1997). *O Engenho e a Arte 19*. Lisboa/Coimbra: Fundação Calouste Gulbenkian. Colecção de Instrumentos do Real Gabinete de Física.

Salazar, António de Oliveira (1937). *Discursos e Notas Políticas*, II: 1935-1937. Coimbra: Coimbra Editora.

Sanches, António Nunes Ribeiro (1959). "Método para aprender e estudar a Medicina"; "Cartas sobre a educação da mocidade". *Obras*. Coimbra: Por Ordem da Universidade.

Santos, J. J. Carvalhão (1991). "Rotina e renovação na faculdade de Medicina: as oposições de 1739", in *Universidade(s). História, Memória, Perspectivas*. Actas. Coimbra, 1, 131-150.

Saraiva, Luís; Figueiredo, Fernando B. (2013). "As Ciências Exactas e Aplicadas nos Concursos da Academia das Ciências de Lisboa (1779-1820): um proto estudo estatístico". *Suplemento do Boletim da Sociedade Portuguesa de Matemática*, 69, 76-79.

Saraiva, Luis. (2014). "A tradução de manuais de matemática nos inícios da Academia Real Militar do Rio de Janeiro", in Nobre, Sergio; Bertato, F.; Saraiva, L. (eds.). *Actas do 6.º Encontro Luso-Brasileiro de História da Matemática*. Natal: RN (SBHMat), 93-137.

Schemm-Gregory, Mena; Henriques, Maria Helena (2013). *Os Braquiópodes da Coleção Krantz do Museu da Ciência da Universidade de Coimbra*. Coimbra: Imprensa da Universidade.

Schubring, Gert (1997) *Analysis of Historical textbooks in Mathematics*. Rio de Janeiro: PUC

Sepúlveda, Christovam Ayres de Magalhães (1927). *Para a História da Academia das Sciências de Lisboa*. Coimbra: Imprensa da Universidade, 12.

Sepúlveda, Cristóvão Aires de Magalhães (1902-1932). *História Orgânica e Política do Exército Português. Provas*. Lisboa: Imprensa Nacional; Coimbra: Imprensa da Universidade, 17 vols.

Serrão, Joel (dir.) (1981-2000). *Dicionário de História de Portugal*. 6 vols. Porto: Livraria Figueirinhas.

Shapin, Steven (2000). *La revolución científica: una interpretación alternativa*. Barcelona: Paidós.

Silva, Ana Cristina Nogueira da (1998). *O Modelo Espacial do Estado Moderno; reorganização territorial em Portugal nos finais do Antigo Regime*. Lisboa: Editorial Estampa.

Silva, Clarete Paranhos da (2002). *O desvendar do grande livro da natureza: um estudo da obra do mineralogista José Vieira Couto, 1798-1805*. Campinas: UNICAMP.

Silva, José Alberto Teixeira Rebelo da (2015). *A Academia Real das Ciências de Lisboa (1779-1834): ciência e hibridismo numa periferia europeia*. Tese de doutoramento, Universidade de Lisboa. http://repositorio.ul.pt/handle/10451/17942

Silva, Maria Beatriz Nizza da Silva (1999). *A cultura luso-brasileira. Da reforma da Universidade à independência do Brasil*. Lisboa: Editorial Estampa.

Simões, Ana; Carneiro, Ana; Diogo, Maria Paula (1999), "Constructing Knowledge: 18th century Portugal and the new sciences. The Sciences in the European Periphery during the Enlightenment", *Archimedes*, 2, 1-40.

Simões, Ana; Diogo, Maria Paula; Carneiro, Ana (2000). "Imagens de Portugal setecentista, Textos de estrangeirados e Viajantes", *Penélope*, 22, 73-92.

Simões, Ana; Diogo Maria Paula; Carneiro, Ana (2006). *Cidadão do Mundo. Uma biografia Científica do Abade Correia da Serra*. Porto: Porto Editora.

Simões, Carlota; Casaleiro, Pedro; Mota, Paulo Gama (2013), "O Museu da Ciência: uma colecção científica do Século das Luzes", in Fiolhais et al. *História da Ciência na Universidade de Coimbra 1772-1933*. Coimbra: Imprensa da Universidade de Coimbra, 117-128.

Simon, J. William (1983). *Scientific expeditions in the Portuguese overseas territories (1783-1808) and the role of Lisbon in the intellectual-scientific community of the eighteenth century*. Lisboa: Instituto de Investigação Científica Tropical.

Sousa, Fernando de (1995). *História da Estatística em Portugal*. Lisboa: Instituto Nacional de Estatística.

Spary, Emma C. (1999). "The Nature of Enlightenment", in W. Clark; J. Golinski; S. Schaffer (eds.), *The Sciences in Enlightened Europe*. Chicago & London: University of Chicago Press.

Subtil, José Manuel (2011). *O Desembargo do Paço: 1750-1833*. Lisboa: EDIUAL.

Tirapicos, Luis (2010). *O Telescópio Astronómico em Portugal no século XVIII*. Dissertação de mestrado. Universidade de Lisboa.

Tirapicos Luis (2016). "Astronomy and Diplomacy in the Court of King João V of Portugal". *Cahiers François Viète (a numéro spécial sur l'Histoire de l'Astronomie au Portugal)*, Série II, 8-9.

Valadares, Virgínia Trindade (2004). *Elites Mineiras Setecentistas, conjugação de dois mundos*. Lisboa: Edições Colibri.

Van Praët, Michel; Mota, Paulo Gama; Byrne, Gonçalo; Pita, João Rui (2006). "Contexto e perspectivas da criação do Museu da Ciência em Coimbra", in Mota, Paulo Gama (coord.). *Museu da Ciência Luz e Matéria. Catálogo de exposição*. Coimbra: Universidade de Coimbra, 20-25.

Varela, Alex Gonçalves (2006). "O processo de formação, especialização e profissionalização do ilustrado Manuel Ferreira da Câmara em sua "fase européia" (1783-1800)", *Revista de História*. São Paulo, 155, 223-260.

Vargues, Isabel Nobre (1999). "Apresentação", in *De Tiradentes às Escadas de Minerva. Exposição biográfica e bibliográfica*. Coimbra: Faculdade de Direito.

Vasconcelos, António (1941). *Escritos Vários*. Coimbra: Arquivo da Universidade de Coimbra, vol. 2.

Vasconcelos, António (1987). "Os colégios universitários de Coimbra (fundados de 1539 a 1779)". *Escritos Vários*. Coimbra: Arquivo da Universidade de Coimbra, 1, 155-295, 2.ª ed.

Vasconcelos, Luís Adolfo P. Walter de (1970). *Aspectos do fomento no reinado de D. Maria I. Obras do Ribatejo e de Estradas que correram pelo Terreiro Público de Lisboa*. Tese de licenciatura. Coimbra: Faculdade de Letras da Universidade de Coimbra.

Vaz, Francisco António Lourenço (2002). *Instrução e Economia. As ideias económicas no discurso da ilustração portuguesa (1746-1820)*. Lisboa: Edições Colibri.

Viana, Hélio (1949). *História da viação brasileira*. Rio de Janeiro: Biblioteca do Exército.

Villas-Boas, Custódio Gomes (1797). "Memória acerca da Latitude, e Longitude de Lisboa, e exposição das Observações Astronómicas por onde ellas se determinarão", *Memórias da Academia Real das Sciencias de Lisboa*, t. I, 305-325.

Villas-Boas, Custódio Gomes; Ciera, Francisco (1804). *Atlas Celeste, arranjado por Flamsteed, publicado por J. Fortin, Correcto, e Aumentado por Lalande, e Mechain*. Lisboa: Academia Real das Sciencias de Lisboa.

Viterbo, Sousa (1899-1922). *Diccionário Histórico e Documental dos Arquitectos, Engenheiros e Construtores Portugueses*. Lisboa: Imprensa Nacional, 3 vols.

Xavier, Ângela B.; Hespanha, A. M. (2008). "As Redes Clientelares". In Mattoso, José (dir.). *História de Portugal, O Antigo Regime*. Lisboa: Estampa 339-349.

Zuquete, Afonso Martins (dir.) (1984). *Nobreza de Portugal e do Brasil. Livro I*. Lisboa: Zairol.

ÍNDICE TOPONÍMICO E ANTROPONÍMICO

Abreu, José M. de: 288-290, 302
Academia das Ciências → Academia Real das Ciências de Lisboa
Academia de Fortificação → Academia Real de Fortificação, Artilharia e Desenho
Academia dos Guardas-Marinhas → Real Academia dos Guardas Marinhas
ACADEMIA DA MARINHA, Rio de Janeiro, Brasil: 79
ACADEMIA DA MARINHA E COMÉRCIO, Porto: 233, 251, 274, 302
ACADEMIA REAL DA HISTÓRIA PORTUGUESA, Lisboa: 241
ACADEMIA REAL DE FORTIFICAÇÃO, ARTILHARIA E DESENHO, Lisboa: 48, 233, 243, 251, 265, 271-276, 280-281, 290, 302, 311 (*vd.* António José Moreira, António Teixeira Rebelo, Francisco Adolfo Varnhagen, José António da Rosa, Pedro Joaquim Xavier, Rodrigo de Sousa Coutinho)
ACADEMIA REAL DA MARINHA, Lisboa: 48, 203, 224, 232-233, 235, 238, 241, 243, 247-249, 251, 261, 263, 273, 276, 278, 300, 302, 311 (*vd.* António Teixeira Rebelo, Francisco Adolfo Varnhagen, Luís Máximo Jorge de Bellegarde, Manuel do Espírito Santo Limpo, Manuel Pedro de Melo)
ACADEMIA REAL DAS CIÊNCIAS DE LISBOA (Academia das Ciências): 40, 102-104, 141, 171, 173, 175-179, 181-185, 187-189, 219, 232-234, 236--238, 241-243, 248-252, 254--258, 260-262, 264-270, 278, 292, 324, 329 (*vd.* António Pereira de Figueiredo, António Rolim de Almeida Tavares, Bartolomeu da Costa, Custódio

Gomes Vilas-Boas, Domingos Vandelli, duque de Lafões, Estêvão Dias Cabral, Fernando Telles da Silva, Francisco Adolfo Varnhagen, Gonçalo Xavier de Alcáçova Carneiro, Charles Marie Damoiseau de Monfort, João António Dalla Bella, João Faustino, João de Loureiro, Joaquim de Foios, José António de Sá, José Bonifácio de Andrada e Silva, José Diogo Mascarenhas Neto, José Francisco Correia da Serra, José Joaquim Soares de Barros, José Monteiro da Rocha, Luís Pinto de Sousa Coutinho, Manuel Dias Baptista, Manuel Henriques de Paiva, Maria I, marquês de Alorna, Miguel Franzini, Miguel Lúcio de Portugal e Castro, Pedro José Fonseca, da Teodoro de Almeida, principal Mascarenhas, Vicente Ferrer da Rocha, Vicente José Coelho Seabra da Silva Teles)

ADAMS, George, construtor inglês de instrumentos científicos: 221, 331-332

ADET, [Pierre Auguste, químico francês]: 99

ÁFRICA: 44, 72, 194, 202, 208, 234 (*vd.* Angola, Cabo Verde, Guiné, Marrocos, Moçambique, S. Tomé)

AGO, Renata:145

AGUIAR, Joaquim António de, lente da universidade de Coimbra, ministro: 49

Aires, Cristóvão: 115, 233, 248

AJUDA, palácio da: 153-154; —, Jardim Botânico da: 97, 157, 170, 188; —, Real Museu da: 157, 170, 323-325, 329 (*vd.* Domingos Vandelli, José I, Júlio Mattiazzi)

ALAGOA, Pernambuco, Brasil: 84

ALAGOAS, Brasil: 76

Albuquerque, Luís de: 96, 195, 232

—, Luís da Silva Mouzinho de, engenheiro, ministro: 311

—, Brites de, casada com Duarte Coelho Pereira: 53

—, Duarte Coelho d', filho de Duarte Coelho Pereira: 53

ALCALÁ, universidade de, Espanha: 27

ALCÂNTARA, Maranhão, Brasil: 82

—, rio, Lisboa: 273

ALCOBAÇA, mosteiro de: 193

ALCÔRREGO, rio: 259 (*vd.* rio Tejo)

ALEMANHA (Prússia): 46, 78, 106, 108 (*vd.* Berlim, Brendel, Burckhardt, casa de Hanôver, Freiburg, Gabriel Biel, Georg Heinrich Zincke, Gotha, Hassen, Henrich Friderich Link, Herschel, Krantz, Jacob Chrysostomus Praetorius, Jauch-Stein, Johann Heinrich Gottlob von Justi, Magdeburgo, Mayer, Prússia, rio Elba, Saxónia, Werner, Wilhelm zu Schaumburg-Lippe, von Zach)

ALEMBERT, [Jean] d', astrónomo, matemático francês: 191, 204, 213, 222, 295

ALENTEJO: 173, 259 (*vd.* Avis, Beja, Elvas, Estremoz, Évora, Fronteira, Joaquim José Torres Salgueiro, José Francisco Correia da Serra, Monforte, Mora, rio Guadiana, rio Sorraia, Serpa, serra do Bispo)

ALGARVE: 241, 264 (*vd.* cabo de S. Vicente, João António Barahona Fragoso, Lagos, Tavira)

Almeida, Joana Estorninho de: 31, 194, 220

—, Francisco José de Lacerda e, astrónomo, matemático: 43-44, 241, 249

—, Lopo de, cónego da Sé de Lisboa: 18

—, Teodoro de, oratoriano: 142, 176-178

ALMEIRIM, Ribatejo: 25

ALORNA, marquês de (João de Almeida Portugal): 176-178 (*vd.* marquês de Pombal, Academia Real das Ciências de Lisboa)

ALTO DOURO, distrito: 250, 270, 306 (*vd.* Barca de Alva, Douro)

ÁLVARES, Baltasar, jesuíta, professor no Colégio das Artes: 26

Amaral, A. R. et al.: 330

—, R. : 271, 320, 327

—, Manuel: 271, 277

AMARANTE, Carlos Luís Ferreira da Cruz, arquitecto, engenheiro: 280, 303, 306

AMAZONAS, rio, Brasil: 148

AMAZÓNIA, Brasil: 249, 324

AMÉRICA DO SUL: 144, 145, 197, 223, 234 (*vd.* Brasil, Buenos Aires, Caiena, Rio da Prata, Sacramento, Peru)

ANDRADA, José Ricardo da Costa Aguiar de, sobrinho de José Bonifácio de Andrada e Silva, deputado brasileiro: 46

ANDRADE, Joaquim Maria de, lente da universidade de Coimbra, astrónomo: 228

Andrewes, William J. H.: 199
ANGEJA, marquês de (Pedro José de Noronha Camões de Albuquerque Moniz e Sousa), mordomo-mor: 151, 154, 157, 167, 168, 170 (*vd.* José I)
ANGOLA: 43, 44, 249, 330 (*vd.* António Pires da Silva Pontes Leme, Joaquim José da Silva, Portugal)
Antonil, André João: 71, 73
ANTONI, Alessandro Papacino d', militar italiano: 275
António Pires da Silva Pontes → António Pires da Silva Pontes Leme
ANTÓNIO PEREIRA, arraial, Mariana, Minas Gerais, Brasil: 72, 83
ANTUNES, Carlos, arquitecto, professor da Universidade de Coimbra: 316
—, *Ermelinda:* 323
AQUINO, S. Tomás de: 16
AQUIRÁS, Ceará, Brasil: 77
ARACATI, Ceará, Brasil: 82
ARANHA, Francisco Xavier do Rego, desembargador: 114, 116
ARAÚJO, Ana Cristina: 11, 87-88, 96, 103, 162, 169, 247, 314
Areia, M. L. R..: 324
ARISTÓTELES: 26

Arnason, J. P.: 90
ÁSIA (Oriente): 70, 202, 208, 234 (*vd.* China, Conchinchina, Índia)
ATLÂNTICO, oceano: 34, 40, 48, 70, 150, 203
Auffdiener, José: 271, 280
ÁUSTRIA: 108, 172, 293 (*vd.* Bürg, Viena)
AUTEROCHE, J.-B. Chappe d', astrónomo : 199
AUZOUX, casa de modelos: 327
AVEIRO, barra de, comarca de: 208, 289, 295, 307
AVICENA, filósofo: 16
ÁVILA, Espanha: 27
AVIS, Alentejo: 259 (*vd.* Ervedal)
AZEDO, Matias José Dias, tenente-general: 280-281
AZEITÃO, Setúbal: 267-268
AZEVEDO, António de Araújo de, [conde da Barca], ministro dos Negócios Estrangeiros e da Guerra: 294, 297

BACON, [Francis, filósofo, cientista inglês]: 195
Bahia → Baía
BAÍA (Bahia), 63-69, 72-74, 79, 81 (*vd.* Alexandre Rodrigues Ferreira, Cachoeira, Cairu, Cotinguiba, Iguape, Ilhéus, Itapagipe, Itapicuru, Jacobina,

Jaguaripe, Manuel Galvão da Silva, Manuel Henriques de Paiva, Maragogipe, Monforte, Muritiba, Nazaré, Porto Seguro, Rio das Contas, Rio Fundo, Salvador, Santa Ana do Camisão, Santo Amaro, Santo Amaro da Purificação, Santo António de Vila Nova, S. Domingos de Sabará, S. Félix, S. Francisco, Valença, Vila Nova de Boipeba)

—, Escola de Anatomia e de Cirurgia da: 40, 51, 75

—, Colégio Médico-Cirúrgico da: 99

BAILLY, [Jean Sylvain], astrónomo: 223

BAIXA CALIFÓRNIA, México: 199

BALBI, [Adriano], geógrafo italiano: 221-222, 242, 254, 283, 299

Baldini, Ugo: 193

BÁLTICO, mar: 203

BANANEIRAS, Pernambuco, Brasil: 84

BANKS, Joseph, naturalista inglês: 156, 181

Baptista, Maria Teresa A. M.: 323

—, Manuel Dias, naturalista: 256

BARBACENA, visconde de (Luís António Furtado de Mendonça e Faro): 45, 102, 115, 166, 169, 175-176, 178, 179-183, 185, 233, 236, 248 (*vd.* Domingos Vandelli, Academia Real das Ciências de Lisboa)

Barata, Carlos: 330

BARBOSA, António Soares, lente da universidade de Coimbra: 176, 178

BARCA DE ALVA: 250, 270 (*vd.* rio Douro)

BARJONA, Manuel José, lente da Universidade de Coimbra: 328

BARRA DO RIO GRANDE, Pernambuco, Brasil: 84

BARRA DO RIO DAS VELHAS, Minas Gerais, Brasil: 72

BARRADAS, Luís António da Costa, naturalista: 44

BARROS, José Joaquim Soares de, astrónomo: 176, 198, 204

Beira → Beiras

BEIRAS (Beira), Portugal: 17, 304 (*vd.* Coimbra, Figueira da Foz)

BEJA, Alentejo: 173 (*vd.* Serpa)

BELÉM, Pará, Brasil: 41, 76, 79, 84 (*vd.* Alexandre de Gusmão, Seminário de Nossa Senhora das Missões)

BÉLGICA: 46, 297

BÉLIDOR, [Bernard Forest de], engenheiro 295

BELLEGARDE, Luís Máximo Jorge de, lente da Academia Real de Marinha: 276
BENAVENTE, Ribatejo: 259 (*vd.* Samora Correia)
Bennett, J. A.: 192
BERLIM, Alemanha: 191, 197, 217, 233
BERNA, (Berne), Suíça: 114 (*vd.* Bernoulli, Berthoud, Bertrand)
Berne → Berna
BERNOULLI, Daniel, [médico suíço]: 295
BERTHOUD, [Ferdinand ou Louis, construtor de instrumentos suíço]: 223,
—, [Louis, construtor de instrumentos suíço]: 332-333
BERTRAND, [Jean, naturalista suíço]: 114
BÉZOUT, Étienne, matemático francês: 213, 214, 222
Biagiolli, Mario: 146, 156, 158
BIBLIOTECA NACIONAL DE PORTUGAL, Lisboa: 315
BIBLIOTECA REAL, Rio de Janeiro, Brasil: 79
BIÈVRE, rio, Paris, França: 260
BIOT, [Jean-Baptiste], astrónomo: 214
BIEL, Gabriel, filósofo alemão: 16

BIRD, [John], astrónomo inglês: 223
BISCAIA, Espanha: 293
BISPO, serra do, Alentejo: 260
BLANC, Francisco Assis, engenheiro: 304
BLONDEL, [Jean-François], arquitecto francês: 258
Bloor, David: 141
BLUTEAU, Rafael, lexicógrafo francês: 148
BOÉMIA: 46, 293
BOERHAAVE, [Herman], médico holandês: 29
Boistel, Guy: 201
BOLONHA, Itália: 145, 148
Borda, J.-C. de: 201, 223, 235, 239
BORDA DO CAMPO, Minas Gerais, Brasil: 82
BORGONHA, canal de, França: 260
Boschi, Caio: 70, 166, 169, 179, 189
BOSSUT, [Charles, matemático francês]: 214, 295
Bots, Hans: 88
BOUGAINVILLE, Louis Antoine de, explorador francês: 240
BOUGUER, [Pierre], astrónomo francês: 223
BOUVARD, [Alexis], astrónomo francês: 231

BOYLE, Robert, cientista anglo-irlandês: 173
BRADLEY, James, astrónomo inglês: 223
BRAGA, Portugal: 25, 74
—, Miguel de Alvarenga, estudante Universidade de Coimbra: 115
BRAGANÇA, casa real de: 157, 180, 285 (*vd.* Catarina de Bragança, Francisco de Bragança, José I, Maria I, Maria Bárbara, Miguel)
—, Catarina de, infanta de Portugal: 25
—, Francisco de, infante de Portugal: 15
Brandão, Mário: 18
Brás, Emanuel: 316, 317
BRASIL (Brazil): 34, 40, 44-45, 47-49, 51-54, 57-59, 69-73, 76, 79, 81, 93, 98, 115, 143, 148, 154, 167-168, 179, 182, 184-185, 202-203, 208, 223, 235, 238-241, 249, 257, 289, 294, 323-324, 327, 329-330 (*vd.* Alagoas, Alexandre Rodrigues Ferreira, Amazonas, Amazónia, Baía, Baltazar Silva Lisboa, Ceará, Espírito Santo, Francisco de Melo Franco, Garcia Rodrigues Pais, Goiás, Hipólito José da Costa Pereira, João VI, João Ângelo Brunelli, João Ferreira de Oliveira Bueno, Joaquim Veloso de Miranda, José Correia Picanço, José Correia Pacheco e Silva, José Feliciano Fernandes Pinheiro, José Silva Lisboa, Jurupixuna, Luís de Almeida Portugal Soares de Alarcão d'Eça e Melo Silva Mascarenhas, Luís Pinto de Sousa Coutinho, Manuel Aires do Casal, Maranhão, Maria I, Mato Grosso, Miguel António Ciera, Minas Gerais, Pará, Paraíba, Paraíba do Norte, Pernambuco, Piauí, Rio Grande do Norte, Rio Grande do Sul, Rio de Janeiro, capitania do Rio Negro, rio Paraguai, Rio da Prata, Sabará, Sacramento, Santa Catarina, S. Paulo, Sergipe d'El Rei)
Brazil → Brasil
BRENDEL, casa de modelos alemã: 327
Brigola, João Carlos: 102, 103, 139, 144, 163, 184, 208, 317, 323
BROTERO, Félix de Avelar, naturalista, lente da Universidade

de Coimbra: 41, 139, 188, 288, 325 (*vd.* Domingos Vandelli)
BRUNELLI, Giovanni Angelo, matemático italiano: 143, 148, 211
BUENO, João Ferreira de Oliveira, político brasileiro: 47
BUENOS AIRES, Argentina: 240
BURCKHARDT, [Johann Karl, astrónomo franco-alemão]: 238
BÜRG, [Johann Tobias, astrónomo austríaco]: 222, 231
Byrne, Gonçalo: 317

CABO CARVOEIRO, Portugal: 286
CABO ESPICHEL, Portugal: 286
CABO FRIO, Rio de Janeiro, Brasil: 84
CABO VERDE: 43, 166, 249 (*vd.* Joaquim José da Silva, João da Silva Feijó)
CABRAL, Estêvão Dias, [jesuíta, matemático]: 269
CACHÃO DA VALEIRA, rio Douro: 250, 270 (*vd.* Alto Douro)
CACHOEIRA, Baía, Brasil: 81
CACHOEIRA DO RIO ARARI, Pará, Brasil: 84
CÁDIZ, Espanha: 222
CAETÉ, Minas Gerais: 82 (*vd.* Vila Nova da Rainha)
CAIENA [Cayenne, Guiana Francesa]: 41

CAIRU, Baía, Brasil: 81
CALADO, Diogo de Morais, estudante da Universidade de Coimbra: 115
—, Justiniano de Morais, estudante Universidade de Coimbra: 115
CALDAS, António Pereira de Sousa, estudante da Universidade de Coimbra: 115
Callapez, Pedro: 327
CÂMARA, Manuel Arruda da, naturalista: 42
—, Manuel Ferreira da: 257, 269, 294
CAMPANHA DE RIO VERDE, Mariana, Minas Gerais, Brasil: 83
CAMPO LARGO, Pernambuco, Brasil: 84
CAMPO MAIOR, Maranhão: 82
CAMPOMANES, [Pedro Rodríguez de] ministro espanhol: 113
CAMPOS, Manuel, astrónomo: 197
—, Rio de Janeiro, Brasil: 65, 66, 84
CAMPOS DE GOITACAZES, Rio de Janeiro, Brasil: 84
CAPASSI, Domenico, jesuíta, astrónomo ialiano: 197
CARBONE, Giovanni Baptista, jesuíta, astrónomo italiano: 29, 197, 240

Cardoso, José Luís: 91, 98, 154, 175
—, *Walter:* 52
CARIJÓS, Minas Gerais, Brasil: 82
CARLOS II, rei de Inglaterra: 217
Carneiro, Ana: 88
—, *Diogo:* 142, 172
— *et al.:* 196
—, Gonçalo Xavier de Alcáçova: 176
Carolino, L. Miguel: 215
Carvalho, Flávio Rey de: 205,
—, *Joaquim Augusto Simões de:* 288-289
—, Joaquim Peito de, engenheiro: 267
—, José Simões de, astrónomo, matemático: 249
—, Luís Gomes de, engenheiro: 280, 308-309
—, *Manuel Jorge Pereira de:* 275,
—, *Rómulo de:* 172, 193, 197, 322
CARY, W[illiam], astrónomo inglês: 221
CASA BRANCA, Mariana, Minas Gerais: 83
CASA DA MOEDA, Lisboa: 99, 288, 302 (*vd.* Gregório José de Seixas, José António Monteiro, José Bonifácio de Andrade e Silva)
CASA PIA, Lisboa: 108

CASAL, Manuel Aires do, padre, historiador: 77
Casaleiro, Pedro: 11, 313, 316, 324
CASSINI, [Giovanni Domenico], astrónomo ítalo-francês: 240, 264
CASTELA, Espanha: 20
CASTELO DE S. JORGE, Lisboa: 220
CASTRO, Columbano Pinto Ribeiro de, magistrado: 304
—, Francisco Rafael de, reitor da Universidade de Coimbra: 283
—, José Ricalde Pereira de, [freire, magistrado], membro da Junta da Providência Literária: 163
—, André de Melo e, conde de Galveias, governador de Minas Gerais: 180
—, Martinho de Melo e (1716-1795), conde de Galveias, ministro de Portugal: 91, 166, 171, 180
—, Miguel Lúcio de Portugal e, [cónego da sé de Lisboa]: 176
CATALUNHA, Espanha 279 (*vd.* Figueiras, guerra do Rossilhão)
CATAS ALTAS, arraial, Minas Gerais, Brasil: 72, 82
Catroga, Fernando: 93

CAULA, Carlos Frederico Bernardo de, engenheiro: 264
CAXIAS, Maranhão, Brasil: 82
CEARÁ, Brasil: 63-66, 82;
—, Real Hospício do: 77 (vd. Aracati, Aquirás, Januária)
CHEVALIER, João, astrónomo: 197
CHICHORRO, José de Abreu Bacelar, magistrado: 304
CHINA: 325
CÍCERO: 93
Cidade, Hernâni: 141
CIERA, Francisco António, matemático, astrónomo: 235, 238, 242, 263-266, 299, 310
—, Miguel António, lente da universidade de Coimbra, matemático, astrónomo, geógrafo: 143, 148, 204, 209, 240-241, 249, 260, 284, 300, 302, 315
CLAIRAUT, [Alexis Claude de] matemático, astrónomo, francês: 191, 222, 237
COCAIS, arraial, [Minas Gerais,] Brasil: 72
COELHO, José Joaquim de Freitas, engenheiro: 304
COIMBRA: 17, 20, 22, 25-28, 31, 49, 93, 100, 189, 227, 269, 306, 315, 319, 332, 334 (vd. Colégio das Artes, Colégio do Carmo, Colégio da Graça, Colégio de Jesus, Colégio dos Militares, Colégio de Pereira, Colégio Real de S. Paulo, Colégio Real de S. Pedro, Colégio da Santíssima Trindade, Colégio de Santo António da Pedreira, Colégio de S. Bento, Colégio de S. Bernardo, Colégio de S. Jerónimo, Colégio de S. João Evangelista, Colégio de S. José dos Marianos, Colégio de S. Tomás, Condeixa, Convento de S. Francisco, Francisco de Lemos, largo/praça de D. Dinis, Louriçal, palácio dos Grilos, Quinta das Canas, Quinta das Lágrimas, Seminário, Sé Nova, rua da Trindade, Universidade de Coimbra)
COLÉGIO DAS ARTES, Coimbra: 25, 39, 193, 196, 316 (vd. André de Gouveia, Baltasar Álvares, Cosme de Magalhães, Diogo de Gouveia, Manuel de Góis, Paio Rodrigues de Vilarinho, Pedro da Fonseca, Sebastião do Couto)
COLÉGIO DE JESUS, Coimbra: 23, 314, 315, 316, 317, 318
COLÉGIO [DE NOSSA SENHORA] DO CARMO, Coimbra: 23

COLÉGIO DA GRAÇA, Coimbra: 23
Colégio da Luz → Real Colégio da Luz
COLÉGIO DOS MILITARES, Coimbra: 23
COLÉGIO DE NOSSA SENHORA DA LUZ, Maranhão, Brasil: 77
COLÉGIO DE NOSSA SENHORA DAS NECESSIDADES, Lisboa: 142, 196-197
Colégio dos Nobres → Real Colégio dos Nobres
COLÉGIO DE PEREIRA [do Campo, Montemor o Velho], Coimbra: 135
COLÉGIO REAL DE S. PAULO, Coimbra: 23, 33
COLÉGIO REAL DE S. PEDRO, Coimbra: 23, 33, 49 (*vd*. Joaquim António de Aguiar)
COLÉGIO ROMANO, Roma: 27
COLÉGIO DA SANTÍSSIMA TRINDADE, Coimbra: 23
COLÉGIO [DO SALVADOR] DA BAÍA, Brasil: 74-76, 78, 196
COLÉGIO DE SANTO ALEXANDRE, Pará, Brasil: 77 (*vd*. casa da Vigia)
COLÉGIO DE SANTO ANTÃO, Lisboa: 194, 196, 197, 244 (*vd*. Giovanni Baptista Carbone)
COLÉGIO DE SANTO ANTÓNIO DA PEDREIRA, Coimbra: 23

COLÉGIO DE S. BENTO, Coimbra: 23, 321
COLÉGIO DE S. BERNARDO, Coimbra: 23
COLÉGIO DE S. JERÓNIMO, Coimbra: 23, 285
COLÉGIO DE S. JOÃO EVANGELISTA, Coimbra: 23
COLÉGIO DE S. JOSÉ DOS MARIANOS, Coimbra: 23
COLÉGIO DE S. MIGUEL, Santos, Brasil: 76
COLÉGIO DE S. TOMÁS, Coimbra: 23
COLLÈGE DE FRANCE, Paris: 106
COMMANDINO, Frederico, matemático italiano: 148
CONCHINCHINA, Ásia: 183 (*vd*. João de Loureiro)
Conde de Oeiras → Marquês de Pombal
Condexa → Condeixa
CONDEIXA (Condexa), quartel de, Coimbra: 303
CONGONHAS, Minas Gerais, Brasil: 64-67
CONGONHAS DO CAMPO, Minas Gerais, Brasil: 82
CONGONHAS DO SABARÁ, Minas Gerais, Brasil: 82
continente → Portugal
CONVENTO DE S. FRANCISCO, Coimbra: 23

CORREIA, Luís, canonista, lente da Universidade de Coimbra: 15
CORUCHE, Ribatejo: 259 (*vd.* Couço, Erra, rio Sorraia)
Costa, A. M. Amorim da: 101, 331
—, Bartolomeu da, naturalista: 176
—, Maria de Fátima: 210, 240
—, José Joaquim Vitorino da, astrónomo, matemático : 249
COTINGUIBA, Baía, Brasil: 81
COUÇO, Coruche: 259
COURCIER, editor, Paris: 225
COUTINHO, Baltazar de Azevedo, engenheiro militar: 276
—, Filipe Neri da Silva, provedor cosmógrafo: 301
—, João Pereira Ramos de Azeredo, [irmão de Francisco de Lemos], membro da Junta da Providência Literária: 163
—, Luís Pinto de Sousa (visconde de Balsemão), governador no Brasil: 151, 154, 157, 183
—, Rodrigo de Sousa, ministro do reino: 91, 184, 186, 242, 283, 289, 294, 298 (*vd.* José Vieira Couto, Monte Rodrigo)
COUTO, José Vieira, naturalista: 186
COUTO, Sebastião do, professor do Colégio das Artes: 26

Coxito, A.: 27
Craveiro, Maria de Lurdes: 320
Cruz, Ana Lúcia R.Barbalho da: 166,
—, Guilherme Braga da: 288, 320
CUIABÁ, Mato Grosso, Brasil: 64-66, 78, 82 (*vd.* Minas do Bom Jesus)
Cunha, Alexandre Mendes: 110
—, João Cosme da, [cardeal, arcebispo de Évora], membro da Junta da Providência Literária: 163
—, José Anastácio da, lente da universidade de Coimbra, geómetra: 232
—, Luís da, diplomata: 29
Curado, Manuel: 241

DALLA BELLA, João António, matemático italiano, lente da universidade de Coimbra: 102, 139, 144, 149, 164, 176, 178, 314, 322
De Ridder-Symoens, Hilde: 21
DECK, José Rollem van, capitão: 323
DELAMBRE, Jean-Baptiste, astrónomo francês: 222-223, 225, 229-231
DELISLE, [Joseph Nicholas], astrónomo francês: 197

Denis, Vincent: 106
Denys, Catherine: 108
DES ESSARTS, [Nicolas-Toussaint, bibliógrafo francês], 109
DESAINT, editor: 260 (*vd.* Paris)
DESCARTES, filósofo francês: 27, 30, 195
Dias, Maria Helena: 242
Dias, J. S. da Silva: 176
DIJON, França: 260
DINIS, Júlio, escritor: 207
—, largo ou praça de D., Coimbra: 285, 320, 334
DIVOR, rio, afluente do rio Tejo: 259
DIOGO DE CASTILHO, prémio de arquitetura: 317
Diogo, Maria Paula: 88
DOLLONDI [Dollond, I. J., fabricante de instrumentos óticos inglês]: 221
Domingues, Ângela: 42, 103, 182
DOURO, rio, região: 17, 208, 250, 270, 280 (*vd.* Barca de Alva, Cachão da Valeira, Luís Gomes de Carvalho, Reinaldo Oudinot)
Dugood, William: 325
DUHAMEL [du Monceau, Henri Louis], naturalista francês, 294
Dunn, Richard: 199
DUNQUERQUE, França: 225

DUPUIS, Luís André, [desenhador francês]: 273

ÉCOLE DES PONTS ET CHAUSSÉES, Paris: 280, 293
Eisenstadt, S. N.: 89-90
ELBA, rio, Alemanha: 295
Elias, Norbert: 155
ELSDEN, Guilherme, engenheiro militar: 219, 284, 285, 320
ELVAS, Alentejo: 259
ENTRE DOURO E MINHO: 242
ERICEIRA, condes da: 18 (*vd.* Henrique de Meneses)
ERRA, Coruche: 259
ERVEDAL, Avis: 259
ESCÓCIA: 293 (*vd.* Sacrobosco)
ESCOLA POLITÉCNICA DE LISBOA: 302, 311
ESCOTO, Duns, filósofo: 16
ESPANHA: 18, 113, 144, 167, 240, 247, 264, 276, 279 (*vd.* Afonso do Prado, Ávila, Baltazar Gracián, Biscaia, Cádiz, Campomanes, Castela, Catalunha, Filipe [III], Francisco Suárez, Galiza, Granada, Madrid, País Basco, Tomás López, tratado de Santo Ildefonso, Segóvia, universidade de Alcalá, universidade de Salamanca)

ESPÍRITO SANTO, Brasil: 74, 81 (Vitória)
ESTOCOLMO, Suécia: 99, 114
ESTRELA, serra da: 102
ESTRELA POLAR: 199
ESTREMADURA: 304
ESTREMOZ, Alentejo: 259
EUCLIDES: 148
EULER, [Leonhard, matemático, astrónomo suíço]: 191, 222, 237
EUROPA: 20, 45, 89, 137, 145, 148, 151, 154, 174, 193, 196, 204, 217-218, 237, 245, 251, 264, 269, 271, 283, 288, 290-293, 297, 309-310, 322 (*vd.* Alemanha, Áustria, mar Báltico, Bélgica, Berna, Boémia, Escócia, Espanha, França, Gibraltar, Holanda, Hungria, Itália, Noruega, País de Gales, Rússia, Suécia, Turquia)
ÉVORA, Alentejo: 20, 112, 113, 193, 196, 301 (*vd.* Filipe Neri da Silva Coutinho, João Rosado de Vilalobos e Vasconcelos)
FABRE, [Jean-Antoine, economista francês]: 295
FÁBRICA DAS SEDAS E ÁGUAS LIVRES, Lisboa: 105

FACCIOLATI, Jacob, reitor da universidade de Pádua: 144, 162
FARIA, Baltazar de, visitador da Universidade de Coimbra: 14
—, Francisco António de, magistrado: 304
FAUSTINO, João, padre oratoriano: 176, 178
FEIJÓ, João da Silva, naturalista luso-brasileiro: 43, 166, 249
FELICE, Fortunato Bartolomeo, [editor enciclopedista]: 110
Felismino, David: 324
FERBER, João Jacob, naturalista sueco: 172
FERNANDES, Vicente Júlio, estudante da Universidade de Coimbra: 115
Ferrão, Cristina / Soares, José Paulo Monteiro: 329
FERRAZ, Manuel Joaquim de Sousa, médico: 41
FERREIRA, Alexandre Rodrigues, [naturalista brasileiro]: 43, 115, 166, 168, 249, 313, 324, 329-330, 333 (*vd.* Domingos Vandelli)
—, *Fernando B.:* 144-145, 235, 328
—, *Gustavo Oliveira:* 11, 139
—, Silvestre Pinheiro, [filósofo, ministro]: 297

Ferro, João Pedro: 116
FIGUEIRA DA FOZ, Beiras: 269, 308
FIGUEIRAS, Catalunha, Espanha: 279
Figueiredo, Fernando B.: 10, 191, 196, 202, 205, 219, 229, 236, 287, 320-321
—, António José, lente da universidade de Coimbra: 102
—, António Pereira de, [teólogo]: 176
Figueiroa, Francisco Carneiro de: 16, 19
FILANGIERI, Caetano, filósofo napolitano: 109
FILIPE II, rei de Portugal e Espanha: 19-20, 25-26 (*vd.* Lopo de Almeida)
Fiolhais, Carlos: 197
FLAMSTEED, [John, astrónomo inglês]: 238
FOIOS, Joaquim de, padre oratoriano: 176, 178
FOLQUE, Filipe, filho de Pedro Folque, matemático: 229-230, 302, 311
—, Pedro, pai de Filipe Folque, matemático: 241, 264, 302
Fonseca, Álvaro Baltazar Moreira da: 250
—, Fernando Taveira da: 9, 13, 51-53, 57, 70, 91, 102

—, Pedro da, [professor no Colégio das Artes, filósofo]: 26--27
—, Pedro José da, gramático, professor no Real Colégio dos Nobres: 176
FORTES, Manuel de Azevedo, [engenheiro-mor do reino]: 241
Foucault, Michel: 106
FOURCROY, [Antoine François, químico francês]: 99, 294
FRAGOSO, João António Barahona, magistrado: 304
FRANÇA: 46, 72, 144, 167, 172, 197, 201, 213, 238--240, 247, 264, 276, 278, 280, 297 (*vd.* Adet, Auzoux, Bailly, Bélidor, Biot, Blondel, Bossut, Bouguer, Bouvard, Burckhardt, canal de Borgonha, canal de Languedoque, Cassini, Charles Marie Damoiseau de Monfort, Clairaut, Collége de France, d'Alembert, Delisle, Des Essarts, Desaint, Descartes, Dijon, Duhamel, Dunquerque, Durand de Saint Pourçain, École des Ponts et Chaussées, Étienne Bézout, Fabre, Fourcroy, Francoeur, Gassendo, J.-B. Chappe

d'Auteroche, Jean-Baptiste Delambre, Jean-Rodolphe Perronet, José Auffdiener, Joseph Lalande, Junot, Lacaille, Lacroix, Lagrange, Laplace, Legendre, Lenoir, Les Fils d'Émile Deyrolle, Lévêque, Louis Antoine de Bougainville, Luís XIV, Luís XVI, Luís André Dupuis, Luis Vives, Mantes, Marie, Méchain, Montalembert, Montesquieu, Montpellier, Napoleão, Neuilli, Orléans, Paris, Pingré, Rafael Bluteau, rio Loire, rio Sena, Vauban)

Francisco de Lemos de Faria Pereira Coutinho → Francisco de Lemos

Franco, Matilde Pessoa de Figueiredo Sousa: 314

FRANCO, Francisco de Melo, médico: 115

FRANCOEUR, [Louis-Benjamin], matemático francês: 215

FRANZINI, Marino Miguel, [filho de Miguel Franzini, militar]: 280

—, Miguel, [pai de Marino Miguel Franzini], matemático italiano, lente da universidade de Coimbra: 116, 144, 149, 164, 176, 178, 263, 284

frei Manuel do Cenáculo → Manuel do Cenáculo Vilas Boas

FREIBURG, Alemanha: 293, 294 (Werner)

Freire, Francisco de Castro: 215, 226, 289-290, 297

FREITAS, António Caetano de, estudante da universidade de Coimbra: 115

—, *Décio Ruivo:* 30, 47

—, Nuno de, estudante da Universidade de Coimbra: 115

Frijhoff, W.: 88

FRONTEIRA, Alentejo: 259

FURTADO, Luís Cândido Cordeiro Pinheiro, engenheiro militar: 303, 306

GALENO, médico grego: 16

GALILEU GALILEI: 158, 173, 195

GALIZA, Espanha: 264 (*vd.* cabo Ortegal)

GALVEIAS, condes de: 179, 180 (*vd.* André de Melo e Castro, Martinho de Melo Castro)

GAMA, Manuel Jacinto Nogueira da, lente da universidade de Coimbra, matemático: 215, 280

GARRETT, João Baptista de Almeida, escritor, político: 48, 49

GASSENDO, [Pierre, filósofo francês]: 30
Gayo, Felgueiras: 180
GEDNER, Christopher, naturalista sueco: 152
Gellner, Ernest / Waterbury, John: 147
GÉNOVA, Itália: 144 (vd. Nicolau Piaggio)
GERÊS, serra do: 102, 326
GIBRALTAR: 240
Gilson, Étienne: 27
GIRALDES, Francisco António Marques, membro da Junta da Providência Literária: 163
GOA: 43, 330 (vd. Manuel Galvão da Silva)
GOIANA, Pernambuco, Brasil: 84
GOIÁS, Brasil: 64, 65, 66, 82 (vd. Goiases, Meia Ponte, Minas de Goiases, Vila Boa)
GOIASES, Goiás, Brasil: 82 (vd. Minas de Goiases, Santa Ana)
GÓIS, Manuel de, professor do Colégio das Artes: 26
Gomes, Joaquim Ferreira: 15
Goodman, Dena: 88
GOTHA, Alemanha: 217, 295
GOUVEIA, André de, humanista, professor do Colégio das Artes: 25

GOUVEIA, Diogo de, humanista, professor do Colégio das Artes: 23
Grã-Bretanha → Inglaterra
GRACIÁN, Baltazar, moralista espanhol: 155
GRAETZ: 99
Grandi, Carlo: 315
GRANADA, Espanha: 27
GREENWICH, meridiano de, Londres, Inglaterra: 191, 199, 217, 219, 223, 236, 237, 244, 264, 295
GRILOS, palácio dos, Coimbra: 221
GUADIANA, rio: 260
GUANARÉ, Maranhão, Brasil: 77
GUARIPIRANGA, Vila Rica, Minas Gerais: 83
Guerrero, Omar: 107
GUGLIELMINI, [Giovanni Battista, físico italiano]: 295
GUIMARÃES, Minho: 270, 282, 306
—, Manoel Ferreira de Araújo, astrónomo: 215
GUINÉ: 330
GUSMÃO, Alexandre de, padre jesuíta: 76
—, Bartolomeu de, padre jesuíta: 76

HAARLEM, Holanda: 99

HALLEY, cometa: 197, 222
HANÔVER, casa de, Alemanha: 277
Hansen, João Adolfo: 158
HARRISON, John, inventor inglês: 200
HASSEN, químico alemão: 99
Hartmann, T.: 324
HENRIQUE (o Navegador), infante de Portugal: 194
HENRIQUES, Júlio, botânico: 325
Henriques, Maria Helena: 327
HERCULANO, Alexandre, escritor, historiador: 48, 274
HERSCHEL, [William, astrónomo anglo-germânico]: 225, 296
Hespanha, António Manuel: 94, 146, 170
HIPÓCRATES: 16
HOLANDA: 46, 144, 167, 297 (*vd.* Boerhaave, Haarlem, Huygens, Leida, Willem Piso)
HOSPITAL REAL MILITAR, Rio de Janeiro, Brasil: 79
HOSPITAL DE SANTO ANTÓNIO, Porto: 286
HOTEL DE CLUNY, Paris, França: 197
HUNGRIA: 46
HUYGENS, [Christiaan, astrónomo]: 195

IGUAÇU, S. Paulo, Brasil: 85
IGUAPE, Baía, Brasil: 81
ILHA DO CATALÃO, Rio de Janeiro, Brasil: 84
ILHA GRANDE, Rio de Janeiro, Brasil: 84
ILHÉUS, Baía, Brasil: 257
ÍNDIA: 149, 235
INFICIONADOS, Minas Gerais, Brasil: 83
INGLATERRA (Grã-Bretanha): 79, 144, 167, 172, 197, 200, 237, 297 (*vd.* Bacon, Bird, Carlos II, Dollondi, Flamsteed, George Adams, Gerard de Visme, Gibraltar, Herschel, Isaac Newton, Isaac Samuda, Jamaica, James Bradley, James Edward Smith, John Harrison, John Muller, John Pond, Joseph Banks, Maskelyne, Robert Boyle, Robert Simson, Thomas Jefferys, W. Cary, William Dugood, William Roy)
INHOMERIM, Rio de Janeiro, Brasil: 84
ITÁLIA: 46, 144, 156, 174, 297 (*vd.* Antoni, Balbi, Bolonha, Caetano Filangieri, Cassini, Carlos António Napion, concílio de Trento, Domenico Capassi, Domingos Scarlatti, Domingos Vandelli, Francesco Maratti, Francesco Saverio Zelada,

Frederico Commandino, Galileu Galilei, Génova, Giovanni Angelo Brunelli, Giovanni Baptista Carbone, Guglielmini, José Teresio Michelotti, Lagrange, Matteo Pellegrini, Milão, Nápoles, Nicolau Piaggio, Pádua, Palermo, Piemonte, rio Pó, Rizzi Zannoni, Roma, Sardenha, Veneza)

ITABERABA, Vila Rica, Minas Gerais, Brasil: 83
ITAPAGIPE, Baía, Brasil: 81
ITAPICURU, Baía, Brasil: 81
ITU, São Paulo, Brasil: 85

JACOBINA, Baía, Brasil: 81
JACUÍ, Minas Gerais, Brasil: 82
JAGUARIPE, Baía, Brasil: 81
JAMAICA: 200
JANUÁRIA, Ceará, Brasil: 82
Jardim Botânico → Universidade de Coimbra
JAUCH-STEIN, casa de modelos alemã: 327
JAURU, rio, Mato Grosso, Brasil: 240
JEFFERYS, Thomas, cartógrafo inglês: 241, 261
JOÃO III (o Piedoso), rei de Portugal: 13-14, 194
JOÃO IV, rei de Portugal: 23, 26
JOÃO V (o Magnânimo), pai de José I, rei de Portugal: 30, 142, 144, 196, 244, 325
JOÃO VI (Serenissimo Senhor Principe, Príncipe Regente), filho de Maria I, rei de Portugal, príncipe do Brasil: 93, 99, 113--114, 116, 136, 138, 171, 188, 226-227, 232, 246, 278, 289
João de Almeida Portugal → marquês de Alorna
JOSÉ I (Augustissimo Rei, Serenissimo Senhor Principe), filho de João V, pai de Maria I, rei de Portugal, príncipe do Brasil: 116, 135, 142-143, 151, 153, 157, 160-161, 166-167, 185, 197, 204, 232, 243, 282 (vd. marquês de Pombal)
JUNOT, [Jean Andoche], general francês: 49
JÚPITER, planeta: 198, 199, 228, 231, 238, 239
JURUPIXUNA, índios, Brasil: 329, 330
JUSTI, Johann Heinrich Gottlob von, economista prussiano: 106, 107, 110
JUVARRA, Filipe, arquitecto: 143

KEW, Jardim Botânico de, Londres, Inglaterra: 182

Koselleck, Reinhart: 89
KRANTZ, casa de minerais alemã: 327
Kury, Lorelay: 91

LABORATORIO CHIMICO DA UNIVERSIDADE DE COIMBRA: 97, 99-101, 167, 313-317, 331 (*vd.* Domingos Vandelli, Manuel Henriques de Paiva)
LACAILLE, [Nicolas-Louis de], astrónomo francês: 200, 201, 214, 223
LACROIX, [Sylvestre-François], matemático, astrónomo francês: 222
LAFÕES, duque de (João Carlos de Bragança de Sousa Ligne Tavares Mascarenhas da Silva), militar, secretário de estado: 172-173, 175-178, 180-181, 233, 277 (*vd.* Academia Real das Ciências de Lisboa, Domingos Vandelli, José Francisco Correia da Serra)
LAGOS, Algarve: 276
LAGRANGE, [Joseph Louis], matemático, astrónomo franco-piemontês: 191, 222
LAGUNA, Rio de Janeiro, Brasil: 85
LALANDE, Jerôme, astrónomo francês: 200, 214, 217, 222-223, 230-231, 260
LANÇÕES, Minas Gerais, Brasil: 82
LANGUEDOQUE, canal de, França: 260
LAPLACE, [Pierre-Simon, marquês de], matemático, astrónomo francês: 191, 192, 222, 223
Lario, Damaso de: 33
LAVRADIO, marqueses do: 179 (*vd.* Luís de Almeida Portugal Soares de Alarcão d'Eça e Melo Silva Mascarenhas)
Leal-Duarte, António: 10, 191
LEÃO, Inácio José, engenheiro: 306
LEGENDRE, [Adrien-Marie], matemático, astrónomo francês: 264
LEIDA [Leiden], Holanda: 29
LEIRIA: 194, 303, 306
Leitão, H.: 193, 194, 195
Leite, Serafim: 74, 75, 77
LEME, António Pires da Silva Pontes, astrónomo, matemático: 44, 241, 249
LEMOS [de Faria Pereira Coutinho], Francisco de, bispo de Coimbra, [irmão de João Pereira Ramos de Azeredo Coutinho], reitor da Universidade de Coimbra: 35, 96-97, 101, 162-163, 166, 169, 174-175, 177, 179-180, 183, 226, 247, 251, 283, 285, 294, 297-298

LENOIR, [Étienne, construtor francês]: 225
LES FILS D'ÉMILE DEYROLLE, casa de modelos francesa: 327
LÉVÊQUE, [Pierre, astrónomo francês]: 201
LIMA, rio, Minho: 257
LIMPO, Manuel do Espírito Santo, [militar]: 280
LINEU (Linnaeus) [Linné, Carl von], naturalista sueco: 97--98, 104, 139, 145, 147--152, 156, 160-161, 164, 172, 186, 189, 256 (*vd.* Domingos Vandelli, José Francisco Correia da Serra)
LINHARES, casa de: 184
LINK, Henrich Friderich, naturalista prussiano: 140
Linnaeus → Lineu
LIPPE, Wilhelm zu Schaumburg-, conde de, militar, príncipe alemão: 271, 276-277
LISBOA: 16, 27, 47, 70, 74, 99--100, 113, 139, 149, 153, 160, 170, 171, 173, 194, 197, 232, 236, 238-239, 247, 274, 276, 278, 297, 300-301, 306, 322, 325 (*vd.* Academia Real das Ciências, Academia Real de Fortificação, Artilharia e Desenho, Academia Real da História Portuguesa, Academia Real da Marinha, Ajuda, Casa da Moeda, Casa Pia, Castelo de S. Jorge, Colégio de Nossa Senhora das Necessidades, Dalla Bella, Escola Politécnica de Lisboa, Fábrica das Sedas e Águas Livres, Lopo de Almeida, Museu Bocage, Palácio da Ribeira, Pina Manique, quinta da Palhavã, Real Colégio dos Nobres, principal Mascarenhas, Real Academia dos Guardas Marinhas, Real Colégio da Luz, rio Alcântara, rio de Sacavém)
—, Baltazar Silva, irmão de José Silva Lisboa, magistrado, historiador brasileiro: 46-47
—, João, astrónomo: 199
—, José Silva, irmão de Baltazar Silva Lisboa, economista brasileiro: 46-47
LOIRE, rio, França: 295
LOMBARDO, Pedro, filósofo: 16
LONDRES, Inglaterra: 29, 182, 219, 331 (*vd.* Greenwich, Jardim Botânico de Kew, Jacob de Castro Sarmento)
Lopes, José Carlos: 159
—, Óscar, historiador: 248

LÓPEZ [DE VARGAS MACHUCA], Tomás, cartógrafo espanhol: 241, 261
LORENA, Bernardo José de, governador de Minas Gerais, Brasil: 186
LOUREIRO, João de, jesuíta, naturalista: 183-184, 186-187, 189
Lourenço, Marta: 324
LOURIÇAL, Pombal: 18;
—, marquês do: 181 (*vd.* Henrique de Meneses)
LUA, satélite da Terra: 199-200, 211, 224, 227-228, 231, 238-239
Luckhurst, Gerald: 181
LUÍS XIV, rei de França: 218
LUÍS XVI, rei de França: 260
Luís António Furtado de Mendonça e Faro → visconde de Barbacena

MACAU: 330
MACIEL, José Álvares, lente da Universidade de Coimbra: 102
MACOMBOA, Manuel Alves, arquitecto: 220, 286-287, 320
Madeira, José António: 230
MADRID, Espanha: 99, 145, 240, 249
MAGALHÃES, João Jacinto, construtor de instrumentos científicos: 331
MAGDEBURGO, campos de, Alemanha: 295
MAGÉ, Rio de Janeiro, Brasil: 85
Maffei, Domenico: 21
MAFRA, convento de: 143
MAGALHÃES, Cosme de, professor no Colégio das Artes: 26
Magalhães, Joaquim Romero: 59, 70, 73
MANIQUE, [Diogo Inácio de] Pina, intendente geral da polícia: 108
MANUEL I, rei de Portugal: 194
MARAGOGIPE, Baía, Brasil: 81
MARANHÃO, Brasil: 64-66, 68-69, 77, 82 (*vd.* Alcântara, Campo Maior, Caxias, Colégio de Nossa Senhora da Luz, Guanaré, Peagim, S. Luís, Viana)
MARATTI, Francesco, naturalista italiano: 172
MARCGRAF, Georg, naturalista alemão: 159
Marcos de Diós, Ángel: 21
MARIA I, rainha de Portugal, rainha do Brasil: 89, 101-102, 108, 113, 135, 152, 166, 170- -171, 181, 185, 232, 246, 249- -250, 262, 285 (*vd.* Academia Real das Ciências de Lisboa, Francisco de Lemos, [frei] Manuel do Cenáculo Vilas Boas, Queluz, Pina Manique)

MARIA BÁRBARA, infanta de Portugal: 143
MARIALVA, marqueses de: 179-
-180 (*vd.* Rodrigo José de Meneses)
MARIANA (Vila Leal do Carmo), Minas Gerais, Brasil: 44, 62, 65-67, 72, 83 (*vd.* António Pereira, Campanha de Rio Verde, Casa Branca, Monsus, Salcelas, S. Bartolomeu)
MARIE, [Joseph François, matemático francês]: 214
Marin, Brigitte: 108
Marques, Júlio F.: 317, 327
Marquês de Ponte de Lima → Tomás Xavier de Lima Nogueira Vasconcelos Telles da Silva
MARROCOS: 177
MARTE, planeta: 198, 228, 231, 239
Martins, Carlos Henriques de Moura Rodrigues: 10, 104, 209-
-210, 219, 233, 245-246, 250, 264, 277, 287, 289, 307, 322
MASCARENHAS, [Domingos José de Assis], principal da igreja patriarcal, Lisboa: 176
—, Luís de Almeida Portugal Soares de Alarcão d'Eça e Melo Silva, marquês de Lavradio, vice-rei do Brasil: 180

MASKELYNE, [Nevil], astrónomo inglês: 200, 223
MATO GROSSO, Brasil: 77 (*vd.* Alexandre Rodrigues Ferreira, Cuiabá, Luís Pinto de Sousa Coutinho, rio Jauru, Santo António)
MATTIAZZI, Júlio, naturalista, intendente do Jardim e Museu da Ajuda: 154, 171, 188 (*vd.* Domingos Vandelli)
Mattoso, José: 170
Mauro, Fréderic: 59
MAYER, [Tobias, astrónomo alemão]: 222, 237
MÉCHAIN, [Pierre François André], matemático, astrónomo: 225, 264
MEIA PONTE, Goiás, Brasil: 82
MELO, Fontes Pereira de, ministro do reino: 310-311
—, Manuel Pedro de, astrónomo, lente da Universidade de Coimbra: 230, 276, 280, 290, 294-297
Mendes, Humberto Gabriel: 209, 242, 260, 264, 267
MENDONÇA, João Bernardo da Costa Falcão e, magistrado: 304
—, José Francisco Rafael Miguel António de, reitor da Universidade de Coimbra: 170

Mendonça, Marcos Carneiro de: 293
MENESES, Alberto Carlos de, matemático: 301, 306, 310
—, Henrique de, marquês do Louriçal, conde da Ericeira: 181
Meneses, José: 322, 324-325, 327, 332
—, Rodrigo José de, governador de Minas Gerais: 180
MERCÚRIO, planeta: 197-198, 211, 220, 227
MERTON, Robert K., sociólogo: 141
MICHELETTI, prémio: 317
MICHELOTTI, José Teresio, cartógrafo italiano: 273
MIGUEL, rei de Portugal: 49
MILÃO, Itália: 222
Milliot, Vincent: 108
Minas, Minas Geraes → Minas Gerais
MINAS DO BOM JESUS, Cuiabá, Mato Grosso, Brasil: 82
MINAS GERAIS (Minas, Minas Geraes), Brasil: 34, 43, 45, 67-69, 71-73, 78-79, 82, 168-169, 179, 182, 186, 257 (*vd.* André de Melo e Castro, António Dias de Oliveira, Barra do Rio das Velhas, Bernardo José de Lorena, Borda do Campo, Caeté, Carijós, Casa Branca, Catas Altas, Cocais, Congonhas, Congonhas do Campo, Congonhas do Sabará, Inficionados, Jacuí, João Inácio do Amaral Silveira, José Vieira Couto, Joaquim Veloso de Miranda, José Vieira Couto, Lanções, Manuel Ferreira da Câmara, Mariana, Minas Novas dos Fanados, Monte Rodrigo, Nossa Senhora da Natividade, Nova Lorena Diamantina, Ouro Branco, Ouro Preto, Paracatu, Piranga, Pitangui, Pouso Alto, Ribeirão do Carmo, Rio das Mortes, Rodrigo José de Meneses, Sabará, Santo António do Tijuco, S. João d'El Rei, S. Pedro do Fanado, Santa Bárbara, Santa Luzia, S. Romão, Serro Frio, Sumidoiro, Tejuco, Tijuco, Vila Boa, Vila Real do Sabará, Vila Nova da Rainha, Vila Rica de Ouro Preto, visconde de Barbacena)
MINAS DE GOIASES, Goiás, Brasil: 82 (*vd.* Santa Ana)
MINAS NOVAS DOS FANADOS, Minas Gerais, Brasil: 83
MINHO: 124, 280, 304 (*vd.* Francisco António de Faria,

Guimarães, Ponte da Barca, Ponte de Lima, rio Lima, rio Minho, serra do Gerês, Viana do Castelo)
—, rio: 261
MIRANDA, Joaquim Veloso de (Veloso), lente da universidade de Coimbra: 43, 102, 166, 168-169, 179-182, 184-185, 189 (*vd.* Domingos Vandelli, Brasil)
—, *M. A.:* 324
MOÇAMBIQUE: 43-44, 149, 330 (*vd.* António Pires da Silva Pontes Leme, Manuel Galvão da Silva, Tete)
MOGIMIRIM, São Paulo, Brasil: 85
MONÇON, Francisco, lente da Universidade de Coimbra: 23
MONCORVO, [Torre de], Trás os Montes: 105
MONDEGO, rio, vale, região: 17, 101, 208, 269, 285, 289, 294--295, 302, 321
MONFORT, Charles Marie Damoiseau de, militar, astrónomo francês: 231, 238-239
MONFORTE, Alentejo: 259
—, Baía, Brasil: 81
MONSUS, Mariana, Minas Gerais, Brasil: 83
MONTALEMBERT, [Marc René de, militar francês]: 277

MONTE RODRIGO, colina, Minas Gerais, Brasil: 186
MONTEIRO, João António, [lente da Universidade de Coimbra]: 99
MONTESQUIEU, [Charles de], filósofo francês: 110
MONTPELLIER, França: 41, 42;
—, universidade de: 79 (*vd.* Manuel Arruda da Câmara)
MONTE ALEGRE, Pará, Brasil: 84
MORA, Alentejo: 259
Morais, Francisco: 52
Moreira, Luís Miguel: 240-241, 262, 281
MOREIRA, António José, lente da Academia Real de Fortificação, Artilharia e Desenho: 275
Mota, Paulo Gama: 317
Moura, Sílvia: 147, 149-150, 152--153, 160
MULLER, John, engenheiro inglês: 275
MURITIBA, Baía, Brasil: 81
MUSEU BOCAGE (Museu Nacional de História Natural e da Ciência), Lisboa: 324, 325
MUSEU DA CIÊNCIA DA UNIVERSIDADE DE COIMBRA: 313--314, 317, 326-327, 334
MUSEU DE HISTÓRIA NATURAL da UNIVERSIDADE DE COIMBRA: 44, 101, 165, 167, 327

MUSEU NACIONAL MACHADO DE CASTRO, Coimbra: 320

NAPION, Carlos António, [militar, engenheiro piemontês]: 273
NAPOLEÃO [Bonaparte]: 45
NÁPOLES, reino de, Itália: 143
Napoli, Paolo: 106
NAZARÉ, Baía, Brasil: 81
NECESSIDADES, convento ou palácio das, Lisboa: 175-176
NEGREIROS, José Manuel Carvalho, engenheiro: 305
NETO, José Diogo Mascarenhas, magistrado, superintendente geral das Estradas: 282, 303, 306, 312
NEUILLI [Neuilly], França: 260
NEWTON, Isaac, matemático, astrónomo inglês: 10, 30, 94, 173, 195
NOSSA SENHORA DA CONCEIÇÃO, Rio de Janeiro, Brasil: 85
NOSSA SENHORA DA ENCARNAÇÃO, Sabará, Minas Gerais, Brasil: 83
NOSSA SENHORA DA NATIVIDADE, Minas Gerais, Brasil: 83
NOSSA SENHORA DOS REMÉDIOS, Parati, Rio de Janeiro, Brasil: 85
NEGRÃO, António Sebastião A. Silva, engenheiro: 304
NIEMEYER, Conrado Henrique de, engenheiro: 266-268, 303, 306
Nobre, João Paulo da Silva Gil: 334
NORUEGA: 293
NOVA LORENA DIAMANTINA, região de, Minas Gerais: 186
Nunes, Maria de Fátima: 89, 113
—, Pedro, lente da universidade de Coimbra, astrónomo, matemático: 193, 194
NUSSANE, José Champalimaud de, engenheiro militar: 306

Observatório Astronómico da Universidade de Coimbra → Universidade de Coimbra
OEIRAS, Piauí, Brasil: 65, 66, 84
OLINDA, Pernambuco, Brasil: 48, 67, 76, 78, 84
Oliveira, António de: 53
—, *Cristóvão José Pinto Correia:* 24,
—, António Dias de, [bandeirante, explorador de Minas Gerais]: 72
—, António Rodrigues de, estudante da Universidade de Coimbra: 116
—, Francisco Rodrigues de, estudante da Universidade de Coimbra: 116

—, Joaquim de, engenheiro militar: 306
—, Joaquim Pedro Gomes de, magistrado, ministro: 266
Oriente → Ásia
ORLÉANS, França: 260
ORTEGAL, cabo, Galiza, Espanha: 264
OUDINOT, Reinaldo, engenheiro militar: 280
OURO BRANCO, Minas Gerais, Brasil: 83, 180
OURO PRETO, Minas Gerais, Brasil: 72
Outran, Dourinda: 152

PÁDUA, Itália: 97, 145, 148, 162, 174, 314, 322 (*vd.* Domingos Vandelli, Francisco Vandelli, Jacob Facciolati, João António Dalla Bella)
PAIS [Leme], Garcia Rodrigues, explorador brasileiro: 72
PAÍS BASCO, Espanha: 113
PAÍS DE GALES: 293
PAIVA, Manuel Joaquim Henriques de, naturalista, médico, mestre de oficina: 99, 100, 114-116, 169, 188 (*vd.* Domingos Vandelli)
PALÁCIO DA RIBEIRA, Lisboa: 244
PALERMO, Sicília, Itália: 217

PALHAVÃ, quinta da, Lisboa: 180-181 (*vd.* Henrique de Meneses)
Papavero, Nelson: 149
PARÁ, Brasil: 61, 63-66, 69, 84 (*vd.* Belém, Cachoeira do Rio Arari, Colégio de Santo Alexandre, Monte Alegre)
PARACATU, Minas Gerais, Brasil: 83
PARAGUAI, rio, Brasil: 240
PARAÍBA, Brasil: 66-66, 76-77
—, Rio de Janeiro, Brasil: 84
PARAÍBA DO NORTE, Brasil: 64--66, 84 (*vd.* Vila Real do Brejo da Areia)
PARANAGUÁ, São Paulo, Brasil: 72, 76, 85
PARATI, Rio de Janeiro, Brasil: 85 (*vd.* Nossa Senhora dos Remédios)
Paredes, Ricardo: 327
PARIS, França: 24-25, 174-175, 184, 191, 197, 213, 217-218, 225, 233, 238, 244, 258, 260, 264, 288, 293, 295, 297, 324, 330 (*vd.* Courcier, Desaint, École des Ponts et Chaussées, Hotel de Cluny, Lenoir, Luis Vives, Ponte Luís XVI, rio Biévre, rio Sena, rio Yvette)
Pataca, Ermelinda Moutinho: 166, 181

Pato, António Vaz: 250
PEAGIM, Maranhão, Brasil: 82
PEDEGACHE [Brandão Ivo], Miguel [Tibério], astrónomo: 197
PEDRO, Desirée, arquitecto, lente da Universidade de Coimbra: 316
Pedro José de Noronha Camões de Albuquerque Moniz e Sousa → marquês de Angeja
PELLEGRINI, Matteo, moralista italiano: 156
PELOTAS, Rio Grande do Sul, Brasil: 64, 85
Pereira → colégio de Pereira
—, António José, lente da universidade de Coimbra: 176, 178
—, *Magnus R. de Mello:* 166, 202
—, Duarte Coelho, casado com Brites de Albuquerque, pai de Duarte Coelho d'Albuquerque, administrador de Pernambuco: 53
—, Gama, comendador: 330
—, *Gilberto:* 315, 318-319
— [Furtado de Mendonça], Hipólito José da Costa, diplomata brasileiro: 47
—, José Maria Dantas, [engenheiro, lente da Academia Real dos Guardas Marinhas]: 238
PERNAGUÁ, Piauí, Brasil: 84

PERNAMBUCO, Brasil: 41, 53, 61, 63-69, 73-74, 76, 78, 83 (*vd.* Alagoa, Bananeiras, Barra do Rio Grande, Brites de Albuquerque, Campo Largo, Duarte Coelho Pereira, Goiana, Luís António da Costa Barradas, Manuel Arruda da Câmara, Olinda, Recife, Serinhém)
PERRONET, Jean-Rodolphe, arquitecto francês: 259-260, 293, 295 (*vd.* École des Ponts et Chaussées, Guilherme Luís António de Valleré)
PERU: 241
PIAGGIO, Nicolau, cônsul de Portugal em Génova: 149 (*vd.* Génova, marquês de Pombal, Miguel António Ciera)
PIAUÍ, Brasil: 78 (*vd.* Oeiras, Pernaguá)
PICANÇO, José Correia, médico luso-brasileiro: 40
Picon, Antoine: 245, 278
o Piedoso → João III
PIEMONTE, Itália: 43, 315 (*vd.* Miguel Antonio Ciera)
PINGRÉ, [Alexandre Gui], astrónomo francês: 223
PINHEIRO, António, [bispo de Miranda, humanista], reformador da Universidade de Coimbra: 14

—, José Feliciano Fernandes, visconde de S. Leopoldo, ministro brasileiro: 46, 48
Pinto, H.: 203, 209
—, *José Manuel Soares:* 317
—, Rodrigo Ribeiro de Sousa, [lente da Universidade de Coimbra]: 215
PIRANGA, [Minas Gerais], Brasil: 72
Pires, Catarina Pereira: 314-315 323
PISO, Willem, naturalista holandês: 159, 161
Pita, João Rui: 317
PITANGUI, Minas Gerais, Brasil: 83
Pitt-Rivers, John: 147
PÓ, rio, Itália: 295
POMBAL, marquês de (Sebastião José de Carvalho e Melo, conde de Oeiras), ministro: 35, 39, 142-143, 148, 151--153, 157, 159, 161-163, 166, 170-172, 175, 177, 182, 202, 204, 232, 273, 277, 313-314, 333 (*vd.* Domingos Vandelli, José I, [frei] Manuel do Cenáculo Vilas Boas, Maria I, marquês de Alorna, Miguel António Ciera, Real Colégio dos Nobres, visconde de Vila Nova de Cerveira)

POND, John, astrónomo inglês: 223, 229
PONTEDERA, [Giulio, lente da universidade de Pádua]: 139
PONTE DA BARCA, Minho: 257
PONTE DE LIMA, Minho: 113, 138, 257;
—, marqueses de: 180
PONTE LUÍS XVI, Paris, França: 293
PORTO: 33, 74, 105, 203, 247, 249, 270, 286, 300, 306, 311 (*vd.* Academia da Marinha e Comércio, Hospital de Santo António, José António de Sá)
PORTO ALEGRE, Rio Grande do Sul, Brasil: 85
PORTO SEGURO, Baía Brasil: 84 (Vila Verde do Prado)
PORTUGAL (reino, nação, continente): 20, 26, 29, 34, 49, 52, 88, 90, 93, 104, 112-113, 121, 122-124, 129, 136-137, 141-161, 167, 173, 175, 177, 180, 183, 190, 192-193, 195, 197, 202, 204, 211, 214, 216, 218, 230, 234-235, 237, 239, 240-241, 243-246, 252, 261, 263, 265, 272-273, 276-278, 281-282, 288-289, 294, 297, 303, 306, 310-311, 323-330 (*vd.* Alentejo, Algarve, Alto Douro, Angola, António de

Araújo de Azevedo, Aveiro, Beiras, Biblioteca Nacional de Portugal, Braga, Brasil, cabo Carvoeiro, cabo Espichel, cabo da Roca, Cabo Verde, casa de Bragança, Coimbra, Domingos Vandelli, duque de Lafões, Entre Douro e Minho, Estremadura, Filipe II, Fontes Pereira de Melo, Goa, Guiné, Henrique (o Navegador), João III, João IV, João V, João VI, João Crisóstomo de Abreu e Sousa, Joaquim António de Aguiar, José I, José Diogo Mascarenhas Neto, José de Seabra da Silva, Leiria, Luís Pinto de Sousa, Macau, Manuel I, Maria I, Minho, Moçambique, Prior do Crato, Queluz, Ribatejo, Rio de Janeiro, rio Douro, rio Guadiana, rio Minho, rio Tejo, Salazar, S. Tomé, serras da Estrela, Setúbal, Timor, Tomás António de Vila Nova Portugal, Trás-os-Montes, Ultramar, Viana do Castelo)
—, Tomás António de Vila Nova, magistrado, ministro: 266-268
POUSO ALTO, Minas Gerais, Brasil: 83

PRADO, Afonso do, castelhano, reitor da Universidade de Coimbra: 23
PRADOS, arraial, Rio das Mortes, Minas Gerais, Brasil: 83
PRAETORIUS, Jacob Chrysostomus, engenheiro militar alemão: 266-267
Prata, Manuel Alberto Carvalho: 54, 97
Prazeres, Tiago Miguel Castanho: 277
PRIOR DO CRATO, [António de Portugal]: 26
Prússia → Alemanha

QUADROS, Manuel de, reformador da universidade de Coimbra: 15
QUELUZ, Lisboa: 94, 136, 179
QUINTA DAS CANAS, Coimbra, 321
QUINTA DAS LÁGRIMAS, Coimbra: 321

Raminelli, Ronald: 103
Ramos, Luís Oliveira: 116
RAZI, [Abū Bakr Muhammad ibn Zakarīyā al- médico persa]: 16
REAL ACADEMIA DOS GUARDAS MARINHAS, Lisboa: 44, 233, 235, 247 (*vd.* Francisco José de Lacerda Almeida, José Maria Dantas Pereira)

REAL COLÉGIO DA LUZ, Lisboa: 48
REAL COLÉGIO DOS NOBRES, Lisboa: 41, 97, 143, 148-149, 151, 162, 211, 214, 248, 314, 322, 325, 331 (*vd.* Alexandre Herculano, Domingos Vandelli, Giovanni Angelo Brunelli, José Diogo Mascarenhas Neto, marquês de Pombal, Miguel António Ciera, Pedro José da Fonseca)
REAL CORPO DE ENGENHEIROS, Lisboa, 209, 233, 251, 260, 272, 277-282, 296, 302, 305 (*vd.* Filipe Folque, José Manuel Carvalho Negreiros, Pedro Folque)
REBELO, António Teixeira, militar, ministro do reino: 275
RECIFE, Pernambuco, Brasil: 67, 84, colégio SJ de: 76, 78
RENDON, José Arouche de Toledo, director do curso jurídico em S. Paulo, militar brasileiro: 48
RIBATEJO: 250 (*vd.* Almeirim, Benavente, Coruche, Rio Maior, Santarém)
RIBEIRÃO DO CARMO, Minas Gerais, Brasil: 62, 83
Ribeiro, José Silvestre: 225, 317
Ribeiro, João Armando: 333

RIBEIRO, João Mendes, arquitecto, lente da Universidade de Coimbra: 316
RIO DAS CONTAS, Baía, Brasil: 81
RIO FUNDO, Baía, Brasil: 81
RIO GRANDE DO NORTE, Brasil: 85
RIO GRANDE DO SUL, Brasil: 65-66, 85 (*vd.* Pelotas, Porto Alegre, Viamão, Vila do Rio Pardo)
RIO DE JANEIRO, Brasil: 40-41, 51, 59, 61, 63- 69, 71-76, 79, 84, 99, 215, 274, 301 (*vd.* Academia da Marinha, Biblioteca Real, Cabo Frio, Campos, Campos de Goitacazes, Hospital Real Militar, Ilha do Catalão, Ilha Grande, Inhomerim, Joaquim José da Silva, José da Silva Feijó, Laguna, Magé, Manoel Ferreira de Araújo Guimarães, Nossa Senhora da Conceição, Paraíba, Parati, Santa Maria de Maricá, Vila do Campo)
RIO MAIOR, Ribatejo: 303, 306
RIO DAS MORTES, Minas Gerais, Brasil: 62, 72, 83 (*vd.* Prados, S. José)
RIO NEGRO, capitania [de S. José] do, Brasil: 43

RIO DA PRATA, América do Sul: 240
RIO DAS VELHAS, Minas Gerais, Brasil: 72
ROCA, cabo da: 261
Rocha, Carla: 327
ROCHA, José Monteiro da, jesuíta, matemático, astrónomo, vice-reitor da universidade de Coimbra: 100, 163, 176, 178, 196, 201-203, 220, 223--226, 229-231, 236-237 241--242, 248, 265, 283-284, 286--287, 291-301, 298-299, 314, 333 (*vd.* Domingos Vandelli, Manuel Pedro de Melo)
ROCHA, Vicente Ferrer da, naturalista: 176, 179, 181
Roche, Daniel: 88
Rodrigues, Manuel Augusto: 16
—, Sebastião, engenheiro: 304
ROMA: 27, 172, 174, 227 (*vd.* Colégio Romano, José Francisco Correia da Serra)
ROSA, José António da, lente da Academia Real de Fortificação, Artilharia e Desenho: 275
ROSSILHÃO, guerra do, Catalunha: 280
Roy, William, astrónomo inglês: 264
Royal Society → Londres

Ruivo, Conceição: 317
RÚSSIA: 29, 147, 293 (*vd.* S. Petersburgo)

SÁ, José António de, magistrado: 104-106, 233, 299
—, Manuel Ferreira da Câmara Bettencourt e, naturalista: 292
SABARÁ, Minas Gerais, Brasil: 64, 65, 66, 67, 83 (*vd.* Nossa Senhora da Encarnação, S. Miguel de Piracicaba, Santa Rita)
SACAVÉM, rio de, Lisboa: 294
SACRAMENTO, colónia do [Santíssimo], Brasil [e Uruguai]: 64-66, 82, 240
SACROBOSCO, [Johannes de, astrónomo escocês]: 194
SAINT POURÇAIN, [Guillaume] Durand de, filósofo francês: 16
SALAMANCA, universidade de, Espanha: 20-21, 27
SALAZAR, [António de Oliveira]: 320-321
SALCELAS, Mariana, Minas Gerais: 83
SALDANHA, Manuel de, reitor da universidade de Coimbra: 26
SALGUEIRO, Joaquim José Torres, magistrado: 304
SALVADOR, Baía, Brasil: 70, 75 (*vd.* Colégio [do Salvador] da Baía)

SAMORA CORREIA, Benavente, Ribatejo: 259
SAMUDA, Isaac, médico judeo-luso-britânico: 29
SANCHES, António Nunes Ribeiro, médico: 29-30
SANTA ANA, Goiases, Goiás, Brasil: 82
SANTA ANA DO CAMISÃO, Baía, Brasil: 81
SANTA BÁRBARA, arraial, Minas Gerais, Brasil: 72, 83
SANTA CATARINA, Brasil: 64-66, 85
SANTA CRUZ, mosteiro de, Coimbra: 18, 23, 193
SANTA LUZIA, Minas Gerais, Brasil: 83
—, Sergipe d'El Rei: 85
SANTA MARIA DE MARICÁ, Rio de Janeiro: 85
SANTA RITA, Sabará, Minas Gerais: 83
SANTARÉM: 26, 74
SANTO AMARO, Baía, Brasil: 81
SANTO AMARO DA PURIFICAÇÃO, Baía, Brasil: 81
Santo Antão → Colégio de Santo Antão
SANTO ANTÓNIO, Mato Grosso, Brasil: 82
SANTO ANTÓNIO DA CASA BRANCA, Minas Gerais, Brasil: 83
SANTO ANTÓNIO DO TIJUCO, arraial, Minas Gerais, Brasil: 72
SANTO ANTÓNIO DE VILA NOVA, Baía, Brasil: 81
SANTO ILDEFONSO, tratado de: 167, 241, 249
Santos, J. J. Carvalhão: 30
—, S. Paulo, Brasil: 61, 63-67, 69, 76, 85 (*vd.* Colégio de S. Miguel)
S. BARTOLOMEU, Mariana, Minas Gerais: 83
S. BOAVENTURA, colégio de, Coimbra: 23
S. DOMINGOS DE SABARÁ, Baía, Brasil: 81
S. FÉLIX, Baía, Brasil: 81
S. FRANCISCO, Baía, Brasil: 81
S. JOÃO D'EL REI, Minas Gerais, Brasil: 62-63, 67, 72, 83 (*vd.* Rio das Mortes)
S. JOSÉ, Rio das Mortes, Minas Gerais, Brasil: 83
S. Leopoldo, Visconde de → José Feliciano Fernandes Pinheiro
S. LUÍS, Maranhão, Brasil: 77, 79, 82
S. MIGUEL DE PIRACICABA, Sabará, Minas Gerais, Brasil: 83
S. PAULO, Brasil: 46-48, 59, 61, 63-69, 76, 78, 85 (*vd.* Iguaçu, Itu, José Arouche de Toledo

Rendon, José Bonifácio de Andrada e Silva, Mogimirim, Paranaguá, Santos, Vila Bela da Princesa, Vila Nova do Príncipe)
S. PEDRO DO FANADO, Minas Gerais, Brasil: 83
S. PETERSBURGO, Rússia: 30, 147, 174, 233
S. ROMÃO, arraial, Minas Gerais, Brasil: 72
S. TOMÉ [e Príncipe]: 330
S. VICENTE, cabo de, Algarve: 264
Saraiva, Luís: 215, 233
SARDENHA, Itália: 108
SARMENTO, Jacob de Castro, médico, exilado: 29
SATURNO, planeta: 198, 222, 228, 231, 239
SAXÓNIA, Alemanha: 293
SCARLATTI, Domingos, compositor italiano: 143
Schaffer, Simon: 141
Schubring, Gert: 212
SÉ NOVA, Coimbra: 321
Sebastião José de Carvalho e Melo → Marquês de Pombal
SEDA, rio, afluente do rio Tejo: 249
SEGÓVIA, Espanha: 27
SEIXAS, Gregório José de, médico, naturalista, provedor da Casa da Moeda: 99, 310
SEMINÁRIO [Maior da Sagrada Família], Coimbra: 321
SEMINÁRIO DE NOSSA SENHORA DAS MISSÕES, [Belém, Pará], Brasil: 77
SENA, rio, França: 293
Sepúlveda, Cristóvão Aires de Magalhães: 260, 278
SEQUEIRA, Joaquim Pedro Fragoso de, naturalista: 269, 292, 294
SERGIPE D'EL REI, Brasil: 64, 65, 66, 85 (*vd.* Santa Luzia)
SERPA, Alentejo: 259
SERRA, José Francisco Correia da, abade, vice-presidente da Academia Real das Ciências de Lisboa: 102, 172, 175-179, 181, 184, 185-188, 233, 237, 254, 263, 283 (*vd.* Domingos Vandelli, duque de Lafões, [frei] Manuel do Cenáculo Vilas Boas)
—, Francisco José Simões da, lente da Universidade de Coimbra: 166
—, Maximiano José da, engenheiro: 267-268
Serrão, Joel: 248
—, *José Vicente:* 98
SERRO FRIO, Minas Gerais, Brasil: 83 (Vila do Príncipe)
SETÚBAL, Estremadura: 261, 263-265, 267, 270, 305 (*vd.*

Azeitão, Conrado Henrique de Niemeyer)
Shapin, Steven: 140
Schem-Gregory, Mena: 327
Silva, Ana Cristina Nogueira da: 270, 304
—, António Carlos de Andrada e, natural de S. Paulo, irmão de José Bonifácio de Andrada e Silva: 46
—, *António Delgado da:* 272, 278, 289, 298,
—, António de Moraes, estudante universidade de Coimbra, brasileiro: 115
—, *Clarete Paranhos da:* 186,
—, Fernando Telles da, conde de Tarouca: 176
—, João Manuel da, engenheiro: 267, 306
—, Joaquim José da, naturalista: 43, 166 (*vd.* Angola, Cabo Verde)
—, *José Alberto Teixeira Rebelo da:* 174-175, 177
—, José Bonifácio de Andrada e, irmão de Martim Francisco de Andrada e Silva e António Carlos de Andrada e Silva, tio de José Ricardo da Costa Aguiar de Andrada, lente da universidade de Coimbra, Intendente Geral das Minas e Metais do Reino: 46-47, 91, 99, 187, 267, 288-289, 292, 294, 301, 310, 328 (*vd.* Alemanha, Bélgica, Boémia, Brasil, França, Gregório José de Seixas, Holanda, Itália, Hungria, Suécia, Turquia, Vicente José Coelho Seabra da Silva Teles)
—, José Correia Pacheco e, político brasileiro: 46
—, José Fernando da, juiz: 257 (*vd.* Ponte da Barca)
—, José de Seabra da, membro da Junta da Providência Literária, ministro: 163, 220, 250, 265, 269, 282, 286, 301, 303, 310, 312
—, Manuel Galvão da, naturalista: 43, 249
—, Manuel Pereira da, membro da Junta da Providência Literária: 163
—, *Maria Beatriz Nizza da Silva:* 40, 42
—, Mário, [lente da Universidade de Coimbra]: 334
—, Martim Francisco de Andrada e, irmão de José Bonifácio de Andrada e Silva: 46-47
—, *Teodoro Marques Pereira da:* 284

SILVEIRA, João Inácio do Amaral, intendente, Minas Gerais: 186
—, José Xavier Mouzinho da, político: 49
—, Tristão Álvares da Costa, [lente da Universidade de Coimbra, militar]: 276
Simões, Ana: 88, 197
—, Carlota: 11, 313
—, Diogo Carneiro: 142, 172-173, 177-189
Simon, J. William: 249, 103
SIMSON, Robert, [matemático inglês]: 148
SMITH, James Edward, [botânico britânico]: 189
SOARES, Eusébio de Sousa, engenheiro militar: 304
SOARES, Pedro Celestino, engenheiro militar, 267
SOBRAL, Tomé Rodrigues, lente da universidade de Coimbra: 49, 315
SOL, estrela: 199-200, 224, 227-228, 231, 238-239, 332
SOR, rio, afluente do rio Sorraia: 259
SORRAIA, rio, afluente do Rio Tejo: 258-260 (*vd.* Guilherme Luís António Valleré, rio Tejo, rio Alcôrrego, rio Divor, rio Seda, rio Sor, rio Tera)

SOUSA, João Crisóstomo de Abreu e, militar, político: 211
—, Luís Pinto de, ministro dos Negócios Estrangeiros e da Guerra: 250, 262, 264, 266, 271, 275-278, 281, 292-293, 304, 308, 310, 312
SOUSA, Manuel Joaquim Brandão de, engenheiro militar: 278, 280, 310
Sousa, Fernando de: 107
Spary, Emma: 91-92
STOCKLER, Francisco de Borja Garção, político: 238, 262, 263, 265
SUÁREZ (o Granatense), Francisco, jesuíta, lente da Universidade de Coimbra: 25-28 (*vd.* Alcalá, Ávila, Colégio Romano, Granada, Roma, Salamanca, Valladolid)
Subtil, José Manuel: 33
SUÉCIA: 46, 149, 293 (*vd.* Christopher Gedner, Estocolmo, João Jacob Ferber, Lineu, Upsala)
SUMIDOIRO, Minas Gerais, Brasil: 83

TAVARES, António Rolim de Almeida, conde de Azambuja: 176
TAVIRA, Algarve: 300 (*vd.* António José Vaz Velho)

TEJO, rio: 259-260 (*vd.* rio Alcôrrego, rio Divor, rio Seda, rio Sor, rio Sorraia, rio Tera)
TEJUCO [Tijuco?], arraial, Minas Gerais, Brasil: 83
TELES, Nuno da Silva, reitor da universidade de Coimbra: 19
TELES, Vicente José Coelho Seabra da Silva, médico, lente da universidade de Coimbra: 99
TERRA, planeta: 198-199, 332
TETE, Moçambique: 44
TIJUCO, [Minas Gerais], Brasil: 65-66
TIMOR: 330
Tirapicos, Luís: 197
TOMÁS, menino: 207 (*vd.* Júlio Dinis, Universidade de Coimbra)
Tomás Xavier de Lima Nogueira Vasconcelos Telles da Silva → Visconde de Vila Nova de Cerveira
TOURNEFORT, sistema de classificação da botânica: 172
TRÁS-OS-MONTES: 304 (*vd.* Moncorvo)
TRAVASSOS, Francisco de Paula, [lente da Universidade de Coimbra]: 276, 280
TRENTO, concílio de, Itália: 14

TRIGOSO, Manuel Pais de Aragão, vice-reitor da universidade de Coimbra, governador de Coimbra: 49
TRINDADE, rua da, Coimbra: 286, 287
TURQUIA: 46

ULTRAMAR: 40, 327 (*vd.* Portugal)
UNIVERSIDADE DE COIMBRA (Jardim Botânico): 8-13, 15, 18-25, 39, 44, 52, 94-95, 99-101, 113, 118-120, 129, 131, 135-136, 141, 144, 161, 163-164, 166-167, 169, 174, 180, 182, 193-194, 202-205, 207-208, 210-211, 214-216, 218, 220-222, 225-232, 237, 242-244, 246, 248, 250-251, 256-257, 260, 263, 265, 273, 276, 278, 282-287, 290-291, 293, 295-297, 300-302, 305, 307-309, 311, 313-314, 317, 320-325, 328-329, 333-334 (*vd.* Afonso do Prado, António Caetano de Freitas, Agostinho Martins Vidigal, António José Figueiredo, António José Pereira, António Pinheiro, António Rodrigues de Oliveira, António Soares

Barbosa, Baltazar de Faria, Carlos Antunes, colégio de São Jerónimo, colégio de Pereira, Desirée Pedro, Félix de Avelar Brotero, Filipe Folque, Francisco António Marques Giraldes, Francisco de Bragança, Francisco José Simões da Serra, Francisco de Lemos, Francisco Monçon, Francisco de Paula Travassos, Francisco Rafael de Castro, Francisco Rodrigues de Oliveira, Francisco Suárez, Gregório José de Seixas, Guilherme Elsden, Henrique [o navegador], Isaac Samuda, João António Dalla Bella, João António Monteiro, João Cosme da Cunha, João Mendes Ribeiro, João Pereira Ramos de Azeredo Coutinho, Joaquim António de Aguiar, Joaquim Maria de Andrade, José Anastácio da Cunha, José Francisco Rafael Miguel António de Mendonça, José Monteiro da Rocha, José Ricalde Pereira de Castro, José de Seabra da Silva, Laboratorio Chimico, Luís Correia, Manuel Alves Macomboa, Manuel do Cenáculo Vilas Boas, Manuel Jacinto Nogueira da Gama, Manuel José Barjona, Manuel Pais de Aragão Trigoso, Manuel Pedro de Melo, Manuel Pereira da Silva, Manuel de Quadros, Manuel de Saldanha, Mário Silva, marquês de Pombal, Miguel Franzini, mosteiro de Santa Cruz, Museu da Ciência, Museu de História Natural, Museu Nacional Machado de Castro, Nuno de Freitas, Nuno da Silva Teles, Paio Rodrigues de Vilarinho, palácio dos Grilos, Pedro Folque, Pedro Nunes, Salazar, Tomé Rodrigues Sobral, Tristão Álvares da Costa Silveira, Vicente José Coelho Seabra da Silva Teles)

Uppsala → Upsala

UPSALA (Uppsala), Suécia: 150, 174

ÚRANO, planeta: 222, 228, 231

Valadares, Virgínia: 170
VALENÇA, Baía, Brasil: 81
VALLADOLID, Espanha: 27
VALLERÉ, Guilherme Luís António de, arquitecto, tenente gene-

ral: 258-261, 277, 293 (*vd.* rio Sorraia)
van Praët, Michel: 317
VANDELLI, Domingos, médico, naturalista, lente da universidade de Pádua, lente da Universidade de Coimbra, membro da Academia real das Ciências de Lisboa, diretor do Real Jardim Botânico da Ajuda, deputado da Real Junta do Comércio: 11, 41--42, 91, 97-102, 115, 139, 145, 148-150, 152-154, 156--159, 161, 163-164, 166-170, 175-176, 178-190, 233, 248, 250-251, 268-269, 301, 314--315, 320, 323, 325, 331 (*vd.* Alexandre Rodrigues Ferreira, Estêvão Dias Cabral, Félix de Avelar Brotero, Francisco José Simões da Serra, Francisco Vandelli, João da Silva Feijó, Joaquim José da Silva, Joaquim Veloso de Miranda, José Álvares Maciel, José Francisco Correia da Serra, José de Seabra da Silva, Carl von Lineu, Martinho de Melo e Castro, Luís António Furtado de Castro do Rio de Mendonça e Faro, Luís Pinto de Sousa Coutinho, Manuel Henriques de Paiva, Nicolau Piaggio, rio Mondego, Rodrigo Ribeiro de Sousa Pinto, visconde de Barbacena, visconde de Vila Nova de Cerveira)
—, Francisco, pai de Domingos Vandelli, professor na Universidade de Pádua: 149
Varela, Alex Gonçalves: 292
Vargues, Isabel Nobre: 79
VARNHAGEN, Francisco Adolfo, [engenheiro, historiador brasileiro]: 48
Vasconcelos, António de: 54
—, João Rosado de Vilalobos e, lente em Évora: 108, 109-111, 113-114
—, *Luís Adolfo P. Walter de:* 250
VAUBAN, [Sébastien Le Prestre de, arquitecto militar francês]: 277
Vaz, Francisco António Lourenço: 103-104, 113
VEIGA, Eusébio da, astrónomo: 197-198
VELHO, António José Vaz, naturalista, cosmógrafo: 280, 300, 310 (*vd.* Tavira)
Veloso → Joaquim Veloso de Miranda
VENEZA, Itália: 43

VÉNUS, planeta: 198, 211, 220, 228
Vergílio → Virgílio
VIAMÃO, Rio Grande do Sul, Brasil: 85
Viana, Hélio: 73
—, Maranhão, Brasil: 82
VERNEY, Luís António de, oratoriano, pedagogo: 30, 142
VIANA DO CASTELO (Vianna do Minho): 124
Vianna do Minho → Viana do Castelo
Vicente Ferrer → Vicente Ferrer da Rocha
VIDIGAL, Agostinho Martins, estudante da Universidade de Coimbra: 102
VIENA, Áustria: 145
VIGIA, casa da, Colégio de Santo Alexandre, Pará, Brasil: 77
VILA BELA DA PRINCESA, São Paulo, Brasil: 85
VILA BOA, Goiás, Brasil: 64, 82
—, Minas Gerais, Brasil: 83
VILA DO CAMPO, Rio de Janeiro, Brasil: 85
Vila Leal do Carmo → Mariana
VILA NOVA DE BOIPEBA, Baía, Brasil: 81
VILA NOVA DE CERVEIRA, visconde de (Tomás Xavier de Lima Nogueira Vasconcelos Telles da Silva), marquês de Ponte de Lima, ministro do reino: 168, 170-171, 179, 182, 188 (*vd*. Domingos Vandelli, Maria I)
VILA NOVA DO PRÍNCIPE, São Paulo, Brasil: 85
VILA NOVA DA RAINHA, Minas Gerais, Brasil: 82 (*vd*. Caeté)
—, Mariana, Minas Gerais, Brasil: 72, 83
VILA DO PRÍNCIPE, [Minas Gerais] Brasil: 65-66
VILA REAL DO BREJO DA AREIA, Paraíba do Norte, Brasil: 83
VILA REAL DO SABARÁ, [Minas Gerais], Brasil: 72
VILA RICA DE OURO PRETO Minas Gerais, Brasil: 64-67, 72, 78, 83 (*vd*. Guaripiranga, Itaberaba)
VILA DO RIO PARDO, Rio Grande do Sul, Brasil: 85
VILARINHO, Paio Rodrigues de, lente da Universidade de Coimbra, principal do Colégio das Artes: 23
VILAS BOAS, Custódio Gomes, geógrafo, astrónomo, engenheiro: 204, 237-238, 241-242, 263-265, 280, 304, 309

—, [Frei] Manuel do Cenáculo, membro da Junta da Providência Literária: 112, 163, 173, 177
Virgílio (Vergílio): 94, 116
visconde Balsemão → Luís Pinto de Sousa Coutinho
visconde de Vila Nova de Cerveira → Tomás Xavier de Lima Nogueira Vasconcelos Telles da Silva
VISME, Gerard de, negociante inglês: 151, 180-181
Viterbo, Sousa: 284
VITÓRIA, Espírito Santo, Brasil: 63-66, 76, 81
VIVES, Luis, editor francês: 28

ZACH, [Franz Xaver] von, astrónomo alemão: 217, 223, 224
ZACUTO, Abraão, astrónomo judeu: 194
ZANNONI, [Giovanni Antonio] Rizzi, geógrafo italiano: 261
ZELADA, Francesco Saverio, cardeal italiano: 172
ZINCKE, Georg Heinrich, jurista alemão: 106
Zuquete, Afonso Martins: 183

Waquet, François: 88
WARD, Bernard: 111
Waterbury, John: 147
WERNER, [Abraham Gottlob] lente em Freiburg, Alemanha: 294
WICKMAN, Daniel, naturalista: 160-161 (*vd.* Lineu)
Wittrock, B.: 90

Xavier, Ângela B.: 146
XAVIER, Pedro Joaquim, sargento mor: 273, 275

YVETTE, rio Paris, França: 260

www.ingramcontent.com/pod-product-compliance
Lightning Source LLC
Chambersburg PA
CBHW050611300426
44112CB00012B/1462